WELSH SETTLEMENT OF PENNSYLVANIA

Charles H. Browning

HERITAGE BOOKS
2007

HERITAGE BOOKS
AN IMPRINT OF HERITAGE BOOKS, INC.

Books, CDs, and more—Worldwide

For our listing of thousands of titles see our website
at
www.HeritageBooks.com

A Facsimile Reprint
Published 2007 by
HERITAGE BOOKS, INC.
Publishing Division
65 East Main Street
Westminster, Maryland 21157-5026

Originally published
Philadelphia
1912

— Publisher's Notice —
In reprints such as this, it is often not possible to remove blemishes from the original. We feel the contents of this book warrant its reissue despite these blemishes and hope you will agree and read it with pleasure.

International Standard Book Number: 978-0-7884-1063-5

CONTENTS.

Arranging Welsh settlement	11- 29
Welsh land companies	33- 42
Thomas and Jones' land patent	45- 59
Merion adventurers	63- 78
Families and lands of first arrivals	79- 92
Families and lands of second arrivals	95-138
Lloyd and Davies' land patent	141-161
John Bevan's land patent	163-173
John and Wynne's land patent	175-193
Lewis David's land patent	195-203
Richard Thomas' land patent	207-212
Richard David's land patent	213-248
Welsh planters and servants	249-276
Welsh Friends' pedigrees	279-302
Annals of the Welsh settlers	305-324
Welsh Tract affairs	327-416
Welsh Tract townships	419-493
Merion, Haverford and Radnor	497-589
Appendix	591-597
Index	599

MERION WELSH FRIENDS' MEETING HOUSE, "BUILT 1695."

WELSH QUAKER EMIGRATION TO PENSYLVANIA

WELSH SETTLEMENT OF PENNSYLVANIA

FRIENDS IN WALES

In Pensylvania, there is no more ancient public building preserved, that is so intimately associated with the settlement of the State, in its provincial period, than the Merion Meeting House, a stone-built house of God. It is one of the very few remaining links suggesting the days of William Penn, and it is the oldest.

The march of public improvement and progress is passing, leaving it the same House, growing older, but not decaying, of hallowed memories, which was the first permanent place for public religious meetings of the first settlers of the region in which it stands, ever an interesting relict of days long passed, of early colonial, or provincial times and customs of the greatest of the American commonwealths.

Its oldest part, completed in the year 1695, as its date-stone tells, the possible successor of a more modest and unpretentious Meeting House, stands as a firm, rock-built, permanent land-mark, in Lower Merion township, Montgomery county, at the intersection of Montgomery avenue, and Meeting House Road, a short distance from the city line.

'Twas on one of those

> "Fair First-day mornings,
> Steeped in summer calm,"

that I made my first visit to this Friends' Meeting. Any day it is worth more than the time you will spend on a visit

WELSH SETTLEMENT OF PENSYLVANIA

there, "for conscience sake," if not out of interest, or curiosity.

You will find a large, double iron gate, just west of the picturesque and quaint "General Wayne Inn, Established in 1704," that yields to pressure, for it's never locked, and admits you to a clean, rolled gravel driveway leading upwards through a well kept lawn to the old building, past the usual shelter for horses, for the merciful are merciful to their beasts, shaded by tall sycamore, or buttonwood trees, native to the soil, ancient you may see, for their girths are near twenty feet, which have witnessed the passing to worship, or to mourn, of many generations of Friends.

You will find that the Meeting House seems to stand on a natural elevation, but the ground is really only a part of the level fields about it, and that it is the bounding roadbeds that here have been cut down to a plane which gives it the apparent elevation. The lawn about the old building has a luxurious growth of clover, and is sufficiently shaded by trees not so old as those you have passed under, and, on the whole, is a restful spot, "far from the madding crowd," that has been enjoyed by thousands in days gone by, and is likely to be for longer, for there is never any lack of funds to keep the place in perfect condition and beauty.

This lawn on which the old house stands, to one side, is of the shape of a triangle, being bounded on two sides by the intersecting public roads, while the third, or base, may be said, rests on an end of the rectangularly spaced grave yard. All about the property is a strong, stone retaining wall, which it was necessary to build when the public roads were cut down and leveled, topped with an iron fence, which gives the grounds a park-like appearance, and, with the Meeting House, makes it notable in this locality, to the thousands motoring and driving on the adjacent avenues.

Outwardly you will find the Meeting House attractive in appearance for it has some architecturally distinctive marks and features, absent in the usually plain, unpreten-

ARRANGING WELSH SETTLEMENT

tious Friends' Meeting Houses, which suggests that its builders were men of refined taste, who could design and erect a meeting house at once plain and unassuming, but at the same time attractive to the senses. Yet, withal, it is a little modest stone building that has withstood the elements for over two centuries, and so will probably remain to the end, an accommodation for all of its congregations, a quaint and charming bit of colonial architecture, with its three gables, and as a whole, a remarkable one, for it is the only Friends' Meeting House erected into the shape of a T, or of a "tau cross," the "crux commissa," which latter design is so incongruous with Friends' taste, it must be considered an accident that this Friends' Meeting House was built cruciform.

In a general description, the Meeting House faces the South, and the transept, east and west, a gable pointing towards three of the chief points of the compass. In the western gable end of the transept may be seen a small stone, set into the wall, above a window, with the legend:

BUILT
1695
REPAIRED
1829

And on the lintel of the window in the Eastern gable may be seen the engraved date, "1829." Of these dates, and what they indicate, will be told further on.

A generous "front-door" on the South side of what may be presumed to be the stem of the cross, opens on a covered wooden stoop, and two side doors are sheltered by the stiff hoods common to the Meeting House of early construction.

Anciently, this may have been an ideal spot for a Friends' Meeting House, but now it seems better adapted for a mission, since its nearest neighbors are a tavern, "where they sell liquor," but a quiet, orderly place, and not unlike the

WELSH SETTLEMENT OF PENSYLVANIA

road-houses of England, and a popular race track. But to maintain the religious atmosphere, its third neighbor is the great convent house and estate of the Sisters of Mercy, a teaching order. Between the walls of the convent grave yard, where Sisters are buried, and the Meeting House, lays the "Friends' Ground," the grave yard of the Merion Meeting, protected from trespass by a stone wall, surmounted by an iron fence.

Passing through its ever open iron gates, unheeding the weather beaten warning, "All Trespassing Forbidden," and going up the long, straight gravel walk, bisecting the grounds, where

> "Round about, the old Friends sleep,
> Grave women, earnest men,"

you may notice that innovation has reached this long-time secluded spot, as it has other Meetings' grave yards, for there are inscribed stones marking graves, something the Founders and early members of this Meeting would not have tolerated. However, these cannot be classed as tombstones, or monuments, for they are little, modest affairs, never taller than two feet which superceded equally low head and foot boards to the graves, and for this reason many have sank as if ashamed, so that the grass hides them, and the simple legends they bear are difficult to read. There are only about 200 graves thus marked, which is but a small percentage of the thousands of people here interred, one above the other, in two centuries, and, singular to relate, one-third of the stones tell they are in loving remembrance of people who died over eighty years of age, thus evidencing, as claimed, that "Quaker habits promote longevity." These modest grave-stones tell the barest details of the departed; only their names and span of life, engraved on the upper edge, in the strata, and for this reason are soon rendered unreadable by the elements of the weather.

As the majority of the stones tell of Friends who died after 1830, it may be presumed it was about that decade of

ARRANGING WELSH SETTLEMENT

the last century, shortly after the Society became divided into two branches, generally known as "orthodox" and "Hicksites," and the latter Friends, who, however, do not recognize this appellation, calling themselves simply "Friends," got control of this Meeting, they being more liberal in their views of such matters, when non-Friends, but descendents of members of the Society, began to be buried here, and the taste and desire for marble marking stones prevailed, for the stones recording earlier decease may have been erected long subsequent to the event, since they do not have the appearance of more age than their neighbors of later dates, and there are several that tell of deaths in the last decade of the 18th century.

And it is also notable that such members of the Friends' families who served as soldiers in the Civil War, are buried here, and bear the little marker-flags placed by the loving hands of their living companions, the members of the Society of the Grand Army of the Republic on Memorial Day.

This spot, hallowed by dear and sad memories, may in a few years be in the midst of a dense population, the overflow from the city, but now, of a summer's day, only the far-off ring of a blacksmith's hammer, or the occasional tap of the convent bell, or the quick rush of an "auto," is the only commotion that disturbs its continual calm.

In some respects, this may be like a hundred other Friends' Meeting Houses, which called for the lines from the Quaker poet, John Russell Hayes:

> "I love the old Meeting Houses,—how my heart
> Goes out to these dear, silent homes of prayer,
> With all their quietude and rustic charm;
> Their loved associations and pathetic solitude;
> Their tranquil and pathetic solitude;
> Their hallowed Memories!"

But the old Merion Meeting, and its house has enough personality to make it distinguishable.

No picture of the neighborhood, in which this ancient House stands, can be painted better by the pen, to compare

WELSH SETTLEMENT OF PENSYLVANIA

its site with what it was in the extreme past, than the commercial statement, the land in its vicinity, which was bought from Penn for only five pence an acre, is now being sold for more than five thousand dollars an acre, and a mile beyond, at Wynnewood and at Ardmore, for fifteen thousand dollars an acre! Which means, the inhabitants of Penn's "City of Brotherly Love," once miles away, and whose buildings could be counted on the fingers of one hand when the Welsh Quakers pitched their tents here, have brought it into sight of the door of the old Meeting House, and have thus enhanced the value of the land about it. The suburban population surrounds it; villages have grown-up about it; it has become accessible by steam and electric cars, and by well-kept avenues, this ancient, vine-grown old stone Meeting House, to which Friends for years came afoot and horse-back, along the bridle-paths and lanes through the wild woods, but whose descendants now roll up to meetings in luxurious limousines.

This Merion Meeting House, as it stands, was not only the first place of public worship erected for the original settlers of the territory west of the Schuylkill river, distant from the limit of the proposed city of Philadelphia, and just without its present bounds, by the Welsh Friends, who began to remove here in the summer of 1682, but the first public house of worship or church building put up in the Commonwealth, and, as may be seen hereafter, it was also the first "town hall' erected in it. And I understand it was the first permanent Meeting House for Friends erected in America.

The story of the experiences of the earliest Welsh settlers in "Merioneth Town," or "Merion Town," as the district in which this Meeting House stands, was at first called, in honor of the shire in Wales from which its first settlers came, or Merion township, as it came officially to be designated, and of the "towns" of "Harfod," or Haverford, and Radnor, contiguous to it, from the year of first settlement,

ARRANGING WELSH SETTLEMENT

1682, will be told by their extant letters written to friends at "home," has none of the thrilling tales of hardship and adventure, of "battle, murder and sudden death," that embellishes, and saddens those of the first comers into Virginia and New England, a half-century earlier, nor those of the pioneers of the Cumberland Valley, the Valley of Virginia, or of Kentucky, when beginning the "winning of the West," a half-century later. Nor did these Friends—"those devil-driven heretics," as the Rev. Cotton Mather, of New England, called the Quakers in his "Magnalia,"—have to suffer from the "sharp laws" of Massachusetts, and New England Puritan intolerance, and any there who did, soon found their way to Pennsylvania.

Writing of these early days, with his facile pen in his "Quaker School Boy," Friend Isaac Sharpless says, "It was a venture, as all emigration is, but the results were happy. There was none of the suffering of Massachusetts and Virginia. The wise arrangement of Penn had made the redmen more than friends. The Quaker home, and children, were left in perfect security, while the adult attended Quarterly Meeting."

And the Welsh Friends were hardly forerunners even in the land, for the way had long been made clear for their peaceful entrance into their purchased lands, and many were able to be seated at the very first on old "Indian fields," and on clearings made by their predecessors, the Swedes, Dutch and early English, who came up here from the old settlements on the lower Delaware. But as these choice spots were, as we may see, soon claimed by Penn as his private property, their tenure of them was brief. That Penn appreciated them highly may be seen from his letter of 16, 8mo. 1683, to the Free Society of Traders in Pensylvania, in which he says, "There are also very good peaches, and in great quantities, not an Indian plantation without them, they make a pleasant drink," hence the "insidious punch" of peach brandy and honey.

WELSH SETTLEMENT OF PENSYLVANIA

The Delaware river country had been opened for fifty-odd years to settlers, on both of its lower banks, and considerable land was being cultivated and farmed, in peace, without fear, though not comfort possibly, as we understand it, when the Welsh Friends removed to Penn's new province, where he "would found a free colony for all mankind that shall go thither," as his land-sale advertisements stated. Therefore, the story of their first years in America is almost devoid of especial interest in respect to what makes that of older colonies here so prominent.

Yet, although it may be only that of domesticity—simply the transfer of "home" across the sea, from one peaceful site to another, with only discomforts incidental to removal and travel, and re-establishment, to enliven it, theirs is the story of active participation in the founding of the Commonwealth of Pensylvania.

They had longed

"For a lodge in some vast wilderness,
Some boundless contiguity of shade,"

and they certainly were accommodated, these Welsh of English nationality, but their settling in Pensylvania was not a complete severance from "home," to which kin and ancestors still bound them for several generations.

Although, like the Swedes of the "South River country," and the Dutch of New Netherlands, the Welsh of the Schuylkill, who, however, ceased coming over in any great number after the "sufferings" were stopped in their native land, or when they learned that Penn had not kept to his promises to the early colonists, as will be explained hereafter; were engulfed, disappearing as a separate race in a few years, in the great flood of English to our shores, and lost their identity, and Welsh characteristics, swallowed up by the cosmopolitan development of our country, and even the use of their distinctive tongue. * The moral influence and teachings

---

*The Welsh language may have been understood, spoken and written and read and preferred by the Welsh Quakers generally in Pen-

ARRANGING WELSH SETTLEMENT

the Welsh members of the religious Society of Friends, "the people vulgarly called Quakers," with their Cymric blood, an industrious, hardy race, were instilled into the community of strangers which grew up about them, and in which they were finally absorbed, grown into the fibre and woof of our great nation, for, there is hardly a present-day family of any prominence, or social pretentions, in Pensylvania, or in the "West," having colonial ancestry, that cannot claim, with truth, an ancestor among the early Welsh Friends of this Commonwealth, and they are proud in being able to do so for reasons that may appear hereafter. ‡ In this connection the late Dr. Levick said in a public address, "The early Welsh settlers of Philadelphia, and its vicinity, belonged to a race which has left its impress, in a very marked manner, on the character of its descendants to the present day."

---

sylvania, for, as will appear, they desired, and expected that the civil affairs of the whole Welsh Tract would be determined by officers and juries "of our language." But English was the prevailing language with the Welsh Quakers in the "Haverford and Merion towns," as the earliest settlers therein were of the upper, educated class of Wales, and were often at London, and among the English. But in Radnor Township there were many Welsh who did not understand English, for, as late as in 1707, the Welsh Episcopalians then petitioned the Bishop of London to send them a rector who could read and speak both Welsh and English. They were the founders of the P. E. Church of St. Davids. In other parts, and in the Gwynedd settlement, however, the Welsh language and customs obtained distinctively for many years, and many of the wills, and documents issued by the people of the latter section were in the Welsh tongue, as, for instance, as late as 1712, the subscription paper passed around, for collecting funds to rebuild the Gwynedd Meeting House, in which House ministers had to speak alternately in Welsh and English, in the same address.

---

‡The Welsh origin for the Pensylvania families of Adams, Apthorp, Arnold, Bevan, Cadwalader, David, Davies, Evans, Ellis, Edwards, Foulke, Floyd, Griffith, Guinn, Gwynne, Hughs, Humphreys, Howell, Hewes, Henry, Harry, Jones, John, Lloyd, Lewis, Morris, Morgan, Owen, Price, Powell, Paul, Penn, Pugh, Richards, Rice, Reese, Roberts, Thomas, Williams, Wynne, etc., can easily be imagined.

WELSH SETTLEMENT OF PENSYLVANIA

And Mr. Benjamin H. Smith, in an interesting article in a recent number of the magazine of the Historical Society of Pensylvania, concerning the lands in Merion of the first coming Welshmen, whose sturdy honesty and integrity he recognized, says, "they were prominent and respected citizens in their own country," and "those who came to Pensylvania took a leading part in the development of the new colony, and many of their descendants have borne distinguished names in literature, science, and public affairs."

Before entering into sketches of the Founders of the Friends' Merion Meeting, and of their Meeting House, and of the people prominently connected with it in its earliest years, and of its present-day members, and the same, incidentally, of the other meetings composing the Haverford or Radnor Monthly Meeting, it should not be uninteresting to review some of the events leading up to its establishing as introductory to them.

Immediately after William Penn was in full possession of the Royal Grant for the territory in America, then named, and so written for fifty years subsequently in public documents, and frequently in preserved private letters of the Quakers, "Pensylvania," he began to advertise, and canvass for purchasers and settlers for it. He first began his efforts within the Society of Friends, of which he was a prominent minister, and well known to thousands, advertising his province as an ideal asylum, or home, for them, with life there everything they might desire, appealing especially to those who were unhappy and dissatisfied, for various reasons, more or less serious, with their conditions in life.

Though it is unnecessary to bring to mind the many, many "sufferings" experienced by the Friends when the "church people" must have studied Collier's "Art of Ingeniously Tormenting," because of dislike to military duties; objections to paying tithes to support the "Established Church," their piety, and especially their public worship, a matter that was positively forbidden by acts of parlia-

ARRANGING WELSH SETTLEMENT

ment, one of these edicts to suppress "seditious conventicles," however, it is proper to mention here, as in it are the names of Welshmen who removed to Pensylvania, or the fathers of others.

This particular "edict" is dated 20 of May, 1675, and is signed by Humphey Hughes and John Wynne, constables. But it is not the notice that these Welshmen "met unlawfully under pretence of religion," and that the constables were ordered to "levy on them by way of distress," but it is the list of names given in the schedule, accompanying it, of those on whom they were to levy the fines, that is of interest.

"The names of those that unlawfully met together att Llwyn y Braner, within ye parish of Llanvaur, upon ye 16th day of May, being Sunday, 1675. Oathes being made they were present formerly in unlawful meetings within three months.

"First conviction on the oathes of Owen D'd, and Thomas Jones.

"Second conviction, and warrant of arrest for the Double fine, on oath of Robert Evans."

(Each of these following was fined ten shillings.)
"John David John, and his wife, of Cilltalgarth.
Hugh Roberts, and his wife, of the same place.
Cadwalader Thomas, of the same place.
Robert David, of the same place.
Robert Owen, of Vron Gôch.
Elin Owen, of the same.
John Thomas ap Hugh, of Llaythgywm.
John ap Edward, of Nanlleidiog.
Evan Edwards, of Cynlas.
Peter Owen, of Bettws y Coed.
Robert John, of Pen maen.
Margaret John, of same place.
Hugh John Thomas, of Nanlleidiog.
His sonne and daughter.

WELSH SETTLEMENT OF PENSYLVANIA

Litter Thomas, of Llandervel.
Jane Morris, of Pen maen.
Edward Griffith, of Llaetgwm.
Edward Reese, of Llantgervel.
John James, of the same.
William Morgan, of Llanecill.
Owen David, of Cilttalgarth.
John William, of the same place.
Anne, verch David, widow, of Pen maen."

This schedule, with the order, is preserved among the mass of MSS. which the wife and widow of John Thomas brought over here in 1683, now in possession of Lewis Jones Levick, Esqr., of Bala, (Philadelphia), who inherited them. It came into John's possession while serving as constable, and he endorsed on it:

"Evan Owen ye son of a widow called Gainor, whose late husband was Owen ap Evan, of Vron Gôch, was convicted by oath to be present at a meeting, though but 9 or 10 years old."

Penn's advertisements of his American possessions (he was his own sales-agent), readily appealed to Friends of every race, but the very first to take advantage of his generous and alluring offers, which he well knew how to make attractive, for he had had only recently some valuable experience in getting settlers for West Jersey when attending to Friend Billing's embarrassed estate there, and which suggested to him the scheme of having a great American territory for himself, and selling it out, giving him a permanent income in quit-rents, were the Friends in Wales.

But, to go back a little of this story of Welsh interests in Pensylvania.

The principal missionary of introduction of the teachings and belief of Friends into Wales was one John ap John, of "Plas Ifa" (Plas Eva, or Plas Evan), at Trevor, a hamlet near Ruabon and Wrexham, in Langollen parish, Denbighshire, then a pastoral country, but now given over to brickyards. He was born at Trevor Issa, about 1625-30, and baptised at the parish church, and became a member of a non-conforming congregation in the parish of Wrexham, in Denbighshire. In some way, the tenets and teachings of the learned apostle of Quakerism, George Fox, had reached this assembly in fragments. The meager reports of the lectures of this eminently successful minister seemed plausible and pleasing, but to be better instructed, the minister of the congregation, the Rev. Morgan Lloyd, sent this John, of "Plas Ifa," with a companion, to attend some of the meetings and make himself familiar with the precepts taught by Mr. Fox, and report them to it. Telling of this John ap John, Mr. Fox says he had been a "minister." He was probably of the Parliamentary party, and may have been a chaplain at "Bewmarres," or Beaumaris, where he lived, in the army in the latter years of the Protectorate.

The result of this mission is thus noticed by Mr. Fox in his "Journal," (p. 123, of London, 1694, edition): "When these triers came down among us the power of the Lord overcame them, and they were both of them convinced of the Truth, they returned into Wales, where John ap John abode in the Truth, and received a gift in the ministry, to which he continued faithful."

Thus it came about that John ap John was the founder of the Society of Friends in Wales. Small Meetings were organized everywhere by him and co-laborers, at first secretly, but it was not till after the "toleration" act of Parliament was passed, that the Society became regularly organized into "Quarterly Meetings," and irregular "Yearly Meetings" were held at Swansea, in 1681, and at Redstone, near Narberth, in Pembrokeshire, on 5 2mo, 1682. But the first Yearly (or Half-Yearly) Meeting regularly organized according to Friends' rules was held at the house of Ellis Morris, at Dolgyn, near Dolgelly, in Merionethshire, on 7, 3mo, 1683. In 1684, the Yearly Meeting was at Haverfordwest, at which William Humphrey, of Llanegryn,

WELSH SETTLEMENT OF PENSYLVANIA

Merioneth, promised and undertook to write up the "sufferings" of the Welsh Friends, in the years past. A subject so enlarged, subsequently, by Friend Besse, that it is only contained in two large printed volumes, since he records the sufferings of Friends in all lands. At the Yearly Meeting at Garthgynvor, near Dolgelly, in 1685, there were in attendance these "gentlemen," who had a part in the founding of the Merion Meeting. Charles Lloyd and Richard Davies, from Montgomeryshire; Roger ap John, and John ap John, and Richard Davies, from Denbighshire. The delegates to the great Yearly Meeting, at London, in 1688, when the Welsh Friends were first represented were Richard Davies, representing North Wales, and James Lewis, South Wales.

And of this John the son of John, the late Dr. Levick, of Philadelphia, said in an address delivered before the Historical Society of Pensylvania, 13 month, 1893*: "He was the Apostle of Quakerism in Wales," and he "was the direct agent, under Providence, in bringing about changes which resulted in the settlement so largely by Welsh emigrants of the Township of Merion."

And this is the good authority for John ap John, the first minister among Welsh Friends, having been the Father of the "Welsh Tract" in Pensylvania, and of the variously called Merion, Haverford, or Radnor Monthly Meeting, in it, and it was natural that he should head the committee of Welsh Friends who first interviewed Penn about buying some of his land in America, and removing thither, and as this was but shortly after he had entered into possession, it is possible that John was in Penn's confidence, and had the earliest information of the consummation of his bargain with the King, and suggested to the Welsh to secure the best lands.

---

*Pensylvania Mag., XVII, 385, etc.

†See further as to John ap John in *The Journal of the Friends' Historical Society*, London, Supplement, No. 6, 1907.

ARRANGING WELSH SETTLEMENT

The material inducements to purchase his land, and remove to it, that Penn offered, no doubt was made to the Welsh Friends through John ap John, and they can be imagined. Surely they were sufficiently attractive, for a committee, probably gotten together by John, and representing Monthly Meetings of a half dozen Welsh shires, decided upon going to London to interview him personally before investing, for the Welsh were ever a cautious race.

The gentlemen,—who may, or may not have gone in a body,—who sought this conference with Penn on the part of themselves, and the Meetings of which they were members, is the first Roll of Honor connected with "New Wales," "Cambria," or "The Welsh Tract," as the lands, in Penn's Province, in which they became interested, were variously known at first.

These delegates, on the part of the Welsh Friends, who went on this mission, gentlemen all according to land deeds, were:

John ap John, of Ruabon, Denbighshire.
Dr. Thomas Wynne, of Caerwys, Flintshire.
Richard ap Thomas, of Whitford Garne, Flintshire.
Dr. Griffith Owen, of Dolserre, Merionethshire.
Dr. Edward Jones, of Bala, Merionethshire.
John ap Thomas, of Llaithgwm, Merionethshire.
Hugh Roberts, of Llanvawr, Merionethshire.
Thomas Ellis, of Dolserre, Merionethshire.
Charles Lloyd, of Dolobran, Montgomeryshire.
Richard Davies, of Welshpool, Montgomeryshire.
John Bevan, of Treverigg, Glamorganshire.
Lewis ap David, of Llandewy Velfry, Pembrokeshire.

There were others, among them Edward Prichard, William Jenkins, and John Burge, who went to talk with Penn about the same time, but the list aforesaid includes the leaders in the movement for Pensylvania land (although there is evidence that John Roberts and Robert Owen, who

WELSH SETTLEMENT OF PENSYLVANIA

came over to Pensylvania, were also present), and who had the interview with Penn, in London, in May, 1681, of which, unfortunately for the Welsh, no written report was kept, and was, as will be explained, the cause of a serious misunderstanding subsequently.

Of these gentlemen, the three "practitioners in physics," and Messrs. Bevan, Roberts, Ellis and Owen, removed to Pensylvania and aided in settling the Welsh people on the lands purchased from them.

What Penn particularly promised these gentlemen, if they would induce the members of their Monthly Meetings to buy his land, and settle upon it, other than its fine quality, and his liberal guarantee of freedom from certain annoyances they had to put up with in Wales, was shortly, and is yet, partly a matter of conjecture and surmise as to its details and particulars, for Penn's promises to them were only verbally made. But these certain great expectations, with which these Welsh gentlemen claimed Penn had lured them to America, had vouching only by slender circumstantial evidence, and hearsay, his English lieutenants and alleged friends in Philadelphia held. Nevertheless, the Welshmen averred, and stuck to it, though little good it did them, as we shall see, that Penn's encouragement was, in part, they should have their whole purchase, the "Welsh Tract," as a "Barony," or State, as it were, within his Province, "within which all causes, quarrels, crimes and disputs might be tried and wholly determined by officers, magistrates, and juries of our language."

However, this committee having engaged to take and try to dispose of by sale to the other Welsh Friends, 40,000, or more acres, of Penn's land, returned to their several Monthly Meetings, and reported, and published Penn's "Articles of Conditions and Concessions" concerning his Province, to which they had subscribed before leaving London,—ideas of settlement he had re-written from the "Articles of Freedom and Exemption" compiled by the Dutch West India Com-

ARRANGING WELSH SETTLEMENT

pany for a like purpose. So alluring were their statements, based on Penn's promises, fresh in their recollections, they had no trouble in getting Friends to subscribe immediately, till their sales, and the lands they themselves would take, amounted to 30,000 acres, and thus it was that these well known, reliable gentlemen, in six Welsh counties, became the first Pensylvania real estate agents.

The men who interviewed Penn, and those concerned with them, were nearly all of the highest social caste of the landed gentry of Wales, as has been frequently proved in recent years on investigation, for it is well known that in Wales the upper class readily embraced Quakerism, through the teachings of John ap John, one of themselves, while in England the gentry did not, as there converts were confined entirely to the "plain people"—the small lease-holding, the yeomandry, farmers, tradesmen, and shopkeepers,—and this fact has occasioned the astonishment that William Penn, an aristocrat by birth and association, against the wishes of his family, became a Quaker. So it may be understood that the committee of Welsh Friends were equals and peers of Penn, and for this reason he may have readily agreed to any propositions they made, though afterwards he certainly was most jealous of concessions.

Surely, he must have been pleased to have the Welsh gentry head his list of grantees, and promise to remove their families to their purchases, for it would have a good effect on his sales, especially when it became known that the best class of the Welsh were going, carrying refinement and education into his Province, for his was a tremendous proposition to undertake single-handed, and the countenance of his scheme by gentry was a great help to him.

It was a great disappointment to all, but John ap John, of "Plas Ifa," who was indirectly the progenitor of the Haverford Monthly Meeting, did not remove to Pensylvania. Concerning him, the late Dr. Levick said in an address, that after a long search he learned that John died on 16, 9mo,

WELSH SETTLEMENT OF PENSYLVANIA

1697, at the residence of his son-in-law, John Miller, of Whitehough Manor, and was buried in Friends' ground at Bashford, near-by, in Staffordshire, where no stone, or memorial marks the grave of this first apostle of Friends' teachings in Wales. He also learned that in 1712, the Friends' Yearly Meeting, of North Wales, desired to collect and acquire his MSS. to preserve them, but they could never be found. Since Dr. Levick's investigations and death, the interest in John ap John, which he started, has continued, and the following further data has been discovered of him.

He married about 1664, Catharine, either daughter of John Trevor, of Trevor Hall, and Valle Crucis Abbey, or daughter of Roger ap John, of Ruabon. About 1653, Roger ap John and John ap John were signers of a positive denial that certain Quakers came into Wrexham to gain proselytes at their meetings, and that "after a long silence, sometimes one, sometimes more, fell into great and dreadful shakings, with swellings in their bodies, sending out skreekings and howlings!"

An extant paper, at the Devonshire House, London, (Gibson Bequest MSS. II, 33), has been discovered, signed by John ap John, saying that, in the year 1653, his "understanding was opened." And, "In my Jvgment I have byn perswaeded vnto the Establishment & setelment thereof & as occasion served, both in Words & praodies J denied ye paement of tithys & becos of ye same Denial i cam to siffer ye loss of corn, hay, lams, peegs, yieves, kids & mvch thretnings with pikyls and other waes."

In another paper he mentions his conversion to Quakerism as follows: "The 2 day of the 5 month, 1673. This time 20 years Agoee was ye time that I John Ap John was at Swart Moore with George ffoox in Lankashire. Yt was ye ffvrst time yt I soe Go ffox."

From sundry mention of him, it is learned that sometimes with Mr. Fox, but more often alone, he traveled all over Wales, preaching to any that would listen to him. But he

ARRANGING WELSH SETTLEMENT

did not accompany Mr. Fox in England. At Brecknock, in 1657, he "was moved of the Lord to speak in the Streets," which occasioned a tumult. At Tenby, he "went to the Steeple House" to speak, which was not unusual at that time, as, when the "priest" had finished his services, the church could be used by Presbyterians, or Independents, but John was arrested and jailed till Mr. Fox got him released. At several other places he was arrested for "speaking through the Town," and at his sometime home, Beaumaris, he was imprisoned "for public speaking." John also traveled through Wales preaching with John Burnyeat, in 1674, after Burnyeat's second return from America. Together, they attended a Quarterly Meeting at the home of Charles Lloyd, at Dolobran. Besse's "Sufferings" of the Quakers, of course, tells more of John ap John's experiences as a minister among Friends, and his are the earliest instances of persecution and annoyance in Wales.

John ap John had only one child, Phoebe, who married, 8, 3mo. 1689, John Mellor, or Miller, of the manor of Whitehough in Staffordshire, at the home of Richard Davies, in Rhuddalt. John ap John, as above, died at Whitehough, where he lived after the decease of his wife, Catharine, who died at Rhuddalt, 9, 11mo., 1694, and was buried at Trevor. Mr. Mellor died 3, 1m, 1718, aged 66 years and his wife Phoebe died 22, 8mo, 1734, at Leek, aged 69 years. Both buried at Basford. They had six children.

According to A Warrt. of our Capt: Thomas Holmes Survey'r Generall. Bearing date the 21st of 9br: 1684 84
members unto me for the Surveying of 2500 Acres of Land for Edward Jones & Company, upon the
said of Shackomaxon: fell Contiguous unto the City Liberty of harfor said and not disturbed the said
quality of Contiguous mentioned pines and unto every man by proportion, as by the Survill figure doth
as at large Appear with Near bounds and courses insert unto it figure by a Scale of 80 perch in an inch;

Da. Powell

Survd. ye Next per me and 241.6m.52 circuit to C.Ffrm
Afts: ye Next: January: 90: and 22.2mo 83. ye takes hhri. Chw ch: 8th: K. 1741

[numbers: 96 / 44 / 64 / 224]

21st: y: 3: m: 84

The Citty Liberty

N:3: W 796 perch
Evan Rees   135.4p   370 p
Jakes Wattkin 76.3p

32p   32p
377p

Lloyd   Thomas Lloyd   1773
                                         440
                                         ———
                                         308

(hand-drawn survey plat of long narrow parcels running between "Shoolkool" [Schuylkill] on the south and "N.E.W. 10 W" line on the north, with "Vacant Land" to the east)

Lot owners (left to right):
- Hugh Jones 76 p. / 318 p.
- William Jones 76½ p. / 256 p.
- Chadwalecler Morgan 76½ p. / Gryzon Robert 76½ p. / 356 p.
- Rees Jones 76½ p. / 316
- Robert Davis 148 p.
- Edward Jones Jr. 153 p. / 290
- Edward Owen 153 p. / Wm. 21 W 678 p.
- Edward Jones 153 p. / N.S.W. 679 p.
- Edward Reed / William Edward 153 p.
- Hugh Robert 306 p. / N.S.W. 65 W 663
- Katherin Thomas ye Relict of John Thomas 612 p. / N.E.W. 87 W 96
- Vacant Land / N.S.W. 71 W 656

Bottom measurements: 39 / 33 / 64 / 48 / 140 / 38 / 118 / 68 / 123
Shoolkool

  40
  13
 120
  96
  53

WELSH LAND COMPANIES

The patentees for 30,000 acres of the "Welsh Tract" lands granted by William Penn, to whom deeds were made out, may be considered self-constituted heads of seven "companies" for the division and sale of this land to the Welsh whom Penn and they hoped would be actual settlers on it, were, with the number of acres each "company" had for sale, as follows:

Co. 1. John ap Thomas, of Llaithgwm, Merionethshire,
    Dr. Edward Jones, of Bala, Merionethshire. 5,000
Co. 2. Charles Lloyd, of Dolobran, Montgomeryshire,
    Margaret Davies, widow, of Dolobran...... 5,000
Co. 3. John Bevan, of Treverigg, Glamorganshire. 2,000
Co. 4. John ap John, of Ruabon, Denbighshire,
    Dr. Thomas Wynne, of Caerwys, Flintshire. 5,000
Co. 5. Lewis ap David, of Llandewy Velfry, Pembrokeshire, ... 3,000
Co. 6. Richard ap Thomas, of Whitford Garne, Flintshire, ... 5,000
Co. 7. Richard Davies, of Welshpool, Montgomeryshire 5,000

It was one of Penn's earliest intentions to sell his land in blocks of 5,000 acres, he having adopted the Dutch plan of "patroon concessions." He certainly made his offer attractive to the Welsh by this "concession." It may not have been stated in so many words, but the purchaser of such block was a "patroon" after the Dutch idea, since those with whom he divided the land settled with him, in his grant, and looked on him as their leader, and it was

WELSH SETTLEMENT OF PENSYLVANIA

not necesary he should remove to, and reside with them on his purchase.

It may be seen that nine of the party of Welsh gentlemen who interviewed Penn, in May, 1681, and engaged to take 30,000 acres of land in his province, became concerned in these "companies," and real estate agents. The balance of 10,000 acres conditionally engaged by them and others present, was disposed of subsequently by Penn himself, or his agents, in small lots to actual settlers, and to parties who bought for speculation only, and 10,000 acres reserved in addition, also in the "Welsh Tract," were taken up in a few years by Welshmen, making their total purchase of 50,000 acres, the extent of this "Welsh Tract."

Excepting for names and amount of land, the patents to the first purchasers from "William Penn, of Worminghurst, in the county of Sussex, Esq.," were nearly all of even date, namely, "the Fifteenth Day of September, in the year of our Lord One thousand six hundred Eighty and one in the CCCIII yeare of the Reigne of King Charles the Second over England".

But there was an important difference in the deeds to these "first purchasers," which turned out to be the cause of considerable trouble in after years, as we may see, and was particularly disappointing to the heads of "Companies" No. 1 and 4, and their grantees. From the deeds of "Thomas & Jones," and "John & Wynne" to their grantees, it appears that they and others made up by subscription the purchase money for the two blocks they took, and that they were only "trustees" in the matter of the purchase, and, like the other subscribers' purchase money, only interested to the amount contributed, whereas the heads of the other five "companies" bought on their own accounts, hoping to sell off what land they did not wish to retain. But Penn, and his representative in Pensylvania, considered all the heads of these companies to be "trustees," and treated them alike, and if they had not been Quakers there would

ADVENTURERS FOR LAND

have been much litigation over land claims. As it was, Penn's commissioners, and the Board of Property, had much difficulty adjusting them.

Penn's deeds to the "trustees" cite the date and consideration, the location of the territory, etc., granted to him, by Royal Letters Patent, 4 March 1681, from which he conveyed to them the various amounts of their purchases, of course, without giving their locations, and the conditions and restrictions under which he made the conveyances. The consideration being £100 sterling for each tract of 5,000 acres located in one lot, "if possible, in his province, and subject to quit-rent of one shilling for every hundred acres of the said five thousand acres att or upon the first day of March for ever."

The deeds to the "companies," as well as those from them to those who bought of them, were long afterwards recorded in Philadelphia County, and were confirmed by Penn's land commissioners. At first, much to their astonishment and disappointment, half of the land called for in "Welsh Deeds" was laid out to the "first purchasers" in the townships of Merion, Radnor, and Haverford, and subsequently the balance was laid out in the townships of Goshen, New Town, or Uwchland in the Tract.

For two years and a half this method obtained, and Penn had given no order to survey the 30,000 acre tract bought, so the Welsh could know exactly its bounds, and if they lay within their rights. Urged by them to do this, Penn gave finally the following warrant for survey, to Thomas Holmes, his surveyor general:—

"Whereas divers considerable persons among ye Welsh Friends have requested me yt all ye Lands Purchased of me by theos of North Wales and South Wales, together with ye adjacent counties to ym as Herefordshire, Shorpshire, and Cheshire, about fourty thousand acres, may be lay'd out contiguously as one Barony, alledging yt ye number allready come and suddenly to come, are such as

[35]

WELSH SETTLEMENT OF PENSYLVANIA

will be capable of planting ye same much with in ye proportion allowed by ye custom of ye country, & so not lye in large useless vacancies.

"And because I am inclined and determined to agree and favour ym wth any reasonable Conveniency and priviledge:—I do hereby charge thee and strictly require thee to lay out ye sd tract of Land in as uniform a manner as conveniently may be, upon ye west side of Skoolkill river, running three miles upon ye same, and two miles backward, & then extend ye parallel with ye river six miles, and to run westwardly so far as this ye sd quantity of land be Compleately surveyed unto ym.

"Given at Pennsbury, ye 13th 1 mo. 1684."

Under instructions from the surveyor-general, dated 4. 2mo. 1684, his deputy, David Powel, laid out the tract, "in method of townships lately appointed by the Governor, att five thousand acres for a township." But it was not until 25. 5mo. 1687, that the bounds of the Welsh Tract were defined, and publicly known.

The next item found concerning the "Welsh Tract," three years later, is a minute of the Commissioners' meeting, held "in ye Council Room at Philad'a ye 25th of ye 5 Mo. 1687". It mentions the "Tract of Land, about 40,000 acres, w'ch was laid out by vertue of a warrant from the proprietary and Governor, bearing Date ye 13th day of the first month, 1684, for the Purchasers of North and South Wales and adjacent Counties of Herefordshire, Shorpshire, and Cheshire, * * * it is bounded:—

Beginning at the Skoolkill [at the Falls], thence running West [by] South West, on the City Liberties, 2256 Perches [a little over seven miles, along Township, or City Line Road] to Darby Creek.

Thence following up the several courses thereof [i.e. Darby Creek] to New Town, 988 Perches [a little over three miles], to a Corner post by Crumb Creek.

ADVENTURERS FOR LAND

Thence down the several Courses thereof [Crum Creek], 460 Perches, [not quite a mile and a half].
Thence West and by South, by a line of Trees, 2080 Perches [six miles and a half].
Thence North [by] North West, by a line of Trees, 1920 Perches [six miles].
Thence East, and by North, by a line of Trees, 3040 Perches [nine and a half miles].
Thence East and by South 1120 Perches [three and a half miles].
Thence South [and by] South East 256 Perches [about a mile and a quarter].
Thence East [and by] North East 640 Perches [not quite a mile and a half].
Thence South [and by] South East 1204 Perches [a fraction over three and a half miles].
Thence East [and by] North East 668 Perches [a little over two miles] to the Skoolkill.
Thence down the several courses thereof [Schuylkill river] to the Place of beginning."

This tract covered 62½ square miles.

So it was not till six years after the Welsh gentlemen engaged to take 40,000 acres, that the tract was surveyed for them. There is a plot of the tract in the Surveyor General's office, at Harrisburg, but it does not agree with the bounds given above. The survey included the townships of Lower Merion, a portion of Upper Merion, Haverford, Radnor, Tredyffrin, Whiteland, Willistown, East Town, Goshen, and part of West Town.

But in all these years, the Welsh were not idle, nor was Penn. All interested were "booming" the land. The Welsh trustees had disposed of their trusts, and Penn had sold a million acres.

This was not the only "Welsh Tract" in Pensylvania. Subsequently lands were sold to other Welshmen, and we

[37]

WELSH SETTLEMENT OF PENSYLVANIA

had "Welsh Tracts" in Chester Co., and at Gwynedd, or 'North Wales," and then in New Castle Co. (Delaware). The Carolinas also had "Welsh Tracts," but with these Penn was not concerned.

The material side of immigration was made as attractive as possible by nicely gotten up pamphlets issued by Penn, or his agents, setting forth, in addition to his advertising, in glowing terms, the general recommendations of his Province and land, the social advantages gained by removal there, and the approximate outside cost of it; in detail, just how to conduct a farm in the new country and make it pay. One of his advertising papers, addressed "to such persons as are inclined * * * to the Province of Pensylvania,"* tells attractively what expense a man with £100 cash would be under if he bought from him 500 acres, and transported himself, wife, a child, and two men servants to his purchase. It being understood that "500 acres of uncleared land is equivolent to 50 acres of cleared English, or Welsh land."

By taking along to Pensylvania certain small articles, cloth, clothes, harness, implements, etc., and selling them there the land would be paid for by the 50% profit derived. The transportation of the party would cost not more than £38.2.6, with new clothes, "Shurtes, Hatts, Shooes, Stokins, and Drawyers," a ton of things to sell, and "four gallons of Brandy, and 24 pounds of Suger for the Voyage." Arriving at the purchase in early summer, encamping and clearing fifteen acres for plowing, cutting out best timber for house, according to directions, planting, erecting the log-cabin, and getting in the crops, brings the experience of this party up to winter, when the prospect is not pleasant, as they have only green wood to burn. The barn is built, and in the spring stock is bought, and first crop sold.

---

*Pa. Mag., IV., p. 331.

ADVENTURERS FOR LAND

Now, the settler takes "account of stock." He finds he has paid out from his £100, in one year:—

"To Passage and Cloaths	£38.02.06
"To House and Barn	15.10.00
"To living expenses one year	17.17.06
"To Stock	24.10.00
	£96.00.00

His receipts and assets, "per Contr. Creditor," he finds as follows:—

Crop valued at	£59.10.00
House and barn, value,	30.00.00
Stock, cost,	24.10.00
Land, with 15 ac. improved,	26.05.00
Remaining cash	4.00.00
Total assets	£144.05.00

It may thus be seen the immigrant has had a good first year, "on paper." The receipts from crops paid for the fifteen-acre field (the profit of goods brought over having paid for the tract), and for the house and barn. Is it any wonder that the humble Welsh willingly removed.

The directions for building the log house are particular as to trees, how to get them ready, etc. It should be "thirty foot long and eighteen foot broad," "with a partition neer the middle, and an other to divide one end of the House into two small Rooms," and a loft over all, the floor of which to be of "clapbord," but "the lower flour is the Ground." "This may seem a mean way of Building, but 'tis sufficient and safest for ordinary beginners." "An ordinary House, and a good Stock, is the Planters Wisdom."

Only three years after immigrants began coming into Pensylvania, there were "evil reports" given out in England "by many Enemies to this new Country," because it promised to be a growing colony of non-conformists, and because others had other colony schemes they were trying to float. Then there were those who could not believe Penn's astonishing statements in his advertisements of his land, and these were as much to be dreaded as the "Enemies."

In order to head-off these aspersions against Pensylvania, Governor Penn asked some of the leading men in the Province to give him their opinions of the country from personal observation and experience. One, Dr. Nicholas More, wrote him, "Green Spring, 13 Sep. 1686," for publication it may be imagined, a long, cheerful account* reciting the "evil reports," "as if we were ready to Famish, and that the Land is so barren, the Climet so hot, that English Grain, Roots, and Herbs do not once come to Maturity, and what grows, to be little worth." This he pronounced bosh. And he gave prices current here for a hundred products and articles, and all possible profits on them.

But what would most appeal to farmers, Welsh or English, was what he wrote of grain crops. He said, "I have had seventy Ears of Rye upon one single Root, proceeding from one single Corn; 45 of Wheat; 80 of Oats; 10, 12, and 14 of Barley out of one Corn; I took the Curiosity to tell one of the twelve Ears from one Grain, and there was in it 45 Grains on that Ear; above 3,000 of Oats from one single Corn." ["Quaker Oats"?], etc. "But it would seem a Romance rather than a Truth, if I should speak what I have seen in these things."

This must have convinced the Welsh farmers.

In referring thus to Penn's advertising his lands, I do not lose sight of the fact that his Pensylvania scheme was "in the course of his pious life,"—"continually and various ways were employed in promoting the happiness of mankind, both in their religious and civil capacity," and attribute any sordid aspects to it. The advertisements

---
*Pa. Mag., IV., p. 447.

are only mentioned to show the method pursued in trying to sell, and to also show that he knew how to "sell without samples," and that he was a pioneer in the real estate business, if not in the "mail-order business," and that as an all-round business man he was "far and away ahead of his time," and would have been the first great "captain of industries" if he had had faithful lieutenants, or, if, in a word, his whole endeavor had not been a chimera.

However, his real estate venture throughout was "clean." There is no evidence of any scandals connected with it. He may have had paid agents to sell his land for him, and he may have paid commissions on sales, and the "trustees" may have sold some lands at advance prices, and some may have bought to speculate, but what of it? Such methods then were as proper as they are to-day.

The "company," some of whose members were the first to come over, and have land laid out in the Welsh Tracts, was that of John ap Thomas and Dr. Edward Jones. This was in August, 1682, a year after Penn's first ship-load of colonists had arrived here, and two months before he himself came on his first visit to America. There has been much told of these very first arrivals in three ships, so it is only necessary here to repeat that the first boat-load arrived in the Delaware in August, 1681, and the third in the following December, and that the immigrants landed at Upland (now Chester), and remained there, supposing it to be the site of the city Penn had said he was going to lay out, till after the first surveyor came over, in June, 1682, up to which time twenty-three other immigrant ships had arrived.

The surveyor, Thomas Holme, after looking around, probably told some one that he was going to recommend that the city be located further up the river, at the Swede's farm, called Wicaco, for in July there was a great scramble of immigrants to that locality. Here Dr. Jones found them when he arrived in August, 1682.

WELSH SETTLEMENT OF PENSYLVANIA

When Penn came in the following October, 1682, he found his first English colonists, like squatters, living in huts and "caves," on the Delaware, where they supposed the city would be laid out, and, as first arrivals, they would have the choice lots. This may, or may not have influenced him to order his city laid out here, but it was months before it was plotted. The site of the new city seems to have been known or well guessed at two months before Penn came, as Dr. Jones mentions "the town of Philadelphia" in his letter, hereafter given, written 13, 6mo. 1682. For this reason it has been believed that the Doctor selected or suggested the site of the city, and possibly named it, as Penn tells it was named "before it was born."

Now, that we have reviewed the inception, founding, and establishing of the "Welsh Tract," on and beyond the Schuylkill, we proceed to consider its first and pioneer settlers, "the company of Thomas and Jones"—the builders of the Merion Meeting House.

MERION FRIENDS' MEETING HOUSE, CIRCA 1830.

THOMAS & JONES' LAND PATENT

Beginning with the Thomas & Jones "Company," and land, which was "ye first within ye tract of land in the Province" to be laid out, we will consider the companies in succession.

There are extant documents like confirmatory deeds, each having the title, "An Indenture where severall are concerned," and bearing date of March 18th, others "The first day of Aprill, in the four and thirtieth year of our sovereign Charles, Second," [1682]. They recite the conveyance of the 5,000 acres of land by William Penn to John ap Thomas and Edward Jones, and that "there have been two severall Indentures, ye one of bargain and sale for one year, bearing date ye 16th day of September in the three and thirtieth year of his majesty's reign [1681]*, the other bearing date ye 17th day of the same month and year," both made between William Penn and John ap Thomas and Edward Jones. And, "that for and in consideration of the sum of One Hundred pounds of good and lawfull money of England to him in hand paid by Jno. T. & Edw. Jones, he did grant [to them] the full portion of 5,000 acres of land, * * * ye first within ye tract of land in the Province," "bearing date ye 11th day of July then last past, paying one shilling for every one hundred acres of ye said 5,000 upon the first day of March forever."

This deed then recites that "others than John ap Thomas and Edward Jones have contributed towards this £100

---

*Charles the Second began his first regnal year in 1660, but as it was his restoration, his first regnal year was called in documents the 12th year of his reign, making his reign date from 30 Jan. 1648-9, the beginning of the Commonwealth. Therefore, in the above deed, the 33 Charles II. was 1681.

[45]

WELSH SETTLEMENT OF PENSYLVANIA

of purchase money," and that "the said John and Edward are as Trustees," they being personally responsible for the amounts to which the others and themselves have individually subscribed. That "for £25 which John ap Thomas has subscribed, he shall have 1250 acres [one-fourth interest], and Edward Jones in like proportion, and that the residue of the land be of equal goodness."

These documents are confirmation that 16 September 1681 was the date of the original grant to John ap Thomas and Dr. Edward Jones, or the "Thomas & Jones Co.," which for convenience, and because its land was the first laid out, and its subscribers the first to arrive here, and founded the Merion Meeting, we will call "Company No. 1."

Company No. 1. There were seventeen Welsh Friends, one a woman, who subscribed to the £100 purchase money for the 5,000 acres in the Welsh Tract, which John ap John and Dr. Edward Jones engaged for them. The names of these subscribers and purchasers are preserved in a memorandum written by John ap Thomas, found among his papers, entitled:—

COMPANY NUMBER ONE

"An account of wt sum of money every ffriend in Penllyn hath Layd out to buy land in Pensylvania & wt quantity of Acres of Land each is to have and wt sum of Quit Rents falls upon every one."

	Pounds.			Acres.	Quit Rent.	
John Tho	25	0s	0d	1250	12s	6d
Hugh Robt	12	10	0	625	6	3
Edd Jones	6	5	0	312 1/2	3	1 1/2
Robt Davis	6	5	0	312 1/2	3	1 1/2
Evan Rees	6	5	0	312 1/2	3	1 1/2
John Edd	6	5	0	312 1/2	3	1 1/2
Edd Owen	6	5	0	312 1/2	3	1 1/2
Will Edd	3	2	6	156 1/4	1	6 1/3
Edd Rees	3	2	6	156 1/4	1	6 1/3
Will Jones	3	2	6	156 1/4	1	6 1/3
Tho Rich	3	2	6	156 1/4	1	6 1/3
Rees John W	3	2	6	156 1/4	1	6 1/3
Tho lloyd	3	2	6	156 1/4	1	6 1/3
Cadd Morgan	3	2	6	156 1/4	1	6 1/3
John Watkin	3	2	6	156 1/4	1	6 1/3
Hugh John	3	2	6	156 1/4	1	6 1/3
Gainor Robt	3	2	6	156 1/4	1	6 1/3
	£100	0	0	5000	£2	10

From this MSS. and from the deeds for this land to the subscribers, we have the names, locations of their residences, their stations in life, and number of acres bought by each of the subscribers to the fund of £100.

"John Tho". "John ap Thomas, of Llaithgwm, gentleman," took 1250 acres, paying £25.

"Edd Jones". "Edward Jones, chyrurgion, of Bala," the partner in the trusteeship, took for himself only 312½ acres, paying £6.5.0.

"Hugh Robt". Hugh Roberts, of Kiltalgarth, gentleman," purchased 625 acres, paying £12.10s.

WELSH SETTLEMENT OF PENSYLVANIA

The following each bought 312½ acres, each paying £6. 5s.:

"Robt David". "Robert ap David, of Gwern Evel Ismynydd, yeoman."

"Evan Rees". "Evan ap Rees, of Penmaen, grocer."

"John Edd." "John ap Edwards, of Nant Lleidiog, yeoman."

"Edd Owen". "Edward ap Owen, 'late of Doleyserre,' gentleman."

The following each bought 156¼ acres, each paying £3. 2s. 6d.:

"Will Edd." "William ap Edward, of Ucheldre, or Ueneldri, yeoman."

"Edd Rees". "Edward ap Rees, of Kiltalgarth, gentleman."

"Gainor Robt". "Gainor Roberts, of Kiltalgarth, spinster."

"Will Jones". "William ap John alias Jones, of Bettws, yeoman."

"Tho Rich". "Thomas ap Richard alias Prichard, of Nant Lleidiog, yeoman."

"Hugh John". "Hugh ap John alias Jones, of Nant Lleidiog, yeoman."

"Rees John W". "Rees ap John ap William, alias Rees Jones, of Llanglynin, yeoman."

"Tho lloyd." "Thomas Lloyd, of Llangower, yeoman."

"Cadd Morgan". "Cadwalader Morgan, of Gwernevel, yeoman."

"John Watkin". "John Watkins, of Gwernevel, 'bathilor'."

As the homes of all of these subscribers were in the hundred of Penllyn, in Merionethshire, it was natural that the township in Pensylvania, where their land lay, should be given the name Merion by the surveyor-general, and subsequently so many settlements in it should be called after Merionethshire places.*

Although the deeds of lease and release from Penn to Thomas & Jones for over 5,000 acres, were executed 16 and 17 September 1681, about four months after they had the interview with Penn in London, the transfers, by deeds, from them, of their proportions, to the several subscribers were not made till the following Spring, as these latter deeds of conveyance (copied into Books C.I and C.II in office of the Recorder of Deeds, Philadelphia), all bear dates between 28 February and 1 April, 1682, and they were not recorded till 22 3mo. 1684, but the confirmative patents were not granted till in 1702-1703. These deeds from Thomas & Jones have the same witnesses who were some of the others of these grantees, excepting, of course, the parties to the deed, and are all drawn very particularly as to facts, containing the "tripping clause," to wit: "Whereas besides the said John Thomas and Edward Jones, chirurgeon, others have contributed some part and proportion of the said sum of £100 for and towards the purchase of the premises, and whereas, though the said John Thomas and Edward Jones

---

*Some of these Welsh Friends of Merionethshire, who were signers of a marriage certificate, in 1mo. 1678-9, at the Penllyn Monthly Meeting, it will be seen came over and settled in the Welsh Tract.

Owen Humphrey.
John Humphrey.
Richard Humphrey.
Humphrey Owen.
Rowland Owen.
John Owen.
Anne Owen.
Elizabeth Owen (*bis*).
Evan John.
Rees John.
Gainor John.
Humphrey Reynolds.
Rees Evan.
John William.

Cadwalader Thomas.
John Thomas.
Elizabeth Thomas.
Rowland Ellis.
Hugh Roberts.
Edward Vaughan.
Ellis Rees.
Ellin Rees.
Gwen Rees.
John Howell.
Daniel Samuel.
Joseph Samuel.
Lydia Samuel.
Rebecca Samuel.

WELSH SETTLEMENT OF PENSYLVANIA

were intrusted to take the conveyances of all the said premises, yet they only intended to have their separate shares and proportions of the said 5,000 acres, according to the said sum they have laid out as part of the said £100 as only Trustees as to the rest of the said 5,000 acres, and for that it was also agreed that no benefit or survivorship should be taken between them." Mr. Thomas had paid in only £25, as mentioned, and Dr. Jones £6.5.0. This identifying Messrs. Thomas and Jones as only "trustees," was a serious matter to them, as will appear.

This distribution cleaned up these 5,000 acres, and reimbursed the trustees, Messrs. Thomas and Jones, for the £100 they had advanced to pay Mr. Penn.

Several of these purchasers did not remove to Pensylvania, but their land was laid out and surveyed along with the rest, and subsequently they sold out to others, who did remove and settle on it, or to their fellow contributors, as will appear later.

The earliest mention found, outside of the "trustee's deeds," which did not, however, give the locations of the lands, which was to be determined "as soon as the 5,000 acres is laid out," as the deeds state, is in a letter of Dr. Edward Jones, dated "Skoolkill River, ye 26th of ye 6mo. 1682," wherein he mentions the 2,500 acres on the Schuylkill as "ye Country lots." From the wording of the Doctor's statements, in this letter, given elsewhere, it would seem he thought his company's land, or at least the half of it, 2,500 acres, should have been laid out in "ye town lot," (in Philadelphia) "called now Wicoco." The earliest location of the land on a map was on that of Pensylvania, made by the surveyor-general of the Province, Thomas Holme, which he began to compile after Penn's first departure from America. But it is here only in outline, and indicates the land of "Edward Jones and Company 17 Families." Next, there is the unsatisfactory original draft of the lands included in this Welsh Tract, preserved at Harrisburg, which desig-

COMPANY NUMBER ONE

nates the land of "Edward Jones and Company, containing 2,500 acres, being 17 devisions." and then Powell's rough draft of the 2,500 acres, on the "city liberties's" line, and the Schuylkill river. Although a block of 5,000 was bought, it was told at the time to Dr. Jones, that because of the great demand for land in the Schuylkill neighborhood, by Penn's order only half of this amount could be laid out there. This, as will appear, was a cause of much dissatisfaction, as only part of purchase would be near the city, and the balance, away off in the wilds of Goshen, where the city of West Chester has grown up.

It is written on this extant draft or plot, preserved at Harrisburg, made by a deputy surveyor, David Powell, of the half of the total purchase made by Thomas & Jones, which lay on the west side of the Schuylkill, from above the Falls and up the river, that the first, or rough survey, was made by Charles Ashcom, on warrant from Mr. Powell, dated 24, 6mo. 1682, and that another rough survey was made on warrant "from ye Gov'r, date 22d 1 mo. 83."

From the Thomas & Jones deeds to each other, and from them jointly to the other parties to this purchase, comes the knowledge that the lots, of whatsoever size, when conveyed, were numbered, and only the number of a deed and the amount of acres going with it were given to the first surveyor, who laid them out accordingly, so the various grantees in this transaction had no part in selecting their land, and it was a lottery in what position, as to the others in this "company," the land would be laid out. The only stipulation on this point in the deeds was, it shall be "land of equal goodness with the residue, or as shall fall out by lot." This was very likely not a satisfactory arrangement, and may account for the many exchanges and sales between these lot holders soon after coming into possession, and getting acquainted with the quality and lay of the land.

Mr. Powell's mem. on the final and extant plot, dated "20th of ye 3d mo, 84," says, "According to A War't from

WELSH SETTLEMENT OF PENSYLVANIA

Capt Thomas Holmes, Survey'r Genrall, Bearing dat the 24th of ye 1st mo. 84, directed unto me for the Subdividing of 2,500 Acres of Land for Edward Joans & Company upon the west sid of Skoolkool above fals Contageous unto the City Liberty. I therefor Laid out and Subdivided the said quantity of Land, 25th of 1st mo. at the befor mentioned place, and unto every man by proportion as by these sevrall figure doth now at large Apeer with their bounds and courses enterd in ye sd figur by a skale of 80 perch in an inch. Da Powell."

In a general way, these 2,500 acres were bounded at first as follows: North, "Vakant Land," East "Skoolkool" river, South, "The Citty Libarty," and West, two tracts of Charles Lloyd and Thomas Lloyd, or Company No. 2.

This first draft of the sub-divisions of the "Thomas & Jones" land is here reproduced. The dimensions of the 17 lots may be given correctly, but the map certainly is not drawn to "skale of 80 perch in an inch." It has been worked out that "the areas of the several lots aggregate 2,444¾ acres," which was a fairly good survey of 2,500 acres at that time, though the area by modern survey would amount to about 3,200 acres. The charges for making the first survey for Dr. Jones was over £25, but he hoped "better orders will be taken shortly about" the bill, and he would not have to pay so much. But from his own account, he was lucky in getting the work done so soon after he arrived, as there were hundreds demanding surveys. To correct this first hurried survey of Mr. Ashcom, in 1682, the draft of Mr. Powell was made in 1684, naming the owner in 1682.

In all of Penn's deeds to the first Welsh companies and to other settlers, and in their deeds to their grantees, there is a safe-guarding clause that protection is guaranteed against Indian claims to the lands conveyed. This was because Penn had not yet purchased the land from the Indians as he proposed doing.

COMPANY NUMBER ONE

After his arrival here, in October, 1682, he began at once to enter upon treaties with the Indian chiefs for the purchase of their domains, taking for granted they were the proper ones to pass the titles, so as to extinguish their rights, and make good the deeds he had issued. The boundaries of the tracts the Indians resigned were, of course, vague, as were the original surveys made of the lands for Penn's grantees, since the stations were natural objects. As to the land bought by Thomas & Jones, and then cccupied by it, and some of the other tracts beyond the Schuylkill:

1683, June 25, William Penn bought from Chief Wingbone, whose "autograph" is extant, all his rights and claims to the land lying on the west side of the Schuylkill, beginning at the Lower Falls, and "up the river," and "backward."

1683, July 16, William Penn brought from the chiefs named Secane and Idquoquehan, all the land lying between the Schuylkill (at Manayunk) and Chester Creek, and as far up the Schuylkill as Conshohocken Hill.

On 22 December, 1701, the minutes of the Commissioners of Property record that grantees of John ap Thomas and Dr. Jones tract were the first of the Welsh to have their deeds confirmed to them, when there was a possibility of losing their lands, of which elsewhere.

Those who appeared, and to whom warrants of resurvey were issued at this time, 1701-2-3, their lands being made up partly of the original purchases, and what was acquired subsequently:—

"To Hugh Roberts for 549¾ acres in Goshen, 482 thereof [bought] of Jno. ap Jno's.

"To Robert Roberts and Owen Roberts 200 acres each, in Meirion.

"To Edward Reese 205¼ acres, in Meirion.

"To Edward Jones' Survey on 200 acres in Goshen, and a Resurvey on 151¼ in Meirion, and 153 in Goshen.

WELSH SETTLEMENT OF PENSYLVANIA

"To Edward Jones, Jun'r, 306¼ acres, half in Meirion. ½ in Goshen.

"Robert David, 274¼ acres in Meirion, and 234½ in Goshen.

"Richard Walter 100 acres in Meirion.

"Richard Rees als Jones, 137½ in Meirion, and 75 in Goshen.

"To Cadwallader Morgan 202 acres and ½ in Meirion.

"To John Roberts, malter, 306 acres and ½, ¾ thereof in Goshen, ¼ in Meirion.

"To Hugh Jones 768 and ¼ acres in Meirion.

"To Griffith John 194 acres.

"To Rob't William 76¼ acres in Goshen.

"To Ellis David 151 acres and ½.

"To Thomas Jones, Robert Jones and Cadwallader Jones, 1225 acres, ½ thereof in Meirion, and ½ in Goshen, left them by their father, John Thomas, the original Purchaser.

"To John Roberts, Cordwainer, of Goshen, 78¼ acres in Goshen."

Only seven of these were original grantees in the tract.

From the Commissioners' "Minutes of ye Welsh Purchasers," we find further as to the distribution of the land of the original contributors, and who got some of this tract:—

Hugh Roberts had by deed, dated 28 February, 1681-2, from Thomas & Jones, 625 acres, laid out, on warrant of 1683, half in Merion and half in Goshen township. He also by deed, 17.6.1694, bought of William Edward 76½ acres, and by deed, 1 April, 1682, from John Watkin, 156 acres. He had in all 842½ acres net. He gave 200 acres out of the 625 acres to his son Robert Roberts on his second marriage, in 1689, and 200 acres out of the balance of the 625 acres and what he bought of Edwards, to his son Owen Roberts on his marriage in 1696. He also sold 100 to Edward Griffith, and 100 to Robert William, and 100 to Thomas Griffith. He further bought 156 acres "of J. Walk"

[John Walker?], and sold 74 acres to Abel Thomas. Reported, that he had sold 776½ acres, and had only 67¾ acres remaining. The land he sold to Messrs. Edward and Thomas Griffith, and Robert William, lay in Merion township, and also all but 67¾ in same place.

William Edward, who bought 153½ acres, through Thomas & Jones, with a questionable right to certain "liberty land," sold 76 acres, as above, and 76 acres in Goshen township, to Robert William.

Edward Rees had deed, 1.2mo. 1682, from Thomas & Jones, for 156½ acres, plus, as supposed, some "liberty land." He sold 76 acres in Goshen township to Ellis David. Of the balance, 78¼ acres and 125 acres he bought from Thomas Lloyd, being out of the purchase of Charles Lloyd and Margaret Davies, and two acres from Dr. Jones, all 205¼ acres located in Merion township.

Edward Jones, the doctor, as above, took for himself only 312½ acres, which came out only 306¼ acres on survey. He sold two acres as above and had 151¼ acres left in Merion, and 153 acres in Goshen township. Later, he bought 200 acres in Goshen from Richard Thomas.

Edward Owen, by deed 1 April, 1682, bought through Thomas & Jones, 312½ acres. By deed, 1.1.1694-5, he sold 150 acres in Merion to Robert David, all he had there. The balance of his land lay in Goshen township.

John ap Edward, by deed 18.1.1681-2, from Thomas & Jones had 312½ acres; half was located in Merion, and rest in Goshen township. His son, Edward Jones, inherited all in 1686-7.

Robert David, by deed 18.1.1681, from Thomas & Jones, received 312½ acres, located half in Merion, half in Goshen. He sold, by deed 1.10mo. 1694, 25 acres of his Merion place to Richard Walter, and had remaining 281 acres, to which he added 156¼ acres, bought, by deed 18.5.1683, of Evan Rees. He also had 150 acres from Griffith Owen. After deductions and allowances and additions and sales, he had

[55]

WELSH SETTLEMENT OF PENSYLVANIA

274½ acres in Merion, and 234½ acres in Goshen. Richard Walter bought as above from Robert David, 25 acres and 75 acres. These parcels lay in Merion township.

Rees Jones, by deed 18.2.1682, bought through Thomas & Jones, 156¼ acres in Merion. He sold 50 acres to Cadwalader Morgan, and by his will bequeathed his land in Goshen to his sons John and Evan, and 100 acres to his son, Richard Rees Jones, who bought from "John Roberts, cordwainer," 37½ acres (part of the Thomas & Charles Lloyd land), which land "the said Thomas [Lloyd] bequeathed by will to the said Jno Roberts, his nephew." So Richard Rees Jones held 137½ acres in Merion township. He also held 75 acres in Goshen township, granted to him by his Uncle, Evan John William, by deed, which lot was a portion of the Richard David purchase.

Thomas Prichard bought through Thomas & Jones, 156¼ acres. By his deed of 16 July, 1684, he conveyed the same to Rees Jones, who then had 306½ acres.

Cadwalader Morgan bought, by deed, 1.2mo. 1682, from Thomas & Jones, 156½ acres. He sold 76½ acres in Goshen to "John Roberts, malter," and retained balance in Merion township. He increased his Merion holdings with 50 acres bought of Rees Jones, and 76½ acres in Merion, which he had by deed 18.4.1684, from John William, so had 202½ acres in Merion township.

Gainor Roberts, spinster, bought by deed, 1.2.1682, from Thomas & Jones, 156 acres. One-half lay in Merion, and "John Roberts, the malter, held balance, in Goshen township. John Roberts, malter, had 75 acres from Gainor Roberts, 75 acres from Cadw. Morgan, by deed of 7.7.1687, and on this date he bought 75 acres from Hugh Jones. So he held 306½ acres, one-fourth in Merion, balance in Goshen.

"Thomas Lloyd (not the Presid't)," was a grantee, by deed of 1 April, 1682, from Thomas & Jones, for 156 acres. He bequeathed his land to his nephew, "John Roberts, cordwainer," who sold of his inheritance 37½ acres to Richard Jones, and 37½ acres to Griffith John, of Merion. So he held 78½ acres in Goshen township.

William Jones' son, John William, inherited of the Thomas and Jones tract, 156¼ acres, three acres was his estimated share of the "liberty land," as in each case of this amount, "liberty land," when allowed always reduced township holding. He sold all his land; to Cadwalader Morgan 76½, and balance to Edward Rees, who sold to Ellis David.

John Watkins received by deed, 1 April, 1682, from Thomas & Jones, 156¼ acres "less 3 acres of liberty land." He sold all to Hugh Roberts, by deed dated 23.4.1684.

Hugh Jones received by deed, 18 March, 1681, from Thomas & Jones, 156¼ acres. He sold John Roberts, malter, 76¼ acres. He and his son held the rest, in Merion township.

Evan Rees received by deed, 18 March, 1681-2, from Thomas & Jones, 312½ acres, "less 6¼ ac. of liberty land." By deeds dated 18.3.1683, he sold out to Robert David and Griffith John. The latter bought 156¼ acres from Evan Rees, and 38 from "John Roberts, shoemaker," of Goshen township.

But these conveyances are given more fully in the sketches that follow of these original grantees. These transfers of land are of much genealogical interest, for they give the names of newcomers, and approximate the time of arrival here.

There is plenty of evidence in the Philadelphia county land records, as may be seen, that the early Welsh Friends made many changes in their holdings in the twenty years following their removal here. Some increased their acreage, some decreased to strengthen the balance, some sold out entirely and settled elsewhere outside of Merion. The land transactions were freqently before the Board of Land Commissioners for adjustment and settlement. It found it

WELSH SETTLEMENT OF PENSYLVANIA

necessary finally, for its own better understanding of the situation in the Welsh "Towns" to learn as near as possible in whose names was the land Penn had granted them. In this matter, the Board, in its Minutes, under date of 22nd 10br 1701, recorded:

"Order issued the 1st inst. for taking some Measures to regulate the Welsh Tract; some of the Chiefs of that Nation in this Province having met and concerted the Methods to be taken in order to the Regulations, it was agreed: That, in as much as the Welsh Purchasers of the Propr'ry were by large Quantities of acres in one Pair, by Deeds granted to one or two Persons only, under which several other Purchasers had a Share, the Gen'l Deeds of one Purchase should be first brought in with an acc't of all other Persons who had a Share in such Purchase, also an account in whose possession the Respective Lands of every under Purchase now are."

"As for the Merion land holders in 1701, "the Propr'ry Deeds to John ap Thomas and Edward Jones for 5,000 acres was brought in with all such necessary acc'ts".

From their statement we learn that about 1,884 acres of their patent was not located in Merion township, but in Goshen township, and that the following number of the original Welsh Friends and descendants only held land in Merion township, the total of their holdings being about 3,000 acres. Newcomers holding about 445 acres.

The Merion holders and acreage being, about January, 1700, n. s.:—

"Robert Roberts, 200.
"Owen Roberts, 200.
"Edward Rees, 205¼.
"Edward Jones, 151¼ and 353 in Goshen township.
"Edward Jones, Jr., 158⅛ and 158⅛ in Goshen township.
"Robert David, 274¼ and 234½ in Goshen township.

COMPANY NUMBER ONE

"Richard Rees Jones, 137½ and 75 in Goshen township.

"Cadwalader Morgan, 202½.

"John Roberts (Pencoid), 76½ and 230 in Goshen township.

"Hugh Jones, 768¼.

"Thomas Jones, Robert Jones, Cadwallader Jones, 612½ (left to them by their father, John ap Thomas); and the same amount in Goshen."

Other land owners in Merion township, at this time, were Richard Walter, 100 acres; Griffith John, 194 acres, and Ellis David, 151½ acres, and in Goshen township, Hugh Roberts, 67 acres; Robert William, 76¼ acres, and John Roberts, the shoemaker, 78¼ acres, who sold inherited land in Merion to "John Roberts, Gent."

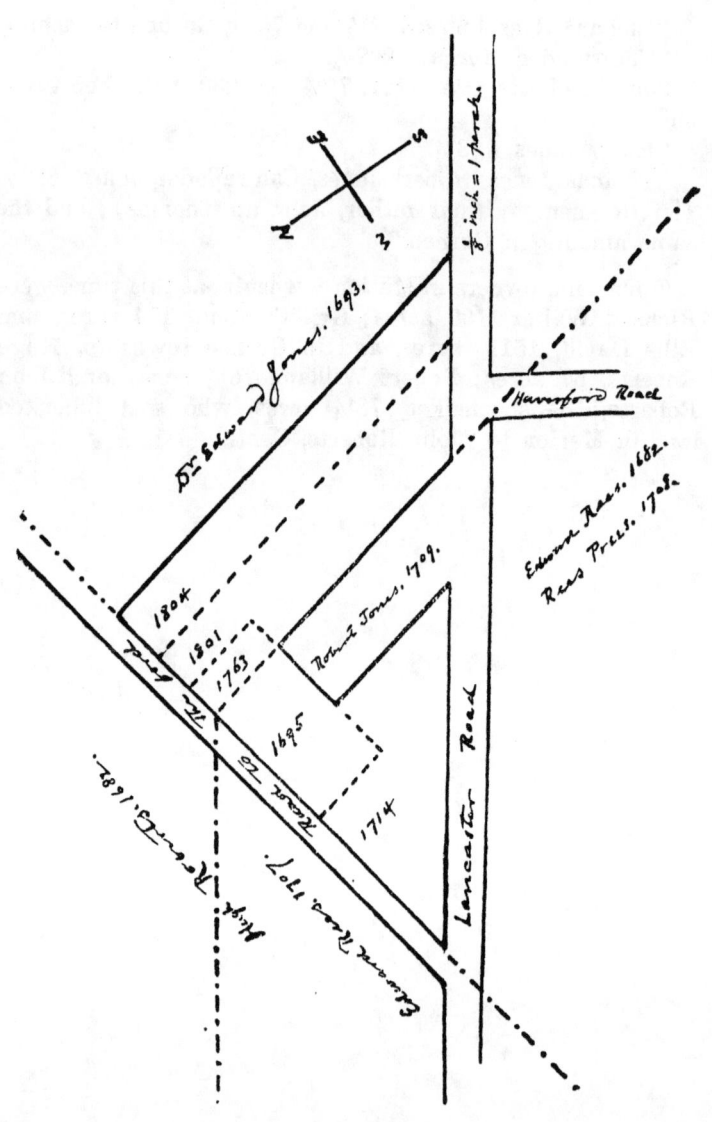

FAMILIES AND LAND OF FIRST ARRIVALS

MERION ADVENTURERS

The following information concerning the aforesaid Welsh Friends, the "first purchasers," "ye first within ye tract of land in the Province" to have their land beyond the Schuylkill laid out, the first settlers in the Welsh Tract, and in Merion township, the founders of the Merion Meeting, has fortunately been preserved, and gathered together from many sources, more or less reliable.

The sketches of these founders are not only of biographical and genealogical interest, for they show the gradual and sure development of Merion, and of the Welsh Tract, now the "garden spot" of Pensylvania, if not of America, and incidentally the part taken by them in laying the foundation of the Commonwealth.

These first four sketches are of the four Welshmen and Friends, and their families, who were the first to remove here from Wales, and arrived at Upland (Chester), on the Delaware, 13 August, 1682, namely, Dr. Edward Jones, William ap Edward, Edward ap Rees, and Robert ap David.

DR. EDWARD JONES. He was described as "chyrurgion," and removed from Bala, in Merionethshire, and was the founder of "Merion in the Welsh Tract." Nothing is preserved of his ancestry, or antecedents. He filed with the Merion Preparative Meeting, or the Haverford Monthly Meeting, on 8. 10mo. 1704, according to its minutes, an account of himself and wife, and of their life before coming over, as all other members did, but such accounts have disappeared from the Friends' archives. His fame was as the one who selected the land to be settled upon by himself and his confrères, and as the founder of the most important settlement in "New Merion."

WELSH SETTLEMENT OF PENSYLVANIA

As told already, he was one of the Welsh gentlemen who visited William Penn in London, in May, 1681, about buying some of his land, and how he was one of the adventurers and trustees, with John ap Thomas, for 5,000 acres, taken up by "Edward Jones & Co.," located part in Merion, on the Schuylkill, and part in Goshen township, because Penn's agent here, according to instructions from Penn, of course, would not survey or lay out so large a tract in one place.

Where Edward ap John, or Edward Jones, studied medicine has not been discovered, but it may be supposed he had medical skill as a barber-surgeon, and practiced his profession among Friends in and about Bala, from whence he came, and later in Merion and Philadelphia.

He and his party, "40 souls," were the first of the Welsh Friends to remove to Penn's Province. The names of all who composed Dr. Jones's party cannot now be determined, and it is only positively known that on this trip of the ship Lyon there were as passengers Dr. Jones and his wife, and two small children; William ap Edward, and his second wife, and two children by his first wife; Edward ap Rees, and his wife, and three children, and Robert ap David, and his wife, and one child, and that they were the "first class passengers."

These four men were the only ones of the seventeen "shareholders," purchasers of the land Thomas & Jones engaged, who made the first settlement in Merion. This accounts for sixteen souls, and the others of the forty were farm-hands and servants.

Dr. Jones, and his party of first Merion settlers, sailed from Liverpool, in the latter part of May, 1682, in the ship Lyon, Captain John Compton, master, and arrived at Upland, now Chester, in the Delaware, 13. 6mo. (August), 1682, two months before William Penn's first arrival.

Among the papers of his "partner," John ap Thomas, brought to America by his widow, is preserved a letter written by Dr. Jones to him, whom he had left very ill at

COMPANY NUMBER ONE

home, thirteen days after reaching his destination. Some extracts from this interesting letter have been give above, but as it was an account of the experience of this first party, as well as the Doctor's earliest opinion of his new home, his letter is given in full. It was written apparently after the men of the party had gone out to inspect the tract assigned to them on the west side of the Schuylkill, at and above the Falls, where subsequently they took their seats close together, and camped with their families, till their comfortable log houses were built, for it was mid-summer, and therefore no great hardship at first.

An account of another family tells that these first comers "dug caves, walled them, and dwelt therein a considerable time, where they suffered many hardships, in the beginning, —the next season being wet and raining about their barley harvest [time]."

It is unfortunate that the Doctor's first letter he refers to has not been preserved, or did not reach John Thomas.

This second letter is addressed in this quaint manner:—

"These ffor his much esteemed friend John ap Thomas of Llaithgwm neer Bala in Merionethshire, North Wales, to be left with Job Boulton att the Boult and tun in Lumber Street London, and from thence to William Sky Butcher in Oswestrie, to be sent as above directed and via London—with Speed."

"My endeared fr'd & brother, my heart dearly salutes thee, in a measure of ye everlasting truth, dear fr'd, hoping that these few lines may find thee in health, or no worster yn I left thee.

"This shall let thee know that we have been aboard eleaven weeks before we made the land, (it was not for want of art, but contrary winds,) and one we were in coming to Upland.

"Ye town [the future Philadelphia] is to buylded 15 or 16 miles up ye River.

WELSH SETTLEMENT OF PENSYLVANIA

"And, in all this time, we wanted neither meate, drink, or water, though several hogsheds of water run out. Our ordinary allowance of beer was 3 pints a day, for each whole head, and a quart of water; 3 biskedd a day, & some times more. We laid in about a half hundred [weight] of biskedd, one barrell of beere, one hogshede of water,—the quantity for each whole head, & 3 barrells of beefe for the whole number—40—and we had one [barrel of beef] to come ashoare.

—"A great many could eat little or no beefe, though it was good. Butter and cheese eats well upon ye sea. Ye remainder of our cheese is little, or no worster; butter & cheese is at 6d per lb here, if not more. We have oatmeale to spare, but it is well yt we have it, for here is little or no corn till they begin to sow their corn, they have plenty of it.

"The passengers are all living, save one child yt died of a surfeit.

"Let no frds tell that they are either too old, or too young, [to come over]. for the Lord is sufficient to preserve both to the uttermost.

"Here is an old man about 80 years of age; he is rather better yn when he sett out. Likewise here are young babes doing very well, considering the sea diet.

"We had one tun of water, and one of drinke, to pay for at Upland; but ye master [of the ship] would faine be pd for 13 or 14 hogsheds yt run out by ye way, but we did not. And about 3 quarters of Tunn of Coales we pd for. We laid in 3 Tun of Coales, and yields no profit here.

"We are short of our expectation, by reason that ye town [future Philadelphia] is not to be builded at Upland; neither would ye Master bring us any further [than Upland], though it is navigable for ships of greater burthen than ours.

COMPANY NUMBER ONE

"Ye name of ye town lots [where they imagined, for some reason, the city would be laid out, as the site was not positively decided till after Penn's arrival] is called now Wicoco. Here [at the supposed town-site] is a Crowd of people striving for ye Country land, for ye town lot is not divided [that is the future Philadelphia was not yet laid out in lots, and was not until the following winter], & therefore we are forced to take up ye Country lots [first].

"We had much adoe to get a grant of it [that is, a warrant to locate and survey the land, from Penn's deputy, young Markham, directed to the official surveyor, Thomas Holme, or Holmes, who had been here only about six weeks, and was filled with engagements]. But it Cost us 4 or 5 days attendance [on the officials] besides some score of miles we travelled [forth and back to the Falls of Schuylkill and to the surveyor], before we brought it to pass [before the site was selected].

"I hope it [the Thomas & Jones lands, and its location] will please thee, and the rest yt are concerned, for it hath most rare timber. I have not seen the like in all these parts. There is water enough besides.

"The end of each lot will be on a river, as large, or larger than the Dye, at Bala. It is called Skool Kill River.

"I hope the Country land [the land the Doctor selected] will within this four days [be] surveyed out. [It seems that Ashcom, a Deputy Surveyor, made a rough survey of this land on 24 August, but probably had not returned when the Doctor wrote this on 26 August.] The rate for surveying 100 Acres, twenty shillings. But I hope betters orders [terms] will be taken [made] shortly about it" [the charge].

At this point there is a long paragraph in Welsh (the major part of the letter being English), and so written to make his remark secret and private, as the Doctor's letter was to be carried to England by the man he referred to, the captain of the ship in which he came over:—

[67]

WELSH SETTLEMENT OF PENSYLVANIA

"We liked him, the Captain, well enough when eating our own victuals; but beware of his provisions [a warning to Mr. Thomas, or any who might sail with him], because it was only bread and salt meat, with little beer, and foul water usually. But he made a great fuss over me and my wife, and over most of those who could talk with him [in English]. There is another Captain living in the same town [Liverpool], and passengers [some of Penn's first colonists] from Carmarthenshire came over with him on his provision, and they spoke well of him, but they paid him £4. 10. 00; early [for young] children, under 12 years of age, 52 shillings, and got plenty to eat, and good drink. The name of this good man is Captain Crossman. It is cheaper to furnish our own provisions than to pay £4. 10.

"I think most of the things [dry goods, utensils, implements, etc., brought over to sell to colonists] will not be sold until you come over, because so many things had previously been brought here."

All these suggestions may have been useful to others coming over. He suggested to bring for sale some white fustian, serges to make clothes, men's hats, saddles, bridles, shoes, etc. "Blue flannel is most called for here, but all colors are used," he wrote. "Don't bring much white flannel with you. Stuff dyed blue we like best."

"Compel the master of the ship to come to the town of Philadelphia with your goods [it appears from this, and Penn said, the town received its name before its site was selected]. I had to pay to the other [another] party 30 shillings for hauling the things up. and be sure to pay for carrying your luggage, and everything else that you start with, to the Captain."

Then continuing in English:—
"The people [about where the tract lay] generally are Swede, which are not very well acquainted [with our language].

COMPANY NUMBER ONE

"We are amongst the English which sent [send] us both venison, and new milk, & the Indians brought [bring] venison to our door for six pence ye quarter.*

"And as for ye land, we look upon it a good & fat soil, generally producing twenty, thirty, & fourty fold. [This may mean that in the tract were old Indian fields of this quality, or reputation.]

"There are stones [for houses] to be had enough at the falls of the Skool Kill, that is, where we are to settle, & water enough for mills. But thou must bring Mill-stones, and ye Irons that belong to it, for Smiths are dear [in charges here]. (This was a useless suggestion, as may be seen elsewhere.)

"Iron is about two and thirty, or fourty shillings per hundred. Steel about 1s. 6d. p. l.

"Ye best way is to make yr picken axes when you come

---

*That is, they were then stopping "in town," and had not yet moved out to "ye country lots," with the squattors on the site where they supposed "ye town" would be laid out, who were living in dug-out caves, on the bank of the Delaware, or in lean-to shacks. Near the Thomas and Jones grant, was Peter Cock, a Swede, who had about 200 acres, west of Mill Creek, *i.e.*, Cobbs Creek, in Blockley tp., Phila. Co. Later the Swansons became neighbors across the Schuylkill, having been forced to exchange their land cn the Delaware, for the city's site, and take land on both sides of the Schuylkill, from Fairmount to the Falls. The one Englishman in this neighborhood was William Warner, who, with his son, held three large tracts of land, extending from the Schuylkill half-way to Cobbs Creek, along the future Haverford Road. It is presumed that Warner came here by the way of New England, and bought land from the Indians, or the poorer Swedes. On 3 April, 1678, the Upland Court confirmed 100 acres to him, and on I June, 1681, he was an applicant to this Court for further confirmations of purchases. After Penn entered into possession, Mr. Warner became a member of young Gov. Markham's Council, 3 Aug., 1681, and on 13 Sep. following, he became a justice, and was a member of the first assembly held in Philadelphia, 10 March, 1683. He called his land, which lay in the "City Liberties," in Penn's time, "Blockley," from the place of his nativity, in Worcestershire, and it gave name to the township in which it lay, extending to the present 52d Street.

over, for they cannot be made in England; for one man will work with ym as much as two men with ours.

"Grindle Stones yield good profit here.

"Ordinary workmen hath 1s. 6d. a day [wages]. Carpenters 3 or four shillings a day.

"Here are sheep [belonging to the settlers on the lower Delaware river], but dear—about twenty shillings a piece. I cannot understand how they can be carried from England.

"Taylors hath 5s. & 6s. a day [wages].

"I would have you bring salt for ye present use;—here is coarse salt; sometimes two measures of salt for one of wheat [in exchange], and sometimes very dear.

"Six penny, & eight penny nails are most in use.

"Horse shoes are in no use.

"Good large shoes [for people] are dear.

"Lead in small bars is vendible; but guns are cheap enough.

"They plow, but very bungerly [here], & yet they have some good stone.

"They use both hookes and sickles to reap with.

"Time will not permit me to write much more, for we are not settled.

"I [send] my dear love, and my wife's unto thy selfe and thy dear wife, and the rest of my dear friends, H. Ro., Rich: P., Evan Rees; J. ap E., Elizabeth Williams; E. & J. Edd., Gainor R., Ro.: On., J.: Humphrey; Hugh J. Tho., and the rest of fr'ds as if named.

   "I remaine thy Lo' friend & Bro while I am,
            "Edd Jones."

"My wife desires thee to buy her one Iron Kettle, 3s or 3s. 6d., 2 paire of shoes for Martha [a little child], and one paire for Jonathan, let them by strong and large [which confirms they had only two children at that time]; be sure and put all yt goods in cases, if they be dry, they keep well, otherwise they will get damp and mouldy [on the voyage].

This is ye 2nd letter, Skool Kill River.
     Ye 26th of ye 6mo. 1682."

COMPANY NUMBER ONE

Dr. Jones, and his companions, Edward Rees and William Edwards, (or the surveyor, Ashcom, assigned the lots to the partners in this purchase, as Dr. Jones gave him the number of acres each bought) selected adjoining lots in their tract, he having laid out to himself here 156½ acres (and the same amount was divided between the other two), which upon Powell's resurvey, he made 153¼ acres, supposing three acres were to be in the Liberties. It was a narrow strip, extending from the river into the back country, 788 perches, or about two and one-half miles, and beyond the present Montgomery avenue, the successor of the Lancaster road. The remainder of Dr. Jones's purchase was laid out in Goshen township (about West Chester) subsequently.

Dr. Jones had two tracts in Goshen of 125 acres and 400 acres, made up of his original purchase, and of land he bought of "Edward Jones, Jr." and Richard Thomas.

"Edward Jones, Jr.," (son of John ap Edward), having procured a resurvey on 306½ acres in two tracts of 153¼ acres, one in Goshen township, the other in Merion township, one parcel was 20 acres over, and the other 28 short, it was ordered 20. 2. 1703, that patent for the whole be issued to "Edward Jones, the elder," to whom "Edward Jones, Jr.," had sold.

On same date, Edward Jones, Sr., it appears had 150 acres in Merion township, and 153 acres in Goshen township, and 200 acres more in same township, which he had purchased of Richard Thomas.

Of these properties, he sold, in 1707, to Robert Williams, 300 acres, and the balance, in 1720, to Ellis Williams. Dr. Jones also owned 160 acres in Blockley township on the old Lancaster road and the Merion line.

From his confirmation patent for this Merion land, where he resided over fifty-five years, dated 22. 4mo. 1703, after the third, and final, survey, it would seem that he had bought from his adjoining lotholder on the South, Ed-

WELSH SETTLEMENT OF PENSYLVANIA

ward Owen, the back half of his purchase of 156¼ acres, and had sold the front half of his own first selection, and on this date, had added 188 acres, purchased from Edward Jones, Jr. (adjoining his purchase from Owen), which land lay on the Haverford and Merion road, going East from near the Merion Meeting House, and extends over the Pensylvania Railroad at Narberth. His deed for his original purchase, dated 1 April, 1682, was from John Thomas, and was witnessed by John and Robert Lloyd, Griffith and Reece Evan, and William John.

Dr. Jones was honored with the appointment of a Justice of the Peace in the Welsh Tract, and was chosen as one of its representatives in the Pensylvania Assembly.

According to Penn, in his long letter addressed to the London members of the Society of Free Traders of Pensylvania, dated at Philadelphia, 16. 6mo. 1683, "Edward Jones, son-in-law to Thomas Wynne, living on the Sculkil," was a good farmer. As Penn says: "He had with ordinary cultivation, for one grain of English barley, 70 stalks and ears of barley."

The Doctor died at his Merion home, in February, 1737. His burial is recorded on books of the Merion Meeting: "Edward Jones, Doctor, aged 80 years," 12mo. 26. 1737.

Friend Thomas Chalkley, of "Chalkley Hall," in Frankford (Philadelphia), in his "Journal" records: "The 26th of the 12mo., 1737, being the first day of the week, there was buried at Merion, Edward Jones, aged about 92 (*sic*) years. He was one of the first settlers of Pensylvania, a man much given to hospitality, a lover of good and virtuous people, and was beloved by them. I had a concern to be at that meeting before I left my home at Frankford, and before I heard of this Friend's death. There were many hundreds at his funeral."

His will, signed 27. 3mo. 1732, was proved at Philadelphia, 2 August, 1738, witnessed by John Roberts and Esther Thomas (marked). He was described as surgeon,

COMPANY NUMBER ONE

and aged and infirm. He named his sons Jonathan, Edward, Evan, Thomas and John Jones, the youngest son, and desired that John should continue to feed, clothe, and support his brother Thomas. His wife Mary was to have his estate during her life, and then it was to go to son John. He gave son-in-law, John Cadwalader, some land in the center of Philadelphia, and negroes to each of the Cadwalader girls, Mary, Rebecca, and Hannah, and one to each grandson, Thomas Cadwalader, and Martha Roberts. He named daughters Martha, Elizabeth, and Mary, and appointed his wife, sons Jonathan, Edward and Evan, and John Cadwalader, executors.

Dr. Jones married, possibly in Denbighshire, Mary, a daughter of Dr. Thomas Wynne, also one of the Welsh adventurers for Penn's land ("Company No. 4"). It is not known when she died. She probably survived her husband, and it is supposed she was buried in the ground of the Merion Meeting. Of her it is said (see "The Philadelphia Friend," XXIX, 396, which dates her decease 29. 7mo. 1726, which is, of course, an error): "She was an approved minister among Friends, and zealous for the promotion of the truth." Of their eight children* named in the Doctor's will:—

---

*Among the present day descendants of Dr. Edward Jones are:

Mrs. Robert R. Corson.
Mrs. Howard Comfort.
Dr. George Smith.
Frank Foulke.
Abraham L. Smith.
Benj. Hayes Smith.
Rodman Wister.
Alex. W. Wister.
Edward Browning.
Mrs. Jawood Lukens.
Mrs. Arthur V. Meigs.
Mrs. Charles Richardson.
Mrs. George B. Roberts.
Mrs. William Cresson.
Mrs. James Yocum.
Mrs. Richard Day.
Dr. Richard Foulke.
Mrs. Charles L. Bacon.
Mrs. Charles W. Bacon.
William Wynne Wister.
Mrs. Richard A. Tilghman.
Dr. Owen Jones Wister.
Mrs. Israel J. Wister.
Robert Toland.
Charles Follen Corson.
Dr. Joseph K. Corson.

WELSH SETTLEMENT OF PENSYLVANIA

Martha Jones, for whom her father asked, as above, two pair shoes be forwarded from Wales, just after her arrival here. She married, seventeen years after coming here, at the Merion Meeting House, on '26. 10mo. 1699, the young school teacher, John Cadwalader** who it is supposed had been living at her father's house for two years. He died 16. 2mo. 1747.

John Cadwalader, although he was never a land owner in Merion, but because of his relationship to many of the families here, and his marriage among them, Merion has ever claimed him as belonging there by rights.

The exact date of his birth has not been preserved, but he was born about the year 1677-78, probably at Kiltal-

---

**Some descendants of John Cadwalader, who are also descendants of Dr. Edward Jones:

Mrs. Henry B. Robb.
Mrs. Edw. Fenno Hoffman.
Mrs. John Hone.
Mrs. Samuel Chew.
Mrs. William Pearsall.
Mrs. John Steinmetz.
Mrs. S. Bevan Miller.
Mrs. Roland L. Taylor.
Mrs. Fred Rhinelander Jones.
Mrs. John Travis.
Dr. Thomas Cadwalader, 1707-1779.
Col. Lambert Cadwalader, 1732-1813.
Gen. John Cadwalader, 1742-1786.
Gen. Thomas Cadwalader, 1795-1873.
Judge John M. Read, 1797-1874.
Col. George A. McCall, 1802-1868.
Judge John Cadwalader, 1805-1879.
Gen. George Cadwalader, 1806-1879.
John Cadwalader.
Dr. Charles E. Cadwalader.
Richard M. Cadwalader.
John Lambert Cadwalader.
Mrs. William Greene Cochran.
Mrs. Samuel L. Shober.

Mrs. Archibald McCall.
Mrs. William Schley.
Mrs. Philemon Dickinson.
Mrs. Richard F. Stevens.
Mrs. Henry J. Rowland.
Wm. Cadwalader Schley.
Mrs. William Woodville, Jr.
Mrs. Arthur S. Johns.
Mrs. Charles W. Ross.
Mrs. George N. Schrew.
Harmon Pumpelly Read.
Mrs. Garret D. Wall Vroom.
Mrs. Samuel Meredith.
Mrs. John Read.
Samuel Reese Meredith.
Admiral Cadwalader Ringgold.
Mrs. William Henry Rawle.
Travis Cochran.
William Cochran.
George Cochran.
Arthur Potts.
Mrs. Samuel E. D. Hankinson.
Mrs. John Graham.

garth, Llanvawr, Merionethshire, where his father lived. He brought his certificate of removal from the Pembroke Quarterly Meeting, dated in 1697, which states he had attended school there. He probably came over soon in this year, and lived in the family of some relative on the Schuylkill, till he received the appointment as a teacher in the Friends' Public School, in Philadelphia, which he had, on motion of Griffith Owen, in the Philadelphia Monthly Meeting, 29. 1mo. 1700, who recommended him as "a person fit for an assistant in the school."

Having received this appointment, he probably moved into town, for in July, 1705, he was admitted as a freeman of the city. In 1718-33, he was a chosen member of the City Council, and of the Pensylvania Assembly, in 1729, in which body he served till his decease, intestate, on 23 July, 1734.

He purchased 200 acres of land in "Ughland," Chester county, on warrant from the Land Commissioners, paying £12. 10s. per 100 acres on 22. 9mo. 1715.

Jonathan Jones, eldest son, who came over with his parents, and for whom his father desired that a pair of strong and large shoes be sent from Wales, although he was only two years old. He was born at Bala, Merionethshire, on 3. 11mo. 1680; died 30. 7mo. and was buried at the Merion Meeting House, 8. 8mo. 1770, aged 90 years. His will, dated 19 May, 1768, was proved at Philadelphia, 1 September, 1770.

Jonathan was given some of his father's estate, and bought from his brother-in-law, Evan Owen, the plantation of about 450 acres, which included the seats subsequently called "Wynnewood," and "St. Mary's," East of Ardmore, and North of the Pensylvania Railroad, which, it being a part of the Charles Lloyd tract, Thomas Lloyd had conveyed by deed, dated 5. 6mo. 1691, to Robert Owen, who settled it on his son, Evan Owen.

WELSH SETTLEMENT OF PENSYLVANIA

Jonathan Jones married at the Merion Meeting Gainor Owen, b. 26. 8mo. 1688, daughter of Robert Owen, of Merion.

This union of scions of two of the most important families of the Welsh Tract, naturally brought to the wedding a great concourse of English and Welsh Friends, as may be judged by the signers of their extant marriage certificate, which is of longer form than now used, beginning:— "Whereas, Jonathan Jones, son of Edward Jones, of Merion, in ye Welsh Tract, Chyrgeon, and Gainor Owen, daughter of Robert Owen, late of ye same place, yeoman, deceased, having declared their intention of marriage with each other before several Monthly Meetings of ye people of God called 'Quakers, in ye Welsh Tract aforsayd," etc., "Now these are to certifie to all whom it may concern, that for ye full accomplishment of their said intentions this 4th day of ye 8th mo in ye year 1705, they ye sayd Jonathan Jones & Gainor Owen appeared in the publick meeting of the said People, and others met together, at the public meeting place at Merion aforsayd & ye Jonathan Jones taking ye sayd Gainor Owen by ye hand did in solemn manner openly declare that he took her to be his wife, promising to be unto her a faithful and loving husband until death separate them & then and there in ye sayd assembly ye sayd Gainor Owen did in like manner declare that she took ye sayd Jonathan Jones to be her husband & promising," etc., The names of the signers are given elsewhere.

They had eleven children, of these:—Mary, m. Benjamin Hayes; Edward Jones, d. unm.; Rebecca, m. John Roberts, Jr., of "Pencoyd"; Owen Jones, (m. Susanna Evans,)* who

---

*Owen Jones, 1711-1793, a provincial treasurer of Pensylvania, and a "Tory," m. 30. 3mo. 1740, Susanna, daughter of Hugh and Lowry Evans, of Merion, had Jane, m. Caleb Foulke; Lowry, m. Daniel Wister; Owen, 1745-1825, d. s. p., Susanna, m. John Nancarro; Hannah, m. Amos Foulke; Rebecca, m. John Jones, d. s. p., Sarah, m. Samuel Rutter, and Jonathan, 1762-1821-2, father of Col. Owen Jones,

COMPANY NUMBER ONE

received 350 acres from his father, and added about 120 acres by purchase from brother Jonathan,—his possessions included much of Wister's "St. Mary's," and "Wister's Woods," and Wynnewood, which had been the estate of his brother-in-law, Evan Owen, and is still, in part, occupied by descendants; Ezekiel Jones, Jacob Jones; and Jonathan Jones, Jr., who received about 120 acres at Ardmore from his father, some of which was owned by the Glenn family, but is now divided among many newcomers.

Elizabeth Jones, wife of Rees Thomas, Jr., of "Rosemont" plantation, in Merion.

Mary Jones.

Edward Jones, Jr., of Blockley township. By gift from his father he had some of his father's land, along with the other sons. His will, signed in the presence of Martha Palmer, John Winne (marked), and Jonathan Hood, 14 November, 1730, was proved 30 September, 1732, by wife Mary. He names children Aquilla, Penelope, Salvenas, Beula, and Prudence; his brothers, Jonathan and John; his father-in-law, William Palmer; Brother-in-law, John Cadwalader; Trustees, Jonathan and John Jones, William Palmer, and John Cadwalader.

Thomas Jones, named in his father's will, 1732, and was probably an invalid.

Evan Jones. He m. first, Mary Stephenson, of New York, and m. secondly, a daughter of Colonel Matthews, of Fort Albany, New York.

M.C., deceased, whose son, J. Awbrey Jones, d. s. p., at "Wynnewood," which property reverted, by the latter's will, eventually to the Toland family of Philadelphia, which was distantly related to him through the m. of Robert Toland and Rebecca, daughter of John Price Morgan, and his wife, Susan, daughter of Lowry Jones and Daniel Wister, aforesaid.

WELSH SETTLEMENT OF PENSYLVANIA

John Jones, of Philadelphia. He received from his father's estate the farm of 188 acres, bought of "Edward Jones, Jr." (son of John ap Edward), as above. This was included in the following sale:

By deed dated 15 October, 1741, "John Jones, late of Lower Merion, and of Philadelphia, yeoman, (youngest son of Edward Jones, late of Merion, Chyrurgeon, deceased), and Mary, his wife," conveyed "to Anthony Tunis, late of township of Germantown, now of Lower Merion," 402 acres of land, "late estate of Dr. Edward Jones," for £812 Pensylvania money. The abutting properties on this land were owned by John Roberts, Hugh Evans, Rees Price, Richard George, and Thomas Davids. "The Road," the old Lancaster pike, was a prominent bound, that is, this property lay "along the Road dividing this land from Edward Price's, south and west, to the Meeting House Ground, thence by the same, south and east, by the Road to Haverford, south and west, by Rees Price's land."

MERION ADVENTURERS

Of the three other gentlemen and their families who accompanied Dr. Edward Jones, and were founders of the Merion Meeting, namely:—
  Edward ap Rees, or Edward Price,
  Robert ap David, or Robert Davis,
  William ap Edward, or William Edwards,
there is preserved the following information. They were all, of course, Friends, and members of the Penllyn Monthly Meeting, and resided in the old country in the same neighborhood, near Bala, where they were free-holders of land, and gentlemen farmers.

EDWARD AP REES, or Rhys, or "Edward Prees," and "Edward Price," as he is variously known (whose descendants assumed the surname "Price"), was a yeoman, and a minister among Friends, and a founder of Merion Meeting, came with his wife and two children, in Dr. Jones's party, from Kiltalgarth, Penllyn, in Merionethshire. He was the son of Richard Rhys (ap Grywwyth), of Tyddin Tyfod, in Merioneth, whose will, signed 26 January, 1685, was proved at the St. Asaph registry, and brother to Jane, wife of Cadwalader Morgan, and to Hannah, wife of Rees John William, all first settlers of Merion.

On request he filed with the Merion Preparative Meeting, of the Haverford Monthly Meeting, on 2. 12mo. 1704-5, according to the minutes, an account of his parentage, his home, marriage, education, &c., which unfortunately has not been preserved, or cannot be found.

His first Merion land, about 76 acres, which he had by deed, dated 1 April, 1682, recorded 11. 4mo. 1684, witnessed by John Lloyd, Robert Lloyd, Griffith Evan and Reece Evan, was not located on the Schuylkill, but back of the purchase of William ap Edward, and between the lands of Dr. Jones and Hugh Roberts.

By deed dated 5. 5. 1691, he acquired 125 acres of the land of Governor Thomas Lloyd, part of Charles Lloyd's purchase from Penn ("Company No. 2"), which adjoined his original land on its west end, and also two acres from Dr. Jones, and received, on resurvey, a confirmatory patent, dated 1 January, 1703-4, for all his land, then amounting to 190 acres here. In 1707, he purchased 222 acres from Robert Roberts, north of his Lloyd land, and 10 acres on Mill, or Cobb's creek, in Blockley township.

The balance of his original purchase, or his Goshen land, 76 acres on Chester creek, and 78 acres which he bought, in 1697, of John William, of Merion (who in 1 mo. 1717-8, had patent for 400 acres on a branch of French creek), he sold, by deed of 9 January, 1708-9, to Ellis David, whose son, called David Ellis, held it in 1735.

Edward Rees resided on his first purchase, some of which lay on both sides of the Lancaster Road, which remained in his family for two centuries, in a stone house, erected about 1695, standing till recently northwest of the Merion Meeting House.

He was, of course, one of the organizers and first members of the Merion meeting. On the northeast corner of his land, and near a path, across his land, succeeded by the old Lancaster road (or Montgomery avenue), was the site selected as best, and most convenient for the public meeting house of the Merion Friends. He sold, for a nominal sum, one-half acre, and by deed, dated 20. 6mo. 1695, conveyed it to the trustees of the Merion Peculiar, or Preparative Meeting, Messrs, Robert Owen, Edward Jones, Cadwalader Morgan, and Thomas Jones, but it is uncertain whether the stone Meeting House, then probably nearly completed, was erected on this lot, or it was land added to the graveyard.

COMPANY NUMBER ONE

Edward Rees was a man of education, and considerable property, as the inventory of his personalty, taken after his decease, shows he owned Bibles and other books of history, in Welsh and English, and considerable cash in his house. Like some others of these early settlers, he revisited his Welsh home, when advanced in years, with Benjamin Humphrey. He was buried at the Merion Meeting House, 6. 13. 1728. His will, signed 6 January, 1727-8, was proved at Philadelphia, 23 November, 1728. Overseers, Jonathan Jones and Samuel Humphrey; witnesses, Robert and Jon. Jones.

He was twice married. He married first in Wales, Mably, or Mabby, daughter of Owen ap Hugh Ievan, and niece of "Thomas ap Hugh, gent," of Wern Fawr, Merionethshire, and married secondly, in 1713, Rebecca, daughter of Samuel Humphrey (ap Hugh), of Haverford. She survived him, and died without issue; her will signed 18. 3. 1732, proved 19 January, 1733; she named as executors, Ellis Price, brothers Daniel and Benj. Humphreys, and sisters Ann Hogg, of New Castle, and Lydia; gave money to school at Haverford.

By his first wife, who came over with him, and was buried at the Merion Meeting House, 23. 8mo. 1699, he had one son and two daughters:—

Rees Price, mentioned as "Rees Rees," in his father's will, *b*. 11. 11mo. 1678. His father conveyed some land to him, by deed of 7 August 1708. He married three times. His children were:—(named in their grandfather's will) Edward Price; Mary, *m*. Rees Harry; and Margaret, *m*. first, ——————— Paschall; *m*. second, William Montgomery; issue by both husbands, and, it is said, Jane, John, and Ellis Price.

He *m*. first, at Radnor Meeting, 6. 10mo. 1705, Sarah, daughter of David Meredith, of Radnor.

WELSH SETTLEMENT OF PENSYLVANIA

He *m.* secondly, at Haverford Meeting, 9. 10mo. 1718, Elizabeth, daughter of Ellis Ellis, of Haverford, and his wife, Lydia, daughter of Samuel Humphreys aforementioned. She was buried at the Haverford Meeting House, 12mo. 5. 1733-4. Ellis Ellis' will, signed 13. 6. 1705, proved 6 April, 1706, names wife and son Thomas only. Overseers; Rowland Ellis, John Richard, Rees Price, and Benjamin Humphrey.

He *m.* thirdly, at Haverford Meeting, 10. 3mo. 1737, Ann Scotharn, a widow, of Darby.

Rees Price was the second landlord of the Blue Anchor tavern, on Dock Creek (now Dock street), Philadelphia, where Penn landed on his first visit to his city, when the tavern, standing by the public landing place, was a little house, 22 feet on Dock (Street) creek, and 12 feet on Front Street, and was kept by Mr. Guest.

His descendant, Esther Price, *m.* at Merion Meeting, 16. 10mo. 1834, Benjamin Hunt, and this, it is claimed, was the last marriage at this Meeting.

Catharine Price, d. an *infant,* and was buried on her father's land, in Merion, 23. 8mo. 1682. This was the first death and burial in this little settlement, at the Falls of the Schuylkill, two months after arrival here.

Jane Price, b. 11. 9mo. 1682. This was the first birth in this settlement, three months after arrival, according to her transmitted birth date. She was buried at the Merion Meeting House, 10mo. 13. 1769, the record saying:—"Jane Mares, widow of George Mares. Born on the banks of Schuylkill in a Stone Hut in 1683. She was the Daughter of Edward Rees, after called Edward Preist, and then Price." She *m.* first, Jonathan Hayes, *d.* before 1727, and *m.* secondly, George Marris, or Mares.

ROBERT AP DAVID, or Robert David, and Davis, as his descendants were called, was living at Gwerneval (Gwerevol) Ismynydd, Penllyn, Merionethshire, when he pur-

COMPANY NUMBER ONE

chased from Thomas & Jones 312½ acres, paying £6. 05. 00, and decided to remove to this purchase in Penn's Province.

He was apparently a young married man, with one child, when he and his wife joined Dr. Jones's party at Liverpool, about the middle of May, 1682, and took passage in the "Lyon," for America. Arriving, in health, like the others of the party, in August he went up the Schuylkill with them, and settled on his land here, which on resurvey amounted to 148½ acres here, the balance of his purchase being subsequently laid out in Goshen township.

He may have been the Robert David, "of Tuyn y nant, Merioneth, who filed Certificate from the Men's Meeting, Penllyn, dated 18. 5mo. 1683, with the Haverford Monthly Meeting, and had sent for it, which was signed by Robert and Evan Owen, Richard Price, Morris Humphrey, Thomas Prichard, Evan Rees, Reece Evan, Roger Roberts, Hugh and Edward Griffith, Griffith and David John, and William Morgan.

His land on the Schuylkill, which had been assigned to him by the surveyor, extended back from the river only 386 perches, to the land allotted to and taken up by John ap Edward, and succeeded to by "Edward Jones the younger." Here he resided as a gentleman farmer for fifty years, the balance of his life. He died in October, 1732, and was buried at the Merion Meeting House.

By deed, dated 1. 1. 1694, he added to his farm, by purchase from Dr. Griffith Owen, the 153¼ acres, extending inland from the river 690 perches to Lloyd's land, and adjoining his original purchase on the North, which was the original purchase of Edward Owen through Thomas & Jones. Of this tract, Robert sold in the same year, 25 acres to Richard Walter.

By deed dated 20. 5. 1683, recorded 28 October following, Robert David bought 156¼ acres (76½ acres of the lot being unimproved land in the Thomas & Jones tract), from Evan Rees, the Penmaen grocer, for £3. 2. 6. Wit-

WELSH SETTLEMENT OF PENSYLVANIA

nesses, Hugh Roberts, John Owen, Ellis Davis, and Maurice Davies. The receipt for the purchase money is in Latin. This land he exchanged for the same amount with Gainor Roberts, which latter land he also sold to Richard Walter, (with the 25 acres which adjoined it,) by deed of 1 December, 1694. Mr. Walter had his purchase resurveyed, and received patent, dated 8. 4. 1703, for 117 acres. The land is all near and on the old Lancaster road, near the City Line.

Robert David's holdings in Goshen township, on Chester creek, were at one time, 346 acres, made up of 234½ acres, his original purchase, and 88½ acres bought of Richard Thomas, Jr., and 23 acres allowed him by the Commissioners.

His final patent, dated 20. 5. 1703, for his Merion land, called for 280 acres and for his Goshen land, 346 acres, although on 12. 2. 1703, he claimed only 275½ acres in Merion, and 243 acres in Goshen, or 509½ acres.

Robert David, of Merion, bequeathed all his estate to his only son, Thomas Davis, by his will, signed 26 April, 1732, witnessed by Robert Evans, Rees Lloyd, and Robert Jones, and proved 18 October, 1732. He mentions his wife, Elizabeth, and daughters Elizabeth and Jane, and grandchildren (Jane's children), and Elizabeth, Jane and Robert, David, kinswoman Margaret Roberts, and his brother Ellis; gave some money for the graveyard at the Merion Meeting House; and named as executors his wife, and daughter Elizabeth, and as trustees, John Cadwalader, Robert Roberts, and Robert Jones. His wife, "Elizabeth Davis"'s will, signed 4 June, 1734, present Thomas and John Cadwalader, was filed 31 July, 1734, mentions son Thomas Davis, daughter Elizabeth Davis, executrix; mentions grandchildren Robert Roberts, Elizabeth Evans, and Jane Roberts.

The brothers, *William ap Edward*, and *John ap Edward*, it has long been supposed, both came over in Dr. Jones's party, arriving here in August, 1682. William, there is good evidence, certainly did come with the Doctor, but John did not, as we shall see.

They were sons of Edward ap John, a free-holder, of Cynlas township, in Llanddervel parish, Merionetshire, and who lived near Bala, and was buried, according to the register, at the parish church, on 1 March, 1667. He had two other sons, Evan Edward, who came over before 1704, and Thomas Edward, of Llanllidiog, in Llanddiervel, 1686.

WILLIAM AP EDWARD, a yeoman, was described as of Ucheldri, and of Nantlleidiog, and Cynlas, and he was sometimes known as "William Bedward," *ap* and *ab* being interchangeable. His descendants assumed the name "Williams." A more particular account of him and his brother, John, we are unable now to learn, as the account of himself and brothers, John and Evan, and their families, and old home life, filed with the Merion Preparative Meeting, by William, 2. 1mo. 1704-5, has disappeared from the Meeting archives.

William ap Edward was twice married, and in May, 1682 with his second wife, Jane, and two daughters by his first wife, Katharine, he embarked for America, with Dr. Jones's party, on the "Lyon," and with others of this company settled on his purchase on the Schuylkill, in the Fall of 1682. Here he lived about ten years only, and sold his 76½ acres in Merion, on the Schuylkill, by deed dated 17. 6. 1694, to Hugh Roberts, whose land adjoined his on the North, and removed to a tract which he purchased in the Liberty Lands, or Blockley township, surveyed 23. 2. 1692, and confirmed by deed to him, 27. 10. 1693. A part of the village of Overbrook is on his land.

His Blockley land was made up of the 100 acres of "Liberty Land," which he bought, (said to have been the same claimed, on account of the purchase of 5,000 acres, by Thomas & Jones), and 30 acres on account of the original purchase of 1,000 acres by William Jenkins, and 20 acres on

WELSH SETTLEMENT OF PENSYLVANIA

account of Jonah Hasting's purchase of 1,000 acres, and this tract of about 150 acres seems to have been all he owned in 12mo. 1701. This land, where he lived and died, subsequently was included in the great estate of the George family—the families intermarried—and "Overbrook Farms."

By deed of 21 January, 1703, he conveyed his 75 acres, on Chester Creek, Goshen Township, to Robert William.

William ap Edward's will, dated 29 December, 1714, was proved by his wife, at Philadelphia, 29 January, 1714-5.

He mentions his son Edward, daughters Mary, and Elizabeth, wife of Thomas Lloyd, Katharine, and Sarah, gives money to the Merion Meeting, and appoints as overseers, his son Edward, and William Thomas Lawrence, Henry Lawrence, and Thomas Lloyd, and friends David Jones and Thomas Jones. Witnesses:—James Hinton, Jenkin David (marked), and Abel Thomas.

He was buried at the Merion Meeting 10mo. 31. 1714. (John George was also buried here on this day). His wife, Jane, was buried here, aged 93 years, on 8mo. 3. 1745.

He *m.* first, Katharine Robert, *d.* in 1676. She was a sister to the Friends' minister, Hugh Roberts, and Gainor Roberts, both of the Thomas & Jones purchasers' colony, and had by her, two daughters, namely,

Elizabeth Williams, b. 14. 3. 1672, who came over with her father. She *m.* Thomas Lloyd, "not the President," who was one of the original purchasers from Thomas & Jones, but resided about a mile North of the village of Bryn Mawr.

Katharine Williams, who came over with her father, and *d. s. p.*

He *m.* secondly, about 1681, Jane, daughter of John ap Edward, (who, of course, was not his brother), a farmer near Bala, and had by her, who came over with him, four children:—

[86]

COMPANY NUMBER ONE

Sarah Williams, b. 20. 8mo. 1685, in Merion. She *m.* Thomas Lawrence, son of David Lawrence, and his wife, a daughter of Thomas Ellis.

Edward Williams, only son, b. 7. 12mo. 1689; he received from his father his Blockley land; will proved at Philadelphia, 21 February, 1749. He was very particular as to bequest to his wife, leaving her "a clothes-press in the parlour," and his "white mare and colt, and new blue-plush side-saddle." He *m.* Eleanor, daughter of David Lawrence, of Haverford. *Issue*: Joseph, father of Rebecca, *m.* Amos George; Eleanor, *m.* Joseph Bond, and Sarah, *m.* Edward George) Daniel, Sarah (wife of Joshua Humphreys) Edward and Jane (wife of Evan Thomas).

Ellen Williams, b. 19. 4mo. 1691, *m.* Henry Lawrence.

Mary Williams, b. 11. 11mo. 1694, *m.* Richard Preston, of Haverford.

JOHN AP EDWARD, the brother of William ap Edward aforesaid, was another of the parties to the "Thomas & Jones tract," but he did not come over with him in the Dr. Jones party, arriving in August, 1682, as supposed. In the testimony before Penn's Commissioners, of Dr. Jones, in June, 1702, taken in the matter of a servant of the late John ap Edward claiming his "time" was up and desiring to be relieved from further servitude, the Doctor declared that this servant man "came to this Province about the year 1683, as the servant of John ap Edward," and there is evidence that John brought over four servants, therefore, if John ap Edward and servants came over with the Doctor in 1682, I think he would have so stated, and not have put his arrival "about the year 1683." Nor did John ap Edward come over in the party of Hugh Robert, bound for the Thomas & Jones tract, because his will is dated 16 October, 1683, when he was very ill, and the Roberts party was then at sea, having sailed in September, 1683. The reference

WELSH SETTLEMENT OF PENSYLVANIA

in John's will that he had brought servants over, is proof that the will was written here after arrival. Nor should I imagine that he arrived in 1683 after Roberts arrived, for, being ill in October, he would hardly have sailed in time to arrive "about the year 1683." Therefore, I judge that John ap Edward arrived here, in some party coming out to Philadelphia, between August, 1682, and October, 1683. The two witnesses to his will were probably servants, possibly his, as the names of only two of his, a man and a maid, have been found.

When John ap Edward arrived, he found his land laid out for him. He had, as we have seen, contributed £6. 5. 0. towards the fund to buy 5,000 acres of Penn's land through Mr. Thomas and Dr. Jones, and that his share amounted to 312½ acres, for which he received the deed, dated 18 April, 1682. When Ashcom roughly laid out the Thomas & Jones purchase into lots, 24 August, 1682, he assigned, by order of the surveyor-general, only half of this purchase (as was the treatment of all the other Welshmen, much to their disgust, for they had been given to understand, and it was not absurd, that the purchaser of each lot would have all of his land in one place), 156¼ acres to John ap Edward, who found it laid out about 1 1/5 mile from the Schuylkill river, and the balance was a right to the same amount to be laid out in Goshen township, miles away, which was not a pleasant surprise for a practical farmer, one that would expect his farm should be in one tract, or at least, in contiguous parcels. However, as this was the misfortune of the other Welsh farmers, John accepted his allotment.

On Powell's map of the Thomas & Jones tract, John is credited with only 153½ acres, as Powell supposed he was entitled to three acres of Liberty Land, and that his land stands in the name of "Edward Joans, Jun'r," who was his son who succeeded to it on the decease of his elder brother. As this draft was made by Powell in 3mo. 1684, Evan, the

COMPANY NUMBER ONE

heir, and his father were then both dead, and Edward, a minor, was the heir apparent.

When John ap Edward came over, he brought with him four servants, possibly three men, farm hands, and his wife's maid. He found his land, though far from the great natural highway, the river, of quality equal to any other's, as was the bargain, and much better than most of it, for we know it lay in the beautiful, rolling country near our Merion settlement. He apparently lived only long enough to see one crop gathered. From his will it may be known that he was a shareholder in the Free Society of Traders in Pa., and was a prosperous man, and a Friend, and a founder of the Merion Meeting.

His will, dated 16. 8mo. 1683, when he was "weak of body"; witnessed by Gabriel Jones and William Morgan (probably servants), was not proved until 8. 2mo. 1686, by his brother, "William Edward, of Merion."

To his eldest son, Evan Jones, he gave the 312½ acres, which he had "purchased from William Penn."

To his youngest son, Edward Jones, he gave "the land due me for bringing over of servants, 200 acres," [that is, he brought four servants, receiving the usual allowance of fifty acres for each], and in addition his interest, or shares, "in the Society Trade of Pensylvania," [i. e., Free Society of Traders], valued by him at £5.

He gave to his daughter, Elizabeth, £15 "of English money," with two feather beds, and bed clothes belonging to them, two brass pans, two pewter dishes, and one large trunk.

The balance of his personal estate, and his interest in the servants, he desired to be sold to pay his debts, and if anything remained, he desired his sons to have it.

He gave ten shillings to "my nephew John Evan."

He appointed "my beloved brethern Evan and William ap Edward, and my trusty friends Hugh Roberts, David Davies, John Roberts, and Hugh John Thomas," to be his executors, (although none but William was in this country, but he had reason to expect they would come), "to whose care I leave my children," as they were minors at that time. He desired that the monthly meeting decide what it was best to do with his estate should both of his sons die young, and without issue. As this will was written a month, or more, before the presumed time of organizing the Haverford Monthly Meeting, he may have expected it, or referred to the Burlington Monthly Meeting, which covered the meetings then in Pensylvania.

"My maid, Mary Hughs, [or Hughes] the sum of two pounds at the expiration of the time of her apprenticeship."

The executed will has not been preserved, but there is a copy of it on file, which shows he marked his will with simply a large E. In the package of testamentary papers connected with the settlement of his estate, at the office of the Register of Wills, Philadelphia, is the original rough draft of the will, unsigned, and undated. Also the original inventory of his personal estate, made as it says by Thomas Ellis, Hugh Jones, and John Roberts, on "the 3 day of the first month 1683-4," which is evidence that John died between 16 October, 1683 and 3 March, following.

It seems that all the personal property was sold in a lump per inventory, after John's death, and that the appraisers filed a copy of the inventory on 20 February, 1702-3, when the heir, Edward, became of age, to show the sum derived from the sale, and stated:—"The Inventory was cast up and found to be £63. 15. 9, according to English money, which being reduced to pensilvania money is £79. 14. 8. five pounds of English money being allowed to the buyer of the said Inventory by the trustees, [which made the sale net] £73. 9. 8."

The value of the unexpired time of the servants is given:—"The Soms of the Servants being £30. 15. 0."

which is in addition to the aforesaid valuation of the personalty. From the inventory, we learn that John was well supplied with agricultural and household implements, bedding, clothing, and some grain, cows, and horses, and harness, and that there were sold his pair of spectacles, children and women's clothing, pewter, a gun, powder, four powder horns, fishing tackle, "leathen dresses," and "lethern waistcoats."

There is also preserved the receipt of Elizabeth Jones, endorsed "no part of the record," that is of the original testamentary proceedings, "Received from William Edward administrator of the Estate of my Father, John Edward, the Summe of fifty pounds, seven Shillings currant silver money of Pensylvania, in full of all bequests and Legaceys bequeathed to me by my sd father in his last will & testament bearing date of sixteenth day of the eight month in the year 1683, and in full of the shars that befell me of my deceased brother Evan Jones his estate, and I do acquitt and discharge the said William Edward his heirs, of all trusts and Legaceys, dues, debts, and demands from the beginning of the world to this day, 22 of 3mo. 1699." She wrote her name "Elizabeth Jones," and was then twenty-eight year of age, and apparently unmarried. The witnesses to this receipt were the same as those to the copy of the inventory mentioned, namely, Hugh Jones (marked), Thomas Jones, and Robert Jones.

The name of the wife and mother of his children of John ap Edward has not been found. She was apparently deceased when he made his will. His descendants assumed the name "Jones." Of his issue:—

Evan Jones, eldest son, b. 2. 2mo. 1677, mentioned in his father's will, died young and unmarried before 3mo. 1684.

Edward Jones, second son, and youngest child, b. 5. 8mo. 1681. He succeeded to all of his father's land when he be-

WELSH SETTLEMENT OF PENSYLVANIA

came of age, in 1702-3. According to a note, he had his father's will copied into the records.

By deed, dated 13. 2mo. 1702-3, he conveyed all of the lands of his inheritance to Dr. Edward Jones, of Merion, giving "Receipt of Edward Jones, of Philadelphia, only son of John ap Edward, deceased, and nephew of William ap Edward, of Blockley," dated 23 January, 1702, Recorded in Philadelphia County Deed Book, No. C. II., fo. 198. His Merion tract of land extended from about the old Lancaster Road (Montgomery Avenue), across the Pensylvania Railroad between Merion station, and the borough of Narberth.

Elizabeth Jones, first child, b. 18. 12mo. 1671. She m. after 22 May, 1699, John ap Robert ap Cadwalader, or "John Roberts," of the Gwynedd settlement. They were the founders of the Roberts family of "'Woodlawn" plantation, in Whitpain township, Montgomery county, Pensylvania.

Sarah Jones, b. 8. 11mo. 1673, not named in her father's will.

FAMILIES AND LANDS
OF SECOND ARRIVALS

MERION ADVENTURERS

The second party of Welsh from Merionethshire, members of the Penllyn Monthly Meeting, who were purchasers of land in the "Thomas & Jones Tract," to remove here, were:

  Hugh Robert.   Cadwalader Morgan.
  Edward Owen.   Hugh John.
  William John.   Katherin Thomas.
     Gainor Roberts.

This is the party generally known as "Hugh Roberts's party."

They came over in the ship Morning Star, of Chester, Thomas Hayes, master, sailing from Mosson, in September, 1683. After a voyage of two months, uneventful, excepting for several burials at sea, they arrived in the Delaware, and at Philadelphia, 16-20 November following.

There was a large passenger list, outside of the Roberts' party, in which there were 50 souls, or more, including servants, Welshmen and their families, coming over to settle somewhere in the great Welsh Tract, who all may have come under Proud's description:—"Divers of those early Welsh settlers were persons of excellent and worthy character, and several of good education, family, and estate."

Of the most noted of those coming in this vessel, at this time, were John Bevan ("Company No. 3"), and his family, and party; John Roberts, of "Pencoyd"; Thomas Owen, who came to open-up Rowland Ellis's land; Rees Thomas, a future man of affairs in the Welsh Tract; Ralph and William Lewis; the Humphreys, Richard, John, and Samuel, the noted men of the Friends' Haverford Meeting;

WELSH SETTLEMENT OF PENSYLVANIA

Griffith John ap Evan, Robert ffloid, William Morgan, Evan John, brother of Rees John William, of Merion, etc., all became land owners, prosperous farmers, "good men and true," in townships of Merion, Haverford, or Radnor, and elsewhere in the Welsh Tract.

HUGH ROBERTS, Hugh Robert, or "Hugh ap Robert, of Kiltalgarth, yeoman," headed the second party of settlers from Merionethshire bound for the Thomas & Jones tract. In his immediate party, were his mother, his wife, his sister, Ganior Roberts, five children, and four servants.

Hugh Roberts was a man of education, a pleasant writer, and an eminent minister among Friends, whom he joined in 1666, and many sketches of his ministerial life have appeared in Friends' publications.

But little is now known of his ancestry, excepting that he was the son of Robert ap Hugh, or "Robert Pugh, gent," of Llyndedwydd, a leased farm, near Bala, and the lake, in Penllyn, Merioneth, by his wife, Katherine Roberts, who, then being a widow, accompanied her son to Pensylvania, and was buried at the Merion Meeting, in 1699. She was the daughter of William ap Owen, of Llanvawr parish, in Penllyn, where Hugh Roberts resided when he set out for America.

Katharine Robert, of Llaethgwn, widow, and her daughter, Gaynor Robert, of Kiltalgarth, spinster, both brought Certificates, dated 18. 5mo. 1683, from the Men's and Women's Meeting, Penllyn, and signed by the same Friends, namely:—Robert, Ellin, and Janne Owen, Richard Price, Evan Rees, Reece Evan, Elizabeth William, Elizabeth John, Gainor John, Hugh and Edward Griffith, Cadwalader Ellis, Thomas Prichard, William Morgan, Roger Roberts, David John, Margaret John, Margaret David, and Margaret Cadwalader.

Hugh Roberts, being so prominent a Friends' minister, in North Wales, suffered annoyances, fines, and imprison-

COMPANY NUMBER ONE

ment. He brought a certificate of membership, for himself, wife, and family, from the Men's Meeting, Penllyn, Merioneth, dated 2. 5mo. 1683.

Some members of this Men's Meeting at this time were:

Robert Owen.	Hugh Griffith.
Evan Owen.	Edward Griffith.
Richard Price.	Morris Humphrey.
Cadwalader Ellis.	Thomas Prichard.
Evan Rees.	David Jones.
Rees Evan.	William Morgan.
Ellis David.	Griffith John.
Thomas Ellis.	Roger Robert.
Rowland Ellis.	Owen Humphrey.

Nearly all of these were signers of Mr. Roberts's certificate, in which he was described as of Llanvawr parish, Merioneth.

He soon became well known in America as a travelling public minister, and in 1688, and 1697-8, made missionary visits to North Wales. On this last trip, he kept an interesting journal of his travels, beginning on 15. 12mo. 1697, which took him to England and Wales by the way of Maryland and Virginia, which is still extant.

This interesting journal, printed in full in the periodical of the Historical Society of Pensylvania, begins:—"In the year 1697, the 15th of ye mo. I set out from home to visit Friends in England and Wales, Samuel Carpenter and John Ascue accompanying me to Maryland." He held meetings *en route*, and in Maryland visited Mordecai Moore, Samuel Galloway, David Rawlins, the Widow Blackstone, "who was no Friend." From her home, where he stopped two days, he went to the Rapahannock river, alone, through the woods, on foot, "to one Captain Taylor, who was very kind to me." Thence "to a friend, George Wilson, a place where I had been before." "Here I had a very open Meeting amongst ye people of ye world." Then to New Kent county, "Where there is a meeting of Friends," and

WELSH SETTLEMENT OF PENSYLVANIA

next day to a Monthly Meeting at Curles on James river, "met dear James Dickinson," "And I went to Edward Thomas at James river, Charles Fleming coming along with me," and attended a Quarterly Meeting at Tenbigh. Then visited Alexander Llewellyn. "We travelled that same day 46 miles, besides keeping ye Meeting, and it was not hard for us to do it because ye Melting love and power of God was set over all." From this Welsh settlement, Mr. Roberts went over the James river to Walter Bartlet's, "and so on to Sevenech, where I had a good meeting at ye Meeting House." Visited to homes of Henry Wiges, William Cook, Richard Ratcliff, Daniel Sanburn, and John Coopland, and held a Meeting at Chuckatuck. Went to the homes also of William Scot, Leven Buffstin, Elizabeth Gallowell, and Elizabeth Hollowell, having Meetings at each house, "from thence on board ye ship, which was to ye mouth of James river, where ye Fleet met, we stayed on board 15 days before we sailed, and had several Meetings from ship to ship, and upon ye 7th day of ye 3d month we sailed." Next, he saw land on 17. 4mo. and arrived at Plymouth on 22. 4mo.

Resuming his travels, Mr. Roberts visited many Friends, and places in England, and at Bristol, "we met our dear friend William Penn, and were not a little glad to see one another." Entering Wales, he visited many Meetings, one at "Trefrug, where John Bevan liveth, and glad we were to meet one another." Together, they made the rounds of many Meetings, at James Lewis's, Rediston; at Owen Bowen's, near Carmarthin; at James Preece's, City Boom. In Radnorshire, he visited Roger Hughes; at Lanole, Ed- From North Wales he travelled to many places in South Wales, then back to Merionethshire, in the North, where ward Jones, David Powel, Thomas Goodin, near Llwyn-du. "Penllyn where I was born and bred," and visited there his he visited Lewis Owen, near Dollegelley, then to Bala, and

COMPANY NUMBER ONE

old friend, Robert Vaughan, and then made another pilgrimage through Wales.

On his return here, he brought over a large party of people from Merioneth, and North Wales. But many died at sea. He arrived at Philadelphia 7. 5mo. 1698, and settled the surviving emigrants, some in Merion, and others at Gwynedd, of which settlement he is considered the founder.

Half of Hugh Roberts's original purchase from Thomas & Jones, by deed dated 28 February, 1681, recorded 16 April 1684, witnessed by Daniel Jones, Robert Owen, William Jones, Reece Evan, Thomas John, and William Apedd (ap Edward), was laid out for him before his first arrival, on the Schuylkill. This parcel of land, surveyed 306 acres, was along the side of the estate of the widow of his dear friend, John ap Thomas, and like hers, extended back to the lands of Thomas Lloyd, the Governor.

For no other reason, as no evidence has been found in either case, than because he was a minister, it is assumed that the Merion Friends held all their Meetings, before the present Meeting House was erected, in 1695, in his house, and that the early weddings took place in the home of the Widow Thomas, because her house was most convenient, and more cheerful. However this may be, there is no documentary proof for the assumptions, and the preserved records of the earliest functions in Merion are described as taking place in the "public Meeting House."

The Pensylvania land records of his day show that Hugh Roberts was a land speculator, as well as a minister, to the day of his death. But space permits only to transcribe a few of his land transactions, especially those connected with the the neighborhood of the Merion Meeting House.

In addition to his original purchase of 312½ acres in Merion, he bought the Merion share, 76½ acres (about the present Overbrook), of John Watkins, 23. 4mo. 1684. By deed of 1. 4mo. 1688, he bought from the Commissioners,

200 acres, in Merion, for which he had warrant to survey, and 100 acres "liberty land." Of this 300 acre lot, 100 acres he had bought for, or did sell to the Widow Thomas, which sale was confirmed to her sons, Thomas and Cadwalader, 22. 12. 1702. By deed of 17. 6mo. 1694, he purchased his brother-in-law's, William Edwards's, original purchase, 76½ acres, adjoining his land, on the Schuylkill.

The aforesaid 100 acres of "liberty lands," were in right of the Richard Thomas purchase from Penn, and lay on Indian creek and the Mill Creek, (now Cobb's Creek). When Penn was here he sold to Hugh 200 acres of liberty land, on the west side of the Schuylkill river, for which he was to pay £150. He gave Penn £60 cash in hand. On 26. 11mo. 1701, he asked for further time, as he could not raise the balance due. The Commissioners ordered him to furnish good bond, and they would give him an extension till 29. 7mo. next.

Hugh Roberts also bought of Peter Young 500 acres, and of Francis Cook 400 acres, that is 900 acres of the original tract of John & Wynne ("Company No. 4"). This purchase lay in Blockley and Merion townships, and in other places. Of his Merion lands, he sold 295 acres to Cadwalader Ellis, and 335 acres were confirmed to his executors, by a patent, dated 26 March, 1706.

Of his Blockley purchase above, 200 acres became the seat called "Chestnut Hill," along the old Lancaster road, which his youngest son, Edward Roberts, inherited. Part of this tract is now included in Fairmount Park. In 1721, a portion, that including what is known now as "George's Hill," in the West Park, was purchased (300 acres altogether) from said Edward by Edward George (son of Richard and Jane George, who came from Llangerig, in Montgomeryshire, about 1707-8), whose descendants, Jesse and Rebecca George, gave it to the city forever for a park. Mr. Roberts also had 300 acres in Radnor in 1717.

COMPANY NUMBER ONE

Hugh Roberts had at one time altogether 1349¾ acres in Merion, and tracts of land in the townships of **Duffryn Mawr**, and Goshen, on Ridley Creek, some of which he disposed of to Cadwalader Ellis.

Hugh Roberts, it has been said, died at the house of John Redman, in Long Island, New York, when on a visit, in 6mo. 1702, and his remains were brought over from Long Island and buried at the Merion Meeting House, on the 20th. August, "after a large meeting was held."

But a letter from Judge Isaac Norris, to Jonathan Dickinson, dated 11. 6mo. 1702 ("Penn-Logan Correspondence"), says:—"Dear Hugh Roberts is, we think, very near his end. I was to see him on First-day, and then took a solemn and tender farewell, his soul being resigned, earnestly desiring and expecting his change; as in his life he was a preacher of Love, so now, in his latest moment does he continue to be so."

Therefore, it is most probable that he died at home, in Merion. The entry on the Merion Meeting minutes is "Hugh Roberts departed this Life 6mo. 18. 1702."

His will, signed 20. 5mo. 1702, was proved at Philadelphia, 7 December, 1702. He names his children, and distributed about 1200 acres in Merion, and 1100 acres in Goshen township, a meadow called "Clean John," &c. He bequeathed £5 to the Merion Meeting. He mentioned his servants, namely, two men, Morris Robert, and John Robert, and boys, Griffith and Morris. He named as trustees, John Roberts (of "Pencoid"), Cadwalader Morgan, Griffith John, and Griffith Owen. Witnesses:—Samuel Bowne, Griffith Owen, and Samuel Jennings.

Hugh Roberts was twice married. He *m.* first, Jane, daughter of Owen ap Evan Robert Lewis, of Fron Gôch, in Merioneth. She was a sister of Robert Owen, of Merion. She came to Merion with him, and brought the certificate above mentioned, and died 1. 7mo. 1686, and was buried at Merion Meeting House. He *m.* secondly, 31. 5mo. 1689, at

WELSH SETTLEMENT OF PENSYLVANIA

the Llwyn-y-Braner Meeting, in Penllyn, Merionethshire, when on a visit, Elizabeth vch. John, or Elizabeth Jones.

His six children, all by his first wife, Jane Owen, who was of Royal Descent, assumed the surname "Roberts." Of them:—

Robert Roberts, b. 7. 11mo. 1673. By his father's will, he and his brother Owen received jointly his Merion land.

On 26. 1mo. 1706, this land was patented to them, in two tracts, of 222 acres, and 31 acres each, and by deed of 16 October, 1707, "Robert Roberts, of Maryland," conveyed his 222 (220) acres, which lay along the Lancaster road (Montgomery avenue) from the Meeting House to the Gulf road, and 10 acres, called "Clean John Meadow," on the "Upper Mill Creek," to Edward Rees.

Robert Roberts was twice married, and is supposed to have removed to Maryland, and died there. He m. first, Catharine Jones, and m. secondly, Priscilla Jones.

Ellin Roberts, b. 4. 10mo. 1675.

Owen Roberts, second son, b. 1. 10mo. 1677. He inherited some land from his father, as above, but entering on mercantile life in Philadelphia, was never a Merion planter. There was in 1716, an "ould Grave Yard" on his Merion property, from which bodies were removed to the ground of the Merion Meeting. He was the worthy son of his father, and was honored by being made the high sheriff of Philadelphia county, 1716-23; the treasurer, 1712-16; collector, 1716-23, a member of the city council, 1712, and of the Assembly, 1711, &c.

He owned 231 acres, of the east end of his father's original land, and by deed of 14 October, 1726, his relict, Ann, then residing in Nantmell township (Chester county), conveyed the same to Jonathan Jones, of Merion.

His will, signed 31. 1mo. 1706, witnessed by Griffith John, Evan Owen, John Roberts, and Robert Jones, was proved at

COMPANY NUMBER ONE

Philadelphia in 1723. He named brother Edward, and appointed trustees, brothers-in-law Evan Bevan and Robert Jones, with uncle John Roberts and Griffith John. He *m.* 23. 1mo. 1696, Ann, daughter of John Bevan, one of the early settlers of Merion, who died after 1723. Issue, six children. His infant son, Owen Roberts, was buried at Merion Meeting, 7mo. 25. 1707, but he had another Owen, *b.* 23. 8. 1711. Other children were Hugh Roberts, *b.* 30. 5. 1699. John Roberts, *b.* 12. 8. 1701, *m.* Mary Jones, and Awbrey Roberts, *b.* 24. 4. 1705.

Edward Roberts, third son, *b.* 4. 2mo. 1680. He received the "Chestnut Hill" place from his father, in 1702, but resided in Philadelphia, where he was a member of the City Council, in 1717, and Mayor, in 1739-40, having served as alderman, and a justice. He used for his seal "a rose, under a crown, between two human hearts." His will was proved 6 May, 1741.

He *m.* first, Susanna Painter, buried at the Merion Meeting House, 10mo. 3. 1707, daughter of George Painter, and *m.* secondly, Martha Hoskins, and *m.* thirdly, Martha Cox. He had four children: Hugh, Jane, wife of William Fishbourne, Mayor of Philadelphia 1719-21; Mary, and Elizabeth Bond.

William Roberts, b. 26. 3mo. 1682; *d.* in 1697.

Elizabeth Roberts, b. in Merion, 24. 12mo. 1683, named in her father's will.

EDWARD OWEN was residing in Dolserey, or Doleyserre, Merioneth, and described as "Gentleman," when he bought, by deed, dated 1 April, 1682, 312½ acres through Thomas & Jones. He was a son of Robert Owen (ap Humphrey), of Dolserey, by his wife, Jane, a daughter of Robert Vaughan, of Hengwrt.

Edward Owen came over in Hugh Robert's party in 1683, and found his land laid out on the Schuylkill, 153¼ acres, adjoining that of Dr. Jones, and the balance in Goshen tp. He probably never resided on this estate, as he sold it to his brother, Dr. Griffith Owen, by deed dated 9. 1mo. 1684-5, and according to it, was then living on Duck Creek, in New Castle Co. (Delaware). His Goshen rights he also conveyed to this brother, who had the land laid out, subsequently, on Chester Creek.

Dr. Griffith Owen, with his wife, Sarah, who survived him, son Robert, d. before 1717, and two daughters, Sarah and Elinor, and seven servants, from Prescoe, in Lancashire, came over (with his parents, and brother Louis Owen, who settled in New Castle Co.), in the ship Vine, of Liverpool, sailing from Doleyserre with a large party bound for the Welsh Tract, and arrived at Philadelphia 17. 7mo. 1684.

Besides the land he had fom his brother, which Dr. Owen, by deed dated 1. 1mo. 1694-5, conveyed to Robert David, whose land adjoined, the Doctor bought some from Richard Davies and John ap John, and the Land Commissioners (of which Board he was a member in 9ber, 1701), in Goshen, and had 775 acres, in one tract, which was confirmed to him, by patent dated 13 Dec. 1703. The Goshen Meeting House was built in the center of this tract, on land donated by the Doctor.

Dr. Owen died in Philadelphia in 1717, aged 70 years, and was one of the earliest physicians here, others being Dr. Edward Jones, Dr. John Goodson, Dr. Thomas Wynne, and Dr. Graeme. His will, signed 3 Jan. 1717, proved 6 Jan. named wife and children, Edward, Griffith (both became "practitioners in physick" in Philadelphia), John (a mariner), Sarah, wife of Jacob Jonathan Coppock, and Ann, wife of John Whitpaine. Son-in-law William Sanders, and "daughter-in-law, Mary, wife of Samuel Marriot."

WILLIAM AP JOHN, or William Jones, a yeoman, and widower, was residing in Bettws, in Merioneth, when he became a purchaser of 156¼ acres, in the Thomas & Jones tract, for £3. 2. 6. Witnesses to his deed, dated 1 April,

COMPANY NUMBER ONE

1682, being John Lloyd, Griffith Evan, Robert Lloyd and Reece Evan.

He came over in the "Morning Star" with the Hugh Roberts party, in 1683, bringing his children, and found 76½ acres laid out for him on the Schuylkill. He had about the same amount assigned to him in Goshen tp. There seems to be no proof that he ever resided on his Merion land, as he died shortly after coming over, his nuncupative will being sealed and proved at Philadelphia on 1. 1mo. 1684-5. He bequeathed his lands to his son, "John Williams," and appointed Hugh Roberts and John Roberts, (of "Pencoid"), trustees and guardians of his minor children. His wife is mentioned in his will as "Ann Reynald, deceased."

Of his children:—

John Williams, as above said, inherited all his father's lands. By deed, dated 18. 4mo. 1694, he conveyed his Merion land to Cadwalader Morgan, whose land adjoined his, and his Goshen land, 78 acres, he sold, 13. 6mo. 1697, to Edward Rees, of Merion, who conveyed it, 9 Jan. 1707-8, to Ellis David.

The other children, "who took the name Jones," were *Alice, Katherine* and *Gwen*, minors in 1685.

CADWALADER MORGAN was residing in Gwernevel, or Gwernfell, Ismynydd tp., Penllyn parish, Merioneth, when he, with his wife and several children, removed to Pensylvania, coming over on the "Morning Star," with the Hugh Roberts party, in 1683.

He brought the usual certificate of membership and removal, from the Penllyn Men Friends' Meeting, dated 8. 5mo. 1683, and signed by Richard Price, Robert and Evan Owen, Evan Rees, Rees Evan, Roger Roberts, Hugh and Edward Griffith, Griffith John, William Morgan and David John. He was a minister among Friends, "though he held no great share of the ministry," was the estimate recorded of him by Eleanor Evans, of Gwynedd, a daughter of Rowland Ellis. But as he had greatly "suffered" in Wales, because of his prominence, and religious faith, he purchased 156 acres through Thomas & Jones, and permanently left Wales.

On arrival, he found part of his purchase laid out on the Schuylkill, and here he erected a dwelling house, near "Pencoid," and passed the remainder of his days. His will, signed 10 Sep. 1711, was proved at Philadelphia, on 10 Oct. following. In it he mentioned his brothers, "Morgan Lewis" and "John Morgan," of Radnor. Cadwalader was therefore a son of James Morgan, who in 1701, had 450 acres in Radnor tp., to which his son and heir, John Morgan, succeeded 1702.

By purchase, he greatly increased his holdings in Merion, originally only 76½ acres, which he had by deed, dated 1 April, 1682, recorded 13. 4. 1684. Witnessed by John Lloyd, Reece Evan, Griffith Evan, Robert Lloyd and William John. He bought by deeds, dated 18. 4mo. 1694, the Merion land, 76½ acres, of Rees John William, of "Rees Joans," and the 76½ acres which John Williams had from his father. William John, an original purchaser of Thomas & Jones, which lands lay on both sides of his, which was backed by the purchase of Gainor Robert, so he now had, by survey of 1701, 223½ acres in Merion, fronting on the river. And, by deed of conveyance, dated 19 Jan. 1707-8, he acquired 92 acres of land, from Hugh John Thomas, or "Hugh Jones," adjoining his last purchase, and this gave him 2,178, or more, feet on the river, near Roberts's "Pencoyd." By deed, 30 May 1709, he sold his last purchases, namely, 223 acres and 92 acres, to Robert Evans, and subsequently it became part of the "Roberts Estate."

The will of "Cadder Morgan, of Merion," signed 10 Sep. 1711, in the presence of Robert Roberts, Moses Roberts,*

---

*Moses Roberts was one of the children of Robert Ellis, who, with his wife, Ellin, and seven children, removed here in 1690, bringing their certificate from the Quarterly Meeting held at Tyddyn y Gareg, and Thomas Jones, was proved 10 Oct. 1711. Executors, sons-in-law Robert Evan and Abel Thomas. Names brother John Morgan (of Radnor), son-in-law Hugh Evans, Cadwalader, second son of son-in-law Robert Evan (of Gwynedd); Sarah, wife of Robert Evan; Elizabeth, daughter of son-in-law Abel Thomas; sister-in-law Elizabeth, wife of brother Lewis Morgan, and her child, not named. Appointed as overseers, Edward Jones, John Roberts, David Jones (of Blockley), and Thomas Jones.

Cadwalader Morgan married Jane, who d. before 1711, daughter of Richard Gryffyth (ap Rhys, or Rees, and Prees, or Price), of Llanfawr, Merioneth, who was of Royal Descent, and a sister of Rees Jones's wife, of Merion, and to Edward Price, of Merion, and had two sons and three daughters by her, who is recorded at the Merion Meeting as buried 7. 19. 1710, "Jane wife of Chadwalader Morgan," namely:

Morgan Cadwalader, b. 23. 6mo. 1679. He was a minister among Friends, and died young, and unmarried.

Edward Cadwalader, b. 22. 6mo. 1682. He died unmarried, before his father.

Sarah, m. Robert Evan, or Evans, of Gwynedd. *Issue*.

Daughter, m. Hugh Evan, or Evans, of Gwynedd.

Daughter, m. Abel Thomas, of Merion. *Issue*. The following entry at the Merion Meeting, 12. 23. 1807: Burial,

---

in Merionethshire, dated 5mo. 28. 1690. Their children named "Roberts" were Abel (*m.* Mary Price), Moses, Ellis, Aaron (*m.* Sarah Longworthy), Evan, Rachel, Jane, Mary, and Gainor. The will of Moses Roberts, of Merion, signed 16. 12. 1715-6, witnessed by John Roberts and David George, was proved 28 Feb. same year. He appoints brother Ellis Roberts, and friend Robert Roberts, executors. Names brothers Aaron, Evan, and Ellis, and sisters Jane, Rachel, Mary, and Gainor Roberts, nieces Katherine and Rachel Roberts, and Margaret Edwards, Elizabeth Roberts, Sarah Dickinson, Jane, daughter of Abel Thomas, John Kelly, and Thomas Bowen.

WELSH SETTLEMENT OF PENSYLVANIA

"Jacob Thomas, son of Abel, with the waggon Load of Stone run over his head."

HUGH JOHN AP THOMAS, Hugh John or Hugh Jones, was living at Nantlleidiog, in Llanvawr parish, Merioneth, and was a widower and a farmer and miller, when he bought 156¼ acres of land, deed dated 18 March, 1681, through Thomas & Jones, and decided to remove to it, and came over with Hugh Roberts's party, in 1683.

He lived several years on his Merion land, 76¼ acres, (the balance of his purchase being laid out in Goshen tp.), which on resurvey on order from the Commissioners, amounted to 92 acres. He paid for and retained the increased acreage, having patent for it, dated 8 Nov. 1703.

By deed, dated 19 Jan. 1707-8, he conveyed his Merion tract to Cadwalader Morgan, whose property then adjoined his, and his holdings in Goshen to John Roberts, of "Pencoid," and removed to the Welsh settlement at Plymouth, where he died in 1727, having had four wives.

He *m.* secondly, at the Merion Meeting, 16. 5mo. 1686, Margaret David, and *m.* thirdly, at the Radnor Meeting, 18. 11mo. 1693, and *m.* fourthly, at the Merion Meeting, 22. 9mo. 1703, Margaret Edwards. It is said that he had issue, and that one of his daughters married after his last marriage, and before 1708, Rowland Richard.

MERION ADVENTURERS

"JOHN AP. THOMAS, of Llaithgwm, Commott of Penllyn, in the County of Merioneth, gentleman," as contemporary manuscripts designated him, was a forefather of the Merion Meeting, and a partner in this, the first, and most notable, company of Welsh Friends that removed to the Welsh Tract, though not destined himself to come over.

He was a son of Thomas ap Hugh (ap Evan Rhys-Goch), a gentleman farmer, or country gentleman, of Wern Fawr, in Llandderfel parish, Merioneth, whose will was proved at St. Asaph registry, in 1682. His brothers and sisters were, Cadwalader Thomas, (mentioned in the will of John Thomas), who resided on a farm at Kiltalgarth, in Merioneth, and died before his father, and whose wife was a sister of Robert Owen, who became one of the most prominent residents of "Merion in the Welsh Tract," one of their sons, John Cadwalader. mentioned in the will of his uncle, John Thomas, was the founder of the well known family of Cadwalader, of Philadelphia and Trenton], Hugh Thomas, of Penllyn; Catherine, wife of Gawen Vaughn, of Hendre Mawr, and Elizabeth, wife of Maurice ap Edward, of Cae Mor.

John ap Thomas was of notable ancestry, according to his pedigree, complied before 1682, which is extant. The late Dr. Levick, of Philadelphia, owned this MS pedigree,* and reproduced it in full in the Pa. Mag. vol. IV. p. 471, but as it is a very extended one, in fact, showing the lineal descent of John ap Thomas from Noah, space for only the last seventeen generations can be given here, which runs: "John

---

*Now in the possession of Lewis J. Levick, Esqr., and loaned by him to the Historical Society of Pensylvania (July, 1910).

WELSH SETTLEMENT OF PENSYLVANIA

Thomas, of Llaithgwm, in the County of Merioneth, Gent., 1682|Thomas ap Hugh|Hugh ap Evan (of Wern Fawr)| Evan ap Rees Gôch|Rees Gôch ap Tyder|Tudor|Evan and county of Denbig|Evan ddu|David ap Eiynion|Eiynion ap Kynrig|Kynrig ap Llowarch|Heilin|Tyfid|Tagno| Ysdrwyth|Marchwysst|Marchweithian, one of the 15en tribes of North Wales, and Lord of Issallet," ap Llud, ap Llen, &c, &c. This Marchweileian, "who beareth guwls a Lyon Rampant Argent, Armed Langued Azure," was the eleventh of the fifteen tribes of North Wales (see "Cambrian Register," 1795, p. 151), who held their lands by Baron's service. He was called Lord of Is-Aled, and owned, or controlled many townships, about A. D. 720.

He was convinced by the Quaker apostle, John ap John, of the truth of the teachings of Fox, "God's Truths," and became a member of the religious Society of Friends, in 1672, and from then till his untimely death, he was a leader and minister amongst Welsh Friends. Hugh Roberts, his life-long friend and neighbor, in an extant sketch of him, tells of his conversion, "though it was a time of great suffering" among the Friends in Wales for being non-conformists.

The members of the Society were beset on every side by paid spies of the "established church," and informers working "on commission," so it could be expected that this prominent gentleman farmer of the neighborhood would be closely watched, and Mr. Roberts records: "The first two meetings he was at, he was fined fifteen pounds [by a magistrate, and refusing to pay] the informer took from him two oxen, and a horse that was valued to be worth eleven pounds, and returned nothing back!" "The appearance of Truth was so precious to him," continues Mr. Roberts, "that he did not only make profession of it, but was also made willing to suffer for its sake, which he did valiantly." This, however, could be said of Mr. Roberts, himself, and of almost every man and woman who fled finally from persecution to the Welsh Tracts in Pensylvania. "When this faithful man first came among us [in Wales], it was the hottest time of persecution that we ever underwent."

So active were informers working for percentage of the fines imposed, that the resourceful John Thomas, records Mr. Roberts, went to one of the county justices, "that was moderate," with strong indorsements, and got the appointment for himself to be the high constable for his district, the position being vacant.

It seems that the procedure against Quakers was for the spy, or informer, to find an alleged culprit, one who did not attend the services of the Established Church, after warning; one who declined to contribute towards the support of that church and its minister, upon assessment; for attending meetings of Quakers; having such meetings held in their homes, and a long list of more petty complaints, sware out a warrant against him before a committing magistrate, which would follow its usual course, be delivered to the high sheriff, who would issue an order to the county jailor to receive and take charge of the prisoner, arrested and brought in by the high constable.

There has been preserved among the papers of John Thomas one of the sheriff's orders to the jailor, and it is possible that it is one of those that came into John's hands when he was high constable, and which he "pigeon-holed."

"Merioneth, SS.

"To Lewis Morris, Keeper of his Majts goale for ye sd County, & to Richard Price and Joseph Hughes.

"Whereas, I have apprehended Cadwalader ap Thomas ap Hugh, Robert Owen, Hugh ap Robert, John David, John Robert David, & Jonett John, spinster.

"By virtue of his Ma'ties writt, issued out of the last great sessions, & unto me directed & delivered, I therefore do will and require you to receive into your custody the bodyes of the said Caddw'r ap Tho ap Hugh, Robert Owen, Hugh Roberts, Jo Robert David & Jonett John, and them

WELSH SETTLEMENT OF PENSYLVANIA

safely to convey to the common geole of the sd County and them in a safe manner to be kept in ye sd geole whom I doe hereby commit, there to remain for the next great sessions to be held for ye sd county on Monday of ye sd sessions, then and there to answer such matters as shall be objected against them on his Ma'ties behalfe, this omitt you not at yr perill, given under my hand & seal of office, the fourth day of May, Anno R. Caroli (di) Angliæ & vicessimo sexto, Annoq dom 1674.

"Owen Wynne, Esq. Sheriff."

These apprehended Quakers were relatives and neighbors of John ap Thomas—one was his brother—so it may be imagined he did not carry out the order. It seems that in John Thomas's neighborhood, the most diligent of the informers, "a cunning, subtle man," was also an applicant for the position John captured,* and it was very evident to him why John sought it, and was glad to get it, so he set out to defeat him and have him impeached, in the following way, as told by Mr. Roberts:

"So the informer went on, and informed against Friends, and when he got a warrant, he brought it to the high constable, according to his orders" [from the magistrate], and John Thomas thereupon would tell him "to go about his business, that he was responsible for them" [the warrants]. So John simply pocketed the warrants, and did nothing. This was just as the informer hoped, for he knew that John was violating the Act of Parliament, and his office, and putting himself in the position to be heavily fined for every neglect. John certainly took great chances, for the informer had nine good cases against him, when fortunately "the King's Declaration came to put a stop to these wicked in-

---

*Among the papers of John Thomas is a letter, written about 1681, addressed to Richard Davies (one of the adventurers for Penn's land), by John ap David, a Friend, mentioned in the Sheriff's order, who also got the appointment of high constable to protect his brethren. It tells of the seizure of the chattels of Robert Evan.

formers," says Mr. Roberts. "Thus this faithful and valiant man hazarded his own estate to save his friends and brethren."

John Thomas wrote out, his notes still extant, many instances of his persecution and teasing, and those of his neighbors, wherein he tells of burdensome fines on the slightest provocations, and of scandalous tithing assessments and collections, all similiar to those related of others in Besse's "Sufferings of Friends." Probably the most disgraceful proceeding in John's experience was when the parish priest of the Established Church came one day to collect John's contribution towards his salary and support of the parish church. John's Mem.,

"In the year 1674, about the 20th day of the 4th month, Harry Parry, parson of Llanthervol, he and his men came to the ground of John ap Thomas, and demanded lambes tithes; and when the said John ap Thomas was not free to give him tithes, he sent his men abroad to hunt for the lambs, and at length they found them in one end of the barn, where they used to be every night, and they took out the best five out of 21 for tithes. And for the tithe corn, they took of the corn I cannot tell how much." John, like many Friends of the days of persecution, made memoranda of raids on his property, hoping a time would come when they could submit them, and be reimbursed.

Another interesting paper that has been preserved with the papers * of John ap Thomas, and which probably came into his hands when he was the high constable, is dated 20 May, 1675, and signed by Humphrey Hughes and John Wynne, justices of the peace, and addressed "To the high and pettie Constables" of Merionethshire, and to the church wardens, and the overseers of the poor in every parish in that county. It is the formal announcement, on informa-

---
*Nearly all of Mr. Thomas's papers are (1910) in possession of Mr. Lewis Jones Levick, of Bala, Pa.

WELSH SETTLEMENT OF PENSYLVANIA

tion from Owen David and Thomas John, of Penmaen, in Llanfawr parish, that certain persons in the county have met together on 16 May, "under colour of pretence of Religion," against the laws of the realm, "in a house called by the name of Ilwyn y Branar, in Penmaen, and orders distraints to be made against them. John ap Thomas is named in the list.

Volumes have been published telling of the persecutions of the Friends, yet the following letter, found among John Thomas' papers,** is interesting in that years after the aforesaid times, the Quakers were still being persecuted. And it was written just at the time the Welsh Friends were arranging to buy land from Penn, and remove to it.

"Dolgelley, ye 25th of the 4th mo., 1681.
"My dear friend John ap Thomas:

"These in haste may let thee understand that the persons undernamed are outlawed, and the Deputy Sheriffe hath writts against them.

"Many of them are dead, those that are alive (I) wish them to look to themselves, untill such time as friends shall come together to confer in their behalfe, that soe friends in their liberty may order some considerable gratuity to the Deputy Sheriffe for his kindness.

"Beside those undernamed, Elizabeth Williams is particularly to look to herself. There is a writt out of the Exchequer against her, as the Deputy Sheriffe informs me.

"Ye names are as followeth, vizt.:
William Prees, de Landervol.
Thomas ap Edward, de Llanvawr.
Litter Thomas, de eadem.
Thomas Williams, de ead.
John Davie, de ead.
Elizabeth Thomas, de ead, widdow.
Lodovicus ap Robt., de ead.

**Inherited by Mr. Lewis J. Levick and now in his possession.

COMPANY NUMBER ONE

Thomas ap Edward, de Llanvawr, Thomas Williams, de ead.
Robt. John Evan, de ead.
Griffith John, de Gwerevol, and Elizabeth his wife.
Hugh Griffith, of the same, & Mary his wife.
Maurice Humphrey Morgan, of the same.
This is att present from thy dear friend and desires to Excuse my brevity.   Lewis Owen."

This letter shows that the persecuted and outlawed Friends had at least one official interested in their welfare. The suggestion that the deputy sheriff be tipped to hold up the writs, has a modern look about it, yet it was a kindly meant suggestion.

Lewis Owen was a member of the Dolgelly Quarterly Meeting, Merionethshire, 2mo. 1684, with Rowland Owen, Humphrey Owen, Rowland Ellis, Ellin Ellis, Owen Lewis, Owen Humphrey, Hugh Rees, Reece Evan, Richard Jones, David Jones, Ellis Davies, Ellis Moris, John William, Kathrine Price, Jane Robert and Agnes Hugh.

"Elizabeth Williams is particularly to look to herself!" This most active preacher among Friends. What a terrible experience hers had been for a half century, and still she had "to look to herself"; stop getting up meetings and exhorting, else she would have to undergo further punishments, and this when she was nearly eighty years old. Nearly thirty years before this last warning, Elizabeth, when 50 years old, with the almost equally celebrated minister, Mary Fisher, nearly escaped execution of some sort in Cambridge, in 1653. Besse, the Quaker annalist, records that "the mayor ordered them to be whipped till the blood ran down their bodies, * * * which was done far more cruelly than with worse malefactors, so that their flesh was miserably torn." They were then driven out of the city.

It has already been told that John ap Thomas was one of the party of Welsh Friends that went to London to interview William Penn, about the land in America, he was of-

WELSH SETTLEMENT OF PENSYLVANIA

fering for sale. There is a letter extant, among his papers, from him to his wife, dated London, 28. 3mo. 1681, telling her that he is well, and that he arrived in London on 21st inst., "without any great difficulty," accompanied by Thomas Ellis, with whom he intended to return home "the next second day," and concludes:

"I lay it upon thee to mind my dear love to my friends, H. R. & his; Robt O. & his; E. Jo. & his; R. D. & his; H. G. & his; G. J. & his; Elizabeth John & hers; Elizabeth Wyn and hers, with all the rest as if named them one by one.

No more at present, but my dear love to thee, and see I

I am JOHN
ap Thomas."

At this time John ap Thomas and Edward Jones secured rights to 5,000 acres of Penn's American land, and upon their return to Merioneth, after themselves subscribing for over 1,500 acres, they conveyed the balance among fifteen neighbors in Penllyn tp., as stated, the majority of whom removed to their purchases.

It was undoubtedly the intention of John Thomas also to remove with his family to his American land, as he was greatly interested in the plan for a refuge for the persecuted Welsh Quakers, and was a shareholder in the Society of Free Traders of Pensylvania, but a little time before the date, in July, 1682, set for the first departure of Welsh Friends, his partner and relative, Dr. Jones, and companions, he became too ill to travel, and never recovered. His old friend, Hugh Roberts, records the scenes of his deathbed, saying: "He took his leave of his friends, giving his hand to every one of us, and so in a sweet and heavenly praise, he departed the 3d day of 3mo. 1683." And of this event, his son, Thomas Jones, entered in the Family Bible, still preserved: "Our dear father, John ap Thomas, of Laithgwm, in the Commott of Penllyn, in the county of Merioneth, in North Wales, departed this life the 3d day of 3d month, 1683, being the 5th day of the week, and was buryed at Friends burying place at Havod-vadog in the said Commott and County, ye 5th of ye said month."

Although his health and strength was poor and failing, John Thomas looked forward to joining his friends in America, and to this end, "sent some effects [with them] and agreed with them to make some provision against his intended coming." This was certainly done, as John's portion of land was located on the Schuylkill, and in Goshen tp., the same as if he were present. In fact, there was an agreement, which is extant, signed by Edward Jones, per David Davies, while John Thomas was so ill, and before Dr. Jones sailed, saying: "And should John ap Thomas happen to die before ye said Edward Jones, that E. J. should take no benefit of survivorship," which probably referred to partnership in goods for sale in Pensylvania, which Dr. Jones took with him.

About four months after her husband's decease, "Katherine Robert," his relict, with her children, sailed from Chester, in the ship "Morning Star," for Philadelphia, with the parties of Hugh Roberts and John Bevan, and arrived 16 Nov., 1683, "and found one-half of the purchase taken up in the place since called Merion, and some small improvement made on the same where we then settled," as her son, Robert Jones, wrote to William Penn.

In a sketch of John Thomas and his wife, by the late Dr. James J. Levick, of Philadelphia, (in the IV Vol., of the magazine of the Historical Society of Pensylvania), he says: "From all that is left on record, Katharine Thomas was a woman of great force of character and of much Christian worth. * * * Great as was the sacrifice, she does not seem to have hesitated to leave her comfortable home for the distant and wild lands beyond the sea."

The certificate she brought from the Friends' Penllyn Monthly Meeting, of which she had been a member for ten years, dated 18. 5mo. 1683, was most flattering, and among

WELSH SETTLEMENT OF PENSYLVANIA

others, bore the signatures of Robert Owen, Richard Price, Cadwalader Lewis and Edward Griffith.

Among the "Thomas Papers" there are letters from Robert Vaughan, "a learned man," to his "loving aunt," Katharine Thomas,—one written in 3mo. 1687, and a letter from her "loving nephew," Edward Maurice, dated "Eyton Parke, Denbigshire, 3 Sep. 1692," mentioning her kin, the Yales, of Plas yn Yale, and other "County Families" of Wales, all suggesting that Katharine was of gentle birth and refined breeding, which is borne out by Friends' endorsements, and the accounts of these families in Nicholas's "Annals and Antiquities of the County Families of Wales."

Many of the Welsh Friends, bound for Merion, came over on this voyage of the "Morning Star," as told before. Katharine's immediate party, her children and servants, numbered twenty. It was a long voyage, even at that time, and only the strongest survived it. Two of Katharine's children died and were buried at sea, namely, daughters Sydney, on 29. 7mo. and Mary, on 18. 8mo. as recorded in the Bible* of Thomas Jones, one of Katharine's sons.

As "some provision against" Katharine's coming had been made on her husband's land, her son records they went there at once, after landing, the place being called, he says, "Geilli yr Cochiaid," or "Grove of Red Partridges."

The "provision" was only a log cabin, and here the family resided till a small stone house was erected on another property she bought. Both of these remained till recently as landmarks near the village of Bala, on the property of Walter Jones. Her property here, as surveyed in 1684, was 612 acres of timber land, and was the furtherest located up the Schuylkill of the purchases through her husband and Dr. Jones, and extended back to north of the present village of Narberth. Adjoining her was her old

---

*This Bible, with its family data, has been presented to the Historical Society of Pensylvania by Lewis Jones Levick, Esqr.

COMPANY NUMBER ONE

friend, Hugh Roberts, who, with his family, had also, as said, come over in this voyage of the "Morning Star."

We can imagine Katharine Thomas to have been of good business acumen, as after getting her 612 acres here into working order, and made crop-yielding, she purchased the following summer 150 acres on the river, between the lands of Barnabas Wilcox and Joseph Harrison, adjoining her husband's land, on which there was "a dwelling house lately erected." On 10 Dec. 1689, took title for a tract of 500 acres north of her first land, on the river, called "Glanrason," from Joseph Wood, (son of William Wood, the first grantee, 30. 7mo. 1684), and adjoining the 500 acre tract, next above on the river of William Sharlow, called "Mount Ararat." * Besides these lands on the river, Katharine also had a tract in Goshen tp., on Chester Creek, being the balance of her husband's purchase for £25, and lots in the "city" and a questionable share of the "liberty land" which went with the original purchase.

About six years after their mother's death, the sons had all of her land that remained to them, surveyed, and it amounted to 679 acres in Merion, and 635 acres in Goshen, for the whole they received a patent dated 3. 11mo. 1703, The Merion land, in a general way, lay north of the town of Narberth, extending from Montgomery Ave. (the old Lancaster Road) to the river, and, from the Price property, west of and near the Merion Meeting House, westward to "St. Mary's" (the Wister, or Chichester property). East of the Ardmore toll-gate, on Montgomery Ave. A part of this Merion tract is still (1910) owned by descendants.

After coming over, Katharine, as executrix to her husband, had his will, a long one, dated 9 Feb., 1682, filed in Philadelphia, 10. 3mo. 1688. It was signed in the presence of Robert Vaughan, Rowland Owen and Thomas Vaughan.

---

*Sharlow's land was wrongly placed on Holme's Map. It was beyond Wood's property.

WELSH SETTLEMENT OF PENSYLVANIA

He desired his tract of 1,250 acres (mentioning the transaction between Penn, Dr. Jones and himself), to be divided equally between his four sons, and left £20 cash to each of his children, providing, of course, for his wife. He named as his overseers, John ap John, of Rhiwabon, or Ruabon, parish, Denbig; Thomas Ellis, of Cyfanedd, Merioneth; Thomas Wayne, "late of Bronvadog," Flintshire; Robert David, of Gwernevel, Merioneth; Hugh Roberts, of Kiltalgarth, Merioneth; Edward Jones, "late of Bala, Chirurgion"; Robert Vaughan, of Gwernevel; Edward Morris, of Lavodgyfaner, Denbig; Robert Owen, of Fron Gôch, and "my son-in-law, Rees Evans, of Fronween," Merioneth.

Katharine Thomas lived fourteen years in "New Merion" among her Welsh friends, and was a regular attendant of the Merion Meeting, her death being thus entered in her son's, Thomas Jones's, Bible: "Our dear Mother Katherin Thomas departed this Life ye 18th day of ye 11 month, 1697, about ye 2d or 3d hour in ye morning (as we thought), & she was buryed next day." Her will, not recorded, dated 7. 11mo. 1697, is mentioned in a deed, executed by her sons —Book G; V., pa. 496.

Her son *Evan* died unmarried a month after she died, in Feb. 1697, leaving a small money gift to the Merion Preparative Meeting.

Of her remaining children, who took "Jones" as their surname:

Thomas Jones, eldest son, was "through school" when he came over with his mother, and there is evidence that his education was a good one. He wrote a remarkably strong, clear hand, and kept a log of the voyage to America on the blank leaves of the Family Bible, and records of his kin. In 1709, he acted as clerk of the Haverford Monthly Meeting of ministers and elders, and was also their treasurer. He became an "approved minister" among the Friends, and was popular in his neighborhood as a guardian, and overseer.

He joined Dr. Jones, his father's co-trustee in the Pensylvania land, in conveying by deed, dated 27. 10. 1693, the 100 acres of liberty land due on account of their entire purchase, to William ap Edward.

He died 6. 8mo. 1727, at his home in Merion. His will, signed 31. 6. 1727, witnessed by Thomas Moore, Richard George and Robert Jones, trustees-"Cousins Robert Jones and Jonathan Jones," was proved on 5 Aug. 1728. He bequeathed lands in Merion adjoining Jonathan Jones, Sr., and in Goshen tp.

He married Anne, named in his will, daughter of Griffith ap John, or Jones, of Merion (a son of John ap Evan, of Penllyn, "old Merion," and a cousin of Robert Owen, of "New Merion"), who owned a 187 acre place northeast of Bala, Philadelphia County, and whose sons, John and Evan, and their descendants took the name "Griffith."

Thomas and Anne Jones had besides John and Catherine, both buried at Merion Meeting in 1706, Evan, Elizabeth, Ann, Mary, Sarah, who *m.* at Merion Meeting 8. 11mo. 1742, Jonathan Jones, (son of Jonathan Jones, and grandson of Dr. Edward Jones), and Katharine, who *m.* Lewis, son of David and Katharine Jones, aforesaid, of Blockley, Philadelphia County.

Robert Jones, named in his brother's will, second son of John ap Thomas, inherited the plantation called "Glanrason," 189 acres, and purchased from David Hugh, 20. 4. 1699, 150 acres (surveyed), 165 acres of Sharlow's "Mt. Ararat," confirmation deed, 12 Feb. 1704, and at one time owned 1,000 acres in Merion, and 426 acres in Goshen. "He was a useful member of both civil and religious society," having been a justice of the peace, and a member of the provincial assembly. He was buried at the Merion Meeting House.

He married 3. 11mo. 1693, at his mother's house, Ellen Jones, sister to David Jones, of Blockley tp., who with his wife, Katharine, had certificate from the Monthly Meeting

WELSH SETTLEMENT OF PENSYLVANIA

at Hendrimawr, Wales, dated 24. 12mo. 1699, signed by Robert Vaughan, Ellis Lewis and Thomas Cadwalader.

Robert's will was dated 21. 7mo. 1746. Of the children of Robert Jones: Gerrad, eldest son, b. 28. 12, 1705-6; inherited "Glanrason," [he m. first, Sarah, daughter of Robert Lloyd and his wife, Lowry, daughter of Rees John William, of Merion, and m. secondly, Ann, (daughter of Benjamin Humphrey, of Merion?) and had eight children, of these Ellen, m. Robert Roberts and Isaac Lewis, and Paul, m. Phoebe Roberts]; Elizabeth, b. 1695, first child, Katherine, b. 1700, m. Thomas Evans; Ann, b. 1702, m. James Paul, of Abington tp., and Robert, b. 3. 6mo. 1709, who received land from his father.

Cadwalader Jones was a shipping merchant in Philadelphia. The Land Commissioners on 23 Feb. 1702, granted him and his brother Thomas, executors to their mother's will, power to take up 100 acres of land (being part of 200 acres sold by the Commissioners to Hugh Roberts "for their mother's use"), which they had laid out in Merion tp., in 11mo. 1712-13, adjoining the lands of Mordecai Moore, John Havid (Havard), James Atkinson, and Owen Roberts.

Cadwalader, and his brothers, Thomas Jones, procured grant and survey of a 34 foot lot in 2d street, and a 20 foot lot in 3d street, in place of one "whole lot" of 51 feet, in 2d street, "of which they have been disappointed."

Katherine Jones m. Robert Roberts, son of Hugh Roberts, of Merion, the eminent minister among Friends, and next neighbor to Katharine Thomas.

Elizabeth Jones, m. before 1662, Rees Evan, of Fonween, in Penmaen, Penllyn, Merioneth. Their son, Evan Rees, came to Pensylvania and his daughter Sydney m. Robert Roberts, of "Pencoyd," Merion.

John Thomas had reserved to himself 1,250 acres, of which 1,225 were in the City Liberties, and 612½ acres in Merion, and the same number in Goshen. On re-survey, it was discovered that his Merion tract contained 679 acres,

COMPANY NUMBER ONE

while that in Goshen came out right. On 19. 2mo. 1703, the Land Commissioners confirmed the land to the brothers, Thomas, Robert, and Cadwalader Jones, the joint heirs under their father's will. It may be noticed all through these notices of Welsh families, that primogeniture was not the custom amongst them. Equal division of the land was made between the sons, and possession given without livery of seizine, that is, immediately. Since it was the practice to divide the land amongst the heirs, especially the improved parts, which they had helped to till, small farms prevailed, and they also became more numerous because they were easier worked.

A SECTION FROM HOLME'S MAP.

MERION ADVENTURERS

GAINOR ROBERTS, a spinster, was about 30 years old, a daughter of Robert ap Hugh, or Pugh, of Llyndeddwydd, near Bala, in Merioneth, (by his wife Elizabeth, daughter of William Owen, of Llanvawr), and a sister of the Friends' minister, Hugh Roberts, when she bought on her own account 156½ acres of the Thomas & Jones tract, and came over to Pensylvania with her celebrated brother, with whom she lived in Kiltalgarth, on the ship "Morning Star," in 1683. Part of her purchase, 76½ acres, was laid out in Merion, back of Calwalader Morgan's land, and the remainder in Goshen tp., and these lands she took to her husband as a marriage portion.

She m. at Merion Meeting, 20. 1mo. 1683-4, whether in the traditional log Meeting House, the predecessor of the present stone one, or at her brother's home, is not known, John Roberts, who came over also on this trip of the "Morning Star." She d. 20. 12mo. 1722, aged 69 years, and was buried with her husband at the Merion Meeting House.

They were the founders of the Roberts family of "Pencoyd," Merion, and theirs was the first marriage in the Welsh tract of record.

John Roberts, of "Pencoyd," though not one of the original purchasers in Thomas & Jones tract, should be noticed here, with the other first settlers of this land, as he was the earliest of Welsh purchasers of the adjoining land, on the river, and became a noted man in the settlement.

In the days of this John there were three, or more, men in the Welsh tract named "John Roberts," and, to distinguish them from the subject of this sketch, their occupation or place of residence, was given with their names in early deeds, as later there was "John Roberts, Skuilkill," buried

WELSH SETTLEMENT OF PENSYLVANIA

at Merion Meeting 7. 28. 1747, and "John Roberts, millwright," buried here 11. 10. 1803.

John Roberts, of "Pencoyd," as he named his seat, and as it is still called, born about 1648, was the son of Richard Robert (ap Thomas Morris), of Cowyn, Llaneingan parish, in Carnarvonshire, and his wife, Margaret, daughter of Richard Evan, of the same parish. He was about 29 years of age when he became a Quaker, in 1677. John Roberts's account of himself, filed with the Merion Meeting:

"John Roberts, formerly of Llyn, being son of Richard Roberts and grandson of Robert Thomas Morris, who lived at Cowyn, in the Parish of Llaneigan and County of Carnarvon; my mother being Margaret Evans, daughter of Richard Evans, of Llangian and county aforesaid.

"Being convinced of God's everlasting worth about the year one thousand six hundred and seventy seven, not by man nor through man, but by the Revelation of Jesus Christ, in my owne heart, Being about thirty miles from any Friends' Meeting in that time when I was convinced but coming into acquaintance with Friends near Dalgelle and near Bala in Merionethshire, I frequented their Meetings while I abode in those parts, but by the Province of God in the year One thousand six hundred and eighty three, I transported Myself with many of my Friends for Pensylvania where I and they arrived the sixteenth day of the Ninth month One thousand six hundred and Eighty three being then Thirty five years old, and settled myself in the place where afterwards I called Pwencoid, in the Township of Merion, which was afterwards called by them being the first settlers of it, having brought with me one servant man from my Native Land, and fixed my settling here. I took to Wife Gainor Roberts, Daughter of Robert Pugh from Llwyndedwydd near Bala in Merionethshire, her Mother being Elizabeth William Owen one of the first that was convinced of the Truth in that Neighborhood. So leaving this account for our ofspring and others that desire to know

COMPANY NUMBER ONE

from whence we came and who we descend from and when we came to settle unto this place where we now abide being then a Wilderness, but now by God's Blessing upon our endeavours is become a fruitful field. To God's name be the Praise, Honour and Glory who is worthy of it for ever and for ever more."

As apparently Mr. Roberts had a good home, and had not "suffered" much, it must be supposed that he only came over to Pensylvania because his lady-love, Gainor Roberts, did. Theirs was probably a long drawn-out courtship, as he was 35, as he states, and she 30, when they came over together, with her brother.

He was living near Dolgelly, and near where Gainor lived, when he set out for America, taking with him only one indentured servant, and his certificate of membership from the Men's Meeting, in Penllyn, dated 18. 5mo. 1683, which described him as of Llun, in Carnarvonshire. On the same date this Meeting issued Certificates to many others bound for Pensylvania, among them Cadwalader Morgan, and Hugh John Thomas, of Gwernfell, Robert David, of Tuyn y nant, Katharine Roberts, of Llaethgwn, widow, and Gaynor Roberts, of Kiltalgarth. All were signed by nearly the same men. Both John and Gainor were members in good standing of the Penllyn Monthly Meeting, as may be seen. It is presumed that John's brother Richard and sister Ann, who came in the Hugh Roberts party, both had issue.

John Roberts probably stayed close to Hugh Roberts and helped put up his house in Merion, in the winter of 1683-4, for in the early spring of 1683-4, he married Gainor Robert. Theirs was the first wedding in the Merion Meeting.

"John Roberts the maltster," as he was known from his occupation, had bought from Richard Davies (Company No. 7), 150 acres by deed dated 30 July, 1682, and this right he had surveyed and laid out to him in "the city liberty" on the Schuylkill, and next east of the land of Evan Rees, in the Thomas & Jones tract. This land he named "Pencoyd," which it has ever since been so called. With the land he had by Gainor, both in Merion and in Goshen, as the marriage portion, this gave him, "on paper," 306½ acres, but on resurvey, (by report of 12. 2mo. 1703), it turned out that he had 108 acres in Merion, and 262 acres in Goshen, which was 25 acres too much in Merion, and 8½ acres too much in Goshen, this over-plus he bought. And on resurvey of another parcel of 150 acres in Merion, this was found 20 acres short, and a resurvey of 60 acres (which had been part of Swan Lum's grant of 400 acres, in 1677, he bought in 1699 of Andrew Wheeler, a Swede, in the "liberties," and Merion tp., "on the westerly side of the Schilckul by the falls," showed 47 acres over, and thus, between the over-plus and shortage, he had to pay for a balance of 60½ acres.

John Roberts bought, by a joint deed dated 8. 6mo. 1702, the land due as head-rights for a lot of servants and others, who had come over about 1683-4, amounting altogether to 750 acres, laid out at his first purchase, among the Swedes, which his son Robert inherited. By deed of 7. 7mo. 1687, he bought from Cadwalader Morgan and Hugh John, 156 acres, in Goshen tp., on Chester Creek. At one time, with his wife's lands, John Roberts owned about 1,250 acres.

1704, 11mo. 5th., according to desire of the Merion Preparative Meeting, extended to all its members, he filed "an account of his place of abode in his native country, his convincement, his removal to this country, his marriage, and other remarkable passages of his life." A copy of this statement is extant in the family of a descendant, and an extract is given above.

He was from the first a prominent man among the Pensylvania Welsh, and was a justice of the peace in the Welsh Tract, and a representative for it in the Assembly, and owned a very large landed estate. He died at his residence in Merion, which now forms a portion of the "Roberts mansion," on the City Line, on 6. 4mo. 1724, aged 76 years, and was buried with his wife, Gainor, in the ground of the Merion Meeting. The record of their burials at the Merion Meeting being "Gainor Roberts, wife of John Roberts, maltster, 12. 23. 1721," and "John Roberts, maltster, 1724, 4mo."

His will, signed 3. 7mo. 1722, witnessed by Edward George, Gainor Jones, and Thomas Jones, was proved at Philadelphia, 31 Aug. 1724. He named "brother Richard and his daughter Margaret," his niece Margaret, daughter of his own sister Ann: grandsons John, Alban, Rees and Phineas. Overseers appointed—Robert Jones, Robert Evans, and Thomas Jones: Owen Roberts mentioned. He bequeathed five pounds to the trustees of the Merion Meeting, for relief of the poor of Merion Meeting.

John Roberts, of "Pencoyd," had only two children, by his only wife, Gainor Roberts, who were named in his will, namely:

Elizabeth Roberts, b. 21. 1mo. 1692, d. unm., 9. 7mo. 1746 She received by her father's will £200, and half of his personal estate.

Robert Roberts, of "Pencoyd," first child, and only son and heir, b. 15. 12mo. 1685. He inherited from his father, the homestead and all his lands, and half of his personalty. He was a member of the Merion Peculiar Meeting, and the Haverford Monthly Meeting, and he and his wife were buried at the Merion Meeting House. He d. 17 March, 1768, leaving a will signed when "antient and Infirm of Body," 4. 7mo. 1764, in the presence of Richard George, Jr., David Lloyd and John Roberts, Jr., proved at Philadelphia 26 March, 1768.

He m. at the Merion Meeting, on 17. 4mo. 1709, Sidney Rees, daughter of Rees Evan, of Penmaen, in Merionethshire (whose mother was a daughter of John ap Thomas, of Llaethgwm, who d. in 1683), and had by her, who d. 29 June, 1764, aged 74 years, the following children named in his will:—

WELSH SETTLEMENT OF PENSYLVANIA

John Roberts, eldest son and heir, b. 26. 4mo. 1710, inherited the homestead farm, about 180 acres, on the City Line, where he d. 31 Jan. 1776. It adjoined land of Robert Evans, on the north, John Griffith on the west, and south, "tp. line road to the Ford road," and land of Rudolph Latch and John Garrett. His will, signed in Oct., 1775, in the presence of John Robert, miller, Rees Price, and Hugh Cully, was proved 7 Feb. 1776. He named all of his children then living. To son Algernon, 50 acres in Blockley, bought of Joseph Abraham, south of the City Line, and north of lands of David George, and the homestead, then 100 acres, laying above and west of the "new road," and adjoining the lands of Thomas Norris, John Leacock, Jacob Bealer, and William Stadleman. To son Jonathan, 27 acres on the river, in Blockley, and money to sons Benjamin, John, Robert, and daughters Elizabeth, wife of Thomas Palmer, and Tacy, wife of John Palmer. Trustees, "loving brothers Owen Jones, Jacob Jones, and kinsman James Lewis Jones, Jr.

He m. at Merion Meeting, on 4. 3mo. 1733, Rebecca, daughter of Jonathan Jones (son of Dr. Edward Jones), of Merion, and had twelve children by her, who d. 8 Dec., 1779. His son Algernon also was the father of twelve children.

Algernon Roberts, who was a lieut. col. of Philadelphia militia, lived and died at the old Roberts homestead. He m. at the Swedes Church, in Philadelphia, 18 Jan. 1781, Tacy, daughter of Isaac Warner, of Blockley, colonel of Philadelphia militia. Of their many children, John 1787-1837, was the ancestor of B. Frank Clapp, of Phila., Isaac, 1789-1859, was the ancestor of the late George B. Roberts, who resided in the old homestead; Algernon Sidney, 1798-1865, was the ancestor of George T., Dr. A. Sidney and Percival Roberts, of Philadelphia, Edward, 1800-1872, was the ancestor of Edward Browning, and Mrs. Arthur V. Meigs, of Philadelphia.

COMPANY NUMBER ONE

Phineas Roberts, *b.* 13. 3mo. 1722. He inherited 30 acres on the river, adjoining the homestead that had been Wheeler's land in Blockley. His wife Ann, aged 80 years, was killed by their insane son, Titus Roberts, in 11mo. 1803.

Sidney Roberts, *b.* 9. 3mo. 1729; *m.* John Paul, who received a portion of the personalty of his father-in-law.

Alban, 1712-1727; Reese, 1715-1755.

"REES JOHN WILLIAM, of Llanglynin," yeoman, or "Rees Joans," or Jones, was one of the seventeen original purchasers, by deed of 1 April, 1682, through Thomas & Jones, but he did not come over till in 1684, when the land on the river was partly cleared and planted, and the "first come-overs," the parties of Dr. Jones, and Hugh Roberts, were well housed on their purchases. He found the land (his deed being recorded at Philadelphia 21. 4. 1684), allotted to him the worst proportioned in the tract, it being a narrow strip, only about 66 feet on the river, extending the full length of the other lots, to the Charles Lloyd land, where it was only about 264 feet wide, in all, here, 76½ acres, and remainder in Goshen tp.

"Rees Jones," as he was generally known, was a son of John ap William, a farmer in Llangelynin parish, Merioneth, who "suffered" considerable with the other Quakers in his neighborhood, 1661, &c. Rees came over with a large party of Welsh settlers in the ship "Vine, of Liverpool," sailing from Dolyserre, near Dolgules, in Merionethshire, which is a maritime county, and arrived at Philadelphia on 17. 7mo. 1684. He was accompanied by his wife and three children.

His sister, "Margaret John William, of Llangyllynin, widow," had preceded him, coming over in the party of Hugh Roberts, bringing a certificate of membership from the Quarterly Meeting, near Dolgelly, dated 27. 5mo. 1683, recorded at the Haverford (or Radnor) Monthly Meeting. As Margaret John she had patent, 18. 1mo. 1717-8, for 400 acres of land on a branch of French Creek.

WELSH SETTLEMENT OF PENSYLVANIA

His brother, Evan John William, or Evan Jones, also came over at that time, with his son, Robert Jones (who resided at Gwynedd), and died soon after, being buried in the ground of the Merion Meeting, in 11mo. 1683. He bequeathed some land in Goshen tp. to his nephews, Richard and Evan Jones. Evan Jones, and Hannah, his wife, and Mary Ellis, his mother-in-law, and Gemima, her other daughter, brought certificate, undated, from the Meeting held at Tyddier y Gareg, in Garthgunfawr, near Dolegelle, Merioneth, to the Haverford Monthly Meeting, signed by Humphrey, John, Robert, and Rowland Owen, Owen, Robert, and Howell Lewis, and Hugh Rowland.

Rees Jones, and his wife, Hannah, also brought the usual certificate of membership and removal, from the Quarterly Meeting, near Dolgelly, dated 4. 2mo. 1684. Rees was described as "of Llwyn Grevill, Clynn parish, Merioneth."

Before coming over, he purchased, by deed dated 16 July, 1684, the original right of Thomas ap Richard, or Prichard, of Nant Lleidiog, to his share 156¼ acres, of the Thomas & Jones tract. The 76½ acres of which that lay in Merion adjoined the back part of Rees's land, and this gave him 153 acres in Merion. The present settlement of Merion, or Merion Station, on Pensylvania Railroad, is on his land, and Rees's dwelling house was near it. By deed of 8. 4mo. 1694, he sold his 76½ acres on the river end, or his original purchase, to his brother-in-law, Cadwalader Morgan, whose land adjoined.

Rees Jones died 26. 11mo. 1697-8, and was buried at the Merion Meeting House. His will, which he signed with his mark, dated 24. 11mo. 1697-8, witnessed by Griffith John and Abel Thomas, was proved at Philadelphia, 4 March, 1702-3. He named his sons, Richard, Evan, and John; and overseers: Cadwalader Morgan, Abel Thomas, Edward Jones, Griffith John and John Roberts.

He *m.* about 1678, Hannah Richards, or Price, *b.* in 1656, sister to Jane, wife of Cadwalader Morgan, of Merion, and

COMPANY NUMBER ONE

to Edward Price, who came to Pensylvania before 1685-6, and daughter of Richard Gryffyth ap Rhys, or Prees, and Price, of Llanvawr, or Lanfor parish, in Merioneth, a member of the Friends' Penylln Monthly Meeting, near Bala, whose will, dated 26. 11mo. 1685, was filed at St. Asaph registry in 1686. His will describes him as of Glanlloidiogin, Llanfor parish. Witnesses were Edward Nicholas, Thomas ap Robert, Lowry v. Thomas Rees Evans, and Cadwalader Ellis. To Edward Prees, alias Price, (of Merion), eldest son; (after he came over here, he sent to Wales for "some intelligence of his Pedigree," which he received about 1700, and is extant); Jane, eldest daughter, wife of Cadwalader Morgan; daughter Hannah, wife of Rees John William; grandchildren William John, and Catherine John, children of John William; and son Thomas ap Richard, the executor, who received all of the estate of his father. Thomas renounced the trust, when the Court gave the administration to Edward Nicholas, of Cynlas.

After Rees's death, Hannah, his relict, *m.* secondly, at the Merion Meeting, on 22. 2mo. 1703, Ellis David, of Goshen tp., a widower, who was buried, *s. p.* 17. 1mo. 1720, and *m.* thirdly, 14. 1mo. 1722. Thomas Evans, of Gwynedd tp.

Rees Jones,* had by his wife, Hannah Price, who was of

---

*Among the present-day people, descendants of Rees John William and Hannah Price, are:

Frank Foulke.
Samuel Marshall.
Hugh Jones Brooke.
Mrs. Charles Richardson.
Mrs. George B. Roberts.
Mrs. Henry K. Dillard.
Miss Mary William Perot.
Mrs. J. Howard Lewis, Jr.
Mrs. Hunter Brooke.
Mrs. George H. Colket.
William T. Brooke.
John W. Townsend.

Mrs. Harrison K. Caner.
William P. Troth.
Henry T. Coates.
William M. Coates.
Joseph H. Coates.
George M. Coates.
Edward H. Coates.
Mrs. Charles Ridgway.
Mrs. Henry S. Harper.
Mrs. John R. Drexel.
Mrs. Edward Y. Townsend.
Henry Troth Townsend.

WELSH SETTLEMENT OF PENSYLVANIA

Royal Descent, the following issue, besides *Margaret*, b. 20. 6. 1697, *Edward*, and *Catharine*, who d. unm.

Richard Jones, b. about 1679. He came over with his parents, and according to the records, filed with the Merion Preparative Meeting, of which he was a member, an account of their ancestry, and life in the Old Country, on 2. 12mo. 1704-5.

He inherited from his father the home-farm of about 100 acres, which he increased to 156¼ acres, and with some land he owned in Goshen, he had 293¾ acres altogether, in 1703. By deed of 8 Nov. 1720, he bought of John Roberts (the nephew of Thomas Lloyd, of Llangower, one of the original purchasers through Thomas & Jones), 39½ acres, adjoining his Merion land.

By deed, dated 26 June, 1729, Richard Jones conveyed all of his Merion land, then 156¼ acres, to Hugh Evans, and removed to his land in Goshen tp. which he had increased by purchase. He and his brother, Evan Jones, bought there a tract of 153¼ acres, which on resurvey was 178 acres. He d. aged 92 years, in Goshen tp., on 16. 7mo. 1771, having been twice married. He had three children by each wife. He *m.* first, 6. 4mo. 1705, Jane Evans, who d. 27. 2mo. 1711, and was buried at the Merion Meeting House, and *m.* secondly, in 1718, Rebecca Vernon, widow of Thomas Garrett. She d. 23. 12mo. 1748.

Lowry Jones, d. in Philadelphia, 25. 11mo. 1762, aged 80 years. She *m.* first, at Merion Meeting, 11. 8mo. 1698, Robert ffloid, or Lloyd, who came over with Hugh Roberts, in 1683, and bought land, some 400 acres, north of Rowland Ellis's seat, "Bryn Mawr," where he d. 29. 3mo. 1714, aged 45 years and was buried at the Merion Meeting House, being the father of eight children. Of these Hannah, 1699-1763, *m.* first, 1720, John Roberts, (son of John Roberts and Elizabeth Owen v. Owen Humphrey); d. 1721; Sarah,

COMPANY NUMBER ONE

1703-1730, *m.* 1729, at Merion Meeting, Garrad Jones, *d.* 1765; Gainor, 1705-1728, *m.* 1727, at Merion Meeting, Mordecai James, *d.* 1776; Rees, 1709-1753; Robert, 1711-1786; and Richard, 1713-1755. Lowry Jones *m.* secondly, at the Merion Meeting, 13. 12mo. 1716-7, Hugh Evans, and had three children by him. Of them Ann, *m.* 1745, (?Samuel Howell); Susanna *m.* 1740, Owen Jones, *d.* 1793.

Evan Jones, b. about 1682-3. He and his brother John inherited from their father 153½ acres of land in Goshen tp. on Chester Creek, which was resurveyed in pursuance of the order of 27. 10mo. 1701. He was also a partner with his brother Richard in some Goshen land. He never married, and was buried at the Merion Meeting, 7. 2mo. 1708. His will, signed 28. 7. 1708, witnessed by Rowland Ellis, Richard Jones, and Robert Lloyd, was proved 1. 25. 1708 He mentions his mother and brothers and sisters, Lowry Lloyd, Richard, John, Edward, Jane, Sarah and Margaret Jones; overseers, Cadwalader Morgan and Abel Thomas.

Janne, or *Jane Jones, b.* in Merion, 15. 9mo. 1635, *d.* 27. 8mo. 1764, and was buried at the Goshen Meeting. She *m.* David Davis, and had nine children by him, four of whom married into the Ashbridge family.

John Jones, b. in Merion, 6. 4mo. 1688, *d.* in Goshen tp., 30. 12mo. 1774. He *m.* at the Gwynedd Meeting, 9. 4mo. 1713, Jane Edward, and had ten children. He and brother Evan shared the lands of their father.

Sarah Jones, b. 25. 7mo. 1690, *d.* 28. 3mo. 1758. She *m.* first, at Merion Meeting, 2. 8mo. 1712, Jacob Edge, 1690-1720, and had four children, and *m.* secondly, 10. 11mo. 1721, Caleb Cowpland, *d.* at Chester, 1757, and had five children by him.

Margaret Jones, b. 20. 6mo. 1697, *m.* first, at Merion Meeting, 16. 10. 1716, Thomas Paschall (and had Margaret,

WELSH SETTLEMENT OF PENSYLVANIA

m. first, Samuel Mather, and Hannah, *m.* Isaac Roberts), *m.* secondly, 6. 1mo. 1729, George Ashbridge, *d.* 1748.

These following Welsh Friends, of Penllyn parish, Merioneth, purchased portions of Thomas & Jones's 5,000 acres, but sold out, and did not come over.

EVAN AP REES, or Evan Price, a grocer, of Penmaen, bought 312½ acres of this tract, for £6. 5s., by deed dated 18 March, 1681, recorded 13. 4. 1684, witnessed by John Lloyd, Griffith Evan, Reece Evan and William Jones. He did not come over, but his son, Rees Evan, did.

By deeds dated 28. 5mo. 1683, Evan Rees conveyed away his Merion land, 153¼ acres, (which on a resurvey amounted to 178 acres) as follows—100 acres to Robert David, one of the original purchasers through Thomas & Jones, and about 54 acres to Griffith John (ap Evan), who also bought the Goshen portion. This Griffith Jones was a cousin of Jane Owen, Hugh Roberts's wife, and came over with them in 1683, and resided in Merion. He was one of the subscribing witnesses to Penn's "Conditions and Concessions to Adventurers for Land," 11 July 1681. His will, signed 26. 4. 1707, witnessed by John Roberts and Robert Jones, was proved 31 Jan. 1707-8, named his sons John and Evan, and son-in-law Thomas Jones, to be executors. Griffith John also bought from John Roberts (nephew of Thomas Lloyd), 37½ acres, and had patent for all, dated 8 Nov. 1703. This land, surveyed 194 acres, lay along the old Lancaster Road, and the City Line, and included, besides the land from Rees, 76¼ acres from each Thomas Lloyd and John Watkin.

THOMAS AP RICHARD, or Prichard, a farmer, of Nantlleidiog, bought 156¼ acres of the tract, of which 76¼ acres were laid out in Merion, and balance in Goshen tp. He did not come over. By deed, dated 16. 5mo. 1684, he conveyed all his lands to Rees John William, or Rees Jones, of Merion.

COMPANY NUMBER ONE

THOMAS LLOYD, a yeoman, (son of John Lloyd), of Llangower, bought 156¼ acres, of this tract, paying £3. 2. 6., but did not come to Pensylvania. It was his intention to come over, but he died suddenly, and by his will, bequeathed his land to his nephew, John Roberts, (his brother Robert Lloyd's son), who came over, and by deeds, conveyed of the part in Merion, the east end, 37½ acres, to Griffith John (ap Evan) in 1700, and dated 8. 9mo. 1720, the west end, 39½ acres, to Richard Jones.

John Roberts also had, with what he received from his uncle, and what he bought subsequently from Evan John William (a part of the Richard Davies tract), 153 acres in Goshen tp.

JOHN WATKIN, who was described as a bachelor, when he purchased, by deed of 1 April, 1682, witnessed by John Lloyd, Griffith Evan, Robert Lloyd and Reece Evan, of Thomas & Jones, 156¼ acres, and a yeoman, of Gwernevel, or Gwernsfel, did not come over, but sold his land. By deed, dated 23. 4mo. 1684, he conveyed all of rights to land, to Hugh Roberts, who sold his Merion portion, 76¼ acres, by deed of 26. 5mo. 1688, to Abel Thomas (who married Cadwalader Morgan's daughter), which land was resurveyed and patented to said Abel, 16 Feb. 1701-2.

This concludes the sketches of the original seventeen partners, purchasers through Thomas & Jones, of 5,000 acres, 2,500 of which were at the Falls of the Schuylkill, and who had the land laid out to them in Merion, on and near the river. It may be seen that four were first settlers, in 1682, one came over in 1682-3; seven were settlers in 1683, and one in 1684, and that four did not come over, but sold their land to the other original purchasers from Thomas & Jones.

It is also worthy of notice that these early settlers were nearly all in some way related to each other. For instance, John Thomas's son married Griffith John's daughter, and a

WELSH SETTLEMENT OF PENSYLVANIA

daughter married a son of Hugh Roberts; Dr. Jones's son married a daughter of Robert Owen; Dr. Jones married Dr. Wynn's daughter; Hugh Robert's son married a daughter of John Bevan; Rees Jones married a sister of Cadwalader Morgan's wife; William Edward married a sister of Hugh Roberts; Edward Rees was brother-in-law to Cadwalader Morgan and Rees Jones; John Roberts married a sister of Hugh Roberts; Robert Owen and Hugh Roberts were brothers-in-law; Robert Owen was a brother-in-law to Cadwalader Thomas; John Cadwalader was a nephew of John Thomas, and of Robert Owen, and a son-in-law of Dr. Jones; both Rees Thomas and his wife were related to John Bevan, and his son married a daughter of Dr. Jones; Hugh Roberts's first wife was sister to Robert Owen, and his son married John Bevan's daughter; Robert Lloyd's wife was daughter of Rees Jones; Thomas Lloyd's wife was daughter to William Edward, and a niece of Hugh Roberts; Griffith John was a cousin to Hugh Roberts's wife, and so on. All of these intermarriages among the leading Welsh families, however, did not establish a long-lived Welsh community, for it has for many years been only a tradition.

Having thus seen the pioneers of the Welsh tract settled, and taken account of these men and women, good Welsh Quakers all, who first ventured into the wilderness, west of the Schuylkill, and discovered the localities of their landed estates, we will take a glance at the people and their lands of the other Welsh companies who followed, many of whom were closely allied by intermarriages and blood with the pioneers.

ADVENTURERS FOR LANDS
IN MERION AND HAVERFORD

LLOYD & DAVIES' LAND PATENT

Company No. 2. The grantees, under the patent for 5,000 acres in the Welsh tract, to Charles Lloyd, gent., and Margaret Davies, widow, both of Dolobran, Meifod parish, Montgomeryshire, to whom, as trustees, they conveyed the land by deeds dated in April and June, 1683, were, in part, as follows:

Joseph Harris, "late of Wallbrook, Middlesex Co."	1,250	acres
And these, all of Montgomeryshire, Wales:—		
Thomas Jones, of Llanwthin parish, yeoman	156¼	"
Edward Thomas, of Llanwthin parish, yeoman	312½	"
Margaret Thomas, of Garthlwlch parish, widow	156¼	"
John Humphrey, of Llanwthin parish, gent.	312½	"
John Rhytherch, of Hirnant parish, yeoman	156¼	"
Thomas Morris, of Marchnant Issa parish, gent	156¼	"
	2,500	acres

It appears that Mr. Lloyd and Margaret Davies each had a half interest in this patent, and that it was her 2,500 acres which were conveyed to the aforesaid grantees, for Mr. Lloyd conveyed his share, 2,500 acres, by deed dated 6. 4mo. 1683, to his brother, Thomas Lloyd, some time the deputy-governor of Pensylvania, much of which was laid out in Merion tp., some north of Haverford,* and some northeast of Ardmore.

---
*"Dolobran," the seat of the Griscom family, is on a part of it. Mr. Clement A. Griscom, though a descendant of Gov. Lloyd, acquired the property by purchase. His wife is a collateral descendant with these Humphrey grantees.

WELSH SETTLEMENT OF PENSYLVANIA

About 1694, the following accounting of the "Lloyd & Davis grant" was filed with the Land Commissioners, showing a difference from the above statement:

"Sales of Charles Lloyd and Margaret Davis":—

"To Benj. Humphries	312½ acres
To Edw'd Thomas	312½ "
To Tho. Jones	156¼ "
To Marg't Thomas	156¼ "
To Tho. Jones & Jno. Rhoderick	312½ "
By Tho. Lloyd to Ev. Owen &c.	340 "
	1,590 acres"

"A new patent was requested for 2,215 acres, making in all 3,805 acres granted."

CHARLES LLOYD, gentleman, the grantee and grantor, of this Welsh Tract land, was born 9 Dec. 1637. He was a son of Charles Lloyd, gent., of Dolobran Hall, in Montgomeryshire, where he was a magistrate, and whose will, signed 17 June 1651, was proved in 1657.

Charles Lloyd was educated at Jesus College, Oxford, became a magistrate and was nominated for the shrievalty in Montgomeryshire. He joined the Society of Friends, about 1662, and erected a public Meeting House near his residence. He and his wife were imprisoned for ten years in the Welshpool jail, on account of their religious principles. He died at Dolobran Hall, which subsequently degenerated into a tenant's house, 26. 11mo. 1698. He married twice. He *m.* first, 11 Nov. 1661, Elizabeth, *b.* 2 Nov. 1633, *d.* 7 Feb. 1685, daughter of Sampson Lort, of Eastmoor (or East Meare), and Stackpole, in Pembrokeshire, high sheriff in 1649, brother to Sir Roger Lort, first Baronet, and *m.* secondly, 8 Feb. 1686, Ann Lawrence, of Lea, in Herefordshire, who *d. s. p.*, 2 March 1708. By his first wife, Charles Lloyd had two sons and one daughter. Two of these were born in jail. They married, and had descendants, but none came to Pensylvania.

COMPANY NUMBER TWO

Charles Lloyd's sister, Elizabeth, married Henry Parry, of Llanfillyn, and his brother, John Lloyd, also educated at Jesus College, Oxon, became "clerk of the petty bag in chancery," 1683-95, and his other and youngest brother,

THOMAS LLOYD, *b.* 17 Feb. 1640-1, *d.* in Pensylvania 10 Sept. 1694. Like his brothers, he was educated at Jesus College, and became a lawyer, and "a Quaker," and "a minister among Friends." In 1681, he and Charles, and other Friends had a celebrated debate, at Llanfillyn, with the Rt. Rev. the Bishop of St. Asaph, about religion, and religious questions, by request of the Bishop, who wished to learn their reasons for becoming non-conformists, and Quakers.

The life and services of Thomas Lloyd as the deputy of William Penn in his Province, and presiding officer of the council, have been frequently printed.

He first, it might be said, came into prominent notice in the Province when he bitterly opposed the Cromwellian soldier, and non-Quaker, Blackwell, whom Penn sent over as another of his experiments, as his Deputy-Governor, having so appointed him on Christmas Day, 1688. At this time, Lloyd had general authority over Penn's affairs, and it hurt him that an outsider superceded him, but Penn continued him as the keeper of the Great Seal, which still, in some things, made him a power Blackwell had always to reckon with, because the royal charter required that to make any law valid it must pass under the Great Seal, which meant Lloyd's consent.

So soon as Blackwell entered upon the duties of his office, Lloyd inaugurated his campaign of opposition by flatly refusing to affix the Great Seal to Blackwell's first commissions, and when declining to do so, sent him a rather insulting note. Only Penn could remove Lloyd from his office, so Blackwell brought charges against him and waited.

While waiting Penn's decision, the election for councillors came off, and Mr. Lloyd was returned as a member. When he went to take his seat, Blackwell ordered him not to enter the room, because he could not be seated while he was charged by him "with high crime and misdemeanors."

Thereupon, Mr. Lloyd, and two others, also elected but refused their seats by the Governor, forced their way into the Council Chamber, and took their seats. Blackwell, presiding, asked them by what right they presumed to do so, and Lloyd, replying for himself, answered insolently, "by special appointment by letter of the proprietor, which was as good as the Governor's commission."

This occasioned great confusion in the Chamber, the Quakers being in the majority, and supporting Lloyd, bitterly denounced Blackwell to his face, "so that he had to flee from the room, nearly all the members yelling at him," and telling him what they thought of him, and, the report says, that "Lloyd being the most clamorous was heard in the street."

Those who supported the Governor, did so from conviction, holding that Lloyd was not altogether within his rights in the matter of the Great Seal, because not one of the engrossed laws then in force, excepting it be the Frame of Government, had passed under the Great Seal. They had been considered "instructions from the proprietor." If Penn had not recalled Blackwell so promptly, on learning what was taking place in his far-off Province, there would certainly soon have been chaos in it. That Penn was "somewhat unsteady in his principles of government, as well as in his matters of carrying them out," was apparent to the thoughtful, so when Mr. Lloyd received the appointment, succeeding Blackwell, there was a great sigh of relief, for everybody was tired of continual misunderstandings, and contentions over the laws and positions. It required the strong will, with his gentle manner, of Governor Lloyd to prevent Penn himself from violating his own laws, which was a cause for "his people" losing confidence in him as a ruler, and of being prejudiced against him.

COMPANY NUMBER TWO

Although Gov. Lloyd never resided in the Welsh Tract, he was strongly in sympathy with the Welsh Quakers in it in their "little unpleasantness" with William Penn and his agents. He was frequently at their meetings as a minister, and they were loyal to him in his difficulties with the Proprietary, for the Welsh stood together, and were always helpful to one another. For years, Gov. Lloyd's was one of the great families of the city, and his sons-in-law were among the most prominent and influential citizens, being mayors and provincial councillors.

He arrived in Philadelphia, in the ship America, 20. 6mo. 1683. His most intimate fellow passenger was the German gentleman and scholar, Fra. Dan. Pastorius, who was coming to settle here, "in this uncouth land, and howling wilderness," as the German described the Province, and of the city, he said, "then Philadelphia consisted of 3 or 4 little cottages, all the residue being only woods, underwoods, timber and trees." Mr. Lloyd's daughters, Rachel Preston, Deborah Moore and Mary Norris, came with him. To them Pastorius dedicated, in 1718, a poem, and in a note told that he could only converse with Mr. Lloyd in Latin, the only language in common between them.

Charles Lloyd, the grantee of Penn, conveyed, as mentioned, the balance of his interests in Pensylvania to his brother, Thomas Lloyd, by deed dated 6. 4mo. 1683.

As above, Charles Lloyd and Margaret Davies jointly, by deed dated 29 June, 1683, conveyed 1250 acres of Margaret's land, for £25, to Joseph Harris, of Wallbrook, near London. Mr. Harris, by deed of 23 May, 1688, conveyed the rights to this tract of Pensylvania land to Francis Smith, "plaisterer," who sold it to Gov. Thomas Lloyd, but he died before the deed was executed, or the papers made out. But his son, William Smith, on 21 Oct. 1693, conveyed it by deed to Gov. Lloyd, and this brought his holding up to 3,750 acres.

WELSH SETTLEMENT OF PENSYLVANIA

Of these lands, Gov. Lloyd sold 1,000 acres, in one tract, to William Cuarton, 200 acres to David Pugh, 118 acres on the Liberty Lands line, to David Prees, or Price, but deed not made till 4. 10mo. 1694, 548 acres to Robert Owen, by deed of 5. 6mo. 1691, and 125 acres to E. Rees. The Governor also owned land in the City Liberties, and sold two lots, 100 acres and 145 acres to B. Chambers, a Philadelphia tavern keeper, and also sold 100 acres, above Merion to Thomas Davies.

After his decease, Thomas Lloyd's* executors, Judge Isaac Norris, of Philadelphia, and Judge David Lloyd, of Chester, had considerable and endless trouble trying to settle his land interests. On 28. 4mo. 1703, they asked of the

---

*Thomas Lloyd of Philadelphia, *m.* first, in Wales, 9 Sep. 1665, Mary, daughter of Roger Jones, of Welsh Pool, Montgomeryshire, and had ten children by her. His will, signed 10. 7mo. 1694, proved 22 Oct. 1694. He left his estate to his second wife, Patience, and his own children named Thomas, Hannah, Rachel, Mary, Elizabeth and Deborah: appointed Executors, his wife, "son Mordecay," son-in-law, Isaac Norris, and "kinsman David Lloyd." Witnessed by Samuel Carpenter, Alexander Beardsley, and John Jones. He names wife's children: Enoch and Marcy Story. His wife Patience's will, signed 14 Aug. 1720, proved 30 June, 1724, "son-in-law Richard Hill," Executor: her son Enoch, deceased; names granddaughters, "Deborah Moor and Patience Story": desired to be buried by the side of her husband, Thomas Lloyd. Signature witnessed by John Weaver (marked), and Charles Osborne. Of his children:

Thomas Lloyd, Jr., 1675-171—; *m.* Sarah Young, who *d.* in Philadelphia, and had issue from which descended the Pensylvania families of Moore, Willing, Wharton, Ridgway, etc.

Deborah Lloyd, 1682-172—; *m.* 12 Sep. 1704, Dr. Mordecai Moore, of Md. (second wife), and had issue, from which descend the Pensylvania families of Morris, Ellis, Collins, Lightner, Waln, Vaux, etc.

Rachel Lloyd, 1668-172—; *m.* 6 July, 1688, Samuel Preston, mayor of Philadelphia, 1711 (first wife), and had issue, from which descended the Pensylvania families of Carpenter, Ellett, Shoemaker, Moore, Wainwright, Preston, Roberts, etc.

Mary Lloyd, m. Judge Isaac Norris, of "Fairhill," *d.* 1735, and had issue from which descended the Pensylvania families of Harrison, McClenachan, Vaux, Logan, Dickinson, Emlen, Norris, etc.

COMPANY NUMBER TWO

Land Commissioners that 500 acres in the Welsh Tract, any way, anywhere, be confirmed to his estate, and that his purchase from his brother, and his sales and leases may be adjusted somehow, (and they never were), for this reason it is impossible to adjust this land account now; but it would seem that Gov. Lloyd got more than his original purchase, and that his estate had 2,215 acres for sale.

These Lloyd lands lay next, and west of the tract taken up by the Thomas & Jones Company, which is quite as interesting a section of the "Main Line." After Gov. Lloyd's death, there are many transfers of his Merion, and other lands, by his executors.

"My Respected friend,

James Logan: I hould my self obledged to give thee an account of those Lands belonging to the purches of Thomas Lloyd where David Lloyd is conecirned, and Likwise of Richard ap Thomas, that is how much is taken up and subdevided to them and sould by them, and what Remaines not disposed of by the sd Thomas Lloyd and the sd Richard Thomas.

	Accres.
Thomas Lloyd had a Richt by his Brother Charles to.	2,500
took up between Mirion and Harford...............	1,100
And one 100 accres he ordered in his Richt to Thomas David the wich was Laid out unto him......	100
	1,200
Remaining	1,300
he allso Bought of ffrancis Smith the Sheare of Margaret Davise to herself being 1250 accres.......	1,250
	2,550
there is I think 100 accres of Liberty Land Laid out to him	100

[147]

WELSH SETTLEMENT OF PENSYLVANIA

The Rest is to be yeat setled, and war'ts to be granted for the subdeviding of it within the Welsh tract.
allso Richard ap Thomas his purchus is............. 5,000

out of wich he sould to Philip Howell.............	700
and 100 of Liberty Land to Hugh Robarts..........	100
and to Robart William........................	300
and I think to Edward Joanes..................	200
	1,300

Remaining to him to have War'ts to himself for...... 3,700
   as to David Lloyd part, there is an Imaginary Survey made one about 1,800, accres but not perfected.

When thou art pleased to order war'ts for them or any others of the said Welsh purches'es I think there ought to be a Recitall of the first war'ts by wich the Land was first bounded by, and the time of the survey, Likwise comanding a Return of the Respective Subdivisions within the bounds of the said tract when not allready subdivided to any other Company, the wich Survey was done on the 28th of ye 8th Mo. 1684, and finished the   day of the 11th Mo. Ensuing.

I Request thee allso to put an end to Philip Howell's business to Ease both myself and the Rest of ye Comiss'rs of his Continuall Importuning, and I think it were best to Let him have that Lott on Thomas Joanes account and Let him pay the money to Joanes, Least the Warr't granted by the Gover'r to Neaison take hould of it, and the Gover'r forced to pay the 35 pounds of Joanes out of his own pocett.

these things I Refer to thy Consideration Leaving it wholy to thee to order it as thou think best and desire thy favor in Leting me have and End to my one business that my most Cordiall freind and Governor Left with thee to do for me Ells I am afraid I shall Suffer for want of it, who am thy Real freind.   D. Powell."
"Dat 5th 12th Mo. 1701."

COMPANY NUMBER TWO

Evan Owen, to whom Thomas Lloyd seems to have sold 340 acres, was a brother of Robert Owen, of Merion. As I do not find Evan was in possession of such a tract in Merion, and the Lloyd land covered the tract Robert Owen subsequently owned, it is probable that Evan only engaged this 340 acres for his brother Robert, as by deed, dated 5. 6mo. 1691, Thomas Lloyd conveyed to said Robert this amount of land, which, with a piece he bought later, on resurvey, 30. 3. 1703, amounted to 450 acres.

Another sale made by Thomas Lloyd, which may have been out of his new patent land, was, by deed of 3. 6mo. 1693, to Richard Cuarton, 200 acres in Merion, with one bushel of good winter wheat as the annual rental. His son, William Cuarton, assumed this land by agreement that he would pay his sister, then the wife of John Moore, seventy pounds, two years after his father's death.

Of the grantees of Margaret Davis, or of her and Charles Lloyd, gent., as they joined in the deeds, when the land was conveyed, all dated 24 April, 1683, and having the same witnesses:— Thomas Lloyd, Richard Davies, Richard Owen, Amos Davies, Rowland Ellis, David Davies, and Solomon Jones, and all recorded at Philadelphia 15. 5. 1684.

Margaret Thomas, of Garthlwlch, Montgomeryshire, widow, who bought 156¼ acres, by deed from Charles Lloyd, appointed, on 14 Aug. 1683, Thomas Jones, of Lanwithin, yeoman, who was also a purchaser of the same number of acres, her attorney to take possession of her grant, and look after the land. He had certificate, dated 31. 5mo. 1683, from the Quarterly Meeting at Dolobran, signed by John ap John, Charles Lloyd, Richard and Evan Davies and Sampson Lloyd. After her death, the Commissioners released him, as his interest in the matter had ceased.

Thomas Morris, of Marchnantissa, Montgomery, yeoman, also a purchaser of 156¼ acres, also gave the like power to him, and on Morris's death, he was also released from this stewardship.

WELSH SETTLEMENT OF PENSYLVANIA

David Rhoderick, or Roderic, succeeded to his brother's, John Rhydd's, land. "John Rhydderch, of Hirnant" parish, Montgomeryshire, yeoman, brought certificate, dated 31. 5mo. 1683, from the Quarterly Meeting at Dolobran, which he filed with the Haverford Monthly Meeting. It was signed by John ap John, Charles Lloyd, and Richard and Evan Davies.

Edward Thomas, of Lanwithin parish, Montgomery, yeoman, appointed John Humphrey, of Lanwithin, yeoman, to be his attorney, in the matter of his 312½ acres, after his decease, and the guardian of his children. Subsequently, Samuel Humphrey, and then his son Benjamin Humphrey, succeeded in this trust. Catherine, wife of Edward Thomas, was buried at the Merion Meeting, 10. 21. 1716.

John Humphrey sold, by deed of 1. 7mo. 1697, 100 acres of his own 312½ acres, to his nephew, Joshua Owen, and gave the balance by will to his nephew, Benjamin Humphrey, whose son, John Humphrey, succeeded to it.

The various Humphreys families, descendants of the first settlers, have always been noted in what was the Welsh Tract, residing on farms about the modern villages of Ardmore, Haverford and Bryn Mawr, and much of their original purchases remain in descendants' hands.

Two brothers, JOHN HUMPHREY, of Llanwddyn, and SAMUEL HUMPHREY, were Haverford land owners, and their cousin, RICHARD HUMPHREY, a purchaser from "Richard Davis Co., No. 7." John and Richard, came over in the "Morning Star," with Hugh Roberts, in 1683, as mentioned.

John and Samuel were sons of Humphrey ap Hugh, of Llwyngrill (1662), and "late of Llwyn du," in Merioneth, *d*. about 1664-5, by his wife, Elizabeth Powel, daughter of John ap Howel (or Powel, who was buried in the parish church of Llanwddyn, in Montgomeryshire, 24 July, 1636), and his wife, Sibill v. Hugh Gwyn, of Penarth.

They were uncles of Rowland Ellis, of "Bryn Mawr," Merion, (whose land adjoined Benjamin Humphrey's land),

COMPANY NUMBER TWO

and also of Robert Owen's wife, Rebecca, (whose farm lay to the eastward on both sides of Montgomery avenue, between Ardmore and Wynnewood), and of John Owen and Joshua Owen, of Merion (1683), (whose property adjoined that of Humphrey), and of Elizabeth, wife of "John Roberts, of the Mill," and "of Wayn Mill," who came from Pen y Chyd, in Denbighshire (whose estate was northward of Humphrey). They were brothers to Owen Humphrey, of Llwyn du, 1625-1695, a J. P. in Merioneth, and a prominent Friend, who was the father of Rebecca, wife of Robert Owen, of Merion, and Elizabeth, wife of John Roberts, aforesaid.

"JOHN HUMPHREY, of Llanwddyn, gent," purchased 312½ acres of the Lloyd & Davies land, by deed dated 24 April, 1683, and witnessed by Thomas Lloyd, Richard Davies, Richard Owen, Amos Davies, Rowland Ellis, David Davies, and Solomon Jones. By deed dated 1. 7mo. 1697, John conveyed 100 acres of this tract to his nephew, Joshua Owen, and by will bequeathed the balance to his nephew, Benjamin Humphrey. He married his cousin, Jane Humphrey (sister to Richard Humphrey, aforesaid).

In 1698-9, John Humphrey was one of the attorneys for Richard Davies, one of the purchasers of Welsh Tract land. His will, signed 22. 7mo. 1699, witnessed by John Roberts and David Llewellyn, was proved at Philadelphia 31 Aug. 1700. He named as executors his nephew, Benjamin Humphrey, his wife Mary, and son John; named friends Rowland Ellis, Sr., and his daughter Jane, Joshua Owen, John Owen, John Robert's children, Robert Owen's son John; cousin Tabitha, Ann, and Joseph Humphrey.

He said, "I give and bequeathe £10 towards putting in the Press the Testimony of the Twelve Patriarchs, in the Welsh tongue, if conveniences can be had for the same in these America pts." Otherwise, he desired this money should be used for the charities of the Haverford Monthly Meeting. This English work, which was to be a reprint in

WELSH SETTLEMENT OF PENSYLVANIA

Welsh, was probably never so printed, as the money was still in the hands of the Quarterly Meeting, in 1702, when Daniel Humphrey and David Lewis tried to have it appropriated for furnishing of the Haverford Meeting House. If the book was printed in the Province about this time, it was the first book printed in the Welsh tongue in America, as Pugh's "Annerch ir Cymru" was not printed till in 1721, by Andrew Bradford, Philadelphia.

John Humphrey, "of Llwundu," and his wife, Joan, brought their certificate, filed with the Haverford, or Radnor Monthly Meeting, from the Quarterly Meeting at Dolyserrey, dated 27. 5mo. 1683, signed by Robert Humphrey and Richard Owen, Griffith and Owen Lewis, John Evans, Hugh Reese, Amos Davies, William Thomas, William, Evan and Rowland Ellis, Ellis Morris, Evan Harry, and Evan Rees.

Richard Humphrey, "of Llanbynin, Merioneth, bachelor," also had certificate of same date from the same Meeting, and signed by the same Friends, with the addition of Humphrey Reinald.

Elizabeth Humphrey, "of Llanegrin, Merioneth, widow," "whose son Daniel is in Pensylvania, the 12 months past," brought certificate, dated 27. 5mo. 1683, from the Merioneth Quarterly Meeting. Her children, Charles, Benjamin, Lidia, Ann, and Gobeithia Humphrey, came over with her to Pensylvania and filed certificate with the Haverford Monthly Meeting. Signers, Owen Humphreys, Hugh and Evan Rees, Humphrey, Robert, Lewis and Rowland Owen, Griffith and Owen Lewis, Rowland Ellis, Evan Will Powel, John and David Evans, Amos and Ellis Davies.

SAMUEL HUMPHREY, the other brother, died in Wales. He was married to Elizabeth Rees, on 20. 2mo. 1658, by Morris Wynne and Robert Owen, both justices of the peace, by Friends' ceremony, and it is believed that this was the first marriage of this kind. They had 8 children. His relict and children removed to Haverford. Of these,

COMPANY NUMBER TWO

Benjamin Humphrey inherited 212 acres of land in Haverford from his uncle, John Humphrey, about where the village of Bryn Mawr, formerly called Humphreyville, stands, and adjacent to Rowland Ellis's land, and resided near the present Bryn Mawr College grounds. He d. 4 Nov. 1738, age 76 years. He m. (1694), Mary, daughter of Morris Llewellyn, of Haverford. Of their children, Ann m. 23. 10mo. 1742, Garrad Jones (son of Robert Jones, a first settler of Merion); Elizabeth, m. John Scarlett; Owen Humphrey m. 29. 7mo. 1738, Sarah, widow of John Hughs, of Merion. The will of John Hughs, of Merion, was signed 2 Jan. 1736, witnesses Griffith and Morris Llewellyn, and William Lloyd, was proved by wife Sarah, 12 Feb. 1736, mentions father-in-law Morgan Herbert, but no children. Trustees, John Roberts and Griffith Llewellyn. Benjamin Humphreys succeeded Rees Price as landlord of the Blue Anchor tavern, on Dock Creek landing, in Philadelphia.

Through Thomas John Thomas, he also had a tract of land, lying east of his other plot, and north of the present Montgomery avenue, at Haverford R. R. Station.

Daniel Humphrey in 12mo. 1701, received warrant for 200 acres of land, which was also located in Haverford, about the present Haverford College grounds, and on resurvey found to be 41 acres "overplus," which he bought, paying 8 shillings an acre. This land was in the right of "T. Ellis, L. David, & J. Poyer," who were grantees of Richard Davies. He also bought, 5. 3mo. 1694, 50 acres "due several purchasers," of the same Davies lands. He lived and died in Haverford, and was appointed to adjust the estates of Thomas Ellis and wife. His will, dated 26. 9mo. 1734, was proved at Philadelphia, 7 April, 1735.

He had thirteen children by his wife (m. about 1695) Hannah, daughter of Thomas Wynne, who survived him, named Samuel, b. 3. 6mo. 1696, first child; Joshua, Edward, Charles, Jonathan, Solomon, Thomas, Benjamin, Hannah, Elizabeth, Martha, Mary and Rebecca, b. 2. 10mo. 1716, last

WELSH SETTLEMENT OF PENSYLVANIA

child, all of record at Haverford Monthly Meeting. His cousins John and David Humphrey, with his first three named sons, were trustees under his will.

Anne, m. (1699), Edward Roberts, son of Hugh Roberts, of Merion.

Lydia, m. (1706), Ellis Ellis, son of Thomas Ellis, of Haverford.

Rebecca, m. (1713, second wife), Edward Rees, of Merion.

Elizabeth, m. (1693), Thomas Abel, of Haverford.

ROBERT OWEN, mentioned above as one of the purchasers of "548 acres" of Lloyd's land, by deed 5. 6mo. 1691, was a minister among the Friends. The Pensylvania historian, Proud, says of him, "he was an eminent preacher, and a very serviceable and worthy person among the Quakers, being a man endowed with many excellent qualities, a skilful peacemaker, and of much service and utility in various respects."

From 1674, he was much persecuted in Wales for being a Quaker, and removed with his wife Rebecca, "and their dear and tender children" to Pensylvania in 1690, bringing a flattering certificate from the Quarterly Meeting at Tyddyn y Garreg, in Merionethshire,* dated 8. 6mo. 1690; which is

---

*The members of the Tyddyn y Garreg Quart. Mtg., signers of the Certificate of Removal:

Evan Owen.	Rees Evan.
Rowland Owen.	Hugh Rees.
Lewis Owen.	Evan Rees.
Griffitt Robert.	Robert Vaughan.
Jane Robert.	Rees Thomas.
Margaret Robert.	David Jones.
Ellis Morris.	Elizabeth Jones.
Hugh David.	Gainor Jones.
Margaret David.	Jonett Johnes.
Rowland Ellis.	Regnald Humphrey.
Ellin Ellis.	Ann Rowland.
John Evan.	Owen Lewis.

COMPANY NUMBER TWO

preserved in the archives of the Haverford (Radnor) Monthly Meeting.

It may be seen he was not one of the original purchasers of land, in the Welsh Tract from the "Adventuring Companies," and it is not known why, nor is the reason apparent why he did not seek refuge from his "sufferings" sooner, since he was nearly related to many of the original settlers.

Robert Owen was born about the year 1657, and was the eldest son of Owen ap Evan Robert Lewis, of Rhiwlas, who resided on the "Fron Gôch" plantation, or farm, near Bala, in Merioneth, and who died before 1678-9 (by his wife, Gainor John), and brother to Jane, wife of the minister, Hugh Roberts, and to Ellin, wife of Cadwalader Thomas, and to Evan Owen, of Merion, b. 1665-6, and nearly related to John and Samuel Humphrey, of Haverford, and others here.

Mr. Owen was one of the signers of the certificate of removal for John ap Thomas, the partner of Dr. Edward Jones, who was fated not to remove here, and was an overseer of his will by appointment, 9 Feb. 1682.

After his arrival, Robert Owen purchased, by deed dated 5. 6mo. 1691, for one hundred pounds, the lands from Thomas Lloyd, variously estimated, according to surveys, at 442, 450, or 548 acres. This land lay west of the present settlement of Wynnewood, towards the village of Ardmore, north of the P. R. R., and was the plantation, which was confirmed to his eldest son and heir, Evan Owen, by the Commissioners, on 8. 12mo. 1704, who conveyed it, by deed dated 31 Dec. 1707, to his brother-in-law, Jonathan Jones.

The original farm of Robert Owen, which is now being sub-divided into little lots for picturesque little country houses, lay in a general way between Thompson avenue, in Ardmore, and the west boundry of Narberth, and north from the P. R. R. to the Mill Creek Road, on both sides of Glenn Road, and Cherry Lane. He left it to his son, Evan Owen, in 1697, who sold it to his brother-in-law, Jonathan

WELSH SETTLEMENT OF PENSYLVANIA

Jones, in 1707, whose son, Owen Jones, 1711-1793, had all of it, three lots, 350, 101 and 20 acres. His sons, Owen Jones, Jr., and Jonathan Jones, next had the property, Owen 350 acres, and Jonathan 101 and 20. Owen devised half of the 350 (on which the stone house stands) to Col. Owen Jones, who also had from his father his 121 acres, and the other half to his sister's son, John Wister, which portion is called "St. Mary's," and was inherited by his grandchildren, two daughters of the late Col. Lewis Wister, and Col. Owen Jones's property, "Wynnewood," went to his son and heir, Awbrey Jones, who, dying without issue, left the place to collateral heirs.

Immediately after he had possession, Robert Owen began the erection of a stone dwelling, which, as the date-stone tells, was completed in 1695. This house, which was built about the same time, apparently of similar materials, and possibly by the same contractor, as the Merion Meeting House, not far away, still stands, somewhat altered, on Montgomery avenue, east of Church road, a noted landmark. Here Mr. Owen resided at the time of his decease, on 8. 10mo. 1697,

Mr. Owen was a justice in Merion and twice chosen as a member of the Assembly, 1695-1697, and was a trustee of the Merion Meeting, in whose ground both he and his wife were buried.

His will, signed 2. 10mo. 1697; witnessed by John Owens, Rowland Ellis and Robert Jones, was proved at Philadelphia, 16 May, 1705. He left his plantation to his eldest son, Evan Owen, only child named, and named as overseers, Messrs. Hugh Roberts, John Humphreys, John Roberts, Griffith John, Robert Jones, Robert Roberts, Robert Lloyd and Rowland Ellis, the foremost men of Merion, and appointed his cousin, Griffith John, sole executor.

The inventory of the personal estate of Mr. Robert Owen was made "ye last day of ye eleventh month, 1697," by John Roberts and John Owen. It is preserved at the Historical

Society of Pensylvania. He had seven cows, valued at £3. 10, per head, two steers at £2. 10, per head, seven young cattle "at £1. 05, ye head," five horses and mares at £4. 10 ye head, twenty sheep valued at £7, twelve swine, £9, and wheat, barley, implements for farming, "books, £3," "bedding, and apparel, £47. 09. 6," "brass, pewter, and other household stuff, £12. 16. 0." Total valuation of the personalty £188. 18. 06. (This John Owen was "ye 2nd son of Owen Humphreys, of Llwyn du," and brother to Joshua Owen).

Mr. Owen married Rebecca Owen, daughter of Owen Humphrey, gent., of Llwynddu, in Llangelynin parish, Merioneth. The marriage agreement, still extant, dated 6. 1mo. 1678-9, was between Robert's mother, Gainor John, his father being dead, and Owen Humphrey. It was signed, as witnesses, by Rowland Ellis, Edward Vaughan, John ap Thomas, and Cadwalader Thomas. The marriage certificate, also extant, is dated 11. 1mo. 1678-9.

Robert Owen had by his wife, Rebecca, who died 23. 8mo. 1697, the following eight children (sic) Pa. Mag. vol. xiii, p. 168, etc.), four, born in Wales, between 1697-1690, coming over with them.

Evan Owen, eldest son, born probably at Fron Gôch, about 1682-3; died intestate in Philadelphia, and power to administer on his estate was granted to his widow and relict. 27 Oct. 1727.

On his request, 3. 3mo. 1703, a resurvey was made of all the lands he inherited from his father, and it was found he had 450 acres in Merion, and 100 acres in Goshen tp. He had no desire to be only a country gentleman, and sold his farms to his brother in-law, as above, and removed into the city, after his marriage.

Like his father, Evan Owen was a man of affairs. He removed into Philadelphia and was a member of the City Council, 1717, a Justice in Philadelphia county, 1723, &c, the treasurer of the city, 1724-27, a member of the Provin-

WELSH SETTLEMENT OF PENSYLVANIA

cial Assembly, 1725, and of the Provincial Council, 1726, and a trustee of the Society of Free Traders in Pensylvania, etc.

He was a member of the Philadelphia Monthly Meeting, where he was married to Mary, daughter of Dr. Richard Hoskins, (then deceased), 1. 10mo. 1711, (53 Friends signed their certificate), and had four children by her, of record at the Arch Street Meeting. One, Esther, *m.* 1743, William Davis, at Christ Church, Philadelphia.

Elizabeth Owen, b. in Wales, in 168-, d. in Philadelphia 22. 10mo. 1753. She *m.* David Evans, of Philadelphia, a deputy sheriff, 1714-21, will signed 27 Sept. 1745, and had six children. Of these, Evan Evans *m.* and had issue, and Sidney, second wife of Joseph Howell, of Chester, Pa.*

Jane Owen, b. in Wales, in 168—. Probably died young.

Gainor Owen, b. in Wales, 26. 8mo. 1688, d. ———. She *m.* at the Merion Meeting, 4. 8mo. 1706, Jonathan Jones, 1680-1770 (son of Dr. Edward Jones, of Merion), and had ten, or more, children, of these, Mary, b. 14. 5mo. 1707, *m.* at Merion Meeting, Benjamin Hayes, (a son of Richard Hayes, of Haverford); Rebecca, b. 20. 12mo. 1709, *m.* at Merion Meeting, 4 June, 1733, John Roberts, 1710-1776 (son of Robert Roberts, of Merion), and had twelve children; Owen Jones, 1711-1793, the last provincial treasurer, *m.* 30 May, 1740, Susanna Evans, 1719-1801, a daughter of Hugh Evans, of Merion, 1682-1772, (their daughter, Hannah Jones, *m.* Amos Foulke, 1740-1791); Jacob Jones, b. 1713, *m.* Mary Lawrence; Jonathan Jones, Jr., b. 1715, *m.* at Merion Meeting, 8. 11mo. 1742, Sarah, daughter of Thomas Jones, of Merion, a son of John ap Thomas, (their daughter, Katherine, *m.* Lewis Jones, of Blockley), and Elizabeth *m.* about 1758, Jesse George, of Blockley.

---

*See "Howell Family," in the American Historical Register, Jan. 1896.

COMPANY NUMBER TWO

Owen Owen, second son, *b.* Merion, 21. 12mo. 1690-91, *d.* Philadelphia 5. 8mo. 1741; will dated 4. 5mo. 1741, proved 11 August. He resided in the city and was high sheriff of Philadelphia Co., 1726, and city coroner, 1729-41. He *m.* 23. 3mo. 1714, Ann Wood, *d.* 4. 2mo. 1743, and had five children. Of these, Jane, *d. s. p.,* wife of Dr. Cadwalader Evans; Sarah, *m.* 3 March 1736, John Biddle, (and had, besides others, Col. Clement Biddle, 1740-1814, who had 13 children), and Tacy, *m.* Daniel Morris, of Upper Dublin tp.

John Owen, third son, *b.* 26. 12mo. 1692, *d.* in Chester Co., Pa., will proved 23 Jan. 1752. He was high sheriff of Chester Co. 1729-51, assemblyman, 1733-43, collector of the port of Chester, 1733-37. He *m.* at Chester Monthly Meeting, 22. 8mo. 1719, (48 Friends signed their certificate), Hannah, *b.* 17. 12mo. 1698, *d.* 1752, daughter of George Maris, of Chester, a provincial councillor, and had five children. Of these, Jane, *m.* Joseph West; Elizabeth, *m.* James Rhoads; Rebecca was the first wife of Jesse Maris, 1727-1811, and Susanna, *m.* Josiah Hibbard.

Robert Owen, Jr., who, with his brother, Evan, was admitted a freeman of Philadelphia in 1717, was *b.* 27. 7mo. 1695, and *d.* about 1730. He *m.* at the Philadelphia Monthly Meeting 11. 10mo. 1716-17, (sixty-one Friends signed their certificate), Susanna Hudson, (she *m.* secondly, John Burr, of Burlington, and *d.* 4. 3mo. 1757), daughter of William Hudson, mayor of Philadelphia, 1726 (by his first wife, Mary, daughter of Samuel Richardson, a provincial councillor), and had three children. Of these, Hannah Owen, 1720-1791, (will proved), *m.* first, 23. 8mo. 1740, at Arch Street Meeting, Philadelphia, John Ogden, widower, of Philadelphia, *d.* 6 Feb. 1742, will dated 31 Jan. proved 12 Feb. 1742, and had William Ogden,* *d.* in Camden, N. J., 13. May, 1818,

---

*See "Owen of Merion," Pen. Mag. vol. XIII, Glenn's "Merion in the Welsh Tract," Browning's "Colonial Dames of Royal Descent," Pedigree XXXVII, Browning's "Americans of Royal Descent, 4th edition, pp. 592-596, and Browning's "Magna Charta Barons and their American Descendants," pp. 373-380.

WELSH SETTLEMENT OF PENSYLVANIA

aged 77 years; *m.* first, 1. 11mo. 1769, Marie Pinniard, and had by her, who *d.* 14. 7mo. 1775, Hannah, 1770-1827, who *m.* first at Christ Church, Philadelphia, 10 April, 1795, Capt. William Duer, drowned in 1800-1, and had Mary Ann, *m.* 5 May, 1825, Lewis W. Glenn, and had Edward, late of Ardmore, Pa., deceased, who *m.* secondly, Sarah Catherine Allen, and had Thomas Allen Glenn, author of "Merion in the Welsh Tract." Hannah Owen *m.* secondly, in 1754, his second wife, Joseph Wharton,* of "Walnut Grove," in Southwark, Philadelphia Co., *d.* 1776, and had issue.

Rebecca Owen, b. 14. 1mo. 1697; buried at the Merion Meeting House, on 21. 9mo. 1697, surviving her mother only one month.

The aforesaid Robert Owen should not be confounded with a contemporary Welshman of the same name. This other Robert Owen, of Dolserau, came over in the ship Vine, of Liverpool, sailing from Dolyserre, near Dolgules, Merioneth, with his wife, Jane, son Lewis, and a servant boy and four maid servants, and arrived at Philadelphia in Sep. 1684. He had been a Justice of the Peace at Dolserau, near Dolgelly, (and near Bala), where he was incarcerated five years in the jail because he was a Quaker. He had been the Governor of Beaumaris, and became a Quaker about 1660. When he came over here, he settled on Duck Creek, in New Castle Co., where his son, Edward Owen, who had come over earlier, in Hugh Roberts's party, in Nov. 1683, was then settled. Both Robert Owen and Jane, his wife, died in the next year. They had altogether nine sons, and all were of age before 1684. Their son Lewis Owen returned to Wales to reside, but their son Dr. Griffith Owen, who bought his brother Edward Owen's land, in the Thomas & Jones tract, Merion, remained here, and became prominent in the Province. The mother of this large family, was Jane, daughter of Robert Vaughan, of Heng Wert, or

---

*See Pa. Mag. Vol. II, "Wharton Family."

COMPANY NUMBER TWO

Hendri Mawr, near Bala, and of Nannau, Merionethshire, and a relative of the John ap Thomas family.

The late Dr. Levick recorded that the Pensylvania historian, Dr. George Smith, was a descendant of the Merion settlers, Dr. Edward Jones, and Dr. Wynne, and also of "Robert and Jane Owen, that brave pair, who, whether as lord and lady of Beaumaris Castle, or for conscience sake, within the gates of Dolgelly jail, commanded the admiration and respect of all about them."

In the ship Vine, of Liverpool, William Preeson master, which sailed from Dolyserre, and arrived at Philadelphia on 17. 7mo. 1684, there were, besides Rees John William, or Rees Jones, one of the purchasers of "Thomas & Jones," or "Company No. 1," and the aforesaid Robert Owen and Jeane, his wife, the following other passengers:

David Davis, and his sister Katharine, and her daughter, Mary Tidey, and one man servant, named Charles Hughes, who had three years to serve. They were from Denbighshire.

Hugh Harris, and Daniel Harris. They were from Macchinleth, or Manhinteth, in Montgomeryshire, as were also the following:

John Richards, Susan, his wife, and daughters Hannah and Bridget, and one servant, named Susan Griffith, to serve six years.

Margaret, the wife of Alexander Edwards, and her daughters, Margaret and Martha, and two sons, Alexander and Thomas.

Rees Prees, and wife Ann, and daughters Mary, Sarah and Phebe, and two sons, Richard and John. From Radnorshire.

Jane Evans, widow, and four daughters, Mary, Alice, Sarah and Elizabeth, and a man servant, named Joseph.

Anne Jones, and her daughter, Ann Jones. From Carmarthenshire.

Griffith Owen, (the physician), his wife Sarah, and children, and servants, from Prescoe, in Lancashire.

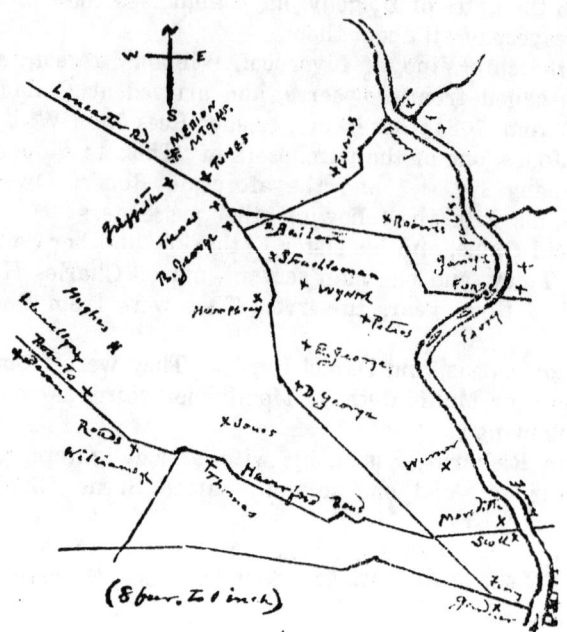

A SECTION OF SCULL & HEAP'S MAP, 1750

JOHN BEVAN'S LAND PATENT

Company No. 3.—The deeds to grantees, who all resided in Glamorganshire, under the patent for 2,000 acres to John ab Evan, yeoman, (or John Bevan), of Trefyrhig, or Trevorrigge, Llantrissent parish, Glamorganshire, were dated after 16 Sept. 1681, and the grantees were, in part, as follows:

Charles ab Evan, (Bevan), of Trevorrigg, and Llantwit Vardre parish, Glamorganshire, brother to John.

John Richard, of Trevorrigg, tailor.

Elizabeth Prichard and Katharine Prichard, of Telcha, Llantrissent, spinsters, whose deed for 250 acres, dated 8 May 1682, was witnessed by Barbara Awbrey, John ab Evan, Jun'r, Evan John, and John Richard.

Matthew Jones, of Carmarthen, Carmarthenshire, Mercer, whose deed, dated 1 Aug. 1682, for 125 acres, was witnessed by Will Broadber, Ch Evans, Ebenezer David, and Jane Miller.

David Jones, of Carmarthen town.

Ralph Lewis, of Eglwysilan.

Eventually John Bevan bought back the lands taken by John Richard, and the Prichards, and Ralph Lewis.

The Commissioners' minutes relating to Welsh purchasers, however, give the following details. After getting deeds for their grant from Penn in Sept. 1681, John and Charles Bevan had laid out to themselves, 980 acres, in three tracts, 750 acres in Marple tp., and 170 and 60 acres in Haverford tp., on warrants, dated 23. 5mo. 1688. By deed of 1 March, 1698, Charles Bevan conveyed all his rights to his brother, John Bevan. Shortly, John sold the 170 acres in Haverford to Evan Williams, and to John Hayes, 275 acres of the

WELSH SETTLEMENT OF PENSYLVANIA

Marple tract, and his "liberty land" to Benjamin Chambers, of Philadelphia, and then had 535 acres left. He then bought, in 1697, 250 acres in Haverford, the purchase of Katherine and Elizabeth Prichard, or Prichit (ap Richard), and about 200 acres in Haverford which he had sold to John Richard, from said John's heir, Lewis Richard, or Richards, in Haverford, and 168½ acres also in Haverford, from "William Howel, and his wife, Mary, relict and administrator of Evan Thomas, who by deed, dated 10 May, 1683, purchased 250 acres of Lewis David." This gave John Bevan three tracts in Haverford tp., or in all 678 acres there, this, with his balance of 475 acres in Marple tp., made him holder of 1,153 acres in Haverford and Marple tps., at one time,— when he sold to the Welsh.

By deed of 16. 5mo. 1684, John Bevan bought of Thomas Wynne 300 acres in Merion, at Wynnewood, which was confirmed to him by patent from the Commissioners, dated 9. 5mo. 1688, and then owned 1,453 acres.

The brothers, Ralph Lewis and William Lewis, relatives of John Bevan, came with their families from Eglwysilan, in Glamorganshire.

Ralph Lewis came over with Mr. Bevan, in 1683, having bought from him 250 acres, which were laid out in Haverford, next to the land of Thomas Rees. He sold part of it back to Mr. Bevan, and a part to David Lewis. He had several children by his wife, Mary. Hugh David, of Haverford, in his will, signed 27 April 1709, present Daniel Lawrence, Thomas James, Robert Jones, and Henry Lawrence, proved by wife Martha, 9 June, 1709, names children David, Ruth, Mary, Jonathan, Caleb, and Samuel, and to be overseers, father-in-law, Ralph Lewis, cousins David Lewis and William Lewis, and Lewis David.

William Lewis, the other brother, arrived in Philadelphia on 11. 5mo. 1686. He purchased, by deed dated 13. 10mo. 1692, a plantation of 120 acres, adjoining his brother Ralph's land, but which had been a portion of the Lewis David

COMPANY NUMBER THREE

("Company No. 5") tract of 3,000 acres. It lay in Haverford, to the south of the present settlement of Wynnewood, and near the old Haverford Road. Subsequently, he bought 50 acres in Radnor, and, by deed, 10. 10. 1698, he bought 300 acres in New Town tp., Chester Co.

William Lewis died in New Town, 9. 12mo. 1707-8. His will, signed 16 Jan. 1707-8, was proved at Philadelphia 12 March following. He had five children by his wife, Ann, namely: David, Lewis, Evan, William and Nathan Lewis, whose son Levi had a son Jesse, father of Levi Lewis, who was a practical farmer in Radnor tp. The latter's son, Tryon Lewis, born in 1839, was of the fourth generation of sons only born at the old Lewis home, and his daughter, Lydia T., was the first girl child born in this branch of the family in five generations.

William Lewis's son, David Lewis, was the father of Amos, who owned the farm near Bryn Mawr, purchased by the late George W. Childs, of Philadelphia, for a country seat. The will of David Lewis, of Haverford, signed 9 Sep. 1723, in the presence of Richard Hayes, John Parry, and John Jones, was proved 23 Sept. 1723, by wife Ann and eldest son William, executors. Other children named, James, Edmond, Amos, Enoch, Elizabeth and Ellen Ann. "To the Quaker Meeting at Haveford." Brothers Lewis, Evan, and William Lewis, and Robert Jones to assist the executors.

The wills of the other two men, in Haverford, having his name, give the following data. "David Lewis, late of Landewi, Pembroke, now of Haverford," marked in the presence of Abraham Hardiman, David Lawrence, and David Lloyd, 26. 3mo. 1697; will proved 22 Jan. 1708. Appoints son James Lewis executor, names son-in-law Peregrine Lewis, and his three children. Codicil 26 Feb. 1707, witnessed by John Maris and David Jones. The will of the other "David Lewis, of Haverford, yeoman," marked 24. 1mo. 1714-5, in the presence of Lewis David (marked), Henry Lewis, Richard Hayes, and Henry Lawrence, proved

WELSH SETTLEMENT OF PENSYLVANIA

28 Jan. 1715, by wife Katherine. Children, Joseph, Susanna, Hannah, James, and Sarah Lewis. Trustees, Lewis David, of Darby, Richard Hayes, Henry and Daniel Lawrence all of Haverford.

JOHN BEVAN, or John ab Evan, who was the trustee for this small company of settlers, was one of the early converts to Quakerism, and became an accepted minister among Friends. He apparently was a well educated man, and belonged to the landed gentry of Wales. He was the son of Evan ap John Evan, of Treverigg, Llantrisant parish, in Glamorganshire, and his wife, Jane, daughter of Richard ap Evan, of Collena, in the same parish.

He and his first wife, Barbara, and their children, "their tender family," and some other relatives, removed to Pensylvania, coming over in the ship "Morning Star," with Hugh Roberts and party bound for the Thomas and Jones land, arrived at Philadelphia in Nov. 1683. He and his wife brought the usual certificates of membership and removal from the Treverigg Friends' Meeting, and the Men's Meeting of Cardiff and Trefrig, dated 10. 7mo. 1683. Among the many signers, William Lewis; Howell, William, Watkins, and James Thomas; Thomas, Edward, Jenkin, and Mireck Howell, John David, John Mays, and his uncle, (his mother's brother), Thomas Richard (or Prichard) ap Evan, of Collena, for whose daughters, Elizabeth and Catherine, John Bevan bought some Haverford land, which he bought back from them as above.

John Bevan left a copy (still extant) of the written account of himself and family, which, at the request of the Merion Preparative Meeting, or the Haverford Mo. Mtg. he had filed with it in 1704, beginning:—"Sometime before the year 1683, we had heard that our esteemed friend, William Penn, had a patent from King Charles the Second for that Province in America, called Pencilvania, and my wife had a great intention to go thither, and thought it might be a good place to train up children amongst sober

COMPANY NUMBER THREE

people, and to prevent the corruption of them here,.... She acquainted me therewith, but I then thought it not likely to take effect, for several reasons." It further tells how he found the way clear to remove; of his voyage; of his experience here; of his travels as a minister into New England, in 1701; and of his final return to his home in Wales in 1704, with his second wife and young daughter, Barbara, as "the aim intended by my wife was in a good measure answered," where they lived the balance of their lives.

Though he lived here, off and on, only about twenty years, or till in 1704, John Bevan was a prominent man of affairs in the Welsh tract. He was chosen one of their representatives, in the Provincial Assembly, by the Welsh, in the years of 1687, 1693, and 1700, and was appointed a justice in Haverford tp., Philadelphia Co., in 1685, and for the same in Chester Co., in 1689.

He visited Wales on private matters, in 1694-5, and married his second wife. An extant letter, dated 29. 2mo. 1695, from Rees Thomas, of Merion to his father-in-law, William Awbrey, says "my unkle John Bevan came over very well, and a good voyage he had." In 1698, he went to his old home again, where he still owned property, and in 1704, went there to remain, as the Quakers were no longer persecuted in Wales, and there was too much unpleasantness in Penn's country.

After John Bevan had made several sales in right to these 2,000 acres he bought from Penn, as explained above, he had remaining, besides 25 acres of the liberty land that went with his purchase, for which he had warrant dated 5. 8mo. 1702, the farm of 300 acres in Merion, and 90 acres adjoining, located in Haverford, constituted his homestead here. This land lay to the south of the present Wynnewood R. R. station, and South of the modern Lancaster Ave., across the old "Haverford Street," and along the lines of

WELSH SETTLEMENT OF PENSYLVANIA

Haverford tp., and of the present Philadelphia Co. Some of this tract belonged to his descendants for about one hundred years,—not after 1810.

John Bevan lived to be about 80 years old, and died at his home, called "Treveyrig," or Treverigg, where he resided after his final return in 1704. His will, dated 1mo. 1724-5, was a very long, and full one, and was witnessed by his brother, Charles Bevan, and was proved at Llandaff Registry, in Glamorganshire, 21 Oct. 1726. Charles Bevan, William Awbrey, of Pencoed, and others, named as the overseers.

To his grandson, John Bevan, he bequeathed his messuage, called "Treveyrig," and a gristmill on this property, and mentions said John's children, his own great-grandchildren, to wit, Richard, Thomas, and Barbara Bevan. He mentioned his 90 acres in Haverford, and his 300 acres in Merion, and two other pieces of land that he had given to his son Evan Bevan.

John Bevan, when a young man, married Barbara, daughter of William Awbrey, of Pencoed, or Pencoyd. She came over with him in 1683, and they returned to the old home in 1704, as he relates in his journal, as follows: "We landed at Shields in Northumberland, and staid over the meeting on first-day, next day we set forward toward our habitation in Wales, having near 300 miles to travel. We had several good meetings in our way, and about the beginning of the Eighth month, 1704, we came to our home at Treveyricke." Telling of his wife's last illness six years later, "in her last sickness she was sensible, she was not likely to recover out of it, she said, 'I take it as a great mercy that I am to go before thee, we are upwards of forty-five years married, and our love is rather more now towards one another than at the beginning,' she quietly departed this life the 26th of the Eleventh month, 1710, aged 73 years, and about 4 months." It has been said that he had two wives, both named Barbara,

COMPANY NUMBER THREE

but this wife was certainly the wife of his youth, as they were married in 1665, he being only 19 and she 28 years old. Of their children:

John Bevan, the eldest. He came to Pensylvania with his parents. He may have been the bachelor of this name, buried at the Merion Meeting 11mo. 13. 1715-6. It is also supposed that he returned to "Treveyrig" with his father, married and died there, before his father, having a son John, who was a gentleman farmer and miller, enjoying the land of his inheritance, and whose children in 1724 were, (named in will of John Bevan, 1725), Richard, Thomas, and Barbara. The father of these children is also placed as a son of Evan, named below.

Jane Bevan, b. about 1667, d. 12. 10mo. 1703; m. at the home of William Howell, in Haverford, 1. 10mo. 1687, John Wood, of Darby, a member of Pensylvania Assembly 1704-1717, a son of George Wood, a J. P., and Assemblyman, 1682-1683, and had seven children, A descendant is John W. Jordan, LL.D., of Philadelphia.

Evan Bevan, from whom all of this surname in Merion descended, was born about 1672. He visited his father at "Treveyrig," and from the Friends' Meeting there brought his certificate, dated 10. 5mo. 1707. He m. at the Darby Monthly Meeting, on 9. 11mo. 1693, Eleanor Wood, who administered on Evan's estate, 13 Aug. 1720, and had eight children. She was a minister among Friends, and d. 28. 11. 1744, and was buried at the Haverford Meeting House.

Evan Bevan resided on his father's Merion land, and died intestate before his father. His father bequeathed his Merion-Haverford plantation to his daughter-in-law in trust for his grandson, Evan Bevan, Jr., 1698-1746, and should he not live to enjoy it, then it was to go to Awbrey Bevan, 1705-1761, or Charles Bevan, other grandchildren of the testator, children of this Evan Bevan. Evan Bevan, Jr., was the father of Charles, who inherited the home farm,

WELSH SETTLEMENT OF PENSYLVANIA

but generally resided in Philadelphia. His estate was administered in Jan. 1800, his wife dead, and two children minors. One of these, Charles, Jr., m. Mary Lippincott, and died intestate, in 1809, in Merion, also leaving two children minors, named John L. and Henry C., who inherited the John Bevan property.

Ann Bevan, b. about 1676-7; m. at the Merion Meeting, 23. 1mo. 1696-7, Owen Roberts, of Merion, (son of the Friends' minister, Hugh Roberts), and had six children.

Elizabeth Bevan, b. about 1678; d. 1739; m. at Merion Meeting 30. 4mo. 1696, Joseph Richardson, d. 1752, son of Samuel Richardson, a Provincial Councillor, and had eight children. Descendants were Mrs. Arthur D. Cross, of San Francisco, and Judge Samuel W. Pennypacker, of Philadelphia, former Governor of Pensylvania.

Barbara Bevan, b. in Pensylvania 5. 7mo. 1696. "She was the only child by his second wife," and went to Wales with her parents in 1704, where she m. William Musgrove.

Charles Bevan, of Lantwit Vardre, had a son Evan Bevan, or "Evan Bevan alias Jeuans," as he signed his name, born in 1678, educated at Oxford, and became a lawyer, and a minister and elder among Friends, and d. in 1745. Testimony as to his good character made in the Monmouthshire Meeting, 17. 2mo. 1746. (See Memoir of him in the "Friends' Library," vol. XIII.)*

* The following item concerns another branch of this family.

A Mrs. Catherine Bevan was sentenced by the Court of New Castle Co. (Delaware), to be burned alive at New Castle, in 1731, for the murder of her husband. It was the intention of the kind-hearted sheriff to hang her by the neck over the pile of fagots, in the hope she would strangle to death before being burned. But some accident happened to the rope—it broke, slipped, or was cut, after the fire was well under way, when she dropped, bound hand and foot, into the blaze. Struggling to free herself from her bindings, she nearly escaped from the pyre, and had to be pushed back into the flames, and held there by the sheriff and the crowd, while she died a lingering and horrible death, in conformity with the sentence of the Court.

COMPANY NUMBER THREE

REES THOMAS, who came over with John Bevan, in 1683, was then a young and unmarried man. Nothing certain is known of his ancestry, but it is presumed he had lived in Glamorganshire, and was a relative of Mr. Bevan. In time, he became a prominent man in the Welsh Tract, a justice of the peace, and an Assemblyman, and a successful farmer.

About two months after his marriage, he bought his first land, some 300 acres in Merion, from Sarah, the relict and widow of John Eckley, by deed dated 15. 6mo. 1692, which land adjoined that of Ellis Hugh, of Merion. Later, he bought 170 acres adjoining this first purchase, from Edward Prichard. These two tracts of land lay about where the village of Rosemont stands, and north and west of the P. R. R. station. From the Land Commissioners' minutes, it appears that "Rees Thomas, of Haverford," by deed dated 4 May, 1713, acquired 500 acres, with the usual bonus of a city lot, and liberty land, from John Clark, of Devizes, Wiltshire, and on 12. 1mo. 1715, he desired warrant of survey to lay out this claim, but it is not evident that this was granted, or that he entered upon this land.

About this time, Rees Thomas and Anthony Morris, Jr., bought from William Awbrey, of London, (a relative of Rees's wife), executor to Richard Whitpain, the right of Whitpain to 7,000 acres "in the country," city lots and liberty land. This tract lay in West Town, Chester Co., in the "Welsh Tract," of that county, a distinct purchase from that of which I write. In 1717, when they applied to have this land laid out to them, they had considerable trouble over it with the relict and heirs of Whitpain, and had to compromise, and on 30. 3mo. 1718, received warrant of survey for only a part, but subsequently were allowed another selection, and had 2,000 acres in Chester Co., and 4,500 acres in Philadelphia Co., and for all this land, they asked for a re-survey, 19. 3mo. 1726.

There is a copy of the following note from James Steel, who was one of the great land-grabbers of the time in the

WELSH SETTLEMENT OF PENSYLVANIA

Lower Counties (Delaware). It is dated 17. 9mo. 1722, "To Rees Thomas, upon his brother's illness: I hereby certify that I did agree with Rees Thomas, on behalf of his brother, William Thomas, for 200 acres of land in Radnor, formerly held by Rees Prees on Rent." The purchase price was £40 for the whole, in consideration that William Thomas also purchase the right in the land of Rees Thomas.

Rees Thomas's will, signed 10 Sept. 1742, was proved 12 Feb. 1742-3. He left the homestead farm, and 200 acres of the "Rosemont" land, bought of Eckley, to his son Rees, and the other tract there to son William.

Rees Thomas married at the Haverford Meeting, 18. 4mo. 1692, Martha Awbrey, who also came over in Mr. Bevan's party, in 1683. She died 7. 12mo. 1726. She was one of the ten children of William Awbrey, who was buried at Llanelyw parish church, in Brecknock, in 1716, aged 90 years, and his wife, and cousin, Elizabeth, a daughter of William Awbrey, eldest son of Thomas Awbrey, gent., of Llanslyw.

In an extant letter, dated 29. 2mo. 1695, Rees Thomas and his wife wrote a joint letter to her father in Wales, telling him about their two children, their farm life, and asked the date of Martha's birth. Mr. Thomas concluded with:—
"I doe understand yt thou were not well pleased yt my oldest son was not caled an Aubrey. I will answer thee I was not against it, but my neibors wood have him be caled my name, being [as] I brought ye Land and I so beloved amongst them, I doe admite to what thee sayes in thy letter yt an Aubrey was better known than I, though I am hear very well acquainted with most in these parts. He is ye first Aubrey in Pensilvania and a stout boy he is of his age being now a quarter."

Of the six children of Rees and Martha Thomas:—

Rees Thomas, Jr., b. 22. 2mo. 1693, who is referred to in the above letter. He *m*. Elizabeth, daughter of Dr. Edward Jones, of Merion.

COMPANY NUMBER THREE

Awbrey Thomas, b. 30. 11mo. 1694, d. s. p. He m. Guleima, only daughter of William Penn, the younger. His mother was a sister of William Awbrey, the son-in-law of William Penn, the Founder.

Herbert Thomas, b. 3. 9mo. 1696, d. s. p. He m. Mary, daughter of John Havard.*

William Thomas, who died at "Rosemont" before 1787. He married and had seven children.

---

*In the will of Lewis John, of Haverford, signed 2. 9mo. 1704, in the presence of Nathan Thomas, John Havard, William Sinkler (marked), and David Powell, proved by wife, Elizabeth, and daughter, Margaret Lewis, the executors, 2 Dec. 1704, he mentions daughter, Elizabeth, wife of John Rees, and "my kinsmen John Havard and Nathan Thomas."

Will of Margaret Thomas, of Merion, widow, marked 23 April, 1719, in presence of James John (marked), Griffith and Mary Llewellyn, names son Owen Thomas, (and his children, William and Hester), daughter Katherine, wife of Robert Pearson, (and their children, Thomas and Mary), and "grandson John, son of James Thomas, and his uncle Nathan Thomas."

Will of Edward Thomas, of Merion, signed 21 Dec. 1729, witnessed by Robert Jones, Hugh Evans, John Bowen, and Owen Roberts (marked). Proved 26 March, 1733, by Thomas Thomas, his son. Other children, Evan, Elizabeth, and Margaret Thomas. Legacy "to the Grave Yard at Merion Meeting." Overseers, Hugh Evans, Robert Roberts, Jonathan Jones, and Robert Jones.

Will of John Thomas Thomas, of Merion, yeoman, marked 25 May, 1721, witnesses Henry Lewis, Jenkin David, Llewellyn (marked), and Evan David. Proved 16 Sep. 1723. Names Margaret, wife of James Mortimer, nephews Thomas Edwards, Morris Thomas, and John Thomas. Cousin Benjamin Humphreys, of Merion, to be executor.

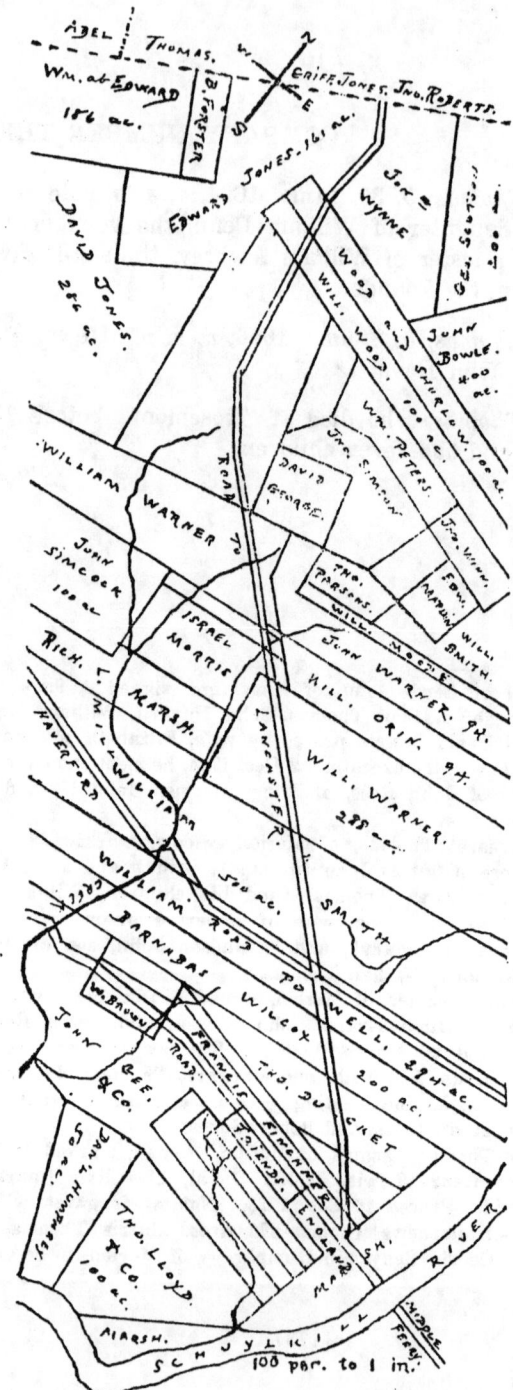

ALONG THE OLD LANCASTER ROAD IN 1773-4. FROM JOHN REED'S MAP OF PHILADELPHIA

JOHN & WYNNE'S LAND PATENT

Company No. 4. The grantees under the patent, dated 14. 7mo. 1681, for 5,000 acres, issued to John ap John, the founder, probably of the Welsh Tract idea and indirectly of the Merion Meeting, and Dr. Wynne, were Denbighshire people, and in part, as follows: It seems that each of these "trustees," John and Thomas, took 2,500 acres of their joint purchase to keep, or to sell, as they thought best.

John ap John, according to a memorandum, in his own writing, says:

"Here is An Account of what I John ap John have sould out of my part of this deed and what remains still in my hands. First, I paid William Penn, by ye hands of Richard Davies and his sonn David Davies, ye sum of Fifty pounds Stl., and for which I have their recets, and I have disposed of ye land as followeth:—

"To Thomas Taylor I sold .... 500 acres
"To John Roberts I sold .... 500 "
"To Treial Reider I sold .... 400 "
"To Mary Fouk I sold .... 200 "
"To Richard Davies .... 250 "
"To Owen Parry .... 150 "
"reserved for myself .... 500 "

"Be it remembered also yt I rebought from Trial Reder aforsd 400 acres.

"So wt remains for me unsold is 900 acres."

But Dr. Wynne left no memorandum of the disposition of his share, but he soon got rid of it.

Some of John ap John's land seems to have passed to the following:

WELSH SETTLEMENT OF PENSYLVANIA

Howel and Philip James, of Philadelphia.

Isaac Wheeldon, of Llanroost, Denbighshire, a glover. His is a very long deed, dated 20 Mar. 1681, for "1 2-30 part, or share of 5,000 acres of land." He assigned his rights, 13. 10. 1695, to Samuel Lewis, of Darby, whose son Samuel, Jr., inherited it.

"Lucien Sixsinth," bought 200 acres.

Owen ffoulke, of Bettws y Coed, Caernarvonshire, a tanner.

Mary Southworth (ffouk?) was also a purchaser from John ap John of 200 acres. Afterwards, she married Henry Molineaux, and the right to this land was sold to John Parker, of Philadelphia, with her right for 300 acres more of her land, bought from Dr. Wynne, for all of which Parker had deeds and warrants, which were accidentally destroyed by fire and he could not locate the purchases.

The dates of the various deeds conveying these lands by John ap John, were, between the first one of 25. 5mo. 1681, and 7. 5mo. 1682.

By deed dated 20. 7mo. 1691, John ap John sold his remainder of 900 acres to Hugh Roberts, of Merion, who had 200 acres of the purchase laid out in Merion, which he sold to Robert Owen, and Robert, by deed of 30. 3mo. 1696, conveyed 100 acres of same to Daniel Thomas, of Merion, and after Robert's decease, 100 acres to Thomas Rees, by deed of 27. 7mo. 1700.

John ap John further sold, of this balance, 482 acres, laid out in Goshen and had about 200 acres left, for which a warrant was issued to him.

"Tryall Rider," never came to Pensylvania. In 1695, with John ap John, he attended a meeting at Tregaron, in Radnorshire. He was a flax dresser, at Wrexham, in Denbighshire.

These further items as to the disposition of the lands of John & Wynne are also of interest.

COMPANY NUMBER FOUR

"Owen Pusey," or "Owen Parry, of Dynullo, Issa, Denbigh, yeoman," named as a purchaser from him by John ap John. It was claimed to the Land Commissioners that he bought 150 acres, by deed dated 17. 5mo. 1682, "of John ap John and Jon (*sic*) Wynne," and it was wished to have same located. No deed, however, could be produced, and said Owen was then dead, yet it appeared that his son had sold the right to this land in 1707, to Owen Roberts, whose executor sold it to John Walter. Jonathan Wynne confirmed this sale, 23 March, 1727. Owen Roberts, and his wife Ann, had certificate from the "Harford," *i. e.* Haverford Monthly Meeting, "held at Merion," addressed to the Philadelphia Monthly Meeting, dated 9. 12mo. 1709-10.

After John & Wynne's purchasers were put into possession of their lands, scattered in the townships of Merion, Haverford, Radnor, Goshen, New Town, Middletown, and in the Great Valley, it was discovered by Jonathan Wynne that 100 acres of their joint transactions were not accounted for. Their land operations were complicated.

When Jonathan Wynne made his application, elsewhere mentioned, and was granted 400 acres on his father's own account, in the "Great Valley," or Chester Valley, it was on condition that he surrender the right to those 100 acres, if such an amount was needed to make up the full acreage of any of John & Wynne's sales to original purchasers; he had to surrender these 100 acres subsequently to one James Steel, who also bought from Jonathan another 100 acres in the Great Valley, paying him £15. 10, and on 14. 7mo. 1736, the Commissioners issued patent to said Steel for 200 acres, as "in old right of John & Wynne."

"Richard Davis," or Davies, had his 250 acres (less 5 acres of Liberty land) laid out in Goshen tp., adjoining the land of Griffith Owen, who subsequently bought it. He had also 312½ acres, laid out "above Newton" (in Chester Co.), which he sold to David Evan, who had bought of "Howel James and son" 232 acres, also "out of the John & Wynne tract," and two lots of 150 acres and 50 acres from William Davies, also of same tract, and supposed he had 744½ acres altogether, but these tracts, upon resurveys, after he had paid for 20 acres over-plus, on an earlier survey, came out only 662½ acres.

Richard Orme (or Orms), who owned 150 acres in the "Letitia Penn Tract," in Goshen tp., above Merion, bought 150 acres in Radnor tp., of "the John & Wynne land," which Jonathan Wynne gave him a deed for, 2. 4mo. 1704. Richard Orme also bought 125 acres of the land in the Welsh Tract, from "Humphrey Bettally," or Betlly, who had 250 acres from John & Wynne, (Jonathan Wynne bought the other 125 acres), and sold the same to "Jonathan Height." It seems that Orme had "located" this land, but someone else also got hold of the same land, for when the Height heirs, (Richard Maris and Elizabeth, his wife, and Evan Lewis, and wife Mary), wanted to sell the land it could not be found. Thereupon, on petition, in 2mo. 1720, the Commissioners granted 120 acres to Lewis Lewis, of Chester Co., to be "located back in the country," and was laid out near New Town.

Thomas Taylor's (he was a resident of Denbighshire), land, 500 acres, which he acquired by deed of 8. 1mo. 1683, was laid out to him in Middletown, Chester Co., next to land of Richard Crosby. His ten acres bonus in the Liberties he sold to William Edwards. Thomas Taylor, Jr., inherited the Chester Co. tract.

The John Roberts, of "Pennyckland," Penytklawe, or Pen y Clwyd, in Denbighshire, yeoman and millwright, to whom John ap John states he sold, for ten pounds, 500 acres, by deed dated 7. 5mo. 1682, when he came to Pensylvania, was known as "John Roberts, the miller," and "of the Wayne Mill," in Merion, where he had a grist mill.

This deed was recorded at Philadelphia 11mo. 16. 1683-4, the grantors being "John ap John, of Ruaben parish, Denbigh, yeoman, and Thomas Gynn, of Cairwis, Flint, Chirur-

COMPANY NUMBER FOUR

geon," Dr. Wynne's signature was witnessed by Richard Davis, Tryall Ryder, Richard Orms, and Mary Southworth, and John's by Richard Davis, and ———— Rogers. The deed recites that the 500 acres conveyed was a part of 5,000 acres purchased from William Penn, and that John ap John and "Thomas Gynn" were co-trustees, and only contributed some part of the £100 to pay for the 5,000 acres, or, quoting the deed, "though the sd John ap John and Thomas Gynn were entitled to take up ye sd conveyances of all ye sd 5,000 acres, yet they onely intended to have their separate shares and proportion of the sd 5,000 acres according to the sume they laid out as part of ye sd 100 pds, and are onely trustees as to ye rest of ye sd 5,000 acres," and that "the said John Roberts hath contributed some part of the said £100 consideracon money towards the purchase of the sd 5,000 acres, that is to say, the sd John Roberts hath laid out Tenn Pounds." This clause in Penn's, and his "first purchasers"'s deeds, was the cause of considerable misunderstanding subsequently, when first purchasers asked to have bonus lands conveyed to them, because it defined them as only "trustees," as may be seen hereafter.

Of his 500 acres, which lay along the "Mill Creek Road" (and ten acres of liberty land he received as bonus, which lot he sold to William Edwards), he sold 100 acres, lying in the upper part of Merion, adjoining the land of Edward Griffith, to Thomas David. He retained two parcels of 250 acres and 140 acres, in the same locality, and these were laid out to him, 12. 2mo. 1685, and 12. 2mo. 1696. In 4mo. 1703, he had trouble with Martha Kcite, or Kite, a neighbor, about division lines. The matter was laid before the Commissioners, who ordered a jury on the case, and a resurvey, and after all the miller lost his suit.

This John Roberts married here a few years after coming over, it is said, Elizabeth Owen, a niece of Owen Humphreys (ap Hugh), of Llwyn du, in Merionethshire, and it has been printed that he was then 60 years old, and the bride

WELSH SETTLEMENT OF PENSYLVANIA

was only 16. His will, signed 18. 12mo. 1703-4, witnessed by James Thomas, Nathan Thomas and John Roberts, Jr., was proved at Philadelphia 13 March following. He names sons John and Matthew Roberts, and daughter Rebecca; nephews Robert, Joseph and Edward Roberts, brothers Edward and Matthew Roberts, and John Owen, his brother-in-law, to be executors, and appointed friends Thomas, John and Benjamin Humphrey, and brother-in-law Joshua Owen,* overseers of his will.

"John Roberts, of the Mill," who was buried at the Merion Meeting House, 27. 2mo. 1721, was his son. His will, "John Roberts, of Merion, wheelwright," was signed 22. 2. 1721, witnesses, John Vaughan, Owen Roberts (marked), and Robert Jones, was proved by his relict, (who was "possibly with child"), Hannah, 17 May, 1721, names aunt Ann Roberts, cousin Robert Roberts and sister Rebecca, overseers, brothers Matthew and Joseph, and step-father, Hugh Evans, and Robert Jones. It has been printed, but without proof, that the "John Roberts, of Merion, miller," who was hung, in Philadelphia, by the order of the President of Pensylvania, for being a traitor to apparently both the British and the Americans, was a grandson of the aforesaid immigrant, John Roberts. Owen Roberts, a blacksmith, of Merion, was of this family. His will, signed 23 July, 1732, witnessed by Joseph Humphrey, John Bowen, and Robert Jones, was proved 26 March, 1733. Names brothers Edward, Robert, Joseph, William, and John; cousin Ann Roberts, but no children; a legacy to the Merion Meeting. His brothers executors.

Ann Humphrey, sister to Owen Humphrey aforesaid, married Ellis Rees ap Lewis, of Bryn Mawr, and was the mother of Rowland Ellis, of "Bryn Mawr," Merion, 1686. Her

---

*Joshua Owen, of Llwyndu parish, Merioneth, bachelor, had certificate, dated 27. 5mo. 1683, from the Quarterly Mtg. at Dolyserry, which he filed with the Haverford (or Radnor) Mo. Mtg., signed by Robert, Humphrey, and Richard Owen, Griffith and Owen Lewis, Rowland Ellis, Humphrey Reinald, etc.

brother Samuel Humphrey was the father of Daniel and Benjamin Humphrey, and three daughters.

JOHN AP JOHN, of Plas Ifa, in Ruabon parish, Denbighshire, as has already been told, did not come to Pensylvania, and died 16. 9mo. 1697, at Whitehough Manor, in Staffordshire, having long before disposed of all his Pensylvania lands.

THOMAS WYNNE (or Gynn, fair haired), was called a "practitioner of physick" in an early mention of him. Watson, in his "Annals of Philadelphia," states that "Dr. Wynne was an eminent Welsh physician," who had "practiced medicine several years with high reputation in London," and that his brother, also a physician, came over with him in 1682, but this brother is not clearly identified, unless he was the John Wynne, a lawyer in Sussex Co. (Del.), in 1687, or was the "John Wynn, chyrurgeon," whose will was proved at Annapolis, Md., in 1684. But the latter may have been the son, or of the family, of Thomas Wynn (son of Gruffydd Wynn, of Bryn yr Owen (ap Richard John Wynn), of Trefechan, near Wrexham, in Denbighshire, who was in Maryland as early as in 1671, and was a sub-sheriff, in 1678, and doorkeeper of the House of Assembly, of Maryland.

In a pamphlet issued by Dr. Wynne, in 8mo. 1679, replying to the attack, entitled "Work for a Cooper," by one William Jones, on his defense of the antiquity of the Quakers, who challenged the claim of Dr. Wynne having any knowledge of the practice of medicine and surgery, saying he was only a cooper by trade, and also "The Ale-Man, the Quack, and the Speaking Quaker," Dr. Wynne tells of his youth, and how he came to be called a physician and surgeon. He says, "my genius from a child had lead me to surgery, insomuch that before I was ten years old I several times overran my school and home when I heard of any one's being wounded, or hurt, and used all my endeavours then to set the fractures and dislocations reduced and wounds dressed."

WELSH SETTLEMENT OF PENSYLVANIA

He says his father died before he was eleven years old, (therefore, the Doctor could not have been identical with Thomas, baptised 1 Feb. 1636, who had a brother John, both living in 1665, when their father, William Wynne's, a son of Sir John Wynne, of Gwydis, Bart., will was proved, as has been suggested), and left his family poor, and "mother not being able to produce so great a sum as to set me to Chyrurgery, I betook myself to this honest and necessary calling he upbraids me with," referring to his having learned the occupation and trade of cooper. "Yet, during all this time (while a cooper's apprentice), I left no opportunity to inform myself in the practice of Chyrurgery, and continued this untill I became acquainted with an honest Friend and good Artist in Chyrurgery, whose name was Richard Moore, of Salop, who, seeing my forwardness to Chyrurgery, did further me in it, and brought me to Defecations in Salop, the Anatomists being men of known worth in practice, whose names are Dr. Needham and Dr. Hallins."

Continuing, he says, after he had learned enough and was able, with the assistance of Dr. Moore, "to set up a Skelliton of a man's bones," the afore-mentioned doctors "thought me fit to be licensed the practice of Chyrurgery, and this is near 20 years ago."

Shortly after being licensed to practice medicine and surgery, Dr. Wynne became too prominent in Quaker affairs, and was arrested and imprisoned for six years in Denbighshire, and when released, he continues: "I betook myself wholly to the practice of Chyrurgery," and says he became a remarkable expert "in the use of the Plaister Box and Salvatory, the Trafine and Head Saw, the Amputation Saw, and the Catling, the Cautery, Sirring and Catheter," . . . "to the great comfort of many, some of them desperately wounded by Gun Shots, others pierced thorow with Rapiers."

Coming over in the "Welcome" he must have been a busy doctor, as nearly all the passengers and the crew were taken ill with the smallpox, and thirty were buried at sea en route for Pensylvania. One of the passengers executed his will, signed 19 Sept. 1682, which was proved at Philadelphia, and with its germs, is preserved in the office of the Register of Wills. It was witnessed by Dr. Wynne, who sealed with a coat of arms, "gules; a three-turreted castle, argent," which arms were his own, but only in American fashion, by adoption, as they were the arms of the first husband of his third wife, Joshua Maud.

In connection with Dr. Wynne's professional life, we have from the minutes of the Quarterly Meeting of Merionethshire, Montgomeryshire, and Shropshire, which met "under the care of Charles Lloyd, Richard Davies, Thomas Lloyd, and Richard Moore," (familiar names in the Welsh Tract), at Dolobran, in 1668, that the said Richard Moore, of Shrewsbury, (who had been the instructor of Dr. Wynne), died in this year, leaving a son, Mordecai Moore, a minor and without money. For the love the Friends had for the lad's father, the Quarterly Meeting appointed a committee to learn what occupation would be suitable for him, and what he "had a taste for." The result was the committee found the "poor boy" had the desire to be a "chirurgeon Barber," so a collection was taken up at the Quarterly Meeting "to bind him as an apprentice to some reliable barber-surgeon." It was decided to send him as an apprentice for seven years to Thomas Wynne, of Caerwys, in Flintshire, and John ap John was instructed to see the arrangement was made, and the boy delivered to Mr. Wynne. Subsequently, this boy came to Maryland, and married Deborah, a daughter of Gov. Thomas Lloyd, of Pensylvania.

From this minute, we learn that Thomas Wynne, in 1668, was a barber-surgeon, or a barber who practiced surgery, and cupping and bleeding, with some knowledge of the use and effect of herbs, and from his own statement, that he never acquired the degree of M.D. from a university.

WELSH SETTLEMENT OF PENSYLVANIA

The place of the birth of Dr. Wynne, and his parentage is unknown, though it may possibly have been in Flintshire, where he resided, in 1682, at Bronvadog, near Caerwys.* The minutes of the Merion Preparative Meeting 5. 11mo. 1704, record that Dr. Edward Jones filed an account of Dr. Wynne, his parentage, home life, conversion, etc., but it has disappeared, otherwise we could know more of him. Dr. Wynne was probably one of John ap John's earliest converts to Quakerism, about 165—, and became himself an accepted minister among the Welsh Friends. He published in 1677, when living at "Caerwys," near the palace of the Lord Bishop, a pamphlet, "The Antiquity of the Quakers," defending Friends' teachings.

The full titles of this pamphlet, and that containing the abusive attack on it, both extant, are quaint, and of the manner of the time:— *The Antiquity of the Quakers, Proved out of the Scriptures of Truth. Published in Love to the Papists, Protestants, Presbyterians, Independents, and Anabaptists. With a Salutation of Pure Love to All the Tenderhearted Welshmen. But more especially to Flintshire, Denbighshire, Caernarvonshire, and Anglesea. By their Countryman and Friend, Thomas Wynne.* Part of it is in Welsh, and "your real friend, Thomas Wynne," wrote it at "Carwys y mis yr ail dydd 1677."

The title of Mr. Jones' effusion:— *Work for a Cooper. Being an Answer to a Libel written by Tho Wynne the Coop-*

---

*If it is any suggestion as to the Doctor's ancestry, his son Jonathan named his seat in Blockley, "Wynnstay," or "Wynnestay," (i.e., Wynne's Field), and there was an estate by this designation near Ruabon and Wrexham, in Denbighshire, in the Doctor's time, in which vicinity he resided prior to removal to Pensylvania. The late Howard Williams Lloyd had the parish Registers, and all the Wynne wills in Flintshire, that would possibly give a clue to the Doctor's ancestry, examined, but got only the information that at that period Wynne, sometimes Gwin, was a common name in North Wales. The most prominent family of the surname was that of Gwydir House, of which there is a printed history, and it was to this family that "Wynnstay" belonged.

COMPANY NUMBER FOUR

er, the Ale-Man, the Quack, and the Speaking Quaker. With a brief Account how that Dissembling People differ at this Day from what at first they were. By one who abundantly pities their Ignorance and Folly.. London. Printed by J. C. for S. C., at the Prince of Wales Arms near the Royal Exchange. MDCLXXIX. The writer thought the Doctor "is ignorant in his very trade of Quack * * * Chyrurgery," and that "he's much fitter to mind his Ax and saw, the Joynter, and the Adz, the Crisle, and the Head knife, the Spoak & the Round Shreve, the Dowling, and the Tapir Bitts, the Tap and Bungbore." This brought out a reply from the Doctor entitled:— *An Anti-Christian Conspiracy Detected, and Satan's Champion Defeated.*

In 1682, he and Charles Lloyd (Co. No. 2), and Richard Davies, (Co. No. 7), who were subsequently also grantees, and "trustees" for large tracts of Pensylvania land, went to Whitehall, London, to see the Secretary of State, and intercede for the Friends of Bristol, who were being badly treated, and received a "fair promise." They themselves had known what it was to "suffer." Joseph Besse, in his book of "The Sufferings of the People Called Quakers," tells that Nathaniel Buttall, Bryan Sixsmith (draper), and Thomas Gwin, and others, "being met together in their own hired house at Wrexham [were] taken to the Common Goal at Writhen," in Dec. 1661. And at another time, when Thomas Wynn and 23 others "were on their way to the Meeting House at White Hart Court, [in London], they were arrested in Angel Court, and sent to prison." On 8. 10mo. they were tried at Guildhall, charged with "being guilty of a riotous assembly, with force and arms," in White Hart Court. All pleaded not guilty, as they had not yet been in White Hart Court, and were only passing through Angel Court. However, as both places were in the same ward, and a woman had preached in the street, they were all confined in Newgate till they raised the money to pay the fines.

WELSH SETTLEMENT OF PENSYLVANIA

He joined the Welshmen who went to London, in May, 1681, to interview William Penn about his Pensylvania lands, and becoming interested himself, became a co-trustee, as said, with John ap John, for 5,000 acres, and from this time he was an intimate of the Proprietary for several years, and came over with him on the ship "Welcome," which sailed 30. 6mo. 1682, and arrived here in the 8mo. following, which was a memorable voyage for many reasons. There were upwards of 100 Quaker immigrants from Penn's home county, Sussex, on the ship.

As to this voyage of ship "Welcome," the *London Gazette*, (No. 1752), in the issue of 31 Aug.—4 Sept. 1682, printed this dispatch:— "Deal. Aug. 30th. [1682]. There are now in the downs, outward bound, two or three merchantships for Pensylvania." And, in issue of 4 Sept.—7 Sept. 1682.— "Deal, Sept. 2d. Two days since sailed out of the downs three ships bound for Pensilvania, on board of which was Mr. Pen, with a great many Quakers, who go to settle there."

Here is an extract from a fictitious letter addressed to John Higginson, written in Oct. 1682, it was said, by the reputedly pious, Rev. Dr. Cotton Mather, of Boston: "There is now at sea a shipp (for our friend Elias Holcroft, of London, did advise me by the last packet that it would leave some time in August), called the Welcome, which has aboard it a hundred or more of the hereticks and malignants called Quakers, with William Penn, the scamp, at the head of them. The General Court has accordingly given instructions to Master Michael Haxett, of the brig Porpoise, to waylay said Welcome as near the end of Cod [Cape Cod, Mass.], as may be, and make capture of Penn and his ungodly crew, so that the Lord may be glorified and not mocked on the soil of this new country with the heathen worshipps of these people. Much spoil may be made by selling the whole lot to Barbadoes, where slaves fetch good prices in rumme and sugar." Signed: "Yours in the bonds of Christ, Cotton Mather."

COMPANY NUMBER FOUR

This alleged "extract" created considerable of a sensation when it was started on the rounds of the newspapers. It was thought it would not have been beneath this devine to take such a fling at the Quakers, therefore the letter, which was addressed to Rev. Mr. Higginson, "at New Port," (Rhode Island), was believed to be genuine. But, after investigators failed to see, or locate such a letter, and on making the discovery that Mr. Higginson was not then living at Newport, but was then established as the minister at Salem, Mass., and knowing that Mather was then only 19 years old, the story of the attempt to kidnap Mr. Penn was pronounced a fake, when several people had the assurance to come forward and each claim, for the fame there was in it, to have been the perpetrator of the "joke on the historians."

It may be presumed that Dr. Wynne passed his first winter here with Penn, at Upland and at New Castle, looking after the small-pox patients, and accompanied him to New York and to Baltimore, on business trips, taking as many of the germs along as possible.

He was chosen by Penn as a member, and his representative possibly, in the first preliminary assembly of delegates from the settlements on the Delaware and Schuylkill, held at Upland, 4. 10mo. 1682, and was appointed a member of the committee to "petition" Penn for a constitution for his Province. And when the first organized Assembly was held in Philadelphia 12. 1mo. 1682-3, he was chosen one of the members to represent Philadelphia Co. in it, possibly by the Welsh, and was selected speaker at the first meeting.

He was present at the first Monthly Meeting of Friends, held in Philadelphia, on 9. 11mo. 1682-3, and was appointed of the committee to select and secure the site for the Philadelphia Meeting House, in Second street, and was a member of the building committee.

It is claimed that his brick dwelling in the west side of Front Street, above Chestnut Street, was the first brick

WELSH SETTLEMENT OF PENSYLVANIA

house erected in the town. The street now called Chestnut was originally called Wynne.

In the 6mo. of 1684, he went to England on a business matter, probably with William Penn, in the ketch "Endeavour," sailing from Philadelphia 12. 6mo. 1684, and, on his return, went to Lewes to reside, which then was a more desirable place than Philadelphia for a residence. Here he became a justice of Sussex County, in 3mo. 1687, and a representative of that county in the Assembly, 3mo. 1688.

He died while attending a meeting of the Assembly, in Philadelphia, on 16. 1mo. 1692, and was buried the next day in the Friends' ground, Philadelphia. His will, dated 16. 1mo. 1691-2, was proved at Philadelphia 20. 2mo. 1692, the overseers named being Thomas Lloyd, the Dep. Gov., and Dr. Griffith Owen, the Provincial Councillor. He named his wife, Elizabeth, his brother-in-law, Samuel Buttall, (to whom he owed £25), and his children as below. The only land he mentioned was what he owned at Lewes, valued at £80, which went to his wife and then to son Jonathan, to whom he also gave 200 acres on Cedar Creek, Sussex Co., valued at £20. His personalty amounted to £430. 1. 3., including 3 negroes, valued at £60, and one "servant."

According to the Minutes of the Provincial Council, 6 Oct. 1693, Charles Pickering (who had been convicted of passing counterfeit money in Philadelphia, by the first Court, see Minute of 28. 8. 1683), "in behalf of the widdow Wynne, having preferred a pe'tion to the Leivt. Governor and Council, setting forth that her Husband, Thomas Wynne, Late of Sussex Countie, deceased, had been Sumoned to the Court of New Castle, to ans'r the Complaint of Adam Short and others. But falling sick, dyed 3 or 4 hours befor Judgm't past ag't him, att the said Court, and that the originall proces ag't her husband was by a wrong name, and therefore requested that the execu'on be stopt, and that the pe'tionr have a fair tryall." The clerk's record of the New Castle Court being produced, and it was found the petitioner's husband's name was written "Thomas Guin." The Council ordered the matter before the next Provincial Court to be held for Sussex Co., and that in the meantime execution be suspended.

Dr. Thomas Wynne* was married three times. He married first, possibly at Wrexham, Denbighshire, Martha Buttall, about 1655-57, by Morgan Lloyd, who sent John ap John to "try out" Fox's teaching. She was the sister of Jonathan Buttall, sugar baker, of the Surry side of the Thames, and was named, with her brother Samuel, in his will, signed 26 Aug. 1695. Her issue was to be his heirs on failure of his own. She died about 1670, and is presumed to have been the mother of all of Dr. Wynne's children.

Dr. Wynne married secondly, a widow named Rowden, who by her first husband was the mother of Elizabeth, who *m.* in Philadelphia Monthly Meeting, 5. 6mo. 1684, John Brock, of Philadelphia. She died in 1675-6.

Dr. Wynne married thirdly, 20. 5mo. 1676 (record of Monthly Meeting of Hardshaw East, in Lancashire), Elizabeth Parr, widow of Joshua Maud, who survived him. When he married her, who came to Pensylvania with him, he was living at Caerwys, Flintshire. Her daughter, Margery Maud, married at Lewes, Thomas Fisher, *a quibus* Fisher family of Philadelphia.

He married Elizabeth Maud, or Mode, of Rainhill, Lancashire, at the dwelling of John Chorley, and among the signers of their certificates were John and Alice Barnes; Bruen, William, and Ester Sixmith; Samuel, Alice, and Margaret Dunbabin; John, Alice, and Mary Southworth.

But his wife, Elizabeth, did not come in the same ship with the Doctor. According to the extant log, 6. 7mo. to 21. 8mo. 1682, of the "Submission," one of the vessels which sailed with the "Welcome," she was a passenger on that ship, and was accompanied by her daughters, Jane and Margery, whose surnames appears as "Mode," and the Doctor's daughter, Rebecca Wynne.

*See further as to Dr. Wynne, in the *Philadelphia Friend*, vol. XXVII, p. 228.

WELSH SETTLEMENT OF PENSYLVANIA

By deed of 3. 3mo. 1688, Dr. Wynne bought for his wife, an island in "the Broad Kill Marshes," in the Schuylkill, near its mouth. After his death, his relict, by deed of gift dated 1. 12mo. 1693, conveyed this island, which, on survey of 5mo. 1701, contained 175 acres, to her daughter, Margery, and husband, Thomas Fisher, and then it became known as Fisher's Island, but subsequently was called Province Island, and was the location of hospitals.

Of the children of Dr. Wynne* by his first wife,

Jonathan Wynne, only son and heir. It is not known when, nor where he was born, nor how old he was when he came to Pensylvania, and it is only presumed he was the youngest child, and that he came with his father, either on his first trip in the "Welcome," or his subsequent trip.

We have seen that Jonathan was to receive, after his stepmother's death, the homestead near the town of Lewes, and 200 acres on Cedar Creek, in Sussex Co., (Del.). After his father's death, he began investigating both the land transactions of "John & Wynne," and his father's personal operations in the Welsh Tract.

He made it out that only 1,850 acres of the 2,500 acres of his father's land had been located and sold by him, and that

---

*These are some of the many present-day descendants of Dr. Thomas Wynne:

Mrs. Stevenson Crothers.
Mrs. Henry Kuhl Dillard.
Mrs. Henry B. Robb.
Mrs. Charles F. Hulse.
Miss Elizabeth Moser Jones.
Mrs. Jawood Lukens.
Mrs. Arthur V. Meigs.
Mrs. Charles Richardson.
Mrs. George B. Roberts.
Mrs. S. Bowman Wheeler.
Mrs. Howard Comfort.
William Penn Humphreys.

Mrs. Thomas Stewardson.
Frank Foulke.
Abraham L. Smith.
Benj. Hayes Smith.
Joseph A. Steinmetz.
Charles Williams.
J. Randall Williams.
Rodman Wister.
Alexander W. Wister.
Miss Martha Morris Brown.
Mrs. Robert R. Corson.
Mary Hollingsworth Stewardson.

All of the descendants of John Cadwalader, 1677-1734, are descendants of Dr. Wynne:

COMPANY NUMBER FOUR

there was thus 650 acres due him, besides 50 acres of the Liberty lands, as bonus; this besides the 100 acres due on the joint account, mentioned above. He went before the Land Commissioners, Edward Shippen, Griffith Owen and James Logan, 18. 4mo. 1705, and presented his claim, as he understood it.

The decision of the Commission as to the 100 acres was made as above, and from the Surveyor General's office it found that 2,125 acres of Dr. Wynne's 2,500 acres could be accounted for. That is, he had sold to Thomas Taylor 500 acres, to John Bevan 300 acres, to Richard Orme 150 acres, to Humphrey Bettly 125 acres, to Richard Crosby 500 acres, and to Cary Southworth 300 acres, and had retained for himself 250 acres in Radnor. The Commission also found some evidence that the Doctor had sold some land to Roger Andrews and to Trial Rider, but not the amount.

Of the Doctor's 250 acres, in Radnor, the Commission learned that it was confirmed to him by patent, dated 29. 5mo. 1684, and that, of this land, he had sold 200 acres to Howel James, of Radnor, by deed of 9. 10mo. 1687 (who sold 100 acres out of the tract to David Evan, and 100 acres to his son, William James, who also sold to David Evan, by deed, dated 26. 11mo. 1689), and had conveyed the balance, 50 acres, to Hugh Williams.

The Commissioners decided to throw out the possible sales to Andrews and Rider, after investigating for two years, and in 7mo. 1707, and granted a warrant to Jonathan for 400 acres even, which he was authorized to lay out in the Welsh Tract if possible, that is, if he could find so much untaken land therein. "The Commission considered that Dr. Wynne's son had all, and more, that was coming to him from his father's grant," was its recorded opinion. This land, 400 acres, was finally laid out in the Chester Valley.

As to the 50 acres of Liberty land, claimed due by Jonathan to complete his father's purchase, the Commission found out that his brother-in-law, Dr. Edward Jones, of Merion, had acquired, in some way not revealed, 10 acres of

WELSH SETTLEMENT OF PENSYLVANIA

it, so a warrant for 40 acres only of this choice land was given him, which was laid out to him in the Liberty lands, or Blockley tp., southeast of the present settlement of Bala, just without the township of Merion. Here Jonathan erected a stone house, which he named "Wynnestay," after the Welsh seat mentioned, or, as is also said, "Wynne Stay," for he proposed to stay here till he died, which he did. The property remained in the possession of this Wynne family till after the close of the Revolutionary War. Since that time it has passed through the hands of several owners, and several years ago was completely "remodelled." In September, 1910, it was leased for Miss Hannah Smedley to Mr. Alvin Ehret.

Jonathan also was granted a lot, 60 by 300 feet, in High (Market) street, in the city, due also on account of his father. This he devised to two of his daughters, Hannah and Mary, to be equally divided between them. He devised to his other three daughters, minors, 400 acres in The Great Valley, "Great Meadows," or Chester Valley, where he had also acquired by purchase 500 acres which he divided between his sons, Thomas and John.

The will of "Jonathan Wynne, of Blockley, yeoman," dated 29 Jan. 1719, was proved 17 May, 1721, by his wife, Sarah. Overseers appointed, "brother-in-law Edward Jones and Daniel Humphreys"; if they died before him, then John Cadwalader and Jon. Jones. The witnesses were Rowland Ellis, Thomas Jones, and Edward Jones. He was buried at the Merion Meeting House, 28. 12mo. (Feb.) 1720-1. His widow, Sarah, was also buried here, 27. 2mo. 1744. He had by his wife, Sarah, whose surname has not been preserved, (unless it was Graves, or Greave, as there is reason to believe), married possibly at Lewes, about 1700-1, eight children mentioned in his will, and a son James, who was buried at the Merion Meeting House, 24. 8mo. 1714, namely, Thomas, his heir, who was to have the homestead (near Bala) after his mother's death, John, Jonathan, Hannah, Mary, Sidney, Martha and Elizabeth.

COMPANY NUMBER FOUR

Mary Wynne, who *m.* Dr. Edward Jones, of Merion. *Issue.*

Rebecca Wynne, who *m.* first, at the Third Haven Friends' Meeting, in Talbot Co., Md., in 3mo. 1685, Solomon Thomas who *d. s. p..* She *m.* secondly, 23. 7mo. 1692, John Dickinson, of Talbot Co., an uncle of Samuel Dickinson, son-in-law of John Cadwalader.

Sidney Wynne, who *m.* in Anne Arundel Co., Md., 20. 10mo. 1690, William Chew, son of Samuel Chew, of this county.

Hannah Wynne, who *m.* at the Merion Meeting, 25. 8mo. 1695, Daniel Humphreys, son of Samuel and Elizabeth Humphreys, of Merion.

Tibitha Wynne, who never came over here, but died in England, after 1692.

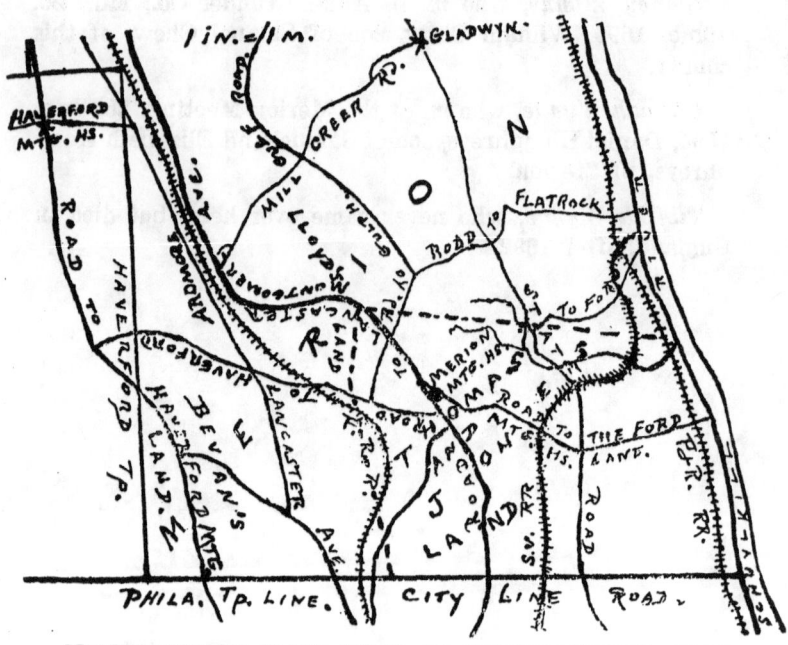

RELATIVE POSITIONS OF THE MERION AND HAVERFORD MEETING HOUSES, AND THE THOMAS AND JONES LAND.

LEWIS DAVID'S LAND PATENT

Company No. 5. The 3,000 acres of land subscribed for by "Lewis David, husbandman, of Llandewy Velfry," in Pembrokeshire, and conveyed to him by deeds, dated 2 March, 1681, for which he paid £60, were taken, under deeds, dated in May, 1682, by the following:

William Howell, Castlebigch, Pembroke, yeoman, 500 acres.

Henry Lewis, Narbeth, Pembroke, yeoman, 1,000 acres.

Rees Rothers (Rotheroe), Lanwenog, Cardigan, yeoman, 500 acres.

Evan Thomas, Lanykeaven, Pembroke, yeoman, 250 acres.

Lewis David retained 750 acres for himself. (24 Oct. 1681.)

His deed from Penn was similar to those of the other "adventurers for land;"—land was to be set out "as provided for in the Concessions, or Constitucons, bearing date of 11th July last past," 1681, "to be holden in free and common socage of him, the said William Penn, as of the signory of Windsore," etc. His deeds to his sundry purchasers, or co-partners, were also, as those of the other adventurers, very explicit as to the tenure, citing the grant of King Charles to Penn, and the latter to Lewis David. In these, he was described as "gentleman." Lewis David was buried at the Merion Meeting, 2. 1mo. 1707-8.

On 16. 12mo. 1701, the following, being grantees, "in the right of Lewis David," of the original company, had their purchases resurveyed and confirmed to them:

Henry Thomas, 400 acres, and 180 acres, in Haverford tp.
John Lewis, Sen., 350 acres in Haverford tp.
John Lewis, Jr., 100 acres in Haverford tp.
Richard Hayes, 260 acres in Haverford tp.

WELSH SETTLEMENT OF PENSYLVANIA

John David Thomas, 210 acres in "Duffein Mawr" tp.
Maurice Llewellyn, 420 acres in Haverford.
David Rees, 260 acres in Haverford.
David Hugh, 220 acres in Haverford.
Nathan Thomas, 81 acres in Haverford, and "100 acres in the upper end of the Welsh Tract."

These further details of Lewis David's purchase are from the "Welsh Minutes" of the Commissioners of Pensylvania land.

He took for himself 750 acres, but by deed of 10 May, 1682, he sold 250 to "Maurice Skurfield," or "Scourfield," who by deed 22 April, 1699, sold the same to Owen Thomas, who by deed, 15. 11mo. 1701, sold same to Ralph Lewis.

William Howel, had deed, dated 10 May, 1682, witnessed by Daniel Humphrey, Rees Henten, and Humphrey Ellis, for 500 acres, which he had laid out in Haverford tp. and Marple tp. He sold 200 acres in Marple to Jonathan Hayes, and by deed of 29. 3. 1697, sold 220 acres in Haverford, to David Hugh. On his own right, and on account of Evan Thomas, whose widow he married, he had 15 acres of the Liberty land, in 1702. Howel sold his 10 acres Liberty land to Benj. Chambers.

Henry Lewis bought by deed, dated 10 May, 1682, 1,000 acres, for which he paid £25. Witnessed by the above witnesses, and William Howell. Part of the tract was laid out in Haverford. His 20 acres of Liberty land, or bonus, he sold to John Ball. He sold, by deed of 6. 12mo. 1684, 250 acres in Haverford to John Lewis, who also had 100 acres, bought of William Rowe, who had same from Thomas Ellis, in Haverford. His son, Henry Lewis, Jr., by deed, 8. 1mo. 1694-5, conveyed 100 acres to John Lewis, Jr. Henry, Jr., also conveyed by deed of 12. 1mo. 1694-5, to Richard Hayes, Sr., 50 acres, who had 50 acres, bought of William Howel, and 160 acres from John Burge.*

---

*Filed with the Haverford (or Radnor) Mo. Mtg. about 1684-5, is the certificate, undated, of "Allice Lewis, daughter of James Lewis,

COMPANY NUMBER FIVE

Henry Lewis, Jr., having right to 180 acres in the Welsh Tract, on his father's account, and 79 acres, bought of John Burge, had same laid out in the Great Valley. On resurvey, this 259 acres was found to be 352 acres, or allowing 25 acres, he had 248 acres there, 68 acres being over-plus. He also had 50 acres over-plus in Haverford, on his 400 acres. He bought the "overs."

Henry Lewis, is probably the best known of this company. He resided at "Maencoch," as he called his seat, or plantation, 250 acres in Haverford. He and his wife, Margaret, removed from Narberth, in Pembroke, in 1682. "As a member of the Religious Society of Friends, he was strict in the performances of his duties, and, during the short period in which he lived after reaching his new home, he devoted much of his time to civil affairs, and acts of benevolence." Before the establishment of the Haverford Monthly Meeting, in 1684, he belonged to the Monthly Meeting of Philadelphia, and was by that Meeting appointed one of a committee "to visit the poor and sick, and administer what they should judge convenient, at the expense of the Meeting." He held the office of "peace maker" for the county of Philadelphia, and was foreman of the first Grand Jury for that county. His will, signed 6. 14. 1688, witnessed by Lewis David, Griffith Owen, and Thomas Ellis, all well known gentlemen, was proved in Philadelphia on 8. 8. 1705.

He was a carpenter by trade, and owned a house and two lots in Philadelphia. He left his homestead to his wife, Margaret, and desired that, after her death, their sons, Henry Lewis, Jr., and Lewis Lewis, should have it. He provided for his son Samuel, and daughter Elizabeth, who married, in 3mo. 1697, Richard Hayes, Jr., of Haverford.

---

of Llardevy, Pembrokeshire," saying she "is clear from all men on ye acc't of Marriage." Signed by Alice, Margaret and Lewis Musgrave, Mary Morce, Mary Bowen, Mary and Henry Smith, Deborah Weston, Margaret and James Skone, Henry and Jone Hilling, Letice Pardo, James, Mary, and James Lewis, Jr., Anthony Tounson, Thomas Marchant, William Garret, John Perrot, and David Morgan.

WELSH SETTLEMENT OF PENSYLVANIA

His father, Richard Hays, Sr., mentioned above, made his will 4. 8mo. 1697, which was witnessed by William Jenkins, Adam Roades, William Howell, Henry and Samuel Lewis, and proved 30 Oct. 1697, leaving his estate to his wife Issat, and then after her decease to his son and heir, Richard Hayes, Jr. He gave legacies to his son John, and "cousin Sarah James," and to the Haverford Meeting. Trustees named: David Lawrence and Rowland Powell. Richard and Isatt were "aged Friends," when they removed from Pembrokeshire, to Haverford, in 1687. Their son, Richard, Jr., resided on the farm first taken. "Having received a better education than was usual among the early emigrants, and being withal a man of excellent business qualifications, he was almost constantly kept in some public employment, yet he managed his pecuniary affairs to great profit and advantage." In company with David Morris and Samuel Lewis, Richard Hayes, Jr., erected, about 1707, a mill on Darby Creek, which for a long time was known as "Haverford New Mill," but now called Leedom's Mill. He conducted the mill at the time of his death, and for many years before, on his own account. He was a justice of the Courts of Chester Co., a member of the Assembly for seven years, and for years was one of the commissioners of the Loan Office. His children were Joseph, Mary, Hannah, Richard 3d and Benjamin.

The daughter Hannah Hayes *m.* at Haverford Meeting, 10. 8mo. 1727, James Jones, *b.* in Wales, 31. 3mo. 1699, a son of David and Katherine Jones, who came over in 1700, and settled on their purchase, 350 acres, in Blockley, bringing certificate from the Monthly Meeting at Hendri Mawr, dated 24. 12mo. 1699, signed by Robert Vaughan, Cadwalader Ellis, Evan Rees, Thomas Richards, Rowland Owen, Edward David, Owen Lewis, Thomas Cadwalader and John Robert, and a certificate from the Men's Meeting, in Haverford West, dated 4. 1mo. 1699-00. David Jones was one of the first that was appointed an Elder in the Haverford

COMPANY NUMBER FIVE

Meeting, "He conducted faithfull, and was approved of, in good esteem to his dying day, which was the 27. 6mo. 1725, and was buried at Merion." His wife, Katherine, appears from the minutes of the Haverford Monthly Meeting to have been called into active service in the Meeting almost immediately after arrival in this country.

Richard, Jr.'s son Benjamin Hayes, m. at the Merion Meeting, 2. 10mo. 1737, Mary, b. 14. 5mo. 1707, daughter of Jonathan Jones (son of Dr. Edward Jones, of Merion), and Gainor Owen, and had Elizabeth, b. 16. 7mo. 1738.

Evan Thomas, who bought by deed, witnessed by Hannah Hardiman, Mary Phillpin, and Henry Lewis, 10 May, 1682, 250 acres, died and left his rights to his children, Daniel Evan, or Evans, and Mary, and his widow, Mary, (who remarried William Howel), who sold it. By deed, 22 Aug. 1700, they sold 75 acres to Nathan Thomas, and 170 acres to John Bevan.

Rees Rothers, or Rytharch, Rutrach and Rotheroe, who bought for £10, by deed, dated 10. 3mo. 1682, witnessed by Samuel Rees, Tho. Ellis, David Lawrence, George Painter, John Humphrey and Morris Llewellyn, 500 acres in Haverford tp., sold 120 acres, by deed, dated 12. 10mo. 1692, to Thomas Rees. Next day, he transferred the same to William Lewis, who, by deed of gift, 6 Jan. 1700-1, gave the same, with 125 acres he had bought of John Bevan, to his son, David Lewis, who subsequently bought 100 acres from Morris Llewellyn, in Haverford. Rytharch also sold 100 acres to George Painter, and, by deed, 6. 8mo. 1695, he conveyed 30 acres to Maurice Llewellyn (who held 390 acres more in Merion, being part of his father's original 500 acres), bought by deed dated 20 Jan. 1681, (100 acres had been sold to David Lewis). The balance of Rytharch's land lay in Dyffrin Mawr tp., and of this, he sold 210 acres to John David Thomas.

Of Lewis David's balance of 500 acres, and 10 acres of liberty land, ("sold to B. Chambers"), he sold 260 acres

[199]

WELSH SETTLEMENT OF PENSYLVANIA

in Haverford to "Peregr. Musgrove," who by deed, 14 Nov. 1699, sold the same to Samuel Lewis, who by deed, 21 March, 1699-1700, sold same to David ap Rees (Prees, or Price), whose son, John Price, inherited it. (Burials at Merion Meeting, Gwenllen, wife of David Price, 6. 20. 1715, and Hannah, wife of David Price, 10. 13. 1727).

Lewis David also sold 30 acres in Haverford, by deed 28 Feb. 1691-2, to William Jenkins, (on account of 250 acres William Jenkins bought of John Poyer,—the Lewis David lands,—he had 5 acres of Liberty land in 1702), who by deed, 24. 6mo. 1698-9, conveyed the same to William Rowe, together with 30 acres he had from John Poyer, out of his 250 acre tract he bought of John & Wynne. William Rowe's executors, Rowland Ellis and Thomas Paschall, by deed of 8. 9mo. 1700, conveyed two lots of 30 acres each to Daniel Humphreys. The will of William Rowe, marked 8. 3mo. 1699, in the presence of John Roberts, Daniel Humphreys, and Lewis Waker, was proved 1 July, 1699. His wife, un-named, was living. He bequeathed his estate to his daughter, Grace Rowe, and legacies to the Haverford Meeting, to David Lawrence and Rowland Howell. Names guardians for daughter, John Lewis, David Maurice, and Henry Lewis.

By the usual deeds of lease and release, dated 24. and 25. Oct. 1681, William Penn conveyed to William Jenkin, or Jenkins, "a Friend who had suffered," of Tenby, in Pembroke, 1,000 acres of land. Of this grant, Jenkins conveyed 500 acres to Francis Howell, of Llancilio, in Caermarthen, by deed of 1 Sept. 1686, which tract was laid out to him in Duffryn Mawr, or Whiteland tp., in Chester Co. The balance of the grant was also located in Duffryn Mawr and laid out to Jenkins, who conveyed 250 acres of it, by deed of 30 Sep. 1686, to James Thomas. But when Jenkins removed to Pensylvania, about 1686, he settled on the 250 acres which he bought of John Poyer, 13 July, 1686, in Haverford. About 1698, William Jenkins removed into Abington tp., then in

Philadelphia Co., and Jenkintown was named for him. In 1691, he was a justice in Chester Co., and in 1690 and 1695, a member of the Assembly. He died 7. 4mo. 1712, aged 54 years, having married, 2. 7mo. 1673, at Tenby, Elizabeth Lewis, died 14. 9mo. 1711, daughter of Lewis Griffith. The births of their four children are recorded at the South Wales Monthly Meeting. Of these, Margaret, *b.* 23. 3mo. 1674, *m.* at Haverford Meeting, 15. 9mo. 1692 (first wife), Thomas Paschall, Jr., of Chester Co., and had eleven children, *d.* 17. 11mo. 1728; and Stephen Jenkins, 1690-1761, *m.* at the Abington Meeting, 14. 9mo. 1704, Abigail, a minister among the Friends, who *d.* 2. 9mo. 1750, daughter of Phineas Pemberton, of Bucks Co., Pa., and had seven children.

Lewis David also sold, 5. 9mo. 1691, 10 acres, and 30. 3mo. 1700, a lot and grist mill, in Haverford tp., which he held with Humphrey Ellis, to William Howel.

Lewis David also held about 190 acres in Dyffrin Mawr tp.

Morris Llewellyn, of Haverford, mentioned above, bought by deed dated 1. 1. 1697-8, for £100, a tract of 500 acres, in Haverford, from the estate of Nathaniel Pennock, (who died 15. 10mo. 1697), the heir to George Collet, of Philadelphia, a glover, who had bequeathed this right, in 10mo. 1686, to Nathaniel, a minor. The said Nathaniel died unmarried, and his father, Christopher Pennock, administered his estate, and conveyed the right to the 500 acres to Llewellyn. This land was a portion of 5,000 acres Penn had sold, 14. 6mo. 1682, to Joshua Holland, of Chattam, Kent, mariner, whose son, John Holland, of same place, a shipwright, had power of attorney to sell 1,000 acres, and therefore sold 500 acres "on West side of river Schuylkil," for £25, by deed of 13. 3mo. 1685, to said George Collet.

The oldest land corner-stone extant, (discovered by Samuel M. Garrigues, surveyor, of Bryn Mawr, in 1889), is on the line of Hannah Llewellyn, to whom descended some of this land, and land of Haverford College, on the north side of Cobb's Creek. This stone, set up in 1683, probably by

WELSH SETTLEMENT OF PENSYLVANIA

Morris Llewellyn, as a deputy surveyor, approximates the date of ownership of land here by the Llewellyns, and marked the corner of the land of Thomas Ellis, on the south, David Llewellyn, on the west, and Morris Llewellyn, on the east, as on the east face of the stone is cut C—D M L, and on the west face C— M D L L— T E — 1683.

Morris Llewellyn's 420 acres in Haverford were surveyed to 490 acres, before 16. 12mo. 1701, when he requested of the Commissioners warrant for the usual bonus of 10 acres of the Liberty land, which was granted, and ordered surveyed to him.

Before the Land Commissioners, 27. 8mo. 1712, "Maurice Llewellyn" produced a deed from James Thomas, of Merion, conveying to him 100 acres in Merion, whereon the said James and his father had been seated. On official survey it was learned there were 137 acres in this place. But when his brother David Llewellyn, surveyed it, he found only 30 acres over, so Morris, taking benefit of all doubt, agreed to pay £15, "at the next Spring Fair of Philadelphia," for 27 acres. The chain of title for this land starts with Penn's sale to Davies, and his conveyance by deed, 10. 6mo. 1686, to one Steel, of Llancillis parish, in Caermarthanshire, and Ellis Ellis, of Haverford, for 410 acres in Merion,

Of this there were conveyed 10 acres to Thomas Ellis, 100 to Francis Howel, 100 to Morgan Davis, 100 to Francis Lloyd, and 100 to James Thomas, of Merion, who gave it to the said James Thomas, his son, (subsequently of Whitland tp., Chester Co.), who sold as above to Morris Llewellyn, of Haverford, by deed of 9 Feb. 1708-9.

Francis Howel devised his 100 acres, 15. 1mo. 1695, to his brother, Thomas Howell, who by deed dated 17 June, 1708, for five shillings and natural affection conveyed the land to the aforesaid Morris Llewellyn. The old farm house of the Llewellyns, called "Castle Br'th," is still standing.

The will of "Francis Howell, of Merion, yeoman," signed 15. 1. 1695, proved 25 Sep. 1696, names wife Margaret sole executrix, names brother Thomas Howell, and sisters Elizabeth, Margaret, Mary and Susan Howell. Legacy to James Mortimer. Witnesses, John Bevan, William Howell and John Humphreys.

The will of his wife, and relict, Margaret Howell, of Merion, was marked in the presence of Edward Jones, David Habard (or Havard), and John Humphreys, 12 Sep. 1696, and proved 25 Sep. following. She names brother James Mortimer, nephew James Mortimer, sister Margaret Thomas, cousin Betty Thomas, brothers-in-law David Jones and David (Haubot?), cousin James . . . . . . and legacies to Lewis David, John Hastings, Katherine Pris, her maid servant, "the residue of her time to be free," to Lewis Waker, to my negro, to John Simons, Nathan Thomas,* Owen Thomas, John, William, and Ann Habart (Habard), Elizabeth and Katherine Thomas, Betty and Margaret Lewis, David Pugh, Mary Waker, John Pris, Mary, wife of Benjamin Humphrey, and her son John Humphrey, Mary, wife of David Morris, and to John Humphrey, Sr., and Jr. Legacies also to the "Meeting Houses of Merion and Haverford." Executors, Morris Llewellyn and James Thomas, Jr.

1713, 22. 5mo., the Commissioners confirmed his land to Morris Llewellyn, amounting to three lots, 100, 130, and 400 acres—bought of Lewis David, gent.

---

*The will of "Nathan Thomas, of Merion, yeoman," signed 6. 2mo. 1710, witnesses, Thomas Howell and David Evan, was proved 4 Aug. 1711. He mentions his mother, Margaret Thomas, and "grandmother Thomas," brother Owen Thomas, sisters Katherine Pearson, and Elizabeth Thomas, cousins Thomas and Mary Pearson, and John and Nathan Thomas.

HAVERFORD TP. EAST OF THE "STREET," 1690.

ADVENTURERS FOR LANDS IN HAVERFORD AND RADNOR

RICHARD THOMAS'S LAND PATENT

Company No. 6—The purchasers of the 5,000 acres of land for which Richard ap Thomas, of Whiteford Garne, subscribed, were not many, and his adventure appears to have been unprofitable. His heir had about the same trouble, as Dr. Wynne's had, in getting his father's land.

From the Commissioners' Minutes 2. 12mo., 1701, we learn that Penn, by deed dated 24th of July, 1681, for £100, conveyed to Richard ap Thomas 5,000 acres, to be laid out "in the Welsh Tract," "of which none has been laid out Saving 600 acres on part of 1.300 Acres laid out to [William] Wood and [William] Sharlow" [or Shardlow, Sharelow, Sherlo, etc.]. This, of course, was "not approv'd of by the Commis'rs". and the "100 Acres of Lib. Land [due, was] taken up by Hugh Roberts." At this Meeting "his Son and Heir, Richard ap Thomas, therefore requets Warr'ts to take up the said Land in the Welsh Tract."

"The said Richard haveing been a Verry great Sufferer by his Father's embarquing for this Province, and deceasing before, or upon his Arrival, by which means he has been reduced to great hardships, 'tis Ordered that a War't be forthwith granted to take up 2,000 A's of Vacant land where to be found in the said Tract, and that War'ts be also Issued for the remainder as fast as he can be accommodated." This was a very fair accommodation all things considered. But on 2. 3mo. 1704, he was assessed the quitrent to run "from the first laying out of the Welsh Tract." Before 7mo. 1702, Philip Howel bought 700 acres from said Richard.

As to the 100 acres in the City Liberties, they were surveyed, 4. 7mo. 1701, "in pursuance of the Proprietor's Warrant, dated 8. 11mo. 1700," to Hugh Roberts, to whom patent for same was issued by the Commissioners 24 Nov. 1701.

WELSH SETTLEMENT OF PENSYLVANIA

This land was located "upon the Indian Creek and the Mill Creek (Cobbs Creek), in Blockley tp., near Adam Rhode's Land," "in Right of Richard Thomas, first Purchaser of 5,000 Acres."

Richard Thomas, Jr., in the Spring of 1703, had considerable trouble about his land, because the surveyor laid it out on a spot that the Commissioners had granted to "R'd Ingels, of Philad'a, Gent." in 2mo. 1686, in the Welsh Tract. On a resurvey, it was found that Ingels had too much land, and with this "overplus" and some unclaimed land adjoining, Richard Thomas was accommodated.

Minute of 8. 9mo. 1703, Richard Thomas, the younger, was granted "a High St. Lott of 132 foot in right of his Fathers Purchase, and 51 foot [lot] in the Front Street."

On 3. 2mo. 1704, Richard Thomas, Jr., made returns of the following sales "of his 5,000 acres Purchased by his Father":—

To Philip Howel, 700 acres.
To Robert Williams, 500 acres.
To Edward Jones, 200 acres.
To Hugh Roberts, 100 acres Liberty Land.
To David Howel, 200 acres.
To Robert David, 861¼ acres.

"In all 1786¼ acres. [He] has taken up and Patented 1,665 acres, which Make 3,451¼, and there remains 1,548¾. To which 320 Being added, allowed to him (for which he is to Pay Rent for the whole 3,200 from the first Location of the Welsh Tract as well P'r agreement), for the 1,665 acres already Patented as for the Rem'd, makes 1,868¾ acres to be Confirmed forthwith, he Paying the said arrears." See also letter of David Powell to James Logan, 5. 12mo. 1701, *super*.

It appears from the Minutes of 1mo. 5th. 1715-16, that the 600 acre part of Richard ap Thomas's original purchase which was sold to Messrs. Wood and Sharlow, was laid out in New Town tp., Chester Co., and that Richard Thomas,

COMPANY NUMBER SIX

Jr. claimed this tract, but the heirs of Wood and Sharlow protested, whereupon the Commissioners issued a patent to him, dated 8. 1mo. 1716-7, for 243 acres in the "Chester County Welsh Tract," "in part of 600 allowed him instead of the like quantity confirmed to him in New Town."

On 8. 2mo. 1717, "Richard Thomas, Son and Heir of Rich'd ap Thomas, haveing formerly obtained the Grant of a Lott of Ground on the River Schuylkill, to be laid out to him in Right of his ffather's Purchase, besides those Lotts laid out to him on Delaware side of Philad'a, which Lott on Schuylkill not being survey'd to him, he now desires that he might risign his Right to the said Lott, and that he would instead thereof grant him one whole Lott in the Back streets on Delaware side. The Comm'rs considers his disappointm'ts in not haveing his Lotts and Lands laid out to him before he came to age, Grants his Request, and a Warrant is signed and dated ye 25 of 7ber, 1717." This was done "for Richard ap Thomas in full of all his Demand."

RICHARD AP THOMAS, described as gentleman, as he was the owner of a freehold of £300 per annum, resided in Flintshire, at "Whitford Garden," or Crossforth, when he first appears in the history of the "Welsh Tract." Nothing is certain of his ancestry. He was one of the early converts to Fox's teachings.

He made arrangements to remove with his wife, and two children, to Pensylvania, but his wife backed out at the last moment, and remained at home with their daughter. It is tradition among their descendants, that Mrs. Thomas was never converted to Quakerism, and therefore was not "inclined for Pensylvania."

Mr. Thomas, with his only son, Richard Thomas, Jr., aged about ten years, and some servants, joined the Hugh Roberts party, and sailed from Mossom, in the ship Morning Star, of Liverpool, in Sep. 1683, and arrived at Philadelphia on 16 Nov. 1683. Mr. Thomas arrived in ill health, and died shortly, in town, without having had opportunity to attend

WELSH SETTLEMENT OF PENSYLVANIA

to the locating of his land, or even the disposal of the goods he brought over to sell. His will, dated 18 Nov. 1683, was probably drawn up just before he died, though it was not proved till 15 Jan. 1695-6, when Richard, Jr., was of age. He devised his lands in Wales and Pensylvania to Richard, his heir, and appointed Dr. Thomas Wynne the executor and guardian of young Richard. To his wife and only daughter, he devised his personal estate in Wales.

Richard Thomas, Jr., lived with his guardian, at Lewes, in Co. Sussex, (Delaware), until Dr. Wynne died, in 1692. In 1693, he had considerable litigation over his Welsh land, attended to by his attorney, Gov. Thomas Lloyd.

The difficulties he experienced, when he became of age, over his Pensylvania grant, are mentioned above. Of his father's 5,000 acres, he sold 1,785 acres to sundry parties. In 1703, he had patents for two tracts, one of 1,065 acres, on a part of which the present city of West Chester stands; the other, 600 acres, laid out in Newton tp., he lost through bad surveys. In 1704, he had a third patent for 1,548 acres, but when it was laid out in Whiteland amounted to 1,869 acres.

In 1699-1700, Richard Thomas, Jr., visited the place of his birth in the old country. His descendant, Col. Richard Thomas, in his memoirs, records that he heard that Richard found his sister "reduced to indigence," and his mother had married again, and was deceased, and that his step-father had dissipated all their joint property.

When Richard returned to Pensylvania, he brought his sister with him, and married her to Llewellyn Parry. They had a family, and descendants may be found in Chester Co., Pa.

After his return, Richard Thomas, Jr., married Grace Atherton, and finally settled in the Chester Valley. In 1704, he is described as of Merion tp., a carpenter, and in 1711, as of Blockley tp.

COMPANY NUMBER SIX

It is of record that Richard Thomas, Jr., was married, by Friends' ceremony, (though there is no evidence that he was a Friend, or member of any Meeting here, so the ceremony may have been performed by a Justice of the Peace), to Grace Atherton, at his own house, in Whiteland tp., on 15. 11mo. 1712-3, and that she was the daughter of Henry and Jennet Atherton, late of Liverpool. Richard Thomas, Jr., died at home, in Whiteland, in 1744, and was survived by his wife, who was buried with him in "Malin's Graveyard," in East Whiteland tp., Chester Co. They had six children, and of these, Hannah, b. 14. 11mo. 1716-7, m. James Mendenhall; Mary, b. 14. 5mo. 1719, m. John Harrison; Grace, b. 9. 7mo. 1722, m. Thomas Stalker; Elizabeth, m. 28. 4mo. 1750, Jonathan Howell, and removed to No. Car., and

Richard Thomas, 3d, only son, heir to the Whiteland homestead, b. 22. 2mo. 1713, d. 22. 9mo. 1754. He m., at the Goshen Meeting, 10. 2mo. 1739, Phebe, daughter of George and Mary (Malin) Ashbridge, of Goshen tp., b. 26. 8mo. 1717, d. 14. 6mo. 1784, and had five children, namely, Lydia, m. John Trimble; Grace, m. William Trimble; Hannah, m. Joseph Trimble; George, (see below), and

Richard Thomas, 4th., of "Whitford Lodge," in West Whiteland tp., b. 30. 10mo. 1744, d. 19. 1mo. 1832. Although a birthright Friend, on the outbreak of the war for independence he entered the army, and became colonel of a Pensylvania regiment, and served throughout the war. He was elected to the Pensylvania Assembly, in 1786, and in 1789, and the State Senate in 1790, and member of U. S. Congress, 1794, '96, and '98, in the 4th, 5th and 6th Congresses. He m. Thomazine, b. 26. 8mo., 1754, d. 4. 5mo. 1817, daughter of Richard Downing, 1719-1803, son of Thomas Downing, the founder of Downingtown.* *Issue.*

---

* Thomas Downing, 1691-1772, a farmer, merchant miller, and a Friend, had also a daughter Sarah, who m. Thomas Meteer, a farmer and paper maker, member of the Falls, Birmingham, Wilmington,

WELSH SETTLEMENT OF PENSYLVANIA

George Thomas, *b.* 21. 12mo. 1746-7, *d.* 17. 8mo. 1793. He inherited 600 acres of his father's estate, in West Whiteland tp., and when the Uwchlan Friends' Meeting House was used as a hospital, during the Revolutionary War, the Friends held their meetings at his house. He *m.*, at the Merion Meeting, on 26. 5mo. 1774, Sarah, daughter of John Roberts, and his wife, Jane Downing, (daughter of the founder of Downingtown), of Merion, *b.* 11. 1mo. 1750, *d.* 20. 2mo. 1840, and had nine children.

---

and Baltimore Friends' meetings, and had Thomas Meteer, Jr., who *m.* Hannah, a daughter of Captain John Quandrill, of the Chester Co. militia, and had Ann Meteer, 1798-1872, who *m.* Eli Sinex, 1797-1830, of Staunton, Del., and had Thomas Sinex, 1820-1899, of Philadelphia, father of John H. Sinex, of Philadelphia, and Edge Water Park, N. J.

RICHARD DAVIES'S LAND PATENT

Company No. 7. The purchasers of the 5,000 acres for which "Richard Davies, of Welshpool, gent.," subscribed and had deed, date 14. 7mo. 1681, were as follows, with the parishes in which they resided, their deeds, bearing dates, 19 June, and 30 July, 1682, give their occupations and station in life.

Merionethshire.

	Acres.
Rowland Ellis, gent, Bryn Mawr	1100
Richard Humphrey, gent, Llan Glynin	150
Ellis Maurice, gent, Dolgun vcha	78
Lewis Owen, gent, Gwanas	183
Rowland Owen, gent, Gwanas	182
Evan John William, gent, Llangylynin	156¼
Evan ap William, gent, Llanvachreth	156¼
David ap Evan, gent, Llanvachreth	156¼
Edward Owen, gent, "Late of Dalserey"	

Carmarthenshire.

James Price, gent, Mothvey	300

Caernarvonshire.

John Roberts, gent, Llangian	150

Unknown.

Ellis ap Hugh, [Pugh], (possibly of Merioneth)	160
Petter Edwards	100

WELSH SETTLEMENT OF PENSYLVANIA

Radnorshire.

David Kinsey, carpenter, Nantmele	100
John Evans, gent, Nantmele	350
Ellis Jones, weaver, Nantmele	100
Margaret James, spinster, Newchurch	200
Richard Miles, weaver, Llanvihangel Velgyen	100
Roger Hughes, gent, Llanvihangel Rhydyithan	250
David Meredith, weaver, Llanbister	100
Richard Corn, glover, Langunllo	50
Richard Cooke, glover, Langunllo	100
Thomas Jones, gent, Glascombe	100
Evan Oliver, gent, Glascombe	200
John Lloyd, glover, Dissart	100
Edward Jones, gent, St. Harmon	250
David James, mariner, Glascram	100

Their purchases were laid out in Merion, Radnor, Goshen and New Town townships, in the Welsh Tract, and the following is his own account of the purchases from Richard Davies.

"Rich'd Davies Purchase & Alienation of 5,000 acres pr Rowl'd Ellis." is the endorsement on the document, owned by the Historical Society of Pensylvania, and is, as its sub-head states: "Richard Davies purchases 5,000 acres as by the original Deed doth appear, sold & subdivided to ye severall purchasers hereafter named."

"Names—first purchasers in England:—

"To Rowland Ellis 1,100 acres as per deed apears, whereof 600 is taken up & setled att Merion; 483 acres att Goshen in ye Welsh tract laid out & both entered in ye Survey'r Generalls Office [&] 17 acres of Lyberty land.

"To John Roberts 150 acres taken up in the Township of Merion, & in's own possession.

"To Richard Humphrey 156¼ acres taken up in ye Township of Radnor—he died, John Humphrey's Executor, did assign right thereto William Tho.

COMPANY NUMBER SEVEN

"To Evan Jno Williams 156¼ acres laid out Goshen in ye Welsh Tract—he died, by's will bequeathed the same to Evan ab William, by's will bequeathed ye same to's son Philip Evan, it being laid out as by patent doth appear in ye Welsh tract—ye s'd Philip died without issue—brother David Evan possess ye same.*

"To Lewis Owen, Rowland Owen, Ellis Maurice, Ellis Pugh, 625 acres, sold to Thomas Ellis their title & interest therein—ye sd quantity was taken up together in Merion—he dec'd, Executor's sold ye same to Joh: William.

"To James Price 300 acres, he sold same to David Price, ye sd David to Henry Rees † the present possessor thereof —in ye Township of Radnor.

"To John Evans 350 acres—out of s'd tract he sold 100 acres to John German now deceased—his widow in possession. Another pt thereof he sold vizt: 100 to John Roberts,

---

*The will of David Evan, of Radnor, signed 16. 12, 1709, witnesses Hugh William, Humphrey Ellis (marked), William Davies, and John Morgan, was proved 17 May, 1710. by wife Mary. Names children Caleb, Joshua, Evan, David, Philip, John, Mary, Gwen, (and her children, John and Gainor), and Sarah. Overseers, Rowland Ellis, Sr. and Jr., Rees Thomas, Rowland Powell, Richard Ormes, and John Morgan.

† The will of Henry Rees, signed 1 Feb. 1704-5, witnesses, Richard Moore and David Evan, was proved 30 June 1705, by wife Elizabeth, names children David, Gwen, and Margaret.

The will of David Rees, (or Reece), of New Town, Chester Co., yeoman, signed 14. 11mo. 1705-6, witnesses, Evan Davis (marked), and John Reece, was proved by wife Eleanor, 30 March 1706. Son Thomas Reece, to be executor. Names son Lewis Reece. Overseers, David Morice, of Marple tp., Henry Lewis, of Haverford tp., and Richard Hayes.

The will of Thomas Reece, of Haverford, yeoman, marked 7. 7mo. 1713; present Rowland Ellis, Henry Lewis, Rowland Powell, and David Morris (marked). was proved 10 Oct. 1713, by son Samuel Reece, executor. Other children, Sarah, Daniel, Mary, David, Isaac, Philip, Miriam, Thomas, and John. Names sister Margaret Reece, of Pembrokeshire. The witnesses, with Rees Thomas, to be guardians and trustees.

the sd John sold the same to John Morgan who has it in possession—the remaining pt ye sd John Evans hath in's possession, all in Radnor.†

"To Richard Corn 50 acres, deceased, his son William Corn convey'd right therein to John Evans as by deeds doth appear & being posses'd thereof, lying in Radnor.

"To Edward Jones 250 acres, one James Morgan purchased's right to ye sd quantity. Late deceased's son & heir John Morgan now possessor.

"To Ellis Jones 100 acres, he assigning's right & title therein to William David, the said William to John Morgan the possessor thereof.

"To Roger Hughes 250 acres, he selling one moety thereof, vizt: 125 acres to Tho Parry, the sd Parry assigning over's right to Richard Moore, ye other half ye sd Roger sold to David Meredith—now in his possession.

---

†The two following wills were probated at Philadelphia. John Evans, of Radnor, marked in the presence of William ap Edward (marked) and Hugh William, 19. 11. 1707-8, was proved 19 Jan. 1708, by his wife, Mary. Names brother Edward Evan. Appointed John Roberts, William ap Edward, Edward Rees, and Hugh William guardians to his children, named Evan, Edward, Mary, and Sarah Johnes.

John Evans, of Radnor, [from Nantmele, Radnor], signed in the presence of Abel Roberts, John Jarman, Evan Rees, David Lloyd, and Philip Howell. 17. 6mo. 1703, was proved by wife, Deliah, 22 Nov. 1707, Names daughters, Mary, wife of David Evan, Sarah, wife of John Morgan, Margaret, wife of Hugh Samuel, Phebe, wife of Edward Jones David, (and "her three children"), and Jane Jones' sons, Rees Jones and Thomas Jones. Brother Edward Evans, and his daughter Elizabeth. Overseers, David Evan and John Morgan.

John Morgan, mentioned in this will, was a brother of Cadwalader Morgan, one of the Thomas & Jones Company. He came over with his father, James Morgan, from Vaenor, Radnorshire, and took up land in Radnor, some of which is still held by descendants. John's daughter, Hannah Morgan, *m.* James Hunter, of Radnor, and their daughter, Mary, 1757-1820, *m.* Hugh Jones, 1748-1796, of Radnor, (and had Mary, *m.* 1804, Nathan Brooke, of Gulph Mills, 1778-1815), son of Hugh Jones, 1705-1790, who, with his father, owned at one time 700 acres, part of it is the farm land called "Brookfield," North of Bryn Mawr, owned by Mr. Wayne MacVeagh.

COMPANY NUMBER SEVEN

"To Richard Cook 100 acres, taken up for him in Radnor.

"To John Lloyd 100 acres, laid out for hime likewise [in Radnor].

"To David James 100 acres, deceased—his daughter Mary James Executrix of ye sd father sold ye title & interest therin to Stephen ab Evan present possessor.

"To Margaret James 200 acres, Samuel James in right of's wife the sd Margaret possesseth ye same.

"To Richard Miles 100 acres, settles thereon.

"To Thomas Jones [100] by his heirs the title thereof was made to William Davies the possessor.

"To Evan Oliver 200 acres, deceased, his heirs sold ye sd quantity to ye sd William Davies the possessor.

"To David Kinsey 100 acres, the Execut's of the deceased Kinsey sold the said tract to James James,* & ye sd James to Lewis Walker, who possesseth ye same.

"To Petter Edwards 100 acres, he sold's title and interest to Thomas Parry, and the sd Parry to Tho Rees, ye present possessor.

"The whole subdivided among ye above named first purchasers in England comes 5,000.

"Whereof 2,656 accers & ¼ is laid out in ye Township Rodnor, the remainder of ye property hath been laid pt in Merion the rest where the [mutilated] lives in ye Welch tract.

"Here followeth some acc more of lands taken up in ye said Township, part whereof by purchase & part rent land:

"David Meredith 250 acres, purchased as by patent doth appear.

"Samuel Miles 100 acres, formerly took up att Rent, sometime after paid for as doth appear.

---

*Will of "James James, of Haverford, yeoman," signed 18. 6mo. 1708, witnesses, Richard Hayes, Rowland Powell, and Adam Roades, was proved 28 Aug. 1708. Wife probably dead. Names children, George, David, Sarah, and Thomas James (executor). Son-in-law David Lewis, and his children, not named.

"John Evans 100 acres, took up att rent, in his possession.

"William Davies 150 acres, formerly took up att Rent.

"Stephen ab Evan 100 acres, hath taken up likewise att Rent.

"all by orders in Radnor Welch tract."

In pursuance of the order made by the Commissioners, 23. 10. 1701, on 16. 12mo. 1701-2, the lands of these grantees of Richard Davis were resurveyed. John Roberts, malter, 150 acres in Merion tp., and William Thomas 153¼ acres in Merion tp., Radnor Tp., John Roberts, malter 150 acres in Radnor tp. The will of "William Thomas, of Radnor, planter," was marked in the presence of Philip Evan, and John Humphrey, 18. 7mo. 1687, and proved 4. 9mo. 1689, by wife Ann, to whom he left his estate, with remainder to William Thomas, if he will come to this country, otherwise his property was to be sold, "and the proceeds equally divided between the children of my brother, and of my sister," unnamed. Legacies to cousin Rees Petter, Ellis Ellis, Humphrey Ellis, David Lawrence, Katherine Morgan, Ellis Pugh, Evan Harry, Hugh Haney, and Daniel Haney. To Owen Morgan* one sow, and his son (Owen's) "to be released after my departure, and if my wife depart before the time of his daughter be over, she also may be released." To brother-in-law David Davies, sister-in-law Katherine Davies. To be overseers, David Lawrence, Rees Petter, David Evan, and John Humphrey.

Richard Davies' "alienation of his 5,000 acres" was long the cause of misunderstanding by purchasers under him, especially as to city lots, and "Liberty lands" which went

---

*Will of Owen Morgan, of Merion, signed 23. 9mo. 1703, in presence of Daniel Thomas (marked), John More, and John Bevan, was proved 26 Feb. 1703-4, by wife Blanche. Names son Humphrey Morgan, and daughters, Katherine Morgan, and Mary Carply. Friends Edward Morgan, and John Lloyd. To be overseers, William Lewis, Ralph Lewis, Ellis Ellis, and John Bevan.

COMPANY NUMBER SEVEN

with such a purchase. Frequently the Land Commissioners had to explain that Richard Davies had no right to such extras on account of the whole purchase, because he had made it only in trust, and had conveyed the tract to parties interested, himself only being one of them, who had taken up lots in several parts of the city according to their shares purchased out of the 5,000 acres grant. And that Davies, himself, was only entitled to a twenty-five foot lot, which he had in High Street and Front Street, Philadelphia, Pa., on account of his share, namely, 1,250 acres of the grant. His Pensylvania land was managed and sold by many mentioned as his attorneys, as Thomas Lloyd, William Powel, Hugh Roberts, David and John Humphrey, Griffith Owen, Rowland Ellis, and David Lloyd.

The Land Commissioners's "Welsh Minutes" give a few further details concerning the distribution of Richard Davies's land. He sold 2,656 acres in Radnor tp., and balance was located in Merion and Goshen.

Rowland Ellis sold, by deed 31 July, 1682, his 17 acres of the Liberty lands, to John Goodson. Of his 600 acres tract in Merion he gave 100 acres "to Edw'd Jones, of London, gent., for settling it," by deed of 6. 12mo. 1687. By deed, dated 11. 2mo. 1702, he bought back this land. Besides this Merion land, he had 483 acres in Goshen tp.

"John Roberts's, gent.," deed for his 150 acres in Merion, dated 30. July, 1682, recorded 24. 4. 1684, was witnessed by Rowland Owen, Ellis Morris, David Evan, Owen Lewis, Sr., and Jr., Evan Harry, and Rowland Ellis. He also held 60 acres adjoining where he resided, which he had from Andrew Wheeler, a Swede, 3 June 1699.

(Will dated 25. 7mo. 1688, of "Jance John Morgan, alias Jane Roberts, of Haverford," left all her estate to "friend John Roberts, of Merion," who was to be sole executor. Signed in presence of William Howell and Blanche Sharples).

WELSH SETTLEMENT OF PENSYLVANIA

Richard Humphrey died without issue, and his 150 or 156¼ acres, located in Radnor tp., were sold by his cousin, heir and executor, John Humphrey, 23. 10mo. 1693, to William Thomas.

Richard Humphrey, "of Radnor, in the Welsh Tract," was the cousin and brother-in-law of John Humphrey, of Haverford. He had resided in the parish of Llangelynin, or Llan Glynin, Merioneth, and had the usual Friends' certificate, dated 27. 5mo. 1683. His will, marked, and witnessed by Theodore Robert (marked), Benjamin Humphrey, and Rowland Ellis, 12. 12mo. 1691, was proved at Philadelphia, 18. 12mo. 1692-3. He bequeathed all his land "to my brother-in-law, John Humphrey," who sold it. He gave legacies to brothers John Humphrey and Owen Humphrey, sister Katherine, or her children, unnamed, cousin John Owen, Lyddie Ellis, Rebecca, Ann, Daniel, Benjamin and Joseph Humphrey, also to the "Friends' Monthly Meeting for the service of Truth."

Rebecca Humphrey and Elizabeth Owen, spinster, also came from this parish, bringing certificates which they filed with the Haverford Monthly Meeting. Elizabeth's certificate was signed by Hugh Rees, Owen and William Humphrey, Robert, Evan, and Humphrey Owen, Humphrey Reinald, John William, Richard, Sr., Elizabeth, and Richard Stafford, Jr. Rebecca's was signed by the same, and Griffith Robert, Edward Ellis, Hugh David, Lewis Robert, Owen Lewis, Lewis Owen, David Edward, Ellis Moris, Robert Richard, Katharine Price, Janne Robert, Ellin Ellis, Anne Hugh, Margaret Robert, and Ann Humphrey.

Evan John William, gent., divided his right to 156¼ acres, laid out in Goshen tp., giving part to his nephew, Richard Rees, and the other to "John Roberts, cordwainer, of Philadelphia, who is Rees Peter's wife's son." "Rees Petter, of Machanlleth, Montgomeryshire" brought certificate, dated 27. 5mo. 1683, from the Quarterly Meeting at Dolyseerey, which he filed with the Haverford Monthly

COMPANY NUMBER SEVEN

Meeting. It was signed by Robert, Humphrey, and Richard Owen, Griffith and Owen Lewis, John Evans, Hugh Reece, Amos Davies, William Thomas, and Evan, William, and Rowland Ellis.

Evan ap William died at sea coming over. A letter of attorney, dated 27 July, 1683, recorded 8. 5. 1684, at Philadelphia, was given by Evan ap William, gent., and David Evan, both of Llanfachreth, to John Roberts, of Langian, Caernarvonshire, in a matter concerning their 312½ acres purchased of Richard Davies. It was witnessed by Tho Ellis, John Humphrey, Evan Ellis, and Rowland Ellis. By his will, his son Philip ap Evan, inherited his purchase, which was laid out near the New Town Friends' Meeting House, patent being confirmed to him, 27. 11. 1687. Philip died without issue, when his brother, David ap Evan, succeeded to the farm. The will of David Evan, of Haverford, was marked in the presence of John Bevan, Evan Bevan, and Elinor Bevan, 16. 1. 1698, proved 20 April. 1706, names his children, Harry, Sarah, and Elizabeth David.

David ap Evan (David Evan) was himself a purchaser of 156¼ acres from Davies, which tract was laid out, 22. 11mo. 1687, along with his brother's tract, at New Town, in the Welsh Tract. In 1701, David Evan had 308 acres in two parcels, in Radnor.

Edward Jones's 250 acres were in Radnor. He, by deed, dated 4 Feb. 1690-1, sold same to James Morgan, who, in 1701, had altogether 450 in Radnor, whose son and heir, John, inherited the place, but John Worrall had most of it in 1703.

Ellis Jones assigned, on 12. 10. 1687, his 100 acres to William David, who sold the same to John Morgan, by deed of 15. 10. 1702, so the said John had 450 acres in Radnor tp. He sold 80 acres to Henry Lewis, of Haverford, who sold the same to John Worrall, or Worrell.

Roger Hughes had deed, dated 20 June. 1682, for 250 acres laid out in Radnor tp. By deed, 11. 7. 1691, he sold

WELSH SETTLEMENT OF PENSYLVANIA

125 acres to David Meredith, who sold to Richard Moore. Roger sold his balance, in 1699, to Thomas Parry, after whose death, Richard Moore had it.

Thomas Parry,* or Thomas ap Harry, a weaver, who bought this land, was the son of Harry ap Rees, of Henllan parish, Cardiganshire, and came to Pensylvania from Llanelwith, in Radnor, bringing a certificate of membership from the Radnor Quarterly Meeting, dated 5. 5mo. 1699. He m. Elinor, daughter of John Edward, of Lanelwi parish, Radnor, and had two sons, Edward Parry, who m. 6. 8mo. 1710, Jane, daughter of Robert Evans, and d. 28. 2mo. 1726, and Thomas Parry, Jr., who m. 27. 8mo. 1715, Jane Phillips, daughter of Philip Philip, of Radnor, (who d. 25. 12mo. 1697), and had ten children.

Roger Hughes subsequently bought 250 acres from the Commissioners, the money being paid to James Harrison. Of this, he sold, 20. 5. 1691, 150 acres to Stephen Evans, who had also 100 acres from David James.

Richard Cooke located his 100 acres in Radnor tp., but did not come over from Wales, and probably lost his rights. Witnesses to his deed, 19 June, 1682, were Ed Jones, Tho Davies, Ric Jones, David Jones, Daniel Morris, Samuel Miles, Evan Evans, and others.

"John Lloyd" remained in Wales, but had his 100 acre right laid out in Radnor tp. This probably should be Francis Lloyd, who died, and his widow, Mary Lloyd, and son, Joseph Lloyd, cordwainer, both of Haverford West, gave power of attorney to Samuel Carpenter, a Philadelphia merchant, and William Howell, of Haverford, to sell the 100 acres, which they did to Mary, widow of David Haverd.

---

*Will of Hugh Parry, of Merion, signed 26 April, 1731; witnesses Hugh Evans, Thomas Lloyd (marked), and Robert Jones; proved 5 June same year, mentions brothers Henry and Robert, and sisters Ellin, Jane, Elizabeth, and Katherine Pugh.

COMPANY NUMBER SEVEN

Cook and Lloyd tried to sell through David Meredith, and Stephen Evans, but they only disposed of their city lots in Walnut Street, near Fifth Street, in 1702, to Enoch Story.

David Jones died, and his only child, Mary, sold his right to 100 acres, to Stephen Evans, in Radnor.

Margaret James, spinster, after receiving deed, dated 20 June, 1682, for her 200 acres, married by Friends' ceremony, and in Welsh, at the house of Ann Thomas, in New Church parish, Radnorshire, 24. 4mo. 1682, Samuel Miles, of Hamhanghobyeholgen parish, Radnor, and they located the land in Radnor tp., removed to it, and bought 150 acres more from Thomas Lehnman. They sold 50 acres to brother Richard Miles, and, in Sep. 1705, had remaining 258 acres in Radnor, which, on resurvey, amounted to 352 acres, the excess they bought, paying 6s. 8d. per acre, and eighteen months' interest on the price of the surplus from the date of the original grant.

Samuel Miles's will, signed in the presence of Edward Rees, Richard Miles, David Thomas, William Davies, and John Reece, 24. 4mo. 1707, was proved by his wife, [Margaret James], not named, 28 Apr. 1708. Names his children, Tamar, Phoebe, and Ruth, [m. Owen Evans]. To be overseers brother Richard Miles, Stephen Bevan, and Edward Reece. Their first child, Tamar, was b. 21 Feb. 1687, and was the first Welsh child born in Radnor tp. She m. Thomas Thomas, of Radnor, and, after 62 years of married life, d. 28. 7mo. 1770, a member of the Radnor Meeting.

Richard Miles also located his right to 100 acres in Radnor, which re-surveyed amounted to 233 acres. He also bought from his brother, Samuel Miles, 50 acres, which was found to be 92 acres on a re-survey, and 20 acres from Ellis Jones, "the Govern's miller." By the first surveys in 12mo. 1701, he supposed he had only 170 acres in Radnor, but the later survey showed he had 325 acres, so he bought the excess from Penn, 155 acres, and paid interest on the cost of the "overs" from dates of the grants.

WELSH SETTLEMENT OF PENSYLVANIA

Thomas Jones, of "Laulanread in Elvel," or Glascombe, Radnorshire, gave his 100 acre right to his nephew, John Jones, who by deed, dated 30 8ber, 1685, conveyed the same to William Davies, who sold it to David Evan, of Radnor tp.

Evan Oliver's 200 acres were sold by his heir to William Davies, who, by deed, dated 18 Jan. 1702, conveyed 50 acres of the same to David Evan, of Radnor, and on 19 July, 1697, 100 acres to Edward David.

David Meredith, besides the 100 acres from Davies, bought 100 from Corn (and on re-survey it was found 37 acres over, which amount he bought, paying a noble an acre), and 125 acres from Roger Hughes, which he sold to Richard Moore. David Meredith, his wife Katherine, and children Richard, Mary, John, Meredith, and Sarah, came from Llanbister parish, Radnorshire, bringing the usual certificate of membership in good standing in the Society of Friends, dated 20. 5mo. 1683.

To Lewis Owen, 183 acres, Rowland Owen, 182 acres, Ellis Morris, 78 acres, and Ellis ap Hugh, 182 acres, were conveyed 625 acres, in proportions named, in four deeds, dated 31 July, 1682. Witnesses to the deeds of the first three, as grantees, were the men of Merioneth, Owen Lewis, Sr., and Jr., Rowland Ellis, Evan Harry, and David Evan, and as grantors, were same, and Morris Ellis, and John Humphrey.

The first three grantees, by deed dated 30 June, 1683, sold their rights to 443 acres for £19. 17. 2, English, to Thomas Ellis, as also did Ellis Pugh,* by deed dated 16 July, 1686. This land, Thomas Ellis had laid out in Merion. By his will, signed 1. 11mo. 1688, he ordered it sold to pay his debts, which was done 5. 7mo. 1698.

---

*Evan ap Hugh (Evan Pugh) made his will 21 May, 1703, and signed with his mark in the presence of Thomas Edward, Humphrey Bate, and John Robert. Proved 7 June, 1704, by wife Ann. Names only son David Pugh, (but had other children) and nephew Hugh Edward. Overseers, John Humphrey, Edward Foulke, and Robert John.

COMPANY NUMBER SEVEN

James Price, who had right to 300 acres in Radnor tp., by deed, 19 June, 1682, rented his land for three year from 16 July, 1684, to David Price, and in case James did not come over to use the land, he could have it forever. "James never came," so David sold the place, by deed 6. 1. 1696-7, to Humphrey Rees. David Price was also granted a city lot, "among the rest of his countrymen in Chestnut Street," between Fourth and Fifth Streets, and this by deed, 7 July, 1693, without even locating the lot, he conveyed to William Thomas, of Radnor, who sold it to Gov. Lloyd, whose executor, David Lloyd, requested confirmation of sale, as said Thomas lost his life by accident before he executed the deed of sale. His widow gave the deed, 27. 2. 1702.

John ap Evan, or John Evans, Sr., received his right to 350 acres by deed of 19 July, 1682, witnessed by Edward Jones, Thomas Davies, David Jones, Richard Jones and David Morris. He located his land in Radnor tp. On resur-

---

Roger Robert, of Radnor, marked his will, 5 July, 1720, in the presence of Robert Jones, Rees Thomas, William Thomas, and Robert Evans, and mentions his children, Robert, John, Owen, and Jane, and grandsons Roger Robert and Roger Pugh.

Will of Thomas Pugh, a mason, signed 3. 3. 1723: witnesses John Roger, Thomas Ellis, Ellis Robert, and Meredith David. proved 1 Oct. 1723, by wife Ann. Mentions brother Job Pugh, and own sons Jesse and Roger Pugh. To be trustees, Robert Jones, of Merion, Meredith Davis, Robert Roger, Job Pugh, and Ellis Robert.

Will of Henry Pugh, of Merion, yeoman, signed 11 June, 1730, proved by wife Katherine, 1 May, 1731. Witnesses, Ellen Thomas (marked) Ellin Jones, Ann Jones (marked), Lowry Evans, Hugh Evans, and Robert Jones. Names children, Hugh, Robert, Jane, Katherine, Elizabeth, Ellen, Henry, and Moses Pugh. Trustees, Thomas Thomas, Thomas Lawrence, Hugh Evans and Robert Jones.

Will of William Pugh, of Radnor, yeoman, marked 19 June, 1705, witnesses Daniel Harry (marked), Susanna Williams, and William Davies. Proved 19 June, 1798. Wife probably deceased. Names son, "Hugh Williams," and his children William, Catherine, Susanna, and Elizabeth Williams. Grandsons, Hugh Jones and Joseph Jones. Mentions "friends Richard and Ann [Roberts,] brother and sister of John Roberts, of Merion, and Jane, daughter of Robert Ellis."

vey it amounted to only 300 acres, and was surveyed again, and came out only 250 acres, and even then he had to buy an "over plus" of 25 acres. By deed, 4. 4. 1688, Evans conveyed 100 acres to John German, or Jarman, whose relict, "Margaret Jermain," held it. On survey, it was made out to be 42 acres over, which her son, John, paid for at a noble an acre. "John Jarman, of the parish of Llangerig," in Montgomeryshire, and his wife Margaret, and children Elizabeth and Sarah, brought certificate, dated 20. 5mo. 1683, from the Radnorshire Men's Meeting, which they filed with the Haverford Monthly Meeting. It was signed by Owen Humphrey, Daniel Lewis, Nathan Woodliffe, David Griffith, Jon Lloyd, Edward Moore, Richard Watkins, Thomas Parry, Edward Jones, Richard Cooke, John Watson, Roger Hughes, John Robert, and Rees ap Rees. At same date (4. 4. 1688), John Evans sold 100 acres to "Jno. Robert, of Haverford, smith," adjoining German or Jarman, on the north. The will of "John Robert, blacksmith," dated 26. 7. 1702, was proved 5 Jan. 1702-3. To daughter Margaret, wife of Thomas Kenderdine, and her children. Mentions his son John, and daughter, Elinor Jenkins, living in Wales. Executors, John Bevan and John Rees. Among the witnesses was William Howell. John Robert, by deed of 9. 1mo. 1699-00, sold same land to John Morgan, who also had 100 acres more of John Evans's land. Edward David, on 19 July, 1697, bought "the remaining 150 acres," and this lot, with 50 acres, he bought of William Corn (the son of one of Davies's grantees), was in Radnor tp., and he sold it to John Evans, "together with 500 acres of 'rent land,' of which he sold 50 to Edward David." In 12mo. 1701, the Land Commissioners supposed John Evans had 2,200 acres in Radnor.

Richard Corn, or Conn, got his 50 acres in Radnor, by deed, 20 June, 1682, his son and heir, William, sold it to John Evans, 6 Jan. 1690.

COMPANY NUMBER SEVEN

By a triparty deed, dated 19. 6mo. 1686, between—
Richard Davies, Thomas Ellis, William Howell.
Francis Howel, Ellis Ellis.
Morgan David.
Francis Lloyd.
James Thomas.
there was conveyed 410 acres of land, for £30, being part of 500 acres out of Richard Davies's 1250 acres, to William Howell and Ellis Ellis (son of Thomas Ellis), that is to say: —for Thomas Ellis, 10 acres, Francis Howel 100, James Thomas 100, Morgan David 100, and Francis Lloyd 100.

The will of David Morgan, "of Merion, yeoman," marked 15. 12mo. 1694, in presence of Robert Owen, Robert Powell, and of John Humphreys, proved 18. 7. 1695, by wife Catherine, sole executor. William Howell, Morris Llewellyn, Francis Howel and David Lawrence, overseers. His estate to go to his two eldest sons, John and Evan, mentions son David. Legacies to daughters Katherine and Elizabeth, and to the Meeting House in Haverford. By deed of 8. 3mo. 1695, the relict and the overseers conveyed David Morgan's 100 acres to James Thomas, who willed the same to his second son, Nathan Thomas. In 12mo. 1701, James Thomas had 100 acres of the Richard Davies patent located in Merion, and altogether, at this time, he held 300 acres in the Welsh Tract.

"David James, from Llandigley and Glaseram [or Glascum] parish, in Radnorshire," and his wife, Margaret, and daughter Mary, wrote to the Radnorshire Men's Meeting, from Pensylvania, in 8mo. 1682, asking for a certificate of membership, &c., which was given, dated 20. 5mo. 1683, and filed with the Haverford (Radnor) Monthly Meeting.

David James had his purchase of 100 acres laid out in Radnor. His sole heir, Mary James, by deed, dated 23. 10mo. 1702, conveyed the same property to Stephen Evans, of Radnor, yeoman, who came from Llanbister parish, Radnorshire, bringing to the Haverford (or Radnor) Monthly

WELSH SETTLEMENT OF PENSYLVANIA

Meeting, his certificate from the Radnorshire Men's Meeting, dated 20. 5mo. 1683.

Stephen Evans bought by deed of 20. 5mo. 1691, 150 acres of David Meredith (who held 350 acres in Radnor, but in 1701, had only 200). Mary James also sold her father's head right, or servant land, to Stephen Evans, whose son John Stephens had the whole surveyed. He declined to pay quit-rent to the land officer, alleging tnat Penn was under some obligation to him for personal services. He probably satisfied the Commissioners, as there is no further mention of this matter.

Roger Hughes, David Meredith, Richard Cook, David (or James) Price, and John Lloyd, had city lots, in Chestnut Street, between 4th and 5th Streets, reserved for the Welsh settlers, granted to them on account of purchases of land from Richard Davies, which lots were resurveyed to them 28. 2mo. 1702. Hughes sold his lot to Meredith. Cook and Lloyd sold their lots to said Meredith and Stephen Evans. By deed of 20. 9mo. 1702, they conveyed the four lots to David Lloyd, who then owned five city lots altogether, in Chestnut Street, between 4th and 5th Streets, which he sold, by deed of 23. 10mo. 1702, to Enoch Story, of Philadelphia.

Stephen ap Evan, or Stephen Evans aforesaid, bought 100 acres from Richard Davies, and, with the two lots purchased as above, he had 350 acres in Radnor, and on resurvey, in 6mo. 1703, it was discovered he had 47 acres "overplus," which he bought, paying Penn a noble an acre. The Land Commissioners found that he owed Mary James £11, and rent-money for her land from in 1684, and ordered this all paid.

Other land transactions in the account of Richard Davies.

David Lloyd bought from attorneys of Richard Davies, 15. 6mo. 1687, 90 a:res, which he sold, 7. 7mo. 1687, to David Powel, who sold it, by deed 10. 10mo. 1687, to Evan Harry, and said Evan Harry also bought 74 acres from Powel, so that in 12mo. 1701, he had 164 acres in one tract, in Radnor. Evan Harry, who had land in Merion—164 acres he bought, which on the survey, amounted to 214 acres, in 4mo. 1704.

Griffith Owen, John Humphrey, Rowland Ellis, and David Lloyd, acting as Davies's attorneys, and Edward Evans, conveyed by deeds of 6. 1mo. 1698-9, and 6. 1mo. 1696, 90 acres to Joseph Growdon.

"Richard Davies *alias* Prees," in 12mo. 1701, held 76½ acres in Goshen tp., part of Richard Davies's 5,000 acres.

Thomas Howell, in 12mo. 1701, held 100 acres in Haverford, being part of Richard Davies's 1250 acres there.

Daniel Humphrey bought 5. 3mo. 1694, 50 acres of "overplus land," due several purchasers of Richard Davies, in Haverford. He also held in Haverford, in 12mo. 1701, 200 acres in rights of "T. Ellis, L. David and J. Poyer."

Richard Moore, in 12mo. 1701, held 245 acres in Radnor, and Henry Price,* 300 acres in same township, bought out of the Richard Davies tract there.

Griffith Owen bought some of this land in Goshen tp., which by first survey amounted to 401½ acres. But on resurvey, in 9mo. 1703, amounted to 775 acres. He was allowed 40 acres "for measure," and promised to pay for the difference.

---

*Price families were numerous in the Welsh Tract.

Will of Isaac Price, signed 4 Sep. 1706, witnesses, David William, Thomas Rees, and Rowland Ellis, proved by his wife, not named, 1 Mar. 1706-7. Names children, Isaac, Mary, and Gwen Price. Overseers same as the witnesses.

Will of Philip Price, of Merion, yeoman, marked 11 Dec. 1719, in the presence of Rees Thomas, Owen Roberts, and Richard Thomas. proved 22 Nov. 1720, by wife Margaret. Names daughter Sarah Lewis, grandchildren Isaac Price, and Samuel, Daniel, Sarah, Mary, David, Isaac, Philip, Miriam, and John, the children of Thomas Rees, "late of Haverford," also grandchildren, ("children of John Lewis, of New Castle, Delaware county"), Elizabeth Stout, Philip, Stephen, Josiah, Sarah, Mary and Ann Lewis. Mentions Joan, wife of Hugh David, Lettice, wife of Samuel Rees, and Rebecca, wife of Thomas Rees. Overseers, Rees Thomas, Norris Llewellyn, and Robert Jones.

WELSH SETTLEMENT OF PENSYLVANIA

Henry Harry, only son of Daniel Harry, grantee of 100 acres in Radnor, in 168—, asked confirmation by the Land Commissioners of this land to him, 25. 9mo. 1724.

"From Macchinleth, in Montgomeryshire, Hugh Harris and Daniel Harris," is recorded on the passenger list of the ship "Vine of Liverpool," which arrived at Philadelphia 17. 7mo. 1684, and from the minutes of the Haverford, or Radnor Monthly Meeting, 8. 2mo. 1686, "William Howell and George Painter are ordered to speak to Hugh and Daniel Harry concerning their Parents money," and, in same, 10, 4mo. 1686, "George Painter & William Howell according to former order did speak with Hugh and Daniel Harry, who have promised yt if any friends would lay out money in England upon their parents account they would out of the Product or growth of this Countrey make them satisfaction." Their surnames, as assumed, were variously Harry and Harris in different families. Hugh Harris, a weaver, and Elizabeth, daughter of William and Ann Brinton, of Birmingham tp., declared their intentions of marriage, at the Chichester Meeting 1. 1mo. 1686. By deed 11. 4mo. 1695, Mr. Brinton conveyed 250 acres of land in Birmingham, to them, where they went to reside, and 19 Nov. 1707, Hugh bought 430 acres in East Marlborough tp., Chester Co. Hugh Harris died in 1708, having nine children. His four sons, Evan, William, Hugh, and John, and their descendants, had "Harry" as their surname.

The will of Lewis Harry, of Radnor, marked 12. 7mo. 1699, witnesses David Davies, Benjamin Humphrey, David Lewis, and Benjamin Lewis, was proved 1 April, 1700, by wife Abigail. Children named Harry, Mary, and Eleanore. The will of his son, Harry Lewis, of Radnor, signed 20 March, 1701-2, in the presence of Peter Worrell, Edward Thomas, and David Evan, was proved 13 April, 1702, by brother-in-law John Worrell, names sisters Mary Worrell, and Eleanor Lewis. His father's servant, Richard Faddery, mentioned in both wills.

COMPANY NUMBER SEVEN

John Evan Edwards, held at one time 625 and 194 acres, in Radnor. He bougth 200 acres of this land from John Williams, by deed of 10. 5mo. 1700, which was a portion of the estate of Thomas Ellis, whose administrator, Daniel Humphreys, had conveyed it to Williams. David Powel conveyed, by deed of 22. 5mo. 1687, to John Evan Edwards 100 acres, which was a part of the 500 acres he received from the Land Commissioners, by patent, dated 4. 4mo. 1686. On resurvey, it was found to be 123 acres, and Edwards bought the difference.

The will of Thomas John Evan, of Radnor, who may have been a son of this landowner, signed 31, 1 mo. 1707, in the presence of friends Rowland Ellis, Sr., Joshua Owen, and Rowland Ellis, Jr., was proved by his wife "Lowry John Evan." Children named, John, Joseph, and Elizabeth.

All of these "Radnor town" original deeds had about the same witnesses, namely, Edward Jones, Thomas Davies, David James, Richard Jones, Daniel Morris, Samuel Miles, John Evans, and Daniel Meredith.

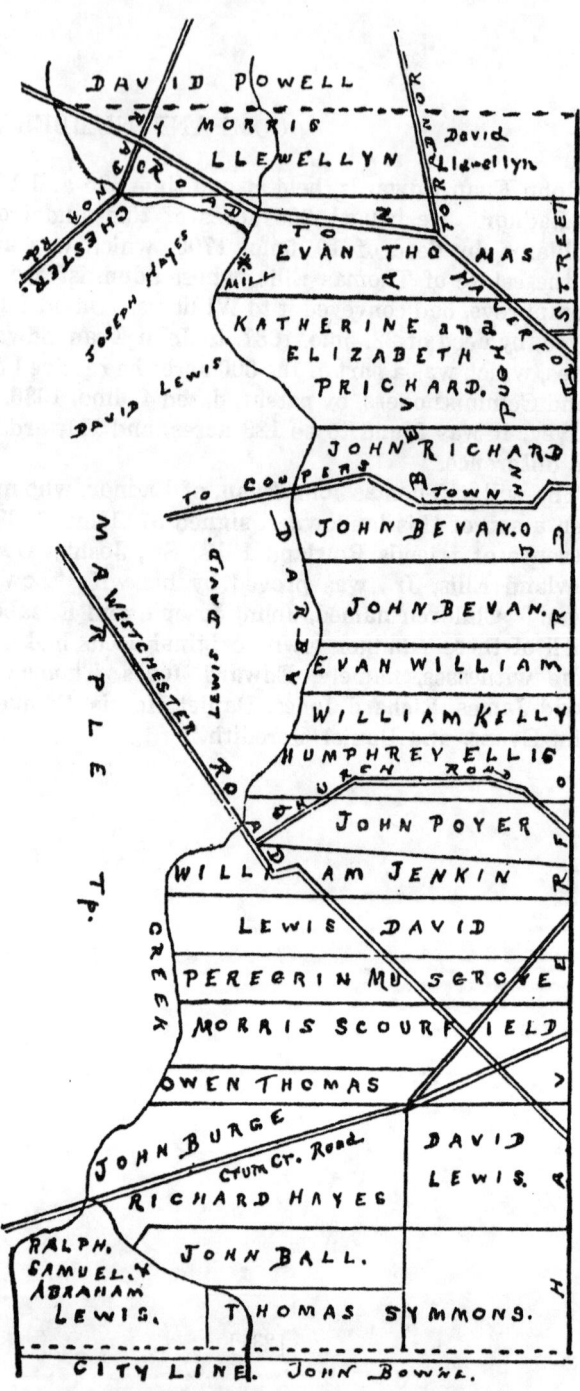

HAVERFORD TP., WEST OF THE "STREET," 1690.

RICHARD DAVIES'S LAND PATENT, II.

RICHARD DAVIES was a recognized minister among the Friends in Wales, and, as it appears, was an active friend of Penn, since he sold so much of his land. But, strange to say, he sold none of it in his home county. "The Journal of that ancient Servant of the Lord, Richard Davies," giving his autobiography, has frequently been printed. He was born at Welshpool, Montgomeryshire, in 1635. His parents were "Church of England people," but being apprenticed to an "Independant," a felt-maker, he became acquainted with Morgan Evan, of South Wales, a minister among Friends, who made the young man a convert to Quakerism. In 1659, he married in London, Tace . . . ., by whom, who died in 1705, he had a daughter Tace, who married ——— Endon, and had a son, David Endon. Mr. Davies died at his home, Cloddan Cochion, near Welshpool, on 22. 1mo. 1707-8.

See the "Friends' Library," vol. XIII., for "An Account of Richard Davies," written in 1708, and a copy of the "Testimonies concerning him," given at the Quarterly Meeting held at Dolobran, 25. 11mo. 1708.

"Rowland Ellis, gent," a minister among Friends, with a good estate, the largest purchaser of land from Richard Davies, and subsequently one of the prominent men of the Welsh Tract, was born about 1650-2, on his father's farm, called "Bryn Mawr," near Dogelly, Dyffrydan tp., in Merionethshire, where he resided till his removal to Pensylvania, having sold the old homestead, a modest stone house, which is still standing in a state of good preservation.

Like other Welshmen who came over to settle here, he wrote out and brought his family genealogy, in Welsh style, still extant in the Evans family, so as to be in touch with "home." From it, we learn that he was the only son of Ellis ap Rees, or Ellis Price, whose father, Lewis ap Sion Griffith, of Nannau, built "Bryn Mawr House" in 1617. And that Rowland's mother, Ann Humphrey, was a daughter of Humphrey ap Hugh, of Llwyngrill, (the marriage settlement dated 1 Jan. 1649), and sister to John and Samuel Humphrey, purchasers of Welsh Tract land from the Lloyds. He is of record, 8. 10mo. 1704, as filing an account of his kindred and life with the Merion Meeting.

Rowland Ellis became a Quaker about 1673, and like other Friends of his neighborhood, suffered imprisonment in 1676, in Dolgelly goal, but, although he bought the largest block of land in the Welsh Tract purchased of Richard Davies, and helped get up his company, he did not remove to his purchase permanently till after sixteen years, when "beyond the Schuylkill" was no longer a wilderness.

In 1683, Rowland Ellis sent in Hugh Roberts' party his farmer, Thomas Owen, who was said to be a relative, and Thomas's family, to have his land properly laid out, some in Merion, and some in Goshen, and to make a settlement on his Merion land, build a house, clear some fields, and begin a farm, and make the usual preparations for the coming of himself and family when convenient. Four years later, Rowland Ellis, then a widower, bringing his son and namesake, came over to look over the situation, with a view of permanently removing with all his family.

On this trip to Pensylvania, he sailed in a Bristol ship from Milford Haven, on 16. 8mo. 1686. Many of his neighbors, about 100, all from about Dolgelly, accompanied him, and they had a long and tedious passage of 24 weeks, as they were obliged to come by the way of the Barbadoes, where the ship was detained six weeks, much to the discomfort of some of the passengers, but the saving of others, for coming, the immigrants generally experienced great suffering from being crowded in a small boat, and from the lack of proper accommodations for so large a party, and as it is recorded, "many died through want of necessary provisions, others from the remaining effects of their 'sufferings' [in Wales] and some that survived never recovered their former strength." If these passengers had not had the opportunity for recuperation at the Barbadoes, it was thought all would have perished before reaching the Delaware, so great was their suffering through bad food and sickness.

Mr. Ellis remained here only about nine months, and then returned to "old Bryn Mawr," leaving young Rowland behind with uncle John Humphreys. So pleased was Mr. Ellis with the outlook in the Province, that he bought a great deal of wild land in various localities at this time, and shortly after, and these land speculations eventually caused his financial ruin.

Mr. Ellis seems to have made his second visit after 1687, and before his second marriage, as he brought a certificate of good standing from some Meeting (not named, and undated), probably the one held at Tyddier y Gareg, near Dolgelley, Merioneth, which he filed with the Haverford (Radnor) Mo. Mtg. It mentions him as "returning to his own country namely Pensilvania." It says that "he was free and clear from any promise or Ingagement up on the account of Marriage, as far as we know when he parted from us." Signed by Robert Ellis, Owen Lewis, Rowland Edward Humphrey, Robert and Harry Owen, Ellis Powell, Owen Humphrey, John Harry, and William Bevan. How long he stayed here is not known.

In 1696, Mr. Ellis resolved to remove altogether, with his family, excepting his daughter Ann, who was left in possession of "Bryn Mawr," and who was then married to the Episcopal clergyman, to his American possessions. He sailed from Liverpool again, with a hundred passengers from his neighborhood, who having the experience of their former neighbors, provided against the discomforts of a long voyage. They arrived at Philadelphia in 4mo. 1697. He brought his certificate from the Garthgynfawr Meeting, dated 7. 11mo. 1696-7, signed by Lewis Owen, Rowland Owen, David Jones, and others.

He resided for several years in the little house erected by Mr. Owen, on his improved land, which he named after his paternal home, "Bryn Mawr," a name perpetuated by a beautiful town and a college, as his farm adjoined the Bryn Mawr College on the North. About 1704, (or was it 1714?), he erected a more pretentious two-story stone mansion on his "Bryn Mawr" farm, which is still standing, but renamed "Harriton" by a subsequent owner.

An interesting and long letter from Mr. Ellis, written in 1698, to his son-in-law, Rev. Mr. Johnson, is preserved, (see Pa. Mag. 1894), and tells considerable about his new home. He wrote:—"Our house lies under ye Cold N. W. wind, and just to the South Sun, in a very warm bottom near a stream of very good water. We have cleared about this run about 10 or 12 acres for meadow land, very good soil, black mould moist over....We have as much more such ground for meadow, when we may have to enclose it. Few, or none of our countrymen have the like conveniency of meadow land. We have above six acres of wheat sown in good order, and an accer and half of ye last summer fallow for barley. We now begin to clear in order for to sow Oats....We are about to enclose with rail fence about 40 accre."

He said his farm property here was about forty perch in length, and four perch in breadth. From his statement, it may be imagined Mr. Ellis had but little of his land under cultivation, and hardly crops enough to sustain his family, and this all seems a very miniature farm, in his great holdings, for from the minutes of the Land Commissioners, 12. 2. 1703, we learn that Rowland Ellis, having purchased of Richard Davies 1100 acres, by deed dated 30 July, 1682, recorded 30. 5. 1684, witnesses being Ellis Morris, Row Owen, Owen Lewis, Sr., and Jr., David Evan and Evan Harry, he had 500 laid out in Merion, and 483 in Goshen tp., having sold 117 acres. And that on resurvey, he had

COMPANY NUMBER SEVEN

in Merion 881 acres, and in Goshen 341 acres, and altogether 1222 acres of land. It was found that he had only 39 acres of "over plus" land, and this he promised to pay for, so patent was issued to him for 1222 acres.

By deed of 24 Feb. 1708, Mr. Ellis, for £180, conveyed to Rees Thomas, of Merion, and William Lewis, of New Town, 300 acres, "wherein the said Rowland Ellis now dwells, with the tract of land thereunto belonging." But Mr. Ellis's residence, still standing, was on the following property.

In 1717-9, Rees Thomas and William Lewis sold 700 acres, (the above 300 acres included), and apparently "Bryn Mawr," which lay on what is known as the Gulf Road, (that is, this road passed diagonally through the South part of the tract, and bounded it on the South-West), to Richard Harrison of Herring Creek, in Maryland, whose second wife Hannah, a Friends' minister, was a daughter of Judge Isaac Norris, and a granddaughter of Gov. Thomas Lloyd. 1719, Oct. 23, Mr. Ellis confirmed by one deed of this date, his whole tract of 718 acres to the said Richard Harrison, and for which he paid £600. The land of John Williams, Hugh Pugh, Thomas Lloyd, Hugh Evans, Owen Roberts, Thomas Nicholas, Philip Price, and Peter Jones, were bounds to Mr. Ellis's land in 1719. On this land is the "Harrison Family Cemetery," where Richard Harrison was buried in 1747-8.

Mr. Harrison's son-in-law, Charles Thomson, the well known secretary of the Continental Congress, lived in Mr. Ellis's stone house, on the Gulph Road, some three miles from Gulph Mill, and changed its name to "Harriton." He was buried in the Harriton Cemetery, in 1824, with his wife. It was while Mr. Thomson lived here, "12 miles from the State House," that Gen. James Potter, of the American army, wrote the following report to President Wharton, of Pensylvania dated 15 Dec. 1777.

WELSH SETTLEMENT OF PENSYLVANIA

"Last Thursday the enemy march out of the City with a desine to Furridge, but it was Nessecerey to drive me out of the way; my advanced picquet fired on them at the Bridge; another party of one Hundred attacted them at Black Hors. I was encamped on Charles Thomson's place, where I staeconed two Regments who attacted the enemy with viger. On the next Hill, I staeconed three Regments, letting the first line know, that when they were over powered, they must Retreat and form behind the second line, and in that manner we formed and Retreated for four miles; and on every Hill we disputed the matter with them. My people Behaved well, espealy three Regements, Commanded by the Cols Chambers, Murrey, and Leacey. His Excellencey Returned us thanks in public orders.* But the cumplement would have been much more substantiale had the Valant Generil Solovan Covered my Retreat with two Devissions of the Army, he had in my Reare, the front of them was about one half mile in my Reare, but he gave orders for them to Retreat and join the army who were on the other side of the Schuylkill about one mile and a Half from me, thus the enemy Got leave to plunder the Countrey, which they have dun without parsiality or favour to any, leaving none of the Nessecereys of Life Behind them that they conveniantly could Carry or destroy."

In those days, fifty years after he left the neighborhood, there were strenuous times about the old home of the mild Quaker minister.

In 1700, Rowland Ellis represented the Welsh Tract, or at least Merion, in the Assembly, and generally he was an active man in Welsh affairs, and because of his sound judgment in all cases, civil and religious, he was highly respected,

---

*"The Commander-in-Chief, with great pleasure, expresses his approbation of the behavior of the Pensylvania Militia yesterday, under General Potter, on the vigorous opposition they made to a body of the enemy on the other side of the Schuylkill." From "Orderly Book," 12 Dec. 1777.

not only by the Welsh Quakers, but in the Province generally. His last attendance at Quarterly Meeting was in Philadelphia on 31. 6mo. 1731.

Mr. Ellis was taken suddenly ill, after attending meeting at Gwynedd, and died in 7mo. 1731, in his 80th year, at the home of his son-in-law, John Evans, in "North Wales," or Plymouth, Philadelphia Co. (where he lived in 1717), and was buried there in the ground of the Gwynedd Monthly Meeting, which Meeting prepared a Memorial respecting him, stating he had "a gift in the ministry which was acceptable and to edification."

About 1672, Rowland Ellis* was married first to his cousin, Margaret Ellis, daughter of Ellis Morris, of Dolgun, and by her had a son and a daughter:

Ann Ellis, "married out," in 1696, to the Rev. Richard Johnson, of the "Established," or P. E. Church, who was the curate of Dolgelly, and had issue. Mr. Ellis was much attached to his wayward daughter, but as she was disowned, he did not know, in 1699, if she was living, and wrote to inquire "whether she is quite dead."

Rowland Ellis, Jr., who came over with his father in 1686-1687, seems to have died without issue. On 19. 3mo. 1725, he requested warrant of the Commissioners for the survey on 3,000 acres which he had purchased, paying £130, by deed, dated 3 April, 1724, of Daniel Warley, Jr., the son and heir of a London wool merchant, who had bought the land in 1695.

Mr. Ellis married secondly, after his second trip to Pensylvania, his cousin Margaret Roberts, daughter of Robert ap Owen Lewis, of Dyffryddan, and had by her, who died at

---

*In her will, marked in the presence of Edward Rees and Rowland Ellis, on 9. 8mo. 1716, proved 19 Aug. 1717, Rachel Ellis, of Haverford, mentions cousin Rowland Ellis and Elizabeth Ellis, and her brother Evan Ellis, and William Ellis, and sisters Elizabeth, Bridget, and Rebecca Ellis.

WELSH SETTLEMENT OF PENSYLVANIA

Plymouth, about 1730, four children, of whom *Elizabeth*, *Robert*, and *Catherine*, b. 1697, died unmarried, and

Ellin Ellis, (or Eleanor) who d. 29. 4mo. 1765, aged 76 years. She married at the Merion Meeting, on 8. 4mo. 1715, John Evans, of Gwynedd, Philadelphia Co., a Friends' minister, (a son of Cadwalader Evans, 1664-1745, of Gwynedd), and had by him, who d. 23. 9mo. 1756, (his will dated 16. 9mo. 1756, proved 22 June, 1757), eight children. Of these the only known grandchildren of Rowland Ellis, of "Bryn Mawr,"—

Cadwalader Evans, 1716-1773, *m*. Jane Owen.
Rowland Evans, 1718-1789, *m*. Susanna Foulke.
Margaret, wife of Anthony Williams.
Jane, wife of John Hubbs.
Ellen, second wife of Ellis Lewis.
Elizabeth Evans, spinster, 1726-1805.
John Evans, 1730-1807, *m*. Margaret Foulke.

Thomas Ellis, of Dolserre, in Merionethshire, having bought a great deal of the Robert Davies land, is included in this section though he was not one of his subscribers, but was originally an independent purchaser from Penn. He was one of the party of Welsh Quakers who interviewed Penn, in London, in May, 1681, about land in his Province, and, being a personal friend of John ap Thomas, accompanied him. Becoming convinced of Penn's representations, he bought from him 1,000 acres, on his own account, and not as a trustee, or "Adventuring Company," which land was subsequently laid out to him in the upper part of Merion.

It is supposed that Thomas Ellis was born in Montgomeryshire, though there is nothing definite known of his people. When he first came into notice, he is a minister among Friends, and travelled much throughout Wales, often in the company of the missionary, John Burnyeat, and was arrested at Machynlleth, and at Aberystwith, for being at meetings and preaching, and was imprisoned, and "suffered" in other ways, and by 1683, he had had enough of Wales, joined the party of Hugh Roberts, and came over to Pensylvania.

He filed with the Philadelphia Mo. Mtg. his certificate from the Dolserre Quarterly Meeting, dated 27. 5 mo. 1683. He also filed with the Haverford Mo. Mtg. his certificate issued to himself, his wife, and family, from the Mo. Mtg. at Redstone, in Pembrokeshire, dated 2. 7mo. 1683, signed by Edward Lloyd, John Poyer, John Bourge, James Thomas, William Jenkins, Evan Rowen, Lewis James, James Lewis, Richard White, David John, David Rees, and Peregrin Musgrave.

Where Mr. Ellis, with his wife and family, resided after settling here, is not known, but from the following letter, of 1685, it was not far from the Haverford Meeting house, and, afterwards, in the city, on account of his public life, and because of his travels. In the Province, he became a man of considerable prominence, even among the English, and, at the time of his decease, he was the register-general of the Province. His speculations in land were extensive and intricate, and on this account his estate was involved in litigation which caused his executor considerable trouble.

There is a rather interesting letter, printed in full in the Journal of the Friends' Historical Society, London, (issue of Nov. 1909), written by Thomas Ellis, while at Dublin, dated 13. 4mo. 1685, addressed "To Phillipp ffoord att Hood an Scarff in Bow Lane, London, for G. ff, these deliv'r with Care." This was the Mr. Ford with whom and his shrewd wife Mr. Penn had certainly peculiar relations, of which elsewhere, and which are fully set out by Mr. Shepherd in his "History of Proprietary Government in Pensylvania."

Mr. Ellis's letter was written on his return from Pensylvania, where he writes he had "left a tender wife and a considerable family of children and Servants well settled and ordered, considering the time, in a good neighborhood."

WELSH SETTLEMENT OF PENSYLVANIA

"Abt 15 families of us have taken our Land together and are to be abt 8 more that have not yet com, we took (to begin) 30 accres a piece, we built upon and doe improve [this land], and the other Land we have for Range to our cattell."

"We have our buriyng place where we intend our [Haverford] meeting house [shall be], as neer as we can to the Center, [of the settlement]. Our first day and week dayes meetings [are] well observed, besides our mens and womens meetings, and another Monthly Meeting [besides the great Philadelphia Mo. Mtg.], both in week dayes, unto wch four townships, [Merion, Haverford, Radnor and Schuylkill] at least belongs."

Mr. Ellis advises Friends to remove from Wales to Pensylvania, because there is no hope, so far as he can see, of their ever doing so well, or of ever being better off than now, in the old country.

"I cam from home since the 12mo. intending to be at the yearly meeting but could not have any shipping for 6 weeks being there was so much winter wether the like was hardly known, and so no seasoning wether for their tobacco, and a sore visitation in Mariland, in so much that hundreds dyed there in this last falls and winter of all sorts of people, 3 or 4 doctors [died] on the easter shore while I was there. dear Thomas Taylor and his wife [of Maryland], and Bryan Mele and Thomas ffurby, and many others, servicable friends, by a violent feaver, but it seems to be well over before I cam thence."

"I suppose you have had an account of Pensilvania affairs by newyork as was intended at the monthly meeting at Philadelphia," he asks Mr. Fox, whom he addressed as "My dear and fatherly friend," and informs him, "the president [Thomas Lloyd] was not then at home, but was expected from newyork."

"Several young people continue to com over without certificates which is a trouble to friends. I am like to con-

COMPANY NUMBER SEVEN

tinue in Wales a while when I would be glad to meet with William Bingley or such.

[Signed] "Thou knowest Tho Ellis."* He requests his mail lying in London be forwarded to him in care of "Peregrine Musgraves, clothier, in Haverford west, in Penbrokeshire, South Wales."

In the "P. S.", Mr. Ellis continues, "I have sent a few lines for W. P."...."dated here abt 4 dayes agoe." "If W. P. [has] not received it let him have part of this" [letter].

Thomas Ellis's first grant, by general description, was 1,000 acres, located in Merion. On survey it came out 819 acres, and on a resurvey only 735 acres, which gives us a fair idea of the ability of Penn's official surveyors at that time.

"Of the Richard Davies purchase Thomas Ellis, gent., of Jsoregenan, in Merioneth, bought of the mesme purchasers," namely, Lewis Owen and Rowland Owen, of Gwanas, Ellis Maurice (or Morris), of Dolgunucha, and Ellis Pugh, 625 acres in Merion, for himself, and 1,000 acres as agent for others. These purchases were conveyed by deeds dated in 1684 and 1686, and witnessed by Owen Lewis, Evan Harry, and John Humphrey, of Llanwddyn. Mr. Ellis took up these lands by warrants, dated 3. 11mo. 1687., and kept for his trouble all of the lands in the city Liberties, due on account of the purchases, besides all of the "overs." From the land records, he seems to have had over 3400 acres at one time, made up of Penn's grant, Davis' land, sundry rights, and "over-plus," but he had only between 800 and 900 acres in various places when he died.

Mr. Ellis was buried in the ground of the Haverford Mtg. By his will, dated 1. 11mo. 1688, he desired that all of his land should be sold by his executors to pay his debts, but those he named as executors declined to act, because

---

*For other particulars as to Thomas Ellis, see George Smith's "History of Delaware County," Pa., and "The Philadelphia Friend," magazine, XXVII.

of the tangled state of his lands. Nor would his relict administer, and settle up his estate, for the same reason, and by her will, threw all this trouble to her executor Daniel Humphrey, and he generously undertook the task with the assistance of the meeting.

As executor, Mr. Humphrey, by deed dated 5. 7mo. 1698, conveyed what was remaining of the Penn grant, about 625 acres, and 194 acres, in Merion to John Williams, and settled Ellis's account with William Penn, as he owed Penn £12.7.9, (being the balance due on the "1,000 acres," or 763 and 84 acres, at 5s. per acre)—with a credit of £30 Penn owed him. Some of Mr. Ellis's land lay in Duffryn Mawr, and Bertha Rowles bought 250 acres out of it, and in 1701, his daughter, Rachel Ellis, held 250 acres there, in his right.

A further account shows that Mr. Ellis had also about 790 acres in Haverford, as there were the following distributions and sales:—To his widow, Ellin, 30; son Ellis Ellis, 200; (and 30 from John Bevan); daughter "Brigid" 100; son Humphrey Ellis, 90; (60, 20 and 10 acres), sold to Daniel Humphrey, 100 (90 only in Haverford); to George Painter, 90; (sold to John Lewis, Sr.); to Daniel Lawrence, 90, (who also bought Humphrey Ellis's 90); to same, 60; to Daniel Humphrey, 20; to William Howell, 10, (sold to Rowland Powel). Or, there was sold 690 acres, and daughter Rachel Ellis had besides 101 acres in Haverford.

In 1700, Daniel Humphrey, of Haverford, held some 200 acres, made up of 90 acres bought (23. 12. 1684) from Thomas Ellis; 30 acres from Mr. Ellis and wife Ellin; 20¾ acres from Humphrey Ellis, son of said Thomas, by deed, 8. 9mo. 1694, and 60 acres from William Rowe, by deed of 30 May 1700.

Thomas Ellis was survived by his wife, Ellen, (surname unknown). Her will to which she put her mark, witnessed by David Llewellyn, Benjamn Humphreys, Theodore Robert, and John Humphrey, 27. 1. 1692, was proved 18. 12mo.

1692-3. She left her estate to daughter Rachel Ellis, and if she died before receiving it, then to the six children, unnamed, of her sisters, Lowry and Gwen. Appoints as executor, nephew Daniel Humphrey. To be trustees, Griffith Owen, William Howell, Edward Jones, John Roberts, Robert Owen, and John Humphreys.

Of their children:—

Ellis Ellis. He received some of his father's land, and held a warrant for re-survey, 18. 12mo. 1701, two parcels; found to be 330 acres, including 63 acres "over plus," which he promised to buy at 7s, 6d. per acre. He *m.* Lydia, daughter of Samuel and Elizabeth Humphrey, of Haverford.

The land deeds of the old Haverford School, and Haverford College, show the college land was originally part of the 410 acres which Richard Davies conveyed, on 19. 6mo. 1686, to Thomas Ellis, gentleman, Francis Howell, yeoman, James Thomas, yeoman, Morgan David, husbandman, and Francis Lloyd, shoemaker. And also that land which Ellis Ellis, of Haverford, yeoman, conveyed, by deed dated 25. 12mo. 1703, to "Robert Wharton, cordwainer," and his wife, Rachel, (a daughter of Thomas Ellis), namely 255 acres of his father's land, for fifty shillings, Pensylvania money, is part of the college land.

Humphrey Ellis, living in 1699.

Rachel Ellis, *m.* Robert Wharton.

"Brigid Ellis," who *d.* in England.

Eleanor Ellis, who *m.* David Lawrence, of Haverford. He came over from Wales about 1683. His will, signed 12. 2mo. 1699, in the presence of John Roberts, Rowland Powell, and John Bevan, was proved 1 July 1699. He left his estate to his wife and eldest son, Daniel. Names sons, Henry and Thomas, and daughters, Margaret, Eleanor and Rachel Lawrence, overseers, "brothers Ellis Ellis and Humphrey

Ellis," and William Howell. Thomas Lawrence* *m.* Sarah, *b.* 1685, daughter of William ap Edward, of Blockley, and his second wife, her sister, Ellen, *b.* 1691, *m.* Henry Lawrence, and their brother "Edward Williams," of Blockley, *m.* Eleanor Lawrence.

John Williams who bought in 1698, the balance of Thomas Ellis's Merion land, as above, sold 10. 5. 1700, some of it to Hugh Jones and John Evans (John Evans held 200 acres of this land, in 12mo. 1701).

Mr. Humphrey, the executor to both Thomas Ellis and his wife, as above, by deed dated 20. 1mo. 1701, conveyed 409½ acres of Ellis's land to Robert Lloyd, and Hugh Jones, aforesaid, and let Robert have 150 acres, which he conveyed to his brother, Thomas Lloyd.

The brothers, Robert Lloyd and Thomas Lloyd, came over in Hugh Roberts's and John Bevan's party, in 1683, from Merioneth, and were young and unmarried. They next appear as subscribing witnesses at the marriage of Robert Roberts and Katherine Jones, at the Haverford Meeting, 5. 3mo. 1696. Robert was one of the overseers to the will of Robert Owen, of Merion.

Robert Lloyd's first purchase of land, as above, was located North of "Bryn Mawr" (Rowland Ellis's tract), and was a portion of the Richard Davies grant from Penn. Robert had 259½ acres of this surveyed and laid out, in 12mo. 1701.

1703, 8mo. 4. Before the Land Commissioners, Robert Lloyd produced return of 432 acres, in Merion, on re-survey, on warrant dated 20. 2mo. 1703, to survey to him 409 acres, "being part of 819 acres out of Thomas Ellis's land." He requested a patent. Granted. And on 6. 12mo. 1707-8, he had title to his land confirmed to him, and this for good reasons, as explained elsewhere.

*From him are descended Abraham Lewis Smith, of Media, and Benj. Hayes Smith, of Philadelphia, who are also descended from Dr. Thomas Wynne, Dr. Edward Jones, Robert Owen, of Merion, Ralph Lewis, etc.

COMPANY NUMBER SEVEN

Robert Lloyd* died 29. 3mo. 1714, and was buried at the Merion Meeting House. His will, signed 30 April, 1714, witnessed by Edward Foulke, William Roberts (marked), and Thomas Albin, was proved 16 Nov. same year, by his wife, Lowry. He names his children, David, Robert, Rees, Richard, Hannah, Gwen, Sarah, and Gainor. Mentions Edward Thomas and Owen Roberts, and his brother Thomas Lloyd, and named as trustees, Robert and Richard Jones, Thomas Lloyd, Jr., and friends Robert Evan, Rowland Ellis, and Robert Jones, of Merion.

He married at the Merion Meeting, on 11. 8mo. 1698, Lowry Jones, who died 25. 11mo. 1762, aged 80 years, and was buried with her husband. She was a child of Rees John William, of Merion. Of their children:—

Hannah *m.* first, John Roberts, Jr., (grandson of Owen Humphrey) and had John Roberts, 3d. *b.* 1721, and *m.* secondly, William Paschall, *issue,* and *m.* thirdly, Peter Osborne, *issue.*

Richard Lloyd, 1714-1755, of Darby, *m.* at Darby Mtg. 24. 9. 1736, Hannah daughter of Samuel and Sarah Sellers, and had Hugh Lloyd, 1742-1832, of Chester Co., colonel of 3d Battalion, presidential elector and associate judge.

Robert Lloyd, *m.* Catherine Humphrey. *Issue.*

Thomas Lloyd, the younger of the brothers, held in 12mo. 1701, the 150 (or 154½) acres in Merion, which had been a part of the Thomas Ellis estate, and lay North of "Bryn Mawr," and by deed, dated 10 Feb. 1709, his brother Robert further conveyed to him 154 acres of his land North of "Bryn Mawr," on payment of £40. He was a farmer, and his will, marked 26. 5mo. 1741, was proved 6 Feb. 1748;

---

*From Robert Lloyd are descended Howard Williams Lloyd, Wm. Supplee Lloyd, and the brothers Samuel Bunting Lewis, Davis Levis Lewis, George Harrison Lewis, and Osborn G. L. Lewis, of Philadelphia, descendants also of William Lewis, who came over in 1686-7. Samuel Marshall, of West Chester, Pa. is also descended from Robert Lloyd, and from Rees John William, of Merion.

[247]

WELSH SETTLEMENT OF PENSYLVANIA

witnesses, David Davids and Richard Lloyd, trustees to be "neighbors Richard Lloyd and Griffith Llewellyn."

Thomas Lloyd was married about 1698, by a justice of the peace, to Elizabeth, *b.* 1672, who survived him, daughter of William ap Edward, or Edwards, of Blockley, by his first wife. They appeared before the Merion Meeting, on 8. 6mo. 1700, and humbled themselves for "marrying out." Her will, signed 2 Dec. 1748, was proved 6 Feb. 1748-9. They had seven children: Thomas, 1699-176-, resided in Bucks Co., Pa.; Sarah, *m.* at Merion Mtg. 8. 9mo. 1721, John Morgan (son of Edward, of Gwynedd); Jane, *m.* first at Merion Mtg. 8. 8. 1725, Lewis Williams, of Gwynedd; John 1704-1770, *m.* at Merion Mtg. 31. 10. 1731, Eleanor, daughter of Henry and Catherine Pugh; Elizabeth, *m.* at Merion Mtg. 9. 8mo. 1728, Joseph Morgan (brother to above John); Evan and William.

Having now brought nearly all of the Welsh "first purchasers," and the early settlers to their new homes in the great Welsh tract, a review of the peculiar claims they made on Penn, or set up for themselves, and how they tried to substantiate them, and, failing in this, see how it was that "the Welsh tract," as a district and indentity was wiped-off the map of Pensylvania should be interesting.

WELSH TRACT PLANTERS

The following is the summary of the foregoing transactions, and others in the Welsh tract, set forth in "D. Powels Acct of ye Welch Purchasers in Genl," in which he gives his personal "Account of the purchasers Concurned in the Welch Tract Granted by the Generall war't by wich the said Tract was Laid out and such Lands as hath bin Laid out by war'ts Dulie Executed within the same and ist of ye ould England Parishes":—

	Acres.		Acres.
Charles Lloyd, and Margaret Davis	5,000	Henry Right	500
Richard Davis, [Davies]	5,000	Daniell Med———	200
William Jenkins	1,000	Thomas Ellis	1,000
John Poy, [Poyer]	750	Tho Ellis for B. Roules	250
John Burge	750	Th. Ellis on ac't Humph. Tho.	100
William Mordant	500	David Powell	1,000
William Powell	1,250	Burke and Simson	1,000
Lewis David	3,000	John Kinsy	200
Morris Llewlin	500	John Kinsy	100
Thomas Simons	500	David Meredith	250
John Bevan	2,000	John Day	300
Edward Prichard	2,500	David Davis	200
John ap John, and Thomas Wyn	5,000	Henry Joanes	400
Edward Joanes, and John Thomas	5,000	Thomas John Evan	250
		John Evans	100
Richard Davis	1,250	John Jormon	50
Richard ap Thomas	5,000	David Kinsy	200
Daniell Hurry, [Harry]	300	Evan Oliver	100
Mordicia Moore in Right of	500	Samuel Mills	100
		Thomas Joanes	50
John Millington	500	David Joanes	100
		John Ffish	300

"The whole Compl'nt 50,000 acres."

As there are only forty-one grants in this list, and Holme's map indicated more than twice this number of land owners

WELSH SETTLEMENT OF PENSYLVANIA

in the Welsh Tract, it may be presumed that Holme did not compile his map as early as he claimed, when testifying before the Council as to the positions of the townships of Haverford and Radnor, as will appear.

In this summary by Surveyor David Powel, without date, we find the names of the first large purchasers of land in Merion township, John Thomas and Dr. Jones, and those of the other six "Companies," or adventurers for Welsh Tract plantations, and also those of the other large independent "first purchasers," some of whose land was laid out in Merion, besides in Haverford, Radnor, and Goshen townships, and it may be noticed that there were very few not strictly Welsh had been granted land in the tract.

Although the acreage given by Powel exceeded the original total of the grants to the Welsh, namely 40,000 acres, and took in much of the supplementary 10,000 acres reserved for them, it did not come up to "the whole Compl'nt 50,000 acres." Mr. Powel, however, may have inadvertently overlooked some grantees, but it appears that he remembered to record a tract of 1,000 acres in his own name, and its future location he had probably selected, for which he had deed from Penn. It seems to have been for services as a surveyor, but the grant was not confirmed to him till in 1705, as mentioned below.

For the above reason, the date of Powel's list cannot be approximated by the mention of his own land, 1,000 acres. For his surveying work for the Land Commissioners, he probably received from them little cash; but he was granted small parcels of land, and realized what he could by the sale of them. He had a patent from the Commissioners, dated 14. 3mo. 1686, for 611 acres, which he laid out in Radnor tp., in two tracts, 500 and 111 acres, and this is his first land-ownership of record. This represented £100 to him. On 22. 5mo. 1687, he sold 100 acres of this patent to John Evans, adjoining the land of Hugh Samuel. On 17. 11mo. 1690, he sold 100 acres more to said Hugh Samuel, (servant to Thomas Ellis), adjoining the land of David

PLANTERS AND SERVANTS

Hugh. On 17. 3mo. 1690, he sold another 100 acres to James Pugh (servant to Steven Bevan), adjoining land of David Pugh, and by another deed of this date, he sold 200¾ acres and closed out his 500 acres, to William Davis and Griffith Miles, the land adjoining Hugh Samuel. Of this land, William and Griffith sold 150 acres to Philip Philips, whose widow, Phoebe, sold the same to David Pugh, and, by deed 22. 6mo. 1690, William and Griffith sold their balance of 50 acres to James Pugh, aforesaid, and here was the "Pugh District" in Radnor.

John Evans, aforesaid, by deed of 10. 5mo. 1700, bought 200 acres in Merion, adjoining Rowland Ellis, from John Williams, who had it from the Richard Davies tract, (Company No. 7), through Thomas Ellis and Daniel Humphrey.

Evan Harry, by deed of 10. 10mo. 1687, bought 90 acres from Surveyor Powel, who received it, 7. 7mo. 1687, from David Lloyd, the lawyer, as a fee, who bought it from the attorneys of Richard Davies, 15. 6mo. 1687. Evan Harry also bought 74 acres more from Powel, and Abel Roberts, son of Ellis Roberts, of Radnor, also bought 100 acres from Powel, by deed of 1. 6mo. 1693, confirmed 9. 6mo. 1703, and these sales exceeded his patents.

In 1704-5, Powel was still the Proprietor's surveyor in the Welsh Tract on the Schuylkill, and receiving no cash for his work, as he states in his petition, he asked the Commissioners, 28. 11mo. 1705, to grant him 1,000 acres he had selected in the Welsh Tract. He asked this, because he had been compensated with only the above mentioned 500 acres. Petition granted, providing he could find any vacant land, which, as an old surveyor in that section, he easily could, and apparently had. His lands were quickly disposed of, as he may have been a good judge of land, and guaranteed his bounds.

The following transportation agreement between **Mr.** Powell and a skipper, suggests that he brought over the passengers to buy land from him about this time.

WELSH SETTLEMENT OF PENSYLVANIA

"Articles of ffreightment, covenanted, indented and made the seventh day of March, 1697-8, between Owen Thomas, of the county burrough of Carmathen, mercer, owner of the good shipp called the William Galley, now residing in the river of Towny, of the one part, and

"David Powell, of the parish of Nantmell, in the county of Radnor, and John Morris, of the parish of Karbardamfyneth, in the said county of Radnor, yeomen, of the other part,

• "Contract to take to Pensilvania after 10th of May, starting with first good wind and weather, from said river Towny, and town of Rhaygsder, to Philadelphia in Pensilvania, with them and passengers and goods." The charge for transportation to be £5 for each adult over 12 years old, persons under 12 years, fifty shillings, sucking children and freight up to twenty tons, free. The head of each family was also charged "fffive shillings encouragement to the doctor belonging to said shipp, and all single persons except servants, to pay one shilling each."

The following is the list of principals in this venture, and how many each paid for in his party:

David Powell paid for 11 passengers.
John Morris paid for 6.
Margaret Jones paid for 3.
Edward Moore paid for 4.
Thomas Powell paid for 3½.
Thomas Griffith paid for 2.
Rees Rees paid for 4½.
Edward Nicholas paid for 4.
Thomas Watts, 1.
Winnifred Oliver paid for 5 passengers.
Evan Powell paid for 5.
Thomas Jerman paid for 3.
John Powell paid for 2.
James Price paid for 2.
John Vaikaw (?) 1.
Lumley Williams, 1.

PLANTERS AND SERVANTS

Ann Lewis, 1.
Walter Ingram, 1.
Benjamin Davis, 1.

"John Burge, of Haverford-West, Pembrokeshire, clothier," mentioned in Powel's list, was another of Penn's personal customers for Welsh Tract land. He bought by deed, dated 24. 8mo. 1681, 750 acres which were to be laid out in Haverford in several tracts. One of these, 250 acres, it was discovered, was laid out on land owned by Humphrey Ellis, and after a litigation, Burge had to look elsewhere to locate this parcel, so he sold the 250 acre right to William Kelly, of Haverford-West, a weaver, who had 141 acres of it laid out in Haverford, and 30 acres in city liberties and lots. On 2. 10mo. 1694, said Kelly sold the 141 acres to Humphrey Ellis, who had also bought 79 acres from John Burge, or from Kelly, which he sold, for £8.9. Pensylvania money, 15 Feb. 1703, to Henry Lewis.

Edward ap Richard, or Prichard, on Powel's list, was another of Penn's personal customers. He took 2,500 acres, deed dated 14 April, 1682, which was confirmed by patent dated 18. 3mo. 1685; 1,250 acres were to be laid out in Merion, and balance in Radnor. Many of his deeds are of record in the office of the Recorder.

John Poyer, on Powel's list, also purchased of Penn, by deed dated 24. 8mo. 1681, 750 acres, and by deed of 3 June, 1686, he sold the rights to 250 acres to Henry Sanders, who had the same resurveyed to himself, on Commissioner's warrant, dated 16. 12mo. 1701, when Owen Thomas requested a warrant to take up this land.

"William Jenkins, of Tenby, in Pembrokeshire, emasculator," (subsequently of Abington tp.), on Powel's list, bought of Penn 1,000 acres by deed dated 24. 8mo. 1681. Of this grant, 245 acres were laid out to him in Duffrin Mawr tp., 12. 11mo. 1689. By deed of 30. 7mo. 1686, he conveyed 250 acres to James Thomas, late of Landboyden, Carmarthenshire, a husbandman, which, on resurvey, amounted to 300 acres, and Penn issued a warrant for that

WELSH SETTLEMENT OF PENSYLVANIA

amount, 2. 7mo. 1701. Afterwards, James was astonished to learn that his purchase was not within the Welsh Tract, and, on 16. 12mo. 1701, requested a new warrant for Welsh Tract land to this amount, which the Commissioners granted, provided he could find such an amount of unclaimed land in the tract. But it seems he could not, as by his will he devised to his son, Nathan Thomas, lands in Duffrin Mawr.

William Jenkins, by deed of 3. 7mo. 1686, sold 500 acres to Francis Howel, of Lancilio, in Carmarthanshire, who devised 300 acres of the purchase to Thomas Howel, which he sold, by deed 1. 7. 1700, to above James Thomas,

From the number of these sales of land, it might be supposed that Penn had no difficulty in getting rid of his land; but he had, even before Ford's persecution cast a shadow on the titles. For some reason the bottom dropped out of his real estate business after the first boom, and when he supposed 100 "barons" in the "House of Lords"—each to buy 5,000 acres, was too small a number to stop at, he suddenly discovered that he might not be able to have even half that number of "Lords." And his order that "no 1,000 acre lot could be increased contiguously, unless within three years there was a family settled on each 1,000 acres," shows how sparsely the country must have been settled at that period.

In the early land records of Chester Co., for the townships of Radnor and Haverford, there are records of the following early grantees.

These had deeds for land:

1681.			Acres.
March	3.	Lewis David	3,000
"	"	Thomas Rowland	1,000
"	"	David Powell	1,000
March	17.	John Bevan	2,000
"	22.	Thomas Ellis	1,000
"	"	Thomas Holme	5,000
"	"	Joseph Powell	250
"	"	Thomas Powell	500
June	16.	Richard Davies	1,250

PLANTERS AND SERVANTS

1681			Acres.
July	13.	Thomas Rudyard	5,000
Sept.	14.	John & Wynne	5,000
"	"	Richard Davies	5,000
Oct.	24.	John Poyer	750
Jan.	19.	Morris Llewelyn	500
"	"	William Sharlow*	5,000

These had patents for land.

Haverford tp.

1684. 11. 29.	Thomas Ellis	791
1688. 5. 23.	Charles & John Bevan	230
1703. 8. 25.	Ellis Ellis	425
1703. 8. 25.	Daniel Humphrey	241
1704. 2. 4.	John Bevan	508
1706. 5. 20.	Henry Lewis	488

Marple tp.

1688. 5. 23.	Charles & John Bevan	750
1694. 2. 21.	Thomas Ellis	330

Radnor tp.

1684. 5. 29.	Thomas Wynne	250
1685. 5. 30.	David Davis	200
1686. 3, 14.	David Powell	611
1687. 7. 9.	David Powell	300
1688. 8. 1.	Reese Prece	200
1689. 3. 26.	David Meredith	350
1701. 7. 30.	Evan Rodderch	122
1703. 8. 25.	John Evan Edward	123
1703. 8. 25.	Margaret Jarmon	152
1703. 8. 25.	David Pugh	174
1703. 8. 25.	James Pugh	162
1703. 9. 1.	Thomas John Evan	340
1703. 9. 1.	Edward David	155
1704. 1. 14.	John Evans	300
1704. 3. 1.	David Meredith	253

* William Sharlow was a London merchant. He purchased from Mr. Penn, by deed dated 2. 5mo. 1683, besides the above, 500 acres, which was laid out and surveyed to him, 30. 7mo. 1684, and named "Mount Ararat." It lay on the Schuylkill, above the Thomas & Jones tract, but not adjoining it, as in Holme's map. Mr. Sharlow's Pensylvania attorney, by deed of 5. 10mo. 1692, conveyed 150 acres of "Mt. Ararat" to Thomas Potts, who by deed of 2. 2mo. 1695, conveyed his purchase to David Hugh, who sold the same to "Robert Jones, of Meirion, Labourer," or "Robert Jones, Yeoman, of Meirion," who was a son of John ap Thomas.

WELSH SETTLEMENT OF PENSYLVANIA

Some of the properties of early settlers were located about as follows:

Along the East boundary, (a line and the Haverford road, about 3¾ miles), of Radnor, in Merion, on the upper side, where are the settlements of Villa Nova and Rosemont, were the great estates of Rowland Ellis and John Eckley. And in Radnor, along and between this line, and where "Radnor Street," (or the present Radnor road, crossing Eagle road, if continued straight to the opposite line), was to have been, passing through the center of the township, North and South, beginning at the upper end, were the properties of Evan Lloyd, Abel Roberts, John and William Thomas, Matthew Jones, David David, Richard Humphrey, John Morgan, Henry Lewis, John Jarman, John Evans, Roger Hugh, David Prees, David Meredith, David James, Thomas Rees and Stephen Evan.

In the same position in Haverford, that is between the line of the proposed "Haverford Street," through the center of the township from North to South, and the Eastern boundary line, about 3½ miles long, were the properties of Hugh David, William Lewis, Thomas Rees, David and Ralph Lewis, Rees Rotherow, William Ellis, Ellis Ellis, Robert Wharton, Thomas Ellis, Lewis David, Daniel Humphrey, William Howell, all lying above the road passing the Haverford Meeting House towards the road to Darby. And below this road, John Lewis, John Havard, Henry Ellis, David Hugh, Henry Lewis, Daniel Lawrence, Richard Hayes, Samuel Lewis. In both townships, West of the imaginary streets, were the properties of some others. And in Merion, along the Haverford township line, at Haverford College station on the railroad, and below Wynnewood station, were the great estates of John Humphrey and John Bevan.

In 1734, the following Welshmen each paid assessments on 100 acres of land in Philadelphia county: Hugh Thomas, Daniel Jones, David George, John Thomas, James Jones, William Roberts, Evan Rees, John Humphrey, George

PLANTERS AND SERVANTS

George, Lewis Jones and Edward Williams; "Robert Roberts, of Mirian," 50; David Morgan, 19, and "Thomas Winne," 50 acres in Blockley.

In an undated paper (1693?) at the Historical Society of Pensylvania, giving "The Valuation of the Estates of the Inhabitants of the Township of Merion," and the amount of tax each was to pay ("one penny on the pound"), we have a list of Merion people, many of whose names are familiar, as follows:—

Merion.	Valuation.	Merion.	Valuation.
John Roberts	£120	Robert Owen	100
Hugh Jones	40	John Roberts "of the Wain"	100
Cadwalader Morgan	90	Robert Jones	72
Rowland Richard	30	David Hugh	60
Robert David [collector]	100	Katherine David	30
Hugh Roberts	150	John Williams	30
Katherine Thomas	100	Benjamin Humphreys	60
Griffith John	110	Reece Thomas	100
Richard Walter	70	Philip and Isaac Price	60
Abel Thomas	30	Peter Jones	30
Reece Jones	60	John Robert Ellis	30
Edward Jones	90	Edward Jones	72
Edward Reece	120	Edward Griffith	72
Richard Cuarton	80	William Cuarton	30
David Pugh	30	Thomas Rees	30
David Price	30	Owen Morgan	30
Daniel Thomas	50	John Moore	30
Evan Bevan	80	Thomas Howell	40
David Havard,		James Thomas, Sen'r	70
"with 200 acres of Land"	82	James Thomas, Jun'r	40

The following men of Merion were each assessed six shillings, without valuations, (which was the tax paid on all estate valuations of £72), and probably were freemen:—

Evan Harry.
Thomas Jones.
David Ryederch.
Meredith Davids.
Joshua Owen.
Edward Edwards.
Robert Lloyd.
Thomas Jones.

William Roberts.
Robert William.
Philip Wallis.
Owen Thomas.
Robert David.
Robert Hugh.
John Owen.
Evan Harry, weaver.

WELSH SETTLEMENT OF PENSYLVANIA

Robert David, who lived in Merion fifty years, was the collector of this tax, and he endorsed on the list, "Paid to James Fox, Recorder." If Mr. Fox was a recorder of Philadelphia County, none of the accepted-as-correct printed lists of them include his name. Mr. Fox was commissioned, 12 Feb. 1697-8, a justice of the Philadelphia county court, and was a member of the Assembly 1688-1699; will proved at Philadelphia, 10 April, 1701.

It is presumed that the aforesaid assessment was made in 1693, because it is known that in this year there was one made in Chester Co., as below, for the same amount of tax, namely, "one penny per pound on Estates," and "six shillings per head on freemen." This was probably the levy noticed in the minutes of the Welsh monthly meeting, 8mo. 1693, "tax levied of one shilling per hundred towards the taking of wolves."

The following names are on the Chester Co. lists for the townships of Haverford and Radnor. The total amounts received were: Haverford, £3.14.5, and Radnor, £2.19.3. The estates in these townships were appraised lower than those of Merion, as may be seen.

Haverford.	Valuation.
John Bevan	£50
William Howell	40
Morris Llewellyn	40
Thomas Reese	30
William Lewis	48
John Richard	30
Humphrey Ellis	30
Ellis Ellis	33
Ralph Lewis	30
William Jenken	45
Daniel Humphrey	40
David Lawrence	36

Radnor.

John Evans	£45
David Meredith	70
John Evans	30
John Jarman	44
John Morgan	32

Haverford.	Valuation.
Lewis David	30
John Lewis	40
Henry Lewis	50
John Lewis, Jr.	30
Richard Hayes	43
Benjamin Humphrey	32
William Howell, for Thomas Owen	72
Richard Hayes, for David Lewis	72
John Bevan, for Evan William	72
Philip Evan	43
David Evan	41
William Davis	31
Samuel Miles	33
Richard Miles	34

PLANTERS AND SERVANTS

William David	31	Evan Prothero	43
Richard Armes	52	John Richard	33
Matthew Joanes	30	Stephen Bevan	45
Howell James	44	Thomas Johns	32

Following the custom long established in Virginia, Penn granted fifty acres for each indentured servant brought into his Providence. In Virginia, this head-right, as it was called there, belonged to the person importing the servant. In fact, the importer, or master, received in Virginia lands, fifty acres not only for each of his servants, but the same amount for each member of his family, or particular party, whose passage he paid. While Penn not only granted (or intended to do so), fifty acres to the servant himself, and gave him a deed, and warrant of survey for the same, at the expiration of his term of servitude, or when his master freed him, but fifty acres to the master for each servant brought. This was a better arrangement, because in Virginia it was notorious that the same servants and other head-rights, were used over and over, often with the same names, to procure lands, hence some of the great tracts of tide-water land in Virginia, held by Colonial worthies.

In neither Virginia or Pensylvania were all of the "servants" of the lowest social class; nor were these, men and women, all servants as we now understand the term. In either colony, many of these servants were relatives of their "masters," even were their children, and frequently were at "home," and here, of equal social standing to their masters. Many reasons can be assigned to account for their servitude, or indenture, and many whose earliest record in America is that of "servant," in a short time became prominent for good in social, religious, or civil life.

According to the Minutes of the Board of Property, 26. 9mo. 1701, it was the intention of William Penn to set aside a township of 6,000 acres, to be used only as "head-land" for servants brought into his Province, in the years 1682-3,

WELSH SETTLEMENT OF PENSYLVANIA

where they could settle when their "time" expired; but this idea was probably abandoned, because it was found the servants nearly always conveyed away for a small consideration their rights to land.

For instance, Philip Howel purchased their head-lands from the following servants, they uniting in a deed for the same to him, dated 18. 2mo. 1702:—

"Humphrey Edwards, servant to John ap Edwards.
"Inemry (?) Osborn, servant to Griffith Jones.*
"Elizabeth Osborn, his wife (born Day), servant to same.
"Jacob Willis, servant to William Cloud.
"Evan Williams, servant to Thomas Ellis.†
"Margaret Williams, his wife (born Richard), servant to John Bevan.
"Edmund MacVeagh, servant to Thomas Holme.
"Alice MacVeagh, his wife, (born Dickinson), servant to James Harrison."

Robert Turner's servants, like himself, were from Dublin, and all named Furness:— John, Henry, Joseph, Daniel, Mary, Sarah, and Rachel. John Furness was Mr. Turner's barber, and in 8mo. 1683, was granted by the Commissioners 350 acres, on account of himself, and the other servants of his surname.

Reuben Ford, servant to John Gibbons, received head-land on his own account, by warrant of 8. 9. 1703.

---

* Griffith Jones was one of the prominent Welsh Quakers of the Province. In 1703, he was chosen as Mayor of Philadelphia, but for some reason he declined to serve, and, as was the custom then, he was fined £20, but did not pay. On 3 Oct. 1704, he was again chosen for the mayoralty, and would have again declined, but being threatened with a like fine, or a total of £40, he accepted the office, and it was such an honour to have him as the Mayor, the first fine was remitted. David Lloyd, another Welsh Quaker, was the Recorder of the city at this time.

† Thomas Ellis came from a hamlet, near Dolgules, in Merionethshire, the name of which was variously written Dolserre, Dolserey, Dolyseerey, Dolyserry, Doleyseere, Dolyserre, Doleyserre, etc.

PLANTERS AND SERVANTS

The following were servants to the prominent families of Merion, the first settlers:—

Edmund Griffith, and Katherine Griffith, "formerly wife to Edmund Griffith," were servants of Hugh Roberts.

John Hugh was servant to Rees John William.

Hugh Samuel was servant to Thomas Ellis.

Mary Hughes was servant to John ap Edward.

John Roberts and William Roberts were servants to Robert David.

William David was servant to John Bevan.

James Pugh was servant to Steven Bevan.

Thomas Rees was servant to Evan Thomas.

Susanna Griffith was servant to John Richards.

Thomas Armes, John Ball (had four years to serve), Robert Lort (had eight years to serve), Jean, Bridget and Elizabeth Watts, and Alexander Edwards (who each had three years to serve), were servants to Griffith Owen, in 1684.

These were servants to Katharine, relict of John ap Thomas, in Merion, Elizabeth Owen, Thomas David, and Ann David.

Frequently servants were given certificates of good character by the Friends' Meetings they belonged to in the old country. There are a number of these preserved on the books of the Haverford, now Radnor, Monthly Meeting, as John ap Evan and family, and Ralph Lewis, from Treverig Meeting, dated 10. 7mo. 1683, and John Richard, and William Sharpless, from the same Meeting, of whom the Certificate describe them "of small abilitie," and "harmless men"; but "ready to hear and Receive the Truth." And that they were "low in the Outward, yett lived Comfortable enough." John Lloyd, a servant to Mr. Bevan, was also thus described.

Servants who claimed to have served their "time," require a strong certificate of the fact before being released. For instance, in the case of Humphrey Edwards, mentioned above; on 9. 4mo. 1702, Edward Jones, William Jenkins, and Philip Howel, declared before the Commissioners, that

WELSH SETTLEMENT OF PENSYLVANIA

Humphrey, "now of Gwynedd, came into this Province about the year 1683, as a servant to John ap Edward, and served his time to him faithfully, and according to Indenture." This occurred on his request for fifty acres of headland.

Thomas Jones also had a servant named Ellis Roberts, who according to the minutes of the Merion Preparative Meeting, 6mo. 6. 1703, was made free, having according to his certificate, which was read to the meeting, as was usual, served Mr. Jones's mother, brother, and himself twelve years.

The certificate of Robert Goodwin, who had been a servant for four years to Evan Harry, was also read in Merion meeting, on 2. 1mo. 1704-5, and, on 4. 6mo. 1704, that of Hugh Humphreys from his master, Benjamin Humphreys, and that of John Roberts from his master, Robert Jones.

A letter from Thomas Jones, of Merion tp., to his cousin, Robert Vaughan, in Wales, tells of Owen Roberts' (son of the Friends' minister, Hugh Roberts), adventures at sea, coming to Pensylvania, and that his company was captured by the French near the mouth of the Delaware, and carried as prisoners to the West Indies. Nine of the servants he was bringing were "pressed on board a ship"; "Morris Richard, the Tailor, died at sea"; but the others finally reached Philadelphia. Among the latter were Humphrey Williams, Thomas Owen, Cadder John, Robert Arthur, Hugh Griffith, Edward Thomas and James Griffith. Thomas Owen died after reaching here. Owen Roberts returned to Antigua, to try and recover his impressed men, but could not find them.

These were some of the servants who came over in the ship Vine, in Sept. 1684, besides Griffith Owen's servants:— Edward Edwards, a boy, Lowry Edwards, Margaret Edwards, Ann Owen, Hannah Watts and Charles Hughes. It appears from the monthly meeting minutes, 11. 2mo. 1695, that Charles Hughs "married out," and that because David Potts, Owen Thomas, and Evan Harry were at the wedding, "which marriage friends had no unity with," "they were dealt with by Robert Owen and Edward Jones, and thereupon gave forth the following paper of condemnation, viz. For as much as we whose names are hereunto written, for want of due consideration have unadvisedly been at the dishonorable marriage of Charles Hughes, and by so doing have transgressed against this good order as established among friends of Truth," &c., hereby acknowledging publicly before the meeting the mistake they made. But in 1722, 5mo. the Radnor Mo. Mtg. was not so certain of its stand as to "dishonorable marriages," as it instructed its representatives to the quarterly meeting "to report that the monthly meeting was concerned whether it was necessary to disown such persons as go to the priest to marry, or only advise them."

The Gwynedd meeting was formed by sanction of the Radnor Mo. Mtg. at the desire of Friends there, and they were "to meet second weekly Third day of every month" beginning in 2mo. 1699. But they were not authorized till in 6mo. 1702, "to keep a preparative meeting among themselves."

Recorded at the Radnor Monthly Meeting is the undated, unsigned, certificate, from some Meeting in Wales, unnamed, of "Treharn David, who hath gone now 13 or 14 months since for Pensylvania with Janne his wife, being noe more in family but they both." "Treharne lived with our friend John Bevan for many years," in Wales.

William Morgan, and his wife Elizabeth, who came over in the "Morning Star," 20. 9mo. 1683, had been "servants," but in the passenger list they were described "both free," having served their "time."

From the burial records of the Merion Meeting come the following particulars about other servants, white and black, of early times, who should not be passed by, for they, like their masters, had a part in the opening and settling of this new country.

1714. 8. 9. "David Lewis, servant of Morris Llwellyn."
1714. 10. 8. "Morgan Thomas, servant to Robert Evans"

WELSH SETTLEMENT OF PENSYLVANIA

1714-5. 11. 16. "Robert Vincent, servant to Jon Jones."
1714-5. 12. 27. "Bumbo, a young negro."
1716. 4. 5. "Catharine Griffith, servant to Evan Harry."
1717. 10. 30. "George Eves, burnt at Edward Jones'."
1718. 10. 14. "Rowland Ellis' tenant," (? Thomas Owen).
1719. 7. 14. Thos. Evans, "living at David Mirick's place."
1719. 10. 27. "Ship, Henry Pugh's Negro."
1720. 1. 5. "William Worm, servant to Hugh Evans"

This Hugh Evans had considerable trouble when he proposed to marry the lady of his choice, according to a minute of the Radnor Mo. Mtg. He desired to marry Lowrey Lloyd, the daughter of Rees John William, of Merion, and widow of Robert Lloyd, of Merion, who died in 1714, but the union was objected to by friends on the ground "of too near affinity," "she being Hugh's deceased wife's mother's sister's daughter." Hugh held that Lowrey was of no kin at all to him, but the monthly meeting thought otherwise, so the matter was referred to the quarterly meeting, which allowed the marriage to take place, and the wedding was at the Merion meeting house, on 13, 12mo. 1716-7.

1720-1. 11. 26. "A young Negro of Edward Reese."
1720-1. 12. 17. "old Bassel, negro to Edward Reese."
1726-7. 1. 13. "Black Hannah."
1745. 6. 2. "A child of Edward Williams' maid."
1746. 9. 2. "Will, a Negro of Edward Price."
1748. 8. 29. "Black Peter."
1749. 10mo. "Old Caesar, Reese Reese's negro."
1749. 6. 28. "A Dutch........from Evan Jones place."
1752. 10. 10. "A Dutch woman from Evan Jones' place."
1754. 11. 20. "A dutchman from Anthony Tunis's."
1754. 10. 22. "Dutch girl from Philip Creakbeam's."
1756. 4. 13. "A Dutch Woman from William Stadleman's. Supposed to be Poisoned by a Dutchman, from Lancaster, who was Tryed & Convicted, but Reprieved"

The Welsh monthly meeting several times issued instructions to the preparative meetings, that as the matter of discharging servants, whose time had expired, was an important one, masters were commanded to give the new freemen certificates as to conduct, &c., as a protection to the community (hence, possibly, our servant's "references"). It also ordered, none should encourage servants to buy their time, by lending them money to do so, or going bond for them without master's consent.

In an advertisement in the *American Weekly Mercury*, Philadelphia, 26 May, 1720, "Samuel Lewis, of Harford in the county of Chester," offers thirty shillings reward for the return to him of his runaway servant, Thomas Roberts, aged about thirty years. The description of the clothes of this servant may give some idea of how his "betters" dressed. "He wore a duroy coat lined with silk, a leathern jacket and breeches."

It is singular but never in all the wills of the ancient Welsh Friends, which frequently mentioned purchased Negroes, and bequeathed them as chattel, have I found an instance of a devisor liberating his slaves. It was the custom of the day to own "blacks," and Penn himself then was only interested in "regulating Negroes in their Morals and Marriages," and in "the regulations of their trials and punishments." His whole interest in the negro was, that "he should receive proper treatment while in bondage." In 1688, the German Friends were the first to protest to the Yearly Meeting against slavery of Negroes, but for fifty years, the Yearly Meeting went no further in the matter than to advise against buying newly imported Negroes, although Ralph Sandiford, a Philadelphia Friend, worked hard in 1730-40, with pamphlets and addresses to suppress slavery altogether in Pensylvania.

Of the second and much smaller "Welsh Tract" much has been printed, but there never seemed to be the same interest in it for the Land Commissioners, which they had in the first and greater, and, in fact, they had no particular reason to watch it, for its settlers made no singular claims, nor were many of its men remarkable in provincial affairs.

WELSH SETTLEMENT OF PENSYLVANIA

Of these "Gwynedd Welsh," it is said they "in general did not at first profess with the Quakers, [being "Baptists"], but afterwards they, with "many others" as the neighborhood increased, joined the religious society with them, and were an industrious, worthy people." One of the longest to be remembered was Ann Roberts, who died 4 June, 1750, aged 73 years, having been a minister among Friends for fifty years.

The nucleus of this second Welsh Tract was a large tract of land in the upper part of old Philadelphia county, owned by Robert Turner, and purchased by people from North Wales, and afterwards was generally known as "North Wales," and the "Gwynedd Settlement." This emigration Mr. Jenkins* places in 1698, and ascribes it to the influence of Hugh Roberts, the minister, who was in Wales the previous year; but why Hugh did not secure these settlers for the greater Welsh Tract, in which he was certainly more interested, rather than for Gwynedd tp., where he owned no land, is not apparent.

On 22 March, 1681, Penn granted by patent of this date, 5,000 acres of Pensylvania land to Robert Turner,† who,

---

*"Gwynedd" by Howard M. Jenkins (1884). P. 22.

† Mr. Turner, who became an important official in Philadelphia, had been frequently roughly handled for being a Quaker. In 1657, "being at Meeting in Londonderry, he was haled out and dragged along the streets by his Armes and Leggs, the Mayor of the City helping with his owne hands, and so turned him out of the City. And about two or three Dais after haled him again in like manner as before, and tied him upon a bare Horse Back with a Hair Rope, and so far their Sport, and Mocking led him at their Pleasure." But Mr. Turner's experience was not singular in Ireland, for there are hundreds of similar "sufferings" of Friends mentioned in the works of Fuller and Holme, (1671); "Sufferings of the People Call'd Quakers," (Dublin, 1731); Stockdale's "The Great Cry of Oppression," (1683); Wight, (1700), in his "History of the People Called Quakers," Dublin, 1751, and Myers's "Immigration of Irish Quakers into Pensylvania."

A score of Mr. Turner's deeds for lands to the Welsh at Gwynedd may be seen in Exemplification Book, No. 7, pp. 381, &c. Recorder's office, Philadelphia.

PLANTERS AND SERVANTS

with Robert Zane, and other Dublin Friends, six years before this, had been a grantee for tracts of West Jersey land, purchased from Friend Byllings, and had started the settlement of English speaking people in that country, which furnished William Penn with the idea for another such scheme for himself. Mr. Turner increased his holdings as follows:—

By deed, 8 Sep. 1685, he bought 2,500 acres which Penn had sold to John Gee, of King's Co., Ireland, and, 29. 7. 1685, 1,250 acres from Joseph Fuller, of King's Co., and 8 March, 1695, 1,250 acres from Jacob Fuller, of King's Co., making Turner's holding in Pensylvania 10,000 acres. Of this Penn confirmed to him 7,800 acres, laid out in Philadelphia County. By deed, 10. 1mo. 1698-9, Turner sold this tract to two Welshmen, William ap John and Thomas ap Evan, of Philadelphia, and they, by several deeds in 1699, sold this land to the following parties, who, on 25. 11mo. 1702, having had their parcels of land resurveyed, according to the order, to find "overplusage" for Penn, rendered the following statement, showing their correct acreage:—

	Acres.	Over.		Acres.	Over.
Ellis, or Da'd Pugh.	220	231	Edward Pugh.*	100	
Evan Hugh	100	110	Cadwall'dr ap Evan.	500	609
John Hugh	500	648	Owen ap Evan	400	538
John Humphrey	450	561	Rob't ap Hugh	200	232
Rob't ap Evan	5,005	1,034	William John	1,900	2,866
Edward Faulk	400	712	Thomas Evan	700	1,049
Robert Jones	500	720	William John	150	322
Robert Evan	200	250	Evan Robert	100	110
Evan ap Hugh.*	400	1,068	Hugh Griffith	200	376
David Pugh.*	200				

*"(Brothers, Evan holds all, other two dead.)"

It may be seen that the overplus on these 7,800 acres was 11,436 acres. No wonder that Penn had new surveys made of old grants. However, he allowed these unfortunates to purchase in all 2,846 acres of the "overs," and, in 11mo. 1702, these Welsh grantees, and their heirs, and those who had bought of them, obligated themselves to pay Penn

WELSH SETTLEMENT OF PENSYLVANIA

the amounts as below. This table also shows the amounts owing, or "continued," after a cash payment:—

	Obligation.	Continued.
Rob't John, Wm. John, Edw'd Faulk	£535.10. 8	£269. 5. 4
Tho. Evan, Cadw. ap Evan, Rob't ap Hugh	140.18.11	80. 7. 5
Owen ap Evan, Robert Evan	216. 5. 3	104. 2. 7
Robert Evan, Evan ap Hugh	134.12. 6	67. 8. 3
Jno. Humphrey, Jno. Hugh	75.00. 3	37.10. 2
Hugh Griffith & Son	22.17. 9	11. 8.10
Robert John		3.00. 0
Owen ap Evan		5.
William John, (Pd by Ja. Logan)		15.
Thomas Evan, (Pd by Ja. Logan)		10.
Robert Evan		10.
John Hugh		15.
Edward Faulk		10.
Evan Pugh		5.

In the latter end of the year 1698, the purchasers of these lands began removing to "North Wales." Among the early arrivals were Thomas, Robert, and Owen Evans, William Jones, Cadwalader Evans, 1664-1745, (an ancestor of Mr. Lewis Jones Levick, of Bala, as elsewhere), Hugh Griffith, John Hugh, &c., as in these lists. Some of these gentlemen subsequently purchased considerable land in the first, or great Welsh Tract, and removed there, having become Quakers, and intermarried with the Welsh pioneer families there, as may be seen in the following chart.

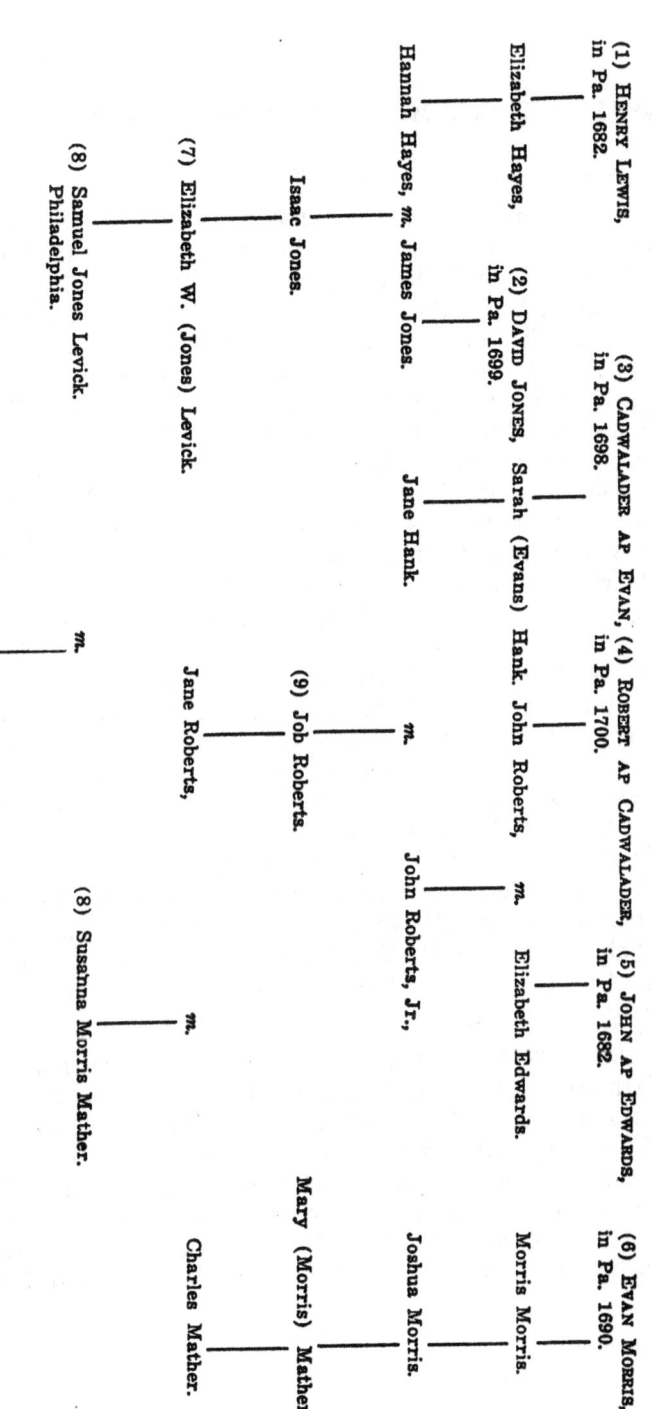

WELSH SETTLEMENT OF PENSYLVANIA

Notes to the aforesaid chart.

(1)—Some account of HENRY LEWIS, and his Welsh Tract land, has been given. He came with his wife Margaret, from Narbeth, Pembrokeshire, in 1682. In 1684, when still a member of the Philadelphia Monthly Meeting, he was of a committee appointed "to visit the poor and the sick, and administer what they should judge convenient, at the expense of the meeting." Besides being the foreman of the first Grand Jury of Philadelphia County, he was one of the three "peace makers," he being the representative from the Welsh Tract, appointed by the county court, an office created by act of assembly, at the second session. Their duty was to determine matters in litigation, and subject to appeal to Court; they were to prevent law suits if possible, and discourage litigation, and "to hear and end differences betwixt man and man." It has been said he was the beloved and trusted friend of William Penn. His daughter, Elizabeth, *b.* at Narbeth, 14. 12mo. 1677, married in 1697 Richard Hayes, Jr., who removed from Ilminston, Pembrokeshire, to Haverford, in 1687, with his parents. His mother, Isatt Hayes, is frequently mentioned in Haverford Monthly Meeting minutes as active in work among the Haverford Friends. Richard Hayes, Jr., was a justice of the court in Chester Co., and member of the Pensylvania Assembly for many years. His wife *d.* 25. 3mo. 1742, and the Philadelphia Quarterly Meeting has recorded the testimony respecting her:— "She was a faithful Elder among us for several years, a good example to the flock."

(2)—DAVID JONES removed from Wales with his wife Katherine and two children, about 1700, and bought 350 acres of land, located in Blockley tp., at Haverford road and 63d street. His sister, Ellen Jones, *m.* Robert Jones, of Merion, a son of John ap Thomas, the associate of Dr. Jones. He was a prominent Friend in both countries. The Friends' minister, William Edmundson, in his Journal (printed), mentions him. He brought his certificate from the Monthly Meeting at Hendri Mawr, dated 24. 12mo. 1699-00, signed by Robert Vaughan, Cadwalader Ellis, Evan Rees, Edward Ellis, Thomas Richards, Edward David, Owen Lewis, Ellis Lewis, Rowland Owen, Thomas Cadwalader, and John Robert. He also had a certificate from the men's meeting in Haverford West, dated 4. 1mo. 1699-00, and among the signers were Andrew Llewellyn, James Lewis, Peregrine Musgrave, Evan Bowen and John Roger. The records of the Haverford Monthly Meeting say of him, "he was one of the first appointed an Elder in the Haverford Meeting." He *d.* 27. 6mo. 1725, and was buried at the Merion Meeting House. His wife was also an active member of this meeting, being "an inspector of conversation," and a "visitor," and represented Haverford in the Quarterly Meeting. After her husband's death, she had a certificate from the Radnor Monthly Meeting to the Philadelphia Monthly Meeting, and *d.* 23. 5mo. 1764. Their Bible, "printed yn Llundian," 1678, records the births of James Lewis, on 8th mo. 10th, 1638, and "Katerin Lewis, ye 25th of 12th month 1640," who may have been the parents of David's wife, Katherine, who had a brother James Lewis, of Llanddewy, whose letters to her are extant. Their son James Jones, *b.* 31. 5mo. 1699, *d.* in Blockley tp. 27. 3mo. 1791, aged 92 years. He *m.* Hannah Hayes, at Haverford Meeting, 10. 8mo. 1727, and had Isaac Jones, who *m.* at Burlington (N. J.) Meeting 26. 11mo. 1778.

(3)—CADWALADER AP EVAN, mentioned elsewhere, came from Fron Gôch, Merionethshire, and died in the Gwynedd settlement, in 1745, age 81 years. He married in Wales, Ellen, daughter of John Morris, of Bryn Gwyn, and their daughter, Sarah Evans, married John Hank, of White Marsh, and had issue as mentioned before.

(4, 5, 9)—The ancestry of ROBERT ap CADWALADER is unknown. He was one of the early settlers of Gwynedd, and his son, John Roberts, who married Elizabeth, daughter of the Merion settler, (5) JOHN ap EDWARD, of whom

WELSH SETTLEMENT OF PENSYLVANIA

elsewhere, was the founder of the Roberts family of "Woodlawn" plantation, Whitpain tp., Montgomery Co., Pa., where seven successive generations of Roberts blood have resided. On this property is another stone mansion, erected in 1715, acccording to the date-stone, called "Woodlawn Farm," which was the home of (9) Job Roberts, who was known as "the Pensylvania farmer," and was the pioneer of scientific farming, on which subject he published a book in 1804. He was a magistrate for twenty-nine years. This family was also remarkable for longevity, as Job Roberts died aged 96 years, his father, John Jr., died at 90 years, and his grandfather, John Roberts, at 96 years.

(6)—EVAN MORRIS was an early settler in the Gwynedd district, and a prominent Friend. He and his wife, Gainor, brought certificates, dated 8. 5mo. 1690, from the Quarterly Meeting at Tyddyn y Garreg, Merioneth, filed with the Philadelphia Monthly Meeting. His son, Morris Morris, gave the land on which the Richland meeting house was built, and also endowed the Friends' school there, which many of his descendants attended. His wife, Susanna Heth, or Heath, was "an eminent minister in the Society of Friends."

(7)—ELIZABETH WETHERILL JONES, (wife of Ebenezer Levick, and mother of the Friends' minister, Samuel J. Levick), whose interesting "Recollections of Her Early Days," in Philadelphia, were printed in book-form, in 1881, was born at No. 17 Pine Street, Philadelphia, her parents' home, on 5. 6mo. 1789. She was the youngest child of Isaac Jones, and his wife, Mary Wetherill, (who is buried at the Merion Meeting House), married at the Burlington Meeting, 26. 11mo. 1778, and died at the home of her son, Dr. James Jones Levick, at 12th and Arch streets, Philadelphia, 21. 11mo. 1886, aged over 97 years and six months, and was buried in Friends' Southwestern Ground, Philadelphia. Dr.

Levick mentioned, was noted for his interest in the Welsh settlement of Pensylvania, and published many valuable articles about the settlers of "Merion in the Welsh Tract." He *d*. 25. 6mo. 1893, aged 69 years. She also had a son, William Manlove Levick, of Philadelphia, a lawyer.

(8)—SAMUEL JONES LEVICK, of Philadelphia, whose Life was written and published, in 1895, by Hugh Foulke, of Philadelphia, was the son of Ebenezer Levick, a Philadelphia merchant, and Elizabeth Wetherill Jones, married at the Pine Street Friends' Meeting, Philadelphia, 1. 5mo. 1816, and was born 30. 8mo. 1819. He was educated at the Friends' Westtown Boarding School, in Chester Co., and according to the memorial of him, prepared for the Philadelphia Monthly Meeting, and approved by the Quarterly Meeting, 2. 5mo. 1889, "he became a public ambassador for Christ in his twenty-first year, continuing in the work of the ministry for over forty-five years. His gift therein was acknowledged by the Richland Monthly Meeting in Fourth month, 1842, and confirmed by Abington Quarterly Meeting of ministers and elders, in Fifth month of the same year."

The memorial tells that Mr. Levick travelled much in the work of the Friends' ministry in all parts of the Union, and that "he was a man of strong and earnest convictions, and very plain and outspoken in the expressison of his views." "He was deeply interested in public affairs, both national and local, active in the work of organized charities in our city." At the time of his decease, he was the secretary of the Society for the Prevention of Cruelty to Animals. In early life, Mr. Levick became an active worker for the abolition of slavery, and was a member of the Junior Anti-Slavery Society. He was also a member of the "Peace Society" of Philadelphia, which, in January, 1839, took up the matter of forming a "Congress of Nations," in which such matters that led to war between nations could be peacefully adjusted, which is a prominent proposition of the present day. Mr. Levick died at his home in West Philadelphia on 19. 4mo. 1885, and was buried at the Merion meeting house, as he desired, when "testimonies were borne by several Friends in the ministry from different meetings," of both branches of the Society of Friends. He was twice married, first to Ellen, daughter of Caleb Foulke, at the Richland Friends' Meeting, on 3. 4mo. 1841; she died in 1842, and he married secondly, on 17. 10mo. 1844, Susanna Morris Mather, who died 9. 4mo. 1904, and was buried at the Merion meeting house. Mr. Levick had by his first wife an only child

Jane Foulke Levick, who *m.* first, Edwin A. Jackson, issue died young. She *m.* secondly, in Philadelphia, 17 Oct. 1910, William W. J. Cooke.

Mr. Levick by his second wife, Susanna Mather, who was the granddaughter of Isaac Mather (and Mary Morris), son of Richard (and Sarah Penrose), son of Joseph Mather and his wife, Elizabeth, only child of John Russell, who purchased several hundred acres of land from Penn, in 1683, in Cheltenham tp., much of which still remains with Mather descendants, had,—

1—Lewis Jones Levick, of Bala, and Philadelphia, *m.* Mary d'Invilliers, of Philadelphia, and had,—
  I. Henry Lewis Levick, of Bala.
  II. Mary Sabina Levick, *m.* Winthrop C. Neilson, of Philadelphia, and had Lewis Winthrop.
  III. Louise Jamart, wife of George B. Atlee.
  IV. Suzanne Levick, of Bala.

2—Charles Mather Levick, deceased. He *m.* Henrietta Wilson, his brother's widow. No issue.

3—Samuel Jones Levick, Jr., deceased. He *m.* Anna E. Bullock, and had,—
  I. Anna Lucile Levick, *m.* Dr. Deemer.
  II. Florence Levick, *m.* Joseph Sullivant.
  III. Elizabeth Wetherill Levick, *m.* William Hicks.

PLANTERS AND SERVANTS

4—William Ebenezer Levick, deceased. He *m.* Henrietta Wilson. No issue.

5—James Jones Levick, Jr., unmarried.

On an abandoned road, near Norristown, which was a short cut between the two Welsh settlements, was the little smithy of Ellis Robert, patronized by people we have heard of, as may be learned from his extant "Day Book," in which it is written that he bought it of Thomas Pugh, a Welshman, and a Philadelphia bookseller, on 21. 6mo. 1703. The blacksmith's first entry in it was on "ye 13th of ye 3rd month, 1703," when he records, "Cadwalader Morgan, dr. 1 day's harvest work, 3s. 6d." And "26th day of ye 4th month, 1703, Ellis David of Goshen, 1 day's work, 1 shilling." In 5th month, next, "For soying with Griffith Jones 12 hundred of Oak & Poplar, £1. 15s. 6d." "ye 18th day of ye 3 month, 1703, Cadwalader Jones dr. for 2 days' work, 3s. 4d." His account book runs into the year 1705, and he had customers of many kinds, and from various places, but principally North Wales inhabitants, and for these he repaired plows, sharpened hoes, mended implements, and harness, besides did some horse shoeing. Among his customers in these years were, Richard Pugh, Edward Jarman, John Williamson, Thomas Craffot, Samuel Brockes, Jacob Cofing, Hernell Cassel, John Good, Morris Roberts, the widow Clancy, John Michinar, Richard Blackham, Matthew Jones, David Hughes, John Meredith, Evan Griffith, William Thomas, John Welles, William Robert Ellis, Thomas Griffith, Rowland Richard, John Morgan, Thomas David, of Valley, John Evans, John Roberts, David Howel, Thomas Louis, John David Thomas, David Harvey Rees, William Thomas Hugh, Robert Williamson, of Goshen, Edward Watgin, John Davis, of ye Gulfe, and John Cadwalader, who "paid for the bell, 4s. 3d. Three pounds remain unpaid." John Cadwalader, who died in Oct. 1742, in the island of Tortola, W. I., where Thomas Chalkley died 4 Nov. 1741, was in debt to

WELSH SETTLEMENT OF PENSYLVANIA

another man, in the following item. The long will, all in Welsh, of Cadwalader David ap Hugh, of Gwynedd, dated 23 Nov. 1700, gives to Hugh ap Edward £18, and appoints brother Evan ap Hugh, and Edward Foulke to be guardians, and overseers. He had considerable money loaned out at interest, although he was a "workingman." Among his borrowers were John Cadwalader, Hugh William, David Evan, of Radnor, Hugh ap William, Edward Griffith, Robert Hugh, and Robert John, for whom he was working when the will was made.

NOBLE AND GENTLE
WELSH FAMILIES

SOME WELSH FRIENDS' PEDIGREES

It has already been remarked that the leading men of the Welsh barony were well educated gentlemen, or yeoman, men of good standing, affairs, and estates, in the neighborhoods whence they came to America, before 1700. Further, some of these were remarkable as to their pedigrees; a matter always carefully looked after and transmitted by Welsh gentlemen, as well as by people of refinement of other nationalities.

Under their ancient local laws, the Welsh in the old country, had good reason for keeping their pedigrees up-to-date. This was because fines and penalties could be levied on the distant relatives of guilty persons, if they were unable to pay. For instance, the "murder fine," (*galnas*), varied according to the status of the victim, and the murderer's kin to the fifth generation of his blood was liable for the payment of the fine. But in case of a mere "insult fine," (*sarhad*), the offender's blood kindred was bound only to the third generation, or third cousins. Then, again, the Welsh were divided into two distinct classes, based upon "pedigree." There were the *bonheddig*, those having a pedigree, men with a lineage (*nobilis*) of the best strain,—pure Cymro on both sides, paternal and maternal, entirely free from bondsman's blood, and even of that of a foreigner, or *alltud*. Of such were the gentlemen of Wales. In the "lower class," was the *taeog*, the villain or the serf; the farm-hand and the yeoman, a freeholder without the requisite "pedigree," and these were the most privileged, the *mab aillt*, of the unpedigreed.

Generally, the pedigrees of Welsh and Irish families are as uninteresting as those of biblical characters, being only strings of names of successive heirs, or successors,

WELSH SETTLEMENT OF PENSYLVANIA

without dates, places of habitation, or records of actions. But these following genealogies of a few of the prominent early planters of the Welsh Tract depart from the ancient method, the usual heir to heir line, and show these particular Welshmen and Welshwomen, Quakers all, to have been of distinguished lineages, and connected by blood with some of the great historic families of England, and being educated, refined men and women, moving from the homes of their forefathers into the wilds of a new country, and new experiences, they naturally brought their genealogies and family histories for the benefit of their descendants. That these Welsh Quakers did bring their pedigrees with them, or in a few years sent home for them, is not singular either, because it is a fact that other immigrants in other parts of the new country did the same, that is when they had any they were proud of, or supposed was worthy of transmission. Therefore, these Welsh Friends were Penn's peers socially by birth, and were not obscure families to whom he had sold his land, under certain promises and conditions, which they clearly recalled, but which he pretended to forget, and certainly ignored, and did not keep.

Robert Owen, Evan Owen, Owen Owen, Jane Owen, wife of Hugh Roberts, and John Cadwalader, identified with "Merion in the Welsh Tract," it appears were lineally descended from the royal houses of France, England, and Wales, in the following lines, as may be seen in Dwnn's Welsh pedigrees, or "Visitations," and Dugdale's "Baronage of England."

1.—HOWEL-DDA, King of all Wales, A. D. 948, had by his wife, Lady Jane, daughter of the Earl of Cornwall,

2.—OWEN, Prince of South Wales, who had by his wife, Lady Angharad, daughter of Llewellyn ap Mervyn, Prince of Powys,

3.—PRINCE EINION, eldest son, who m. Lady Nesta, daughter of the Earl of Devonshire, and had:

GENEALOGICAL DATA

4.—TUDOR-MAWR., Prince of South Wales, who had by his wife, Lady Gwenlian,

5.—RHYS, Prince of South Wales, who had by his wife, Lady Gwladys, daughter of Rhiwlalon, Prince of Powis,

6.—GRIFFITH, Prince of South Wales, who had by his wife, Lady Gwenlian, daughter of Griffith ap Cynan, Prince of North Wales,

7.—RHYS, "Prince of South Wales," who, as "Lord Rhys," was the chief justice of South Wales (see Burke's "Ancestry of the Royal House of Tudor"). He had by his wife, Lady Gwenlian, daughter of Madoc, feudal lord of Bromfield,

8.—RHY-GRYD, feudal lord of Yestradtywy. He m. Lady Joan, daughter of Richard de Clare*, fourth Earl of Hertford, &c., one of the celebrated twenty-five Sureties for the Magna Charta, 1215, and had:

9.—RHYS-MECHYLLT, feudal lord of Llandovery Castle, whose son,

10.—RHYS-VAUGHN, was feudal lord of Yestradtywy. He m. Lady Gwladys, daughter and heiress of Griffith, feudal lord of Cymcydmaen, and had:

11.—RHYS-GLOFF, who succeeded to the estate of his maternal grandfather. He m. Lady Gwyrryl, daughter of Maelywn ap Cadwalader, and had:

12.—MADOC, who had, by his wife Tanglwyst, daughter of Gronowy ap Einion,

13.—TRAHAIRN-GOCH, lord of Llyn, Grainianoc, and Penl-

---

*This RICHARD, Earl of Hertford, was the son of ROGER, third Earl of Hertford, second son of RICHARD, de Clare, created Earl of Hertford, son of Gilbert de Tonsburg, in Normandy, by his wife, Lady ADELIZA, daughter of Hugh de Monchi, 2d Count of Clermont, and his wife, Lady MARGUERITE, daughter of Hildwin IV., Count of Montdidier, lord of Rameru, &c., and Count de Rouci, by his wife, ADELA, Countess de Rouci, daughter and heiress of Eblo I., Count of Rouci and Reims, and his wife, Lady BEATRIX, daughter of Rainier IV., eleventh Count of Hainault, by his wife, Princess HAVIDE, daughter of HUGH CAPET, KING OF FRANCE, 940-996.

WELSH SETTLEMENT OF PENSYLVANIA

lech, who had by his wife, Lady Gwyrryl, daughter of Madoc ap Meirig,

14.—DAVID-GOCH, lord of Penllech, in 1314. He *m.* Maud, daughter of David Lloyd ap Cyrveloc (see Browning's "Americans of Royal Descent," fourth edition, p. 95, for his pedigree), and had:

15.—IEVAN, lord of Grainianoc and Penllech, in 1352. He *m.* Eva, daughter of Einion ap Celynnin, of Llwydiarth, Montgomeryshire, a lineal descendant of Bleddyn Cynfyn, king of Powis, 1046, and had:

16.—MADOC, lord of Grainianoc, or Grainoc, whose son,

17.—DEIKWS-DDU, had by his wife, Gwen, daughter of Ievan-ddu, a lineal descendant of Maelor-crwm, chieftain of the seventh Royal Tribe of Wales, in 1175,

18.—EINION, lord of Grainoc, who *m.* Morvydd, daughter of Matw ap Llowarch, and had:

19.—HOWEL, who *m.* Mali, daughter of Llewellyn ap Ievan, and had:

20.—GRIFFITH, who *m.* Gwenlian, daughter of Einion ap Ievan Lloyd, and had:

21.—LEWIS, lord of Yshute, who *m.* Ethli, or Ellan, daughter of Edward ap Ievan, of Llanoddyn, parish Montgomeryshire, by his wife, Catharine v. Gryflyth Llewellyn Einion ap David, the feudal baron of Cryniarth, in Edermon, also of Royal Descent, and had:

22.—ROBERT, lord of Rhiwlas, who *m.* Gwyrryl, daughter of Llewellyn ap David, of Llan Rwst, in Denbighshire, and had:

23.—EVAN ROBERT LEWIS, of Vron Goch farm, Merioneth, lord of Rhiwlas, by his wife Jane, five sons, Owen, Evan, John, Cadwalader, and Griffith. Of these:

1.—OWEN AP EVAN, of Vron Goch farm, *d.* 1669, had by his wife, Gainor John,

GENEALOGICAL DATA

I.—ROBERT OWEN, 1657-1697, who m., 1678, Rebecca Humphrey (see below), and removed in 1690 to Merion, as mentioned elsewhere.†

II.—JANE OWEN, who m. Hugh Roberts*, the Friends' minister, and removed to Merion, as already mentioned, p. 96, &c.

III.—ELLEN OWEN, 1660-169-, who m. Cadwalader Thomas Hugh, of Kiltalgarth, Merioneth, and had:

JOHN CADWALADER, who m. at the Merion Meeting, 29 Dec., 1699, Martha Jones, see p. 74.

IV.—EVAN OWEN, a Welsh Tract land owner.

V.—OWEN OWEN, a Welsh Tract land ower.

---

†Among the prominent descendants of Robert and Rebecca Owen are: Mrs. Clement Acton Griscom, Mrs. J. C. W. Frishmuth, Mrs. Arthur V. Meigs, Mrs. Charles Williams, Mrs. Walter S. Wyatt, Mrs. Howard Wood, Alexander Biddle, Abraham L. Smith, Mrs. George M. Conarroe, Benj. Hayes Smith, Mrs. Lewis Allair Scott, Mrs. Moncure Robinson, Jr., Mrs. Eugene Blackford, Mrs. Arthur E. Poultney, John Barclay Biddle, Mrs. Andrew A. Blair, Alex. Williams Biddle, Jr., Charles Meigs Biddle, Arthur Biddle, Mrs. John B. Thayer, Mrs. William D. Winsor, Mrs. William R. Philler, Mrs. Samuel Bettle, Mrs. Clement S. Phillips, Mrs. Daniel F. Shaw, Mrs. James D. Winsor, Algernon S. Roberts, Mrs. Edward Browning, Sr., John Browning Clement, Thomas Allen Glenn, Mrs. Charles C. Royce, Thomas Dunlap, Jr., Marquise de Potesdad Fornari, Henry Williams Biddle, James Wilmer Biddle, Princess d'Aragon, Mrs. de Grasse Fox, Rodman Wister.

*Their son *Roberts Roberts* (see p. 102), d. in Calvert Co., Md., 11 Nov. 1728. He m. secondly, 3 Dec. 1703, Priscilla, b. 21 Mar., 1681, d. 16 Apr. 1725, dau. of Richard and Elizabeth (Kensey) Johns, and had ten children by her. Of these:—*Elizabeth* m. Edward Parrish, Jr., see below; *Isaac*, b. 4 Feb. 1711, m. Hannah Paschall; *Patience*, b. 1 Feb. 1725, m. 1, Samuel Gray, m. 2, Isaac Howell; and

Richard Roberts, b. 21 Nov. 1706, m. Elizabeth, dau. of Benjamin and Elizabeth (Tongue) Allen. Of their children:—*Richard*, b. 10 Apr. 1735, m. 29 May, 1770, Mary (Thomas) Harris (for descendants, see Mackenzie's "Colonial Families," p. 438); *Hugh*, b. 26 Jan. 1745, m. Hannah West Moore; *Elizabeth* m. Thomas Tongue, and

Robert Roberts, b. 12 Jan. 1741-2, d. 18 June, 1791; m. 6 Apr. 1773, Catherine, dau. of David and Mary (Le Fèvre) Deshler, and had, *Elizabeth*, 1781-1868, m. 19 May, 1803, James Canby, 1781-1858, of Wilmington, Del. *Issue.*

WELSH SETTLEMENT OF PENSYLVANIA

2.—EVAN AP EVAN† of Vron Goch farm, Merionethshire, who had:

I.—THOMAS EVANS,‡ 1651-1738, removed to Gwynedd.
II.—ROBERT EVAN. removed to Gwynedd, *d.* in 1738.
III.—OWEN EVANS, 1659-1723, removed to Gwynedd.
IV.—CADWALADER EVANS, 1664-1745, removed to Gwynedd in 1698. He *m*, Ellin, daughter of John Morris, of Bryn Gwyn, Denbighshire, by his wife, Ellin, daughter of Ellis Williams, of Caifadog, also of Royal Descent, and had:

SARAH EVANS, who *m.* at the Gwynedd Meeting, 11, 10mo. 1711, John Hank, of White Marsh, will dated 12 Dec. 1730, proved in May, 1731, and had besides other children:

1.—JOHN HANK, JR., *b.* 1712, who sold his farm near Reading, Pa., in 1787, and removed eventually to Fayette Co., Ky., where his daughter, NANCY, *m.* Thomas Lincoln, and settled in Larue Co., Ky., and here was born their only child, ABRAHAM LINCOLN, twice President of the United States.

Edward and Elizabeth (Roberts) Parrish, aforesaid, had
John Parrish, who *m.* Mary, his cousin, dau. of Edward Roberts, p. 154 (son of Hugh Roberts, p. 103), and had *Mary*, *m.* Stephen Collins, and had *Elizabeth m.* Richard Bland Lee (son of Col. Henry Lee, and his wife Lucy Grymes, also of Royal Descent, see Browning's "Americans of Royal Descent," fourth edition, p. 724, and seventh edition, Pedigree CXIII), and had *Zaccheus Collins Lee*, who *m*, Martha A. Jenkins, and had *Richard Henry Lee*, only son, *m.* Isabella George Wilson, and had *Richard H., J. Collins; Robert E.*, and *Elizabeth Collins Lee*, of Baltimore.

Also descended from Hugh and Jane Roberts are Henry C. Baird, Mrs. Louis Starr, and Mrs. Edward T. Canby.

†Among his descendants are Allen Childs, Mrs. Levin Hill Jackson, Miss Helen Erben, Jacob Sperry Willing, and John M. Whitall, Jr.

‡Descended from Thomas Evans's son Hugh, and wife Lowry, are Mrs. Jawood Lukens, Mrs. Howard Comfort, Mrs. Robert R. Corson, Mrs. Geo. Mason Chichester, Mrs. Edgar W. Baird, and Mrs. Charles P. Keith.

GENEALOGICAL DATA

2.—JANE HANK, who *m.* John Roberts, Jr., of "Woodlawn," Penllyn, and had, JOB ROBERTS, of "Woodlawn," who *m.* Mary Naylor, and had JANE, who *m.* Charles Mather, of "Woodlawn," and had, SUSANNA MORRIS, who *m.* Samuel Jones Levick, of Philadelphia, for many years a well-known minister among Friends, and had, besides other children, LEWIS JONES LEVICK, of Bala, who *m.* Mary d'Invilliers, of Philadelphia and had Henry Lewis; Mary Sabina, wife of Winthrop C. Neilson; Louise Jamart, wife of George B. Atlee, and Suzanne.

The Humphreys family, Rowland Ellis, of "Bryn Mawr" farm, and Rebecca Humphreys, wife of Robert Owen, of Merion, were descended as follows from the Royal Houses of England and France.

1.—HENRY III., KING OF ENGLAND, *m.* Lady Eleanor, daughter of Raymond de Berenger, Count of Provence, and had by her:

2.—EDMUND, Earl of Leicester, lord high steward, who had by his second wife, Lady Blanche, widow of Henry I., of Navarre, and daughter of Robert, Count of Artois, second son of LOUIS VIII, King of France:

3.—HENRY, Earl of Leicester and Lancaster, who *m.* Lady Maud, daughter of Sir Patrick de Chaworth, by his wife, Lady Isabel de Beauchamp, daughter of William, first Earl of Warwick, also of Royal Descent, and had:

4.—LADY ELEANOR PLANTAGENET, who *m.* secondly (his second wife), Sir Richard Fitzalah, K. G., Earl of Arundel and Surrey, and had:

5.—SIR RICHARD FITZALAN, K. G., Earl of Arundel, who had by his first wife, Lady Elizabeth de Bohun, daughter of William, first Earl of Northampton, K. G., also of Royal Descent:

6.—LADY ELIZABETH FITZALAN, who had by her third husband, Sir Robert Goushill, Kt., of Hault Hucknell manor, Derbyshire:

WELSH SETTLEMENT OF PENSYLVANIA

7.—LADY JOAN GOUSHILL, who *m.* Sir Thomas Stanley, K. G., Lord Stanley, lord chamberlain of England, and had:

8.—LADY MARGARET STANLEY (her brother, Sir William, crowned Henry VII. on Bosworth Field), who had by her second husband (see Dugdale's "Baronage," vol. II., p. 248), Sir William Troutbeck, lord of Prynes Castle, Cheshire, who was slain in the battle of Bloreheath:

9.—LADY JANE TROUTBECK (see Omerod's "Cheshire," vol. II., Collins's "Peerage," III., p. 40), widow of Sir William Boteler, who *m.* Sir William Griffith, lord of Penrhyn Castle, Caernarvonshire, chamberlain of North Wales, "made a Knight of the Bath on St. Andrew's Eve, 1489, at the coronation of Prince Arthur, and of his Bayne," and had:

10.—SIR WILLIAM GRIFFITH, lord of Penrhyn Castle, knighted at Touraine, Christmas, 1513, "after the king came from mass, under the banner in the church"; chamberlain of North Wales, 1520. He had by his second wife, *m.* in 1522, Lady Jane, daughter of John Puleston, lord of Caernarvan Castle (see Dwnn's "Visitations of Wales," vol. II., 154-59, or Pedigree CXLIX):

11.—LADY SIBILL GRIFFITH, who *m.* Owen ap Hugh, of Bodeon, high sheriff of Anglesea in 1563, and 1580, *d.* 1613, and had:

12.—JANE OWEN, who *m.* Hugh Gwyn, of Penarth, high sheriff of Caernarvonshire, in 1600 (see Dwnn's "Visitations of Wales," II. 172), and had:

13.—SIBILL HUGH, who *m.* before 20 Sep. 1588, John ap Howel-goch, of Gadfa, Llanwddyn, Montgomeryshire, who was buried in the parish church, 24 July, 1636, and had:

14.—ELIZABETH POWELL, who *m.* Humphrey ap Hugh Howel, of Llwyn-du, Llangelynin, in Merionethshire, *d.* 1664-5, and had:

1.—OWEN HUMPHREY, of Llwyn-du, eldest son, 1625-1699, a justice in 1678. He had by his wife Jane,

GENEALOGICAL DATA

Rebecca Humphrey, who m. in 1678, Robert Owen, of Vron Goch farm, and removed to Merion in 1690, as mentioned above.

2.—Samuel Humphrey, of Portheven, Merionethshire, who bought land in Haverford and removed here in 1683, but died in Wales. He m. in 1658, Elizabeth Rees, and had eight children,* who settled in Haverford with their mother.

3.—John Humphrey, who m. his cousin, Jane Humphrey (sister to Richard Humphrey, who was a Haverford land owner), and bought land in Haverford, and removed to it.

4.—Anne Humphrey, who m. Ellis ap Rees Lewis, or Ellis Price, of Bryn Mawr, in Merionethshire, 1649, also of Royal Descent, as explained in another page, and had:

Rowland Ellis, 1650-1729, of "Bryn Mawr" farm, in the Welsh Tract. His daughter Eleanor, m. in 1715, John Evans,† of Gwynedd, also of Royal Descent as above.

5.—Daughter (name not preserved), m. Owen ap ———, and had the following children who removed to the Welsh Tract.

I.—Elizabeth Owen, second wife of "John Roberts, of Wayn Mill," Merion, d. 1703-4, who removed from Pen y Chyd, or Clwyd, in Denbighshire.

II.—John Owen, a land owner in Merion in 1683-1703.

III.—Joshua Owen, a land owner in Merion, unmarried in 1683-1703.

---

*One of his children, Daniel Humphreys, m. Hannah, daughter of Dr. Thomas Wynne, and from them descended Joshua Humphreys, a celebrated naval constructor, Mrs. Thomas Stewardson, William Penn Humphreys, &c.

†Among their numerous prominent descendants are Mrs. John Henry Livingston, Gouveneur Morris Ogden, Mrs. Alfred T. Mahan, Glendower Evans, Howland Evans, Allen Evans, Edmund Cadwalader Evans, Hartman Kuhn Evans, Mrs. Charles Mather, Mrs. Franklin T. Haines, William Elbert Evans, Mrs. Henry S. Huidekoper, William W. Erwin, Manlius Glendower Evans, Cadwalader Evans Ogden, David B. Ogden, Cadwalader Evans, &c.

WELSH SETTLEMENT OF PENSYLVANIA

John Bevan, another of the prominent Welsh Tract land owners and settlers, also had ancient and distinguished lineage; one of his ancestral lines showing his lineal descent from kings of England and France, as follows:

1.—HENRY III., KING OF ENGLAND, had:

2.—EDMUND, Earl of Leicester, who had:

3.—HENRY, Earl of Leicester, who had:

4.—LADY ELEANOR PLANTAGENET, who m. secondly (as in the "Humphrey" Royal Descent, above), Sir Richard Fitzalan, K. G., Earl of Arundel and Surrey, and had:

5.—JOHN FITZALAN, Lord Maltravers, second son, d. 15 Dec. 1379. He m. Lady Eleanor Maltravers, d. 20 Jan. 1405, granddaughter and sole heir to John, Lord Maltravers, and had:

6.—JOHN FITZALAN, feudal lord of Arundel, heir, but d. v. p. His youngest son, brother to the twelfth Earl of Arundel,

7.—SIR THOMAS FITZALAN, Knt., m. Lady Katherine, daughter of Sir John Dynham, and sister to Sir John, Lord Dynham, K. G., and had:

8.—LADY ELEANOR FITZALAN, who m. Sir Thomas Browne, treasurer of the household to King Henry VI., and had:

9.—SIR ANTHONY BROWNE, standard-bearer to King Henry VII., whose daughter,

10.—LADY ELIZABETH BROWNE, m. Henry Somerset, second Earl of Worcester, d. 26 Nov. 1549, and had:

11.—LADY ELEANOR SOMERSET, who m. Sir Roger Vaughan, Knt., of Porthaml, Talgarth, Glamorganshire, and had:

12.—WATKIN VAUGHAN, of Porthaml, Talgarth, who m. Joan, daughter of Evan ap Gwilim Yohan, of Peytyn Gwyn, and had:

GENEALOGICAL DATA

13.—SIR WILLIAM VAUGHAN, of Porthaml, Talgarth, Knt., d., 1564, who *m.* Catharine, daughter of Jenkin ap Havard, of Tredomen, and had:

14.—CATHARINE VAUGHAN, who *m.* David ap Evan, of Neath, high sheriff of Glamorganshire, in 1563, and had:

15.—MARY DAVID EVAN (widow of Edward Tuberville, of Sutton), who *m.* secondly, Thomas Basset, of Miscin, and had:

16.—CATHARINE BASSET, who *m.* Richard ab Evan, of Collenna, Glamorganshire, and had:

17.—JANE EVANS, who *m.* Evan ab John, of Treverigg, Llantrisant parish, Glamorgan, and had:

18.—JOHN BEVAN (John ab Evan), who removed from Treverigg, in 1683, to the Welsh Tract, with his wife, Barbara Awbrey, and family.*

Edward Rees, and his sisters, Hannah, wife of Rees John William, or Rees Jones, and Jane, wife of Cadwalader Morgan, all of "Merion in the Welsh Tract," were also of distinguished ancestry through their father's family, as follows:

1.—JOHN, KING OF ENGLAND, had by his second wife, Lady Isabella Taillefer, daughter of Ademar, Count of Angouleme.

2.—LADY ELEANOR PLANTAGENET, who *m.* secondly, Simon de Montfort, Earl of Leicester, and had,

3.—LADY ELEANOR DE MONTFORT, who *m.* Llewellyn Gryffyth, Prince of North Wales, and the last sovereign Prince

---

*Among the prominent descendants of John Bevan are John W. Jordan, LL.D., Hon. Samuel W. Pennypacker, Annesley R. Govett, Mrs. John Thomas Bell, Charles W. Sparhawk, Mrs. Duncan L. Buzby, Mrs. Thomas McKean, Mrs. Arthur Dudley Cross, of San Francisco; James Aull, Walter Bevan, Henry Clay Pennypacker, Henry Clay Bevan, Aubrey Bevan, Robert Annesley Govett, Isaac R. Pennypacker, Francis Jordan, Jr., Walter Jordan, William E. Bevan, and Andrew J. Bevan, Francis K. Wainwright, Clement R. Wainwright.

WELSH SETTLEMENT OF PENSYLVANIA

of all Wales, killed on 11 Dec. 1232, son of Llewellyn the Great, and had,

4.—LADY CATHERINE, heiress, who *m.* Philip ap Ivor, lord of Iscoed, in Cardigan, and had,

5.—LADY ELEANOR, heiress, who *m.* Thomas ap Llewellyn Owen, of Trefgarned, lord of South Wales, and had,

6.—LADY ELEANOR, co-heiress, who *m.* (see Burke's "Royal Families," vol. 1. Ped. LII), Gryffyth Vychan, fourth lord of Glyndyfrdwy, whose descent from Bleddyn Cynfyn, King of Powys, 1046, is in Ped. CX. Burke's "Royal Descents," and "Royal Families," II. p. LXI, see also Lloyd's "History of Powys Fadog," vol. IV. 118, and had,

7.—TUDOR AP GRYFFYTH VYCHAN, lord of Gwyddelwern, killed 15 May, 1405, brother to the celebrated Owen Glendower. He *m.* Maud, daughter of Ieuf Howel ap Adar, and had,

8.—LADY LOWRY TUDOR, heiress, who *m.* Gruffydd ap Einion, of Cors y Gedol, Merionethshire, and had,

9.—ELLISSAU AP GRUFFYDD, who *m.* Margaret, daughter of Jenkin ap Ievan (also descended from Kings of England), and his wife, Leiki, daughter of Llewellyn ap Edneyfed, of Sonby, in Maelor, and had,

10.—LOWRY, who *m.* Reinaullt Gruffydd ap Rhys, of Branas Uchaf, Llan Drillo Plas Ynghrogen (see Dwnn's "Visitations of Wales," II. 126), and had,

11.—MARY, who *m.* Robert Lloyd, of Gwern y Brechtwyn, and Glanllyn, also of Royal Descent, and had,

12.—THOMAS LLOYD, 1520-1612, of Nant y Friar, who *m.* Catherine, daughter of Robert ap Griffith, by his wife, Margaret, daughter of Cadwalader ap Rhys Lloyd, of Cydros, and had, Evan, 1555-1640, and

13.—MARY LLOYD, who *m.* Richard, of Tyddyn Tyfod, Merioneth, and had,

14.—RHYS AP RICHARD, whose son,

GENEALOGICAL DATA

15.—GRIFFITH AP RHYS, of Tyddyn Tyfod, was the father of

16.—RICHARD PRESS, of Glanlloidiogin, Llanfawr parish, Merionethshire, will dated 26 Jan. 1685-6, proved at St. Asaph registry, in 1686. His daughter,

1.—HANNAH PRICE, b. 1656, who was mentioned with her children in her father's will. She m. Rees ap John ap William, or Rees Jones, who d. in Merion, 26, 11mo. 1697. Their children assumed "Jones" as their surname.*

2.—EDWARD REES, of Merion, 1682.

3.—JANE, wife of Cadwalader Morgan, of Merion, 1683.

The above pedigree is partly made up from a quaint letter, extant but undated, and unsigned, but apparently written by a friend, or relative in Wales to Edward Prees, or a member of his family, who had curiosity about his forefathers. Much of it is faded and undecipherable.

"My old friend, Edward Prees, hath w   in his letter to Thomas Lloyd, requesting to send him some intelligence of his Pedigree. I know but little thereof at this time but give him this much while he stays for more. Edward Prees son of Richard son of Griffith son of Re   no more than this of his Father's side these were own   of that Land where you have seen William ap Robert   and the name of that land is Tyddin Tyfod. And the mother of Rees Princhard was Mary the D   Thomas son of Robert David Lloyd the son of D   Vaughan son of

---

*Their daughter, Lowry Jones, 1682-1762, m. first, Robert Lloyd, of Merion, d. 1714, and was the third wife of Hugh Evans, of Merion, 1682-1772 (also of Royal Descent), m. 13 Feb. 1716, by whom she had Susanna Evans, 1719-1801, who m. 30 May, 1740, Owen Jones, Sr., of Merion, 1711-1793, also of Royal Descent (an ancester of Mr. Rodman Wister of Philadelphia), son of Johnathan Jones, of Merion, 1680-1770 (and grandson of Dr. Edward Jones, of Merion, and greatgrandson of Dr. Thomas Wynne of Merion), and his wife, m. at the Merion Meeting, 4 Oct. 1705, Gainor Owen, daughter of Robert Owen and Rebecca (both of Royal Descent), of Merion, their daughter, Hannah Jones, 1749-1829, m. 1779, Amos Foulke, 1740-1791, of Philadelphia, also of Royal Descent, *Issue.*

WELSH SETTLEMENT OF PENSYLVANIA

Griffith son of Evan Son of Madock the son of Ierwith the son of Madock Flidd of Glan y Llyn these followed further by Ann John Vaughan of Mein y .The mother of Mary the daughter of Thomas lloyd of Gwern y Brychdwyn was Catharine the daughter of Robert the son of Griffith the son of Coch the son of Ddu the son of David the son of Einion the son of Canwrig Vaughan the son of Canwrig the son of Heilin the son of Tyvid the son of Tago the son of Ystwyth the son of Marchwyth the son of Marcheithian of the fifteen tribes of Gwynedd North Wals from the Lord Is Aled.

The mother of Catharine vch Robert was Margaret the daughter of Cadwallader son of Rees Lloyd of Cydros lineally descending from Enion Ardudwy, the mother of Robert the son of Griffith was married the daughter of Tudor the son of Ewan lloyd of the Upper Plasin Llanfair. The mother of Griffith the son of Evan the son of Coch was Gwenhwyfir the daughter of Thomas David of the Court in Fenel Hill.

Lineally ing from the Lady Dulas Gray. The mother as, the son of Robert Lloyd of Gwern Brychwyn the dau of Raynold, the son of Griffith the of Upper Branas, the mother of Richard Griffith llian, the daughter of Rees of the House where wen Lived."

The brothers Charles Lloyd, (who did not come over), and Thomas Lloyd, the deputy-governor, large land owners in the Welsh Tract, also had remarkable ancestry, in part as follows,

1.—EDWARD I., KING OF ENGLAND, had by his second wife, Princess Margaret, daughter of PHILIP III., KING OF FRANCE,

2.—EDMUND, Earl of Kent, who m. Lady Margaret, daughter of John, Lord Wake, and had,

3.—LADY JOAN PLANTAGENET, the Fair Maid of Kent, (who was the mother of King Richard II., by her third hus-

GENEALOGICAL DATA

band, Edward the Black Prince), *m.* secondly, Sir Thomas de Holand, K.G., Earl of Kent, captain-general of Brittany, France and Normandy, and had,

4.—Sir Thomas de Holand, K.G., second Earl of Kent, earl marshal of England, who *m.* Lady Alice, daughter of Sir Richard Fitzalan, K.G., Earl of Arundel and Surrey, *d.* 1357, and had,

5.—Lady Alianore de Holand, widow of Roger, Earl of March, who *m.* secondly, Sir Edward de Cherleton, K.G., fourth Lord Cherleton, of Powys castle, *d.* 1420, and had,

6.—Lady Joan de Cherleton, who *m.* Sir John de Grey, K.G., created in 1418, Earl of Tancarville, killed at battle of Baugy Bridge, 1420, and had,

7.—Sir Henry de Grey, second Earl of Tancarville, *d.* 1449, who *m.* Lady Antigone, daughter of Humphrey, Duke of Gloucester, regent of France, and had,

8.—Lady Elizabeth de Grey, who *m.* Sir Roger Kynaston, *d.* 1517, and had,

9.—Humphrey Kynaston, of Morton, Salop, *d.* 1534, who *m.* Elizabeth, daughter of Meredith ap Howell, of Llansilin, Denbighshire, and had,

10.—Margaret Kynaston, who *m.* John Lloyd Wynn, of Dyffryn, (son of Evan Lloyd, of Dolobran), and had,

11.—Humphrey John Lloyd, of Dyffryn, whose daughter,

12.—Katherine Lloyd, *m.* John Lloyd, of Coediowrid, 1575-164-, a magistrate at Dolobran, also of Royal Descent, and had,

13.—Charles Lloyd, 1613-1657, of Dolobran Hall, Meifod parish, Montgomeryshire, a magistrate, who *m.* Elizabeth, daughter of Thomas, son of Sir Stanley, Knt., of Knockyn, in Salop, and had,

WELSH SETTLEMENT OF PENSYLVANIA

14.—CHARLES LLOYD, of Dolobran Hall, and Dep. Gov. Thomas Lloyd,* the Welsh Tract land owners.

Martha Awbrey, who came over with the family of John Bevan, "being engaged to be married to one Rees Thomas, who had gone to Pensylvania," and married him at the Haverford Meeting, 18 April, 1692, was also one of the early settlers of Merion, who had a remarkable pedigree, as follows,

1.—GRUFFYDD AP CYNAN, KING OF NORTH WALES, *d.* 1136, had a daughter,

2.—LADY GWENLLIAN, sister of Owen, Prince of Wales, who *m.* Rhys ap Tewdwr, Prince of South Wales, and had,

---

*Some of the prominent descendants of Deputy Governor Thomas Lloyd: Mrs. George Emlen, Jr., Miss Ellen Emlen, Mrs. Richard Vaux, Thomas Wister, M.D., Mrs. Travis Cochran, Mrs. Richard Willing, Mrs. Richard H. Reeve, Mrs. Benjamin C. Reeve, Mrs. Augustus W. Durkee, Samuel B. Wheeler, Edward Shippen Willing, Countess Emily de Ganay, Mrs. Alexander C. Fergusson, Mrs. Charles C. Harrison, Mrs. S. Bowman Wheeler, Frank L. Neall, Clement A. Griscom, Countess Ellen van Cuelebroeck, Mrs. Stiles Huber, Preston Carpenter, Mrs. Andrew Wheeler, Mrs. Charles E. Noblit, Mrs. John Jacob Astor, Hon. Lloyd C. Griscom, Mrs. Charles F. Hulse, Mrs. Malcolm Lloyd, Mrs. Robert B. Haines, Henry H. Collins, Jr., Richard M. Gummere, Mrs. Philip Trapnill Allin, Woodruff Jones, Mrs. James S. Merritt, Mrs. Frank N. Hickok, Henry Morris, M.D., William Morris Collins, Mrs. Ludwig Wilhelmi, Edward Hacker, Mrs. Thomas S. K. Morton, Mrs. Henry Carey Baird, Mrs. Charles J. Churchman, Mrs. John B. Bispham, Charles Ellet, John Jay Smith, Samuel Rhoads, M.D., Mrs. Philip B. Chase, Benj. Raper Smith, Mrs. James B. Morson, Adm. Louis M. Goldsborough, Henry Ewing Pope, William J. Wainwright, Mrs. William H. Gardiner, Robert H. McClenachan, Mrs. Edward K. Rowland, Mrs. James A. Lowell, Mrs. Burnet Landreth, Jr., Mrs. Levi Morris, Mrs. Charles E. Smith, Rt. Rev. Benj. W. Morris, Mrs. William J. Hardy, Jr., Mrs. John Lowell, Jr., Mrs. Walter Abbott Wood, Mrs. Jacob Shoemaker Waln, Edward Waln, Mrs. Richard B. Jackson, Mrs. Nathaniel Burwell Marshall, Isaac Norris, Charles Perrin Smith, Mrs. Charles Wilson Peale, Mrs. C. Emory McMichael, Mrs. Tench Francis Joseph Parker Norris, Daniel Clark Wharton.

GENEALOGICAL DATA

3.—LADY ELIZABETH, who *m.* Edmund, feudal lord of Cayrowe, and had,

4.—SIR EDGAR DE CAREW, lord of Cayrowe, who had,

5.—JOHN DE CAREW, feudal lord of Carew, whose daughter,

6.—ANNE DE CAREW (also called Nesta), *m.* Thomas Awbrey, son of William Awbrey, of Aberkynfrig and Slough, in Brecknockshire, and had,

7.—THOMAS AWBREY, of Aberkynfrig, constable, and ranger of the forest of Brecon. He *m.* Johan, daughter of Trahaerne ap Einion, lord of Comond, and had,

8.—THOMAS AWBREY-GOCH, of Aberkynfrig, who *m.* Nesta, daughter of Owen Gethyn, of Glyn Taway, and had,

9.—RICHARD AWBREY, of Aberkynfrig, who *m.* Creislie, daughter of Philip ap Elidor ("Phe ab Elerd"), and had,

10.—GWALTER AWBREY, of Aberkynfrig, second son. He *m.* Johan, daughter and co-heiress of Rees Morgan, of Llangadog, Carmarthenshire,* and had,

11.—MORGAN AWBREY, of Aberkynfrig, who *m.* Alice, daughter of Gwatkin Thomas ap David Lloyd, and had,

12.—JENKIN AWBREY, of Aberkynfrig, who *m.* Gwenllian, daughter of Owain ap Griffith, of Tal y Llyn, and had,

13.—HOPKIN AWBREY, of Aberkynfrig, who *m.* Anne, daughter of John ap Griffith, of Gwyn, and had,

---

*His pedigree (see Libscome's "Buckinghamshire," vol. I. p. 67) compiled in 1681, was as follows:

ALFRED, KING OF DUBLIN, *m.* Lady Eva, daughter of Dermot, King of Leinster, and had,

SUTTRICK, King of Dublin, who *m.* Lady Nesta, daughter of Theodore-mawr, Prince of South Wales, and had,

IDEO WYLLT, Lord of Clwye, in Brecon, who came out of Ireland into Wales with a band of soldiers to the assistance of Rees ap Theodore against the Normans." He *m.* Eleanore, daughter of Drympenog, lord of Cantre Seliffe, and had,

"CADWGAN HEN, Esq., descended from Ideo," whose son,

"GRIFFITH AP CADWGAN, lord of Llangadog, Esq.," had, CADWGAN-GOCH, who had, HOWEL-GOCH, who had, EINION, who had, MORGAN, father of REES MORGAN, aforesaid.

14.—WILLIAM AWBREY, of Aberkynfrig, d. 27 June, 1547. He had by his second wife, Jane, widow of Thomas Lloyd, and daughter of Sir Richard Herbert, feudal lord of Montgomery castle, a gentleman usher to Henry VIII., by his second wife, Jane, daughter of Gwilim ap Rees Philip, of Llwyn-howell,

15.—RICHARD AWBREY, of Aberkynfrig, eldest son and heir, d. 1580, after selling his paternal estate. He m. Margaret, daughter of Thomas Gunter, of Gileston or Gillston, and had,

16.—RICHARD AWBREY, of Llanelyw, Brecknockshire. He was buried in the parish church 25 Sep. 1646, with an inscribed monument. He m. Anne, daughter of William Vaughan, of Llanelyw, and had,

17.—THOMAS AWBREY, of Llanelyw parish, third son, whose son,

18.—WILLIAM AWBREY, of Llanelyw parish, d. 16 Dec. 1716, aged 90 years, and was buried with his ancestors in the parish church, under an inscribed stone. He m. in 1646, his cousin, Elizabeth, daughter of William, eldest son of Richard Awbrey, d. 1646, aforesaid, and succeeded to the farms in Llanelyw. Their daughter,

19.—MARTHA AWBREY, b. 166-, became a Quaker, and m. 18 June 1692, at the Haverford Meeting, Rees Thomas, who became a J. P. and member of the Pensylvania assembly, will proved 12 Feb. 1742-3. Issue.*

Rowland Ellis, of "Bryn Mawr," in the Welsh tract, besides having the Royal line given in another page, had also further remarkably distinguished ancestry, as follows, being descended from Lady Mary Kynston, a sister of Humphrey Kynaston, the ancestor of Dep. Gov. Thomas Lloyd.

---

*Among their prominent descendants are Mrs. Charles Richardson, Mrs. George B. Roberts, Mrs. Henry K. Dillard, Miss Mary William Perot, Mrs. Nathan Brooke, Hunter Brooke, Jr., Mrs. George H. Colket, William Thomas Brooke, Mrs. J. Howard Lewis, Jr., Hugh Jones Brooke, and Mrs. Harrison Koons Caner.

GENEALOGICAL DATA

1.—EDWARD I., KING OF ENGLAND, had by his first wife, Princess Eleanor, daughter of FERDINAND III., KING OF CASTILE AND LEON,

2.—LADY JOAN OF ACRE, who *m.* first, his second wife, Gilbert de Clare, Earl of Hertford and Gloucester, and had,

3.—LADY MARGARET DE CLARE, who *m.* secondly, Hugh, second Baron D'Audley, created in 1337, Earl of Gloucester, and had,

4.—LADY MARGARET D'AUDLEY, who *m.* Sir Ralph, second Baron Stafford, K.G., created in 1351, Earl of Stafford, and had,

5.—LADY JOAN DE STAFFORD, who *m.* John, second Baron Cherleton, of Powys Castle, chamberlain to Edward III., (see Jones' "Feudal Barons of Powys"), and had,

6.—SIR EDWARD DE CHERLETON, K.G., fourth Baron Cherleton, of Powys castle, who *m.* Lady Alianor, daughter of Sir Thomas de Holand, K.G., second Earl of Kent, earl marshal, also of Royal Descent, and had,

7.—LADY JOANE DE CHERLETON, who *m.* Sir John de Grey, K.G., created in 1418, Earl of Tankerville, killed 22 March, 1420, also of Royal Descent, and had,

8.—SIR HENRY DE GREY, second Earl of Tankerville, *d.* 1449, who *m.* Lady Antigone, daughter of Humphrey, Duke of Gloucester, regent of France, and had by her,

9.—LADY ELIZABETH DE GREY, who *m.* Sir Roger Kynaston, *d.* 1517, also of Royal Descent, and had,

10.—LADY MARY KYNASTON, who *m.* Howell ap Ievan, of Gnya y Maen-gwyn, and had,

11.—HUMPHREY HOWELL, who *m.* Lady Anne, daughter of Sir Richard Herbert, of Colebrook, and had,

12.—JANE HUMPHREY, who *m.* Griffith ap Howell, of Nannau, in Merionethshire, 1541 (see Dwnn's "Visitations of Wales," II. p. 226), a descendant of Bleddyn ap Cynfyn, a prince of Powys, and had,

WELSH SETTLEMENT OF PENSYLVANIA

13.—JOHN GRIFFITH, of Nannau, second son, who *m.* Elizabeth, daughter of David Lloyd, of Trawsfynedd, or Tawrynydd, and had,

14.—LEWIS JOHN GRIFFITH, of Dyffrydan tp., Merionethshire, who *m.* Ellen, daughter of Howell Griffith, and had, *Owen Lewis,** and

15.—REES LEWIS, who *m.* Catherine, daughter of Elisha ap David Owen, and had,

16.—ELLIS AP REES LEWIS, or Ellis Price, of Bryn Mawr, Merionethshire, 1649, who *m.* Anne Humphrey, daughter of Humphrey Hugh Howell, and his wife, Elizabeth Powell, also of Royal Descent, (as in another page), and had,

17.—ROWLAND ELLIS, of "Bryn Mawr," in the Welsh Tract, *d.* 1729. *Issue.*

As members of the Foulke family, Welsh Quakers, which settled in Gwynedd Tp., intermarried with several Merion families, its pedigree is of interest here. To a certain point it is the same as those of Rowland Ellis, Gov. Thomas Lloyd, and Edward Rees, Hananh, wife of Rees Jones, and Jane, wife of Cadwallader Morgan, and is as follows:

1.—EDWARD I., KING OF ENGLAND, had by the Princess Eleanor, of Castile,

2.—LADY JOAN, who *m.* first, Gilbert, Earl of Hertford, and had,

3.—LADY MARGARET DE CLARE, who *m.* Hugh, Earl of Gloucester, and had,

---

*OWEN LEWIS, *m.* Mary, daughter of Tudor-vaughn, of Caer y Nwch, in Merionethshire, and had,

ROBERT AP OWEN LEWIS, who *m.* Margaret, daughter of John ap Lewis, and had,

LEWIS ROBERT OWEN, who had by his wife, Mary, family unknown,

ELLIS LEWIS, who removed into Ireland, and came to Pensylvania, bringing certificate from the Friends' Meeting at Mt. Mellick, in Queen's Co., dated 25 May, 1708. He settled in Kennett tp., Chester Co., Pa., where he *d.* 31 Aug. 1750, his will proved 29 Oct. following. He *m.* first, in 1713, at the Concord Mo. Mtg., Elizabeth Newlin, and had issue.

GENEALOGICAL DATA

4.—LADY MARGARET D'AUDLEY, who *m.* Ralph, Earl of Stafford, and had,

5.—LADY JOAN DE STAFFORD, who *m.* John, 2d Lord Cherleton, and had,

6.—LADY JOAN DE CHERLETON, who *m.* John, sixth Baron Le Strange, of Knockyn Castle, also of Royal Descent, *d.* 1397, (see Lloyd's History of Powys Fadog, vol. IV., 48), and had,

7.—LADY ELIZABETH LE STRANGE, who *m.* Gruffydd ap Madoc Vychan, third feudal Baron of Glyndyfrdwy, and lord of Rhuddalt, (see Burke's "Royal Families," vol. II, fo. LXI), and had,

8.—LADY ISABEL GRIFFITH, who *m.* Goronway ap Gruffyth Madoc, and had,

9.—TUDOR, feudal lord of Penllyn, who had,

10.—HOWEL TUDOR, whose son,

11.—DAVID-LLWYD TUDOR had,

12.—LADY GWENHWYFAR TUDOR, who *m.* David ap Ievan-vychan, of Llanuwchllyn, in Penllyn, descended from the feudal Barons of Penllyn, (see Dwnn's Visitations of Wales), and had,

13.—DAVID-LLWYD, who *m.* Lowry, daughter of Howel-vaughan, and had,

14.—ROBERT-LLWYD, of Gwerny Brechtwyn, who *m.* Mary, daughter of Reinaullt, of Branas Uchaf, and had,

15.—THOMAS ROBERT-LLWYD, 1520-1612, of Nant y Friar, or Nanfreur, in Penllyn, Merioneth, buried in the parish church of Llandderfel, 21 May, 1612. He *m.* Catherine, daughter of Robert Griffith Evan-goch, who was descended from Ievan-goch, of Cwm Penaner, Denbigh, an ancestor of John Cadwalader, the Philadelphia school teacher, and of John ap Thomas, of "Company No. 1" (see Dwnn's Visitations of Wales, 1585-1603), and had *Mary*, wife of Richard, of Tyddyn Tyfod, and

16.—EVAN AP THOMAS LLOYD, 1555-1640, buried at the Llanderfol church. He *m.* Dorothea Evans, buried with her husband, in Feb. 1619, and had,

WELSH SETTLEMENT OF PENSYLVANIA

17.—THOMAS EVAN LLOYD, high sheriff of Merionethshire, 1623, d. Nov. 1649; m. Catherine, daughter of William David, of Llanderfel, and had,

18.—FFOULKE AP THOMAS LLOYD, bapt. at Llanderfol, 14 April, 1623; m. Lowry, daughter of Edward David Ellis, of Llanvor, Merioneth, and had (see Jenkins's History of Gwynedd),

19.—EDWARD FOULKE, 1651-1741, he removed from Coed y Foel, 2 Feb. 1698, to a tract of 700 acres of land which he had bought in Gwynedd tp., Philadelphia county, with his family. He m. Eleanor or Ellin Hughs, (also of Royal Descent, as below), daughter of Hugh Cadwallader Rhys, of Yspytty, or Spytu parish, Denbighshire, and had by her, who d. in 1733, nine children.*

1.—JOHN, KING OF ENGLAND, had by his second wife, Queen Isabella,

2.—LADY ELEANOR PLANTAGENET, who m. secondly, Simon de Montfort, Earl of Leicester, and had,

3.—LADY ELEANOR DE MONTFORT, who m. Llewellyn Gryffyth, the last sovereign Prince of Wales, 1232, and had,

4.—LADY CATHERINE, who m. Philip Ivor, lord of Iscoed, and had,

5.—Lady Eleanor, who m. Thomas Llewellyn, of Trefgarned, and had,

6.—LADY ELEANOR, who m. Gryffyth Vychan, lord of Glyndyfrdwy, and had,

7.—LOWRY VAUGHAN, sister to the celebrated Owen Glendower. She m. Robert Pyllesdon, or Puleston, lord of Emral manor, Caernarvonshire, and had,

---

*Among the prominent descendants of Edward Foulke are Edward Jeanes Foulke, Howard M. Jenkins, Frank Foulke, Charles Francis Jenkins, Richard Foulke Beirne, Warren M. Stansbury, James Cresson, Thomas Corson Yocum, Mrs. Jawood Lukens, Mrs. Howard Comfort, Mrs. Robert R. Corson, Geo. Rhyfedd Foulk, Wm. Parker Foulke, Mrs. Henry Carvill Lewis, J. Roberts Foulke, Linford Foulke, Mrs. Richard H. Day, Richard C. Foulke, M.D., Allen Childs, Jacob Sperry Willing, and John M. Whitall, Jr.

GENEALOGICAL DATA

8.—JOHN PULESTON, of Emral, heir, who *m.* Angharad, dau. of Griffith de Hanmer, and had,

9.—MARGARET PULESTON, (see Dwnn's Visitations of Wales), who *m.* David Ievan ap Einion, of Cryniarth, constable of Harlech Castle, in 1468, and had,

10.—ANGHARAD DAVID (sister to Einion David, of Cryniarth, in Edermon, mentioned above), who *m.* Gwilym ap Gruffydd Robert, of Coch Willym, high sheriff of Caernarvonshire, and had,

11.—GWENLLIAN WILLIAM, who *m.* David ap Meredydd (or Meredith) ap Howel, of Bala, Merionthshire, and had,

12.—HOWEL LLOYD DAVID, of Bala, *m.* Mallt vch. Howell Tychan, of Llnyaiarth, Montgomeryshire, and had,

13.—THOMAS GETHIN HOWEL, of y Danyfaen, Denbigshire, *m.* Catherine v. David ap Ievan, of same place, and had,

14.—MARGARET THOMAS, who *m.* Hugh Thomas ap David, of Cae Fadog, Ciltalgarth tp., Llanfor par., Merionth, and had,

15.—WILLIAM HUGH, of Cae Fadog, *d.* before 1627-8, His son,

16.—ELLIS AP WILLIAM, or Ellis Williams, *d.* at Cae Fadog, where his personal estate was inventoried, and administered, 26 Feb. 1645, by Margaret John, his relict, at St. Asaph Registry. Of his children:—*

*An extant memorandum, made about 174-, which is copied into the records of the Haverford Mo. Mtg., says, "Ellis Williams of Caifadog had four Daughters, viz: Margaret, Douse, Givenn, and Ellin. The said Ellin married John Morris of Brin Gwin in Denbigshire, by her had one Daughter named Ellin who married Cadwalader ab Evan late of Gwynedd deceased," (he *d.* in 1745). "Givenn (another Daughter of the said Ellis Williams) had 3 children who came to Pensilvania," as given above. And also: "Evan Robert Lewis was an honest, sober man, lived in Fron Goch, [p. 155], he had five sons, viz: 1. John ab Evan, 2. Cadw'r, 3. Owen ab Evan, 4. Griffith ab Evan, and 5, Evan ab Evan. The first John ab Evan had 3 Sons & three daughters by his first wife."

WELSH SETTLEMENT OF PENSYLVANIA

1.—ELLIN WILLIAMS, *m.* John Morris, of Bryn Gwyn, Denbigh, and had,

    ELLIN MORRIS, *m.* Cadwalader Evans, 1664-1745, removed to Gwynedd tp., in 1698, elsewhere mentioned.

2.—GWEN WILLIAMS, *m.* Hugh Cadwalader Rhys, of Yspytty parish, Denbigh, alive in Dec. 1688, and had,

    I.—JANE HUGHS, *m.* William John, who removed to Gwynedd tp., in 1698, a son of John Evan, of Penmaen.

    II.—JOHN AP HUGH, or John Pugh, removed to Gwynedd tp., *m.* and had *Ellis Pugh*, of Gwynedd.

    III.—ELLIN HUGHS, *d.* 1733, who *m.* Edward ffoulke, 1651-1741; to Gwynedd tp., in 1698, also of Royal Descent, as above. One of their children, *Jane Foulke*, *d.* 8mo. 7. 1766; *m.* 4mo. 5, 1718, Ellis Hughs, 1688-1764, of Exeter, Pa., and had, *William Hughs*, of Exeter, 1716-1760, from whom descends Mrs. Walter D. Mansfield, of San Francisco, see Browning's "Colonial Dames of Royal Descent," p. 389.

EARLY DAYS
IN THE WELSH TRACT

FRIENDS GOING TO MONTHLY MEETING.

ANNALS OF WELSH SETTLERS

Having seen the Welsh Quakers put in possession of their land purchases in their tract beyond the Schuylkill, and the settlements begun, we will now listen to the stories of some of them, as told in letters by themselves, or by their grandchildren, or Pensylvania annalists, of their experiences in early days here, and learn something of their habits, and environments in the time of the beginning of the city, and of the Commonwealth.

As to these first comers, it was Proud's opinion, and his opinion applies as well to the Welsh as the English, "they appear to have been provident and cautious in their removal, so that rashness and inconsideration, so common in new attempts of this kind, was not for the most part much observable among them. Many of them brought servants, and had provided themselves with food and raiment for such a space of time after their arrival as it might reasonably be supposed their care and industry would afterwards procure necessary subsistence in the province, besides sufficient quantities of household furniture, utensils, implements and tools." And "notwithstanding the precaution, which many of these adventurers had used, in bringing provisions and other necessaries with them, for a certain time, yet it cannot be reasonably supposed that the arrival of such a large number of persons, in a wilderness, within the space of two or three years, would not necessarily be attended with inconveniencies and difficulties," and then tells of cases of suffering. "Besides," he continues, "these adventurers were not all young persons, and able to endure the difficulties and hardships which are mostly unavoidable in subduing a wilderness, nor as equally regardless of convenient accommodations as young, healthy, and strong men, accustomed to

WELSH SETTLEMENT OF PENSYLVANIA

labour and disappointment, but there were among them persons advanced in years, with women and children, and such as, in their native country, had lived well, and enjoyed ease and plenty."

"Their first business, after their arrival," says Proud, writing out, in 1797, the annals descended to him from Caleb Pusey, the "Governor's miller," whose recollections easily went back to 1681-2, and applied to the Welsh, as well as the English, "was to land their property, and put it under such shelter as could be found; then, while some of them got warrants of survey, for taking up so much land as was sufficient for immediate settling, others went diversely further into the woods to different places, where their lands were laid out, often without any path or road to direct them, for scarce any were to be found above two miles from the water side [Delaware], not so much as any mark, or sign of any European having been there. As to the Indians, they seldomed travelled so regularly as to be traced, or followed by foot-steps, except, perhaps, from one of their towns to another. [This statement contradicts many 'old Indian path' claims in the Welsh tract]. So that all the country, further than about two miles distant from the river [Delaware] was an entire wilderness, producing nothing for support of human life, but the wild fruits and animals of the woods." Yet there must have been some cleared grounds across the Schuylkill, since there are mentions of "old Indian fields" in land records, and these Penn particularly claimed for himself.

"The lodgings of some of these settlers were at first in the woods. A chosen tree was frequently all the shelter they had against the inclemency of the weather. The next coverings of many of them were either caves in the earth, or such huts as could be most expeditiously procured. [havod-un-nos, as the Welsh term them], till better houses were built, the Welsh hendree, the stone house, in a hill-sheltered spot, near a good spring of water], for which they had no want of timber." The finest log cabins were built of barked,

SETTLERS' EXPERIENCES

and hewn logs of equal thickness, with stairs, or a ladder on the outside to reach the upper chamber, the first floor was pounded earth, as was the floors of all the early meeting houses. "The appearance of a wild and woody desert, with which they had now to encounter, among savages, must have created in them very sensible ideas, and made strong impressions, at first, on their minds. That likewise the consideration of the long and painful labour, and inevitable disappointments and hardships, which are naturally inseparable from such undertakings, and for a series of years must necessarily be endured, before a comfortable subsistence could be procured in a country, and a sufficient portion of land brought into proper order for that purpose, must undoubtedly have been very affecting to a thoughtful people, in this new, remote, and solitary situation." "These first comers, after their arrival, soon cleared land enough to make way for a crop of Indian corn, in the succeeding spring, and in a year or two, they began upon wheat, and other grain. Thus they went on improving till they got into a comfortable way of living."

While not a Welshman, "The Testimony of Richard Townsend, showing the providential hand of God, to him and others, from the first settlement of Pennsylvania," is not without interest in this connection. He relates, that having settled his business in London, where he dwelt, he and his wife and child embarked with William Penn, on the "Welcome," "about the latter end of the Sixth-month," 1682. After referring to the passage as "properous," during which nearly every passenger had the smallpox, and thirty died, as others recovered, they landed and "found the New World a wilderness, and the chief inhabitants Indians," and some Swedes, "who received us in a friendly manner, though there was a great number of us. The good hand of Providence was seen in a particular manner, in that provisions were found for us by the Swedes and Indians, at very reasonable rates. Our first concern was to keep up and main-

WELSH SETTLEMENT OF PENSYLVANIA

tain our religious worship, and, in order thereunto we had several meetings in the houses of the inhabitants, and one boarded meeting-house was set up [Oct. 1681] where the city was to be, near Delaware, and after our meeting was over, we assisted each other in building little houses for our shelter. After a time, I set up a mill [belonging to Penn's milling company] on Chester Creek, which I brought ready framed from London, which served for grinding corn, and sawing of boards, and was of great use to us. There not being plenty of horses, people generally brought their corn on their backs many miles." This was when the Welsh Friends were forbidden by Penn to have mills of their own, convenient to their homes.

As there were always a considerable number of Welsh in Philadelphia, it may be presumed that some abandoned their country lots, or sold them, and removed to the "city," and that there were others who never got into the country, being tradespeople, and not farmers. The city life was becoming attractive, for the town grew rapidly. In 1683, William Penn wrote, "from my arrival in 1682, to date hereof, being ten months, we got up four score houses at our town, from that time to my coming away, which is a year, within a few weeks, the town advanced to 357 houses, divers of them large, well built, with good cellars, three stories, and some balconies." John Goodson, 24, 6mo. 1690, telling of Philadelphia, wrote, "They build all with stone and brick now. Except the very meanest sorts of people, which build framed houses with timber and fetheredge-boards without side, two stories high." And there were seven "ordinaries" or taverns, in the town, as early as in 1683. Davis's Queen's Head tavern in Water Street, being the meeting place of the non-Quaker Welsh in town, where they had religious services in the Welsh tongue. In 1685, Robert Turner wrote of the town, "There are about 600 houses [put up] in three years' time." And Logan wrote, 2, 6mo. 1684, that 800 Friends attended the Philadelphia meeting.

SETTLERS' EXPERIENCES

Although the information contained in the following letter, written about 1710, is hearsay, for its writer, John Jones, was born in Pensylvania, it is interesting. He was a son of a Thomas Sion Evan, (or Thomas Jones), who came to the South River, or Delaware country, from near Bala, Merionthshire, in April, 1682, and subsequently settled in what became Radnor township, whose will, signed 31, 1, 1707, was proved at Phila. 23, 7, 1707; to be guardians and overseers, Rowland Ellis, Sr., Joseph Owen, and Rowland Ellis, the younger. The date of this interesting letter, entirely in Welsh language, is uncertain, but it was written after 1707.*

"My Dear Kinsman, Hugh Jones,

"I received a letter from you dated May, 8th, 1705, and I was glad to find that one of my relatives in the old land of which I have heard so much was pleased to recollect me. I have heard my father speak much about old Cymru; but I was born in this woody region—this new world."

Then, mentioning many places in Wales he had heard his parents talk affectionately about, "and the kind-hearted and innocent old people who lived in them," he continued, "And now, my friend, I will give an account of the life and fortunes of my dear father, from the time he left Wales to the day of his death."

"He was at St. Peter's fair, at Bala [10 July, 1681], when he first heard of Pensylvania, three weeks only after this, he took leave of his neighbors and relatives, who were anxiously looking forward to his departure for London on his way to America.

"Here [in London] he waited three months for a ship; and at length went out in one bearing the name of "William Penn." He had a very tempestuous passage for several weeks, and when in sight of the river Delaware, owing to adverse winds and a boisterous sea, the sails were torn, and the rudder injured. By this disaster they were greatly disheartened, and were obliged to go back to the Barbadoes,

---
*Printed in the *Cambrian Magazine*, 1833.

where they continued three weeks, expending much money in refitting the ship. Being now ready for a second attempt, they easily accomplished their voyage and arrived safely in the river Delaware, on the 16th of April, being thirty weeks from the time they left London. During this long voyage, he learned to speak and read English tolerably well.

"They now came up the river 120 miles, to the place Philadelphia is at present situate. At that time, as the Welsh say, there was 'na thy nae ymogor,' [neither house nor shelter], but the wild woods, nor any one to welcome them to land. A poor outlook this for persons who had been so long at sea, many of whom had spent their little all.

"This was not the place for them to remain stationary. My father, therefore, went alone where chance led him, to endeavor the means of subsistence. He longed much at this time for milk.

"During his wanderings, he met with a drunken old man, who understood neither Welsh nor English, and, who noticing the stranger, by means of some signs and gesticulations, invited him to his dwelling, where he was received by the old man's wife and several sons, in the most kind and hospitable manner. They were Swedes. Here he made his home till he had habitation of his own.

"As you shall hear, during the summer of 1682, [October], our governor, William Penn, Esq'r, arrived here, together with several from England, having bought lands here.

"They now began to divide the country into allotments and to plan the city of Philadelphia (which was to be more than two miles in length), laying it out in streets and squares, etc., with portions of land assigned to several of the houses. He also bought the freehold of the soil from the Indians, a savage race of men, who have lived here from time immemorial, as far as I am able to understand. They can give no account of themselves, not knowing where or whence they came here; an irrational set, I should imagine, but they have some kind of reason, too, and extraordinary natural endowments in their peculiar way; they had neither towns nor villages, but lived in booths or tents.

"In the autumn [August] of this year [1682], several from Wales arrived here—Edward ab Rhys [Edward Prees], Edward Jones of Bala [the doctor], William ab Edward, and many others.

"By this time, there was a kind of neighborhood here, although, as neighbors they could little benefit each other. They were sometimes in making huts beneath some cliff, or under the hollow banks of rivulets, thus sheltering themselves where their fancy dictated.

"There were neither cows, nor horses, to be had at any price. Yet no one was in want, and all were much attached to each other.

"During this eventful period, our governor began to build mansion houses at different intervals, to the distance of fifty miles from the city, although the country appeared a complete wilderness.

"At this time, my father, Thomas Sion [John] Evan, was living with the Swedes [possibly the Swenson or Swanson family], and intending daily to return to Wales. But, as time advanced, the country improved. In the course of three years, several were beginning to obtain a pretty good livelihood, and my father determined to remain with them.

"There was by this time no land to be bought within twelve miles of the city, and my father having purchased a small tract of land [in Radnor] married the widow of Thomas Llwyd [Lloyd] of Penmaen, [a poet]. He now went to live near the woods. It was now a very rare, but pleasing thing to hear a neighbor's cock crow.

"My father had now only one small horse. In process of time, however, the little which he had prospered, so that he became possessed of horses, cows, and everything else that was necessary for him. During the latter years of his life, he kept twelve good milch cows. He had eight children. He was a muscular man."

WELSH SETTLEMENT OF PENSYLVANIA

The writer of this letter, which is a fine advertisement of some school in Radnor tp., was the eldest child. He and his brother, Joseph *b.* 28. 2. 1695, each received a farm from their father, as also did his sister Elizabeth, *b.* 8. 11. 1691, she married, as stated, in the letter, Risiart ab Thomas ab Rhys. His mother, Lowry, he says, was then 75 years old.

Probably one of the most valuable and interesting letters of the first Welsh settlers preserved is that of Dr. Edward Jones, the leader of "Company No. 1," of Pensylvania adventurers, the first settler of Merion, since it was written 26 Aug. 1682, thirteen days after landing here. It is what may be defined as a chatty letter, and a letter of advice to immigrants, and is full of interesting items showing the state of affairs and prices current, in the home of their adoption as viewed by a man of education and refinement, to his partner, in this land adventure, John ap Thomas. It confirms much that John Jones told in the aforesaid letter.

"Ye name of town [Philadelphia] lots," he wrote, "is called now Wicoco. Here is a Crowd of people striving for ye Country land, for ye town lot is not divided, & therefore we are forced to take up ye Country lots. We had much adoe to get a grant of it, but it cost us 4 or 5 days attendance, besides some score of miles we traveled before we brought it to pass, [this was locating the 5.000 acre share of the general purchase from Penn, and which became 'Merion,' or (Lower) Merion township]. I hope it will please thee, and the rest yt are concerned, for it hath most rare timber. I have not seen the like in all these parts, there is water enough besides. The end of each lot will be on a river, as large or larger than the Dye at Bala, it is called Skool Kill River."

The expected discomforts of the first settlers of Merion, is further recorded in an old Bible by someone who probably had heard the immigrants relate them, thus:—

"In the fall of 1682, William ap Edwards, with his family, Edward Jones, Edward Rees, Robert Davies, and many others, settled on the west side of the Schuylkill, Six or seven miles distant from the city, there dug caves, walled them, and dwelt therein a considerable time, where they suffered many hardships in the beginning. The next season being wet and rainy, about their barley harvest [time], they could not get their grain dry to stack before it swelled, and it began to sprout, rendering it unfit for bread. They were in their necessities supplied by the natives with venison and wild fowl. Their first cows to milk were obtained from New Castle, and divided among the neighbors, and not having inclosures for them, they were obliged to tie them with rope of grape vine, some to a tree, or a stake driven into the ground, there being plenty of grass and sweet weeds. The Lord blessed them, and enabled them to bear their difficulties for a time, and blessed their labor with great success in raising grain, and every support they could wish for."

However, we have William Penn's word for it that the first winter, 1682-3, the Merion settlers lived here, was the coldest in the memory of "the oldest inhabitants," (White, or Indian). It may have been that being unprepared for weather colder than a winter in Wales, they "suffered many hardships," having only poor shelters for dwellings, and only green wood for fires. In Penn's letter to London shareholders of the Free Society of Traders, he wrote from Philadelphia, on 16. 8mo.* 1683, when he had been here almost a year. He said he had then "lived over the coldest and hottest times that the oldest liver in the province can remember," so this first year must have been one of extreme of temperature. In general, what were Mr. Penn's experiences this year, were those of Dr. Edward Jones, and his neighbors, on the bank of the Schuylkill, who had been

---

*The date of this letter shows that Penn did not always begin the year with "the month called March," the then "First Month," for the letter is dated "8th month," which according to the then custom would make it written in October, and he was writing in August.

WELSH SETTLEMENT OF PENSYLVANIA

here just one year. Penn says that from the time of his arrival in October, up to December, the weather was mild, "like an English mild spring," and "from December to the beginning of the month called March, we had sharp, frosty weather, not foul, thick, black weather, [as in England], but a sky as clear as in summer, and the air dry, cold, piercing and hungry," and tells that the Delaware river was frozen over for a few days. We can imagine what sort of a winter he passed through, but he was writing an advertisement of his province to be published in England, so why tell of "zero weather" to possible customers used only to a mild winter. (Rowland Ellis was more candid in his description of a Pensylvania winter, in a letter quoted further on). "From March to June," Penn continues, "we enjoyed sweet spring, gentle showers, and a fine sky." "From thence to this present month, we have had extraordinary heats."

Thomas Ellis, of Haverford, in a letter dated 13. 4mo. 1685, tells of the hard winter in Pensylvania he had just passed through. He says no ships could leave Philadelphia in February, "being there was so much winter wether ['twas certainly a bad spell of weather], the like was hardly known, and so no seasoning wether for tobacco."

The make-shift protections against storms and freezing weather which the first settlers used in their necessity, naturally influenced the accounts of their first winter in America. It is notorious that the first settlers on the Delaware, where they supposed Philadelphia was to be, lived in "caves," dug in the river bluff. And it also may be presumed that the Welsh Friends on the Schuylkill did the same. These artificial grottoes were by no means poor accommodations, excepting that the occupants must, in many large families, have been greatly cramped for room, and there could not have been any opportunity for privacy. But they were no worse off than the Western pioneers in their cabins. The description of one of the best "caves"

SETTLERS' EXPERIENCES

has come down to us as follows. First, a pit was dug, three feet deep, and twelve by fifteen feet in extent, in the river bank, well up from the water. The side towards the river was levelled and left open. The side walls were carried up from the ground to the height of the tallest man standing erect, with interlaced and thatched saplings, and the roof over all was also made this way. The floor was beaten earth. So it may be imagined these temporary abodes were fairly comfortable, when the family was in the open much of the time, and certainly they were substantially put up, as in the city some were rented to party after party of new comers, and some became boarding houses, and worse, and, becoming a scandal to the city, all were extirpated.

In the country, it is said some of these caves were in existence* many years after the log cabin was put up, and became stables, and in many cases the old log cabin, replaced by the stone house, was left standing and used for servants' quarters, or for storage. There are a few of these cabins still standing in the Welsh Tract, at least it is so claimed, which were the early home of the founders of our most prominent families.

---

*The only instance known to me of the original "cave dwelling" of an early settler being preserved, or identified, in the family of a present day descendant, is the one belonging to the Lownes family, in Springfield tp., now in Delaware Co. Hugh Lownes, and his wife Jane, and four children, sailed from Chester, England, for Pensylvania in 1685. They were Friends. Mr. Lownes had been imprisoned because he was "a practicing Quaker," and contracted a disease in jail from which he died at sea. His widow took up his land in Springfield tp., and farmed it, and a portion of the old place is owned by descendants. On this property is the cave, a natural rock grotto, which served as the home for the widow and her children, till the log cabin was built, which in turn was followed by the present stone mansion. The cave has been carefully protected all these years, and is marked on a tablet, "Jane Lownes's Cave and Dwelling, 1685." Watson, in his "Annals of Philadelphia," mentions that the "cave," made and used by the Quaker family of Coates, was incorporated in the cellar of their brick house, erected at Front and Green streets, and survived till his day (1830).

WELSH SETTLEMENT OF PENSYLVANIA

A preserved letter,* written in the spring of 1698, by Rowland Ellis, of "Bryn Mawr," gives us a good view of the progress Merion had made in ten years, and customs of its people in their new home. Mr. Ellis had shortly returned from Wales, where he went in the spring of 1688, after having been here about a year, so his letter may be considered one of an observant man considering contrasts.

"They begin now to build the houses with Stone, & many with brick, whc may be made in any place here. * * * * There are but few natives now. Not 1 to 10 as formerly. As many as there is, are very quiet.

"A new comer may supply himself with horses, cows, and sheep, as many as he wants—good horse £4 with you, may cost £8 more or less; Good Cow here, £5, or 6; beef ye last fall 2½ per pound; pork 3d; cheese 7d; butter 10d. to 1s. per pound; mutton 5d. also; wheat 8s; Rye 6s; Malt 6s. ye bushell. All other things are very dear, accordingly all things, whether foreign, or country commodities, will fall.

"We had a very cold winter, such another people here cannot remember; hard frost, & deep snow, which continued untill ye beginning of this month; we bore it I think as well as most, we had an indifferent good house, very good & large chimney; we made fire night & day. * * * * It has been very sickly season here ye last fall & winter; several died of our Countrymen."

Proud, in his History of Pensylvania, says further of these first colonists and early settlers, "Among those adventurers and settlers, who arrived about this time [1682-3], were also many from Wales, of these who are called Ancient Britons, and mostly Quakers, divers of whom were of the original, or early stock of that society there. They had early purchased of the Proprietary, in England, 40,000 acres of land. Those who came, at present, took up so much of it, on the west side of Sculkil river, as made the three townships of Merion, Haverford, and Radnor; and in a

---

*Pa. Mag. of His., 1894.

few years afterwards, their number was so much augmented, as to settle the three other townships of New-town, Goshen, and Uwchland."

"Divers of these early Welsh settlers were persons of excellent and worthy character, and several of good education, family, and estate; chiefly Quakers, and many of them either eminent preachers in the society, or otherwise qualified and disposed to do good, in various capacities, both in religious and civil, in public and private life. Of some of them there are particular and extraordinary accounts in manuscript, both respecting their eminent religious services among the Quakers, &c., and also of their great usefulness among their neighbors, in settling the province, and in regulating and managing the civil affairs of the government; as persons highly and justly esteemed and distinguished both in private and public station."

In his notice of these Welsh who were active in public life, and in the affairs of the Province, as well as in those of the Friends, Proud named as the most prominent only Rowland Ellis, Robert Owen, Hugh Roberts, and Ellis Pugh. But there were a few others of the Welshmen who were quite as prominent in the affairs of Philadelphia county, and who represented it in the assembly, before 1709, namely Thomas Lloyd, Griffith Jones, David Lloyd, Griffith Owen, John Bevan, Thomas Wynne, Rees Thomas, John Roberts, etc.

In the very first meeting of the assembly, in Philadelphia, on 10 and 12, 1mo. 1683, out of the nine representatives from Philadelphia Co. two were Welshmen, Dr. Wynne and Dr. Owen. But in 1684 and 1685, no Welshman represented Philadelphia Co., in which the entire Welsh Tract was then located, nor in 1690, but in other years there was always found some Welsh Friend willing to sacrifice some of his time for the public good, and sit in the general assembly.

The early Welsh Friends seem to have been soon interested in education, as among the petitioners for a charter for the first Friends' Public School, in Philadelphia in 1697, which was a Latin and grammar school in 1689, were David Lloyd and John Jones. In his final patent for this school, dated 29 Nov. 1711, Penn nominated as overseers of the public school, among others, Griffith Owen and Rowland Ellis, of Merion. This institution is still maintained, as the William Penn Charter School.

During the "Keith Disturbance," at a general meeting of Friends, in Philadelphia to denounce and disown the disturber, Keith, among the signers of the "Declaration of Denial," 20, 4mo. 1692, were the Welshmen from over the Schuylkill, Robert Owen, and Hugh Roberts, and in town, Thomas Lloyd, and Griffith Owen. Mr. Keith came to Philadelphia as the first headmaster of the aforementioned Latin school.

Penn in his letters frequently manifested his regard for individual Welshmen of Merion, which he did not have for the Welsh collectively. For instance, in a long letter dated London, 16. 1mo. 1684-5, to his Deputy, Thomas Lloyd a Merion Welshman, he concluded, "Dearly salute me to dear friends, particularly Thomas Ellis, G. Jones, H. Lewis, T. Howel, J. B., [John Bevan] and the rest of the Welsh Friends, Captain Owen, &c., with their families."

Oldmixon, writing in 1708, said of the Welsh Tract, " 'Tis very populous, and the people are very industrious, by which means this country is better cleared than any other part of the country. The inhabitants have many fine plantations; they are looked upon to be as thriving and wealthy as any in the province, and this must always be said of the Welsh, that wherever they come, 'tis not their fault if they do not live, and live well, too, for they seldom spare for labour."

Since we thus have their own evidence, and that of contemporary writers, there is no occasion for one to draw any imaginary picture of the first years here of the Welsh Friends; nor to imagine what manner and quality these settlers were. As experienced farmers, they were well able to take care of their families. The soil was good we know,

SETTLERS' EXPERIENCES

the seasons in general were not unlike those of Wales, and there was nothing to prevent them from exercising their industry and ingenuity. That they made no attempt at commercial farming, or cultivation of their plantations on a scale larger than to supply home necessities, is not surprising, since the early large landowners here had been gentlemen farmers in the old country, and they only resumed the life here.

Nor is there evidence there were "country stores" in the Welsh Tract till many years after its settlement, so it may be presumed the Welsh Quakers did the buying of necessaries they could not raise, or find, at the Philadelphia stores. In the years 1700, &c., the largest general store in Philadelphia was conducted by William Trent, and his extant account books show that the country people brought him peltry of all kinds and got in exchange dry goods and groceries. Among his Welsh customers, who had accounts with him, were Richard Anthony, "John Andrew, ye shrieve," (1705), William Bevan, Mary Bevan, his widow, Owen Davis, Francis Ellis, Edward Evans, "Evan Evans, ye minister," Thomas Griffith, Thomas Harriss, Thomas Howell, "Evan Harry of Morgan," (bought a negro for £60, in 1708), John Jones, Sr. and Jr., Nicholas Thomas Jones, Griffith, Edward, Samuel, Moses, and Richard Jones, David Lloyd, Griffith Owen, "Ro Owen ye ministr," John Powell, John Richard, Elizabeth Roberts, "John Thomas, ye tailor," Richard and Lewis Thomas, and John Vaughan.

Some of the household and economic features of the times I write of, are not without interest here. While the Welsh Friends were "plain people," they liked to have about them, and evidently did according to inventories, the best of all solid-wood furniture in their houses, modest though these were. But, if we could inspect one of the better class of these, the things we would not see would impress us more than what we did. We would see no carpets, nor rugs; but hardwood floors, holy-stoned, or polished, and nearly always sanded; the clean creek sand brushed into curious designs by the housewife, an artistic labor in which they had great pride. We would be pleased to see no wall paper, for the walls of rooms would be half, or wholly wainscoted and panelled and, if in hard wood, waxed and polished in natural color, but if only in pine wood, then painted white. We would also be pleased to see no stoves, only the large fire places, with pictured tiles about them. There would be a mantle-board, but never a marble mantle. If there was a mirror, it was in sections, framed in polished mahogany, or in black-painted wood. Of pictures, there were none mentioned in inventories. Of course, we would see the chests, the high nests of drawers, the high-boys and the low-boys, peculiar to the times, the tall clock, the corner-cupboard, the hinged tea-table, the dresser, but no easy chairs would greet us; possibly not even the "winsor" ones, but many with rush seats, and always high backed, and uncomfortable, companions of the high-backed bench. Candles in plain "sticks," never in girandoles, gave the artificial light; but they were dipped candles for ordinary use. At meals, if there was silver, it was solid, for plated ware was unknown, and the coffee, or tea service was of china, as it was considered more elegant. Delft-ware was held in reserve for grand occasions, and earthen-ware, and plates and platters of pewter, and wooden trenchers, were in ordinary use, and it was long subsequent when silver waiters, for serving, succeeded wooden trays. There were glasses for wine, but not glass tumblers. But different times made different ways, and the Welsh Friends followed the fashions, as much as their convenience, and the war of the revolution, as did the civil war, for us, marked distinct changes in their manner of living and furnishing, for innovations and luxuries invaded their dwellings and habits, and the general primitiveness, the relative differences, remained about the same from Penn's day till after the revolution's influence was experienced, just as our customs and needs are changed from our ante-bellum days. It is worthy of notice here, however, that the first carpet in Philadelphia was laid, 1750, in the city dwelling of the Welsh Friend, Owen Jones.

It is true that as a class the Indians were peaceable when the Welsh removed here, and were not murderers and scalpers, but yet there were some "bad Indians" then, as well as nowadays. There is evidence that some of these roamed the forests of Haverford and Radnor, apparently on innocent wild game hunting, but, at the same time, were frightening the Welsh so they were obliged to complain to the Council, for there is a minute 16. mo. 1686 of "The Complaint of ye friends Inhabitants of Hertford against the Indians, for ye Rapine and Destruction of their Hoggs." Thereupon, the Provincial Council ordered that "Ye respective Indian kings with all speed" should be summoned to appear before it, and "be made to desist" the raids on farm live stock.

During the French and Indian war, some outlying families, apparently, had to abandon their plantations, and come into the more thickly settled part of Merion. For instance, the following entry of a burial at the Merion Meeting, 5mo. 4, 1756, "Joseph, son of Joseph Conlin, who left their plantation for fear of the Indians."

In the early books about America we find many statements that are silly, or amusing, as we may look at them from our point of view, and with our experience and knowledge. For instance, the Rev. John Campanius, a Swedish Lutheran minister, who was here for six years, 1641-46, and was the first missionary of religion among the Delaware Indians, took notes from which he hoped to write a book, but died in 1683, aged 83 years, without doing so. His son, Thomas, who was here when a lad with his father, re-wrote his father's notes on America, and added much information, and is the one responsible for their exaggerations, and printed the whole in Swedish, in 1702, the title translated being, "Brief description of the Province of New Sweden, now Pensylvania."

WELSH SETTLEMENT OF PENSYLVANIA

What is particularly interesting to us, is the information recorded of the country about the Falls of the Schuylkill, where the minister had been to visit the Indians. He tells of the abundance of walnut, chestnut, peach, and mulberry trees, of wild plums, wild grapes, and hemp and hops everywhere. And of that wonderful gourd, "calabash," which, when dried hard, is fashioned into dishes and cups, tipped with silver, some being so large they hold a gallon.

But what is recorded of our familiar fire-fly is news indeed. "There is a kind of fly, which the Indians call 'cuouye,' which in the night gives so strange a light that it is sufficient, when a man is travelling, to show him the way, one may also write and read the smallest print by the light which they give. When the Indians go in the night a hunting, they fasten these insects to their hands and feet, by which they can see their way as well as in the daytime. One night these flies frightened all the soldiers that were on guard at Fort Christiana [Wilmington, Del.]; they thought they were enemies advancing towards them with lighted matches!" "There is also," about the Falls, "a large and terrible serpent, which is called a rattle-snake. It has a head like a dog, and can bite off a man's leg as if cut with an axe! * * * These snakes are three yards long, and thick as the thickest part of a man's leg." What a life of wonder, and anxiety the ladies of Dr. Jones's settlement at these Falls must have led!

It is a well known fact that the Quakers never proselyte, but a few years after the first settlements were made "out of town," the Welsh who then removed to Pensylvania were generally "Church of England" people, for when the annoyances ceased in Wales, the well-to-do Friends stopped coming over. These "Churchmen" from Wales, having acquired the habit at home, resumed it here, and made attempts to proselyte the Quakers of Radnor, but there is no evidence that they made any remarkable headway.

SETTLERS' EXPERIENCES

William Penn, in his "Agreement" with these later emigrants promised them they should be at liberty to worship as they wished, and, if a body of settlers desired a minister, they were at liberty, as far as he was concerned, to ask the Bishop of London to send them one. The Churchmen in the Welsh Tract had been visited by missionary ministers; but imagining the influence a regular congregation, and a "steeple-house," would have in the community, about a hundred Welsh Episcopalians, in Radnor, Haverford, and Merion, petitioned the Bishop of London for a permanent minister, one who could speak both Welsh and English, and particularly one "who could be sober," "hoping to recover to the Church the non-conforming Quakers."

Their petition was granted, and the congregation was united, and the church erected in Radnor, and called St. David's. It may have been only a small log building, as the present little stone church was not erected till 1717. The records of this earliest Episcopalian Church, West of the Schuylkill, begin only with the baptism, on 8 June, 1706, of Elizabeth, child of Morgan and Elizabeth Hughes, but there were regular services held here before this. It is estimated that about fifty families attended this church in 1707-8-9, but it is not until 1721-2 that there was recorded a list of members, when we find that among the communicants were David Howell and Evan Harry, the wardens, and Thomas Edwards, James Price, Thomas James, David Thomas, George Lewis, Francis Lewis, Owen Hugh, Philip David, John David, William Owen, Evan Jones, Richard Hughes, &c.

In the "North Wales," or Gwynedd settlement, was another Church of England congregation, holding services at Oxford and Evansburg. The Rev. Evan Evans, of Christ Church, in town, included all the little out-of-town churches in his parish, and visited them at stated times, holding services and preaching in both Welsh and in English, but the

WELSH SETTLEMENT OF PENSYLVANIA

Quakers were not disturbed, and their meetings were held regularly in the Welsh Tract proper, at three, or four meeting houses, and at Plymouth, Oxford, Gwynedd, &c.

At Gwynedd, where the majority of the early Welsh were "Churchmen," and met at the home of Robert Evans, where his brother, Cadwalader Evans, 1664-1745, conducted the services as lay-reader. The prominent Welsh Quakers in that neighborhood at that time were John Hughes, John Humphrey, and Thomas Evans.

THE WELSH BARONY
OF PENSYLVANIA

WELSH TRACT AFFAIRS. I.

Now, as did these Welshmen, we, too, will look back on the conditions on which this land, the great Welsh Tract, was purchased and seated by them, for we have reviewed the reasons for their removal, and see that promises verbally made by grantor to grantees had no recognition subsequently by the proprietary and deputies, since they were not "so nominated in the bond."

That William Penn promised to these Welsh gentlemen, his peers, that their individual purchases each should lie in one body; that they so understood him; (that these farm lands were divided in halves by miles of waste, or sparsely settled territory, we have seen); that he repudiated his verbal agreements with them, this we will see.

That their great, joint tract of land was to be exclusively to their use; that it was to be controlled and governed by themselves, and through laws of their own enacting; that such was their understanding and expectation from promises made by Penn; that this claim was ultimately denied and refused by him, that we will also see.

Unfortunately for the Welsh Friends there could be no appeal from Penn; his word in such matters was final.

When William Penn received from Charles the Second the royal charter for the American territory, which his father had tried and failed to get, conditions for William's success being more favorable, dated at Westminster, 4 March, 1681, for which William, as his father's heir, had petitioned the previous year, in lieu of a debt of £16,000, and interest thereon, due his father from the Crown for disbursements in the Victualling Office, and over which granted territory he was constituted "absolute proprietary," captain-general, and lord high admiral, with only allegiance to the

WELSH SETTLEMENT OF PENSYLVANIA

Crown, and to hold the same forever by fealty only, on a trivial, or nominal annual payment, this territory was erected into a seigniority, and named the Province of Pensylvania.*

But it still continued to be territory of the kingdom, and subject to provisions set forth in the royal charter, yet Penn's power within it was virtually feudal, though subject to these limitations, which defined his authority and legal status. His province he was to govern by the general laws of England; but he could form a constitution for it, with such scope he thought necessary for his domain, and enact laws for it covering peculiar cases or that were necessary under different conditions, with the assent of the freemen and land owners, if he saw fit to ask and consider their wishes, which did not conflict with those of the kingdom. That is, he had full power to form a government to suit his ideas. (With his inexperience in such matters, it is not surprising that when Fletcher superceded Penn as Governor, he declared, after investigation, "the constitution of their Majesties's government, and that of Mr. Penn are in direct opposition, one to the other.")

Penn in full control was more than "absolute proprietary," in the sense that every freeholder is, as he appointed his courts and officers for the proper government of his territory, or province, and was authorized to erect counties and townships, incorporate boroughs and towns, and establish ports in his province. His deputy, residing in the province, ruled in his name the same as the king's lord lieutenant, or governor-general, and Penn was virtually his

---

*See the Pensylvania Colonial Records, vol. I. for the full text of the principal papers relating to the beginning of Pensylvania, namely, the Royal Charter of Charles II. to Penn; Penn's "Conditions and Concessions to Adventurers for Land"; Penn's "Frame of Government," for his province, in its several shapes, as he would like to have had it, and as he had to have it, in the years 1681, 1683, and 1696, and the "Laws agreed Upon." Also Pa. Archives, fourth series, vol. I.

sovereign, for it was in his name councils and assemblies were called and dissolved, and these had no power to initiate legislation for his minature kingdom, and existed only to see that his laws, his wishes, his whims, were carried out in his domain, which he thought to govern from London, as a monarch did his outlaying territory, or as his king then did Virginia, New York and Georgia. Or as he expressed the conditions, "out of my great love and kindness," he had granted the people a charter * * * to ratify his bills.

Penn deriving his authority over his province from the Crown, and, fortified by the Royal Charter, ordered his subjects, the freemen and freeholders, to choose from themselves delegates to an assembly, to make them appear like men of affairs; but they were for a time, only by courtesy "an advisatory body" to him, and really only voiced the wishes of their constituancy, for the province was palatine, even regal, in its nature, and William Penn, the Proprietary, was the petty king, the sovereign count-palatine of feudal times, and he fully expected his dignity would be supported by the revenue from rentals, quit-rents, customs, and taxes, paid into his treasury, willingly, or if not, forcibly, by his subjects, for he is on record under his own hand, that he "must be supported in state and proper magnificence," when residing in his Province, else he would not live here! While Penn may have been sometimes a good Quaker, he certainly "put on airs," and was at first, a stickler for style and pomp he supposed due his exalted position as a minor monarch. However, Quakers in his domain thought differently, and as mild as was the tribute he exacted, arrows, roses, skins, grain, shillings, etc., incorporated in his land patents, very little was willingly paid him, so he is found everlastingly writing that he got no income from his investment, and that his speculation, grandly conceived, but poorly considered, was his ruination. "Prepare the people," he wrote his agent once, "to think of some way to support me. So I may not consume all my substance to serve the Province." But when his "ungrateful assembly" would make no provision for him, he wrote in disgust: "I will sell the shirt off my back before I will trouble them any more." His idea, which he backed with his fortune,—and lost, be it considered only a chimera, was a great "experiment," as he called it, if not a grand scheme, and he had all possible liberty from the Crown to carry it through, and may be would have done so with confiding Quakers, in an entirely Quaker colony, but he never took into consideration the possibility of a mixed population in his province, and that he could not keep it exclusive, or have the "Meeting" paramount.

Some other man, with the backing and freedom he had, might have done better, and made the province into a paying concern, which was his dream, for, although it may in charity be claimed he was "far removed from mercenary consideration in founding Pensylvania," yet there are many instances to the contrary. "Though I desire to extend religious freedom, yet I must have some recompense for my trouble" he wrote. But this "province business" was a new one, in the way he proposed to carry it through, and he had no training to carry through such an undertaking. Other American proprietaries did business on different plans not better. But the chances against Penn's winning were like theirs in a measure, and none won out. Each could lay their undoing and loss to different causes. One of Penn's was, his humanitarian project in mind, that he carelessly, or unwittingly made promises to grantees, that subsequently were urged vigorously, and caused his agents much trouble, and him nearly the cancellation of his royal grant, which he frequently forgot was still in the power of the Crown to do under certain circumstances.

Penn always an idealist, was certainly to be pittied, for with all sorts of claims, "trumpt-up" and legal, coming with every day, the general and necessary confusion of a new settlement, made up of many sorts of settlers and speculators; defective titles, and lapping grants to be straightened out; his money going out in a steady stream, and no cor-

WELSH TRACT AFFAIRS

responding in-flow, were a few of the causes of daily occurence that could have made a less warm hearted and "longer headed man" than William Penn "the greatest Englishman of his time," break under his responsibility. But if Penn had not been so vacillating in his promises, or forgetful of them, when not "so nominated in the bond," his Welsh grantees would have had a higher opinion of him, or have retained their respect for him, and we will see the reasons for their loss of faith. Even his agent here had to remind him he had better carry out his contracts with the grantees, and avoid further troubles.

His career has been more studied than any other man of his day, and because he was no ordinary man, many of his deeds arouse inquiry, therefore, from some points of view, it looks as if Penn had particular spite against the Welsh Friends, and we can believe this to be a fact from the records preserved to us of his treatment of them. His unfair treatment of them, and his pretended ignorance of verbal promises, till he succeeded in humiliating them, and through sundry devices recovered without payment much of the lands they purchased or engaged in good faith from him, are matters so interwoven that they can hardly be classed for separate consideration, so we will only consider the main features of what might be called his persecution of or his unfair dealing with his Welsh settlers.

Even though Penn held to the opinion that the Welsh purchasers had no privileges different from his other grantees, he did not accord them equal rights. Their grant was made to them for a valuable and sufficient consideration and conditions embodied in the lease and release were satisfactory, but this was not all there was to the transaction. We have seen they bought in blocks of 5,000 acres, and under his plan their property as "first purchasers," was "a propriety," subject to a nominal quit-rent, with his free-gift deed, given with each such purchase, of a promise of a certain amount of extra land in the city liberties, or suburbs, and a varied number of lots in the city, and this was a part

WELSH SETTLEMENT OF PENSYLVANIA

of the bargain he made with the Welsh "first purchasers" one they could understand very well, as under a *gwarthal*, it was a Welsh custom.

But Penn tried to annul this gratuity, claiming that the Welsh gentlemen who bought in 1681-2, were only "trustees," and, although they individually may have engaged to take 5,000 each, yet, he learned subsequently, they were only agents and trustees for the real buyers, or co-partners in the purchase, whose purchases out of these "allotments" were at best only a few hundred acres to each, therefore, these "trustees" had no claim to gifts of liberty lands and city lots, as no one of them bought whole tracts of 5,000 acres, there being always two or more concerned in *such purchases. There was no appeal. Purchasers held immediately of William Penn, not of the king. They had to accept the fact that the grant of 40,000 acres was not to one man, or to a corporation, but in fee to a number of individuals, some of whom represented themselves only, while others were trustees for themselves and others, as we have seen, all by separate deeds of conveyance. This hair-splitting in the case of the Welsh purchasers was more evidence of Penn's unfairness to the Welsh Quakers, and they thought him *diwyneb*.

---

*It appears from the minutes of the Board of Property (Book G), 14, 7mo. 1709, the "The Swedes, who presented that abusive Petition in the Assembly, concerning their lands, having desired a meeting with the Commissioners, divers of them met at the secretary's office, and it being demanded what it is they complain off, they Said that the Prop'ry, at his first coming Into this Province, Promised them that he would be as a Father to Them, and that he Came not to Lessen or Take away their Rights, but to confirm Them to them, but that soon after he demanded a Sight of all their Pat's, which were delivered to him, that these had been detained from them, and that many of them had lost a Considerable Patent of the lands they hold of these Pat's taken from them. & that they were obliged To Pay for the Lands they held Greater Q't Rent than they had formerly Paid, which they Conceived to be greatly to their Wrong".

WELSH TRACT AFFAIRS

In another way Penn showed unfair treatment of the Friends from Wales when he exacted more quit-rent from them than he was justified either by his agreement with them, or by the terms of his deeds to them.* The title to the land were not alloidial, for the land was held of Penn by socage tenure, or payment of quit-rent annually, which was a well known fact.

But Penn raised the question inadvertently, particularly with the Welsh Friends, when he was hard pushed for cash, years after they were settled in their new homes, as to when the payment of quit-rent should begin. He insisted it should start from the date of the original grant, to enlarge his revenue, but it was evident to the grantees that the payment was due only after full and legal possession of purchases was had, which could not be till after the final survey of the land, confirmation of title, and receiving of the deed, and this was a matter of several years difference, and, of course, larger payment.

Penn had decided the first surveys were only primative; made only to approximate the locality and extent of the purchases, and that the final surveys, which he ordered, when he suspected there was much overplus land, (which he took to himself, and sold at great advantage, for prices had advanced because of the settlement and improvement of the "country lots"), constituted the completion of the titles. That is, he would have it supposed that he ordered the final survey only to perfect the title, when, in fact, he made the order only to gather to himself the excess land, which he was entitled to.

But this subterfuge re-acted on him, for when the quit-rent question came up, the Welsh, who had by this time considerable "inward light" on such matters, reminded him of his former decision, and held that not till the "final survey" was made did they have legal possession of the lands

---

*See Reed's "Explanation of the City and Liberties," also Shepherd's "Proprietory Government in Pensylvania."

[333]

WELSH SETTLEMENT OF PENSYLVANIA

standing in their names, and from that date the assessment and payment of quit-rent should begin. However, they had to pay from the time of the date of the grant, for the "law," that is Mr. Penn, so decided, for he held it was a matter of indifference to him whether they paid from the date of a grant and called it quit-rent, or paid him ordinary rental of his land, the overplus they used, from the date of the grant up to the time of the "final survey," and then commenced paying quit-rent on their holdings. Being Quakers, there were no suits at law in this matter, and there could be no appeal, for Penn's word was the last.

Still another example of Penn's unfair dealing with the Welsh Friends was when he made the date of the original, the approximating survey, as the date to reckon from when he enforced his "Condition" that "in three years" the purchaser must seat his land, otherwise, Penn could confiscate it, and sell it again. He made the concession; the then holding grantee, however, should have the refusal of it for a "short time," to arrange to buy it over! This rule was particularly aimed at the Welsh Tract land holders.

His "condition," to which many Welsh gentlemen subscribed, 11 July, 1681, was that "a family must be seated in three years," in each purchase of 1,000 acres in the "country lots." This was when he verbally declared to his interviewers from Wales, that no one could purchase more than 1,000 acres, excepting under this condition, and with this understanding.

The question was raised by the Welsh Friends, when Penn notified them of his intention of enforcing this particular "condition," as to when it was proper to begin to reckon the "three years" time. Penn ruled, as in the quit-rent case, "the three years must be reconned from the time of the survey."

"Which survey?" the Welsh inquired, for there had already been several, one of which was the "final survey,"

WELSH TRACT AFFAIRS

"certainly not the first one, nor the second, Friend William, for thee declared the 'final survey' was the only legal one, and we think the three years previlege should be reckoned from the date of it."

"From the first and original one," was Penn's laconic reply.

As in the previous instance of the arbitrariness of Penn, there could be no appeal from his last word in this matter, so the Welsh had to hustle for tenants, or lose their purchases, which had increased much in value, for we have learned from John Jones' letter that "there was no land to be bought [in 1685] within twelve miles of the city," and Dr. Edward Jones, in 1682, wrote that there was "a crowd of people [in Philadelphia] striving for ye Country land."

Another grievance the Welsh Friends felt was theirs, a thing much to their chagrin; but not pecuniary loss, however; was when Penn divided the great Welsh Tract into three parts, or the townships of Merion, Haverford, and Radnor, and subsequently erected others.

Penn certainly had authority, under the Royal Charter, to erect townships by patents, describing the bounds, number of acres in each, locations, and names, which should be recorded, (which, however, was never done), and grant power to the inhabitants of each "to chuse anealy a Constable, Overseer of ye Poor, and Overseer of ye highways for the Township." It seems the Welsh were not allowed "to chuse anealy" their township officers, which was their right, as they understood it, as they were appointed by the County Court.

In this connection, it is of interest to hear what Penn wrote "at Worminghurst Place, 12. 10mo. 1685," in his "Further Account" of his sumoirous province. "Our Townships lie Square, generally the Village in the center; the Houses either opposit, or else opposit to the middle, betwixt two Houses over the way, for near neighborhood. We have another Method, that tho the Village be in the Center, yet after a different manner; 500 acres are allotted for the Village, which, among ten families, comes to 50 acres each. This lies square, and on the outside of the Square stand the Houses, with them 50 acres running back, where, ends meeting, make the center of the 500 acres as they are to the whole. Before the Doors of the Houses lies the Highway, and across it, every man's 450 acres of land, that makes up his complement of 500, so that the Conveniency of Neighborhood is made agreeable with that of the Land. I said nothing in my last of any number of Townships, but there are at least 50, settled before my leaving those parts, which was in the Moneth called August, 1684. I visited many of them." "We do settle in the way of Townships, or Villages," he also wrote, at another time, "each of which contains 5,000 acres, in Square, and at least Ten Families; the regulation of the Country being a Family to each 500 acres. Some Townships have more."

But Robert Turner, in a letter from Philadelphia, 3. 6mo. 1685, to Penn, to be sent out as an advertising circular of the Province, to influence sales of land, was even more "enthusiastic" than Penn, when he wrote, "As to the Country, the Improvements are Large, and settlements very Throng by the way of Townships and Villages"! Most of Penn's "Further Account" of his Utopia we know was "a pipe dream." There is no question but that his idea was to have townships of 5,000 (or 10,000) acres extent, with a village in the middle, and five (or ten) families at least, in each township. But when he wrote the "glowing account" above, there were few families in any township, and these, with the exception of in Merion, (and there the Thomas & Jones party had settled in one corner, and although this township had the largest number of settlers in 1685, it was very far from being "throng"), were seated so scatteringly through any 5,000 acre tract, that a whole township was long called a "town," as much for this reason as for abbreviation.

WELSH SETTLEMENT OF PENSYLVANIA

The Welsh Friends contended that it was agreed their 40,000 acres of land would lie in one undivided tract, or "town," and not be cut up into sections; but, if now there must be townships in the Province, their tract should be only one township, in conformity with the desire which they had expressed, and Penn had agreed to, and that they alone should have the right "to chuse" its officers, and from among themselves, as was also promised, and to expend within it the local taxes collected.

But this municipal district plan did not suit Penn, so the Welsh Tract was arbitrarily divided into three townships, and his Council appointed the first officers, and tried to collect the tithes, and thus the Welshmen were not allowed to have and support their own government within their territory. However, the Welsh continued to exercise some civil authority through their monthly meeting, and held "town meetings" among themselves at the several Friends' Meeting houses, to regulate certain matters of their "towns" which they did not wish to take into court. But of this further. This solid township idea is what has come to be known as the "Welsh Barony."

When you come to review the "Welsh idea," you may note that whatever the Welsh, when purchasing, wanted, Penn promised, and that they realized only disappointments out of their expectations. (And this was the experience of the Germans, too.) Their hopes for a township, or a "barony," in one tract, for themselves alone, their tract to be separate and distinct from every county, to have courts and magistrates of their own, for there is the testimony of one Welshman, that when they called upon Penn in London, they "asked that in our tract, within which all causes, quarrels, crimes, and disputes [arose], might be tried and wholly determined by officers, Magistrates, and Juries of our own language"; * its inhabitants not to do jury duty outside

---

*If the Welsh Friends had enforced some of the old laws peculiar to themselves in their State, there certainly would have been trouble, but probably no more than we are now experiencing in our "united"

WELSH SETTLEMENT OF PENSYLVANIA

of the "Welsh Town," which should be represented as a "barony" in the Provincial Council, and in the Provincial Assembly, by men of their own selection from among themselves, although they claimed to have their own Assembly in their Monthly Meeting, to pay taxes raised only for the use of their Towns, they had reason to expect to enjoy, for they heard the "Great Man" promise, and for these, and other conditions, they often petitioned for confirmation.

Because there was no deed from Penn to the Welsh covering a solid tract of 40,000 acres of Pensylvania land, he, and his agents, took advantage of this oversight, and champions of Penn have claimed there was no authority for supposing the several grants should be laid in one body. Yet, there is Penn's personal instruction to his surveyor-general,

---

States where each has laws of its own choosing, especially in marital matters. The Welsh would have had the wife's dower (*agweddi*, or *gwaddol*), or marriage portion, remain her property, but would have "compensated" the husband by having the bride's father pay him the "maiden fee," (*amobr* or *gobr merch*), if she married by his consent. But not to be excelled in courtesy, the bridegroom would pay the father something, generally live stock, for the "loss" of his daughter's services in his household. And then further, on the morning after the marriage, "if the bride proved to be what he had a right to expect," the groom presented her with *cowyll*, a gift of money for her own use; but this only once, and this was her *cyvarwys*, or perquisite. And if the Welsh Tract, or *cymwd*, had really been as they hoped, that is a *gwlad*, and held by the Friends organized into a polity, their Welsh "land laws" would have conflicted with Penn's. No *ebediw*, nor *gobr estyn*, no inheritance tax, nor investure fee would have been paid, providing all the land had been paid for by the decedent. Then there were peculiar "regulations" as to *gorvedog*, and *mach*, or bail bonds, and security for debt. But it is not clear how their law of *marwdy*, would work, for by it a house and contents "reverted to the lord" when the owner died intestate. Possibly Penn, as the *pennaeth*, or petty king, would have claimed it. But their laws as to *trevtad*, or patrimony, land, cattle, crops, etc., would certainly have made this "State" singular. The law as to horse trading was certainly peculiar; "Whom shall sell a horse or a mare let him be anserable for inward disorders, to-wit, 3 mornings for the staggers, and 3 months for the glanders, and a year for the farcy. Let the person who shall buy it look to an outside blemish."

in his warrant of survey, instructing him to do the very thing the Welsh claimed, and confirming what the Welsh said they understood him to promise them, and this warrant was issued but a short time after the date of their purchases, when the conversation could have been fresh in Penn's recollection. Certainly, it was before he began to be unfair to his Welsh friends. But a stronger argument for unity of the Welsh Tract, and the larger purchasers in it, may be seen in the "condition" of 11 July, 1681, under which he sold to them: "That whenever any number of purchasers, whose acres amount to 5,000 acres, desire to sit together in a township, they shall have their township cast together." However, it was not that the tract was intersected by other tracts, or that part of a Welshman's farm was in one place, and miles off there was some more of it, for it really lay contiguously, and the complaint of the Welsh was that it was subsequently made to lay part in one county and part in another, so, as far as the unity of the tract was concerned the county line might as well have been a many mile wide strip.

Their complaint of "division" also concerned another case within the greater one, but there was nothing to substantiate it, unless Penn's "conditions" of 11 July 1681, covers the case, and in part it does. This was the splitting up of the grants of 5,000, 3,000, and 1,000 acres of land, as we have seen was the case, for nearly all the Welsh Tract parcels, bought from the "trustees," were laid out part in one township, and the balance in a distant one, although within the Welsh Tract. And this affected not only the large tracts, but the small purchasers, for we have seen 150 acre lots, half, the maenor, in Merion, and half in Goshen. The evidence seems to be against any cause for supposing that the grants to the trustees, or companies, should lay contiguously. The deeds to them all read the same, differing of course as to names and acreage, saying "the full quantity of Five Thousand Acres to be allotted and set out in such places, or parts of the said province," etc., as had been or may be agreed upon. There appeared to be no guarantee that the trustees's tracts should be located in one place. This the Welsh overlooked to have in the deeds, never imagining a purchase, or a *cantrev*, would not be all together.

But Penn was particular to have his own 10,000 acre tracts, which he reserved out of each 100,000 acre lot he sold, lie contiguously. This was the plan of "tenths" which he introduced into West Jersey, when he was managing the Byllyngs domain, which, by the way, was not an humanitarian venture, though the sales were at first made to Quakers almost exclusively, and led up to Penn's personal "holy experiment."

There seems always, and particularly so in recent years, to have been considerable misconception about the Welsh Tract having been erected by Penn into a "barony," with all the honors and power pertaining to such a state.

Just as had William Alexander, the poet and court favorite, in Nova Scotia, the proprietors of Maryland, and of Carolina had authority to create a nobility, and the latter only used it. But Penn overlooked, or missed such a concession, or, more likely, he never insisted upon it, for he knew it would not be to the taste of the plain people of his faith, to whom he hoped to sell his land. So, he missed of his own accord being "the fountain of honour, as well as the source of office," yet he was the seignior, with a court, administering and dispencing justice in his name.

Penn, presumably, had no authority given him to create a baronage, and consequently to erect a barony of any degree in his domain, (yet he conferred on a Scotchman the "barony of Inverie," in 1685), or to establish a semblance of an order of nobility. This only king and parliament could do, after he got his charter, and there was no suggestion that such would ever be their intention, or to delegate power to him, a dependent, to create a nobility, which would be feudatory to the Crown only through him, for this would have been what a baronage then meant, whether in Pensylvania, or England.

WELSH TRACT AFFAIRS

Even his 10,000 acre reservations though called manors were never such, for this was only their courtesy title.

Penn's instructions to his surveyors-general to lay out the 40,000 acres of land, (they took altogether 50,000 acres), which the Welsh Friends purchased, "as in a barony," was only a "figure of speech" so far as the tract was concerned. He employed the same expression in the same sense when formulating his assembly; "one representative from each purchase of a 5,000 acre baronage." That is, as to the Welsh Tract, he desired it laid out in a barony-like tract; "may be lay'd out contiguously as [like] one Barony," was the wording of his instruction. He meant all of the purchases of the seven, or more, Welsh "companies" should lie contiguous, in one body, a large sweep of land, or "broad lands," and this did not even suggest that the purchases lying contiguously should be a parish, or a precinct, but only "as one Barony." Penn owned property in Ireland, and had been there, and was probably familiar with the scheme of the plantation of Ulster, and with King James' "Orders and Conditions to be observed by the Undertakers upon the Distribution and Plantation of the Escheated Lands of Ulster," (these Orders, and the "Concessions and Agreements of the Proprietors of West Jersey," 1675-6, Penn must have consulted when he wrote his own "Conditions and Concessions to Adventurers for Land," as he copied their ideas, and expressions some places), which instructed that the ten "townlands" of 5,000 acres each should constitute a barony, and this term is still used in Ireland for every ten townships lying contiguously, or a precinct of 50,000 acres in size, which was the acreage of the Welsh Tract.

I don't think the Welsh Friends, the pioneers, had any notion that Penn meant their tract of land should be "a real barony," under ancient conditions, as has often been claimed. All they were interested in was having their purchases "lie contiguously as in a barony," or whatever such a whole tract of land may be termed, and that Penn should

WELSH SETTLEMENT OF PENSYLVANIA

keep his promises to them, especially as to the entire control and management of it through their meetings, or their monthly meeting.

And I do think that the "true barony" idea originated in the fertile imagination of some zealous, enthusiastic modern descendants of the Welsh Quaker pioneers. They imagined that the "barony" carried with it the feudatory right to sit in Parliament, overlooking the fact that the dignity of a baron, a lord of Parliament, was then, as now, a personal matter; not a territorial adjunct, but an honor conferred by the king and confirmed by a writ of summons to Parliament.

A "true barony," the descendants' idea, I can imagine would have been an ineptly bestowed concession, if the ancient custom had obtained, and Penn had power to inaugurate it. Who among the Welsh Quakers can you imagine would have been the Welsh peer who would sit in Parliament? Who would issue the fee simple grants within the Welsh barony? From whom would have been held the land if at that time a baronage had been a territorial dignity? Whoever he would have been, who would have selected him?

The nearest, the final, or acceptable Royal Charter came to giving Penn power to erect a dignity resembling a baronage was where it gave him a baron's power to erect manors in his province, with all the authority peculiar to them, namely court-baron, "to hold view of frank pledge for the conservance of the peace," "to be fully exercised by the lords of the manors for the time being." Such manors may have been "a feudatory of the prince," for Penn at first had the authority of a petty king, but it did not carry with it the right of the manor-holder to sit in Parliament as a baron, though he was the "lord of the manor for the time being." His Royal Charter also gave Penn's grantees "power to erect any parcels of land within the province into manors," "and in every such manor to have and to hold a court-baron, with all things whatsover which to a court-baron do belong."

WELSH TRACT AFFAIRS

Sydney George Fisher, writing of these times in Pensylvania, has a view of them that is hardly justified by the facts. He said, Penn "had promised them [the Welsh Quakers] a tract of 40,000 acres, where they would have a little government of their own, and live by themselves." "They insisted that their 40,000 acres constituted a barony, or county palatine, and it was known as the Welsh Barony until modern times changed it to Welsh Tract." "It was a manor, with the right of court-baron, like the one occupied by the Moravians on the Lehigh, and, if circumstances had been favorable, it could easily have been developed into a sort of a palatine." The Moravian "barony," was only a reservation, within one of Penn's "manors, and baronial rights, if any ever existed, were never exercised." A better suggestion of Penn's elastic grants was the one to Eneas Macpherson, a Scotchman of course, in 1685. Though it was similar in conditions to the grants to the Welsh "first purchasers," it was manorial, since it gave Mr. Macpherson power to erect his 5,000 acre lot "into the barony of Inverie," with privilege of court-leet, court-baron, &c. He further directed his Land Commissioners to grant large tracts of land with the same conditions, but, somehow they overlooked this order, which was very careless of them. This idea of manors, with court-baron, and even the Board of Land Commissioners, was the same King James employed when dealing with the undertakers for Ulster.

Penn knew better than to experiment with a petty nobility in his refuge for Quakers, and, as said above, he considered his manors were simply divisions of his territory for his own convenience. That is, his own manors were the lands kept in his own hands, for his personal use, or that of his family, and the "lord" of such manors, was simply his steward, appointed, or removed by him, at will.

But it was not Penn's fault that there was not the order of nobility in Pensylvania. Although not himself of the nobility he was an aristocrat, and so were some who assisted him in framing his government. But others, not living in

WELSH SETTLEMENT OF PENSYLVANIA

aristocratic atmosphere, advised him, if he wished to realize on his land, and interest the "plain people" in it, he should change his "Frame," and eliminate the nobility idea from it.

We have seen that one of his schemes was to sell land in lots of 5,000 acres, with the "patroon idea" of settlement. This idea he held on to when he early planned the "Parliament" for his Province. He wanted a "House of Lords," composed of owners of 5,000 acre tracts of land, and a "Lower House," made up of their tenants. That is, the Upper House of Parliament, or House of Lords, should be composed of fifty "barons"; and to be eligible to it, or to be a baron, one must be a married man and own 5,000 acres, or "a propriety." The right to sit as a "baron" was to descend from heir to heir, so long as the "barony" was not reduced below 2,000 acres, in such a case the "baronage" should cease. This was a great advertising card for Pensylvania if Penn had not been argued out of distributing it. It seemed such a good thing to him, that another draft of the same "Frame" makes the number of "barons" 100. The "lords and tenants" were to be organized into standing committees, with, of course, the "Lords" in the majority, which should attend to all matters of "church and State."

In Penn's draft of the charter, the one he would have liked the king to grant, but which was discarded, he mapped out for himself extraordinary powers. He was to have the usual and magnificent powers of a count-palatine of feudal times, or an independent principality, with homage and fealty only to the king. It gave him powers to coin money, confer titles receive and spend all the revenue, control all the courts, etc., and be dictator in everything within his domain. The conferred royal charter was very much modified, probably to Penn's chagrin.

It cannot be denied that from the first the Welsh Friends had large ideas about the status of their tract, or "towns," for all along there are suggestions that they presumed on what might be considered manorial, or baronial rights and privileges within their tract, and attempted to

WELSH TRACT AFFAIRS

enjoy them. Their chief offense in this respect against the supreme authority of the proprietary was the use, if not organization of the monthly meeting into an alleged local court, to settle disputes arising in the tract, generally civil disputes arising among themselves, but probably not criminal cases, and there is suggestion that "taxes" were levied within their bounds for the use of the community, through the monthly meeting. And further, that they claimed that their "towns" should have delegates of their own selecting sit in the general assembly, and, if possible, one member from the tract in the provincial council. The "Welsh idea" of a tract exclusive to themselves, be it a barony, manor, or state, within Penn's province, may have been crude and impracticable, but certainly, if we are to believe Hugh Roberts, they originally had some encouragement from Penn in the matter of self-government, or that he held out some such inducement when effecting the sale of the land, and without actually committing himself to the scheme by signing any agreement to this effect. Penn himself did create one barony, or manor, we know, and did instruct his commissioners to do the same for him, so I do not doubt but that he made the promises to the Welsh Friends, which they claimed he did as late as in 1688-89.

Pastorius, the German scholar, who bought 15,000 acres of Penn, in London, on 5 June, 1683, for himself, and "an aggregation of individuals," all Germans, known as the Frankfort Company, came over to Philadelphia, arriving 20 Aug., 1683. It seems they experienced almost the identical troubles the Welsh Friends had about lands, and concessions. His letters tell of the difficulty he had to get the land located and surveyed, after he had paid for it, and William Penn, "of his princely bounty," had granted it, and how he had to be satisfied with any location for the purchase the surveyor would give him, which we know was out on the hills of the present Germantown, across from the "Welsh Town." Pastorius may have supposed he should have had better treatment from Friend Penn, because Penn was part Dutch himself, his mother "Dutch Peg," (as Pepys called her), having been a Dutchwoman, and Penn spoke the Teutonic language well enough to express himself in both Dutch and German, and preached in both lands.

A minute of the Provincial Council, 5. 1mo., 1700-1, records that Pastorius presented a petition in behalf of the German corporation, "setting forth, That by the Proprietaries advice and Directions, they had seated themselves so close together that they Scarce have room to live. But Especially, That the Propriet'ry by his Charter in the Year 1689, had granted Several Considerable Privileges to the Germans of the Said Town by making them A Corporation by virtue of which they looked upon themselves exempt from the Jurisdiction of ye County Court of Philad'ia, and from all Taxes & Levies of the Same, having a Court of Record & Magistrates within themselves, and Defraying all the Public Charges of their Said Town & Corporation without any Assistance from the rest of the County. Therefore, they requested to be exempt from general County levies. A copy of their Charter being produced, It appeared by it that they had full Power of holding Court of Recording, and of trying Cases Judicially within themselves, but had no other grant for Representatives to Sitt in Assembly, than what ye rest of the County had." Several reasons were advanced why they should not share and contribute to the Philadelphia county taxes, one being that the roads and bridges the county maintained near their bounds, were enjoyed more by them than any people, and therefore they should help pay for them. On the contrary, they replied this was offset by keeping at their own charge the roads and bridges within their bounds, which were used by the whole country. From this it may be seen that not only the Welsh experienced Penn's capriciousness.*

---

*Even the beneficiaries under his will of his old friend, the noted apostle of Quakerism, George Fox, had an unpleasant experience with Mr. Penn. By deed of lease and release, dated 21 and 22 Oct. 1681 (which was not recorded till 21 April, 1767), George Fox bought

WELSH TRACT AFFAIRS

It may have been for this reason that some of the leading English Quakers considered the Germans, as new settlers, were not acceptable. In 1717, Judge James Logan complained of "the great number of palatines pouring in upon us, without any recommendation, which gives our country some uneasiness, for foreigners do not so well among us as our own people."

This German community kept together till about the year 1707, not so long as the Welsh one, and the cause of disintegration in both "towns," or settlements was the same, for the Germans, like the Welsh, presumed on too much, when they supposed they were to live by themselves, have a government of their own, under laws they had been accustomed to, and in their own tongue, and be represented in the general assembly of the province as a distinct "German State," for Pastorius, their leader and "Moses," says

---

from Penn 1250 acres of land, to help along his "experiment," paying £25, for which amount Penn gave him a receipt, witnessed by Harb't Springette, Tho Coke, and Mark Swaner. Fox was, as bonus, to have a city lot of twenty acres, or if he preferred, 16 acres of Liberty Land among the Welsh Friends, and two good city lots, and to pay one shilling per 100 acres in ground rent. Fox died in 1690, without having had his patent recorded, but he devised the "city lots" for the use of Phila. Friends, and this gift was confirmed to Friends Carpenter, Hill and Morris, as trustees, by patent dated 26. 6mo. 1705. The remainder of his right, Mr. Fox devised to his wife's sons-in-law, Thomas Lower, John Rouse, and Daniel Abraham. Said Abraham, and Nathaniel Rouse, son and heir to John, by deed dated 21. 4mo. 1715, for £8, released their interest in Fox's lands to Mr. Lower, who requested warrant to lay it out, which was granted, 22. 9mo. 1717. The above trustees had Fox's city lots, ' for the use of Friends located at the corner of High and 2d Streets, and on this property a meeting house was erected in 1695-6. This "annoyed" Penn greatly (see the Penn-Logan Correspondence, letters of Oct. 1703, and Sep. 1705), as he claimed these were lots he wished to reserve for his family, and that Markham had given them away without his permission. This, too, was a reflection on the trustees, but as they had had other similar experiences with the Founder, they let him fume, and did not surrender the lots, but had them confirmed to them as above.

WELSH SETTLEMENT OF PENSYLVANIA

(just as the Friends minister, Hugh Roberts, also said), he so understood Mr. Penn promised him at the time he bought and paid for the land, when, "not respecting his own profit, but the welfare" of the Germans, he was "graciously pleased to distribute" the lands of his province "to them as shall seek the same." As late as in 11mo., 1693-4, these Germans, like the Welsh, wanted to know if their grant, or charter, did not exempt their "town" from paying two sets of taxes, their own, and to Philadelphia County.

Penn evidently made some promises, possibly "with a mental reservation" not to keep them if they did not suit him ultimately. Therefore, it is not surprising that we do find him "changing his mind" about having independent states within his province. Once, he might have supposed this plan practicable, but, as he wrote in his "Frame of Government" (1682), a most wonderful document, even if compiled from the ideas of previous promoters, but it had defects, yet it has "excited the enconiums of many historians," "I do not find a model in the world that time, place, and some singular emergencies have not necessarily altered," so changed his mind. It is history that nearly every one of his ideas of government, on trial, turned out dreams, and failures, and were easily replaced by the carefully thought-out Charter of Privileges, in 1701. The practical men on the ground rather than Penn, the almost stranger, knew what the province required.

Penn was not only vacillating in the manner of disposing of his land, and promises made concerning it, for at the very first, he had no fixed rule for either mode, or extent of his grants; they were in consequence of an irregular, and informal nature, but even in the little matter of selling "whiskey," or intoxicating liquor to Indians.

At a meeting of the Provincial Council, 21. 1mo., 1683-4, at which he presided, it was left to him "to discourse with the Indians concerning an agreement with them about letting them have Rum." On 10. 3m. following, Penn in person informed the Council that he "had called the Indians together, and proposed to them to let them have Rum, if they would be contented to be punished as ye English were [when they became noisy-drunk], which they did agree to, provided that ye law of not Selling them Rum be abolished," which we all know was a distinct departure from Penn's original ideas as to rum for Indians.

Less than three years after the successful settlement of the great "Welsh Tract," the English of the province became jealous of its advancement, and started in to wreck it. Their procedure was not systematic, but in point of date, the matter of having a new boundary line for Chester county, particularly between the counties of Philadelphia and Chester, that would be directed so as to place the "towns" of Haverford and Radnor within the county of Chester, when a big slice would be cut off from the tract, was the first move, in 1685, and deserves first consideration. Upon this first occasion, the Chester people were not so much vexed over the irregular and uncertain bounds of their county, as they were concerned in extending their territory, and increasing their tax list, and consequently, revenue.

From Minutes of the Provincial Executive Council, 1. 2mo., 1685. Thomas Holme (or Holmes), the surveyor general, acting president, and present, the following matter was introduced:

"WHEREAS, The Gov'r in psence of John Symcock and William Wood, was pleased to Say & grant, That ye bounds of the Countys of Chester & Philadelphia should be as followed, Viz't:—

"That the bounds should bigin at the Mill Creek ["Darby Mill Creek," or Cobbs' Creek], and Sloping to ye Welch Township, and thence to Scoolekill, &c., in obedience thereto and Confirmation thereof,

"The Council having Seriously Weyed & Considered the same, have and doe hereby Agree and Order that ye bounds betwixt the said Countys shall be thus: That is to Say, 'then

WELSH SETTLEMENT OF PENSYLVANIA

follows the description of the lines proposed for Chester County laid down so as to take into it the Welsh townships of Harford and Radnor,' mentioning in the courses 'the land of Andros Boone & Co.,' the 'Severall Tracts of Land belonging to the Welch & Other Inhabitance,' 'Land belonging to Jno Humpheris,' and 'land of Jno Ekley.'*

"The Question was put, whether the afore mentioned Creeks, Courses, and Lines, shall be the bounds betwixt the Countys of Philadelphia & Chester, according to ye Gov'rs grant as aforesaid; Unanimous Carried in ye Affirmative."

No Welsh Quaker was a member of the Provincial Council at this time. No notice, or warning was sent to the Welsh that question of throwing their "towns" of Haverford and Radnor out of the Welsh Tract, and Philadelphia county, into Chester county, was sent to their leading men. The Irishman, Mr. Holme, was presiding that day over the meeting during the absence in New York of Thomas Lloyd,† and advantage of this was taken by the Chester members, as it was well known that Mr. Lloyd did not favor this transference. Symcock and Wood, who brought up this matter at the meeting, represented Chester county, and it was upon their statements that the matter was considered, and there thus could never have been a more favorable chance

---

*By deed dated 30 Oct. 1682, Edward Prichard, of Almeley, Hereford, glover, for £25, sold 1250 acres, a part of his 2500 acres in the Welsh Tract, to John Eckley, of Kimbolton parish, Herefordshire, yeoman. Prichard also sold 312 acres, for £6.5.0. to John Vaston, of Docklow parish, Hereford, yeoman, and 312 acres to Elizabeth Good, of Kimbolton parish. Both deeds dated 1 Nov. 1682.

---

†There is a letter from Mr. Lloyd, preserved by the Pa. Historical Society, written in New York about this time. And there is one from Penn to Lloyd, dated London, 21. 2mo. 1686, saying, "Thyn from N. York of Novemb'r last is come to my hand." Lloyd apparently intended to desert Pensylvania and take up his residence in New York, for Penn wrote at this time, "Since the Lord has cast thy lott else where, I am glad thou affordest the Province thy presence Some times."

WELSH TRACT AFFAIRS

to introduce it, and have it acted on to satisfy their constituents of Chester.

However, although the resolution had been properly passed in the Executive Council, it could not become operative until it had the sanction of William Penn, or of his deputy governor, and Mr. Holme would not presume on using all the power of the latter entrusted to him. Therefore, at the next meeting of the Council, a week later, or on 8. 2mo., 1685-6, the subject was again introduced by the Chester members, who urged the acting president to forward the resolution to Mr. Penn, to get him to ratify it, owing to the continued absence of President Lloyd.

But by this time, the scheming of the Chester county people had become known to the Welsh Quakers across the Schuylkill, and they did considerable lobbying and wire-pulling, as their efforts against the proposition would be known to us, and through their influence it was decided by the Council that the bounds of all the counties should be adjusted and determined, for the purpose of properly collecting taxes, and defining sheriffs' jurisdictions, before sending the resolution as to the Chester line to Penn, and when all the counties had been bounded to send the descriptions together to him. It was decided to consider the bounds of Bucks county at the next meeting, and, in due time, the bounds were considered, and laid down, but no other county was reached before adjournment, which was just what the Welsh hoped would happen. At the next meeting, Mr. Lloyd presided, and for reasons of his own the matter of county boundaries was dropped. Whatever was the nature of Mr. Lloyd's influence over the Council and with Penn, it must have been strong, for the Chester line matter lay dormant for three years, although the resolution passed on the 1st of 2mo., had been sent by Holme to Penn, when Mr. Lloyd declined to confirm it.

Up to March, 1689-90, the Welsh Tract was left in a peculiar position, with thanks to Mr. Lloyd, Mr. Eckley,

WELSH SETTLEMENT OF PENSYLVANIA

and Mr. Turner, the majority of the five commissioners. Its large "towns" of Haverford and Radnor had been transferred from Philadelphia county to Chester county by the resolution of 1 April, 1685, and this was acknowledged by the Philadelphia county authorities, as they made no attempt to collect taxes in these townships for Philadelphia county uses. And, although attempts were made to induce them to do so, they had paid no taxes, or assessments for the expenses and support of Chester county, the resolution aforesaid not having the sanction of Penn, nor had it been confirmed by him or his deputy governor. The Welsh Quakers did not care how long this state of affairs lasted. In fact, this being separate and distinct from all county organizations, was what Penn had given them to understand would be the status of their whole tract in the province, so they could only suppose they had come so far into their own (it was as near as the tract ever came to being a real "barony"), and accordingly, in these years, carried on the affairs of the two "towns" through their monthly meeting, and collected assessments, and contributions within them for the use of the whole "barony."

But unexpectedly, on the morning of 25. 1mo., 1689-90, the Chester line matter, and the assignment of Haverford and Radnor, was suddenly revived in the meeting of the Executive Council, Captain John Blackwell, the then deputy governor, presiding, by a motion to consider.

Information as to this soon reached Thomas Lloyd, the attorney and champion for the Welsh in the "line matter," so he went to the Chamber, and inquired of the Governor as to the rumor. The Governor assured him, saying, "No such thing was yt brought before them, but that if any such thing were, wherein it should be found requisite to hear them [the Welsh Quakers] they should have notice thereof."

That very afternoon, the justices, and some inhabitants of Chester county, appeared by appointment before the Council, and presented a petition, stating:—

WELSH TRACT AFFAIRS

"WHEREAS, Ye said County [Chester] is but a Small tract of Land, not above nine miles Square, & but Thinly seated, whereby ye said County is not able to Support the Charge thereof [the illproportioned tax put on it for the support of the Provincial Government]. Upon our humble Request to The Proprietor & Goer'r, and his Serious Consideration of our weak Condition, was pleased out of Compassion to us, to grant an Enlargement of ye same, in manner following, viz: to runn up ffrom Delaware River, along darby mill Creek, ye severall Courses thereoff, untill they took in Radnor and Herford Townshipps."

The Chester county people thereupon again prayed for the confirmation of the bounds named in the resolution of 1685, so their county would be large enough to be able to defray the charges against it, and the justices urged that the new line be run and recognized, on the ground of general jurisdiction and assessments.

The Governor, John Blackwell, then demanded the Chester county committee should put in writing, as a matter of form, and submit to the Council, "their allegations" as to the bounds of the county, and proof that the Proprietor said that Radnor and Haverford townships should be included in Chester county, for the object they claimed, as there was no documentary proof of it.

John Blunstone, of Chester Co., wrote: "A few days before Govern'r Penn left this Province that upon ye bank by John Simcock's house, I moved him to decide this matter," . . . . "who then, before me and Others, did Declare that" . . . [the new bounds should] "take in the Townds of Herford & Rudnor," &c., "then I asked him if he would be pleased to give it under his hand, to avoyd further Trouble," and he said that Penn told him to see him the following day. A Chester Co. man, Blunstone continued, was sent the next day to see Penn, and came back without getting the order, "what then obstructed I am not certaine," said Blunstone, and Penn sailed to England two days later, without leaving directions.

WELSH SETTLEMENT OF PENSYLVANIA

Randall Vernon, of Chester Co., testified in writing, that, "some time since William Howell, of Harford [he served on the petty jury 28, 8, 1683], Signified unto me, and gave it under his owne hand, yt some time after they there Settled that he asked ye Govern'r to what County they should be joyned, or belong unto, & The Govern'r was pleased to answer him that they must belong to Chester County."

Thomas Usher, the sheriff of Chester Co., testified, that in conversation with Penn, the Governor said to him, "Thomas, ... I intend that ye bounds of Philadelphia County Shall Come about 3 or ffour miles on this side of the Skoolkill."

To clinch the "evidence," a map of Pensylvania,* "made for the Governor" by Surveyor Holme sometime after it was voted, in 1685, at the Council meeting over which Holme presided, that Haverford and Radnor should be included within Chester county, was produced, and examined by the President. It showed these two townships located in Chester county, of course, for that was where Holme wanted them, and he had the resolution of 1685 as his "authority" for so placing them (that the "bounds of Chester county should begin at the [junction of Darby Creek and] Mill creek [now Cobbs creek] and sloping to ye Welsh township [line], and thence to Schoolkill," in a straight line, thus throwing the townships of Radnor and Haverford, and the lands of "Rowland Ellis & Company," "John Eckley &

---

*"Thomas Holme's Map of the Province of Pensylvania, containing the Three Counties of Chester, Philadelphia, and Bucks, as far as yet surveyed and laid out," was the title of this map. The bounds are in different colors, and the statement is made: The divisions or distributions made by the different coullers aspects the settlements by way of townships." The map is drawn to scale of one mile to an inch. The information on the printed map is 'First printed and sold and dedicated to William Penn by John Thornton and Robert Green, of London.' The original map is in the Philadelphia Library. In 1845, 200 opies in facsimile, by "the asastic process," were made from the original, for Mr. Lloyd P. Smith.

WELSH TRACT AFFAIRS

Company" into Chester county, while originally the dividing line began at the mouth of Darby creek, and a straight line, with Haverford and Radnor Towns on the East side of this line, and New Town on the West side, continued to the uppermost line of the Welsh Tract), so it was taken for granted by the President that it was Penn's desire, although there was no evidence that he had confirmed the resolution of 1. 2mo., 1685.

Ever since then there has been mystery surrounding the date of Holme's map, as it bears none, yet it is certainly an interesting, if not valuable one to us. In October, 1690, certain Welshmen reported in a petition (quoted thereafter) to the Executive Council that there were at that time "near four score" settlements in the whole Welsh Tract, which they desired should be understood as a fine showing of population after eight years' possession. But according to Holme's map, alleged to have been compiled in 1683-4, or in 1685, he mentions in it as settlements, or seated plantations, in the Welsh Tract, forty in Radnor, thirty-two in Haverford, and thirty-two in Merion, that is 104 in all. He did not name the settlers of Haverford and Radnor, but did those of Merion, excepting the "17 lots" in the "Thomas & Jones" tract. He, being a surveyor and acquainted personally, or through his deputies, with this section, must have been certain of his statements. Therefore, from the statement of 1690, it looks as if Holme made his map long after 1685, and about 1689, when it was displayed to convince Blackwell, and when the actual seats numbered near eighty, the other score, or more, being names of land owners only.

" 'Twas asserted," by someone, "that the Welch Inhabitants had Denyed themselves to be any part of The County of Philadelphia, by refusing to bear any Share of Charges, or [to] serve in office, or Jurys, And the like as to ye County of Chester." "That the pretence thereof was," said

WELSH SETTLEMENT OF PENSYLVANIA

another, "they were a distinct Barrony, wch [and this] they might be, yet [that] severall Barronys might be in one and ye same County." This was in 1689.

The members of the Council present "Declareing themselves satisfied Concerning their [Haverford and Radnor] being a part of Chester County, upon ye grounds alliged and proved as aforesaid," were going to confirm the bounds, when they were informed that Thomas Lloyd was without, and had something to say against this.

On being brought into the Council Chamber, Mr. Lloyd again said he "understood something had been moved about adding ye Welsh Towns, or tracts, to the county of Chester, and if anything was proposed, desired they would give him an opportunity to speak."

So, he was invited to come next morning and "shew cause why they should not be Declared to be of the County of Chester, as the Proprietor had promised." "Otherwise, the Evidence seemed so full as that they should proceed to Declare their judgment therein."

The following morning, 26 March, 1689, "At the Councill in the Councill Room," the minute of the Council, "touching the ascertayning the dividing lyne betweene the Countys of Philadelphia & Chester, dated ye 1st day 2. Mo. 1685," was read. Samuel Carpenter and William Yardley thought the Welsh of Philadelphia Co. should have a longer time to consider the boundary question, but the Governor thought the matter was so plain, there was no need debating it further. However, if there was anyone without who wished to say anything at once, he would hear him if brought in. The Secretary, William Markham, was sent from the room to inquire, and brought back the attorneys, Thomas Lloyd and John Eckley. "The Governor asked them if they had anything to object (on the behalf of ye Welsh people), against the Running of the lyne as appeared by the map, which added them to ye County of Chester."

"Tho. Lloyd sayd, 'the Proprietor assured them their Barony should not be divided, and had given them grounds

WELSH TRACT AFFAIRS

to Expect they should be made a County Palatine.' The Govern'r inquired if any such thing had beene past? [recorded]. Nothing appeared." Apparently, Gov. Lloyd did not produce the warrant of survey as voucher that the Welsh tract was to be as in a barony.

"Tho Lloyd asked the Govern'r by what authority these dividing Lynes were drawne? The minute on this matter, of the day before, was read to him as answer; to which Tho. Lloyd declared his opinion: That some more time should have been allowed for their appearing to make their Exceptions." "He also demanded of the Gover'r whether the Proprietor had power of himself to divide the Countyes, or whether the Proprietor & Councill. The Govern'r answered that by ye said Depositions, minutes, & map, it appeared to be done by both in this case."

"John Eckley declared he had nothing to say, but that he thought further time might be allowed in the matter."

After the attorneys for the Welsh has retired, the question was put in Executive Council as to accepting the bounds of Chester Co., "Expresst by the dividing line marked in the large map of the Province, dedicated to ye Proprietor, and being according to the Order of the Provinciall Councill, dated ye 1. of ye 2d month, 1685." The motion was "carried by a rising vote. Carpenter and Yardley voting contrary, because they thought the Welsh ought to have had a longer time for making their defence."

Friend Thomas Lloyd, who had good reason for not liking Gov. Blackwell, and the Governor had no liking for him, as he was one of the men he could not control, or bring into his way of thinking, was not only exceedingly annoyed at the loss of his "case," but was angry over the "snap judgment." Whether, or not, he wished to annoy the Governor, Col. Markham, the secretary of the Council, tells that Thomas hung about the Council Chamber door harranguing a crowd so loud about the injustice to his clients that the Governor could not proceed with business in Coun-

WELSH SETTLEMENT OF PENSYLVANIA

cil, "and desired ye sayd Tho Lloyd would forbeare such lowd talking, telling him he must not suffer such doings, but would take a Course to suppresse it, and shutt ye Doors, So he went away." And the Governor, the erstwhile Cromwellian, remarked, "Seems we have two Governors, one inside the Council Chamber, and one outside," thus recognizing the great influence the Welsh Quaker, Mr. Lloyd, had in the city, and the Province.

After the Governor's decision, the regulation of Haverford and Radnor was left to the Chester Co. Court, and it had a hard proposition before it to make the Welsh Quakers submit to its authority. The first attempt to organize the townships with proper officers, was when the Court made the order appointing as constables, John Lewis for Haverford, and John Jarman for Radnor. But as they declined to appear at Court and qualify, the Court ordered that warrants of contempt be "directed to the sheriff to apprehend the bodys of Lewis and Jarman for their contempt in not entering into their respective offices of Court, ... when thereunto required by this Court." Lewis does not appear to have surrendered, but Jarman was, in a few months, attested constable for Radnor by the Court. David Lawrence was drawn as a grand juror from Haverford, and declining to serve, "was mulct in ten shillings fine," William Jenkins for the same reason was also fined, and finally consented to serve. As early as in the June term of Court, William Howell, mentioned above by Vernon, was appointed the justice of the Court, in Haverford, but would not accept the commission, "But he did afterwards subscribe to the solemn declaration prepared by the 57th chapter of the great Law of this province." In 1mo., 1689-90, John Blunston, mentioned above, was rewarded for his efforts in the "line matter" by being returned by Chester Co. to represent it in the Provincial Council for three years. But being unable to serve, William Howell, of Haverford, was elected in his place, but he, too, sent a letter "setting forth his Incapassity of giveing Such attendance as is

WELSH TRACT AFFAIRS

Requisite to that Service." Like the others of the Welsh Quakers, he was stubborn, and could not be conciliated even by high office, and the supposition is, Vernon misquoted him at the hearing. The Court at Chester presented "the want of the Inhabitants of the townships of Radnor and Harfort and the Inhabitants adjacent they not being brought in to join with us in the Levies, and other public services of this County." But in about a year, the jurisdiction of the Chester Court was recognized, and the Welsh "towns" had the proper officers in 1690, when the civil authority exercised by the Monthly Meeting was supplanted by the usual township government.

In fact up till now, no Welsh Quakers would accept appointments from the Chester Co. Court, else it would be construed an acknowledgment by the Welsh that Haverford and Radnor were parts of the county of Chester. It was such continued refusals in past years that forced the Chester Court and inhabitants to bring the line matter up again before the Executive Council, as above related, and this is the proof that the Chester Court had considered the action of the Council, on 1. 2mo., 1685, as final, but to make the resolution valid, wanted the new Governor's confirmation, as Penn, nor Lloyd, would not give it.

I don't suppose there ever was a better sample of fake evidence winning a cause than that of this use of "Holme's Map of Pensilvania." Gov. Blackwell, a stranger here, it would be charitable to believe was "easy" and credulous, and had no suspicion that Holme was always unfriendly towards the Welsh, and had made his map, in 1685, or later, after the Council meeting, on 1. 2mo., 1685, at which he acted as presiding officer, showing Haverford and Radnor, located in Chester Co., and the Welsh Tract bisected, for the very object in which it was used.

What was Penn's part in this suspicable transaction? When he received the map in England, if he examined it, he must have supposed that his surveyor-general had placed the two Welsh "towns" in Chester Co. only to let him see

WELSH SETTLEMENT OF PENSYLVANIA

what the proposed county line would do, if he sanctioned it. He certainly knew that the Council passed the "line resolution" in 12mo., 1685-6, for it was sent to him, and also that he, or his Deputy Governor, never confirmed the action. But as there was no protest from Penn on file, Governor Blackwell, with the map dedicated to Penn before him, could have presumed it was just as Holme, and the Chester justices, and principal inhabitants of Chester Co. assured him, for although Lloyd and Eckley must have been familiar with the situation, they only asked that the Welsh have "more time to consider" about giving their consent. However, we have only the scanty Council minutes on this matter as authority for this. But there was more behind this "line affair" than "the county sheriff's jurisdiction," and "assessments," that showed the personal interests of Holme, et al.

At this time there was an election shortly due for councillors and assemblymen, and there was to be returned for Philadelphia county, in which the Welsh Tract lay, one councillor and six assemblymen. There were two sets of candidates—the Governor's tickets, and that of the Quakers. With the Welsh Tract Quakers voting solid against the administration's candidates, there was no hope of their election. Therefore it was the scheme of the political supporters of the administration to force the acceptance of Holme's Chester county line before the election. If they gained their point, as we see they did, this would throw the votes of the two big Welsh townships of Radnor and Haverford into Chester Co., and with the lost of the sixty Welsh Quaker votes in these townships, or 72 votes, if we are to believe Holme, who, on his map, has this number of land owners in these townships, the power of the Welsh Tract would be broken. Further, the casting of these Welshmen's votes in Chester Co. would make no difference

WELSH TRACT AFFAIRS

in that county, as it was overwhelmingly in favor of the administration.

But when the election took place, the transplanted Welsh Quaker freemen declined to recognize the new dividing line, and cast their votes as with Chester Co., but voted for their candidate for councillor, John Eckley, with Merion township, as of Philadelphia county, with this solid Welsh Tract vote Eckley was elected to represent Philadelphia Co. in the Executive Council, and the administration candidate was defeated.

The Deputy-Governor and the Council immediately considered this feature of the election, the irregularity of which was reported by the sheriff, 1 Sept., 1689, and threw out the entire Welsh Tract vote for Mr. Eckley, declaring "yt ye Election of Jo Eckley was not a good Election according to ye Charter," and ordered a new election.

Then arose a momentuous question. The Council debated the proper manner of choosing the candidate, and conducting the election, as all were not of one mind, and the "Form of Government," and the "Charter" were ambiguous and uncertain on this subject, so "the usual custom" had to be considered as the rule, whether the election must be "by vote or by ballot," a distinction being made in these methods, that is, "by vote" the expression of choice was *viva voce*, and "by ballot" the proceeding was comparatively secret.

In the second election ordered, the freemen, uncertain which was correct, generally "voted" by both methods, for the same candidates, in different counties, so the proper manner of voting was not settled, nor was the result of the election changed.

In this new election, the Welsh freemen of the three townships of the Welsh Tract, voted together again, and this time *viva voce*, and again elected Mr. Eckley unanimously.

But the Deputy-Governor and the Executive Council would not accept this second election, because "the Haver-

WELSH SETTLEMENT OF PENSYLVANIA

ford and Radnor freeman voted in the wrong county," and because "all the polls were not taken uniformly," and a new election ordered, although the administration could be defeated without Haverford and Radnor voting in Philadelphia and refusing to vote in Chester Co.

This brought up again the discussion between the freemen and the Council, over the manner and method of choosing at a poll. It was on this occasion that Griffith John, or Jones (the father-in-law of Thomas Jones, of Merion, son of John ap Thomas), deserted the Welsh column, and took side against the views of the Welsh Quakers beyond the Schuylkill.

One Mr. Curtis claimed, in the debate, "it was a very fayre Election. In other places we are generally chosen by the Vote." Another gentleman said, "the balloting box is not used in any other place but this country." And Griffith Jones replied, "this was a mistake, for it is used at Upland, and all the Lower Countyes, by black and white beans put into a hatt, wch is a ballotting in my sense, and cannot be denyed by the Charter when it is demanded." (Pa. Col. Rec. I. 282.)

The above gives a good idea of primative elections for officials in Pensylvania in 1689. But the manner, I don't think, agreed with the instructions in the 1683 "Frame of Government," which was to use a written ballot, as was the custom in West Jersey, since 1676, and in the New England colonies, following the ancient Roman institution.

So bitter was the feeling against Mr. Eckley that the doors of the Council Chamber were shut to him, and he would not be allowed in the room even only as a spectator. But then spectators had the privilege of injecting remarks, expressing their opinions, if not actually taking part in debates. Nor was Thomas Lloyd permitted to enter the Chamber, because he annoyed the Governor even by his presence. Nor was Samuel Richardson, because he refused to recognize Blackwell's authority over the Welsh Friends in the "barony." Mr. Lloyd urged him to enter one morn-

WELSH TRACT AFFAIRS

ing, but the Governor had him forcibly ejected from the Chamber. Captain Blackwell's tenure of office was as unpleasant to himself as to the people generally, and when he was ordered home, he thanked God for his removal, for "he was sick of the Pensylvania mess." Thomas Lloyd again received the appointment to Governorship, and succeeded him, much to the delight of the Friends, in Jan., 1690-91.

The Council refusing to accept the election of Mr. Eckley, the opinion of the Court of Chester was sought, as to the status of the Welsh Quaker votes, and manner of voting in Chester county. But as Mr. Lloyd shortly returned to the Deputy-Governorship, he settled the questions satisfactorily out of court.

Of course, after the Welsh Quakers of Haverford and Radnor found they were irrevocably located in Chester Co., they accepted county offices for their own protection, but as the Executive Council, or the Court of Chester had no control over their spiritual matters, the Haverford and Radnor Welsh Friends continued their allegiance to Merion Friends, and the three meetings continued as the Haverford (or, subsequently, Radnor) monthly meeting, and in the jurisdiction of the Philadelphia quarterly meeting, ignoring altogether the Chester quarterly meeting, in spite of its protests, and this situation still obtains.

In this connection, the following note from the Haverford Monthly Meeting, addressed to the Chester Quarterly Meeting, preserved with the papers of John ap Thomas, in the Levick family, of Bala, is not without interest:—

"To ffriends of the Quarterly Meeting in Chester County.

"From our Monthly Meeting held at Haverford, the 10th of the 8th month, 1700. Dear friends, In the Truth of God our Salutation is unto you, desireing we may be one in it forever.

"The proposal Layd before our monthly meeting of friends appointed by your Quarterly meeting, viz. that our

WELSH SETTLEMENT OF PENSYLVANIA

monthly meeting should be Joyned to your Quarterly meeting, was Laid before the Quarterly meeting at Philadelphia, by the friends of our monthly meeting appointed to attend the same, And their unanimous desire & sence, and also the generall sence of this our monthly meeting is, That being we Joyned to their Quarterly meeting from our first Settlement, That therefore & for other Reasons we Should So continue, which in answer to your desire we thought fitt to Signifi unto you.

Signed by the approval
of the meeting,
By Thomas Jones".

Sometime before the alleged final decision as to the positions of Haverford and Radnor, the Chester County Court cited all the freemen of the county, inhabitants of these two townships included, for not paying their taxes into Court. But these Welsh towns paid no attention to the command. When it was supposed there was no longer any question where they were, the Chester Court cited the Welsh Quakers alone to pay, not only current taxes, but "back taxes" even from the 12mo., 1685, when it was assumed they were transplanted into Chester Co. Long and bitter was the contest over this fought out by Judge David Lloyd;* and

---

*Judge David Lloyd had more than the interest of a paid attorney in this matter, for though he was not an inmate of the Welsh Tract, he owned some land therein, and was a Welsh Quaker, and a relative of Gov. Thomas Lloyd. He and his wife, Sarah, a native of Cirencester, in Gloucestershire, came over in the ship Amity, of London, to Upland, or Chester, and arrived on 15. 5mo. 1686. He was born in Manavan parish, Montgomeryshire, in 1656. In Pennsylvania and in England he had a reputation as both a shrewd politician and a learned lawyer, and in 1690, he was mentioned in a proclamation of Queen Mary, as a suspected conspirator against King William. In 1700, he was appointed attorney-general of the province, and was Penn's champion in his troubles with the Quarry-Moore faction. But in the next year, he turned and became opposed to the Penn-Logan party, and so stood when Penn died. He also served the province as speaker of the assembly, and was the register, and recorder of

it all goes to make up the sum and substance of the harsh treatment of the Welsh Quakers. Judge Lloyd argued that payment was due only from the time of the decision as to in which county Radnor and Haverford were, and gained his case. Some inhabitants of these townships had paid taxes into Philadelphia County. They were indemnified. Patents describing Haverford and Radnor lands as in Philadelphia County, were changed in the records to read as of Chester County.

Yet, for all this, the arrangement at that time was only tentative,—accepted by the Welsh Friends because of their aversion at this time to "fighting the case in court," for in June, 1720, the dividing line question had not been settled definitely, for once more it was up before the Provincial Council to give opinion on the division line between the counties of Philadelphia and Chester, as the "inhabitants of the South side of Schoolkill" had been assessed in both counties. Nor was it settled in the next year, when it was again asked that a proper adjustment and re-survey of the whole division line be made. And on this matter, on 26 March, 1722, David Lloyd, the lawyer, appeared for the Commissioners, and also the petitioners. He declared that up to this time no regular division between the two counties "had yet appeared to this Board" of Commissioners, and "tax collectors did not know what to do, as an injunction stood," till the line was positively determined. Mr. Lloyd was thoroughly posted in this matter, having been concerned in it from the first. He mentioned the beginning of

---

Philadelphia county, and was chief justice of the Supreme Court when he died, in 1731, aged 75 years. He was buried at Chester, where he resided in the mansion called "Green Bank," built in 1721, as a tablet in west gable said, subsequently owned and occupied by Como. David Porter. In Feb. 1882, this old house, which had degenerated into a fire-works factory, was destroyed by fire. Judge Lloyd also had a Philadelphia residence, where the Bank of Pensylvania was erected. His second wife, Grace Growden, died in 1760, aged 80.

WELSH SETTLEMENT OF PENSYLVANIA

the trouble in 1688-9, and earlier, but he said that the records of the early surveys and proceedings therein, excepting the slight mention in Council minutes, could not be found, and therefore the Board was unable to determine the matter till these papers could be produced. He knew that they had passed from official into private hands years ago, but who now had them he did not know, so an order was given to try to find them.

One of the earliest annoyances the Welsh Quakers had was that a Chester Co. man, as Deputy-Surveyor, was continually making lands, which he laid out for non-Welsh, adjoining the Welsh Tract, overlap the Welsh lands. So frequently did this occur, that the Welsh finally complained to the Executive Council.

17, 7mo., 1685. Minute of the Council, Thomas Lloyd, president:

"Complaint being made by Henry Lewis, John Bevan, and others, in ye behalfe of ye Welch friends, that their Lines runn out Regularly, according to ye Gov'rs Warr't, were notwithstanding, by Charles Ashcome, Deputy-Surveyor of Chester County, his undue Execution, of several Later Warrants, prevented from ye quiet Enjoym't of ye tract that was legally laid out for them.

"The Board [of Land Commissioners], upon ye hearing of ye same, ordered yt Charles Ashcome be required to prepare and bring in to ye Council a Draught by a scale of a 160 perches in an inch, for all ye Lands Surveyed and Laid out by him Westwardly of ye N.N.W. line, runn by Ralph ffretwell and himselfe, and to attend the Councill & Comiss'rs with it ye next Third day, by ye hour in ye forenoone, for ye Speedy Composing ye Differences & ascertaining ye lines between ye Chester friends and others, and ye Welch friends, & in the meantime to Survey no more Land until further Or'd."

At the Meeting, 22, 7mo., 1685, Ashcome appeared bringing "a Draught of ye Settlement upon ye West side of ye

WELSH TRACT AFFAIRS

line Runn out, ye Councill upon perusall and observation of ye same, and Comparing the lines thereof with a Draught made up by ye same Scale by David Powell, of ye Tract surveyed by him in behalfe of ye Welch friends, have recommended by adjustment of ye disputed bounds, and accomodating the Differences thence arising & further likely to Ensue, unto ye Council and Comiss'rs Joyntly, at their next sitting."

At this meeting, Thomas Holme, the Surveyor-General, stated, to excuse himself, that he only kept Ashcome as a deputy-surveyor "on order of Gov. Penn, verbally, and by letter." Ashcome was asked to explain the faults of his surveys; his answer not being satisfactory, he was suspended by Thomas Lloyd.

Along in the next year, according to the minutes of the Commissioners of Land, the Welsh across the Schuylkill began to have other trouble about their Tract, not only with squatters within their bounds, and, as above, with influential English patentees for whom land was surveyed overlapping their Tract, but, what was more disappointing, with Penn's Commissioners, and even with the Proprietary himself.

Pressure was brought on him by those who coveted the fertile lands beyond the Schuylkill, and by those desiring the breaking up of the Welsh Tract, to dispossess the Welsh of their unoccupied land, and put it up for sale again. To satisfy the new applicants, realizing, by doing as they suggested, he could raise money,—he then needed it badly,—he established some new rules as to holding land; the one aimed directly at the Welsh was embodied in the following Proclamation, "Given at Worminghurst Place in old England the 24th of the 11th Month, 1686":—

"Since there was no other thing I had in my Eye in the Settlement of this Province next to the advancement of Virtue, than the comfortable Situation of the Inhabitants herein and for that end, with the advice and consent of the

WELSH SETTLEMENT OF PENSYLVANIA

most eminent of the first Purchasers, ordained that every Township consisting of five thousand Acres should have tenn familys at least,* to the end that the Province might not be like a Wilderness as some others [West Jersey?] yet do by vast vacant tracts of Land, but be regularly improved."

He commanded his Commissioners "that they inspect what Tracts of Land taken up lye vacant and unseated, and are most likely to give cause of exception and Discouragement to those yt are able and ready to seate the same, and that they dispose of them, if not seated by the present pretenders within Six Months after the Publication hereof."

This was followed by another proclamation by Penn dated 1. 12mo., 1686-7, which contained many new rules jealously guarding his lands and rights, and thereby limiting those of the first comers. For instance, "no warrants of resurvey be granted for Land within five Miles of the River Delaware, or any Navigable River." In this document, he acknowledges that "I formerly granted a warrant for 40,000 Acres for the Welsh People to lie contiguous on the West side of ye Schoolkill," yet it was the experience of the grantees that they could not have their purchases within the tract "lie contiguous."

Penn further claimed "one share" for himself in every township, "with all ye Indian Fields that are in the townships." The Welsh were undoubtedly sore over this rule, for it not only cut up their tracts, or farms, but took away from them cleared land, that the Indians had cultivated, but they could only protest, and that to no relief.

This was mentioned in taking notice of a survey of 4,000 acres to Thomas Barker & Co., that over-lapped the Welsh Tract, concerning which trespass Messrs. David Powell, Hugh Hoberts, Griffith Owen, Edward Jones, William

---

*This sounds very like the instructions to the Council of New Amsterdam, over thirty years before,—to have "Colonists settle themselves with a certain number of families in some of the most suitable places, in the manner of towns."

WELSH TRACT AFFAIRS

Edward, Price Jones, and Rowland Ellis, the most prominent Welshmen, appeared before the Commissioners "in behalf of ye Welsh friends," on 13. 3mo., 1687. A matter that was settled to the partial satisfaction of the Welsh.

Some years after the Welsh Friends had settled on land, for which they paid according to the acreage described in their deeds, their holdings being defined by rough surveys, marked by natural objects, Penn concluded to have all the grants of land carefully resurveyed, and laid out according to the deeds, for he felt sure, on certain information, that his grantees held more land, or acreage, than their deeds called for. To this end, he included in his proclamation of 1. 12mo., 1686-7, the notice:—"All overplus Lands upon Resurvey be reserved to my use, and Disposal."

Penn was within his rights in this order, but when it was found that nearly every Welshman had more land in his possession than his deed called for, and that Penn informed them they could have the "overplus," but only by paying for it, at then current prices, they became very indignant, and felt much abused; but Penn was obdurate. If we may be allowed to judge from the results of the resurveys of Turner's grantees, given above, where resurveys showed great overplusage, and I have mentioned many other instances, Penn was right in discovering what belonged to him, and also in selling it at the best advantage, though it was considered a hardship to have to pay the advanced prices for land which had been improved by the holder, so this order, probably, should not be included in the catalog of Penn's unjustness towards the Welsh Quakers, at whom the notice seems to have been particularly aimed, although it was one of their grievances.

All these sundry curtailments of gifts, promises and rights by William Penn, caused the Welsh Friends, not only mortification and annoyance, but loss of property, standing and respect, and these injuries brought out the following petition, written in English, but now almost illegible:—

WELSH SETTLEMENT OF PENSYLVANIA

"Philadelphia, the 23rd, 3d mo., 1688."
"To the Proprie^try," Etc.
"The humble petition of the Inhabitants of the Welsh Tract, Showeth,
"That, whereas William Penn, Propriet'y" &c., &c. Because, not understanding with English tongue, and court proceedings," . . . . . "he gave his most solemn word before they removed from the land of their nativity, that they, ye petion^s, should have abt forty thousand acres of land contiguously laid out as a Barony, and that they should not be obliged to answer nor sweare in any court whatsoever, but should have Courts and Magistrates of their own, wherein justice should be ministered according to the laws of the Govern^mt," or to that effect.
"In consideration whereof, and for a manifestation of ye pet^s Love & gratitude to the Govr and his Govern^mt, they came over to this Province.
"And Whereas, these Proprietary, in pursuance of his former promise, Did grant a Warrant for Surveying the tract accordingly.
"And thereupon, further, that y^r petion^rs should enjoy the said previledges in manner aforesaid, and be exempt from attending all others [?], save only that they should maintain members to serve in the Councils and Assembly.
"And, also, whereas, this Tract extends to the county of Philadelphia, and therefore [? is as in a county or barony]. Y^r pet^rs have been summ^d to the County Courts of both these Counties to serve on juries, and are likewise to be taxed in both places, to their great imposition.
"Now, for as much as the priviledges & exemptions aforesaid so [?] proposed by the Gov^nr, is most thankfully acknowledged as a peculiar kindness to y^r Pet'^rs, Nevertheless, they desire to improve the same to no other end than to have their Courts & Magistrates of and among themselves, as they had in Wales, and to be governed by the laws of Pensilvania here as they were by the laws of England

WELSH TRACT AFFAIRS

there; and [in order] that good rule and order may both better be kept amongst them, and are [make them] amiable with those English and others [our] neighbors."

Further, they hoped especially that their monthly, and other Meetings may not be separated, and asked "what had been granted them by parole may now be confirmed to them, and other purchasers, and inhabitants of said tract."

This "autograph petition," (preserved at the Pa. His. Soc. among the "Penn MSS.") beautifully written, in quaint expression, with some words uncertain, was signed, in autograph, by the following prominent gentlemen of the Welsh Tract:—

Thomas Ellis.	John Humphrey.
Griffith Owen.	Samuel Rees.
John Bevan.	Morris Llewelyn.
Hugh Roberts.	John Roberts.
Henry Lewis.	Daniel Meredith.
William Howell.	Richard Moor.
John Evans.	Rees Peter.
Robert Davies.	Hugh Jones.
Francis Howell.	David Evan.
William Jenkins.	John Fairman.
Phylyp Evan.	

On the reverse, the petition is endorsed:—"The petioners are worthy and are very earnest about it, but John Symcock much against, [and] as [to] also laying another County [the Welsh] beyond this," [Philadelphia].

It is almost impossible to imagine what the political development in the "Welsh Barony" would have been, if the Welsh Quakers—if so there had been enough of them, and there never was,—had had their rights as they understood them; an independent State within the Province, with only one party in the field, and therefore no party struggles, an arcadic condition. But this could not have continued.

WELSH SETTLEMENT OF PENSYLVANIA

There would have always have been a changed condition to face, and the crisis would come when non-Quakers became in the majority in the "Barony," unless the Quakers had intended putting a Chinese-wall of immigration laws about their State, for the Quaker yoke, though mild to Friends, would be galling to non-Quakers,* as was the Mormons's to the Gentiles. Spiritual authority and control might have been tolerated so long as the majority were Quakers; but this condition had been, and has been tried, never with success, as it never obtained long, unless the little commonwealth of San Marino, which originated from a religious community, may be the exception, but the Welsh Tract Quakers did not for long constitute a singular community, either of all Welsh, or of all Quakers.

Or, if it would not be the religious atmosphere and authority in the "Barony," that would be repugnant to newcomers, who were not of the Society, then it would have been the owners of the small farms, and the sense of freedom the General Assembly gave, and universal suffrage, would have dragged down such suggestions of feudalism in their midst, as being dictated to by the owners of the princely estates. But this is only a trite conclusion, for it is a fact that "revolutions do not arise from discontent of the rich," and there was bound to be many small farmers in the Welsh Tract, because Penn had omitted the feudal law of primogeniture from his plan of government for his social and "holy experiment," since he was one of the advanced in thought who believed it the moral and religious duty of a parent to provide equally for all of his children, the laws of England, of course, preventing him from following the conviction in his own case. The benefits,

---

*Or, as Mr. Isaac Sharpless says of the general government of the Province, in his work, "A Quaker Experiment in Government," "Had all the inhabitants been Friends and amenable to their discipline, very little civil government would have been needed in internal affairs, * * * * and the courts of law would have been shorn of nearly all their criminal and much of their civil business."

WELSH TRACT AFFAIRS

or discomforts, with or without primogeniture had often been thrashed out in his time, and apparently good found concealed in both plans, so it is only necessary here to observe that the incessant sub-division of property, that began in Penn's day, has not resulted in any remarkable general misery and poverty and barbarism as predicted would be the condition in Pensylvania in a hundred years by the prophets opposed to the revolutionary principal he recommended. We have seen the great estates of the Welsh Tract pioneers divided in the second generation among all the sons, and sub-divided in the third, and then again cut up, all to the advantage of the general community.

In inspecting the members' lists of the Welsh Tract Preparative Meetings, and the minutes of the Welsh Monthly Meeting of Friends, when it was the "Baronial Assembly," it can be seen that the Friends's ministers and the elders were not only the leading men in the meetings, but were also the largest land holders, and the wealthiest men. So it can be imagined that in the Meeting-Assembly the patricians would be the "potent power of authority," and whether it was an Assembly, or an irregular Town Meeting of Freemen, the ministers and elders would control and direct the proceedings. Such was the case in the Swedish settlement down the Delaware; in Dutch one of New Netherlands; in that of the Waloons, on Long Island, and notably among the Puritans of New England, the minister was the chief man, just as the abbot was the "potent power" in the monastic "Towns" of England. Possibly, the only difference was that the Friends's ministers in the Welsh Tract were the richest men there. As late as in 1701, in a minute of Penn's Commissioners, they were all Friends's ministers, those men from the Welsh Tract, "some of the Chiefs of that Nation in this Province," who appeared as we shall see, before this Board on a matter of the affairs in the Welsh Barony.

WELSH SETTLEMENT OF PENSYLVANIA

I have read that these Quakers transplanted into their Towns their Welsh "customs" and "laws," but they were never so distinct that they could be identified after the Revolutionary War, and there is only evidence that they hoped they would prevail in the Towns. The supposition that peculiar Welsh laws had been in force in the Welsh Tract may have had its origin from what Minister Hugh Roberts said, in a letter quoted hereafter, Penn promised in respect to corporate rights in the "Barony." But certainly Penn gave the Welsh no charters to establish "Towns" as they understood such, therefore, at the best, they could only assume they could have town officers and ordinances of their own selecting and making. And, whatever they were, it is likely the Welsh laws were similar to and as good as the English, for few laws of an old country are adapted to conditions peculiar to a new one, and certainly not without revision or amendment, and if Penn's "Laws" were traced back to their birth place it may be some were derived from the ancient Cymric code, though there is good evidence that Holland was the original home of his "Concessions, or Constitucons," and his "Frame."

Apparently, the Welsh Quakers of the "Barony" enforced no peculiar Welsh code of laws, for the "Friends's customs,"—committees on suffering, relief, peace, discipline, &c., were the working machinery of their "Assembly," and these were common to all monthly meetings. Whatever other intentions for self-government they may have had, they were never developed; the independent State was too short lived. So far as the "customs" could go, they were good and useful, but there were many matters they could not touch or cover, and, possibly the first to come up of this class of "annoyance," would have been suffrage privileges, and voting qualifications, when it came necessary to send delegates to the General Assembly to look after the interests of the Welsh "Towns," when they were hoping to enjoy representation without taxation, and their singular desire that their "State" was to flourish in the atmosphere,

WELSH TRACT AFFAIRS

—not in the protection, for Penn made no provision, or martial arrangement even to protect his Province from any possible enemy,—of a general government, without contributing to its support.

This little territory of "62½ square miles" the Welsh Quakers thought would be the acme of comfort to have it all by themselves,—to which they fled from "sufferings," and where they hoped for complete release and rest from all the unpleasantnesses of that "high civilization" that then prevailed in the old country, and to be let alone, all of which might have been granted by Penn if they had not tried unusual political conditions, and not satisfied to be similar to the chartered New Netherland Company on Manhattan, and simply privileged to support themselves. But, as will be seen, they wanted more privileges, greater concessions than Penn could afford to allow, hence, as we shall also see, this was the cause of downfall of the Welsh Tract as a distinct settlement, a Welsh Utopia.

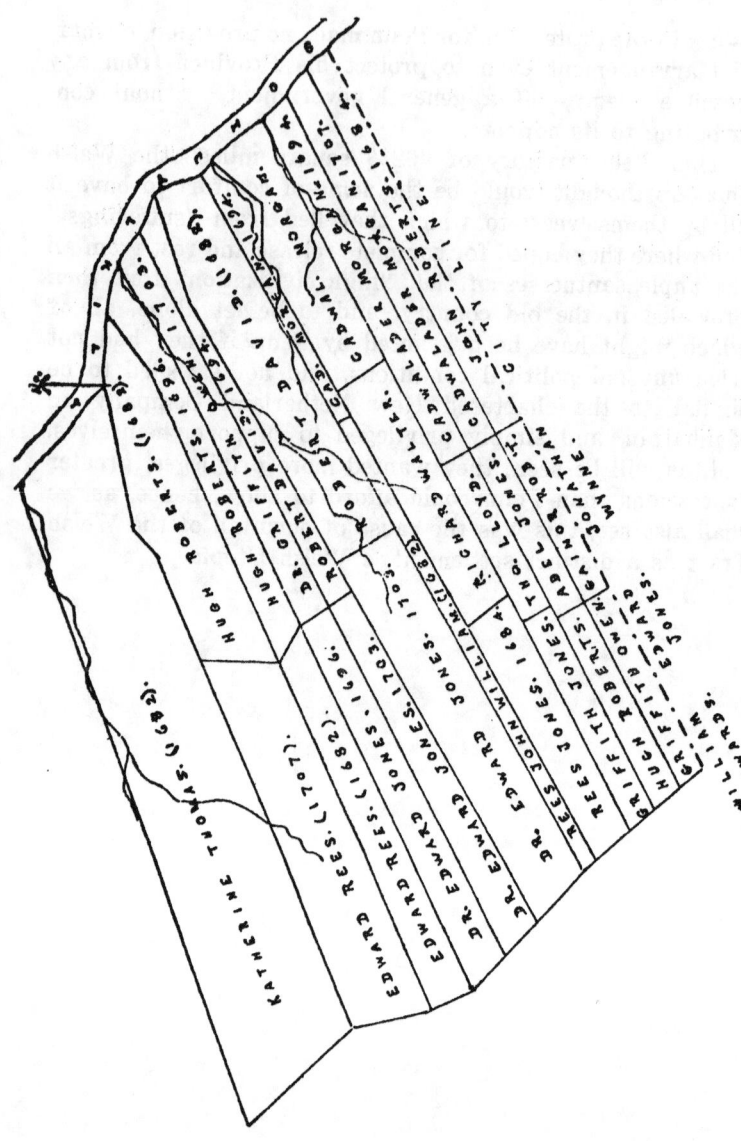

"THOMAS AND JONES TRACT TWENTY YEARS AFTER SETTLEMENT."

WELSH TRACT AFFAIRS. II.

Possibly, the greatest dissatisfaction among the Welsh Friends beyond the Schuylkill was occasioned by the new order as to "unseated lands" in the Province, mentioned before, for there can be no question but that they held the greatest part of such land. It was a fact that the seven adventuring Welsh land companies, the so called "land trustees," when disposing of the 40,000 acres, did sell much land to speculators, or to some who held for a rise in values, but, all the same, the vendors knew the purchases had been made in good faith, and that they were in honor bound to protect them.

A resolution passed by the Land Commissioners, Messrs. Markham, Turner, Carpenter, and Goodson, (not Welshmen), under Penn's warrant of 24.11-1686, began the campaign to get away from the Welsh Friends as much of their 40,000 acres as possible, at a sitting on 25 Oct. 1690, when they "took into Consideration the Great Quantity of Land lying waste and unsettled within a tract of about 40,000 Acres, Commonly known by the name of the Welsh tract, the want of Seating and Improveing of which has been of great Dammage to the Proprietary and of Exceeding Loss and hinderance to the well seating and Strengthening the Province. Several Honest, able and Substantiall persons haveing either Leaft it for want of such convenient Seates that are unsettled in that Tract, or hindered from Seating Such as have been formerly layd out unto them in it.

"Resolved, that notice be given unto David Powel, or some other purchaser concerned in the said tract, that they show cause why the land, not laid out, or not seated and Improved, within the said tract, according to regulation, may not be disposed off as other Lands within this Province." The hearing was set for 19th of November following.

On this date, 19 Nov. 1690, the Minutes record:—"Griff Owen with several other Purchasers who have an Interest in the Welsh Tract, was this Day with the Commiss'rs, according to notice sent to David Powel, bearing date the 25th of ye Last Month. They requested a longer time to Give their answer to the Commiss'rs' Proposall, which was granted untill the 13th of ye Next Month."

On this date, "13th of 10ber, 1690," the Minutes record: —"Griff. Owen, with several others, Inhabitants of the Welch tract, Came and gave in a Paper to the Commiss'rs, which follows verbatim:—

"Wee, the Inhabitants of the Welch tract in the Province of Pensylvania, in America, being Descended of the Ancient Britains, who always in the land of our Nativity, under the Crown of England, have Enjoyed that Liberty and priviledge as to have our bounds and Limits to ourselves, within the which all cause, Quarrels, Crimes, and Tittles were tryed and wholly Determined by officers, Magistrates, Juries of our own Language, which were our Equals.

"Having our faces towards these Countrys; Made the Motion to our Gov'r that we might Enjoy the same here, which thing was soon granted by him, before he or we ever came to these parts.

"And when he came over, he gave forth his Warr't to lay out 40,000 acres of land, to the intent we might live together here, and Enjoy our Liberty and Devotion in our own Language, as before in our Country.

"And so the 40,000 acres was Surveyed out, and by his own Warr't, Confirmed by several orders from the Commiss'rs of ye Propriety and Settled upon already with near four score Settlements, and, as we have good grounds to believe, if the way had been Clear from troubles, there might had been so many Settlers upon it, by this time, as in Reason it could Contain.

"And besides, it is well known, there was several Scores of our men Serv'ts who was very desirous to have out their head land, according to promise, but could have none with any convenientcy that was worth to settle upon, whereby many are like to Desert the province and go to other Countrys.

"Also, some of our Friends that have Concerned themselves with the first that came over to this Country, have lived a while here, and Returned again to their families.

"Friends and Relations, that had Disposed themselves to come over with all speed, if Providence had permitted, and, as far as we are given to understand, are Still waiting for the opportunity to their great Dammage.

"And now to Deprive these of their lands and Libertys, which they Depend upon when Coming here (and that in their absence), Wee Look upon it to be a Verry Unkind Dealing, like to Ruining many Families, as also a Subtill undermining to Shutt that Door against our Nation, which the Lord had open for them to come to these Countrys.

"For we can declare, with an open face to God and man, that we Desired to be by ourselves for no other End, or purpose but that we might live together as a Civill Society, to endeavour to deside all Controversies and debates amongst ourselves, in a Gospell order, and not to entangle ourselves with Laws in an unknown Tongue, as also to preserve our Language, that we might ever keep Correspondence with our friends in the land of our Nativity.

"Therefore, our request is,

"That you be tender, not only of violating the Governor's promises to us, but also of being Instrumental of depriveing us of the thing, which were the Chief Motives and Inducements to bring us here, and that you would be pleased, as far as in you lies, to preserve us in our properties, by removing all such incroachments as are made upon the Lines and Boundarys of our said tract, and by Pattent, or otherwise in Due form of Law, to Establish and Confirm

WELSH SETTLEMENT OF PENSYLVANIA

the same to us, so that we may not by any further pretences be interrupted in the peaceable Enjoyment thereoff, according to the Governor's true intent.

"And then we shall with all readiness become responsible for the Quit-rent accruing to the Proprietor, the Commencements whereoff we shall referr and submitt to his Consideration. and if these our reasonable desires be not answered, but our antagonists Gratifyed by our being exposed to those uncertainties that may attend, wee shall choose, rather than Contest, to suffer, and appeal our Cause to God, and to our friends in England."

As four years passed before his Land Commissioners in Philadelphia, began to act on Penn's order about the idle lands of the Welsh, over the Schuylkill, it may be presumed, if the order was published in 1686-7, that the Welsh tried to meet Penn's wishes, and failed, or that the Commissioners suppressed the Proclamation till they got the Welsh "just where they wanted them," and then began their attack, when they could make out a clear case against them, or when would-be purchasers were clamoring for this valuable land. Anyway, it was a well planned procedure.

The reply of the Welsh, it may be seen, was dignified, and in part it was just and proper in their interest, though of quaint expression. It may be noticed, they claimed Penn promised them, before they bought his land, the right to govern themselves, in the manner they had been accustomed, within their tract on the Schuylkill, (just as he also promised the German settlers, as we have seen), else, possibly, they would not have removed.

That their 40,000 acre tract was to be an independent "Welsh State," a "Civil Society," a municipality, governed by laws of its own making, and by men chosen from among themselves by themselves, all within Penn's Province, which has been noticed elsewhere, was a chimera, of course, but I do not imagine these intelligent Welshmen would have made this ascertion had they not known it to be the truth, as

WELSH TRACT AFFAIRS

they understood it, so it may be presumed Penn did agreed verbally to their plan of a State, for he was then selling his land.

It may be also noted, they claimed there were only near 80 homesteads, or "settlements," in the whole tract after eight years ownership, (Holme's map of about this date says 104), so it is likely that four years before there were not ten families seated to each 5,000 acre lot, "town," or township, when Penn issued his order that so astonished the Welsh, and from this, it may be supposed, he had not seen the map made for him by Holme.

But as to the excuses for no greater seating, they are both good and poor. There is other proof that the intelligent Welsh were timid about removing, because of rumors of the uncertainty of land tenure in the Welsh Tract. Then, too, the Welsh had ceased coming over, conditions at home having improved, for the "toleration act" had ended their physical sufferings, and teasings, though their political disabilities remained. But why, in this great, fertile tract, the few servants could get no good land is not apparent. They seem to have been entitled to some land, after serving their time, so the question is, had many served-out even their passages? Certainly, Penn could not be blamed for this. Nor, that some early settlers had tired of farm life, and had returned to Wales. And, it was only a possibility that those who had bought, and had not removed, would do so.

But quit-rent was the crux of this matter, as much as was cash money through sales. Evidently there had been some effort by the Commissioners to collect the quit-rent due Penn from the Welsh, and they had not paid (in fact, few, possibly none, paid in the province, and this was one of the causes of Penn's mortification, and shortness of money), because it was not agreed when the rentals should begin, but now promised to do so, under the conditions mentioned in the reply, and when it was determined from when the payments should date.

WELSH SETTLEMENT OF PENSYLVANIA

"1690, 20th of 10ber." The Commissioners again met, and took up the reply of the Welsh, particularly as to quit-rents. They read it over again, "and haveing Considered of the same and found not to answer the propositions made by the Commiss'rs to them, Ordered, that the Commiss'rs propositions be Drawn up in writing to be Delivered to them, which follows Verbatim:—

"By the Proprietary Com'rs.

"To the Inhabitants of the Welch tract:—

"The Proposition that was made to you by us was,

"That, there being 40,000 acres of Land actually Surveyed and laid out and known by the name of the Welch tract, and there being Regular Returns thereof made in form and Manner as other purchasers Lands by which we know (and by no other means can) how to charge each Tract of Land with its Quit-rent, and, therefore, in course and according to the Method which has hitherto been used, we have Charged the said Tract of 40,000 acres as other tracts of the like purchase are. But least it should Surprise you, or give Suspition of an unneighbourly, or unfriendly act, we gave you time notice for a conference with us about it, and afterwards a Considerable time to make your answer; which you gave in writing the 13th Instant.

"The which we have very Deliberately Considered, and find the Maj'r part of the writing not Cognissable by us, Or within our province, which is only to Confirm and grant Lands, &c., and settle the affairs of the Proprietor's Revenue, nor, Indeed, does any part of it answer our proposition, but Verry Obliquely, and with much ambiguity, which shows more of Skill and Cunning, then a Direct and Sincere answer.

"Whatever the Proprietor hath promised, we Question not but he will perform; and in whatever he has given us power we are Ready to doe, and when you please to Demand, willing to Confirm to you the said tract by Pattent, as we doe unto other purchasers, according to the warr't and Survey

WELSH TRACT AFFAIRS

the which, if you Refuse, and others accept, You Cannot think it hard if we grant your Refusal to them, who have Equal right with you by purchase to take up land.

"To this we desire you will be speedy and plain in your Answer, as we are with you in our proposition, for we are Resolved what in us lyes, God willing, to Remove all Rubs and hindrances in the way to a quiet and easy Settlement off the Proprietor's Revenue within his Province.

"Dated at Philadelphia, the 20th of 10th Mo. 1690."

By this, the Welsh were allowed more time to consider the demand of the Commissioners, and their conclusion is found in the following Minute; but there is no suggestion that they had appealed to Penn over the heads of his agents.

"At a Meeting of the Commis'rs ye 2nd of the 3rd Month, 1691."

"This being the Day appointed for the Welch friends to give their answer to the Commiss'rs's propositions of the 20th of December, Last, there appeared in behalf of the Welch, Griffith Owen, Hugh Roberts, Robert Owen, John Bevan, with many Others.

"The Welch Friends' answer is: that they are willing to pay hence forward Quit-rent for the whole 40,000 Acres, but not since the Date of Survey.

"The which answer not being Satisfactory, or Direct, to our proposition:

"Resolved, that the Lands already laid out in the Said Tract unto other Purchasers, Be Confirmed unto them."

This was a terrible blow to the Welsh, for it opened up their large tract to strangers, people of any nationality, and any religion, who had money to buy from Penn. and it rudely awakened them from their dream of an independent Welsh State, and quite shattered their confidence in William Penn.

However, from the Minutes of the Commissioners, or Board of Property, 27th, 4mo. 1691, we learn that the Welsh made one more attempt to justify their claims, and to have

WELSH SETTLEMENT OF PENSYLVANIA

the quit-rent payable only from the time of the final survey of their tract, and not from the date of the grant, several years difference, or about £100 total difference, which was then quite as large a sum to Penn, as to them.

This final attempt was another petition addressed to Penn himself, dated 15. 3mo. 1691 (the document is at the Historical Society of Pa.), which went over the same ground and statements, covering three large pages, they did on 13 Oct. 1690.

But this last petition has as its important feature and statement, that it was to Hugh Roberts, of Merion, the celebrated Friends' minister, that Penn personally made these promises, before the Welsh Friends would buy and leave their native country. Hugh Roberts was one of the signers —the third—of this second petition, and therefore subscribed to his statement included in it, namely, "before we came from our native country, we desired a tract of land from you, ... and you promised Hugh Roberts it should be a barony, or corporation apart from others, but to fall under the Gen'l Gov^{mt}, and desired him to communicate it to Friends."

And all those prominent Welshmen, who signed this petition, "with the unanimous consent of all ye Welsh concerned in ye tract," had every confidence in the statement of Hugh Roberts, and in the man himself.

This document, a guarantee of the veracity of Hugh Roberts, as much as it was a petition, endorsed at the time, "Petition of Griffith Owen, R. Owen, and others," was signed in autograph, and in three columns, as follows:—

Lewis David.	David Meredith.	Griffith Owen.
John Bevan.	Stephen Evans.	Robert Owen.
John Humphreys.	Ellis ap Hugh.	Hugh Roberts.
Francis Howell.	John Gorman.	John Roberts.
William Howell.		Robert Davies.
David Lawrence.		Cadwalader Morgan.
John Lewis.		Will Edward.

WELSH TRACT AFFAIRS

Edward Jones. Thomas Jones.
Rees Jones.
Hugh Jones.
Edward Jones, Jun.
Robert Owen.
Griffith Jones.
Abel Thomas.

All but ten of these signers were Merion men, neighbors of Hugh Roberts, and the others lived in Haverford and Radnor. Seven of them were signers of previous petition, 23. 2mo. 1688, and some who had signed it were dead in 1691.

The minutes of 27. 4mo. 1691, record that:

"Griffith Owen, with several of the Welch Friends, appeared for themselves, and other Inhabitants and those concerned in the Tract of Land of about 40,000 acres called the Welch tract, and did offer to pay quit-Rent from hence forward for the Whole 40,000 acres, and thereupon Challenged a Patent for the whole to themselves.

"The Commiss'rs Ordered the Minute of the 2nd. 3rd mo. last [1691], about the same business to be read, which was accordingly done, and [informed] them it was now too late for them to alter that result, having passed their words Already to Confirm those Tracts to the purchasers that have been laid out within the said 40,000 acres, who are ready and willing to pay their quit-Rent from the time of [first] Survey.

"Whereupon, it was Ordered a Warrant for takeing of the Caveats entered in Surveyor General's Office of the Lands within the said tract."

Even while the Welsh Friends were present in the chamber, the Commissioners issued orders to a surveyor to lay out land in the Welsh Tract, for a dozen applicants, named in the minutes, thus adding insult to injury. The first who were accommodated were the pressing creditors of Penn, and it was thus he cancelled some of his obligations. The

WELSH SETTLEMENT OF PENSYLVANIA

Commissioners also took some of the tract for themselves and friends, as also did the surveyor.

This was the end of the "Welsh Tract."

The hopes and plans for the New World, expressed in their several extant petitions, the Welsh Friends had to surrender and forget "greatly in the cross."

When the unoccupied land was put on the market, after the rush of the "insiders," there was a steady demand for it. Among the first to enter the tract, were Richard Snead, of the city of Bristol, linen draper, for 1,500 acres, William Pardoe, a merchant, and Francis Fisher, a glover, both of the city of Worcester, each buying 1,250 acres. But Penn, fearing that these English purchasers might be no more desirable than the Welsh speculators, issued an order not to sell more than 500 acres (and "no faster than it could be improved") to one purchaser, hence these and hundreds that followed had to be satisfied with that amount:—Thomas Brascy, John Hart, John Moore, John Finchner, &c.

At this time, the original Welsh Friends became frightened even as to the tenure of the places they were then farming, and living upon,—their homesteads, and went before the Land Commissioners, asking confirmation of their deeds, which, under the circumstances, was a wise thing to do.

The Commissioners' minutes, 1 Dec., 1701, record their awakening, "for taking some Measures to regulate the Welsh Tract." "Some of the Chiefs of that Nation in this Province having met and Concerted the Methods to be taken in order to the Regulations. It was agreed (states the Minute of 22 Dec. following) :—

"That, in as much as the Welch Purchasers of the Propr'ry were, by large Quantities of acres in one Pair of Deeds, granted to one or two persons only, under which several other Purchasers had a Share, the Gen'l Deeds of one Purchase should be first brought in, with an acco't of all other Persons who had a Share in such Purchase, also an account in whose possession the Respective Lands of every under Purchase now are, and that, because all the Lands hitherto laid out (or most of them) in the said Tract were by Vertue of one Gen'l Warrant; particularly Warr'ts of Resurvey should be granted to every Man upon what he now possesses, and that an exact account of all their Titles should be taken in distinct Minutes from these presents, to be kept fair in a Book or Papers for that Puropse."

Accordingly, at this meeting many of those who bought of Dr. Edward Jones and John Thomas ("Company No. 1"), appeared before the Commissioners, and had their deeds confirmed. And in Nov., 1702, these following also had their deeds examined and reconfirmed:—Rowland Ellis, for 577 acres; Edward Jones, Sr., 402; Edward Jones, Jr., 125; Griffith Owen, ———; Hugh Roberts, 338; John Roberts, 262; Robert David, 346; Hugh Roberts, 441; Richard Jones, 157; Evan Jones, 361; Ellis David, 409; Rees Jones, 587; Cadwalader Ellis, 310, &c.

In Oct., 1701, Griffith Owen became a member of the Board of Commissioners of Property, when Penn ordered that each first purchaser should be deeded a lot in the city, hence, after this, we find the Welsh Friends city lot owners.

The first surveys were roughly made,—land then was so abundant, but nearly ten years after the Welsh Friends were seated, accurate surveys of their lands were ordered for the tracts they claimed, because it was found that more land was claimed under the original surveys than the deeds called for, and this "overplus" reverted to Penn. The claimants, however, were generously permitted to buy the surplus from him at an advanced price. But if a located farm fell short of acreage called for by the deed, the owner was privileged to buy enough, wherever it could be had, and make it up after having once paid for the full amount! Then frequently, in surveys of adjacent properties, none of the farms took in certain pieces of land (called "concealed land"), yet one or the other of the abuttors supposed it was his,—this Penn took, too.

WELSH SETTLEMENT OF PENSYLVANIA

Another unpleasant experience the early Welsh Friends had was over grist mills and saw mills they had erected.

When the Welsh settlers for the Falls lands came, they brought enough wheat flour to last them, they supposed, till they could raise a crop, and build a water-mill on the creek, or at the Falls, for themselves. But great was their astonishment, when they learned that private grist and saw mills were *taboo* in the Province, and that "William Penn & Co." had the monopoly of all kinds of milling, and when the Welsh wanted grain ground they would have to pack it miles off to the Chester Creek to the "Proprietor's Mill."

This, the Welsh felt was an imposition, but, as it was "not in the bond" that they should have water-mills, there was nothing for them to do, but to submit to Penn's greed.

One of the earliest acts of Mr. Penn was to secure all mill rights to himself. He organized a milling corporation in 1682, with thirty-two shares of stock (the celebrated Philip Ford subscribed for five shares), and allowed the man who was to set-up the "Government Mill," and the man selected to manage it, called "the Governor's Miller," have a few shares in payment for services, at prices fixed by himself. And, in 1682, he brought over Richard Townsend, with all the materials required to construct a grist and saw mill, to superintend its building, and then appointed Caleb Pusey, who had been sent on ahead to prospect, and was here when Penn and Townsend arrived, to manage it, collect the tolls, and remit to him. This mill was put up on Chester Creek, on "reserved mill land," protected by Penn's warrant. This was the first of the company's mills, and the start of a short lived "trust."

Caleb Pusey may have been the official "government miller," but as he was a last maker by trade, it may be presumed that Mr. Townsend attended to the practical part of of the Government Mill. He made enough money for himself out of this mill to build a good, old fashioned stone house. But it was the governor's miller, Mr. Pusey, who erected the "mansion house" (still standing, and tenanted

WELSH TRACT AFFAIRS

by Negroes at last account), about 1683. Even in the time of Pusey and Townsend, Pusey's house was not a good example of American "colonial architecture," it may be imagined, if we have any clear conception of what that style of architecture really was. Its beauty was certainly not enhanced by the hipped roof added by Samuel Shaw shortly before the '76 war.

When the Welsh Friends found they had to patronize Penn's establishment if they wanted bread, those among them, who had lawyers's minds, thought they had found a way out of this method of paying tribute to their grasping over-lord, who enjoined all water-mills, and began to erect grain-grinding wind-mills! But Penn declared this was but a subterfuge; an endeavor to evade paying him his income, and threatened the undertakers with the jail if they did not desist. But he gave them something to hope for, and to look forward to, when he graciously informed them that just as soon as the mills, in which he was a partner, were on a good paying basis, and the plants were paid for by the profits, he would possibly issue generally warrants for mill-rights, on terms yet to be determined by him. But in time, this mill matter regulated itself, and the Welsh had mills of their own.

Besides the grist and saw mills on Merion's Mill Creek, and the Schuylkill, there were two small ones in Haverford. The one on Cobb's Creek and the road which passed the Haverford Meeting House, is of record as early as in 1688. It must have been a small one, as, in 1695, it was valued for assessment at only £20, by the Grand Jury of Chester Co., while the Darby and Chester mills were valued at £100 each. In that year, there were only five mills in Chester county. There was a second mill in Haverford, in 1703, on Darby Creek, where the Radnor and Chester road comes in, and it may have been there earlier, and have had the "mill way" lead to it which was ordered by the Chester Court, in 8mo., 1688, to be cut in Marple township.

WELSH SETTLEMENT OF PENSYLVANIA

Another little unpleasantness, and near the last, between Penn and the Welsh Friends beyond the Schuylkill arose from Penn asserting his right was exclusive to any and every ferry across the Schuylkill, which ferries must be a source of revenue to him, either through receipts from leases, or ferriage. The wonder is that he did not place toll gates on the paths through the woods.

Ever since the Welsh had settled on their land, they had had communication with the city, if they did not boat down the river, either by way of a ferry at the Falls, or, one at the end of the Haverford road—"the upper ferry," thence by path to where they wished to go, or by a path on the west side of the river, to opposite the Schuylkill end of the city, and then across the river, and through the woods to the village on the Delaware. This was known as the Center, or Middle Ferry, where the Welsh Friends, or their Monthly Meeting, had a subsidized ferryman, and a flatboat to carry them, and their teams, forth and back, to market-fairs, and the assembly.

But of course this could not go on long without someone coveting such a valuable franchise, or without Penn demanding a share of the receipts. Therefore, on 29 April, 1693, the Middle Ferry rights were granted by him to a Philip England (whose land laid nearest this ferry, and on the south side of the "road," adjoining the burial ground of the Welsh Friends, or Schuylkill Meeting, on the west side of the river), for which England was to pay him yearly, by way of lease, seven pounds. He got his ferry into working order promptly, but had to compete with the Welshmen's ferryman, who still continued doing business at the old stand, much to his annoyance and loss.

But Philip did not put up long with this infringement and interference, and carried his protest into the Provincial Council, and according to the minutes, 7 Feb., 1693-4, he "petitioned," stating that he was "lawfully impowered" "to keep an ordinary and ferry att Skuillkill by the Proprietor, 16. 8mo., 1683, and that no one else was to trans-

WELSH TRACT AFFAIRS

port any one over the river for money, or gain, or reward, att or near his ferry." And then he told that the franchise was granted on a lease to him, 29 April, 1693, and "that from the first he conducted the ferry properly, transferrying people, Baggage, and Horses," and cited William Powel, a Welsh Friend, who owned 300 acres in "West Philadelphia," as a trespasser on his rights, because for a long time he had ferried here for money.

Mr. Powel was sent for, and appeared before the Council on 18 July, 1693, and told the Councillors he was not the man they wanted, as he had sold out his boat and business "to certain people," who employed "Nathaniel Mullinox" (or "Mull," as the clerk wrote it), to ferry them over the river. England urged that all this was still in contempt of his grant.

But, according to the subsequent Council Minutes of 27 June, 18 July, and 29 September, the matter was not yet settled to England's entire satisfaction, for he made the Council believe that Powel had not told the truth about his selling out, as he still acted so often as the ferryman. Finally, the Council got "Nate Mullenex" before them, and when asked who employed him, replied "that most of the people of Harford and Merion, and some of Darbie employed him to ferry, and that they were to pay him wages, and knew no reason why he ought not to earn a living this way." "And after some time, he brought in a list of names of some that employed him, namely—Evan Brothero, William Howell, Thomas Smith, William Smith, Morris Luellen, David Meredith, John Rhodes, William Warner, Humphrey Ellis, Ellis Ellis, Hugh Roberts, Robert Owen, Jno. Apowen, Richard Hayes, Adam Rhodes, Christopher Spray, David Lues, Lues David, David Ewer, John German, Hugh Shone, Evan Hendrie, William Garret, John Bennstone, and Samuel Lewes."

As the Council knew that in this list were the names of some of the most respectable people of the Welsh Tract, and the adjoining Liberties, it convinced them that the extent of

WELSH SETTLEMENT OF PENSYLVANIA

Nathaniel's custom was a great injury to Philip, therefore, "it was ordered the sd Nathaniel Mullinux be committed to the Common Goale of this County till he give Good and Sufficient security to the Lieutenant Governor that he shall ferrie no more persons, horses, or cattle, over the Skuillkill att William Powell's for gift, hyer, or reward, directlie or indirectlie. And that the said boat be forwith Seazed and secured by the Sheriffe till the owners thereof appear before the Lieuteant Governor, or give the like Securitie."

1693-4, February 27th, the minutes state, "Appeared Robert Owen, and others of the Inhabitants beyond the Skuillkill, and claimed interest in the Boat, and stated that the transportation of themselves therein over the river did not procede from least Contempt to Authority, and requested the return of the Boat, so they would go to Meetings, fairs, markets, elections, &c., and attend the Assembly."

"Lest they pretend they were hindered from coming to election the Lieutenant Governor ordered the boat returned, and they could use it only for themselves, and take, or give no pay, untill the Governor came and decided. For which the committee returned William Markham, Lieutenant Governor, heartie thanks," and waited for Governor Fletcher's return to town.

On 11 June, 1694, Governor Fletcher forbade the Welsh even using their own boat to cross the river, as Penn's ferry right should be observed. The Welsh asked for another ferry along side of England's with Mullineaux as ferryman, under a grant from Penn. This was referred to Penn's Commissioners, and pigeon-holed, and it was some time before Mullineaux was released.

Four years after this, as Penn lost his milling monopoly, so he lost his ferry rights. It is of record that a town meeting of the Welsh was held at the Haverford Meeting House, in 1694, to regulate certain matters of the Towns, and particularly the one of the Schuylkill ferry, at High Street.

WELSH TRACT AFFAIRS

It may be supposed that this monthy meeting moved the General Assembly to take some action in matter, because from its minutes, 24. 3mo. 1694, we learn that a committee was appointed by the Assembly "to inspect the Aggrievances of the Inhabitants, reported, That there was not more than one ferry allowed over the Schuylkill. That the seizing, or taking away the boat belonging to the Inhabitants of Haverford, Radnor, Merion, and Darby, is an Aggrievance, and of ill-tenancy to the Inhabitants of this Province."

Subsequently, the minutes of the Haverford monthly meeting prove that this ferry was conducted, in 1698, by the Haverford Monthly Meeting (composed of the peculiar meetings of Merion, Haverford, and Radnor), and that the revenue from the ferry was paid to this monthly meeting by the ferryman, "Nathaniel Mullenex," who was employed on a salary. The ferry was subsidized by these meetings, and any loss shared between them. On the last page of one of the minute books of the Haverford Mo. Mtg., is preserved "The Recept of Nath Mullinex, 1699, of the Inhabitants of Haverford, Radnor and Merion full satisfaction for my service at the ferry, and I do acquitt and discharge them in General and every of them in particular of the same."

It was not until in 1721-2 that the Philadelphia city council awoke to the need of a well regulated ferry over the Schuylkill, when a committee was appointed to examine a route "to the Middle Ferry of the Schuylkill through the woods," (probably the original woods beyond Broad Street, because on 2 Feb. 1705, it was ordered that "the city between Broad Street and the Delaware be grubbed, and cleaned from all its rubbish, in order to raise grass for pasture.") On 4 February, 1722, the city council ordered as to the "Schuylkill middle ferry" that "the Assembly be petioned for an Act to vest it in the city corporation, which should have sole management of it." This granted, the city council gave order to fix on a site for "a public ferry at the Schuylkill end of High Street." Shortly, in this year, a wharf-boat, or landing was placed on the city side, and

WELSH SETTLEMENT OF PENSYLVANIA

another on the "country side," and a license was given to John Maultsby to conduct this ferry under city control. In the Weekly Mercury, 18 December, 1728, Maultsby offered for sale the lease of "the Sculkil Ferry on High Street," saying the lease had sixteen years to run. But it was not until 30 September, 1723, that the city council ordered High Street opened to the "New Ferry," (only a few years previous to this, "the seven streets of the city," on the Delaware side, were ordered "to be staked-out, so that people would not build houses in the streets.") The upper and the lower ferries still continued as private property. In 1762, there was still a ferry at High Street, over the Schuylkill, but during the Revolution, a floating-bridge was maintained.

One other "little unpleasantness" (referred to elsewhere) between Penn and the Welsh purchasers, especially the original ones, those who interviewed him in May, 1681, and who bought, as they thought with the full understanding of the "Conditions," some of whom, if they did not help compile them, signed them, was about the land bonus, or concession of land, in the "great Town," or Philadelphia, in with their country purchases, the promise being, that every one who bought and paid for 500 acres in the country, should receive gratis ten acres in the city, "if space therein would allow it," that is, two per cent. on purchases of 500 acres, or more, would be given to buyers of "country lots."

After the sale of the 40,000 acres was made to the Welsh Friends, Penn saw the impossibility of giving away so much land in the city, as "space did not allow it." This was mortifying to the Welsh gentlemen, the first purchasers, the buyers of 5,000 acres in "country lots," or "one share, called a propriety." But to conciliate them and some others, Penn ordered 10,000 acres to be laid out "contiguous to city's site, as liberties," and in the said "town" (*i.e.* township), lying between the Schuylkill and the present city line on the west be agreed to give them 100 acres, with each purchase of 5,000 acres in the country, "out of that 10,000 acres," and one small city lot.

WELSH TRACT AFFAIRS

But when some of the Welsh gentlemen came to ask the benefit of these new concessions, and that the bonus-land be conveyed to them, they experienced a surprise. They were informed that they were not purchasers on their own accounts of 5,000 acre "country lots," but only acted as "trustees," or agents, for the real purchasers, and that their shares, or those of their principals, none of them, of course amounted to 5,000 acres. This they could not deny, when they studied their deeds, so these received no bonus-lands, in large quantities, only some single city lots, on the south side of Chestnut Street, between 4th and 5th Streets, "reserved for the Welsh."

Naturally, as in any colony, made up from all walks of life, there were some people who had better have not come for many reasons, and some who were disgruntled, and fault finding, and, of course, some too lazy to work and support themselves, and even some who thought they had been vulgarly cheated by William Penn. In this connection the two following extracts from letters are interesting, as they are the opinions of two men who passed through all the troubles experienced by the Welsh Friends in Pensylvania.

Mr. Hugh Roberts, in one of his letters to William Penn, wrote,

"My dear frd, it is well known unto thee that many of our ffrds in England, had hard thoughts of thee and we, because of our removal from that to this country, and I doe not thinke but they had som cause, for here cam som peopel that had not a right end in their removals, some for fere of persecution, som that were discontented with their brothern where they were, and others that promised to themselves to be great in the world.

"I believe all these meet with great disappointments and som of them cam back unto England, others of you did send very bad reports, both of the cuntry and ffrds, for they were not contented with ffrds here, no more than they were in their native Land, and so when som ffrds in England heard and perceved these things, some were redy to conclude that they had not mist in their first thoughts of us, but for all this I know here is many hundreds that cam here in the integrety of their hearts, and in a true sence of what they did, and never to this day had cause to repent nor repin, though they were very hard put to in the outward."

And, in 1698, Mr. Rowland Ellis, of "Bryn Mawr," wrote to his son-in-law:

"I desire yt none may take occasion by any word yt discovers, nor suppose if I do nor did repent of my coming, for be it far from me from encouraging any to venture ymselves, and what they have, furtherly they live comfortably in their native country, to ye danger of ye seas, and many more inconvenience yt may happen, and on ye other hand, discourage any yt hath any real inclinations to transport themselves into ye hands of providence. Some came here might have better staid in their own country, and it is my thought yt great many more would have done better here yt ever they are like to do in their own country."

In a general way the principal is responsible for the acts of his agent, so the blame for all of the disagreeable features of the first eight years of the experience of the Welsh in Pensylvania has been put on William Penn following contemporary public records, and statements in private letters.

Well, it may have been Penn's fault indirectly, and often times directly, that the Welsh Friends were badly treated, but, as all of his provincial affairs were mismanaged by him, during the time mentioned by this reason all of his colonists had to experience different degrees of annoyances.

What was the reason William Penn lost his grip on his "province business," for certainly he started out brave enough? The answer I find to this, which is a matter concerning the Welsh Friends as much, if not more, as any, is that there was in these first eight years some greater and personal matters on his mind, besides the happiness of the Welsh.

WELSH TRACT AFFAIRS

One was the gay life he was leading in the King's company, as we shall see, the other, there was "a skeleton in his house" about which he worried, knowing that, sooner or later, it would be discovered, when it would be imagined that he had been living a double-life and trying to account for it, be suspected of having done a thing that was quite in keeping with the then customs of the "high life" he was born to.

The dread of the revelation was on his mind for years, for the peculiar position he held among Friends would make his conduct more reprehensible when it became general gossip. This was "eating the very heart out of him," but it was years before his friends knew it and more before they knew the reason. They discovered what he let them see; if they supposed they saw more, they kept to themselves and his "greater secret" died with him. Anyone is at liberty to imagine what it was or if there was one; but here I give only the story of the "effect," as known to only a few when he told it, but which is now generally known. It is that of an alleged dishonest employee, one Philip Ford.

The story goes that Ford, a young Quaker, had been an unsuccessful merchant in London when he applied to Penn for aid, and that Penn, taking pity on him, made him his steward for his Irish estates, at the salary of £40 a year, in 1669, and from then was most intimate with the Fords, though they were not his social equals.

This may have been the cause of one of Penn's mottoes: —"Guard against encroaching friendships."

In the summer of 1682, a few days before Penn set out for Pensylvania, Ford submitted a memorandum to him, claiming that Penn owed him a balance of £2851. 7.6., "On account salary arreares, money advanced, and expenses." Without taking time, as Penn subsequently confessed in Court, to examine the account, on Ford's suggestion, he also said, not having the money to pay, he signed, without even reading, "a due-bill and an acknowledgment of the debt,"

WELSH SETTLEMENT OF PENSYLVANIA

as he supposed, which, much to his astonishment, he discovered subsequently was a deed of lease and release, dated 24 August, 1682, for a grant of 300,000 acres of land to be laid out in Pensylvania, which conveyance should stand good unless he paid Ford £3.000 "within two days." And, for full security for the payment of this sum and interest it would draw, Penn also executed a bond in double the amount.

Since Penn wrote James Logan, twenty-three years afterwards, when this matter was still unsettled, for him not to worry, as "Ford's business is only a mortgage," it may have been that Penn did suppose if he thought anything about it, that £3.000 (the indebtedness "in round number"), with bond and mortgage security. That is, a bond in double the amount of the "loan," and the mortgage on 300,000 acres, which valued at the price he then sold land, namely 5,000 acres for £100, would equal the debt, and claimed to have had no knowledge that he would forfeit the land if the money was not paid within two days after date. Penn sailed on 31 Augsut, 1682, therefore he had time to take up the note, but did not do so.

Here is where the queer part of this transaction is first introduced. It seems that without foreclosing this mortgage, or cancelling the bill, Ford sold rights to the land in lots for a total of £8.000, and kept the money, and Penn said, when he returned to England, in 1684, Ford told him he then still owed him a balance of £4.293.3.0! Penn says he thereupon gave him £500 in cash on account, and, as security for the mysterious balance, after many delays, signed a note, dated 10 June, 1685, for £5.000, with interest, payable on or before 21. 1mo., 1686-7, giving as security, what he supposed was an ordinary mortgage, but which was in fact a straight deed for 300,000 acres of land in Pensylvania, besides the grants of the manors of Pennsbury and Springettsbury, a manor in Chester Co., an island in the Delaware, and city lots, and all the revenue from the Pensylvania quit-rents!

WELSH TRACT AFFAIRS

No one has ever thought William Penn was a fool, nor suspected him of being ignorant of the simple forms of business papers and transactions, for there are too many instances to the contrary. At least, he has been supposed to have been gifted with considerable business acumen. Then, why did he allow himself to be imposed upon? Why did he tie himself up so with promisory notes, and convey away his property by deeds in this manner, are questions that have never been answered. The excuse of "implicit confidence in Ford" has been suggested. If so, it was an act of credulity past the understanding of worldly people.

Looking at the matter from another point, the question is, did Ford and his wife have knowledge, since they were well acquainted with Penn, of some incident in his life, which would ruin him if exposed? And, for this reason, they proceeded to blackmail him? Or, if this was not the nature of influence they possessed, was it hypnotic control? Whatever it was, it caused Penn much unhappiness, for he was continually fearful of exposure, and he was ashamed to let his most intimate friends know that "he was in the clutches of a brace of sharpers," as the Fords have somewhere been defined.

Because, after Ford's death, his widow was so vindicative towards Penn, it has been presumed that she was all along the master mind in getting Penn into this compromising position, and that Mr. Ford acted under her instructions.

When Philip Ford, "late of Alisbury, County of Bucks, near London," applied to his meeting, the Upper Side of Bucks monthly meeting, on 4. 7mo., 1672, for a certificate of good character addressed to the men's meeting, London, having declared his intention of marriage with one Bridget Gosnell (Gosnel, or Gosnold, as her name was variously written), of London, William Penn was one of the signers of it.

WELSH SETTLEMENT OF PENSYLVANIA

Penn attended their wedding, on 24. 8mo., 1672, at the Bull and Mouth meeting, in London, of which Philip and Bridget were members.

Ford stood high in the estimation of English Friends from this time till his death. In 1676, he was one of the Friends in Hereford, appointed by the yearly meeting, to whom Friends in the county "afflicted with sufferings" should report. And from the minutes of the Upper Side of Bucks monthly meeting, 1679, 11mo. 7, and 1680, 2mo. 7, it appears he was the one selected to take the contributions to James Claypool, in London, and, as late as 1686, 9mo., he was one of the Friends appointed by the yearly meeting, at London, to receive contributions from monthly meetings. According to a circular of the Free Society of Traders in Pensylvania, dated 25 March, 1682, "Philip Ford in Bow Lane, near Cheap Side," London, was their agent to receive subscriptions to the shares of this company, so dear to the heart of William Penn, because it advertised and "boomed" his province land sales. Therefore, Friends of all classes must have had great confidence in Ford, and the "mighty secret" between him and Penn was kept well hidden.

*This company, often referred to, was organized for the purpose of "trade, manufacture and commerce in and with Pensylvania." Its first meeting was held in London, in 3mo. 1682. Future meetings were "to be held on the first Thursday in November, in the Capital city of Pensylvania."

This "society of traders" had extraordinary privileges. Among these, it was invested with "the lordship of the manor of Frank," and was to have three representatives sit in the Pensylvania Assembly, under its original charter, mapped out by Penn himself, for it was one of his pet schemes by which to sell his land, and build up some outside trade for his province, even "with the Emperour of Canada," besides among the Lenni Lenapes, which was ratified in London, 5 May, 1682, by the largest land purchasers, at the same time, with Penn's consent, when they "adopted" the Laws he had proposed for them for the better government of his Province. The capital stock was £5400, and although the shares were put "on the market" in March, 1682, they were all subscribed for by 26 April following. £50 subscribers, or purchasers of two shares, were each to be entitled to a vote on the management. But anyone living in The

WELSH TRACT AFFAIRS

To resume the story, when the note of 10 June, 1685, came due, 21 March, 1686-7, Penn did not pay it, and on 11 April, 1687, gave another note for £6.000 (as the "balance due," Ford told him, was £5.282.9.8), without receiving the previous note, he said. For security of the payment of this new note, payable one year from date, Penn executed a bond, and a deed by which he gave Ford a "Welsh mortgage," on his entire Province (without destroying the previous mortgages), at the quit-rent of one peppercorn annually. Neither did Penn take up this note. All this time Ford was acting as Penn's "Irish agent," and paying himself out of receipts. Penn must have been dumbfounded, when on 11 October, 1689, Ford rendered an account to him of his stewardship, and Penn learned from it that he owed Ford a grand total of £20.333.19.2! However, Penn marked the account O. K. and ratified the obligation. Then Philip and Bridget let Penn alone till in August, 1690,

---

Province, who owned there 1,000 acres of "inhabited land," and who subscribed £100 was to be entitled to two votes; £300 subscribers could vote three times. However, when the charter came before the Pensylvania Assembly for confirmation, the grandure of the Society was considerable curtailed when it was made Free, and it was so "free" to do as it, or Penn had hoped and the final facts are, that, though great promises were made towards the development of the commercial side of Penn's domain, the only act positively accomplished was to buy 20,000 acres of country land from Mr. Penn, and 400 acres in his city, laying between the two rivers, below Walnut street, and selling on long credit some cargoes of goods for which the Society had paid "good money," the bills for which were never paid, because being strict Quakers they were not "sued out," and by May, 1684, the Society had no money in its treasury, and no income so it "went out of business," and it was wound up officially by the Pensylvania Assembly, in 1722-3, without ever declaring a dividend. Several times before this, certain English shareholders publicly demanded an investigation and accounting of the Society, but there could not be found anyone on whom to "serve the papers." The promoters of the Society apparently got rid of their holdings while the "boom was on," for they strongly recommended the shares for permanent investment, and the inventories of their personal estates do not show that they had any of this company's stock.

when for further security for the debt, which accumulated fast, because Ford compounded the interest every six months, and charged Penn commission on both receipts (which he kept) and expenditures managing the Irish estates, they demanded, and received the release from Penn of all equity of redemption in the mortgage of 10 April, 1687. In the following month, Ford demanded that Penn pay him on account £6.900 cash. However, as Penn could not raise the money, Ford induced him to make to him a conveyance of his entire Province without defeasance! Was it blackmail, hypnotism, or credulity that influenced Penn?

At this time, Penn seemed to be letting Ford manage for him. In his advertisement of 1690, headed Some Proposals for a Second Settlement in the Province of Pensylvania, telling "there being above One Thousand Houses finished" in Philadelphia, put out when trying to dispose of the shares in the proposed sister city out on the Susquehannah, which could be reach easily via "boat on ye River Scoalkill," that those desiring shares, should direct their applications "to Robert Ness Scrivener in Lumber-Street in London for Philip Ford." In letters, 6. 4mo., 1687 and 10. 4mo., 1691 to Thomas Lloyd, Penn desired him to send reports directly to Ford.

In 1693, when the Provincial government became a scandal, and Penn was under suspicion at Court, and his Province was taken charge of by the Crown, with Fletcher appointed Governor ('twas then the Welsh Friends sent a letter facetiously addressed, "William Penn Improprietor of Pencilvania," &c.), the Fords thought it a trick of Penn's to shake them off, and commanded him to raise £10.000 cash within six months, and on payment thereof they promised they would give him a receipt in full of all accounts (as he had paid them cash on account at divers times, and thus reduced the £20.000 considerably, in spite of the compound interest, &c., and at the same time confirmed the

WELSH TRACT AFFAIRS

debt), otherwise they "would expose him,"—whether in the matter of this "debt," or some other particular, it is not known.

Thereupon in this emergency, Penn wrote an old friend in Philadelphia, Robert Turner, and begged him to persuade one hundred of the Pensylvania Friends to each contribute £100 towards a purse of £10.000, and lend it to him, as he was "hard pushed for cash just then," because his "Irish affairs were wretched." After some correspondence, nothing came of this request. The "city Friends" in the Province wanted security, which Penn could not give, and the rich Welsh Friends of the "barony" had too many grievances to be adjusted by Penn to listen to his troubles.

However, when Penn told the Fords of his failure to raise the money, they did not "expose him," but instead took new notes, with interest due every six months (which was his choice, possibly), until the total sum was appalling to Penn. This blackmail, or debt went on piling up for four years, Penn feeding cash to the Fords when able, or until Parliament laid the tax on money at interest, in 1697, when Ford told Penn he would either have to pay the tax, or give him as security an indenture of absolute release and confirmation, and turn over to him the Royal Charter, and the deeds of enfeoffment, making the conveyance of Pensylvania absolute, when Ford would lease the Province to him at an annual rent, equalling the compound interest reckoned each six months on the accrued indebtedness, all well secured, and that this transaction should be kept secret; Penn still appearing as sole owner, and himself continue the sales of land, but to turn over to him (Ford) the proceeds as received, and in this way Penn could evade the tax. Penn may have protested this duplicity, but he agreed to this arrangement on 1 April, 1697, as he stated in Court.

This was the state of Penn's affairs when he arranged to visit Pensylvania the second time. When he went to say farewell to Mr. and Mrs. Ford, in August, 1699, they insisted that he give them, which he did, a signed statement, saying in effect, that he had carefully examined all of Ford's accounts against him, and all transactions between them, and had never found any errors, or misstatements, in them, and that by this document he released Ford from all obligations to him.

Shortly after Penn arrived in Pensylvania, Philip Ford died. By his will be devised to Bridget, his wife, and executrix, and trustees, all of the province of Pensylvania, and its territories, and instructed that the "province" be sold for the benefit of his wife and children, unless Penn paid his executors within six months, £11.194.8.3 (Ford was always particular to include shillings, and even pence, in his claims, to make them business like), and all debts, and arrears of rent of the Province, interest, &c. Should Penn do this, then the Province, &c., would be reconveyed to him. But if William Penn himself was then deceased, his heir should not have this privilege, or any equity of redemption.

Mr. Ford's son and heir, Philip, Jr., now took up the system of blackmailing Penn, under his mother's instructions it is presumed, and frequently, in America and in England, went to Penn and demanded cash, always threatening to "expose him" if it was not given, and it always was. This went on, with variations, until Penn simply could not stand it any longer, and in 1705, had to acknowledge before the London Yearly Meeting that he needed advice on a private matter. A committee was appointed, and to it Penn complained that Bridget Ford was annoying him about a little money he owed her, and was just them unable to pay, and asked that the committee should request her to desist from persecuting him, until the matter could be adjusted. "Only this, and nothing more." But the Fords, although Friends in good standing, positively declined to be interfered with by the committee, in the collection of money due them, so they were promptly "silenced" until they yielded, or were more "tender."

WELSH TRACT AFFAIRS

This brought out from Penn a partial statement of his secret affairs to the committee, and on their advice, though against "teachings," proceeded against the Fords by a bill in the Court of Chancery. He pleaded "fraud," and extortion; admitting he owed them something, but that he did not owe them anything like the amount they claimed, and by the greatest liberality the balance of his debt was then only £4.300, and this he was willing to pay, and no more, and requested the release of all security he had given upon payment.

But the Fords backed up their claim with the paper Penn in fright, had signed in Aug. 1699, acknowledging their accounts were correct in every particular, so the matter of fact Chancellor decided against Penn, and put the costs of the suit on him, and required him to enter bond for payment. Penn appealed, but again lost, as can be imagined for his evidence was meagre. Now, the Fords considered themselves in complete ownership of Pensylvania, and instructed David Lloyd, and others in Philadelphia, to remit rents, &c., only to them, and to sell the "Province" at the best advantage. At home, the Fords entered suit in the Common Pleas Court against Penn for arrears of rent of the Province since April 1697.

It was at this juncture of this remarkable affair that Judge Isaac Norris came over from Philadelphia to learn the true nature of Penn's difficulty with the Fords, for Philip, Jr., had been in Philadelphia, and had told some queer stories about "Father Penn." The Judge does not seem to have learned from Penn the "true inwardness" of the difficulty; but he told Penn he must give good security guaranteeing the titles to all the land he had sold since 1 April, 1697, else trouble would arise for him when it was discovered he had concealed the gravity of his affairs. (Penn even deceived his most intimate friend, James Logan, for as late as in 1705, he wrote him, "Ford's business is only a Mortgage.") Penn replied to Norris, that there was no occasion for this, as "Ford approved of all his sales."

WELSH SETTLEMENT OF PENSYLVANIA

While Judge Norris was in London, the Fords won their last suit, and got judgment for about £3.000, for rental due, on account of "Penn's Province." and as Penn could not pay, or furnish security for this sum, he was committed to the Fleet prison till he could do one or the other. It is said he led an humble life in the Fleet, holding almost daily meetings.

The next move of the Fords was to petition the Queen, asking to be confirmed not only in possession of Pensylvania, but in the government of the province. On advice of her council, the petition was dismissed, for a technicality, and "political reasons," and this was the beginning of the end of the persecution by the Fords, for shortly afterwards, Judge Norris, after many rebuffs, prevailed on Bridget, and her son, to come to terms, and accept a certain sum in cash, which he raised among eight Friends, in England and Ireland, to whom Penn executed a "blanket mortgage" on Pensylvania for security, and on 5 Oct. 1708, executed a deed of release for Pensylvania, when Penn was liberated not only from jail, but from the clutches of Bridget, and his heart-sickness.

What was William Penn doing with himself all these years, that his time was so occupied he could not consider the complaints of the Welsh Friends in his province, or even had time to investigate Ford's accounts, or block his blackmail, if it was that? In a letter, dated London, 28. 1mo., 1688, Penn wrote to Gov. Lloyd, "I am here serveing god."

There is good evidence that during the remaining four months of Charles' reign, after Penn returned from his first visit to his American possessions, he was a prominent figure in the inner circle of his gay court, for, although not ennobled, Penn was of the elect, being the governor of a province of the Crown. At this time, having the ear of the king, the Friends in difficulties, and there were hundreds of these in England, Wales, and Ireland, being harrassed and imprisoned on slight provocations, naturally made appeals through him, but as Charles was inimical towards all dissenters, Penn, fearing his displeasure, made them only promises of aid. This did not take up much of his time, though it made him feel his importance. During these months, and subsequently, as a "pardon broker" it may be presumed, and there is evidence of its being so, that he only used his influence with the king on condition that the petitioners bought land from him, his *quid pro quo*, for those forgiven for their offenses soon transported themselves and families to his province, following his good advice.

Through these months, Penn followed his queer life,—publicly a courtier, privately a minister among Friends; or, outwardly a provincial potentate, prominent in the gayest Court of Christendom, otherwise, an accepted preacher at Quaker Meetings, held secretly in obscure places; living openly in great style, though vexed by poverty, and all the time in the clutch of Bridget Ford. Penn was then not forty years old, and according to description, still debonnaire, and of youthful, handsome presence, and a thorough aristocrat.

During these months, King Charles' brother James, Duke of York, and one of the greatest American land owners, a strict Romanist, was Penn's intimate at Court, and when he unexpectedly succeeded to the throne in Feb. 1685, Penn's position at Court was assured, so he continued his "high life" and "humble teachings" without interruption, incidentally corresponding with his far-off "holy experiment," for he dearly loved letter-writing and dictating to his colonists, and permitting himself to be everlastingly fleeced by the Fords. But, as this is not a biography of the great William Penn, it is unnecssary here to give the details of his life in the Roman Catholic atmosphere of James' Court, and show how he allowed himself to be used by the Brethern of the Society of Jesus to carry out their plans for reinstatement, craftily, if not legally, in England, through the king with whom they knew he had influence, while it is alleged he supposed he was doing only great service to the Quakers, as their go-between and pardon broker. At least this is what he wished the Friends to believe of him, for this was when he was being suspected, possibly justly, of a leaning, if not conversion, to Jesuitism, because of his marked intimacy with the Catholic monarch, and the leading Jesuits. The suspicion was so general that even his "friend," Philip Ford, put out a "broadside" (London, 1683), headed "Vindication of William Penn from late Aspersions spread abroad on purpose to Defame him." Ford denied that Penn had become a Catholic.

To be a courtier and the king's intimate, Penn was obliged to live the life. He resided in a great mansion, the Holland House, which he rented furnished from the Earl of Warwick, and rode in his "coach of four," and gave expensive entertainments at his mansion to fellow courtiers, "top-company" as he used to call these guests. Then, doffing his silk and lace, he would simplify his clothes to something similar to recognized "Quaker garb," and slip off to a meeting and lecture on the doctrine of humility. He was in the zenith of his enjoyment when his far-away colonists urged him to come over, live among them, and exercise his gubernative authority in his province. But he had no intention of going, unless, as he wrote, he could transplant and continue his surroundings, the colonists to furnish the money to pay for it all, servants, coaches, barges, wines, and company, for this petty king would have a court circle.

Several times when Penn had slipped off to attend secret Quaker meetings in London, he was captured there, along with the others, and taken before a magistrate, and paying the usual fine, returned to his mansion, his fellow courtiers, or the Court, as if he had had no adventure. The Jesuit Fathers, of course, knew of his dual life, but it was no business of theirs, since in obtaining exemptions and privileges for the Friends, and other non-conformists, was the same as if he worked for the Catholics, for they participated in them directly. These concessions meant more to them than to the Quakers and others, and in time led up to the important Declaration of Indulgence, granted by the King, in 1687.

WELSH TRACT AFFAIRS

Penn's companions were as varied as his life, at this period. He was intimate with the Catholic King (on 17. 7mo., 1687, he wrote to the Commissioners, Philadelphia, "I am just come off a Progress with ye King through ye west & northwest part of ye kingdom"); with the prominent Jesuits; with the notorious Earl of Sunderland; with the scheming, crafty Father Petre, and was used to do the plotting for James, the Romanist, at the Court of William, the Protestant, and at the same time, he was chummy with Henry Sydney, who plotted to oust James and seat William of Orange, and with Algernon Sydney, the executed anarchist. But Penn's adherence to his old friend, the Catholic king, is notorious, for there is his pamphlet entitled "Good Advice to Roman Catholics and Protestant Dissenters," as evidence. That he aided and abetted Catholic ascendency in England in getting relief for Friends was unfortunate, as it placed him in a peculiar position, for the American Friends openly accused him of being under Jesuitical influence, and asked him if it was, as rumored, "have you become a Roman Catholic?" (In after years, when the disputes began and prevailed between two branches of the Friends, the believers and followers of the teachings of Elias Hicks, and those who did not believe in the matters of faith and doctrine which he preached, it was advanced by the former section, as an arguement that Hicks was in the right, and his teachings was the belief of the original Friends, those of the apostles George Fox, John ap John, &c., which he hoped to re-establish, else why were the Friends of Penn's day so worked up when they thought he leaned towards the teaching of the Church of Rome, and was so intimate with the Jesuit priests?)

During these days of political intriguing, pretending to work in Friends' interests he was laboring for those of the Catholics, or *visa versa*, whichever way you choose to look at the employment, what did Penn care that the Welsh Friends on the Schuylkill were disappointed in him. He ignored their complaints. What did he, living in kingly company, with his head in royal clouds, care whether or not, the Welsh had to go miles to have flour made, were deprived of their ferry, had their lands confiscated by his agents, were juggled out of bonus, or liberty lands, and city lots, or, whether or not, the Welsh Tract was cut to pieces, and divided between two counties. All items of almost vital interest to the Welsh Friends in his province, and which, through his indifference lost them the autonomy which they had good reason to think should have been assured to them. But all he thought of then was "William Penn," first, last, and all the time, in these days of his pomp and pride, how to keep up appearances, how to find the money to meet the expenses of Court life, and how to support the machinery of his province in proper style, so that his "holy experiment" should appear successful to his fellow courtiers, and not give them opportunity to ridicule him. The wonder is, whence came the money to meet all of these expenses, the necessities along with the luxuries? Ford, as his steward, he subsequently testified in Court, stole all the revenue from the estates of his inheritance, and also for years during this period, appropriated as his own, the bulk of the receipts from Pensylvania land sales, for it has been figured out that previous to 1712, Penn personally received in cash from land sales only £10.645. But two conditions can be imagined, either that Penn was fairly wallowing in debts through the reigns of Charles and James, or what he said of Ford was false, unless we wish to imagine a third, namely, as the secret agent at Court of the Pope he had an assured income to pay for all these luxuries.

When James was deposed in the Revolution, and William and Mary seated, Penn, the "Jacobite Quaker," spoke freely of the liberty and peace the Friends had enjoyed under James through his efforts, and ridiculed the charge that he was tricked, and used to negotiate Catholic interests in England, when he got relief for the Quakers. He wrote a celebrated letter to the Committee on Trade and Plantations, in reply to one from its secretary, accusing him of being a Jesuit. It was a manly explanation of his position at the Court of St. James, but his position among Friends was weakened because he had put himself in a situation that required explanation, and it took years of altered living to regain their esteem.

Penn's first experience under the Protestant king was unpleasant. He was arrested and taken before the Privy Council to answer the charge of treason, and of "being a Jesuit and a Papist." He was placed under bond to stand trial, but for some reason, possibly the lack of witnesses, the case was not reached before the Toleration Act ended all persecution on account of religion. However, though this charge was dropped, Penn was no longer a *persona grata* at Court, because of his continued intimacy with the deposed James, in France, and the Jesuits in England.

A year after this, in the Spring of 1690, a letter from James to Penn was intercepted and read, in which the former king asked him "to come to his assistance," in what matter the Privy Council was uncertain, but determined to find out, so Penn was ordered before it to explain. The out-come was as in the previous case. But in July following, when plots against William and Mary were prevalent, Penn was made the special subject of a royal proclamation, and again arrested, as before, "on suspicion of being a traitor." He was imprisoned, but not brought to trial for want of sufficient evidence, and was finally released, but placed under surveillance, because he persisted in saying James was his dearest friend, and the good angel of the Friends.

Penn now not being a courtier, but a suspect, and having nothing to entertain him, again turned his attention to lecturing among the Friends, and preached Fox's funeral sermon, on 16 Jan. 1690. During the services, he got the tip that a warrant was out for his arrest again, and slipped away from this function, went into hiding, and did not come out into the open for three years. Why he fled and

WELSH SETTLEMENT OF PENSYLVANIA

hid, can only be guessed,—he let the people of his province suppose it was on account of the same old thing, his religion, although Quakers were not being persecuted then. Where he went to, and laid concealed these three years, a fugitive, he gives us no definite information. He certainly was frightened this time, for he knew that one of the men arrested with him, the last time he was captured, was executed for treason on slight evidence. Then, too, at this time, there were many Jacobite plots afloat, known to the Privy Council. The Government knowing that Penn was personally acquainted with these schemers, easily imagined that he might know the plans of the leaders, and when these men were captured, and executed for treason, declared that "Penn the Quaker" was one with them, knowing this, he thought it best to abscond, lay low till possibly James would come to his own again.

Wheresoever Penn hid may have been known to very few, but he secretly kept in touch with certain Friends' Meetings, and the leading men of his province, and was in secret correspondence with relatives at Court, asking them to beg the king to stop hounding him, and let him live the life of a harmless, peaceful Quaker.

Now it was that Penn found himself so pushed that he threatened to turn at bay. [Penn was the true son of his father, a man of spunk always, as witness his reproof, in 1683, of Jasper Yates, a captious Quaker, who complained of the authority Penn claimed in Pensylvania, writing, "No, Jasper, thy conceit is neither religious, politic, nor equal, and, without high words, I disregard it as meddling, intruding, and presumptious"]. His menace being, that if the king did not desist he would have "reason to regret his action." What was the nature of this threat has not been preserved, but it was more likely a political than a personal matter. Unfortunately, there are many gaps in the public records of this period.

Whatever was the ultimatum Penn had in mind, it either fell flat, or may be suggested in the following item of an extant diary of that day, under 18 Sep. 1691, "William Penn the Quaker is got off from Shoreham in Sussex, and gone to France." ("Diary of Narcissus Lutteral," II. 286). Many have guessed where in France, or on the continent, Penn went, and what company he kept there, but this year of his life is a blank as far as we are concerned, as he left no details relating it. The first we hear of him after his departure is in a letter to Robert Turner, Philadelphia, dated at London, 29 Nov. 1692. "I have been above these three years hunted up and down, and could never be allowed to live quietly in city or country," wrote the fugitive in another letter, undated, on matters of faith and religion.

Old-time friends of Penn by this time had risen to favor at Court, and through them Penn petitioned, and they convinced the king that he was not the dangerous man the Privy Council would have him thought, so we read again in this same Diary, under 5 Dec. 1693, "William Penn the Quaker, having for some time absconded, and having compromised the matters against him, appears now in public, and on Friday last held forth at the Bull and Mouth [a Friends' Meeting was there], in St. Martin's [parish, London]."

Penn, in a letter written at this time, says:—"From the Secretary [of State, after his "compromise," or acquital] I went to our Meeting at the Bull and Mouth, thence to visit the sanctuary of my solitude," the secret place of refuge "from justice" where he hid so long, and which has never been discovered. Even Ford did not know where Penn was, as it may be seen there was no "transactions" between them in these several years, but the interest went on piling up day and night. From this time, Penn, although having the *entree* at the Court of Anne, returned to, or rather assumed the mode of life exampled by the religious Society of Friends, and meddled no more in national politics.

This little sketch of Penn's life, during seven early years that Ford and wife dominated, if not black-mailed him,

WELSH SETTLEMENT OF PENSYLVANIA

shows no excuse for his allowing them to go on as they did, nor any for his turning his back on the Welsh Friends he had induced, by certain promises to remove to his province. But the last three years, when he was a fugitive, should be an excuse for him in both cases. After this, when he became "a living Quaker," his life yields no excuse, so far as the Welsh are concerned, and we have seen what happened in the Ford's matter.

As a summary to the aforesaid statements, it may be of interest to read here what the editor of the History of Haverford College (1892), wrote of the same, "These worthy people" [the Welsh] he said, "had emigrated to the new world with the desire to live quietly and apart from the people around them. Gov. Penn had given them some reason to expect their wishes would be gratified. In a letter of instruction to the surveyor-general, he directed that the Welsh tract should be laid out in accordance with the understanding with them, *i. e.* contiguously as one barony; the intention of the Welshmen being to conduct their own affairs separately from the rest of the colony, and in their own language, as a county palatine. Tempted by the prospect of peace and quietness in the new land, the settlers swarmed over. * * * During the sad days of financial distress which darkened Penn's declining years, however, he wrote to his agents to be vigorous in the collection of the quit-rent, whereupon, in their zeal, the rents were assessed upon the whole 40,000 acres, heretofore exempt, * * * and in spite of the original assurance of the Proprietary himself, a line was run between Philadelphia and Chester counties, which divided the Welsh Tract in two parts. A pathetic appeal was made from what they at least regarded as a grave act of injustice. * * * Their spirited claim did not avail, and the reservation was thrown open for settlement by others. Doubtless it seemed to them an act of glaring wrong, and seriously marred their pleasant pictures; but it is a striking commentary on the obliterations wrought by time, that these ancient Britons are now

WELSH TRACT AFFAIRS

completely merged, and all lines between them and their English speaking neighbors have vanished; no distinction remaining save the old Welsh names. The early dissensions, probably, account for the quiet obscurity of the annals of this part of the colony, of which we hear little, and the Welsh settlers were not, perhaps, much in accord with William Penn."

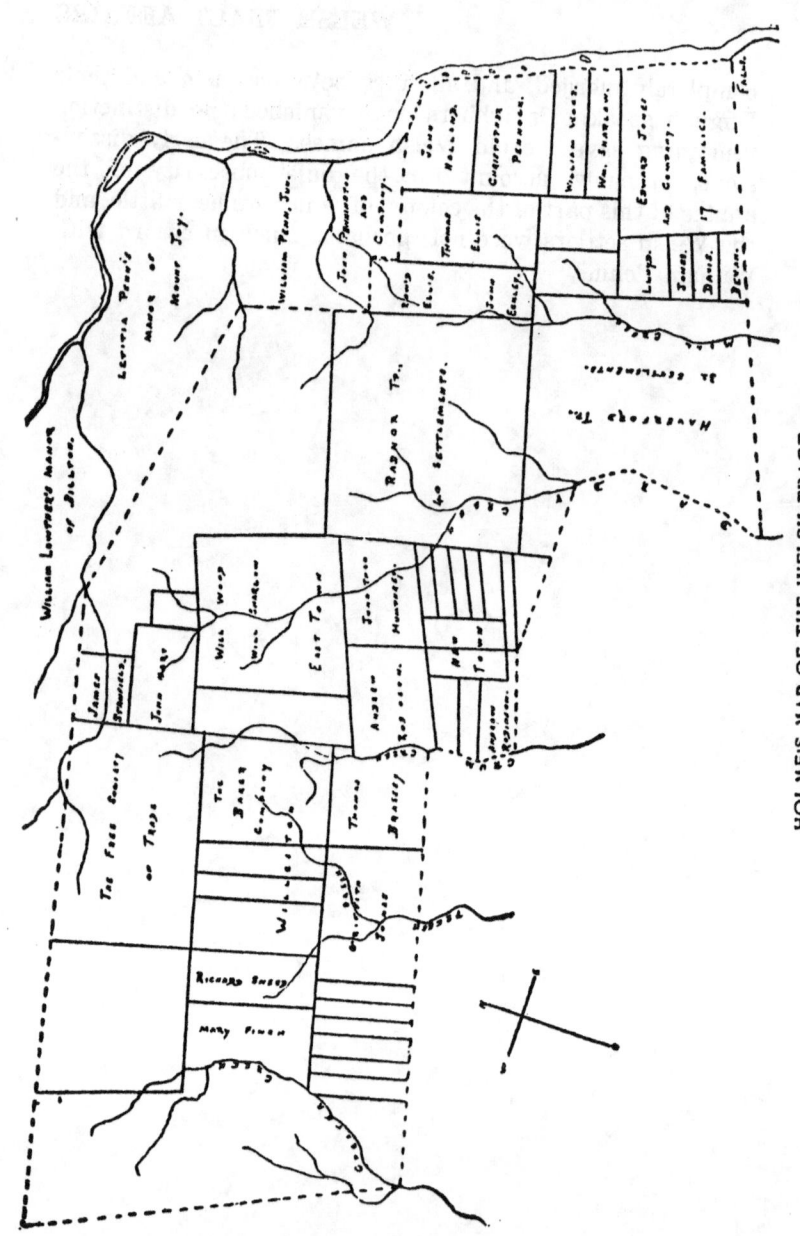

HOLME'S MAP OF THE WELSH TRACT

ALLIED WELSH TOWNS
OF PENSYLVANIA

WELSH TRACT TOWNSHIPS.

While reviews of these origins are interesting, we should not forget that much quite as engaging in other ways has occurred in the same localities, since the Welsh settlement was made, in more than two centuries, when Evan Oliver was the official wood-ranger in Merion, and when ear-marked cattle and swine roamed at large in the fenceless wilds of the plantations beyond the Schuylkill. In this cradle, under Welsh Friends' influences and teachings, were nursed the Welsh forebears of many noted men and women, who helped in various ways to uplift the Commonwealth and its metropolis, the names of hundreds of whom it should be invidious to relate, whose descendants returned, after many years, with riches and refined tastes, to the "old home," and bought back the desirable portions of their Welsh ancestors' holdings,—the "home fields" of the pioneer planters, and beautified them till the "Main Line" district has become justly celebrated for its improvements the world over. And these descendants are more proud of these Welsh farmer, Quaker ancestors than any of their others of equal date, for always has there been more pride in a farmer ancestor, was he a small or a large land owner, than in one following a trade.*

---

*From the Philadelphia tax list, for the year 1771-2, preserved at the Pa. Historical Society, can be learned the kind of trade, for they had to "live," of the progenitors of a multitude of Philadelphia families, more or less prominent, and this old book should be valuable data for family historians. Space permits only a few extracts, but I can give enough instances to suggest that there were very few in the city who wrote themselves "Gentleman" in 1772:—Gunning Bedford, James Bringhurst, Benjamin Loxley, Edward Stretcher, John Keen, Benjamin Shoemaker, William Lownes, Josiah Matlock, Richard Armett, Joseph and Samuel Wetherill, Edward Bonsell, James Shars-

WELSH SETTLEMENT OF PENSYLVANIA

Lying adjacent to the city of Philadelphia, (or Penn's Liberties, or old Blockley township's 7,580 acres), which has grown to its bounds,* the lands of the Welsh settlers it may be seen are naturally advantageously situated for great and greater improvement. And to further enhance the value of these lands bought from Penn for a few shillings an acre, and to make them most accessible as a residential section, within a few minutes of the heart of the business district of the city, there are two great "steam roads," an "electric road," a "trolley line," and two broad, well-kept avenues for "limousines." Yet, strange to relate, these advantages and possibilities in the "country lots," received general recognition only a few years ago, and the greatest changes in the "Seven Companies'" tracts have occurred only in the last twenty-five years, when farms dis-

---

wood, James Cresson, Isaac Lobdale, &c., were carpenters; Joseph Bringhurst, and William Shippen, coopers; Joseph Claypoole, Benjamin Horner, Thomas Cuthbert, Jr., Jonathan Wainwright, and David Bacon, were hatters; William Lippincott, Christopher Sellers, Robert Bailey, James Welch, John McCalla, &c., tailors; Benjamin Rundolph, Alexander Frazier, George Claypoole, were joiners; John Guest, Andrew Filler, John Hood, Jr., and Benjamin Paschall, were cordwainers; John Spencer, the butcher; John Drinker, and Thomas Hallowell, bricklayers; Henry Neill, Joseph Frazier, Thomas Middleton, and Henry Lisle, were bakers; William Bedford, the sadler; James Claypoole, the glazier; Isaac Snowden, and Benjamin Sharpless, tanners; Benjamin Shoemaker, distiller; Jonathan Shoemaker, blacksmith; John Biddle, and Abraham Wayne, tavern keepers; John Snowden, potter; Thomas Cuthbert, mast maker; Philip Syng, goldsmith; and some of the shopkeepers were George Sharswood, Blair McClanachan, William Turnbull, Edward and George Bartram, Clement Biddle, Geo. Anthony Morris, &c.

*Pownall in his journal, journeying from Philadelphia to the Susquehanna in 1754, says:—Crossed the Schuylkill at Coalters' Ferry. "All plots of this town represent it as extending from the Delaware to the Schuylkill. That this town should ever have such an extent is impossible. It does not now extend one-third of the way, those, therefore, who bought lots on speculation were much deceived."

MERION, HAVERFORD, RADNOR

appeared, and "country places" succeeded, and these in turn are being "cut up into lots to suit purchasers," hence a multitude of small holdings and a greater population.

This is the present state of the "Thomas and Jones" tract, and those adjoining of the other Welsh companies, and back from the river line, and along the river front of the pioneer company, called for convenience Number One, starting at the Falls of Schuylkill, there are the great plants of the American Bridge Company, and the Pencoyd Iron Works, conducted by descendants of the first Welsh settlers, while across the entire Thomas and Jones tract is the roadway of the Philadelphia & Reading Railroad. Here also are the properties of the West Laurel Hill Cemetery, on lands of Robert David and Edward Owen, or Dr. Griffith Owen, or Robert David and Dr. Edward Jones, and Dr. Griffith, proprietors at various times, and of the Westmoreland Cemetery, on land of William ap Edward, or of Hugh Roberts, while the settlements of Belmont Heights and Ashland Heights are laid out on the lands of Katherine Thomas.

With the disappearance of the "Welsh Tract" as a distinct territory in the Province, begin the annals peculiar to the townships that lay in this tract. Some of those of the townships called Merion, Haverford, and Radnor, the original settlements of the Welsh Friends, with their preparative meetings, one in each township, by whose names they were and are still known, united in a monthly meeting called Haverford at first, and subsequently Radnor, that met alternately in its earliest years with these three meetings, are of especial interest, because of the many Welshmen, prominent in provincial affairs, who resided within their bounds.

Of these three adjoining "towns," as at first they were called, first attention is given to "Merion in the Welsh Tract," which it needs no imagination to believe, and which has before been said, was named for the Welsh shire whence came its first Welsh settlers, the party of Dr. Jones, in the summer of 1682. This township in its early days was some-

WELSH SETTLEMENT OF PENSYLVANIA

what larger than our present "Lower Merion" portion of it (which is in dimension, 6½ by 4 miles, or about 14,500 acres), but not so large as with the whole of the present "Upper Merion" portion joined to it, as the "Upper" section in 1695, was a portion of the private land of Letitia Penn, or the Mount Joy manor, and the center was private land of William Penn, the younger, and these were not included in any "town." Then "Merion" extended inland from the Schuylkill river to the land of William Penn, Jr., and included the land adjoining his, belonging to an English adventuring land-company, headed by John Pennington, which the Welsh looked upon as invaders of their tract, just as they did the Swedes, who bought from Penn some 5,000 acres of the unsettled, confiscated "Welsh Lands," along the river from present upper line of Lower Merion to Bridgeport, opposite Norristown.

From the following list of subscribers for the shares of the Susquehanna Land Company (preserved at the Historical Society of Pensylvania), about 1690, we get the names of probably the most substantial of the early inhabitants of the old Welsh Tract, in the "town" of Merion, as well as those of Haverford, and Radnor, judging from the amounts subscribed for shares. This, too, may furnish some information of their prosperity at that time.

This subscription was taken when Penn had a scheme to found an interior city in his province, on the river Susquehanna, about 1690-1697. He designed well, but unlooked-for events prevented the consummation of his plans, which got no further than getting the subscriptions, and selling a few lots in the plot of the proposed interior "city," at the rate of three hundred acres for one hundred pounds. The Welsh subscribed liberally, as may be seen, and also purchased building lots extra.

It can hardly be said that Penn compelled the Welsh to invest their money in this undertaking of his, but he certainly influenced them to do so, and when it failed, it became another matter that tended to unfix their faith in him,

MERION, HAVERFORD, RADNOR

at least as a promoter of their welfare and wealth, but it is common knowledge now that in the province their gratitude was displaced by complaints, and it was as written, through the ill-treatment they had at his hands that caused the loss of his "fatherly influence" over the Welsh Quakers, else he might have persuaded them out of their conceit about their "barony;" conquered their obstinacy about paying Philadelphia county-tax; doing court duty in that county, in which their "barony" lay, and having magistrates and laws of their own adoption.

The key, and annotations, to the following "Susquehanna Subscribers" may, in many instances, be found in the notices of the early settlers.

MERION TOWNSHIP.

John Roberts, of "Wayne Mills"...... £5.	Thomas Howell .... £5.
John Bevan .... 25.	Daniel Thomas .... 5.
Hugh Roberts .... 20.	Ellis Pugh .... 5.
John Roberts .... 20.	Robert Lloyd 2.20
Cadwalader Morgan .... 15.	Edward Jones [glover].. 5.
Robert David .... 15.	Edward Griffith .... 3.
Griffith John .... 10.	Thomas David 1.10
Edward Rees .... 15.	Peter Jones .... 5.
Edward Jones .... 10.	James Thomas, Sen...... 5.
Rees Jones .... 6.	James Thomas, Jun'r.... 5.
William Edward .... 6.	Evan Harry .... 5.
Hugh Jones .... 5.	Joshua Owen .... 5.
Robert Owen .... 8.	Benjamin Humphrys .... 5.
Thomas, Robert, Evan and Cadw'd Jones .... 20.	Thomas Jones, Sen'r..... 2.10
David Hugh .... 5.	David William .... 4.
John Humphrys .... 10.	John Owen .... 5.
Margaret Howell .... 10.	John William 2.10
Dan Thomas [cancelled]. 8.	Abell Thomas 2.10
Rees Thomas .... 8.	Katharine David .... 5.
David Havord .... 10.	Sarah Evans .... 5.
	Philip Price .... 5.

WELSH SETTLEMENT OF PENSYLVANIA

HAVERFORD AND RADNOR TOWNSHIPS.

William Lewis	£10.	Thomas John Evan	£5.
David Lewis	5.	Henry Rees	2.10
William Jenkins	10.	John Evan Edward	2.10
John Lewis	5.	Thomas Parry	2.10
David Lawrence	5.	Evan Prothero	8.
Morrice Llewellen	10.	Hugh Samuel	2.10
Ellis Ellis	5.	Owen Evan	2.10
William Howell	6.	Daniel Chivers	2.10
Daniel Humphrey	10.	Rees Henton	10.
Henry Lewis	5.	William David	2.10
Samuel Lewis	5.	Richard Moor	2.10
William Row	5.	Samuel Miles	6.
Lewis David	5.	William David	5.
John Evans	6.	John Morgan	2.10
David Meredith	10.	Thomas Owen	3.
John Jarman	2.10	David James	5.
David Evan	8.	William Thomas	2.10
Richard Orms	10.	Elizabeth Jones	2.10
David Morice	5.		

The following list of fifty-two land owners in Lower Merion, in 1734, is also interesting, although their acreage is not given. It was made for the use of Gov. Thomas Penn, when he was putting the Pensylvania Land Office in proper shape for its duties. Up to his time, the land records had been a scandal.

John ap Mathias Roberts.
Hugh Evans.
Robert Jones.
Robert Roberts.
Robert Evan.
Rice Price.
Edward Jones.*
Abel Thomas.
Benjamin Eastburn.†
Jonathan Jones.

Catharine Pugh.
Rees Philip.
Joseph Tuker.
James John.
Thomas John.
John Lloyd.
Griffith Lewellen.‡
Robert Roberts.
David Jones.
William Walton.

---

*He was the captain of the Merion Associators, or militia, during the Revolution.
†He married at the Abington Mtg., 1722, Ann Thomas.
‡He was commissioned a justice in Phila. Co., April, 1744.

MERION, HAVERFORD, RADNOR

William Havard.
Richard Hughes.
Morris Llewelyn.
Benjamin Humphrey.
John Humphrey.
Joseph Williams.
Joseph Roberts.
John Roberts. (Pencoyd).
David Price.
Isachar Price.
John Evans.
Rees Thomas.
William Thomas.
Peter Jones.
Humphrey Jones.
John Griffith.

David Davis.
David Price, Jr.
Lewis Lloyd.
John David.
Robert ap Peter Jones.
Thomas David.
Owen Jones's plantation.
Eleanor Bevan.
Evan Harry.
Samuel Jordan.
James Dodmead.
John Roberts, carpenter.
Nicholas Repy.
Evan Rees.
Edward Edwards.
Garret Jones.§

The regular assessment lists of 1740-43, show 101 taxables in Lower Merion. The collector was probable more diligent, and let none escape him.

That there was particular confidence in the Welshmen may be judged by the fact that so many of them were named to sign and number the Exchange Money, or Bills of Credit, for the trustees of the Loan Office of Pensylvania, in November, 1755, as among the signers were Hugh Roberts, Daniel Williams, Christopher Jones, Joseph Morris, Owen Jones, Jonathan Evans, and Evan Morgan.

There has also been preserved a list of the taxables of Lower Merion, without date, but apparently about the year 1780, which gives the following inhabitants of the old "town," who were of Welsh extraction, and the number of acres they owned, out of a total of 153 names on the list. But in Upper Merion, at the same assessment, there were apparently only thirty-six having Welsh names out of 173 taxables. That is, among 326 taxables in the stronghold of the Welsh Friends, there were only 63 apparently of Welsh extraction, in their paternal lines. It may be noted

---

§He "perished under the snow," and was buried in the Merion Friends graveyard, 3mo. 30. 1765. See p. 134-5.

WELSH SETTLEMENT OF PENSYLVANIA

that at this time there were no very large farms in Lower Merion, but at all times here the farms of the Welsh, who succeeded the pioneers, were small, as primogeniture was not a custom among them. Each son received land, often in equal proportion.

Thomas David Estate	280	Eleanor Lloyd	50
Peter Evans	280	Thomas Morgan	100
John Evans (tailor)		Edward Price	200
Nehemiah Evans	50	Rees Price	15
Isaac Hughes	70	Henry Pugh	50
Thomas Humphreys (smith)		Joseph Roberts	150
Jesse Jones	100	Hugh Roberts (bach.)	130
Francis Jones	50	Algernon Roberts	224
John Jones	50	John Roberts	50
Hugh Jones	334	Jesse Thomas (smith)	40
Jacob Jones	230	Abel Thomas	40
Paul Jones	130	Walter Walter	80
Silas Jones	140	Lewis Thomas (wheelwright)	
John Llewellyn	350		

Lower Merion, still the most populous of the three old Welsh "towns" (in 1910, it was over four times that of Haverford tp.), and the richest "township" in the world, according to assessments, at the period of our '76 Centennial, contained only 1,200 taxables in a population of 5,000. This cannot be considered a wonderful growth however, for this country, since in 1800, Lower Merion had a population of 1,422. That is, in seventy-five years the population had only a little more than trebled itself, but following this period it took only thirty years to treble it again. At this writing Lower Merion, according to the 1911 report from the Bureau of the Census, has a population of 17,671. This is a gain of 4,400 over the census of 1900, and an increase of 7,200 over that of 1890. The figures do not include the students of the colleges and boarding schools in the township. The valuation of property for taxation in Lower Merion, in 1876, was $4,000,000, but in 1911, it is $17,621,130, and this being only at the "farm rate" is not a fifth of the true value of the properties.

MERION, HAVERFORD, RADNOR

Lower Merion, and the other "Welsh townships," even in the memory of some present-day men, were distinctively agricultural districts, and contained no towns, or even villages, as there was no occasion for them, for farmers do not need them. There were only little groups of a few houses, hamlets, about a grist mill, or a smith's shop, or an inn. These have grown into villages, and towns, but only by the overflow of population from the nearby city. Of stores, there were a very few. Even at the time of our national centennial, Lower Merion had not developed in this direction, as within its bounds there was only one drug store, one confectioner, one stove store, and one shoe store. Here primitive life and customs prevailed among the Welsh Friends, though it was the nearest to the city, and the most advanced of the three Welsh townships, fifty years after its settlement.

It was not till in 1830, that there was a post-office in Lower Merion, and thirty years later, there were only three. One at the General Wayne Inn, the first established, a near neighbor of the Merion Meeting House. The Inn had accumulated a blacksmith shop, a little country store, and a few dwellings, and the whole was dignified as the village of General Wayne, but this growth had been only since the Revolution. Another post-office was at Merion, Lower Merion, or Merion Square, as variously called, a village now, called Gladwyne. Here too the inn was the nucleus for some dwelling houses and a store. In 1860, the other post-office was at a cabinetmaker's shop, about which were some dwellings, and the whole known as Cabinet, or Cabinetville, and later Athensville, a stopping place of the first railway through the township. This gave it some importance, and soon it became the largest of Merion's villages, having in 1860, 28 houses, three stores, and a new tavern, the Red Lion, rebuilt in 1856, on the site of an older inn, on the Philadelphia and Lancaster Pike. In recent years, this settlement was re-christened Ardmore, and has become a town with about 6,000 inhabitants. These places were so in-

WELSH SETTLEMENT OF PENSYLVANIA

significant they had no mention in the *State Gazetteer* of 1832, though Humphreyville, on the pike, now Bryn Mawr, was recorded as a village, but in 1875, it had only twenty-one houses.

In Provincial times, and almost to recent years, the "freemen" of the Welsh Tract were put to great inconvenience when balloting for Philadelphia county officials. Before the Revolution, there were successive election days, as in England, when all of the voters of the Welsh Tract were obliged to go to the inn opposite the State House, in Chesnut street, Philadelphia, to cast their votes. When the British occupied the city, the men beyond the Schuylkill were obliged to go to Germantown, and cast their ballots at the tavern of Jacob Coleman, and continued doing this at each election till by Act of Assembly, 17 Sep. 1785, when the Merion voters, and others west of the Schuylkill, who did not reside in Philadelphia county, went to the court house of the newly created county, Montgomery, at Norristown, to vote, as Merion was from that time a part of this new county. By Act of 31st March, 1806, Merion tp. became a separate voting district, when its elections were held at the tavern of Titus Yerkes, the General Wayne Inn, till in 1867.

Although Lower Merion was known as a "farm country" till it became a "suburb," from its earliest settlement its main stream, now called Mill Creek, but in early days, Upper Mill Creek to distinguish it from another Mill Creek to the South, whose name was changed to Cobb's Creek,* furnished the

---

*This "Lower Mill Creek" was called Karakung, and Kakara Kong by Indians, and Carcoen Creek by the early Swedes. The Swedish Governor, Printz, had his gristmill built at the ford, or at the old Blue Bell tavern, in Paschallville. When the territory became Penn's he took over this mill, and established William Cobb as the miller, and the concern became one of the properties of Penn's monopoly Milling Company. It was patronized by the Welsh Friends at great inconvenience till the downfall of Penn's monopoly, as related herein. From this it may be seen that this Mill Creek got its present name from Penn's miller, William Cobb.

power for many manufacturing industries. After Penn's milling monopoly was broken, there was a grist mill erected on Upper Mill Creek by the Welsh, which was well patronized by settlers in Dr. Jones's, and the other plantations.

After the Revolution, and during it, it is believed, there was an important gunpowder mill on this creek, carried on by Messrs. Young & Homes. It seems to have been a rather unfortunate concern, for according to entries of burials at the Merion Meeting House, there were numerous accidental explosions in it, when workmen were killed. As the Burial Records state:—8mo. 2. 1788, "Richard Gill [entered again as Still]. Powder mill blode up"; Nov. 1804, "Two men, blue up at Young and Homes powder Mill on Mill Crick, [buried] in Strangers Yard"; Jan. 1805, "Two men, burnt in Young & Homes powder house on Mill Crick, [buried] in Strangers Yard;" 5mo. 10. 1806, "miller, killed [by] the Blowing up of Young & Homes Powder Mill." Written under this entry; "and they gave out makeing," which it may be supposed was a note by the clerk of the meeting, that because of so many accidents, Young & Homes discontinued powder making.

In 1785, there were four saw mills and five grist mills, along Mill Creek, and in 1800, there were seven paper mills, and two others in the township elsewhere, but at this time there were only three saw mills and three grist mills on the creek. The water power of Mill Creek was used by a dozen small concerns each employing from six to twelve men, up to a few years before the Civil War. Beginning at the mouth of the creek, there were Joseph Stillwagon's paper mill, William Chadwick's lampwick factory, and his grist mill and seven dwellings, Daniel Nippes's "manufactury," William Todd's carpet-fillings factory, Hannah Hagy's woolen yarn factory, Charles Greaves's Kentucky jeans factory, Evan Jones's carpet-yarns factory, Samuel L. Robeson's saw mill, Samuel Croft's brass mill, a concern of three factories, and a half dozen dwellings, Francis Sheetz's paper mill, Charles Humphreys's woolen mill, and factory for agricultural implements, and Levy Morris's grist and saw mill. A notice of Roberts's Pencoyd Iron Works, at the Falls, just before the Civil War, says the concern employs sometimes as many as thirty-six men! Also in the Thomas and Jones tract, at this time, Isaac Wetherill had a cotton factory, and Grimrod a grist mill on Frog Hollow Run, and on a little tributary to Mill Creek, James Dixon had a diaper factory. The Merion Furnace, at Matson's Ford, Schuylkill, was also a wonder in the middle of the last century, for "it employs as many as thirty men sometimes." The other streams of Merion, Trout Run, Indian Creek, Rocky Hill Creek, Gully Run and Arrowmuck Creek, have ever been small affairs, but Cobb's Creek in Haverford tp., and Darby Creek, its western boundary, in times past ranked with Mill Creek as water powers.

No sooner were the first Welsh settlers seated than they began to plan convenient roads in their proposed "barony," or borough, connecting their meeting houses, and themselves with Philadelphia. But, at first, naturally, the stream bordering one side of their tract, which the Indians called Manaiunk or Manayunk, and the Swedes, Skair Kill, the Dutch, Skulk Kill, and the English, Schuylkill, was the only thoroughfare from the tract to the great town on the Delaware. This stream, before the erection of the dam at Fairmount, was sometimes navigable for flat-bottom boats up to the falls, or the southeast corner of the Welsh Tract, and possibly the earliest settlers in the Thomas & Jones lands at the falls removed their effects up the stream from the Delaware to the Falls of Schuylkill, in preference to using the narrow Indian trails over the hills. But the necessity of convenient intercommunication must have been felt soon, for a year after the first arrivals the Welsh had fairly good communications between their little settlements, and with Philadelphia, though these ways were at best only bridle-paths through the woods, and no wider than single wagon

MERION, HAVERFORD, RADNOR

tracks,* the principal ones were called "streets" by courtesy or custom, and not known as public roads till after the rights of ways were surveyed, laid out, and confirmed, which was after the Provincial township organizations had been established, and each township had its highway supervisor, and when directions of public roads were determined by road-juries. Besides these "streets," the great highways, there were many lanes and by-ways in different directions through the tract, over private property, used as short cuts, connecting the "streets" which had their beginnings when needed, only a few of which came to be confirmed roads in after years. In all cases, the dates of confirmation are only suggestions as to the ages of public roads or the dates were only those of the time of their matureness.

A fairly complete sketch of the old wagon roads of the Welsh Tract would be the annals of its townships, and for this reason I will notice only the main "streets"; those decided upon by the Welsh, in 1683, and these were Merion Street, through Merion township, connecting with the road leading through Blockley to the "middle ferry" of Schuylkill (at High, or Market Street), known subsequently by several names, and best as "the old Lancaster Road"; "Haverford Street" through Haverford township, and also to the middle ferry; "Radnor Street," through Radnor township, and via Haverford road to the middle ferry, and the highway between the Welsh Friends' meeting houses of Merion, Haverford, and Radnor "towns." Early, there were the

---

*Possibly this order "By the Co'rt of Upland," (Chester), 12 Nov. 1678, concerning the public highways, was continued in force, and, though the method was crude, communication was opened through the country. It ordered that every person, "as far as his Land Reaches, make good and passable ways, from neighbour to neighbour, w'th bridges where itt needs, To the End, that neighbours on occasion may come together." Another order instructed "the highways to be clensed as forthwith, viz.: The waye bee made clear of standing and lying trees, at least ten feet broad, all stumps and shrubs to be close cutt by ye ground. The trees mark'd yearly on both sides."

WELSH SETTLEMENT OF PENSYLVANIA

"cross streets" connecting Merion meeting house with Haverford meeting house, and another connecting both with "the ford in Schuylkill," above the falls.

The "streets" of Merion and Haverford apparently had official recognition by Penn's government, and may have been surveyed routes, in 1683, as in land deeds of that date, and later, they are called "settled roads," without names. The "Haford," "Harfod," Haverford Street, or road, through the townships of Haverford and Blockley to the Schuylkill, surveyed in 1683, apparently, laid out in 1703, and confirmed as a public highway in 1704, has changed but little from its original course and grade. It does not have the same sentiment and "history" connected with it, that its twin, the "Merion Street," or old Lancaster Road has. Nor has the Merion to Radnor road, a "cross street" as early as 1683-4, and laid out and confirmed in 1713. Nor what is known as the Radnor to Chester road, dating from 1687. Nor that other landmark road from Merion to the Darby road, through Haddington, or the "Haverford and Darby road," passing Narberth and Overbrook, an official highway as early as 1687.

Other "historically inconspicuous" Welsh Tract roads: 19 Dec., 1693, "the Inhabitants of Radnor petitioned for a Road to be laid out from upper part of sd township to the Merion Ford." The request was granted. (On same date, there was "request of confirmation of the Road that is from Merion Ford to Philadelphia," and that "it come into the third street in the sd town. Ordered.") In 1696, it was ordered that a road be opened "from David Meredith's to Haverford meeting House" (this passed White Hall inn, and Haverford College on the west), and in 1697, a road "from Humphrey Haines's in Marple tp. to Haverford Meeting House," was opened.

But the fact that a "side road" was officially "opened" did not always keep it open to general use. If it was one opened in the Welsh Tract through English influence, or for the particular convenience of "English invadors," a Welshman, with an abutting farm, would not hesitate to plow and plant the ground taken from him, and *visa versa*. Merion seemed to be free from such troubles, but Haverford, and particularly Radnor, with its mixed, as to creed and nationality, population, had some difficulty in having "the right of way kept open," and had to appeal to the Provincial Council for assistance. As an instance of this, on 6mo. 18. 1687 (Council Minutes), "upon ye Reading ye Petition of ye Inhabitants of Radnor complayning yt part of ye road yt lades to the ferry of Philadelphia is ffenced in, & more likely to be" [continued so]. This was where an abuttor ran his fence across the opened road and took the road bed back into his farm. In Council, it seemed to be a question whether the trespass should be overlooked, and a new course selected for the road, or otherwise, as "it was Ordered yt John Bevan, Henry Lewis, David Meredith, John Evans, Barnabas Wilcox, and Thomas Ducket meet within 4 daies to view, or agree upon as Conscientiously as may be, a Road from ye Place aforesd to ye ferry, and return ye same to the Board ye next sittinge."

Some of the Welsh Tract public roads now designated as old, are not so in fact compared to those mentioned above. We hear of the "old Mill Creek Road." It was, as a public road, quite modern, since the petition for it to be opened "from John Roberts's mill to Rees Edwards' Ford," bears date of 1766. (This was "John Roberts, of Wayne Mill," as often found in print, but who was really of the "Vane Mill," so known from its wind director, and not a property of the well known Wayne family, any more than the "Wynn Mill, in another part of the tract, was the property once of Dr. Wynne, or his family, because once it was only a wind mill.) The same of the "old Gulph Road," the "old Ford Road," and the "old Levering Road," &c. This Levering Road, from Anthony Levering's mill, on the Schuylkill, connecting with the Lancaster Road (Montgomery Ave.), by another road through Academyville, and past the Belmont Driving Park (where Hugh Roberts lived), and the

WELSH SETTLEMENT OF PENSYLVANIA

Merion Meeting House, is referred to elsewhere as the "Ravine Road" to Rock Hollow. It was not made a public road till about 1785, on the petition of the miller Levering. This connecting road is now a handsome driveway, known as Meeting House Lane, but was in its earliest days known in deeds as simply "the road to the ford." For this reason it is often confounded with "the old Ford Road." This latter highway was quite another ancient institution of Merion and Blockley, but its identity is almost obliterated, for one end of it has been swallowed by an avenue of West Fairmount Park, and the other end by what is known as the State Road, in Merion. Yet its route can be described as from an olden time Schuylkill ford, about where Laurel Hill Cemetery landing is located (of course, before Fairmount dam was built), through Fairmount Park to the City Line road, or City Ave., then crossing the Schuylkill Valley Railroad, near Bala station, thence through Merionville, or what was known as Bowman's Bridge, till it is lost in the State Road. It has been supposed that the continuation of the "Ford Road," or its counterpart on the east side of the river, was an Indian trail from the Delaware river to the Schuylkill, passing between the two Laurel Hills to the landing.

The greatest and most prominent thoroughfare through Merion, passing the Friends' meeting house, our beautiful Montgomery Ave., is such a road, for it is tradition that once it was only an Indian path, from the Delaware to the Susquehanna, widened in part by the Welsh. Taken officially, this road is a mere infant compared with some other Welsh Tract highways. But of this road hereafter.

The "old Gulph Road," or the Gulf Road going westward to Gulf Mill and Paoli, from the old Lancaster Road, near the Merion meeting house, through the Merions, seems old because it has the Penn family coat of arms on its milestones, and it certainly was a "line of communication" as early as 1690, yet it was not officially a public highway till

MERION, HAVERFORD, RADNOR

it was surveyed and opened in 1748, when it is presumed, the milestones were placed under the direction of Richard and Thomas Penn, the joint governors of the Province.*

What we now know as the West Chester Pike, is the result of a petition, 16. 9mo. 1703, of Humphrey Ellis, Daniel Lewis, and fifty-eight others, inhabitants of the Welsh Tract, for a public road from Goshen tp. to Philadelphia, past the Haverford meeting house. It was ordered that it be laid out "from William Powell's ferry on Skuylkill & passing by Haverford meeting House to the Principal part of Goshen Township."

All of these country roads were primarily for the convenience of farmers marketing their produce, as it is likely that few people travelled in vehicles in the Welsh Tract till after the Revolution since no Welshmen's inventories of estates earlier than this period, mention any. At the time of the Revolution, there were only eighty-five vehicles of all kinds in the whole Province, and in 1760, in Philadelphia, there were three coaches, drawn by four or six horses (the Proprietor's, the Governor's, and William Allen's), two landaus, drawn by four horses, eighteen chariots, or two horse carriages, and fifteen one horse chairs, volanties, sulkies, and chaises. In the years just before the end of the

---

*The annalist Watson mentions in his MS notes (at Pa. His. Soc.) the mile stones he saw in 182-, along the Gulf Road, and the Haverford Road, particularly one on the latter, at White Hall Inn, (the water station on the old Columbia Railway), and one on a line of the "Harriton" farm, at 12 Mile Hill, which he records, "was marked 12 in front, with the Penn arms on the rear." (This stone, without figures, is now stored in the cellar of the Pa. Historical Society building. "These stones," says Watson, presumably referring to those on the Haverford Road, "were placed by the Mutual Association Fire Company, [Green Tree] of Philadelphia, as the price of its charter." The 11 Mile Stone was also on the "Harriton" farm, as the Gulf Road (and the Mill Creek) traversed it. The 10 Mile Stone was where the road crosses Mill Creek, and at its junction with the road to Merion Square (Gladwyn). The 9 Mile Stone was on the old Gaskill place, and the 8 Mile Stone on the old Lancaster Road, about 800 feet east of where the Gulf Road joins it.

eighteenth century, there were a thousand of all kinds of private vehicles in use. William Penn owned a coach and a calash when last here, but could not use either because of the "dreadful roads." Thirty years later, there were only five four-horse coaches, and three two-horse four-wheeled chairs in the Province. It was horseback for all but a very, very few till after the Revolution.

The present fine road passing the Merion Friends' meeting house from the city, was in its earliest times described only as "a settled road," in deeds concerning abutting lands, and may then not have had a name, as it had not become the King's Highway, for it was only a courtesy way across private grounds, having never been officially laid out, nor dedicated, excepting by implied consent, to public use by the Welsh Friends, owners of the land, for their own convenience in going to and from the city, by way of the "Middle Ferry," through the woods. Unless this could be considered as Penn's imaginary "Street" through Merion, there is no clear conception of what and where "Merion Street." was. Nor is the western terminus of this road in earliest days certain. Pioneer roads always led to a definite spot. This one, after connecting Merion Meeting people with Middle Ferry, possibly united with what we know as the Gulf road, and continued on to "the mill at Gulph," for in 1740, it only had the reputation of a "settled road" from the Merion meeting house towards the city, when it was known as the "Blockley and Merion Waggon Road," and the "Merion Road to Middle Ferry," and, of course, was only a mud road, for Macadam was not yet born. In after years, when it came to be widened, extended, and improved, and a part of a great highway, and was confirmed as a connecting link between Lancaster, or the frontier, and the city, it was known as the "Road to Lancaster," and was the principal thoroughfare of Merion. Its original route from Ducket's place, or the Friends' Schuylkill meeting place, near the Middle Ferry, out our Market Street and Lancaster Avenue,

MERION, HAVERFORD, RADNOR

to our 52d Street, does not appear to have been altered. But from 52d Street, and the Pensylvania Railroad, and in Merion, there were some changes made in direction and in grades, when the way over it to Lancaster was confirmed, and this Welsh enterprise came under the immediate protection of Philadelphia county, and after 1784, under that of Montgomery, beyond the new Philadelphia county line. Anciently, as now, the route in Merion, in a general way, of this historic road, over which our soldiers of six wars have marched, and only in one was their way contested, was via Merionville, past Daniel Morgan's place now the site of the great convent and school of the Sisters of Mercy, past the General Wayne tavern, the Merion Friends' meeting house, and westward for miles.

The beginning of this road in its present course and shape was when, on 20 Jan., 1730-1, the Provincial Council was petitioned by the settlers of Lancaster county for a road "from Lancaster town till it falls in with the high road [the King's High Road] in the county of Chester, leading to the Ferry of Schuylkill at High Street." The Council thereupon appointed a committee of Lancaster and Chester county men to select a route. On 4 Oct., 1733, this committee reported a route in their counties to the Council, which ordered that it be vacated and cleared in those counties, and also directed, to extend it to the ferry, and that the "road in Philadelphia county leading to the Ferry be searched" by a committee consisting of Messrs. Richard Harrison, Hugh Evans, Robert Roberts, Samuel Humphreys, David George, and John Warner. But eight years passed without any report from this Philadelphia county committee; and the Lancaster and Chester people had to petition again to have "a road from John Spruce's, on the Chester line to the High Street ferry," and thereupon a new Philadelphia county committee was appointed by the Council, namely Richard Harrison, Griffith Llewellyn, William Thomas, Edward George, Hugh Evans, and Robert Jones.

WELSH SETTLEMENT OF PENSYLVANIA

On 23 Nov., 1741, this committee reported a route with courses and distances made out 10 Nov., for the Lancaster road extended, which, in a general way was, in Philadelphia county, from near the homes of Rees Thomas and David James, on the Chester county line, over the "Conestoga Road" (surveyed on 20 July, 1741), beginning at Spruce's through Whiteland tp., to the Pektang road, to Kinnison's run, to Robert Powell's house, "then leaving the old road, and on George Aston's land" thence "to Willistown, to the west bounds of Burge's tract, to William Evan's smith shop, through Tredyffryn tp., to the Sign of the Bull, through East Town tp., to Radnor's upper line, and near John Samuel's place." Past the Radnor Friends' meeting house, "to Samuel Harry's lane, and his house, to James's house and lane, to the county line." Thence from the Radnor line to the Merion line, "past David Rees's shop." Over the Chester county line "to Benjamin Humphrey's upper line (being the Philadelphia county line), to the Gulf Mill road, thence through the lines of Benjamin and Edward Humphreys, to Richard Hughs's upper line and house, to Evan Jones's lower line, past the Merion Meeting House, and into the Ford road, and through Richard George's property, to the Blockley line." Then "near the house of Edward George, over David George's lane and run, to the Haverford road, past Peter Gardner's house to High Water mark at end of the Causeway at west side of High street ferry." It was ordered that this route be opened and cleared.

Going back over this road, in earlier days, there was coming from the ferry, the lands of Edward Prichard and Thomas Ducket, and a survey of the latter's land here shows the Friends' burying ground as a bound, and that the land of Francis Fincher was also a boundary for Ducket, and a deed shows that Fincher's land was bounded on the west by a street or road, the one to the ferry, and that he also bought land bounded on the south by this road. That is, Fincher had 35 acres on the upper side of Market

MERION, HAVERFORD, RADNOR

Street and across the street was "the Haverford Friends' burying ground," that is the graveyard of the Schuylkill Preparative Meeting, and the land of Philip England.

The road passed through 200 acres, next to Ducket's, owned by Barnabas Wilcox, thence through William Powell's 294 acres, William Smith's 500 acres, William Warner's 288 acres, the lands of Israel Morris, William Warner (again), and [Hugh Roberts's] 200 acres, William Woods's and Wood & Sharlow's claim of 200 acres, and by the land of Jonathan Wynne (lying between 161 acres of Edward Jones and 200 acres of George Scotson), across the city line, and through the land of John Roberts, whose neighbor to the southwest on his side of the line was Griffith Jones, and next to the latter was Abel Thomas, opposite to whom, across the city, or liberty line, was William ap Edward, and where these two properties were, now grows the village of Overbrook. Adjoining William Edwards' 186 acres, and Edward Jones' 161 acres, on the southeast was the 286 acre farm of David Jones. On 19. 12, 1700-1, Penn issued "warrant to survey unto David Jones, late of Merionethshire, 250 acres of my land on the west side of Schuylkill within the bounds of the liberties of Philadelphia, to be bounded to the eastward with the land seated by Hugh Roberts, to the northward with William Edwards, to the south'd with the line of William Warner, and to westward with my vacant land, reserving 50 acres on the northeast corner, adjoining to Jonathan Wynne and Hugh Roberts."

The commercial value of this roadway, or "public utility," was not fully appreciated, or recognized till the end of the century. In the fall and winter, 1786-7, the Assembly minutes record consideration of the improvement of the road, and the diary of Jacob Hiltzheimer, 6 Dec. 1786, says:—"the order of the day was brought forward concerning the new road to be made from the middle ferry on Schuylkill to Lancaster. All the speakers in the House debated upon it for some time." And 31 March, 1792, the

WELSH SETTLEMENT OF PENSYLVANIA

Assembly "finished with the bill for the turnpike between Philadelphia and Lancaster," and the Governor appointed as the Lancaster Turnpike commissioners, Messrs. Adam Reigert, Gen. Hand, Andrew Graff, Jacob Graff, A. Witmer, and Thomas Boude, of Lancaster, and Philip Wager and Capt. Faulkner, of Philadelphia, and entertained them at dinner on 19 Oct. 1792. But on 10 April, 1791, its right of way and roadbed had been granted and confirmed to some Philadelphia capitalists and promotors, who organized a stock company to improve and operate it by charter, granted 9 April, 1792, the corporation being called the Philadelphia and Lancaster Turnpike Road Company. The company's shares were readily sold, and there was "money a plenty," yet little was laid out on the old road to improve it, and it still went straight to given points without regard to hills and valleys. Mr. Hiltzheimer say that on 7 Aug. 1793, he "drove ten miles up the Lancaster road to the widow Miller's, to see the new turnpike, about a mile of which is laid." But the revenue of the road was conscientiously attended to, for in the 62 miles between Philadelphia and Lancaster there were nine tollgates when the road was opened in 1795. Gate No. 1, was two miles west from the Schuylkill, and collected for three miles; gate No. 2, was five miles west from the river, and collected for five miles; gate No. 3, was ten miles west from the river, and collected for seven miles. Mr. Hiltzheimer was appointed to inspect the new road, and Nov. 1795, he records that in driving over it, he frequently measured it, and found it full 21 feet wide, coming from Lancaster to the 14 Mile Stone.

As this road was still "paved with mud," the "Rules of the Road" are quite as primitive. "No waggon, or other carriage with wheels, the breadth of whose wheels shall not be four inches, shall be driven along said Road between December 1st and May 1st following, with a greater weight thereon than two and a half tons, or with more than three tons during the rest of the year." If loads were over three tons, the wheel tires must be proportionately wider. The old English "law of the road" still obtained, and drivers "kept to the left," up to the taking-over of the road by the stock company, when by general understanding and consent the teamsters reversed the rule, for it appeared to them, as well as all Americans,

> "The law of the road is a paradox quite,
> In riding or driving along,
> If you go to the left you are sure to go right,
> If you go to the right you go wrong."

This road, incorporated, now became the passenger and freight route of great importance, not only to Pensylvania shippers, and New York and New England merchants, but to the development of "the old Welsh Tract." The traffic in each of these industries was at first controlled and operated by alleged subsidiary concerns of the corporation, but as there shortly seemed to arise great rivalry between "lines" travelling the road, it is presumed the original scheme of close monopoly was abandoned, or was lost control of, or the carriers became independent. But what was known as the Line Wagon Company, owned by directors of the corporation, was long the monopoly freighter over the pike. It had warehouses and repair shops along the route, with extra wagons, horses, drivers, harness, &c. The Pike Stage Company, carrying passengers, the mail, and the newspapers, was the sister monopoly, also owned by the directors, "on the side." It maintained relays of teams, and extras, at such taverns along the road, and where meals were taken which gave the company the best percentage on travellers' fees. Through bad example of these monopolists, it is tradition not without foundation, that after they lost their control, the old stage drivers and the teamsters, working independently, practised "graft" to perfection, on the proprietors of road inns, the "wagon houses" and the stage taverns, distinct concerns, when also it was not unusual for teamsters to hold up the public stages by blocking the narrow road, and demand payment from the driver, who collected the "fee" from the passengers, and kept a "rake-off," to "go on and turn out." This method of "highway robbery" was also practised by teams, and even stages, on individuals in private vehicles. This state of affairs was the forerunner of another "controlling interest" on the pike. It was not long before old stage drivers and boss teamsters combined, and persecuted and drove from the road, or levied blackmail and tribute on any invaders of the pike, and stopped opposition and rivalry, and ended "rate cutting," and monopolized to themselves the traffic of the pike, charging exorbitantly. Nowadays we hear much about the chivalrous, "gentlemanly, though rough," stage drivers of ye olden time!

In its best days as the great thoroughfare to Lancaster and the West, the "Merion Street" of the Welsh Friends, when teams of four or six horses dragged heavily loaded Conestoga wagons over it, there were mile stones to regulate their journeys, as well as the amount of toll to pay. These reckoned the distance from the old court house at High and Second Streets, Philadelphia. At the 5 Mile Stone, in Merion, just across the Philadelphia county line, was the first important stopping and watering place for stages and teams coming from the city, Stadelman's Black Horse Tavern. Here also wagoners tarried to fix up their loads before entering the city. Near it, behind his great stone barn, was his starch factory, on the west side of the pike, near a "never failing spring." This was a long established inn, and was indicated on Scull's map of 1749-50. Pownall mentions it in his extant Journal, kept on a trip, in 1754, from Philadelphia to the Susquehanna:—"To Shadling's, the Black Horse, 4½ miles." Thence "To Meeting House [Merion], 1¼ miles." "To Richard Hughes', The Three Tuns, 2½ miles, To Ann Miller's, the Buck, one mile. To Richard Bury's, the Plow, 2¾ miles. To G. Ashton's, the Vernon [Warren?], 3¼ miles. To White Horse (Hambright's), 2¾ miles. To the Ship (Thomas Park's), 8¼ miles," &c. Stadelman's was a fair road-house, and had good custom till about 1798, when Col. Edward Heston built a tavern for his son, Abraham, on the pike in Blockley, east of Meeting House Lane (which is now 52d Street), which he named Columbus Inn. On the pike, opposite the 4 Mile Stone, was another good inn, called White Lamb. It is also still standing, back from the road, near Wynnefield Ave. Near it is a little stone blacksmith shop that was patronized by travellers long before the "settled road" became a turnpike. Near this inn, Thomas Wynne conducted a rope-walk, and at the edge of the woods was the snuff-mill of John Adams, a son-in-law of Thomas Wynne, 3d. At the 7 Mile Stone, on the pike, the old Columbia railway crossed the pike, at Bowman's Bridge. The 8 Mile Stone stood on Price's land, about a hundred perches beyond the Merion Meeting House. Other road houses in Merion were the General Wayne, the Red Lion, and the Eagle, and beyond was the Spread Eagle, the Paoli, and the Sorrel Horse, all popular in stage coach days, and all still operated. In all, between the Schuylkill and Lancaster, there were sixty inns of importance along the turnpike.

The "Turnpike Road," greatly improved, prospered as a tollroad till the canal and the railroad took away its business, when it became a disreputable affair,—a broken-down plankroad along its eastern end, and its western worse. The eastern end was then known as the West Philadelphia Plank Road, long ago only a memory, yet while it lasted may have been a reputable institution, but it was "too good to last," for its life was only between 1855 and 1858.

About 1876-7, the old Lancaster road became a menace to the paralleling Pensylvania Railroad, for the management of the latter corporation feared that street-car lines might be extended from the city out the old road into the growing suburbs, and cut into its local passenger business. Therefore, to protect itself from opposition the railroad bought the pike through a subsidiary company, in April, 1880, from 52d Street to Paoli, about seventeen miles, for $20,000,

WELSH SETTLEMENT OF PENSYLVANIA

and got a charter, under the name Lancaster Avenue Improvement Company, A. J. Cassatt, president, to operate it as a tollroad. Subsequently, this company sold and abandoned that part of the road that would not be likely to menace the railroad, west of Bryn Mawr, and retained the eastern portion, in Montgomery Co., re-naming it Montgomery Ave., and continuing to operate it as a tollroad, through a re-organized corporation called the Philadelphia, Bala, and Bryn Mawr Turnpike Company. However, this as the "old Lancaster Road" will always be "the first and most interesting macadamized road in the United States."

Of the aforementioned inns along the old Lancaster Road in the Welsh Tract, the General Wayne deserves particular mention here, as it is still a noted landmark in Merion. The inducement for changing what was a little stone dwelling into an inn, was that it stood on the great highway near two well-used side roads and a long established blacksmith's shop. That it was located so close to the Merion meeting house, was undesirable from Friends' viewpoint, yet they could, at several times, have purchased the lot on which it stands, surrounded on three sides by the meeting house land. This location of the tavern endorses the statement of De Foe:

> "Where ever God erects a house of prayer,
> The Devil always builds a chapel there."

This inn, about which there is misconception as to its age, as there seems to be about its nearest neighbor, the Merion meeting house, was originally, as may be seen, a small stone house, which was erected by Robert Jones, a son of John ap Thomas, sometime after 1709, the year in which he became the owner of the lot on which it stands, and was not "established" as an inn, as its sign now states, "in 1704," and did not so become till about 1776, as will appear from extracts below from deeds concerning the property, but for many years was only the home of the smith whose

MERION, HAVERFORD, RADNOR

shop was across the road. It also may be noted that Pownall, travelling this way, in 1754, did not mention an inn, or tavern here, though he noticed the Meeting House.

It has already been stated that Edward ap Rees (or Price) had 76½ acres, of the Thomas and Jones tract, in 1682, located back of William ap Edward, with Hugh Roberts on the north, Dr. Jones on the south, and Thomas Lloyd on the west; and that in 5mo. 1691, he bought 125 acres of land from said Lloyd on the west end of his first land, and in the same year bought "two acres" of the back end of Dr. Jones's first land, and that these several parcels of land were resurveyed and patented to him, in 1704, amounting in total 190 acres. And that Dr. Jones bought 76½ acres, adjoining his first land on the southwest, and along the Merion and Haverford road; and that he sold the river end of his original land, and in 1704, bought 188 acres south of his last purchase, and then had about 340 acres on both sides of what was afterwards Lancaster pike, and both sides of the road from here to Haverford meeting house.

Edward ap Rees, by a tri-party deed, dated 7 Aug. 1708, conveyed to Robert Jones (son of John Thomas), and "David Meredith" (or Meredith Davis), of Plymouth (father-in-law of Rees Press, whose first wife, Sarah, was the only daughter of Meredith), of the second part, and his son Rees Prees (Price), of the third part, two tracts of land, the above 190 acres, and 220 acres he had bought of Robert Roberts, a part of Hugh Roberts' estate. The two tracts adjoined, but would now be separated by the "Road to the Ford," and were surveyed together, but only the first part of the survey concerns the land of interest here namely, "beginning at a corner in Edward Jones's land, and by the same E. 15°, N. 156 per., N. 16°, W. 28 per. by Jones's land, to a stake in Jones's land, 1. 18°, N. 64 per. to a stake, ... 14°, W. 24 per. by land of Robert Jones, and thence by the Meeting House ground, W. 13°, S. 5¼ per.,

[445]

WELSH SETTLEMENT OF PENSYLVANIA

then N. 14°, W. 7 (7¾) per., then by land Edward ap Rees bought of Robert Roberts, and by lands of Evan Owen, Evan Harry, and William Cuarton."

The "two acres" which Edward Rees had bought of Dr. Jones, as above, went to make up the 190 acres, but Rees had promised them, half to the Merion Meeting, as will appear, and half as follows:

By deed, 23 April, 1709, he conveyed to Robert Jones, aforesaid, "one acre" (where the tavern stands), for twenty shillings Pensylvania money. Described:—"beginning at the southeast corner of the Meeting House stable, thence to a settled road" (Lancaster pike); thence S. S. E. 24¼ per. to a stake by the road to Haverford, in the line of Edward Jones; thence by said Jones' land and line, W. S. W. 5¾ per. to a stake; then by "line dividing it from said Edward Rees's land" (the lot on which the meeting house stands, which was still in Rees's name), N. N. W. about 24¼ per., to a chestnut tree; thence "by the Grave Yard belonging to the meeting aforesaid,'" E. N. E. 5¾ per. to the beginning. On this lot, as appears in a subsequent deed, Robert Jones "built a house, and made other improvements."

The above tri-party deed is quoted in another tri-party deed, dated 31 May, 1753, between Garret (or Garred) Jones (eldest son of said Robert Jones), of the first part, Rees Prees, of the second part, and John Prees (a son of Rees Prees), of third part, concerning the above 190 acres. Described:—beginning at Edward Jones' corner, E. 15°, N. 146 per. to a post; thence N. 16°, W. by Edward Jones 28 per., thence by Edward Jones E. 18°, N. 64¼ per., thence N. 14°, W. by Robert Jones 24¼ per., "thence by Meeting House ground," W. 13°, S. 5¼ per., thence N. 14°, W. 7¾ per. by same; thence by land bought by the said Edward Rees of Robert Roberts,* W. 13°, S. 206 per., &c., by Evan Owen, Evan Harry, and William Cuarton.

---

*This land was conveyed, "for £300 silver," to Edward Rees, 16. 8mo. 1707, and deed acknowledged 17. 2mo. 1708, by Robert Roberts,

MERION, HAVERFORD, RADNOR

Robert Jones* died, and by will dated 21. 7mo. 1746, devised "my house and lot of ground near the Merion Meeting House, with all its appurtenances," to his grandson, Silas Jones, of Darby, grazier, who by deed, dated 25 March, 1768,† sold and conveyed this house and lot to Benjamin

---

of Calvert Co., Maryland. It was a tract of 200 laid out to Hugh Roberts, which on re-survey amounted to 220 acres, and was bounded by lands of Jonathan Jones, Thomas Jones, Owen Roberts, and Edward Jones, and the ten acre meadow, called "Clean John."

The 125 acre lot, in the 190 acre tract Edward Rees bought of Thomas Lloyd, by deed of 5. 5mo. 1691, (witnessed by Robert Owen and David Lloyd), was bounded on W. S. W. by Richard Cuarton; on N. N. W. by Evan Harry, (or Harries), on E. N. E. by Robert Owen, and on S. S. E. by Ree's land.

*By his will, signed in the presence of Jonathan Jones, Jr., Edward Price, and Sydney Roberts, proved 17 Oct., 1746, he gave his son Gerrad Jones the plantation where he lives, 223 acres, bounded south by David Evans, his own home-farm, and cousin Evan Jones's land; west by his son Robert's plantation; north by some of his (Robert, Sr.) own land; east by Schuylkill river. To son Robert Jones, Jr., the plantation where he lives, 325 acres, bounded south and west by land of cousin Evan Jones; north by land of the late William Sharlow; east and south by son Gerrad's land; east and north by his own farm. To daughter Elizabeth Jones the plantation called "Mt. Ararat," which he bought from David Hugh, 165 acres, and an adjoining tract of 66 acres, bounded by son Robert's land, and on the east by the plantation called "Glenrason." This "Glenrason" farm, 189 acres, bounded north by "Mt. Ararat" (formerly Sharlow's land); west by Elizabeth's land and Robert's land; south by Gerrad's other land; east by the Schuylkill, he devised to son Gerrad. Besides the "tavern lot," he gave to grandson Silas Jones ten acres "where the hempmill stood." He gave his lands in Goshen tp., 426 acres, to son Robert, to sell and remit the price to daughter Ann and her husband, James Paul. To granddaughters Sarah and Katherine Evans £50; to granddaughters Ellen and Ann Jones, £10 each. To daughter Elizabeth his "large Bible," and £20. Trustees Cousins Robert Roberts and Evan Jones, and friend Edward William.

†It is presumed that during the interval between 1746 and 1768, Anthony Tunis also bought land adjoining in 1741, rented the property and kept "open house," as the place was about this time, and down into the time of the Revolutionary War, called "Tunis' Ordinary."

Jones, of Philadelphia, blacksmith. This deed recites Penn's confirmation to Edward Rees of the 190 acres, in which was included this acre, in 1704 (this is the only excuse for advertising that this tavern was "established in 1704"), and Edward Rees' deed, 1709, to Robert Jones, and again describes the bounds of the one acre, as "beginning at the southeast corner of the Meeting House stable, thence to a settled road, S. S. E., about 24¼ perches," &c., and that "Robert Jones here built a house, and made other improvements, and by will devised the same to his grandson, Silas Jones," &c., Deed recorded at Norristown C. H. 25 Sep. 1883.

Benjamin Jones, blacksmith, then of Coventry tp., in Chester Co., and wife, Tacy, by deed, dated 1 April, 1775, for £115, Pensylvania money, acknowledged 3 Aug. 1776, recorded with above deed, conveyed this "house and one acre lot" to Abraham Streeper (and Streaper), blacksmith. He built an addition to the old stone house, and made other improvements, and is the first occupant of record who conducted the place as a stage house and tavern, and this was throughout the Revolution and till his decease, in 1794. He was tax collector of Lower Merion, in 1779. He died intestate, and much in debt, and the court appointed his daughter, Mary Streaper, spinster, and Joseph Price, to administer, and sell his property and pay his debts. By order of the Orphans Court, the tavern and lot were sold at public sale, 4 April, 1795, and deed given for the property by Joseph and Mary, on 20 April, to Edward Price, who "bought it in" for £405 Pensylvania money. This deed to the lot describes it:—"beginning at the southeast corner of the Merion Meeting House Grave Yard Wall (supposed to be the corner of the said Meeting House stable)"; thence along John Dickinson's land, and the land of Robert Holland, S. 16°, E. 30 per. to a stone in said Holland's land and line; thence along the same S. 67°, W. 5¾ per to a stone; thence along John Price's land, and the land of the Meeting, N. 16°, W. 30 per. to said Grave Yard wall; thence

MERION, HAVERFORD, RADNOR

along the same, N. 67°, E. 5¾ per. to beginning. By deed dated next day, 21 April, 1795, Edward Price conveyed the tavern and lot to Mary Streaper. These deeds recorded at Norristown, 8 Nov. 1802. Mary leased the property first to a Mr. Taylor, and in 1806, to Major William Methey, who was the landlord till about 1824, when he was succeeded by Jacob Castner, who also had a store in connection with the tavern. Mary Streaper married Titus Yerkes, and by deed, dated 23 Sep. 1854, they conveyed the tavern property to their daughter, Mary, wife of Joel Cook, of Philadelphia, grandfather of the late Congressman, Joel Cook. By deed, dated 25 Sep. 1854, Joel and Mary conveyed the tavern and lot in fee to David Young, innkeeper, who died, and by will, dated 21 Sep. 1858, gave the property to his wife; and her heirs, Rees Young, farrier, and Matilda and Harriet Young, sold the tavern and lot to James Baird, of Haverford, steward, by deed of 8 Sep. 1883, which describes the property:—as "a lot with a two and half, and three story stone hotel, stone stable," &c., and the lot:—"beginning at the S. E. cor. of Merion meeting house grave yard wall, supposed to be the corner of the said meeting house stable"; thence along land now, or formerly, of John Dickinson, and land now, or formerly, of Robert Holland, S. 16°, E. 20 per. to a stone in the last mentioned land; thence along the same S. 67°, W. 5¾ per. to a stone; thence along land now, or formerly, of John Price, and the said meeting house land, N. 16°. W. 30 per. to the said grave yard wall, &c. Baird also bought from same party, two lots on the opposite side of the pike, about 82 sq. per., "beginning at a point in the middle of the Blockley and Merion plank road. The General Wayne Inn next passed, in 1891, to Edward Odell, as owner.

It is tradition, that at one time this tavern was called the William Penn Inn, and at another, Wayside Inn, during the Revolution, and was alternately occupied by officers of each army. When Gen. Wayne was a popular hero, and returned triumphant from his expedition against the Ohio

WELSH SETTLEMENT OF PENSYLVANIA

Indians, the inn was named for him. He was received at the inn, on 6th Feb. 1796, by three troops of Philadelphia Light Horse, and escorted to a greater reception in the city. When Castner was the host, it is an unverified tradition that Gen. Lafayette was entertained at the inn, while travelling through the country as the Nation's guest, in 1824-5. When Mr. Young bought the inn, he fitted it up as a summer hotel for rich Philadelphians, and it was well patronized for many years. When it became the location of the first postoffice in Merion, David Oram Young carried the mailbag to Paschall's Landing, or Gen. Wayne station, on the railroad, subsequently called Elm station, and now Narberth. In 1876, the inn was enlarged by the addition of its frame portion, and was a popular summer boarding house, but of late years it has degenerated into simply a "barroom."

In so fertile a country as the Welsh Tract, lying between the contending armies during the Revolutionary War, its prosperous Quaker farmers did not escape the forced levies of both the Americans and the British, and each side helped itself freely and liberally to Quakers' property, for it was thought if they would not fight they should contribute of their stores. It has been said that the British were more welcome to what they could find in their raids, because if they paid at all, they always paid in gold for whatever they took. On the other hand, the Americans paying, gave only due-bills, or promissory notes, or orders on their migratory treasurer, so their visits were considered depredations. When the Americans lay through that terrible winter of 1777-8, at Valley Forge, just without the Welsh Tract, and prolonged their existence with the little that could be found in the neighborhood, there are several severe, sharp orders extant, issued by Gen. Washington, aimed directly at all non-combatants, and suspected tory farmers in his vicinity, for there were not a few of these in the region "seventy miles of my headquarters," as Washington described it in an order about them, dated at Valley Forge.

MERION, HAVERFORD, RADNOR

Either there must have been a misrepresentation concerning the British liberality, or the "cash" story was imported from elsewhere, for there is evidence that the Welsh Tract farmers complained bitterly about the British while they held Philadelphia. After their departure from the city, they reported their total losses to both armies, through the assessors appointed by the Americans to rate damages, amounted to £3212, the several Friends' Meetings in the Welsh Tract having kept alleged accurate accounts of their losses. There was taken from the members all kinds of live stock, and all sorts of household goods, but mixed with these claims were, as may be seen, the money value of other grievances.

In the Radnor Mo. Mtg. (Men's Meeting) records there are preserved several schedules of losses, as "An account of Effects taken from sundry friends of the Haverford preparatory meeting by the contending armies, Taxes, &c."

"Taken from Isaac Davis of Haverford, by a Detachment of the British army, commanded by Earl of Cornwallis, the 12mo. 12, 1777, £284, 10. 2. From the same by the army under George Washington, £5. 17. 0."

"Taken from John and Samuel Gray, for the use of the army commanded by George Washington, £6. 12. 6."

"From Isaac Bartram and Abraham Liddom, for ditto, £3. 0. 8. And from same by British, £48. 16. 0, on 12mo. 12, 1777. And on same day from Abraham Liddom, £47. 14. 9."

"And from friends of Merion preparative meeting, in 1777, and beginning of 1778, from John Roberts (the miller), by army under George Washington, horses, cattle, &c., about £500."

"From Isaac Lewis for a demand of £22. 7. 6, for the non-attendance in the militia, by Isaac Williams, collector, 28. 7mo. 1778, £30."

"Taken, 8mo. 6. 1778, for a demand of £24. 7. 6, for substitute money, and non-attendance in the militia, from Amos George, of Blockley, by John Ellis, collector, £33."

WELSH SETTLEMENT OF PENSYLVANIA

"Taken, 9mo. 16. 1778, for same and same, from Edward George, of Blockley, by the same, a young mare, sold at vendue on 19th, £70."

"Taken from Jesse George, 9mo. 16. 1777, of Blockley, by Thomas Rhoads, William Rees and Henry Alexander, militiamen, with fixed bayonets, three blankets, £1. 17. 6."

"8mo. 6. 1777. Taken from Jesse George, of Blockley, £24. 7. 6, substitute money, &c., by John Ellis, &c. (sold on the premises by public vendue the 12), £28. 19. 6."

"9mo. 14. 1777. Taken from Thomas George, of Blockley, by Isaac Kite, Jr., and two others of the militia with fixed bayonets, two blankets worth...."

"9mo. 19. 1778. Taken for a demand of £1. 7. 6, for non-attendance in the militia, from Thomas George, by John Ellis, collector, a heifer which he sold the same day for £13."

"From Radnor Friends:"

"8mo. 1777. From Daniel Maule, of Tredd. (Tredyffrin), for demand of £3. 10. 0, for non-associating, by John Maxwell, collector, £10."

"6mo. 1778, from same for the Provincial Tax, by John Lloyd, collector, £2. 17."

"8 & 9 mos. 1778. Taken from same for a demand of £55 substitute money, & by David Briggs and Jeremiah Eardley, by order of Lewis Gronow, £68. 14. 5½."

"3mo. 1778, for a demand of £31. 10. 7½, for substitute money, &c., from Evan Lewis, of Radnor, by D. B. and J. E., by order of L. G., £72. 4. 0."

"12mo. 1777, from Evan Lewis for use of army commanded by George Washington, £8. 15. 6. By same, from Jesse Meredith, for same, £34. By same, from Abijah Richard, for same, £29. By same, from John Jones, for same, £29. By same, from James Espen, for same, £29. 5. 0."

Many other Radnor Friends "suffered" in this way, "for their country's good," some having to meet demands of £120, £60, &c. The Walkers, and Richards, Quakers, were

MERION, HAVERFORD, RADNOR

the greatest "sufferers." One Michael Smith claimed his property was damaged to the extent of £451, but by which army the record does not tell. These sufferings of the sons and grandsons of the first settlers, must have given them an impression of what their forefathers had to endure in the old country up to the time they emigrated, of which they had often heard, and of which much has been printed.

I don't know that the Friends as a class were "Tories," nor did they appear to have been "obnoxious partisans," but in their "quiet way" they favored the patriots, their countrymen, and as testimony of this a speech by Elias Boudinot, in Congress (second session of the first); 22 March, 1790, is of interest. "The indiscriminate abuse that has been thrown out against Quakers, without distinction, has not comported with the honour, or dignity of this House. Not only their characters, but their very names, have been called upon, and private anecdotes, relating to individuals, been mentioned on the floor. Many of the Quakers I have long lived in the habits of friendship with, and can testify to the respectability of their characters and the regularity of their lives. Their conduct in the late war has been arraigned, and they have been condemned in a lump. I have known many of them during the war, and impartial justice requires it from me, to give some official information on the subject. I had the honour of serving the United States at the commencement of the war as commissary-general of prisoners. Congress not being able to afford them supplies, those unhappy men in this town were reduced to the very depths of distress, without food, or raiment, without blankets or firing, they suffered everything that human nature could bear. In this situation many of the Quakers of this city exercised such humanity towards them as did honour to human nature. The miserable prisoner not only felt the happy effects of their exertion in his favour, but participated in their money, their food, and clothing. Nay, such were the jealousies created by this conduct, in the British army here, that an armed force

WELSH SETTLEMENT OF PENSYLVANIA

entered the house of one of them, seized his books, and though a man of great property and large commercial dealings, on finding that he had loaned large sums of money to our distressed prisoners, he was turned out of their lines, and with his family was a refugee during the whole war afterwards, separated from his business and property. To whom was the care of our prisoners in Philadelphia committed? To a Quaker, and I have been witness to the just tribute of gratitude and thankfulness paid by great numbers of our unhappy fellow-citizens to that gentleman for his kindness and humanity. * * * * I rejoice to say that our cause was not carried on by fanaticism or religious zeal, but a general struggle for the rights of human nature. Then why all this abuse of this particular sect without discrimination?"

The teachings of the ancient Friends naturally would prevent them from taking any active part in any war, even that for freedom from British tyranny, but it was not so with some of their sons, who had not learned to restrain the fighting blood of their ancestors, the Britons, and self-protection they fully believed in. This may be known by there being a company organized in Merion, during the French and Indian war, or for the "war scare" of 1747. In Feb. 1747-8, a company of Associators was recruited and organized in Lower Merion, and Edward Jones was appointed the captain, Griffith Griffith first lieutenant, William Coates, second lieutenant, and James Ritchie, ensign. This was a "home-guard" company, and did not "see service," but it may be supposed it would willingly have gone into battle if called upon.

Subsequently, Edward Jones became the colonel of a regiment of eight companies of associators, and in 1756, he was captain of the Merion Troop of Horse, Lynford Lardner being the lieutenant.

During the Revolutionary War, the following Merion "Welshmen" served in the Philadelphia county militia, Peter Richards, and Abel Morgan, as sub-lieutenants, and

Peter Evans, and Algernon Roberts, as commissioners of purchases.

The seventh battalion of Associators of Philadelphia county was recruited in Upper and Lower Merion and Blockley. The regimental officers, commissioned 6 May, 1777, were at first, colonel, Jonathan Paschall, of Paschallville;† lieutenant-colonel, Isaac Warner,* and major, Matthew Jones. The regiment then was only four companies. In the Pensylvania Packet may be seen orders signed by Samuel Dewees, the Sub-Lieut. of Philadelphia county, calling out the companies to drill, similar to the following:—"Norrington, July 24th, 1778. Notice is hereby given to the inhabitants of the Townships of Upper Merion, Lower Merion, Blockley, and Kingsessing, that an Appeal will be held at the house of William Stadleman, in Blockley Township, for the fourth and fifth Classes of Militia, on the 31st day of July, at ten o'clock in the forenoon."

Subsequently, this militia regiment was re-organized, and recruited up to eight companies, of eight "classes" each, when Isaac Warner was the colonel, and Algernon Roberts, the lieutenant-colonel. The First Company was composed of all Lower Merion men, with Llewellyn Young, captain; David Young, 1st lieutenant; Isaac Williams, 2d lieutenant, and William Addihi, ensign. In 1780, Matthew Holgate was lieutenant-colonel, commanding this battalion, and John Bethell was the major.

The young Friends within the jurisdiction of the Radnor monthly meeting, who joined either side during the Revolution, were reported to their several preparative meetings as "violating the testimonies of Friends," and many forfeited membership in the Society rather than leave the

---

†Col. Paschall was descended from Thomas Paschall, a pewterer, who bought 500 acres from Penn, 26 Sep. 1681, and arrived here in following Feb., and died in 1718, aged 83 years.

*Isaac Warner, the colonel aforesaid, was a son of William Warner, mentioned elsewhere as the founder of the "State in Schuylkill." He married in 1757, Lydia Coulton, and died in 1784.

WELSH SETTLEMENT OF PENSYLVANIA

army, and humble themselves. The men's meetings disciplined not only for entering into military service, but for agreeing to attend "classes," or military exercises; for learning military exercises; for assisting in collecting forage for soldiers; for associating with soldiers; for paying tax to support war; for buying a substitute for the army; for paying money to redeem horses or cattle taken by the soldiers; for paying muster fines for not attending drillings; for taking the "test oath," &c. And these rules obtained as well in the "1812 War," and the Civil War.

The known Revolutionary War soldiers from Merion, who were of Welsh Quaker blood, buried in the ground of the Merion meeting, were Lt.-Col. Algernon Roberts, Thomas Roberts, Joseph Roberts, William Roberts, Jacob Hoffman, John Wells, John Price, Isaac Davis, Lieut. Thomas Wynne, Daniel Williams, Nehemiah Evans, Jesse George, William Holgate, Benjamin Holland, Jonathan Jones, Col. Isaac Warner, John Zell, Richard Jones, and Edward George, who all served in the Pensylvania militia. "A soldier. Died at David Gillis', buried 1mo. 6. 1781," is the record of an unknown soldier buried at the Merion Meeting House, but in which army he served is now unknown.

Of course, there are many more Revolutionary War soldiers buried in other cemeteries in Lower Merion. For instance, in the Bicking family graveyard, near Mill Creek and Righter's Road:—Frederick and Richard Bicking, and John Kuhn; "Harriton" graveyard, back of Bryn Mawr:—Major William Cochran; the Baptist cemetery on Gulf Road, back of Bryn Mawr:—Samuel Davis, William Thomas, Joseph Wilson, John Wilson, James Wilson, John Elliott, John Young, Jacob Morris, John Cornog, Jacob and John Righter, Griffith Smith, John Wilfong, Christopher Shubert, Francis Conrad and Benjamin Sheetz, George Coulter, and in the German Lutheran cemetery, Ardmore:—Col. Philip Lowry, Casper Weest, John Brooks, John Philler, Martin Miller, John and William Smith, John Goodman,

MERION, HAVERFORD, RADNOR

Jasep Grover, William Wagner, David and Llewellyn Young, Peter Ott, Sr. and Jr., Peter Trexler, George Horn, Sr. and Jr., John Horn, Daniel McElroy, Ludwick Knoll, Martin Wise, Adam Grow, Jacob Waggoner, Jacob Latch, Michael Simple, John and William Fiss, John Maurer, Nicholas Pechin, Obadiah Wildey, J. Righter, and possibly others, and nearly all of German blood. Among the "1812" soldiers buried here are Col. Conrad Krickbaum, Col. William Pechin, Adam and Simon Litzenberg, and John and Jacob Stadleman.

During the Revolutionary War, not only were there scions of the Welsh Quaker families serving in the American army, but there were several who were prominent members at that time of the "Pensylvania Lodge," "Lodge No. 8," or the "Schuylkill Lodge," of the Brotherhood of Free and Accepted Masons. This lodge had no habitat, as most of its members were serving in the army of the patriots, and for this reason it is presumed it was really the celebrated "military lodge" which had its meetings at Valley Forge, when the Americans encamped there, in the farm house used as headquarters by Gen. Pulaski. This particular masonic lodge existed till about 1789-90, when it is last of record advocating to make the Friends' meeting house, at 5th and Race Streets, Philadelphia, the meeting place for the Pensylvania Grand Lodge. Among the members of this alleged "military lodge," or Lodge No. 8, at that time were the following men of Welsh Quaker blood:—John Davis (master of the lodge), John Cadwalader (secretary of the lodge), James Morris (the treasurer), David Thomas, Jesse Roberts, Isaac Thomas, Joseph Price, Abel Morgan, and John Richards. (See "Freemasonry in the Continental Army," *American Historical Register*, March, 1885.)

The "Harriton" graveyard mentioned above, was the private burial ground of the Harrison and Thomson families, who, in 1719, succeeded by purchase to the "Bryn Mawr" estate (and gave it the name "Harriton"), of Row-

WELSH SETTLEMENT OF PENSYLVANIA

land Ellis, the early Welsh settler, in what is known now as Morris' woods, not far north from the Bryn Mawr College.

From the will of Richard Harrison,* dated 11 Sep., 1746 (he died 5 Aug. 1747), we learn that he erected on this ground "a certain meeting house, or place of worship," * * * * * "It is my will, and I do hereby declare that the said meeting house, together with a square piece of ground containing by estimate two acres, adjoining the said house, where several of my children lie interred, shall not be sold by my trustees, but that the same house and grounds shall forever be excepted and reserved out of my said tract of land, and shall remain for the use and service of a meeting house, and a place of interment forever."

This house, primarily a school house, was intended by Mr. Harrison for the use of an "indulged meeting" of the Welsh Friends, and to be used only on occasion of interment in its graveyard. The house was not kept in repair by the Friends, and the attention of the Radnor monthly meeting was called to this neglect in 1792, when a committee composed of James Jones, Jr., of Blockley, and Jonathan Roberts, of Merion, was appointed to look into the matter, and report. On 7. 10mo. 1792, Mr. Roberts wrote to Mr. Jones that Charles Thomson (the secretary to the Continental Congress), had written to him that he considered the Harrison heirs to be the legal trustees for the meeting house and graveyard, and as the Friends had not held meetings in there for many years, a Presbyterian congrega-

---

*Richard Harrison was a Quaker, and had a certificate from the Clifts Meeting, Maryland, dated 11mo. 1729, which he presented at the Phila. monthly meeting, in that year. His wife, Hannah Norris, daughter of Judge Isaac Norris, and granddaughter of Gov. Thomas Lloyd, was an accepted minister among Friends. Under date of 11mo. 14. 1730, permission was given by the monthly meeting that Mr. Harrison and other Friends have liberty to keep a meeting on the First Days, for the winter season, at said Richard's school house. The same was extended in several subsequent years, when afternoon meetings in the summer were also allowed, and continued till in 1757.

MERION, HAVERFORD, RADNOR

tion had applied to him for leave to repair the house and use it, which request he had granted, and they held religious services there occasionally. Mr. Thomson also wrote he had no objection to the Friends building a meeting house on the property, and would sit with them if they did do so. Subsequently, the Presbyterians abandoned the house, and it fell in ruins, and was removed, and the Friends did not take advantage of Mr. Thomson's offer.

This little private graveyard, with its two dozen graves, remained unnoticed in its solitude till in 1838, when an item appeared in the *Philadelphia National Gazette*, stating that, "on Second Day morning, 13th of eight month," the graveyard was entered stealthily by four men, and the graves were opened by them till they found the bodies of Charles Thomson (who died 16 Aug. 1824), and his wife, and carried them away; the farmer in charge protesting. On 16 Aug. Mr. Levi Morris, the owner of "Harriton" advertised in the paper, "Upon conviction of any person, or persons, who may have been concerned in this outrage, a suitable reward will be paid." The *Gazette* called attention editorially to the scandal, saying, "What adds to the heinousness of the offense is that the interment was made there in accordance with the wish of the deceased." * * * * * "It is hoped that every means will be taken to discover who committed the offense."

A few days later, the *Philadelphia Daily Advertiser* contained the statement as to the removal of Mr. Thomson's body, that "it is proper that the public should be informed that it was done under the direction of the nearest relatives of the deceased, for the purpose of placing it in a situation more consonant with the feelings of the family," and that the removal was made by "an experienced undertaker, with proper care, and were reinterred in the new Laurel Hill cemetery." This called out a rejoinder, protesting "against the right of any persons, in a clandestine manner to remove the body to a public cemetery," "for the purpose of giving eclat to a particular locality, as there is strong reason to believe has been done in this instance." This brought out a long reply from John Thomson, nephew and executor of Charles Thomson, dated New Ark, Delaware, Aug. 24th, 1838. He explained that the body lay at "Harriton," virtually an abandoned, out of the way grave yard, unkept and brier-grown, and that he had been refused the privilege of erecting a stone to mark the grave, therefore he deemed it his duty to remove it to a more suitable place, and erected a suitable granite monument (which he did immediately, Watson writing the inscription). He feared, he said, that the original burial place would be in time diverted from its original use, in spite of the will of Mr. Thomson, and his letter to Jonathan Roberts. This brought out a sharp rejoiner from Mr. Levi Morris, dated 8mo. 31, printed in the *U. S. Gazette,* saying he had been approached as to the removal of Secretary Thomson's remains, and declined to give his consent, because Mr. Thomson's body was in the spot he himself had appointed for its burial. He contradicted that the burial plot was ever brier-grown and neglected, on the contrary kept it in good order, as was natural for him to do, since his child, and his father-in-law were buried there. Mr. Morris had built a stone wall round part of the lot, and his widow left money to complete it. In time the Philadelphia newspapers* and the public became reconciled to the removal, and decent re-interment of the Secretary's remains.

To correct and amplify the statements made in regard to the beautiful seat of "Bryn Mawr" or "Harrison" (*ante* pp. 236-7), in which I followed Mr. Glenn's theories (*vide* "Merion in the Welsh Tract"), I have the following more lucid information from the venerable Friend and antiquarian, Mr. George Vaux,† to whom the property belongs, and

---

*See *Phila. Evening Bulletin,* 15 Sep. and Oct. 1886.

†Mr. Vaux's interest in this property is, genealogically, as follows: Richard Harrison, Jr., of "Harriton," *m.* in 1717, Hannah, 1696-1774, daughter of Judge Isaac and Mary (Lloyd) Norris, of Philadelphia, and had Thomas Harrison, (whose sister, Hannah, *b.* 1728, *d.s.p.*

where he resides in the summer time, who has been personally acquainted with the farm since 1856. He says that when he was a young man, he examined the date-stone in the wall of the house, which much to his regret has been taken out and carried away by some person unknown years ago, and it showed plainly the figures 170-, and that the last figure was apparently a 4, and that the 0 was, without question, distinct. He also says that there is no doubt about it that the 300 acres surveyed 24 Feb. 1708, to Rees Thomas (p. 171),* and William Lewis (Jr., p. 165), included the land on which the old house stands. This tract of 300 acres was at the southeast end of plantation, and that the northwest line was far to the northwest of the house, in which Rowland Ellis lived in 1708. Mr. Vaux's statement is substantiated by the recorded facts that Rowland Ellis' son, by his second wife, Robert Ellis married Margaret, daughter of William John, of the Gwynedd settlement, 3. 9mo. 1705, and died about two years later, leaving his wife and an infant daughter, Jane Ellis. Rowland Ellis had settled 380 acres and one moiety of the dwelling house, the orchards, fields, &c., of the plantation, on his son Robert, and after Robert's decease, his widow and relict, Margaret Ellis, claimed her dower and portion for her child out of the 380 acres. For some reason unknown, the widow could not get a settle-

---

1807, *m.* 1 Sep. 1774, Charles Thomson, secretary of the Continental Congress), of "Harriton," 1729-1759, who *m* Frances Scull, and had, Amelia Sophia, *d.* 1820, who *m.* Robert McClenachan, of Philadelphia, *d.* 1822, and had, Charles McClenachan, who *m.* Mary Thomas, and had Naomi, who *m.* Levi Morris, of "Harriton," and Philadelphia, and their daughter, Sarah, was the wife of Mr. George Vaux, of "Harriton" and Philadelphia.

*Mr. Vaux says that Rees Thomas lived a little north of the north corner of the Roberts road and the Lancaster road, in a stone house, which existed till about 1872. As he recollects it, it had lead window sashes, and that the interior plaster was combined with straw instead of hair, and that wooden pegs were used instead of iron nails, and in the living room was a very large fire place, flanked by two large settles.

ment with her father-in-law, so the claim was laid before the Welsh Friends, of the Haverford Mo. Mtg., for arbitration, who decided that Mr. Ellis should pay to Jane Ellis, his granddaughter, £180, when she became of legal age, and other arrangements were agreed upon for the widow. To secure the payments, 300 acres of "Bryn Mawr" were conveyed to Rees Thomas and William Lewis, in trust. In Oct., 1719, when Rowland Ellis sold "Bryn Mawr" to Richard Harrison, the conveyance was for 718 acres, less 20 acres reserved, or 698 acres,* and included the trust land of 300 acres; Thomas and Lewis joining in the conveyance, which was made by two deeds, recorded 22 Dec., 1719, giving full title to Mr. Harrison.

So prominent a road as the Lancaster, from the city into the disafforested fertile country beyond the Schuylkill, it is natural should have been the scene of some military operations during the Revolution. Within Merion's bounds, however, they were few, and not of great moment. Hiltz records, 24 Aug., 1777, Sunday, "Our army commanded by Gen. Washington, marched through the city, crossed the bridge over the Schuylkill, proceeded four miles, then turned back." From the Journal of the American officer, Lieut. James McMichael,† under Sunday, 14 Sep., 1777, we learn: "9 A. M., we marched from camp near Germantown, N. N. W., for a few miles up a good road, from Philadelphia to Reading, then turning W. S. W., we crossed the Schuylkill in the center, between Philadelphia and Swedes Ford, eight miles from each. We reached the great road to Lancaster, at the Merion Meeting House, and proceeded up that road, then we camped in an open field, being denied every desirable refreshment."

It has been decided that this camping ground was on the land of Edward ap Rees, or his descendants, the Price family, near the 8 Mile Stone. At that time, there was a

---

*See *Pa. Mag.* Vol. XXI. 119.
†See *Pa. Archives*, 2d series, XV. 221, and *Pa. Mag.* XVI, 156.

MERION, HAVERFORD, RADNOR

Price mansion house, recently demolished, in this field, beyond the Meeting House, and another belonging to the same family, nearby, across the road, still standing. It is presumed that it was at these homes of "strict Friends" this young lieutenant and soldiers were denied "desirable refreshment" on Sunday. It may be noticed they were not refused refreshments, so the supposition is the young man was over fastidious. The wonder may be that his men did not try to get something more desirable, but this they would not dare do, as there were orders positively forbidding any raiding, or depredations, and there are no complaints extant that dwellers along the route were annoyed in any way when Washington moved his army from Germantown over the Schuylkill, and up the ravine, or the Rock Hollow road, and Meeting House Lane, past the rear of the meeting house, and out the Lancaster road, on his way "to get between the enemy and Swedes Ford."

Pickering, in his Journal, tells of the movement of Washington's army, the day following the defeat at Brandywine:—"Marched to the Schuylkill (12 Sept. 1777,), part crossing and marching to our old camp by the Schuylkill Falls," on the east bank. He says that on the next day, "the rest of the army crossed, and the whole collected at the old encampment."

Washington's Orderly Book, under Saturday, 13 Sep. 1777, records the army as "At Schuylkill Falls, Philadelphia," but the General issued his address to his troops, complimenting them on their gallant conduct at Brandywine, dated "Head Quarters, at Germantown, Sep. 13th," and his order of march to "Swedes Ford," dated 14 Sep., was from same headquarters.

From Pickering's Journal, we have the further information that, on Sunday, 14 Sep., "the army marched up a few miles [from the old camp], and re-crossed the Schuylkill at Levering's Ford, the water being up to the waist. We advanced about five or six miles that night." This ford was at Green Lane, two miles above the falls, but according to

WELSH SETTLEMENT OF PENSYLVANIA

historians, the crossing was made at Matson's Ford (Conshohocking), some six miles beyond the falls. In her diary, 14 Sep., 1777, Elizabeth Drinker also wrote: "It is said that G. Washington has left the city and crossed the Schuylkill this day."

On Sep. 15th, Monday, Washington wrote a letter dated "at Buck Tavern, 3 P. M.," to the President of Congress, saying, "We are moving up this road [Lancaster road], to get between the enemy and Swedes Ford," Norristown. This tavern, now a private house, in Haverford tp., just across the Merion line, was eight and a half miles from Second Street. That day, Sep. 15th, the army went thirteen miles further up the Lancaster road, to its junction with the Swedes Ford road, and that night, Washington lodged at the house of Joseph Malin, near the White Horse Tavern.

A few days after this, or on 19 Sep., 1777, the American Congress became frightened and packed up its documents, loaded them on wagons, amid great excitement and confusion, and considerable trepidation, and before daylight the gentlemen of Congress, with their luggage, fled from Philadelphia, out High Street, over the middle ferry, as best they could (for, by request of Washington, the Supreme Executive Council of Pensylvania, 14 Sep., had ordered the bridge of boats at this ferry "be effectually and immediately removed, and bring it away into the Delaware, and boats be hauled up on land"), thence out the historic road to Lancaster, when it became evident that the British were sure to capture and enter the capital city, and hardly rested in their flight till Lancaster was reached. A fair idea of the extent of the scare may be had from the minutes of the Supreme Executive Council, which, on 11 Sep., was so alarmed that it commanded all shops and factories to be closed, and all men to assemble under arms, and as many as possible to "rendezvous at the Falls of Schuylkill," "as the enemy is near at hand, and this minute engaging our army under the command of his Excell'y Gen'l Washington." It was ordered to "press waggons in Radnor." Its documents, some fourteen boxes and two trunks of deeds, mortgages, bonds, etc., were sent to Easton, but the Council did not flee to Lancaster till 23 Sep., where it and the Council of Safety next met on 1 October.

Taking Lieut. McMichael for good authority, the site of the encampment of the army, on the night of Sep. 14th, was in Price's field, beyond the meeting house, where the Lancaster and Gulf roads meet, this event in the neighborhood has been marked by an inscribed granite tablet, four feet high, located at the junction of the roads, on Montgomery Avenue, stating:—"On this and adjacent / ground Washington's army / encamped September 14, 1777. / Erected by Merion Chapter / Daughters of the American / Revolution, September 14, 1896, / Ground presented by / Samuel R. Mc Dowell."

Further down the Lancaster road, towards the city, about the Black Horse Tavern, near what was then the boundary line of the "liberty lands," or Penn's public lands, since 1784, known as the City Line, and as City Avenue, there was a hot skirmish between the Americans and the British, in Dec., 1777.

A letter from Gen. James Potter, a gallant, though illiterate officer, to President Wharton, of Pensylvania, who was then at Lancaster with Congress, dated "Headquarters, Chester Co. Camp, 15 Dec., 1777," gives an account of this affair,* "Last Thursday [11 Dec.], the enemy marched out of the city with a desine to Furridge, but it was Nessecerey to drive me out of the way; my advanced picquet fired on them at the Bridge [the floating bridge over the Schuylkill, at Market St.], another party of one Hundred attacted them at the Black Hors." Lieut. McMichael, in his Journal, says, "the enemy having crossed at the Middle Ferry, attacked a party of militia under Gen. Potter. The losses were inconsiderable on both sides."

---
*See *Pa. Mag.* XVII. 423.

WELSH SETTLEMENT OF PENSYLVANIA

From other reports it would appear that this was a reconnoissance in force by Gen. Howe, as he went out as far as Matson's Ford, and returning, passed the night of Dec. 11th, at the Humphreys Mansion House, "a hipped roofed, stone and brick house, with lead window frames," &c., which stood on Cobb's Creek, not far from the Haverford meeting house. The mansion was then occupied by Charles Humphreys (born in 1712), who was a prominent member of the Pa. Assembly in 1763, and a deputy to the First and Second Congresses. In his diary, Christopher Marshall says, 12 Dec., 1777:—"News of the day is that Gen. Howe is come out again from Philadelphia, with an army; crossed Schuylkill at middle ferry; marched up Lancaster Road to the Sorrel Horse, thirteen miles from the city, and then returned yesterday." And in the same, 15 Dec., 1777, "Upon the rumor yesterday of Gen. Howe's army being on the Lancaster Road it's said that the papers and records belonging to the Executive Council were packed up and sent by wagons to York Town, [Pa., from Lancaster]. Its said that the English army is returning to Phila."

Further down the Lancaster road, within the Liberties, or in Blockley tp., across the present city line, about "Wynnestay," the old home of Dr. Wynne's son, Jonathan, who died here in 1719, there took place several skirmishes between outposts of the contending armies, when the Americans tried to cut off from the British in the city, their supplies of good things out of Merion. The house at that time was occupied by the family of Thomas Wynne, a "fighting Quaker," a lieutenant in the Pensylvania Flying Camp, who was then in the field with the army.

The extant diary of Robert Morton tells of frequent raids by the American troopers on the "British ferry boat, operated by a pully rope, at the middle ferry." They generally succeeded in taking the guard prisoners, and in cutting the rope, setting the boat on fire and adrift, much to the annoyance of the British, and would then retreat out the Lancaster road. But on 3 Nov., 1777, Major Clark wrote to Gen. Washington, that the British were building three bridges of boats, or rafts of logs and boats, at the Middle Ferry, so they could drive wagons over the river and fetch fire-wood. These bridges had draws, in two places, to allow boats to pass on the river.

It was when his army encamped for the night, 14 Sep., 1777, on the Lancaster road, that "Tunis's ordinary," or Streater's, got the reputation of being a sleeping place of Gen. Washington. It's possible he lodged here, of course, for his army was encamped only a half mile away. But it is also claimed that he spent the night, with Lafayette, at the Price house, about which his army lay. It is also claimed that Gen. Howe slept in both of the Price houses, and the inn, at various times and this is also possible. Unfortunately for antiquarians' satisfaction, none of these heroes have made mention in their writings of these events, so important to the Prices, and the reputation of the Gen. Wayne Tavern. And it's not surprising that the old Black Horse Tavern has also similar traditions as to prominent men of the Revolutionary times. In June, 1783, this tavern was one of the public houses, on the "great highway," raided by the mob of dissatisfied soldiers, when they walked from Lancaster to Philadelphia, and stormed the State House where Congress was assembled, and so frightened this body that it broke up its sitting, and fled to Trenton. After Braddock's defeat, 1755, the shattered regiments of Dunbar and Hacket passed down the Lancaster road, and crossed the Schuylkill, and went down "Conestoga Road" to High Street, in the city. The ferry charges for carrying these regiments over the Schuylkill amount to £12, and in 1757, the ferryman, Coultas, was trying to collect this bill from the Philadelphia City Council.

Near the Black Horse Tavern, but about a quarter of a mile up the road, still stands the dwelling, somewhat enlarged, of the Whig Quaker, Robert Jones, a dealer in lumber in Revolutionary days. His house was probably built

WELSH SETTLEMENT OF PENSYLVANIA

after Scull made his map in 1749-50. Mr. Jones was buried at the Merion Meeting House. His only son, and heir, died unmarried, and eventually the property, called "Lilac Grove," came to Margaret, daughter of a Capt. James Boyle, of Chester Co., who took it as her marriage portion to Edward Harvey, who was for twenty-eight years a J. P. in Merion, when they wedded on 16. 6mo. 1808, at the Merion Meeting, where they were both buried.

Of the twenty-nine persons in that part of Philadelphia county, which is now Montgomery county, mentioned by name in the proclamation of the Supreme Executive Council of Pensylvania, 8 May, 1778, "who have severally adhered to, or willingly aided and assisted the enemies of this State, and the United States of America," and who were ordered to surrender themselves to a justice of the peace of the county, on or before 25 June following, to stand trial for adhering to the British, there was only one in the list who resided in Merion, namely, "John Roberts, late of the Township of Lower Merion, miller," and his was a peculiar case in itself, so there must have been some mistake about the wholesale sympathy of the Welsh Quakers, those of Merion anyway, with the "red coats." These following from Haverford tp., were mentioned in the proclamation of 25 June, 1778, as having joined the British army:—Robert Kissack, weaver; John Brown, wheelwright; James Gorman, and Enoch Gorman, cordwainers, and Michael Crickley, laborer. None of these were Welsh Quakers, nor prominent men.

And there was only one of Welsh extraction from Merion among the Friends suspected of being British sympathizers who were arrested and exiled to Winchester, Va., in 1777. This unfortunate was Owen Jones, Jr. It seems that he was arrested and caused to "suffer" in mistake for his father, the provincial treasurer (p. 158), who was a pronounced Tory. But according to subsequent revelation, he was far from loyal to the Americans, as a disloyal letter from young Owen, at Winchester, addressed to John Musser, Lancaster, Pa., was intercepted by the patriots.* This letter revealed a scheme concocted by these men to depreciate Continental money. On this discovery the Board of War transferred the Quakers from Winchester to Staunton, Va., so they could be further away from the seat of war, and placed young Owen Jones in the jail, and refused him writing materials, nor was he allowed to communicate with any Friends, till all danger was past. Owen Jones, Jr., died in Philadelphia. His will, dated 15 June, 1822, proved 14 May, 1825, gave his Merion land, 350 acres, to his nephews, Owen Jones and John Wister.

This single instance of discovered disloyalty and of being a British sympathizer in 1778, as said above, fell to the lot of Mr. John Roberts, a wealthy miller, and a Friend, aged about 60 years, a member in good standing of the Merion Meeting, and one who was of unquestioned integrity among Welsh Quakers. He was always a man of affairs:—in 1773 he was appointed by the General Assembly one of the commissioners to improve the navigation of the Schuylkill, and in 1775, he was a delegate to the convention in Philadelphia, which considered the prohibition of future importation of Negroes for slaves.

The story of his alleged treason has been told variously, in fiction with much embellishment; in history with many unsupported allegations, because the court record of his trial was destroyed, or hidden so it has not been found, it is said, as were also the personal notes of the chief justice who tried his case. In a general way, his capital crime was, that he remained loyal to his king and country, and was considered to be a too zealous partisan for so prominent a man. There was no suspicion of his being still loyal at heart to the Crown till the British occupied Philadelphia, when he removed into the city from his home in Merion. This would only have caused him to be mistrusted, and if

---

*See *Pa. Archives*, Vol. VI. 53; the Journal of Thomas Gilpin, or "Exiles in Virginia," and Christopher Marshall's Journal, 11 Dec. 1777.

he had been captured he would probably have been only exiled, as other Quakers were. But it is said, when he was seen accompanying the British superintendent of police, Joseph Galloway, in raids for provisions on the Whig families of Merion, and apparently leading him to the best stores in Merion, he was considered as bad as a traitor, if he was not one. As to this, he claimed in his trial, it has been said, that Galloway forced him to accompany them, and show the way.

As the report of the trial, and the notes of the judge have not been preserved, we are able to learn a little of it from the extant written notes of the sentence of the Court upon Mr. Roberts pronounced by the chief justice, which upon request he sent to the Supreme Executive Council, Oct. 29, 1778, and which is printed verbatim in the Pensylvania Packet newspaper, 7 Nov., 1778. It seems that when some Pensylvania Friends, suspected of being British sympathizers, were arrested and were about to be sent in a body, under guard, in exile to Winchester, Virginia, as mentioned above, Mr. Roberts asked the British General Howe, it was alleged, for the loan and command of a troop of horse so that he might try to release the Friends, and that Gen. Howe declined this request, not being willing to risk the loss of his troop, and because these Quakers were of no more use to him than to Gen. Washington. This was made the principal evidence of Mr. Roberts' being guilty as charged, according to Judge McKean's notes of the sentence he passed on him. That Mr. Roberts, who was known to be a Quaker, offered to command the cavalry and try to rescue other Quakers known to be adherents of the enemy, convinced the trial judges that Mr. Roberts was certainly not loyal to the Americans, and possibly also influenced the jury which found him guilty of aiding the enemy, and being a traitor.

Mr. Roberts may have supposed the British would never leave the city, and much less lose the colonies, so he stayed on with them in Philadelphia. But when they began to evacuate the city, he realized his mistake, and, since he had considerable property in Merion, he decided that he had better get the good will of the Americans, and under their protection again. Therefore, so the story goes, he hurried out to Washington, at Valley Forge, on getting the first intimation of the evacuation of the city, and gave him the news, saying he had learned it while he was on a secret visit to the Middle Ferry, or the floating-bridge, over the Schuylkill, at High, or Market Street.

But Washington had previous information about the proposed movement of the British, and he had also some as to Roberts, while it might have amused him to see the old Friend turning his coat and skipping from one shelter to another, if he had not had good information that Mr. Roberts had been an aggressive "traitor" while sojourning in the enemy's camp. Before the end of June, 1778, Mr. Roberts was arrested, under the proclamation mentioned, on suspicion of disloyalty to the American cause, and adhering to the enemy. On this charge he was shortly brought to trial before Chief Justice McKean, in the State House, Philadelphia, and after trial before a jury, on the testimony of many witnesses, judging from the notes (printed in "Penna. Archives," Vol. VII, p. 44, etc.), of the trial of Abraham Carlisle, of Philadelphia, a house carpenter, who was also tried and convicted of being a traitor by this court. He was found "guilty of being a traitor to his neighbors, his kith and kin, and the just cause of his native land," was sentenced by Judge McKean to be "taken back to the jail, and from there to the place of execution, and then to be hanged by the neck until dead." As the Judge did not set a date for the execution, it may have been left to the convenience of the sheriff. Justice McKean says in his "Sentence" that Roberts's counsel moved for a new trial, which he disallowed.

Mr. Roberts' lawyers were Ross and Wilson, of the Philadelphia Bar, but it seems the honors of the legal contest were carried off by the Commonwealth's council, the attorney-general, and Sergeant and Reed, of the Philadelphia Bar, because at first the case against John Roberts was weak, and was won by methods which would not be tolerated in times of peace and common sense. That is, Mr. Roberts was arrested, and put on trial for high treason against the Commonwealth, under the Act of the Pensylvania Assembly of 1777. The only charge against him, with specifications, or his particular act of treason was that he tried to *persuade* a man to enlist in the English army, "an enemy at open war with this State," and therefore, was guilty of high treason. But the law defining the Act:— "there must be an *actual enlistment* of the person *persuaded* to constitute the offense of treason." And the Court said:— "the word *persuading* in the Act means to succeed, and that there must be an actual enlistment of the person persuaded, in order to bring the defendant within the intention of the clause."

The person Roberts persuaded and attempted to prevail upon to enlist in the British army was produced as a witness against him. He said Roberts *persuaded* him (which Roberts confirmed), but did not *convince* him, so he did not enlist. This, under the Judge ruling, should have ended the prosecution. Next, it was tried to convict him on his confession, but as it was not supported by evidence, the confession was insufficient, the Court ruled. But at length it was legally and satisfactorily proved he "aided and assisted" the enemy "by joining them," and therefore, he was guilty of treason.

In Oct. 1778, immediately after the conviction, and sentences had been pronounced on Roberts and Carlisle, petitions and memorials were showered upon the Supreme Executive Council of Pensylvania, signed by hundreds of prominent citizens, and army and navy officers, asking "from feelings of Humanity," respite of the sentences till the close of the next session of the Pensylvania General Assembly, desiring that body's opinion of both cases, although the signers were "sensible that the unfortunate John Roberts

MERION, HAVERFORD, RADNOR

and Abram Carlisle most justly merit the Sentence which the Law has lately pronounced against them, and of the fairness of the trials." They told of the good characters of the men, and, because the enemy had left the State, and were never likely to return again, these men would never again have opportunity to do as they had done, they asked the respite, not hoping for pardon, of course, but at most for term imprisonment. Prominent Friends individually, and ten members of the Grand Jury came before the Council and asked for mercy for Roberts and Carlisle. A heartrending appeal for pardon was sent in signed by Mr. Robert's wife and children, and their nearest relatives, the families of Meteer, Downing, Baldwin, Roberts, Howell, Wister, Jones, Biddle, Lloyd, Whelen, Van Lear, Bond, &c. Other petitions for mercy came from inhabitants generally of the counties of Philadelphia and Chester, and from inhabitants of the Welsh Tract townships. One hundred "Beneficiaries of John Roberts" asked his pardon, "because he used his influence with the British, and stopped them from plundering them." Even ten members of the jury that sat in their cases and convicted them, addressed a petition to the judges of the Supreme Court and prayed for respite till the General Assembly should consider the cases, and the judges who sat in the trials, McKean and Evans, recommended, on 18 Oct. that the jury's request be complied with.

When the many memorials, and particularly the petitions of the judges and the jury, who tried the cases of Roberts and Carlisle, were presented in the Supreme Executive Council, it decided to review the cases, and, accordingly, on 21 Oct., wrote the Chief Justice, McKean, "The Council have now before them the cases of John Roberts and Abraham Carlisle, the determination of which is highly interesting, not only to the criminals, but also to the public. Council therefore wish to be favoured as soon as possible with your notes taken on the trial. They are the more desirous of this from the recommendation of the Petitions of divers of the Jurymen, signed by you, and the Hon'le John Evans, Esq., in the case of John Roberts. They remark that you have not mentioned any equitable circumstances which ought to be allowed weight in their determination in this case."

Judge McKean, it may be presumed, sent his rough notes on both cases, though, as said above, only those on the trial of Mr. Carlisle have been preserved, and they were consulted in the meeting of the Council on 2 Nov., on which day it received petitions, asking for mercy, if not pardon, from Mr. Roberts and his wife, and Mr. Carlisle and his wife. This "Court of Last Resort," the Supreme Executive Council of Pensylvania, adjourned, without reaching a conclusion, considering both cases separately, till the following day, 3 Nov., when they resumed the matter, "and after solemn consideration," say the minutes, "and the Question being put:—Shall a Reprieve be granted to John Roberts and Abraham Carlisle, or either of them. The same was Carried in the Negative." Then, this serious matter being concluded, the gentlemen of the Council turned their attention to finding out how many planks were actually needed to repair a bridge in Kensington.

There is nothing in the minutes to show if the decision was unanimous, or how each member voted, but it does tell that Messrs. Arndt and Hambright were not present when the vote was taken, and that those present and probably voting were Messrs, Hart, Mackay, Will, Scott, and Smith, and the vice-president, George Bryan, presided. On the day of execution, 4 Nov. the minute is only "Council met," and it may be presumed adjourned, as there is no record of business. That day, Wednesday, must have been one long remembered in Philadelphia, for all of its prominent citizens thought Roberts and Carlisle should have had a hearing of their cases by the Assembly, but it was "war times," and captured and convicted and sentenced "traitors" must be summarily punished for examples to others.

The Philadelphia tri-weekly newspaper, *The Packet*, of

5 Nov. 1778, gives only three lines of space to this sad event, saying, "Yesterday, Abraham Carlisle* and John Roberts were executed on the common of this city, pursuant to their sentence." Other Philadelphia "newspapers" of that week did not mention the affair, although it was the "feature" of the week.

Mr. Roberts was buried† with his ancestors and relatives in the graveyard of the Merion Meeting, on 6th. 11mo., his burial being recorded, without comment, under this date, "John Roberts, miller."

The Radnor Monthly Meeting had refused to interfere in behalf of Mr. Roberts, because as a body of Friends it could not sanction many of his actions, especially wishing to lead the British troop into a battle with the guards conducting the Quakers beyond the State. This probably was agreeable to the desire of the superior meeting, as in the minutes of the Radnor Mo. Mtg., 8. 8. 1778, "the case of John Roberts, miller," was under consideration, when it was decided to apply to the "meeting for sufferings," in Philadelphia, "for advice and assistance in his distressing situation," and the following Friends were appointed to attend to this, John Gray, Jacob Jones, Evan Lewis, and Jesse George. Individually, however, the members did their utmost to save the life and honor of their old neighbor, born and raised among them.

Mr. Roberts' great property was confiscated by the State, on order of the Court, and sold at public sale, in Philadelphia, 21 June, 1780. The proceeds of the sales were handed over to the University of Pensylvania for educational purposes. Of his estate, thus confiscated, there were farms

---

*In her Diary, Elizabeth Drinker tells of the incidents connected with the hanging of Mr. Carlisle, who was her neighbor in Philadelphia, and of his funeral, and that George Dilwyn and Samuel Emlen spoke at the grave. See also Sabine's "Loyalists of the American Revolution."

†John Thomas Peggy, the official gravedigger of Merion Meetings, who prepared his grave, was buried near him, on 7. 7mo. 1779.

WELSH SETTLEMENT OF PENSYLVANIA

amounting to 318 acres, his mansion house, north of Ardmore, on Mill Creek, and two gristmills, a sawmill, tenaments, and 300 acres of land on the Schuylkill, with three dwelling houses, a sawmill, a powdermill, an oilmill, and other property.

Remains of parts of the roadbed and cuts of the old "Columbia Railway," which traversed Merion tp., years before the first of the four tracks of the great "Pensylvania" were laid, are, with a few old mills and cabins, the only "ruins" of interest in the Welsh Tract. A brief sketch of this first railway is appropriate here, because the Welsh Tract was the part of the State first to have a railroad, and because a Welshman, Oliver Evans, of Philadelphia, was the first inventor who conceived the idea, as early as in 1773, of propelling carriages on land by steam power, though he only utilized it on his automobile earth excavator till in 1805, when he gave exhibitions of his steam propelled vehicle, and took passengers around Center Square, Philadelphia. From that time, there were many imitators and improvers of his idea—Leiper, Stevens, and others.

John Stevens (John ap Stephen), of Welsh extraction, was the father of the railroad system of the State. The legislature on 31 March, 1823, passed an act permitting the laying and operating a railway from Philadelphia to Columbia, at the request of Mr. Stevens and others. But this act was repealed and supplanted by another with more liberal scope, approved 7 April, 1826, incorporating the "Columbia, Lancaster and Philadelphia Rail Road Co." (which came to be known simply as "the Columbia Railway"). In 1828, the shares in this Company having been sold, the legislature passed an act providing for the constructing of the road. It was opened for traffic in Sep. 1832, but only from Broad and Callowhill Streets, in the Northern Liberties, to Paoli.* At

---

*Hazard's Register, Philadelphia, 7 Feb. 1829, contains the full report of the Engineer, Major John Wilson, on laying out, cost, &c., of the railway from Columbia to Philadelphia, Broad and Vine Sts., in Aug., &c., 1828. See also *Pensylvania Railroad Men's News*, June, 1896.

first, the Schuylkill was reached only by stages from Broad Street, and passengers and light freight were ferried over the river to the "rail cars," at Callowhill Street, which horses dragged to the "Belmont incline," and then from the top of the hill up to Paoli over the rails. But this method of travel obtained for only a few weeks, when the "locomotive engine" was put into service, and the route much extended, west and to Broad Street, but it was not until in April, 1834, that the road was completed to Lancaster. The finished portion was formally opened on 9 Dec. 1833, as well as a spur from Vine to South Streets, on Broad Street, and the big red, wooden bridge over the Schuylkill.

This pioneer railroad had features of its own. Its light iron rails were laid in iron chairs, bolted to sills of stone about 22 x 14 x 12 inches in dimension. When much of the original roadbed was abandoned for the present one, these stones went to other uses. Sometimes we see them doing duty as carriage steps by driveways.

In a general way, for the old road simply meandered through Merion tp., with many curves and digressions to avoid hollows and hills, and of course tradition has it,

> "Columbia's iron rails
> Lay on Indian trails."

The route, before it was vacated, was through the ancient Liberty Lands, or Blockley tp. and what is now Fairmount Park to the base of Peter's Hill, near "Tom Moore's cottage," where the carriages were drawn up on an "incline" of about 180 feet, by a stationary engine and cable to "Belmont," the home of the Peters family.

Thence the route, over the George property, crossed the county, or city line, on the old south line of "Pencoyd," and a half mile north of the old road to Lancaster, then through Jacob Stadleman's property, and across the lands of Joseph Evans and the S. Stadleman estate, crossing the old Lancaster road, at the old McCalla store, and paralleling it,

WELSH SETTLEMENT OF PENSYLVANIA

past the General Wayne Inn and the Merion Meeting House, crossing the properties of Bowman, John Wainwright, John Underwood, William Thomas, Edward Price, to Libertyville, where it again crossed the Lancaster road, and parelleling it again, passed over the lands of Owen Jones, and over Cherry Lane, and through the old farm of John Wister, beyond which, at the Montgomery Avenue tollgate, and where Church road intersects this avenue (the old Lancaster road), passing the new High School building, it again crossed the Lancaster road, and thence southwestwardly, between what is now Coulter avenue, and the tracks of the Pensylvania Railroad Company, it continued through Athensville (now Ardmore), and so on, crossing the Philadelphia and Lancaster pike, passing between Founders Hall, of Haverford College, and the old Haverford Meeting House, to White Hall Inn to Paoli, and out of our district towards Lancaster. When the Pensylvania Railroad Company took over the "Columbia Road" it vacated the route to Athensville, and established the one now used, but for years it used the balance of the old roadbed, passing White Hall Inn.

A poster advertisement of the "Through Line from Philadelphia to St. Louis," the "Pioneer Fast Line," dated Philadelphia, April, 1837, advertised, with pictures of an engine and one passenger car, and a canal boat, drawn by three horses: "By Rail Road and Canal Packets, / from Philadelphia to Pittsburgh, / through in $3\frac{1}{2}$ days, / and by Steam Boats, carrying the United States Mail, / from Pittsburgh to Louisville, / starts every morning, from the corner of Board & Race St. / In large and splendid eight wheel cars, via Lancaster and Harrisburg Rail Roads, arriving at the latter place, at 4 o'clock, in the afternoon, where / passengers will take the Packets, which have all been fitted up in a very superior manner, having been built expressly for the accommodation / of Passengers, after the most approved models of Boats used on the Erie Canal, and are not surpassed by the / Boats used upon any other Line. / For speed and comfort,

MERION, HAVERFORD, RADNOR

this Line is not excelled by any other in the United States. / Passengers for Cincinnati, Louisville, Natchez, Nashville, St. Louis, &c. / Will always be certain of being taken on without delay, as this Line connects with the Boats at Pittsburgh, carrying the Mail. / Office, N. E. corner of Fourth and Chestnut St. / For Seats apply as above, and at No. 200 Market Street; at the White Swan Hotel Race Street; at the N. E. Corner of Third and Willow Street; / No. 31 South Third Street, and at the West Chester House, Broad Street. / A. B. Cummings, Agent. / "

The list of advertised stopping points in 1850, on the "Central Pensylvania," its successor, also give an idea of the direction of the "Columbia Railway" beyond the river. These were Merion, or Merionville, Libertyville, Athensville, Haverford, Whitehall, West Haverford, Villa Nova, Morgan's Corner, Eagle, Reesville, Paoli, &c. The city depot was then at Broad and Cherry streets. Before the junction with the new road at Columbia, the old railway in the year 1849, carried 90,250 passengers, but after the connection with the "Pensylvania," the Columbia is credited with 146,320 passengers, in 1852, and 162,136 in the next year, and its freight increased proportionately, showing the value of the route extended.

The following few items from the 1860 issue of "The Business Guide of the Pensylvania Railroad" give us some knowledge of the "Main Line" and its stations at that time. It says that West Philadelphia is the first station on the road, and that here "locomotive engines" are attached to trains, the carriages having been drawn there by mules from the city. The next stops are at Hestonville, 3 miles, and City Line, 5 miles, but these were only flag stations. The next stops were at Merion and Libertyville. But they were also only "flag stations for the convenience of a thickly settled country, principally the country residences of Philadelphians." The post office for these points was at General Wayne. Of our thriving town of Ardmore, then called Athensville, that it is $7\frac{1}{2}$ miles from the city. "It has no

WELSH SETTLEMENT OF PENSYLVANIA

railroad agent," and the post office is Cabinet, with Joseph Pearce as the postmaster. Of Haverford: "the post office for this station, and for Whitehall, is West Haverford. Charles Anhurs has a fine large boarding house here, well patronised by Philadelphians in summer." Whitehall, "this is the first regular station on the Road, ten miles from Philadelphia." West Haverford was a flag station, and had no railroad agent, but had a post office, with John G. Henderson as postmaster. Villa Nova, too, was only a flag station, and its post office was "Radnor," which was also the post office for Morgan's Corner, another flag station, thirteen miles from Philadelphia. Eagle was the next regular stop after Whitehall, and Eliza Lewis was the railroad agent. The post office was "Spread Eagle," Paoli, "20 miles from Philadelphia, and 600 feet above tide water," was the third regular stop.

When George B. Roberts became the president of the Pensylvania Railroad, being a lineal descendant of the earliest settlers of the Welsh Tract, and interested in its annals, he renamed a few of the stations of the railroad in the Welsh property for places in Wales from which came the first settlers, hence we have Bryn Mawr for the home in Wales and here, near where the station stands, of Rowland Ellis, Rosemont for the name of the seat near the station of Rees Thomas, Merion, Haverford, and Narbeth, or Narberth. But Ardmore, for some reason unknown, was substituted for Athensville from a town in county Waterford, Ireland. But as few of the Welshmen came from the county of Anglesea, he was not obliged to name a station after its celebrated village, Llanfairnwllgwyngyllgogerywyrndrobwllilandyssiliogogogoch, much to the comfort of the conductors.

The first substantial improvement in Lower Merion, of the old Welsh lands, along the "Pensylvania Central," or our "Main Line," that was the beginning of the making "along the Main Line" celebrated for its villages and coun-

[480]

try seats, was Humphrysville, the Bryn Mawr settlement. It was plotted in 1868-9, to extend from the Philadelphia and Lancaster turnpike northward to the Gulf Road, and from Roberts' Road eastward to old Lancaster road, on lands purchased from Messrs. Robert N. Lee, Benjamin Tilghman, Hugh Barrett's estate, Charles J. Arthur, Joseph C. Turner, Thomas Humphreys. "Windon," Nicholas Hart, Benjamin Shank, and others, and deeded in 1868 to William H. Wilson. This was land originally patented by William Penn, 13. 1mo. 1684, to Edward Prichard, in two tracts, 1,200 acres (adjoining "Rees Radrah's" land), and 1,250 acres (adjoining land of John Humphrey). The latter tract, on which much of the town stands, Prichard sold in fee to John Eckley, who sold, 1. 3mo. 1685, to Launcelot Lloyd 100 acres, (adjoining Rowland Ellis on the east northeast, and John Humphrey on the south southwest), being "one mile in length and fifty perches in breadth." This land Lloyd sold, 20. 5mo. 1691, to Philip Price. Eckley devised, by his will 17 July, 1686, the balance to his wife Sarah, who by deed, 15. 6mo. 1692, conveyed 300 acres (adjoining Ellis Hugh) to Rees Thomas. And Prichard conveyed, 25 Nov., 1701, to said Rees Thomas 325 acres. After this, these lands passed through many hands till conveyed in 1868 to Mr. Wilson.

The value of these lands increased rapidly after the Civil War. For instance, Rees Thomas 3d., died intestate, and seized of 308 acres, and improvements, appraised in 1788 at £1423. In 1864, Robert N. Lee paid $21,000 for about 59 acres of this farm land, and in 1868, sold 40 acres of the same, lying on Buck Lane and Gulf Road, to Mr. Wilson for $28,573, and Wilson paid $10,469 for 14 other acres of Thomas's land, and for 6 acres which Hugh Barrett sold, in 1865, to Nicholas Hart for $2,212, Mr. Wilson had to pay $6,225, in 1868; but he paid only $31,184, for another tract of 146 acres which had belonged to the Morgans. In

WELSH SETTLEMENT OF PENSYLVANIA

1850, these Bryn Mawr lands, outside of Humphreyville, were owned by Benjamin and Thomas Humphreys, Louisa Evans and William Hesson.

The "old Lancaster road" also led, by the way of the older Haverford road, which crossed it, to the Upper, or Scull's Ferry, opposite Fairmount. At this ferry lived Mr. Scull, the maker of a valuable map of the city of Philadelphia and vicinity, published in 1750. At that time, Scull's neighbors were the families of Meredith and Warner, just above him, on the west side of the Schuylkill. This Warner family descended from Capt. William Warner (son of John, of Draycot), who was baptized at the Blockley church, in Worcestershire, 8 July, 1627. He was a settler beyond the Schuylkill before Penn received his royal grant, (having come here from Connecticut, it is supposed), and was here to welcome the first Merion settlers. His will was proved in 18 Oct., 1706. His eldest son, by wife Ann, namely Isaac Warner, will proved in April, 1722, married on 30 Nov., 1692, Ann Craven, and had William Warner, of "Eaglesfield," on Schuylkill, who was the founder of the celebrated State in Schuylkill Fishing Company, the oldest social club in Pensylvania. His will was proved in Sep., 1766.

This club was started in May, 1722, with a select few of Mr. Warner's neighbors. He leased the club an acre of land on the river, for the nominal rental of three sun-perch per annum, payable in the Spring, and the payment thereof to the "Lord of the manor" was always a ceremonious function. On this lot, which was enclosed by a high fence, the "Company" erected its "castle," having organized itself into a "State" of independent colonists, with a governor, assembly, sheriff, etc., in 1732. (Was this intended as a parody on the Welsh Quakers' "Barony"?) After the Fairmount dam was built, and ruined the sport here, the "fishermen" removed the "castle" to Rambo Rock, below Gray's

MERION, HAVERFORD, RADNOR

Ferry, in the Schuylkill, where it still stands, the scene of memorable annual fish-dinners, and the concocting of the still more celebrated insiduous "Fish-house Punch."

In 1750, according to Scull, coming from town on the then so-called Lancaster road, "only a dirt-road, corduroyed in low places," the first dwellings met were those of David and Edward George, in Blockley tp., on the upper side of the road. Further on, on the lower side, was the Humphrey's house, and nearly opposite, in Blockley, was Jonathan Wynne's "Wynnestay," still there, with "Stradleman," or William Stadleman's and Bailert's (?) beyond, near the old road that led to the ferry, (at the "Wissahickon creek"), down which road was Hugh Evans's house. On the lower side of the Lancaster road was Richard George's home, near Anthony Tunis's. On the road, beginning opposite Tunis's, leading to Garrig's, and the falls ferry, was the John Roberts house, still there. Beyond Anthony Tunis's, across the road, was Joseph Tunis's house, but the alleged old inn was not placed on the map between Tunis's and the meeting house. Opposite the Merion meeting house was Griffith's house. Along the old Haverford road, about two miles out from where it crossed the Lancaster road, was a Thomas home, on the lower side, then came Rhoads', back of whom was Williams' and Moore's. Further along this road, on the upper side, were the homes of Roberts, Hughes, and Llewellyn, and opposite a Bevan. None of the houses on this map were located exactly right.

Long before the Civil War, Philadelphians had handsome summer homes along the old Lancaster road, and the opening of the Columbia railway, some six miles through the township, gave further great impetus to Lower Merion as a summer residential district. But the Philadelphia and Reading Railroad, opened in Dec., 1839, going about 7½ miles through the township, passing over the river ends of the land taken up by some of the Thomas and Jones Company, never was particularly beneficial to Merion in this respect, though its stopping places were Pencoyd, Mill

WELSH SETTLEMENT OF PENSYLVANIA

Creek, and Spring Mills. But the Pensylvania Railroad, the worthy successor of the "old Columbia railway," has certainly been the making of towns in the Welsh tract. I refer, of course, to those along its route, for the settlements distant from it, yet using it, as Merion Square, or Gladwyn, General Wayne, Libertyville, Academyville, Cooperstown, Garretsville, &c., are but little grown in fifty years, and in half that time nearly a dozen thriving villages have grown up in the township along "the Pensylvania," several being three times as large as the combined towns of the township in 1860.

Naming farms, as gentlemen named their seats in England, (and not as in Maryland, retaining the name given a tract by the surveyor, for his convenience, on making the original plot), was a fashion early imported into the Welsh Tract. A map of sixty years ago shows the following named farms in Lower Merion, a few of which still bear their old names, and the mansion houses are still standing, Green Hill farm, 214 ac., Israel W. Morris; Red Leaf, 276 ac., Thomas P. Reming; Fair Hill, 64 ac., Henry C. Bevan; Poplar Grove, 40 ac., Thomas Bealer; Maple Grove, 78 ac., Josiah Hunting; Twine Grove, 24 ac., Thomas Bealer; Clover Hill, 100 ac., James L. Paiste; Penn Grove, 72 ac., Stephen Paschall; Wynne Wood, 269 ac., Owen Jones; St. Mary's, 167 ac., John Wister; Walnut Grove, 130 ac., Anthony Zell; Rose Hill, 80 ac., Jacob Latch; Juniper Bank, 25 ac., Mary Bowman; Pencoyd, 50 ac., Isaac W. Roberts; Marble Hill, 111 ac., Anthony L. Anderson; Ashland Hill, 27 ac., Paul Jones; Narrows Hill, 88 ac., David Jones; Glanrason, 163 ac., Silas Jones; Green Dell, 100 ac., Abraham Levering; Harriton, 594 ac., Levi Morris; Eagle Farm, 100 ac., John Supplee; Brookfield, 336 ac., Frederick W. Porter; Green Bush Farm, 87 ac., Benjamin B. Yocum; Prospect Hill, 120 ac., Joseph Crawford; Walnut Hill, 135 ac., Eleanor Curwen; Windon Farm, 147 ac., Thomas Humphreys; Fountain Green, 52 ac., Wm. J. Underwood; Rock Hill, Henry K. B. Ogle; Mine Hill, 133 ac., Heydock Garrigues; Break Neck Hill, 58 ac., Joseph Kirkner; Federal Spring, 15 ac., John Underwood; Elm Hall, 35 ac., John Wainwright; Green Bank, 114 ac., Dr. James Jenkins; Lilac Grove, 40 ac., Edward Harvey; Homeworth, 25 ac., Mary Jones;* Penn Cottage, 73 ac., Mary Penn-Gaskell; The Orchard, J. George Kiess.

The Welsh Friends were the first settlers who "Built God a Church" in the township of Merion, and their meeting house was the only place for public Christian worship in it for seventy-five years.

> "The sound of the church-going bell,
> Thou, valleys and rocks, never heard,"

till about 1770, when the German Lutherans erected a little stone church, part of which is now standing in their cemetery at Ardmore.

The earliest evidence of the existence of this religious society was in Oct., 1765, when the trustees of the German Lutheran Congregation, Messrs. William Stadelman, Frederick Grow, Stephen Goodman, Christ. Getzelman, George Baasler, and Simon Litzenberg, purchased 66 acres of land, at £4.3.0, per acre, from John Hughes, who had bought the same at sheriff's sale, on 3 Sep., 1765. This was to secure a location for a burying ground, and a church site (as, like the early Welsh Friends, the German settlers had held their religious meetings in private houses in Merion), for all German Protestants,—the German Reform and Lutheran

---

*Mary Jones, wife of Jonathan Jones, whose old house "Homeworth" is still standing, (on the McFarland property), off of Church Road, Ardmore, near and north of the railroad, has left an interesting account (see *Pa. Mag.* XXIV, p. 231), of an entertainment of Granville John Penn, a descendant of the Founder, by Mary Penn-Gaskell, (born McClenanchan, wife of Thomas Penn-Gaskell, who was a cousin of the guest), of "Penn Cottage," on the old Gulf Road, at the nine-mile stone, given 1mo. 31. 1852. She had at five o'clock dinner all of the relatives and descendants of William Penn, and there came in the evening descendants of many of the Welsh Tract pioneers, and first prominent families of Philadelphia.

WELSH SETTLEMENT OF PENSYLVANIA

Congregations,—conjointly. The dwelling house on this property was used as a church by the Germans till in 1769. In this year, the 66 acre lot was conveyed to Stephen Goodman, who thereupon conveyed 133 perches of the same to the trustees of the Society of Lutherans of Merion. Forty years afterwards, the Society increased its holdings for interments, and, in 1810, put up the stone wall about the cemetery.

In 1769, the Society built a log church on the 133 perches, which was used thirty years. In 1787, it erected a stone school house, still standing. In 1800, it built a stone addition on the east end of the school house, and used the whole for church purposes until the present St. Paul's church was built on Lancaster Avenue, in 1833. The records of the Merion German Lutherans begin with the baptism, on 17 Oct., 1765, of three infants, Jacob, son of Jacob and Margaret Schlonhouse, (sponsors, Tobias and Barbara Taumiller), Jacob, son of John and Annie Leix, and John, son of John and Catherine Leix, (sponsors, John Getzelman, and Elizabeth Stadelman). In Sep., 1767, there were 43 communicants in this congregation, which suggests that Merion was receiving a fair share of the German emigrants at that time. Among the surnames of these Germans in Merion, besides those mentioned above, were Sorg. Schlerman, Prinz, Fimbel, Hoffman, Horn, Negler, Heller, Graner, Wagner, Keller, Hass, Heidle, Seibert, Mowrer, &c. Some of these names may still be heard in Merion but like the Welsh, the Germans lost their identity in the greater English population in this section.

The church of the Merion Baptist congregation, at the intersection of the Gulf Road and Roberts's Road, on the Harrison-Morris-Vaux land, was not built till in 1800. Descendants of early Welsh Friends, and of the Gaskills, descendants of William Penn, have been buried in the graveyard of this church. But a much older Baptist congregation, all Welsh, built a church in Montgomery tp., before 1720, and of its members were John Evans, William,

MERION, HAVERFORD, RADNOR

Thomas, and Josiah James, James Lewis, Edward Williams, and James Davis. And an older one than this was the Baptist congregation of Welsh in the English settlement of Plymouth, members of which, before 1703, were David Meredith, Thomas Owen, Isaac Price, Ellis Pugh, and Hugh Jones. A Welsh minister, Malachi Jones, gathered the first congregation of Welsh Presbyterians, at Abington, among the Quakers, in 1714. In all of these churches the sermon and hymns were in the Welsh tongue till the time of the Revolutionary War, and, at only a short time before this, the population of what is now Montgomery Co., was nearly one-half Welsh and "half Welsh." Or, according to assessors' returns in eight townships of this district, made in 1734, there were 155 distinctively Welsh surnames to only 37 English.

Nothing of particular interest has come down to us about the early schools of the Welsh Tract. Mr. Isaac Sharpless, in his little book, "The Quaker Boy," only refers to them in a general way. That there were Friends' schools in early days, there is no question, as the extant meeting minutes are generally nicely written, and well expressed, and that they had sessions in their old meeting houses, for some of these have preserved some of the old school desks, and then there are entries in meeting records of the burials of teachers. At Merion Meeting, "Buried, James Marks, schoolmaster, 7mo. 15. 1742," and "Garret Hodnut, schoolmaster at Blockley, 8mo. 16. 1753." Elsewhere is noted the school house, built back of the Merion meeting house, about 1765, on a lot on the S. E. corner of Rees's land, and corner of Lancaster road and Meeting House Lane, (indicated on Levering's map of Merion, in 1851), which this meeting bought from Rees, in 1765. Down the Rock Hollow road, and near the Meeting House Lane, Jacob Jones, a Welshman by descent, founded in 1812, the Lower Merion Academy. It was a pay and free school, for boys and

WELSH SETTLEMENT OF PENSYLVANIA

girls, boarders and day scholars. Many prominent Merion men and women began their education at this academy, which gave name to the hamlet here, Academyville.

The general lines of the great tract of land bought by the Welsh Friends for themselves, have already been given. It included eleven and a half of the present contiguous Pensylvania townships, in the counties of Montgomery, Delaware and Chester, these being Lower and Upper Merion, Haverford, Radnor, Tredyffrin, East and West Whiteland, Willistown, East and West Goshen, East Town, and a part of West Town. The north and west lines of Whiteland township, are the old Welsh Tract lines. The Welsh Tract's north line separated Tredyffrin tp. and Whiteland tp. from Schuylkill, Charlestown, and Uwchlan townships, and the west line of the Welsh Tract separates West Whiteland, West Goshen, and the borough of Westchester from East Caln and East Bradford townships. Its northwest corner being the northwest corner of West Whiteland township.

The first three original townships, Merion (Lower), Haverford,* and Radnor, have been treated of, and of the others there are the following items concerning their Welsh settlers. Of this celebrated tract of land, geologists who have been investigating its structure for years, but have not come to a verdict. One set of gentlemen holding that the Welsh Tract may once have been on the side of a mountain 25,000 feet high, and the other, it may have been the bottom of the ocean, a thousand feet below the waves, and in support of this guess, they show the "Bryn Mawr gravel," which is the regular sea gravel, bedded 400 feet

---

*Haverford tp. taxables in 1715:—Richard Hayes, Henry Lewis, Samuel Lewis, John Havard, Daniel Humphrey, David Llewellyn, Rowland Powell, Henry Lawrence, Thomas Lawrence, Humphrey Ellis, Samuel Reese, Martha Hughs, Gaynor Musgrove, Hugh David, Robert Wharton, Lidia Ellis, Owen Thomas, John Parry, Daniel Lawrence, David Lewis, and Mireck Davies. Freemen, Jacob Jones, and Evan David.

above present tide water. But they concur that after the Welsh Tract was dry land, a great glacier coming from the northward scraped the Welsh Tract level, and left the huge limestone blocks, brought miles and miles from their natal bed and left them near the Chester Valley and in Blockley tp., about Race and 66th streets, Philadelphia.

When we go into Upper Merion, we are on ground made sacred by memories of the American Revolution, as many of the military events previous to the army's occupation of nearby Valley Forge farms, in 1777-78, happened within its bounds, though not all occurred in what had been a part of the great Welsh Tract. Swedes' Ford, Flat Land Ford, Matson's Ford and other Schuylkill river crossings of that period, are still landmarks of those strenuous times, when Washington and Howe marched up and down, crossed and recrossed the river, trying to get the advantage of each other, as also are North Valley Hill, Red Hill, Gulf Hill, (or Conshohocking Hill as it was known to the earliest Welsh settlers), Gulf Creek, Gulf Road, and the "old Gulph Mill," built in 1747, near which, in an unidentified farm house, Washington had its headquarters, his army being encamped here a week, 13-19 Dec., before taking possession of Valley Forge.*

Upper Merion's population never approached that of Lower Merion, and in 1741, had only 52 taxables, but in 1857, it had as many post offices, and they were located at Port Kennedy, King of Prussia, and Gulf Mills. At that time, the only public library, besides the Friends' inter-meeting one, in the two townships, was a little affair at the King of Prussia, conducted by Mr. C. J. Elliott, at the intersection of the Gulf and State roads, and three other roads, and near the tavern where the township elections were held.

In 1734, under the direction of Thomas Penn, when organizing the Land Office, a list of the landowners in Upper

---

*See "Camp by the old Gulph Mill," *Pa. Mag. of His.* XVII, p. 414.

WELSH SETTLEMENT OF PENSYLVANIA

Merion was taken, and in it were named the following Welsh, some of whom were of the families of the earliest settlers of Lower Merion, who had bought land there, and removed:

Hugh Hughes, Morris Edwards, Owen Thomas, Griffith Philips, Owen Jones, Thomas Junkin, John David, Hugh Williams, Benjamin Davis, Isaac Rees, Richard Bevan,* David Jones, William Rees, Edward Roberts,† Matthew Roberts, Thomas Rees, Harry Griffith, Hannah Jones, Griffith Rees, David Lewis, John Rees. The other landowners were Swedes, possibly excepting William George, and John Moor.

Although the Abraham family is not in this list of Upper Merion landowners, yet there is evidence that a Sarah Abraham, widow, came from Wales, with her three sons, James, Enoch, and Noah Abraham, and that she bought land from the Letitia Penn estate, in Upper Merion, about 1730, and settled there. The sons married, but Enoch had no issue. James married Margaret Davis, and had a number of children, one of whom, Isaac Abraham, born 28. 4mo. 1717, married Dinah Havard, and from them there are many descendants living in what was the "Welsh Barony."

Whiteland township (East and West Whiteland tps. after 1704), was also originally a part of the Welsh Tract, and in 1704 David Jones was its constable. The extant tax list of 1715, shows the following Welsh were then among its landowners, James Thomas, Richard Thomas, Thomas James, Owen Thomas, Thomas Owen, Llewellyn Parry, David Howell, Rees Hughs, Rees Prichard, James Rowland, Griffith Philips, Evan Lewis, David Meredith, and John

---

*He lived near Gulf Mills, and in 1751, advertised in the *Pena. Gazette*, July 24th, as having for sale, "a likely negro man, about 30 years of age, fit for town, or country business," and also a negro girl, aged 15 years. In 1790, there were 114 negro slaves in Montgomery Co., but in 1830, only one.
†He was the 'Squire, 1726-41.

MERION, HAVERFORD, RADNOR

Martin. Early township officers were James Thomas, Lewis William, David Meredith, Sr., Evan Lewis, Rees Richard, Thomas Owen, James Rowland, James David, Thomas James and Griffith Howell. A petition from this township in 1731, addressed to Richard Hayes, president justice of the Chester Co. Court, shows that there were still many Welshmen in it.

Willistown township landowners in 1715, according to the tax list, were all English people, although this "town" was a part of the Welsh Tract, which was to have been entirely for Welshmen. Thomas Garret was the constable in 1704.

East Town township, another section of the Welsh Tract, had for its constable in 1704, William Thomas, and the 1715 tax list shows names of Welsh landowners, Edward Hugh, Ellis Hughes, Hugh Jones, Morgan Hugh, Philip David, David Davis, John Harris, John David, Evan Thomas, Owen Hugh, Richard Evans, and Thomas Edwards, and non-residents, John Pugh, and Owen Humphrey, and William Sharlow.

West Town township had earlier organization than the other distant "towns," but only a portion of it was within the Welsh Tract bounds. Its settlers were all English. Daniel Hoopes was its constable, in 1700, and possibly earlier.

Tredyffrin township, in Chester county, was also a portion of the original Welsh Tract. The Welsh knew this "town" as Tre yr Dyffryn, (the town in the wide valley, that is the great and beautiful Chester Valley), according to the extant tax list of 1722. The English knew it as Velleyton, in 1708. This township was organized about 1707, when it appears that Thomas David, a Welshman, was the constable. Among the landowners in the Great Valley, in 1722, were James Abraham, Morris David, Hugh David, James David, Sr., John David, Henry David, Thomas David, James Davies, William Davies, Timothy Davies, Stephen Evans, Lewis Evans, William Evans, John Howell, Griffith

WELSH SETTLEMENT OF PENSYLVANIA

Jones, Sr. and Jr., Thomas Jermon, Thomas James, Jenkin Lewis, James Parry, John Robert, Thomas Martin, Thomas Godfrey, Samuel Richard, John Richard, all Welshmen, and Daniel and Lewis Walker, Thomas Hubbert, Mark Hubbert, &c. It seems that in early days, the landowners, residents of a "town," took turns in being the constable. In this township there served this office, 1707-1753, Thomas David, Griffith John, Rowland Richard, John David, Owen Gethen, Stephen Evans, John Roberts.

The earliest road supervisors were also Welshmen, among them, David John, Thomas James, John David, Thomas Martin, Stephen Evans, &c. The extant tax list for 1715 for this township shows that the following Welsh were land owners in it: Thomas Jarman, Sr. and Jr., Stephen Evans, Rowland Richard, Griffith John, John Roberts, James David, Margaret Walters, John David, John David Howell, Thomas Rees, Owen Gethen, John David Griffith, Llewellyn David, James Parry, Henry John, David Evan, Thomas David, Thomas Martin, Thomas Godfrey, and Thomas Hubbert, and Lewis Walker. The non-resident holders were Capt. Nordant, Benjamin Davies, Mordecai Moore, and William Evans.

Over the roads of this township portions of the contending armies of the Revolution maneuvered for positions, and it was while Gen. Howe's division was in this township, he sent Gen. Grey in the night to surprise and attack Gen. Wayne, near Paoli Inn, when Wayne was surprised and 150 of his soldiers were killed and wounded, and 80 taken prisoners, and his cannon and baggage carried off by the British.

Goshen township, (divided in 1817 into East and West Goshen township), though originally a portion of the great Welsh Tract, and where nearly all of the early Welsh Friends had to accept as the location of half of their purchase from Penn, was too far away to become settled till nearly twenty years after the first coming of the Welsh, and, for some reason, but few of them settled there. The township is presumed to have been organized about 1704, as this is the time when it had its first constable, Cadwalader Ellis, a Welshman. The oldest extant tax list is of 1715, and there are few Welshmen mentioned, namely Ellis David, Cadwalader Ellis, Ellis William, Thomas Evans, and the following non-resident landowners, Dr. Edward Jones, Dr. Griffith Owen, Thomas Jones and Robert Jones. Gov. Lloyd owned considerable land in the southwest part of the township. His executors, in 1706, sold 797 and 850 acres here. In 1702, they had sold 965 acres to John Haines, a resident of West Jersey, and the city of Westchester stands, made a borough in 1788, on part of this tract, and on a part of a 1,100 tract owned by Richard Thomas, of Whitland. His land lay east of High street, and Lloyd's south of Gay street. East of Richard Thomas's land was 346 acres owned by Evan Jones, and 350 acres owned by Ellis David. Next was a tract of 635 acres owned by John ap Thomas's sons, Thomas Jones, &c. The first Welshman to settle in Goshen is supposed to have been Robert Williams. An extant petition, dated 1731, shows only the following apparently Welshmen out of thirty-two signers, Thomas Evans, David Davies, Ellis Williams, Richard Jones, and Thomas Price. On the extant tax list of 1753, only the Welsh names of David Davis, Thomas Evans, and Amos Davis are among the taxables, and in the 1774 list, not so many.

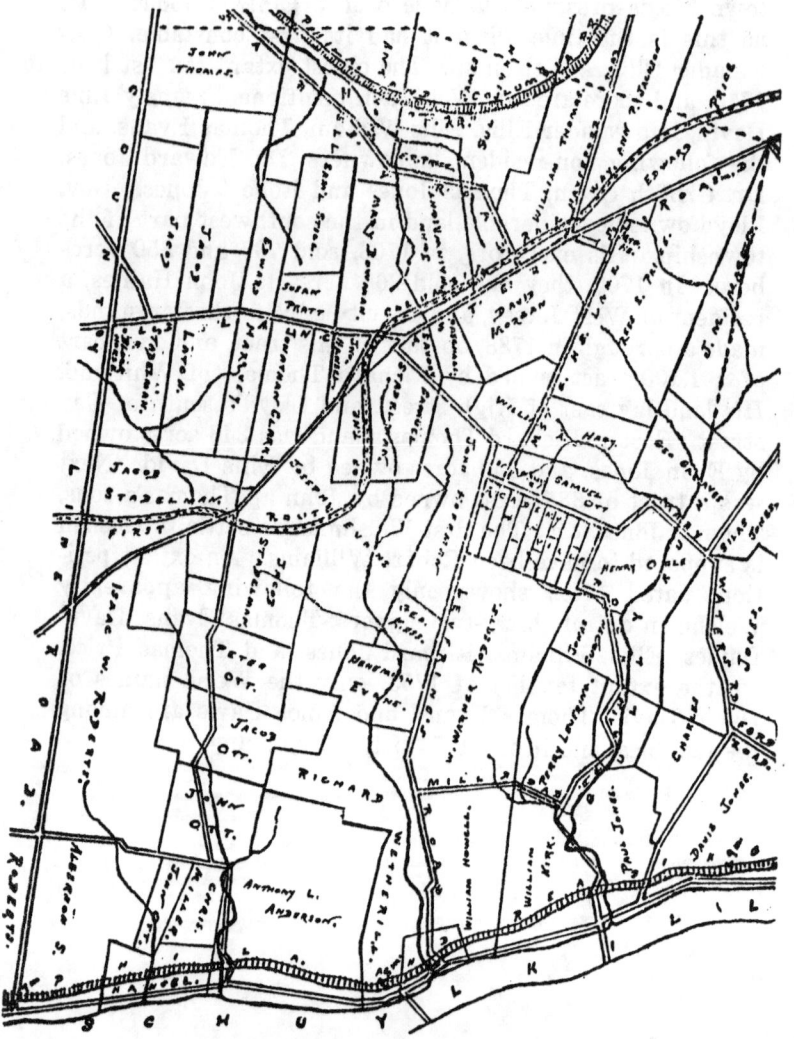

THOMAS AND JONES TRACT IN 1850

FRIENDS MEETINGS
OF THE
WELSH TRACT

MERION FRIENDS' MEETING HOUSE, *CIRCA* 1830.

MERION, HAVERFORD, RADNOR

The Welsh Friends being of course pious, and in full appreciation of the liberty their new home gave them to meet for worship without molestation, joined together for thanks and communion as soon as they became in a manner settled. These first meetings upon their land at the Falls of the Schuylkill, were beneath the great trees of the primeval forest about them, in pleasant weather, and, otherwise, at the primitive home of a family in their settlement, be it then a cave, tent, or a lean-to shelter, and subsequently in the dwelling houses they immediately erected.

This was the experience in each Welsh township—Merion and Haverford, and subsequently in Radnor, Goshen, and the others—where the little settlements were far apart, for several years, till the inhabitants increased in such number, that central, convenient public houses for worship were required.

At this period, these two contiguous settlements of the Welsh Friends, in Merion and Haverford, with a third one, mostly of English people, in the Western city liberties, adjoining the great Welsh Tract, held their meetings independently, not yet being large enough to effect the organization peculiar to the Society.

In Philadelphia, where there was soon a large population of Friends, and there being several small peculiar, particular, or preparative meetings, then amenable and subordinate to the Burlington monthly meeting, the necessity for the proper local organization was sooner experienced and accomplished. The first conference of resident "city Friends" for this purpose was held on 9. 11mo. (Jan.) 1682-3, when it was ordered that those present, and other Friends in town, bring their certificates of membership and removal, vouching their good standing, issued to them by the meetings of which they had been members in the old country, and submit them for examination and record, at the business meeting to be held on 6. 12mo. following. This was accordingly done by a great number, and on 6. 1mo. (March) 1682-3, the distinctive Philadelphia monthly and quarterly meetings were regularly instituted.

As the initial meetings in Merion and Haverford were composed of those who had been friends and neighbors in the old country, and belonged to the same monthly meeting, there was no occasion, till long afterwards, for a call for certificates as to the standing of anyone, hence, there are few recorded early in the books of the Haverford (Radnor) monthly meeting, unlike that of Philadelphia, which was in a great measure a congregation of strangers.

The following are some of the earliest Welsh Tract settlers who brought certificates from meetings in Wales and England to the Haverford (Radnor) monthly meeting: Evan Jones; Mary Elis, widow; Rowland Ellis; Treharn David; Evan ap William Powell; David Powell and wife Gainor; Philip Evan; Elizabeth Owen; Rebecca Humphrey; Alice v. James Lewis; Thomas Duckett and wife, and his sister Mary; Hugh Roberts; Cadwallader Morgan; Hugh John Thomas; John Robert of Llun; Robert David; Katherine Robert; Gaynor Robert; John Jarman; David Meredith; Stephen Evans; David James, Rees Petter; John Humphrey; Richard Humphrey; Elizabeth Humphrey, widow; Joshua Owen; Margaret John, widow; John Rhydderch; Thomas Jones; Thomas Ellis; John Bevan; Ralph Lewis; John Richard; Rees John; Griffith Owen; Sarah Hearne; Howell James; Owen Morgan; Mary Tyddur; Matthew Holgate; Ellis Pugh; Robert Tuddur; Robert Ellis; Jane Griffith; Anne Jones; Griffith John, widower; Robert Owen and wife Rebecca; David Price's children; Maud Richard; John Rice, &c.

It is of interest that certificates of the following Welsh Friends were among the earliest filed in the Philadelphia monthly meeting: Henry Lewis, Lewis David, and William Howel, from the Redstone meeting, in Pembrokeshire, dated 6. 6mo. 1682. They became of the founders of the preparative meeting of Haverford. Samuel and James Miles, from Montgomery-llainhangel meeting, in Radnorshire, dated 27. 5mo. 1683, who settled in Haverford. Thomas Ellis from the quarterly meeting, at Dolyserre, in Merionethshire, dated 27. 5mo. 1683, a large Welsh Tract landowner. Evan Morris, and his wife Gainor, from the quarterly meeting at Tyddyn y Garreg, Merionethshire, dated 8. 5mo. 1690. They settled at Gwynedd. Evan Powel, a weaver, and his wife Gwen, from Nantmell, Radnorshire, dated 20. 3mo. 1698. Thomas Powell and Edward Moore, from Landwdaen parish, Radnorshire, dated 20. 3mo. 1698. Lumley Williams, from Radnor Town, dated 20. 3mo. 1698. These Welsh Friends, all from Radnorshire, came over with Penn, in the "Welcome": Thomas Jones and Evan Oliver, and his wife Jean, and their children, David, Elizabeth, John, Hannah, Mary, Evan, and "Seaborn."

As said, in the first year, the three small separate meetings for the Welsh Tract, and the Liberties, had no further organization than as independent preparative meetings. In Merion Town, there were, in the year 1682, only five families, those of Dr. Edward Jones, Robert David, William Edward, Edward Rees, and John Edward; in Haverford Town, only the families of Lewis David, Henry Lewis, William Howell, and George Painter, and in the adjoining "city liberties," only those of Thomas Duckett and Barnaby Wilcox, while in far off Radnor Town, there were no families at all, (although by his map, Surveyor-General Holme would have it believed there were forty settlements in Radnor tp., and thirty-two in Haverford, in the following year). Therefore, it can be said, Friends' families across the Schuylkill, in 1682-3, were "few and far between."

In June, five months after the Philadelphia Friends' families were numerous enough to separate themselves from the Burlington monthly meeting, and organize the Philadel-

WELSH SETTLEMENT OF PENSYLVANIA

phia monthly meeting, we learn from the minutes of the latter, under 5. 4mo. 1683, that the English Friends living over the Schuylkill river, nearest the city, had a small meeting which gathered at the home of Thomas Duckett. This memorandum, made when the Philadelphia monthly meeting was considering the settling of the preparative meetings in Philadelphia County, says, it was "agreed that there be a first-day publick meeting at Philadelphia, and a first-day publick meeting at Skuylkill." And "agreed that every other first-day there be a publick meeting of friends for the worship of the Lord at the house of Thomas Duckett, on the other side of Skuylkill, and that the meetings in these two places [Philadelphia and Duckett's house], make one monthly meeting."

From this, it might be presumed that the "English Friends living over the Schuylkill" were numerous, (but they were only two families), and that the Welsh Friends were not recognized by the Philadelphians. But other minutes clearly show that the Welsh met with these English at Mr. Duckett's, so it may have been only convenience to designate all the little meetings over the Schuylkill, as "Duckett's meeting," for, when the Philadelphia quarterly meeting was established, composed at first of the Philadelphia, "Duckett's," Tackony, and Poquessin meetings, in Philadelphia County, it appears that Welshmen and Englishmen represented "Duckett's meeting," or "Skuylkill meeting," as it was variously called. But it was not until the Philadelphia quarterly meeting of December, 1684, that the Welsh meetings were distinctively recognized, although they "belonged to the quarterly meeting" from the first.

It has been presumed that after Hugh Roberts arrived here with his family, in Nov. 1683, accompanied by four families for the "Thomas & Jones tract," namely those of the widow Thomas, William Jones, Cadwalader Morgan, and Hugh Jones, and John Bevan's, and some other families, that settled nearby, or in Haverford, he set out to organize the two Welsh preparative meetings into a monthly meeting; but this arrangement was not consented to by the Philadelphia quarterly meeting till the following spring, when, in the minutes of the Philadelphia monthly meeting, under 4. 1mo. 1683-4, is the statement:—"It being proposed to this meeting that the friends of Wales, beyond Skuylkill, belonging to the Quarterly meeting, may be allowed to keep a weekly and a monthly meeting amongst themselves. The meeting agreed, thereunto."

This was the birth of the Welsh monthly meeting, known for several years only as the "Skuylkill monthly meeting," but which was called both the Merion, and the Haverford monthly meeting later, and subsequently, when the preparative meeting of Radnor was added, the union became known as the Radnor monthly meeting, and ever since has been tributary to the Philadelphia quarterly meeting, an arrangement positively decided upon in 1698, after the Welshmen's "boundary line troubles," when these Welsh meetings refused to be within the jurisdiction of the Chester monthly, or the quarterly meeting, although located in Chester Co., and in this stand they had the consent and support of the yearly meeting, as elsewhere stated.

The cause of there being several names for the Welsh Friends' monthly meeting may be found in the early custom of these Friends to hold their monthly meetings alternately with each preparative meeting, those of Merion, Haverford, and Schuylkill, as the little meeting in the Liberties was called, the gatherings being at the dwellings of members of the Society, and, from the minutes of these meetings, the men's and the women's, it is learned that wherever a monthly meeting was held, it was called by the name of the "town" in which the dwelling used was situated. This was, of course, before the permanent name "Radnor" was adopted. As late as 26. 6mo. 1706, the Chester monthly meeting minutes record that the Newtown meeting had received "from the Merion Monthly Meeting," a general certificate,

WELSH SETTLEMENT OF PENSYLVANIA

recommending William Lewis, Sr. and Jr., Evan Lewis, Lewis Lewis, Rees Howell, William Bevan, and William Thomas.

It would be natural to suppose that this new monthly meeting had borne permanently the name of "Merion," when the designation "Schuylkill" was dropped, in honor of the eldest of the original meetings in the Tract; but in deciding upon the name, it was the unanimous wish that it should bear the name of "Haverford," (and for the same reason it subsequently was called "Radnor"), because of the brave opposition that meeting put up against the plot of the Chester people to divide the Welsh Tract, and refusing courteously but flatly to be in the jurisdiction of the Chester monthly meeting.

The extant minutes of the monthly meetings held at the dwellings of Friends in the Western Liberties, Merion and Haverford, till in 1698, open with the minutes of the first four "men's meetings," and seem to be complete for these early years, but then comes a gap of seven years in them, without any known reason, and when the record is resumed, the monthly meeting is no longer called "Haverford" but "Radnor," without any suggestion why the change of name took place. This hiatus is provoking, as it occurs at an important time in the life of the Welsh colony, the period of its contention for autonomy. And then, too, we might have found reliable information concerning the date of building the stone meeting house for Merion, and what accommodations were had for meetings in Merion and Haverford before their houses were erected, aside from meeting once a month at dwellings.

Or, more particularly, the minutes of the men's monthly meeting are from 10. 2mo. 1684, to 12. 6mo. 1686; 15. 5mo. 1693, to 12. 8mo. 1699; 1709 to 9. 9mo. 1704, and from 10. 10mo. 1712. (Originals at No. 140 N. 15th St., Philadelphia.) And the minutes of the women's monthly meeting are 12. 1mo. 1684-5, to 1740, and from 1746. (Original at No. 142 N. 16th St., Philadelphia). Minutes of the men's

WELSH FRIENDS' MEETINGS

meeting Merion, 1701-2, 12mo. 6 to 6. 5mo. 1705, and of women's meeting, Merion, 1702-1705, both at No. 140 N. 15th St. Philadelphia. Records of Radnor monthly meeting from 23. 8mo. 1682 (births, marriages, deaths, certificates, &c), originals at No. 142 N. 16th st. Philadelphia.

The first entry in the records of the "Haverford monthly meeting," of the Welsh Friends, in its "old limp-leather book," is under "2d month, 10th., 1683-4," telling that at the men's meeting, held at Thomas Duckett's house, "two couples passed." These were Thomas Stampford and Joane Hooding, and Humphrey Ellis and Gwen Rees, who "declared their intentions of marriage with each other." Each monthly meeting of these Friends appointed a place for the holding of the next meeting, of course, always at some neighbor's dwelling. "Weekday meetings" were also held at Mr. Duckett's on each "third day," and "at Haverford" on 4th days, and "at Merion" on 6th days.

It is not till long after minutes began to be kept that it may be known from them who acted as clerk, overseers, and trustees of the "Welsh monthly meeting." On 13. 4mo. 1695, the clerks of meetings were, John Jarman, (Radnor), William Howell, (Haverford), and Robert Owen, (Merion). In 5mo. 1693, the monthly meeting overseers were John Roberts and Edward Rees, and in 7mo. 1694, Robert Owen and Edward Jones. John Bevan, Rowland Ellis, William Howell, David Lawrence, Humphrey Ellis, Richard Orms, and Edward Jones, were the "peace makers" of the early years.

The first delegates appointed to attend the quarterly meeting, held in Philadelphia, between 13. 9mo. and 11. 10mo., 1684, were Griffith Owen and Mary Jones, for Merion; John Bevan and Margaret Lewis, for Haverford, and "widow ffinger," for Schuylkill. On 11. 10mo. 1684, the Welsh Friends ordered Evan Harry to make a copy of all the papers brought from this quarterly meeting, for the use of the Haverford Monthly meeting.

WELSH SETTLEMENT OF PENSYLVANIA

The "little unpleasantness" between the Welsh Friends and the Chester monthly and quarterly meetings, which has been several times mentioned herein, and about which much has elsewhere been printed, may be seen in detail in the minutes of the Radnor monthly meeting, in 6mo. 1698. That the Chester Friends were exceedingly jealous of the supposed rights of their monthly meeting within Chester county, may also be seen in many instances in its records. As, for instance, when the little preparative meeting of Newtown was started, or, when (in 11mo. 1696), "William Lewis and some others, proposed to settle a meeting at Newtown meeting," the Haverford monthly meeting, on 11. 14. 1696, considered and consented to there being such a meeting for Newtown, and, as is customary, so formally notified the Chester quarterly meeting, which became very indignant upon the receipt of this communication, and took the matter of the so called presumption of the Haverford body before the yearly meeting at Philadelphia. The Friends in yearly meeting, after sober debate and subsequent investigation, compromised and settled this dispute, by ordering, in 12mo. 1701, the Newtown preparative meeting, in Chester county, "to remain as it is," and that "for the future, ye said Welsh friends may set up no meetings further within the sd county of Chester, without ye approbation of the Chester quarterly meeting." This certainly was a victory for the Welshmen. The Newtown meeting continued a part of the Haverford, or Radnor monthly meeting for several years, but in 1705, consented to transfer its allegiance to the Chester monthly meeting. In 1700, the Chester quarterly meeting was still concerned about the preparative meetings of the Welsh Friends living in Chester Co., "which appear not at this meeting, but go to Philadelphia quarterly meeting." But it does not appear that the Chester Friends interfered with the jurisdiction of the Welsh Friends over those in the Chester Valley, as in 11mo. 1698, "Friends in upper end of Merion, complain they live too far from the settled weekly meeting. Ask to have weekly meeting among themselves. Approved," by Haverford monthly meeting. This was the beginning, it may be presumed, of the Valley Meeting, but it was not till many years after when these Friends had a meeting house, as a minute in 12mo. 1730, says, "arranged to erect a meeting house for Valley friends" and in 1 mo. 1730-1, "decided to build a meeting house at the graveyard of Lewis Walker, deceased, which was left by him for this purpose." The following entry in Haverford, Mo. Mtg. records, as to summer arrangements, which is not without interest, 1701, 2mo. (April), "the dais now growing long, ffriends made known their intention to keep afternoon meetings." The Newtown Friends to meet at Lewis Lewis's; the Haverford Friends at their meeting house; the Radnor Friends at their meeting house, and at Rees Thomas's and Ellis Pugh's; the Merion Friends at their meeting house, and at John Bevan's and Cadwalader Morgan's, and the Gwynedd Friends at Hugh Griffith's.

The ship "Vine," arriving on 17. 7mo. 1684, bringing many Welsh families to settle in Merion, Haverford, and Radnor, increased the population of the Welsh Tract so that it was almost immediately necessary to erect appropriate houses for public worship, therefore, probably, two log houses were put up at first, one in Merion, and the other in Haverford, (though there is evidence that the Friends in this township continued to meet for some time at the home of John Bevan), in localities most convenient to the majority of the settlers' families, and most accessible by the bridle paths, or trails, through the woods, for as yet there were no roads, nor need of them; but the Schuylkill meeting continued to be held at the house of Thomas Duckett in the "liberty lands," near the river, (on Market Street). But there seems to have been no occasion for a meeting house in Radnor before 1717.

The increase of inhabitants in the Welsh Tract also called for proper, and central places for burials, and to this end the Haverford monthly meeting minutes record:—

WELSH SETTLEMENT OF PENSYLVANIA

"Att our monthly meeting held at John Bevan's house at Haverford, the 9th of the 8th month, (1684), it was ordered as followeth: This meeting haveing taken to their consideration the necessity of a burying place, it was ordered that Thomas Ducket and Barnaby Willcox,* for Schoolkill; Hugh Roberts and Robert David, for Merion; George Painter and William Howell, for Haverford, should view and set out convenient places for that purpose respectively, for the meetings they belong to, as aforesaid."

This was done, following up the permission given by the quarterly meeting, according to its minute, 2. 7mo. 1684, to wit: "Agreed that the monthly meeting at Skuylkill shall take care for a burying place, and its Enclosure." At this meeting, "Skuylkill friends being called, there appeared Thomas Duckett and Barnaby Wilcocks" only, and the Welsh were not represented. At the next monthly

---

*Both of these men served on the grand jury, 27 12mo. 1683-4. Mr. Willcox, who was a justice in 1687-9, and assemblyman, 1685, had been a member of the Bristol monthly meeting, in England, where the births of some of his children are recorded, namely, "George, 1667, 6. 22, son of Barnebe and Sarah Wilkox"; Joseph, 1669, 4. 19; "Hester, 1673, 6 30, daughter of Barnabus and Sarah Wilkcox"; "Abigael, 1679, 7. 28, daughter of Barnabas and Sarah Willcox." The will of Sarah Willcox, widow and administrator of Barnabas, dated 4th mo. 20, 1692, was proved at Philadelphia, 9mo. 30. It is not known when and where they married. It was the above Joseph Willcox (mayor of Philadelphia, in 1705), when an alderman of the city, who in the "historical fray," or "drunken brawl," as the occasion is described (see minutes of the Provincial Council), between the Founder's son, William Penn, Jr., and companions, and the "city watch," in Sept. 1704, at a tavern in Philadelphia, came to the rescue of the watchmen, and "fell upon young Penn, and gave him a severe beating."

Mr. Duckett was a maltster, and brought his certificate, dated 4. 4mo. 1683, from the "Monthly Meeting for the East Part of the County of Wilts," where the first men's meeting, or monthly meeting of record, was held 10. 2mo. 1684. His will, signed 20. 3mo. 1699, was proved by his widow, Ruth, 24 June, 1700.

meeting of Welsh and English Friends, held in 9mo. 1684, reports were made that the burying places had been selected and laid out respectively for Merion and Haverford.

These minutes do not mention a graveyard for the use of Duckett's meeting, or "the Skuylkill meeting." But in the minutes of the Philadelphia quarterly meeting, 2. 1mo. 1684-5, inform that "the meeting appoints Barnaby Wilcocks and Thomas Duckett to apply to the Governor's commissioners for a grant of two acres of Land for a burying place on the other side of Skuylkill." This land was granted, and became the graveyard, near Duckett's house, and along the south side of the "settled road," about where Market and 32d streets now intersect, and is part of the Pensylvania Railroad property. It was used as a general burying place for Friends, after the Duckett meeting was abandoned, or about 1688-9, and was known as the "Lower Burying Ground," and "Haverford Friends' Ground." In 1809 there was a committee of the Pensylvania Legislature appointed to pass on the validity of Friends' title to this land, and it was reported that the graveyard had been used up to that time for 120 years, and their title good. But the Pensylvania Railroad effected some arrangement, and took the ground in 1850 for tracks, and the bodies were removed.

It might seem more natural that the ground selected for the burials should be at the meeting houses, than that these buildings should be subsequently erected near the graveyards, hence it could be presumed there was at first at least a log meeting house in Merion, if not in Haverford. But as to the latter, there is the contemporary statement, "we have our burying place where we intend our meeting house." The Philadelphia monthly meeting, which first took into consideration the erection of a permanent house for its meetings on 9. 11mo. 1682, did not take up the matter of a graveyard for itself till 4. 7mo. 1683. It is notable that the Welsh Friends, Thomas Wynne and Lydia Grif-

WELSH SETTLEMENT OF PENSYLVANIA

fith Jones were appointed to the building committee, and that Dr. Wynne and Henry Lewis served on the Philadelphia graveyard committee.

In later years, when there was much uncertainty about the quality of Penn's deeds for land, and in fact about the tenure of land generally in the Province, the leading Friends, of all nationalities, influenced the Pensylvania assembly, in Jan. 1706-7, to request of the provincial councillors that the titles to land of meeting houses and graveyards be confirmed, but for some reason the council did not grant this request for several years.

From the records of the Haverford (Radnor) monthly meeting, it appears that the English families of Warner, Kiete, Willcox, Saunders, Griffith, Duckett, Gardner, Clayton, and Hearne, were members, in 1684-5, of the Schuylkill preparative meeting, and that their children's births were recorded as of this meeting up to 6mo. 19, 1685. While the general records did not begin so early, the entry of the first birth is 8mo. 29, 1680. In these years, the "Burials att Skoolkill Buring Place West Side," were only five, namely,

1683. 7mo. 8. Janne Duckett, widdow.
1684. 7mo. 10. Mary Duckett, Daughter of Thomas and Mary.
1685. 6mo. 11. Mary Duckett, Wife of Thomas.
1685. 9mo. 27. John Rhydderch.
1685-6. 1mo. 3. Mary Keite Wife of Thomas.

After 2. 7mo. 1684, the Welsh Friends' meetings, their monthly meeting, were regularly represented at the Philadelphia quarterly meetings, sometimes under the designation "Friends for the Welsh friends, and Skuylkill," or as "the Skuylkill Meeting," "Friends for the other side of Skuylkill," "Friends appearing for Skuylkill monthly meeting," "Friends from the monthly meeting on the other side Skuylkill," and "Skuylkill Meetings," and it was not until after 1688-9, that the designation Haverford monthly meeting was used in Philadelphia quarterly meetings.

WELSH FRIENDS' MEETINGS

The delegates from "over the Skuylkill Meeting" to the quarterly meetings were the prominent men of the meetings. For instance, in 10mo. 1684, Thomas Ellis, Griffith Owen, Thomas Duckett, Henry Lewis, Barnabas Wilcocks, and John Bevan; in 4mo. 1685, Barnabas Wilcocks, George Painter, and William Howell. At this session, Duckett and Wilcocks were placed on the committee to oversee the building of the new meeting house, in Center Square, Philadelphia, to be "50 by 35 feet, and 14 feet to roof." In 7mo. 1685, Thomas Duckett, John Bevan, John Humphreys, Edward Jones, and George Painter, "for the other side of Skuylkill, appeared for the service of the yearly meeting." In 1mo. 1685-6, Griffith Owen, George Painter, John Bevan, Edward Jones, Thomas Duckett, and Paul Saunders. In 4mo. 1686, John Bevan, George Painter, Hugh Roberts, Edward Jones, Thomas Duckett, and John Warner. In 10mo. 1686, Paul Saunders, George Painter, John Jermin, John Warner, Richard Orme. The latter was appointed official grave digger in Philadelphia at two shillings a grave, "if not a big one," by the Philadelphia monthly meeting, 12. 7mo. 1685. After his marriage in this meeting, in 12mo. 1685, to "Mary Tedder, of Harford," Mr. Orme resigned, and Thomas Howell was appointed, 17. 4mo. 1686.

At the quarterly meeting, 7. 1mo. 1686-7, "appeared for the other side of Skuylkill," John Bevan, William Howell, John Roberts, John Evans, and David Meredith. At the next quarterly meeting, Griffith Owen, Hugh Roberts, John Warner, Henry Lewis, David Lawrence, Richard Orme and John Jermin were the representatives. At the next quarterly meeting, held, 3. 7mo. 1687, as before, at "the meeting house on the front of the Delaware," William Howell, Edward Jones, John Roberts, John Bevan, and David Meredith, represented "the Welsh meetings," when the "Harford meeting" contributed £5 toward a fund to give assistance to a Friend whose home was destroyed by fire, and "Merioneth Meeting," gave £6.7.0 for same object, but Radnor could only promise 32s. 6d. Griffith Owen,

WELSH SETTLEMENT OF PENSYLVANIA

Hugh Roberts, John Evans, David Meredith, William Jenkins, and William Howell, attended the next Quarterly. Mr. Duckett as usual representing his meeting. The minutes of the next quarterly meeting, 5. 1mo. 1687-8, "Friends appeared, to attend the meeting:—from Harford, John Bevan, and David Lawrence; from Radnor, Richard Orme, and Reese Peters; from Merrioneth, Edward Jones, and John Roberts; from Skuylkill meeting; Paul Saunders." At the next Quarterly, "William Jenkins, and William Howell, from Harford; David Meredith and John Evans from Radnor;" but "Merryoneth" was not represented. At the quarterly meeting, 2. 6mo. 1688, the German Friends, of the Germantown Friends' meeting, had their first delegation; but none of the Welsh Friends attended this meeting.

The second men's meeting, or monthly meeting, of the Merion and Haverford Welsh Friends, was held at the home of William Shaner, in Radnor, "on the second fifth day of the third month," 1684, when the Radnor preparative meeting was authorized.

The third men's, or monthly meeting of record was held at the house of Hugh Roberts, in Merion, "on the second fifth day of the fourth month," 1684, and the next one, in 5th mo. at the home of John Bevan, in Haverford.

In the earliest years, in fact for twenty-five years, the Welsh "men's meeting," or the monthly meeting for business, was transitional. A minute says, "At our monthly meeting held at Haverford, 22d of 2d month (1698), it is considered that the monthly meeting for business be kept in course here, at Merion, and Radnor." This changing of the place of assembly was the cause of the Welsh monthly meeting being variously named, as before suggested, since the name of the place it was held at was given to that particular men's meeting, hence we find the "Merion Monthly Meeting," the "Haverford Monthly Meeting."

The Welsh Friends of course had monthly meetings for worship, and what they called "First Day Monthly Meetings," and "General Monthly Meetings." It may be that some of these Welsh people could not understand English, and there is a suggestion that Rowland Ellis acted as interpreter sometimes in meetings; but as a whole they were probably an English speaking people, for all their surviving documents are written in English, and well done, both as to writing and expression. Yet, in one of their petitions they said it was their desire "Not to entangle ourselves with laws in an unknown tongue."—Penn's laws in English.

There is evidence that the monthly meeting of the Welsh tract exercised the same authority over its members, as did the Englishmen's monthly meetings elsewhere, and not only had it care of the piety of the Welsh Friends within its jurisdiction, and of ecclesiastical matters, having particular care to find if there were "any loose livers," or "disorderly walkers" among them, but also, as was Friends' custom of old, endeavored to adjust or settle disputes between neighbors, who were members of a Welsh preparative meeting, to prevent them going into the county court with their trouble, for Friends have always had a "testimony against" law courts. The men's meeting of the Welsh Friends maintained committees, or tribunals, to consider personal differences, after the matter between them had been attempted to be adjusted by reference to disinterested parties, members of the meeting; this method failing, the difference was laid before the men's meeting, which endeavored to reason with the disputants, and settle the misunderstanding. Whatever the decision of the meeting was, the two Friends must abide by; but should one of them refuse the arbitrament, the only thing left for the "unruly one" to do was to withdraw from the Society, or for the monthly meeting to "disown" him. Of course, if one of the disputants was a non-Quaker, and spurned the decision, the meeting could go no further in the case, and it generally found its way into court. But the "Quaker method" was more often acceptable, since lawyer's and court fees were avoided.

The Welsh monthly meeting also had cognizance of members "going backward in their outward concerns." It

WELSH SETTLEMENT OF PENSYLVANIA

insisted that business engagements must be kept, and debts paid, and the way of the defaulter was hard indeed, if he was a Welsh Friend. The Welsh "men's meeting" also made it its business to watch the reckless, and if anyone was discovered "venturing too much in the judgment of the elders," be it buying too much land, or what not, he was warned in a friendly spirit, and steered out of the danger of bankruptcy. Everything was done to avoid calamity to the Welsh Friends, especially if it was possible that it might bring a scandal to the meeting. These were the lessons they had learned in the old country, and they transferred these rules into the new. And this was what the Welsh Friends meant when they wrote the President:—"we can declare with an open face to God and man, that we desire to be by ourselves for no other end or purpose, but that we might live together as a civil society; to endeavor to decide all controversaries and debates amongst ourselves in a gospel order, and not to entangle ourselves with laws in an unknown tongue."

And this was the reason these Welsh Friends also sat in their meetings as the legislative assembly of their "barony," and looked after its civic affairs, while nursing the claim they made as a State distinct from every county. But it cannot be proven that the Haverford men's meeting, as a body, ever meddled with the provincial politics, or made up county "tickets," or selected candidates for election, outside of their territory, unless it may have been in the case of Eckley's candidacy, mentioned elsewhere.

The following is an example of the Acts and Orders of this Legislative Meeting, when taking care of the "constituancy." "It is Ordered by the Meeting and consent of the Inhabitants of the Townships of Haverford & Radnor in pursuance of a Law in that Case made yt ye Inhabitants of ye sd two Townships should pay 1 shilling per hundred [? acres] towards ye takeing of woolves."

Other "Acts" concerned line and division fences, stray cattle, and the utilities of the "State." But, when it would seem necessary to have to use force in making an arrest, or in protecting property, the Meeting-Assembly went to the Provincial Council, and handed over to it such matters, as, for instance, to stop Indians from killing the Friends' hogs, mentioned elsewhere.

The Welsh Tract "Assembly" also did police duty for itself, and tried to keep out undesirable inhabitants, as, for instance:—"Our friend John Bevan, haveing laid before this Meeting That divers Persons came over here, and left debts unpaid in those parts and places yt they came from, and the Creditors complaining against ye sd Persons that they did not receive any satisfaction from them for ye sd debts, the ffriends yt are appointed by this Meeting to see to such affairs, are desired to deal with them, if there be any such belonging to this Meeting." How they were to "deal" with these fugitives from obligations is not of record, but the interesting part of this item is that the Assembly-Meeting was the first to govern through "standing committees," which is a recognized and most important portion of the machinery of all of our present-day legislative bodies, and some others. This monthly meeting further assumed to itself the authority of the "General Court," with legislative and taxing power in the "Welsh Towns," and as an Orphans' Court, it appointed guardians for minor children, and if not administrators looked after testamentary proceedings; assisted in settling estates, or apportioning of property, especially land, to heirs, as in the case of the adjustment of the estate of Thomas Ellis, 1688-1698, mentioned elsewhere.

The following matter, one as much secular as canonical, also had the earnest attention of this monthly meeting. We all know, and Butler ("Hudibras," II, 2) confirms it,

"Quakers (that, like lanterns, bear
Their light within them), will not swear,"

And that it is now a long established and proper custom in our courts that anyone having conscientious scruples may select to "affirm," instead of taking a prescribed oath.

WELSH SETTLEMENT OF PENSYLVANIA

But it may not be generally known that the Friends of the Haverford monthly meeting had a considerable part in bringing about this concession, and that they were obliged to help buy it.

In 1704, the statute of 1694-5, by which Quakers were not permitted to testify in any case in court, particularly in criminal cases, where evidence was given under oath, or to serve on juries, or even to hold any office of profit in the government, was confirmed by an act of parliament.

It was understood that the provisions of this act extended to Pensylvania, and disqualified Quakers here, as well as elsewhere. At that time, the important offices in Pensylvania were held by Quakers, and they were in the majority in the assembly; but as they did not hold their positions from the general government of the kingdom, the act did not effect them, yet it did the business of the courts, as the supreme court of Pensylvania held the act extended to Pensylvania, therefore, criminal cases could not be tried. Many important ones* were held-over, and even alleged murderers were released on bail.

This state of affairs obtained for years, until in 1724-5, when the provincial council and the assembly passed what was known as the "Affirmation Act," enabling Quakers to

---

*One of these was that of Hugh Pugh, a millwright, and Thomas, a laborer, charged in Oct. term, 1715, Chester Co. Court, with the murder of Jonathan Hayes, of Marple tp., a justice of the peace, and member of the assembly. (The Welsh Friends, John Parry, Caleb Evans, and David Parry, were fined by the Chester court for refusing to aid the constable in arresting Hugh Pugh, they having conscientious scruples in such matters.) This case, the first for homicide, was tried 17 April, 1718, before David Lloyd, chief justice, and associates, at Chester, and the men found guilty, and sentenced to be hung on 9 May following. On May 8th, they petitioned the Governor for a reprieve, till the King should be heard from as to the legality of their conviction and sentence, claiming that seventeen of the grand jury, and eight of the jury which tried their case were Quakers, and only affirmed contrary to the statute. There is no proof that they were hung.

WELSH FRIENDS' MEETINGS

testify. But as this Pensylvania act had to receive the King's approbation before it was legal and should be in force, the Pensylvania Quakers started out to learn if His Majesty, George the First, would give it freely, if not, what they should do to persuade him. They were not long in learning that the King's apprcvement would have to be purchased from him personally. Thereupon, the Pensylvania Yearly Meeting gave notice to every monthly meeting that collections should be taken up within their jurisdictions to make up a purse for the mercenary monarch.

The part that the Haverford monthly meeting took in this matter is of record in its minutes, as follows:

1725. 13. 3mo. "This meeting refers to the consideration of ffrds:—getting of money to pay for negotiating ye late affirmation act in Great Britain."

12. 6mo. "Lewis David, Thomas Thomas, and Edward William are desired to take frd's contributions in Cash to defray the Charge of having the Royal assent to ye affirmation act & make report thereof at next meeting."

9. 7mo. "The friends appointed to receive ffrd's contributions towards having ye Royal assent to ye Affirmation Act is continued, and advised to press friends to bring it in as soon as may be, in order to be paid to Richard Hill before ye yearly meeting."

9. 10mo. "Edward William produced a Receipt signed by Richard Hill for £8. 18, received of him and Thomas Thomas, towards negotiating the affirmation act, for account of this meeting."

That these first settlers, pioneers in Pensylvania, Welsh Friends all, were sensible of the part they were taking in building a new world, and wished to appear to posterity at their best, both as to their acts and themselves and families, may be presumed from two of their contemporary records.

First, in the minutes of the Haverford (Radnor) monthly meeting, under date of 12. 11mo. 1698, a committee, consisting of John Bevan, Hugh Roberts, Rowland Ellis, and John

WELSH SETTLEMENT OF PENSYLVANIA

Humphreys, who were among the leading men of the Welsh Tract, were appointed "to inspect and view over the [book of] minutes of this monthly meeting, since our arrival here, that it may be placed in order to enter upon Record for the service of generations to come." By entry in 9mo. 1697 it may be learned that this monthly meeting "decided to buy a book in which to enter testimonies concerning ffriends of this monthly meeting." This we take to mean that our Welsh Friends were proud of their acts and proceedings, and wished future generations to profit by not only their teachings, but their experiences.

Secondly, in the minutes of the Merion preparative meeting, under date of 3. 9mo. 1704, "Ordered to file accounts of themselves, Children, servants, and families, and their removal to this country, their place of abode in their native country," &c. "to be kept in Remembrance to Generations to come." Members of the meeting were commanded to bring such accounts to the next meeting. At this sitting, it was also ordered to procure a book in which to enter the births, marriages, deaths and burials of members of the Merion meeting.

That many accounts of members and their families were presented and copied into a book, appears on the minutes of this meeting, but the book into which they were entered as "Remembrance to Generations to come," is said to have been "lost" when the clerk of the Merion meeting carried off its record books at the "separation." But several families kept copies of the accounts filed, and they have been preserved to the present day. These accounts, written by themselves, of the antecedents of the first settlers, supplemented by the certificates of removal from Friends' meetings in the old country, and in several cases by "long drawn out" genealogies in the Welsh tongue, are what makes the pedigrees of these early settlers so substantial.

It appears from the minutes of the Merion meeting that the following members filed sketches of themselves. 1704, 8. 10mo., Dr. Edward Jones, Rowland Ellis, and his uncle,

WELSH FRIENDS' MEETINGS

John Humphrey, "per R. Ellis"; on 5. 11mo., John Roberts, Dr. Thomas Wynne, "per E. Jones"; on 2. 12mo., Edward Rees, Rees John, "per son Richard Jones, of Llwyn-Gwrill, Clynin parish, Merioneth," and on 2. 1mo. 1704-5, William Howard, John Edward, "per brother William Howard," Evan Edward, "per brother William Howard," and Richard Walter.

The below data as to the birth dates of some of the earliest settlers in the first "Towns" of the Welsh Tract, in this connection is of interest. It is from a paper which passed through the hands of Jesse George, and who indentified it, on 1. 22. 1775, as having been memoranda made by Edward Roberts (a son of the minister, Hugh Roberts), when on a visit to Merionethshire, from the original records. Mr. George says that David George was appointed in 1750, by the Radnor Mo. Mtg., to record the births of children of members of the meeting, and that Hugh Roberts, a son of the aforesaid Edward Roberts, gave him this paper. In 1758, Jesse George was appointed to record the births, and he copied Edward Roberts's data into the proper book, "which was all in the British language." It may be noticed that Edward did not give to some of the children the surnames they afterwards used.

Children.	Born.			Parent.	(See page).
Elizabeth Edward,	12.	18.	1671.	John.	91
Sarah Edward,	11.	8.	1673.	"	91
Elizabeth Edward,	3.	14.	1672.	William.	85
Catherine Thomas,	6.	20.	1673.	John.	122
Robert Roberts,	11.	7.	1673.	Hugh.	102
Evan Thomas,	5.	8.	1675.	John.	120
Ellin Roberts,	10.	4.	1675.	Hugh.	102
Catherine Edward,	11.	29.	1676.	William.	85
Evan Edward,	2.	2.	1677.	John.	90
Mary Thomas,	8.	8.	1677.	John.	120
John Evan,	8.	11.	1677.	Robert.	..
Owen Roberts,	10.	1.	1677.	Hugh.	102
Jane David,	2.	28.	1678.	Robert.	83
Martha Jones,	3.	10.	1678.	Edward.	74

WELSH SETTLEMENT OF PENSYLVANIA

Children.		Born.		Parent.	(See page).
Hannah Jones,	7.	22.	1678.	William.	105
Cadwallader Thomas,	11.	4.	1678.	John.	122
Morgan Morgan,	6.	25.	1679.	Cadwallader.	107
Rees Rees,	11.	11.	1678.	Edward.	80
Catherine David,	1.	25.	1680.	Robert.	83
Edward Roberts,	2.	4.	1680.	Hugh.	103
Jonathan Jones,	11.	3.	1680.	Edward.	75
Catherine Rees,	12.	1.	1680.	Edward.	81
Edward Edward,	8.	5.	1681.	John.	90
William Roberts,	3.	26.	1682.	Hugh.	103
Edward Morgan,	6.	22.	1682.	Cadwallader.	107
Sydney Thomas,	6.	14.	1682.	John.	120
Rachel Ellis,	1.	27.	1675.	Robert.*	..
Abel "	1.		1677.	"	..
Moses "	10.	5.	1679.	"	..
Ellis "	12.	2.	1681-2.	"	..
Aaron "	8.		1685.	"	..
Evan "	1.	1.	1687-88.	"	..
Jane "	4.	24.	1690.	"	..

The scope of the "business" of the leaders of the Welsh monthly meeting seems to us to have been very wide, even limitless as far as the concerns and conduct of its members were concerned, for the ministers and elders were the guardians and monitors of the people. But, whatever may be said, or supposed of any other Friends' meeting, in no minutes of theirs does it appear that the ruling Welsh Friends used their authority to the limit. It is the diversity only of their official employment that would be most remarkable, if it was not known they were controlling and regulating immigrants in a new country. And this was the first experience of Quakers in living entirely under the control of the Meeting, for at home surroundings were different, and one might evade "the rules," many of which for this reason were "dead letter" there, but here were enforced, where

---

*"Arrived with their family in Pensylvania about the beginning of the 10mo. 1690. The said Robert [Ellis] died in 10mo. 1697, and his wife [Ellin] within two weeks after."

WELSH FRIENDS' MEETINGS

there was nothing but "Quaker Rules." It was obey, or suffer,—not corporal punishment,—but just the inward suffering that hurts more than any bodily pain. Here, comparison between the Friends and the Puritans, in like conditions, would suggest partisanship. But in time, changed conditions has curtailed the great responsibility of the Friends' ministers and elders.

In addition to the variety of the work put on the monthly meeting, or the leading men and women of it, already mentioned, it may be learned from the records of the Haverford Mo. Mtg. that sometimes matters which should have been settled at home, in the family circle, were laid before the meeting, and incorporated in the minutes, as, on 4. 11mo. 1702, the trouble her father had with Hannah Jones, because she persisted in "keeping company with Rees William," after her father had warned her not to have anything to do with him. He asked aid of the meeting (Women's Radnor Mo. Mtg.), to influence Hannah to obey him. A minute, in 1693, shows the concern of the monthly meeting on account of the tendency of certain Friends, and neighbors, "to follow the vain customs of the world," therefore, a committee from the three meetings, Merion, Haverford and Radnor, was appointed to have "inspection" over these back-sliders, and bring them the sense of the right way they should behave.

In 1695, "disorder at Friends funerals" claimed the attention of the Haverford monthly meeting, for it was reported that some mourners were "remarked for immoderate speaking," and others "for want of seriousness and gravity." And in 2mo. 1703, "it is friends desire that friends be not Restless in meetings, and stand up in Meetings, and turn their heads to Publick friends when they are bearing Testimony; that such be spoken to." In 1696, there was much concern in the monthly meeting because David Powell posted on the meeting house door certain accusations against other Friends (unnamed), "before they were dealt with according to Gospel order." This seems to

WELSH SETTLEMENT OF PENSYLVANIA

indicate that it was the custom at that day to place "testimonies of denial" in prominent positions at a meeting house. In 1726, the representatives to the Philadelphia quarterly meeting from the Welsh meetings are instructed to report "that things amongst us is not as well as we could desire; but a remnant hopes to obtain the victory." This refers to some now unknown disagreement between the majority and the minority in the Haverford Mo. Mtg., and the smaller party was the ministers and elders. On 8. 8mo. 1713, we have an example of arbitration by the monthly meeting, when "Friends appointed to end the differences between David William and John Robert Ellis, reported they have agreed to an award, or determination between them." On the same date, we have a different example of the "work" of the monthly meeting, when "the Merion overseers bring a complaint of Edward Rees against Joshua Owen that he does not take care to pay him some money that has been due to him several years. Edward Jones and John Roberts appointed to speak to him to take care to pay his just debts." In 9mo. 1717, the matter of "regulation of weddings at private houses considered, on advice of the yearly meeting, which desired marriages to be only in the meeting house, excepting by permission of a monthly meeting,"—this rule was an echo of their ancestors, members of the Church of Rome, and one still enforced by "the greatest hierarchy on earth."

The matter and manner of courtships and marriages among these Welsh Friends was one of the first consideration, and their rules were firmly maintained, and impressed on the young and their elders. The rite was clean. Betrothals carelessly entered into, resulting often in "broken engagements," were not possible, and "membership" be retained, for even there were rules of courtship to be observed, and they were enforced, therefore, though the country was thinly settled, and homes of the betrothed far apart, bund-

WELSH FRIENDS' MEETINGS

ling was not tolerated, as it was at that time in other American colonies, and long subsequently in this, "up the State."*

In this matter, the Haverford Mo. Mtg. has the following minute, "That all young men among Friends make known their intentions to their parents, or guardians, before they acquaint the woman's relations, and make it known to the woman's parents, or guardian, before they speak to them [that is, before the young couple ask consent together], and if any do otherwise, they shall condemn the same."

---

*From the Men's and Women's minutes of the Concord monthly meeting, 4. 2. 1740, Women Friends complained of "Mary Wright, now House," as follows "for going to be married by a Priest, and marrying in a very uncommon way, by putting off her Close and putting on a shift, in order to screne her husband from her former husband's debts." Mary for this, and "marrying out," was disowned, 3. 4. 1741.

This seems to have been a way of evading the Provincial law as to certain old debts, and the celebrated statesman, Benjamin Franklin, says in his Autobiography that he just "took to wife" the young woman (a presumed widow who passed as his wife, and was the alleged mother of Franklin's bastard son, Gov. William Franklin, of New Jersey.—See Pa. Magazine, Sept. 1911), and who was the mother of Mrs. Sarah Bache after this "wedding," and no marriage ceremony was performed, although he was then, and afterwards, connected with Christ P. E. Church, Philadelphia, else he could have been compelled to pay his wife's former "husband's" debts, which were considerable when he disappeared, although this "husband" had a wife living when he "married" Franklin's subsequent "wife." He must have known of the trick of shifting such debts, but preferred to have only a "common law wife," which turned out to be a very disagreeable reminiscence for some descendants of his daughter,—his son had no issue.

Mr. Watson, in "Annals of Philadelphia," also mentions that in 1734:—"A widow of Philadelphia was married in her shift, without any other apparel upon her from a supposition prevalent then that such a procedure would secure her husband in the law from being sued for any debts of his predecessor," and that "Kalm, in 1748, confirms this fact as a common occurrence when her husband dies in debt. She thus affects to leave all to his creditors." The same traveller tells of a woman going from her home to the house of her intended husband in her shift only, and he meets her on the way and clothes her before witnesses, saying, "I lend these clothes."

WELSH SETTLEMENT OF PENSYLVANIA

But, this order obeyed, did not release a Meeting from appointing a committee to find out the moral standing of the candidates for matrimony, and also, if possible, to learn if both were "clear" to marry. "Having declared their intentions of marriage before this Meeting," a committee of several elderly members was "ordered to inspect as to their Clearness, and to bring an account thereof to the next Meeting." There never was any question but that the candidates were thoroughly "inspected," for if there were ever any cases of bigamy among Friends, they never made a minute of it. A month after this "declaration," the couple, "having laid their Intention of Marriage the second time before this Meeting, and nothing but Clearness found on each side," the candidates are "left to their freedom to proceed therein," and stand up and make their vows one to another and that they took each other in marriage, when the "Spirit moved them" to do so before any Public Meeting of Friends.

This orderly proceeding in the matter of the second important event of life, had everything to do with the orderly, clean life in the Welsh Tract, in the years it was virtually under the care of Welsh Friends.

Whether all young Friends approached marriage in the solemn manner that the following young Quaker did, I do not know, since there are not enough similar confessions preserved to decide, but this one certainly went about it deliberately. Richard Davies, of Cloddean cochion, and Welsh Pool, (or Walsch Pole, as Leland wrote the name), in Montgomeryshire, who was one of the subscribing witnesses, on 11 July, 1681, to Penn's "Conditions and Concessions to Adventurers for Land," and who had a patent from Penn, dated in June and July, 1682, for 5,000 acres of the Welsh Tract land, as set forth elsewhere as "Company No. 7," tells in his autobiography how "the Good Lord alone provided an help-meet" for him, after, as he says, "I prayed unto Him that she might be of His own providing, for it was not yet manifest to me where she was, or who she was."

His is an unconventional love-story:—

"But, one time, as I was at Horslydown Meeting, in Southwark, I heard a woman Friend open her mouth, by way of testimony against an evil, ranting spirit that did oppose Friends much in those days.

"It came to me from the Lord that that woman was to be my wife, and to go with me to the country, and to be an help-meet for me.

"After Meeting, I drew somewhat near to her, but spoke nothing, nor took any acquaintance with her. Nor did I know when, or where I should see her again. I was very willing to let the Lord order it, as it seemed best to Himself, and therein I was easy.

"In time, the Lord brought us acquainted with one another. She confessed she had some sight of the same thing that I had seen concerning her.

"So, after some time, we parted, and I was freely resigned to the will of God.

"When we came together again, I told her, if the Lord did order her to be my wife, she must come with me to a strange country, where there were no Friends but what God, in time, might call and gather to Himself.

"Upon a little consideration, she said, if the Lord should order it so, she must go with her husband, though it were to the wilderness.

"Being somewhat sensible of the workings of God upon her spirit in this matter, she was willing to consider in her mind as to what He wrought in her. But by harkening to one who had not well weighed the matter, she became disobedient to what God had revealed to her, which brought great sorrow and trouble upon her.

"I went to see her in this poor condition, and rested satisfied with the will of God in this concern, being freely resigned if the Lord had wrought the same thing in her, as was in me, to receive her as His gift to me.

WELSH SETTLEMENT OF PENSYLVANIA

"After some time, we waited upon the Lord together.

"She arose, and declared before me, and the other Friends who had begot doubts, and reasonings in her mind, that, in the name and power of God, she consented to be my wife, and to go along with me, wither the Lord should order us.

"I said, in the fear of the Lord, 'I receive thee as the Gift of God to me.'"

"So I rested," concludes Mr. Davies, "satisfied with the will of God, for a farther accomplishment of it," that she would not back out again, but would marry him. "They were married, and lived happily ever afterwards," and had a son, David Davies, who was living at the time Mr. Davies signed the "Concessions."

The solemn, stilted style of "the greatest Quaker of them all," in his love-making letters, when he was past 51 years, to the homely woman, over 30 years old, who became his second wife on 11 Nov. 1695, are reproduced to show the acme of Friends' love-letters of the period. However, we should make some allowance for Friend William, as he had been schooled in "the gayest Court of Christendom." As these two letters were sent to Hannah's father to read first, before handing them over to her, it is evident that Mr. Penn himself now bowed to the custom prevalent among the Friends, which the Haverford monthly meeting insisted upon being observed, as above.

"1st. 12mo. 1694-5.

"I cannot forbeare to Write where I cannot forebeare to Love as I love my dearest Hannah and if yt be a fault, till she ceases to be so lovely, I need no Apology for it. Receive, then, my Dearest Heart, the Embraces of the best love I have, that lives & flows to thee every day, with Continual desires for thy felicity every way: more especially in the best things wch setts all to rights, & gives a peace above the little & low interruptions of this world. Suffer not anything of it to disturbe or abate thy satisfaction, but feel thy peace bottom'd upon that which is unchangeable. o meet me there, myn own Dearest, in thy retired walks & recesses from the world; & lett our fellowship be enlarged in that nobler Relation, wch time cannot dissolve; which gives us Courage, Sweetness, affection, truth & Constancy in the discharge of our Lower relation. The Lord in his wisdom & goodness,

WELSH FRIENDS' MEETINGS

bless comfort, fortefy & settle thy minde & spirit more and more, above every careful thought, and anxious and doubtful reflection, with wch the most worthy, tender, & humble spirits are too often assaulted and but too incident to disquiet themselves with. In all which, my heart still loves & embraces thee above every other worldly comfort, of which thou haust a proof in thy last receipt, wch, tho I held the lower part too neer, & made it in part illegible I read enough to be sensible & Concerned with most endeared affection for my poore deare H. and rejoyced yt last time it seemed over. * * * Now, my Dearest, I will say no more, only remember the receipt for the eyes, & apply it, and at all times, & in all conditions remember thou art sure of the love and friendship of Him that is more than he could ever tell thee. Thyn Whilst.,
"WM. PENN."

"10th. 7mo. 1695.

"Most Deare H. C.

"My best love embraces thee wch springs from ye fountaine of Love & life, wch Time, Distance nor Disapointments can ever ware out, nor ye floods of many & great Waters ever Quench. Here it is dearest H—— yt I behold, love, and vallue thee, and desire, above all other Considerations, to be known, received & esteemed by thee. And Lett me Say, that the loveliness yt the tendring & blessed Truth hath beutified thee with, hath made thee amiable in my eyes, above many, & for yt it is my heart, from the very first, has cleaved to thee. Did I say above many, ay, above all, & yt is my confidence in this thing at all times, to my Selfe and others. o let us meet here, most Dear H! the comfort is unspeakable, and the fellowship undesolvable. I would perswade my self thou art of the same minde, tho it is hard to make thee say so. yet yt must come in time, I hope & beleive; for why should I love so well & so much where I am not wellbeloved? Take it not amiss: I have no other way of Convers, let my letters have some place if I deserve any; tho I hope thou art sensible of me in yt in wch we can never be seperated; but the time draws neer, in which I shall enforce this subject beyond all scruple, yet till then I must tell thee, & ever that thou art most entirely beloved of
"Thy unchangeable FRIEND W. P."

Although the Welsh may be, and were, of musical tastes, and, like the Irish, had a harp peculiar to themselves, there is not even a tradition that the Welsh Friends over the Schuylkill were inclined to music, singing and dancing, and so it is safe to imagine that music and fine arts, and classic

WELSH SETTLEMENT OF PENSYLVANIA

literature were not parts of their life. Yet, they were far removed from boors, and had literary taste along congenial lines for it is on record that the Radnor monthly meeting voted "£40 by the year to encourage him [William Bradford] to continue in the art and practice of printing," and this was a very liberal subsidy considering the scarcity of cash at that time.

On 5mo. 14, 1720, there is a minute, in the Radnor Mo. Mtg. records, as to the printing, at his wish, of the MS left by Ellis Pugh, who "in the time of his long sickness had composed divers religious points contained in a few sheets accommodating to the understanding of illiterate, mean people, which he earnestly desired might be published in the British tongue, and sent to his native country, as Friends might see Service." Twelve Friends were appointed by each of the monthly meetings of Haverford and Gwynedd, to consider this weighty matter, "they reported unity and satisfaction, and recommended the publication." Thomas Pugh, a Welshman, was a bookseller in Philadelphia in 1702.

It is elsewhere noted that John Humphrey, of Haverford, in his will, dated 1699, gave £10 towards the expense of reprinting, in Welsh, "The Testimony of the Twelve Patriarchs, and The Sons of Jacob." Up to 1702, this had not been done, as the money was then loaned to the Haverford Meeting. And in 1723-4, the Radnor monthly meeting subscribed for fourteen copies of Sewell's "History of the Quakers," for the members of the preparative meetings of Merion and Radnor.

It does not appear that the Welsh Friends experienced trouble here in their first years as they had had in the old country on the hat question, so it may be presumed they sat "covered" in the Provincial Court, without creating comment. That Friends chose to wear their hats in places where others removed theirs, as a mark of respect for the law, or the service, be it in court, or in church, was not a fad which they clung to obstinately, for the general explanation of their custom is that the hat is as much a garment as any of the clothing of a man, and that it is just as senseless to uncover the head as to take off the coat, or the shoes, in court, or church, or meeting.* And, if we are to believe Pepys, in the seventeenth century, in his day, it was not remarkable that men sat in the "steeple house" wearing hats, for he records: "To church and heard a simple fellow open the praise of church musique and exclaiming against men wearing their hats on in the church." and again, that he saw a minister "preach with his hat off, . . . which I never saw before." At that time the hat was an integral part of a man's costume, and Pepys himself apparently wore his hat all the time, excepting in bed, for he records: "caught a strange cold in my head by flinging off my hat at dinner."

However, from 1707-8, when the country began to be peopled with promiscuous inhabitants, especially descendants of those who had persecuted Quakers in the old country, the "burning question," "Had Quakers the right to wear their hats in the Court of Chester?" was a popular one in non-Quaker Chester Co. The final answer, and settlement of the query, came about in this way in 1720. One day, in the Chester Court, the Quaker lawyer's, John Kinsey's, hat was knocked off by a tipstaff, when he refused to remove it upon

---

*John Churchman, of Philadelphia, a Friends' minister of the Gospel, in his Journal, 1738, tells of being joined in his journey in Maryland, by Mr. John Browning, of Cecil Co., "a Friend from Sassafrass" meeting. He relates that Mr. Browning, "some time before, had been convinced of the blessed Truth"; that he had been a member of the Church of England, and a vestryman; that "he had felt a scruple in his mind about taking off his hat when entering the church yard, so called, fearing it was superstitious adoration of the grounds from its supposed holiness, but would take it off when he entered the worship house, and walk uncovered to his pew. But after a time could not uncover his head until what they called Devine Service began." On his death bed, Mr. Browning told his wife to have the Friends place the tomb-stones, which he had prepared for his parents' graves, for hearth stones in the new brick house he was then having built, which was what he intended doing himself, as he, as a Friend, did not approve of monuments.

WELSH SETTLEMENT OF PENSYLVANIA

the announcement of the opening of the court. The Quakers of the country were very indignant, and the matter came formally not only before the Chester monthly meeting, but the Haverford monthly meeting, which presented a remonstrance to Gov. Keith, signed by Richard Hayes, Morris Morris, Anthony Morris, Evan Evans, Rowland Ellis, Reese Thomas, &c. The Governor ruled that Friends, should they so desire, may wear their hats in Court, and especially in the Court of Chancery.

This reminds me that visitors to the old Merion meeting house are shown a wooden pin in the wainscoting above the elder's benches. About this pin itself, or its location, there is nothing remarkable, but the guide will inform you that it was on a similar pin, that used to be in the same position, William Penn hung his hat whenever he addressed this meeting. So much was said about this at the bi-centennial, that some rascal stole William Penn's hat pin, and, therefore, the similar, new peg in the wall.

Of course, it is possible that William Penn visited the Merion meeting, when he was the second time in his province, but I have seen no contemporary record of it, and only know of the tradition, the same that connects him with the house built by Robert Owen, it is claimed about 1695, which is that he "often made it his stopping place whilst travelling through these parts." For this reason the old house has been known in late years as "the Penn Cottage."*

But the good evidence that he was present at least once at a meeting of the Haverford monthly meeting may be found in the Journal of Thomas Story, the English Friends minister who came over here on a visit in 1698-99, stopping

---

*This once little stone house, told of elsewhere, which stands on Montgomery Ave., back of Wynnewood RR station was changed from its original appearance about 1873, and subsequently to its present appearance, yet the walls of the original house remain. When Col. Owen Jones's father built the mansion house near the Owen house, and removed from the latter into it, the older house became the farmer's house, but before that, every occupant of it held a prominent

WELSH FRIENDS' MEETINGS

most of his time with Samuel Carpenter, in Philadelphia. He records:—"I remained here [Philadelphia] till the 2d of the 11th mo. [1699], and then went in company of the governor and other friends to a general meeting at Haverford, among the Welsh, wherein we met with great refreshment. . . . After the meeting, the governor returned to Philadelphia, and I staid at a Friend's house, accompanied by my near friend, Dr. Griffith Owen, who, with our valued Friend Hugh Roberts, and some others, went with me the next morning to a meeting at Germantown."

Mr. Story says he was again, on 5. 1mo. 1699, at a very large gathering at the Haverford monthly meeting, and returned after it directly to Philadelphia. On 13. 10mo. 1699, he records that he was with Penn on a visit to Chester, that they dined with Caleb Pusey, two miles off, and they went to lodge with John Blunston, eight miles off. And on 20. 10mo. without Penn, he went "to 4th day meeting, which fell in course at Haverford-West, among the Welsh Friends, and Griffith Owen was with me. The meeting was small, no Notice being given, but comfortable. And that night we lodged with John Bevan. The next day, Radnor meeting falling of course, we went to it. It was small, for want of Notice of our coming, and because of the Badness of the Weather, for it rained and froze at the same time. That night we lodged with Richard Orms. The day following we took Merion meeting, also in course. It was large and heavenly, for Friends had heard from the former meetings that we were going that way, and several from thence met us there likewise. After meeting, we went with John

---

social and official position in Merion. In the builder's time, it could have been called the local court house, since as the magistrate, the judiciary head of the township, Robert Owen, here held his court for the hearing of cases that were not such that the monthly meeting could adjust. His son, Evan Owen, inherited his father's judicial mind, but was a magistrate in Philadelphia, and Robert Jones became His Majesty's Justice in Merion.

WELSH SETTLEMENT OF PENSYLVANIA

Roberts, and lodged at his House that night, and the next morning returned to Philadelphia." On 19. 1mo. 1699, Mr. Story attended the Burlington meeting with William Penn.

Not only were the men of the Welsh, or Haverford or Radnor monthly meeting active in what could be termed "church work," but the women also had a large part to perform. For it is in the records of the Women Friends of this monthly meeting, after 1684, they were obliged, occasionally, to take up collections of corn, wheat, &c., for the relief of unfortunates in their midst, who had to be helped along when their crops failed, or were the newcomers who needed assistance till their time of harvest and plenty. Or a loan would be made by the monthly meeting, "to collect [for] him, out of each meeting, effects to buy him a Cow and Calfe at Spring, provided he doth repay it, if he be able, hereafter. It being his proposall to ffriends when he requested the same." Or, "It was ordered as followeth: That Three pds of the Collection of Haverford & Merion is ordered by this Meeting to be paid to assist . . . to build him a Home, vizt; Thirty shillings of each Township." "At our Women friends meeting, held at Haverford, ye 17th of 1st month, 1697-8, it is ordered thirty Shillings out of the Collection for John Cadwalader to help him att his p'sent necsity." And in another instance, "it was ordered by this Meeting that Cadder Morgan and James Thomas do receive the voluntary gift of Meirion Meeting to assist . . . . . in his present distress, he having sustained loss by fires, that Richard Ormes and Stephen Bevan, for Radnor, and Maurice Llewellyn and David Humphrey, of Haverford, to receive the voluntary subscriptions of each of the sd Townships, to the sd use." Such items show that there was in early days of first settlement that neighborly interest in the Welsh Tract common later among the pioneers of the "middle west."

But the charities of this monthly meeting were not confined to local needs, as it contributed £60. 14. 11. collected by John Roberts, and sent the money, towards aiding desti-

WELSH FRIENDS' MEETINGS

tute Friends in and about Boston, Mass., when being persecuted by the fanatics there. And on another occasion, sent £10. 10. 4. towards a fund raised for the redemption of the wife and children of John Hanson, who were carried off by Indians in New England, in 1724. This monthly meeting was also generous towards weak preparative meetings, and always prompt in payment to the quarterly meeting its proportion, and upon the erection of "the new Meeting House," in the city, the contributions of the preparative meetings were Merion, £6.5.0, Haverford, £6.0.0, and Radnor, £1.7.6. This indicates the relative ability of these meetings to raise money, and possibly the extent of membership in each.

From the earliest times, the meeting houses were recognized as centers of information in the Welsh Tract, and we find that on the first establishment of the postal service, notice of the time of departure of mails was ordered to be tacked on meeting house doors, where also were placed the notices of the time and place of receiving quitrent, notices of strayed domestic animals, &c.

At the very first, the Haverford Monthly Meeting began being careful about those coming from abroad asking to be admitted into membership. In all cases the old World Friends' custom of requiring Certificates of Membership in good standing, and orderly removal, and transference from the meeting the applicant had claimed to be connected with, were required and demanded, and the old world meetings sustained Haverford Mo. Mtg. in this. It may be seen there was good reason for this cautiousness in early times from the following extract from one of the earliest certificates filed with the Haverford monthly meeting, though it is undated, and without stating what meeting gave it, but evidently one in Merionethshire, and possibly one near Dolgelley (phonetically written Dolgethle by Leland). It is that of "Evan ap William Powell, late of the parish of Llanvaehreth, Merioneth," who removed with his wife, Gwen, and two sons, David, then married, and Philip, and

WELSH SETTLEMENT OF PENSYLVANIA

his daughter-in-law, Gainor, with her two small children:—
"Whereas, Likewise many have been known to transport themselves, or were transported upon account of their Evill doeings, as theft, murther, Debts, or running away in passionate discontentedness with parents, wifes, or the like," therefore, this Meeting took pleasure in giving this family a clean bill. This description of some of the early Pensylvania settlers, not from Wales, as the signers were unlikely acquainted with the class of immigrants from elsewhere, was signed by Messrs. Evan and Hugh Rees, Ellis Davids, Evan, Lewis, Rowland, David and Robert Owen, William and Owen Humphrey, Humphrey Howell, Griffith Ellis, Griffith and David John, Rees and John Evans, and Richard Davies.

These certificates, originally intended as vouchers for the good character of the bearers, have become valuable genealogical assets for descendants of the Quaker immigrants, since they indicate the home of the immigrant, and often told something of his people. The certificates, and the written accounts of immigrants required to be filed with meetings by them, are the sources of much genealogical data, hence through these papers we can identify almost any family of Quaker settlers. This fact appears of more importance when we read in Mr. Diffenderffer's "German Immigration into Pensylvania, 1700-1775," that descendants of these immigrants bewail the dearth of information as to the antecedents of the Germans, and a knowledge of the towns, and districts even whence they removed, for they brought no genealogy with them, so back of the German settlers, with very few exceptions, their family history is as blank as a negro's.

MERION, HAVERFORD, RADNOR

As already noted, the Welsh Friends of Merion and Haverford, in Nov. 1684, selected sites for their burial places. Up to this time, there had been in Merion only two deaths in 1682, five in 1683, and none in 1684. But there is no similar minute preserved which records that these Friends considered the erection of meeting houses for their neighborhoods, at so early a period. From their minutes, we learn that from 4mo. 1684 to 22. 2 mo. 1698, the monthly meetings were at the private houses of Hugh Roberts and John Bevan, when they began to take place at the Merion meeting house. But from this, we are not to imagine there was no public meeting place in Merion before 1698, as there are a few items, as below, that proved the Merion Friends had a meeting house as early as 3mo. 1689. It may have been a log house, or a stone building, but no record has turned up guaranteeing its material, or its quality, nor the location of such a meeting house, unless as tradition says, it stood just east of the present house. And, if we are to have any confidence in Friends' records, there certainly was some building used for public worship here for the accommodation of the Merion preparative meeting, as there is the record, under 19, 3mo. 1693, of a wedding "in a solemn and public assembly in our public meeting place at Merion." A private house would hardly be thus described.

From the minutes of the Merion Women Friends' meetings, 1689, 3mo. "Paid towards the meeting house, one shilling, and 4½ bushel of wheat, @ 3s. 6d per bushel."

1689, 8mo. "Paid towards the meeting house."

1690, 11mo. "2 bushel of wheat paid to B. S. for swiping [sweeping] the meeting house."

1693, 10mo. "Paid Blainch Sharplus for cleaning ye meeting house, 8. 0." [This Blanch Sharpless, the caretaker of

WELSH SETTLEMENT OF PENSYLVANIA

the Merion meeting house, was a widow at that time, and on 11mo. 23, 1694, she married at the Haverford meeting, Owen Morgan, widower, of Haverford, and was succeeded as caretaker by "Tho Phey."]

During the days of the commemoration of the present stone meeting house of Merion Friends, or the bi-centennial of its commencement or completion, there was, as could be expected, since the question was not settled in the minds of some, and there was some petty jealousy on the part of members of some other meeting whose meeting house is supposed to rival that of Merion in age, inquiry as to the true date, or proof of date when the Merion meeting house was erected, and this while above the heads of the disputants was the positive assurance that it was "Built in 1695." Of course, it is evident that the present date-tablet was made and placed in the gable wall in the year 1829, on the order of the "Hicksite Friends," after they came into sole control of the property, when they repaired the building. This should strengthen the claim as to "1695" being the correct date of completion, for who would accuse the then trustees of the meeting of manufacturing and transmitting a false date. For this reason, this date-stone cannot be classed with "tombstone evidence," which is never reliable unless we know by whose authority the inscription was made, and the quality of his integrity and veracity. Apparently there was once another, smaller date-stone in the front gable, about the size to state "BUILT IN 1695, which was stolen, as was the one from the old Rowland Ellis house back of Bryn Mawr. In both cases the niche in which it rested is prominent.

Though it is of little or no consequence now whether the Merion meeting house, as it stands, was, as its date-stone says, built in 1695, or was not, and whether, or not, the so-called Hicksite Friends can make good their statement, the fact is, that it was on this spot, in this house, or its predecessor, that the Welsh Friends held their early "town meet-

WELSH FRIENDS' MEETINGS

ings"; first considered together formally the needs of their "barony," after attending to their spiritual needs, and both under the leadership of their ministers and elders, for here, no less than in any of the American colonies, the "Church" was paramount at the beginning, yet it is a subject interesting archeologically.

Of this date tablet, which from its position it may be supposed records the year of completion of the building, although it is not a cap-stone, just as a "corner-stone" would have told the time of its beginning, the two deceased local authorities, William J. Buck, and Dr. George Smith, are on record as saying that "this was the means of leading many astray, they supposed the present edifice had been erected at that date [1695], whereas, it was the date of the erection of the original building whose place it supplanted eighteen years later." And further, "this has now been so long and widely published that the impression will not be so readily removed." These archeologists decided, "the first meeting house was of wood, built in 1695, and used till 1713, when the present one [of stone] was built." They agreed that the date "1829," also on the tablet, referred to the time when the rough stone of which the house was built were overcast with cement to make them appear like something better, or uniform, and when the building was generally overhauled and repaired by the Hicksite branch when it entered upon possession.

Unfortunately, the minutes of the Merion Men's Meeting are wanting in the very years so necessary for data of the first meeting house, as the minutes between 6 mo. 1686 and 5 mo. 1693 have been lost. But, thankful for the little that has survived concerning the Merion meeting, and its house, in the earliest years, I here assemble what data there is extant in relation to the meeting house that came before Merion men Friends in their meetings, but first giving two little items, of some importance in this discussion, from the extant minutes of the Merion Women Friends' meetings,

WELSH SETTLEMENT OF PENSYLVANIA

"In ye year 1694, an account of what was laid out of Merion Women's collection: [paid] Tho Phey 2 bushels and half bushels of wheat for cleaning ye meeting house, 8. 0."

"1695, 3mo. 9th. For cleaning ye [meeting] houses, having received 3s. of collection. Lay'd out £1. 13, 2. Contributions in wheat, bushels and half bushels."

There is no question that there was a "Merion meeting house" about the year 1700, as Friend Thomas Story, in his Journal, under 15. 10mo, 1699, records, "this day held a large meeting at the Merion meeting house." And the extant minutes of the Merion Men Friends' meetings, in 1700-1705, tell that these assemblies were held regularly in the meeting house of Merion, and that in 1700-1702, an addition was built to the Merion meeting house, and paid for. and in 1702-3, sundry items of hardware, &c., for the Merion meeting house were ordered and paid for. And all these little items suggest they were procured for a newly built house. But the minutes of the Merion Men's Meeting between 5 mo. 1693 and 8mo. 1699 are extant and accessible, and it was within these years that the present stone house, the "Hicksites" advertised, in 1829, on the tablet, was built, yet the minutes up to 1699, record nothing whatever of such work, which would be looked after by the men Friends of the meeting. In order to appreciate this, it can be seen in the extant minutes of the same body, as below, that it was the custom at that time, to record in their minutes items the like we would expect to find in them between 1693-99, if building the present stone house, before, or about 1695.

1702-3, 4. 12mo. A minute under this date, of the Merion Men's Meeting, records a call for cash contributions to pay for an addition to the meeting house, the minute reading: "griffith John is continued [as collector] to speak to those that have not paid their subscriptions towards building the addition to the meeting House, and to receive it, and to bring account thereof to the next meeting." In the absence of any details as to this addition, it is presumed it referred to building the stone kitchen and warming room for the females, which adjoined the meeting house, on the west side, and was there many years for the accommodation of Friends coming from a distance, and spending a whole day at a meeting in cold weather. According to these minutes, the usual meetings for worship and business were held in the meeting house during the year 1700-1705, therefore, whatever this "addition" was, the work of building it did not interfere with the use of the main building, and it may have been the kitchen that was the "addition," as supposed, and not the "transcept," as has also been claimed by those who imagined the "nave" was first portion of the meeting house built. But expert builders have examined the building to see if there was anything in this idea, and have declared the house was built all at one time, and just as it now stands, excepting the stucco embellishment inflicted on it in 1829, and interior partitions, a uniform and choice little piece of architecture.

Apparently, the subscriptions referred to did not come in satisfactorily, or the cost of the "addition" was more than the estimate, for there was not money enough to pay off the charge in the year 1706, when, in the 2d and 3d months of that year, Evan Owen (son of the Friends' minister, Robert Owen, deceased), Edward Cadwalader, Moses Roberts, Evan Jones, Jonathan Wynne and John David, desired permission of the Merion meeting to add their subscriptions to the collection to help pay for the "addition." The list of subscribers to this building fund has not been preserved.

In themselves, they are little things, but the following acts were of sufficient interest at the time to be noted, and like many trivial matters, they have been preserved to us, while those of great importance to us have not been. On 5. 1mo. 1702-3, the Men's Meeting "ordered that Robert Roberts make a cubord [cupboard, or closet] in ye meeting House to the use of ye Meeting to keep ffriends Books or papers." Robert seems to have filled the order, but not as well as he should, or something had happened to "ye cubord," for, on 7. 3mo. 1703, Thomas Jones was ordered to

WELSH SETTLEMENT OF PENSYLVANIA

get hinges and a lock for this meeting house closet. It looks as if a burglar had visited the Merion meeting house, as on the same day, Owen Roberts was ordered to speak with David Maurice, (who may have been the caretaker), "concerning securing the meeting house," and John Moore, (probably a blacksmith), was ordered "to make hooks and staples to the meeting House Windows." John was also commissioned "to make a grybeing how [grubbing-hoe] to the use of the meeting." This was in the month of May, and the ground about the probably new building would need to be graded. Or possibly there had been no trespass on the meeting house, and the new hooks and staples were necessary for the new building, for, under the same date, 7 May, 1703, Owen Roberts and Robert Jones were "to gett boardes sowed for Benches, and for the Loft." From this item, it looks as if a new building was being slowly completed and fitted up. John Moore was certainly slow about his work, for a month later he had not filled his order, nor had Thomas Jones, and were so reported to the Men's Meeting, but they were "continued," and in the following month, Thomas had fixed the book closet, but Maurice had not "secured" the house, therefore, on 3. 7mo. Sept. John Roberts, Owen Roberts, and Robert Jones were appointed to see carpenters "to secure the meeting House," This may not have been, however, to make the meeting house "burglar proof," but may have meant anything from stopping leaks to putting a roof on a new or old meeting house.

If these extant items refer entirely to an addition to the new meeting house at Merion, it will be seen they are few, and that they refer to a period after "1695," and are the earliest references to any work on a new meeting place for the Merion meeting. It further appears in the minutes of the Merion Men's monthly meeting, that John Roberts acted as the treasurer of what we may suppose was the building fund, and that this money was accumulated by subscriptions from individuals and from other meetings, but whether all for the "addition," or in the most for the new building, it is only a guess. However, whatever was built, was finished and partly paid for before 6mo. (August), 1703, for on 6 August, this year, John Roberts reports, his account showing the "balance due ffriends £2. 19. 11," and of this amount he himself owed £1. 8. 5, (probably the balance of his subscription), which he proposed to cancel with his bill "for Sawing upon ye account of ye meeting," as he conducted a sawmill. As to the balance, or £1. 11. 6, he said it would have to be determined whether he, or the executors of Robert Owen, deceased, should pay this to the meeting, as the balance due it from contributors. He said if it was his obligation, he would let it also go towards paying his bill for sawing out timbers, for the meeting owed him this much. He also reported that he had paid himself "out of ye poores taxe, £2. 10. 0," "in sawing in behalf of ye Meeting." The following is the only other accounting that is extant, made by Mr. Roberts to the Merion Men's meeting, and it may be seen is all in the matter of the "addition."

1703, 3d. 1mo. Paying for work on House
                for the addition to it.

Presented accts of
Richard Thomas, due him for work   £1. 12. 0.
Received from Margaret Thomas   10

Richard Thomas   Bal. £1 02. 0.
Robert Thomas for work on meeting House 05. 0.
Moses Roberts   "   "   "   "   03. 9.
Evan Griffith   "   "   "   "   01. 8.
    All paid. (7. 3mo. 1703).

It seems that Griffith John who was continued as collector of "slow" subscriptions, in Feb. 1702-3, was replaced by Thomas Jones, as the latter reported, on 3. 10. 1703, "he hath fully paid what remains in his hands of the subscription monies he was appointed to receive." This balance is not stated. It was probably paid to John Roberts, as treasurer, as he endorsed, "the accounty viewed."

WELSH SETTLEMENT OF PENSYLVANIA

Messrs. Buck and Smith, and others following them, decided, as above said, that "the first meeting house was of wood, built in 1695." This, by the extracts from the extant minutes of the Merion men's monthly meeting, we can see was wrong, for there was a Merion meeting house long before 1695. They also held that this wooden meeting house was "used till 1713, when the present one [of stone] was built." As to "1713," anon. As to the wooden building being the meeting house in 1695-1713, it does not seem probable in the face of some data of record. We shall see that the date "1713" was at the wrong end of the life of the stone house, for that was the year in which it was entirely finished.

From the items I have furnished, and from some yet to give, I am of the opinion that the stone meeting house of Merion was begun as far back as in 1691, when it was possible for the Merion Friends to begin building on land they owned; that the date "1695" was only presumed as the building date, because that was the year in which this meeting had its deed for the burial ground, as we shall see; that the stone house was built slowly, and as the money was contributed, we have evidence; that about 1695, it was so far advanced that it could be used under favorable conditions; that up to this time, a one-story log building was "our public place of meeting," as was the case in other parts of the country; that the "addition" to the meeting house, in 1702, was either the kitchen, or addition meant to build some more of the house under construction; that "securing" the meeting house, in 1703, meant roofing what was finished; that in May, 1703, it was far enough progressed to put in the benches, and floor the loft. But that it was then far from finished, may be seen by the following items, in the following year, and up to 1713.

From the minutes of the Merion men's monthly meeting.
1703-4, 2mo. 7, and 4mo. 2. "Edward Rees, Edward Jones, Owen Roberts, Evan Harry, Rowland Richard,

WELSH FRIENDS' MEETINGS

Robert Jones, and John Roberts, ordered to see for stones to build a meeting house, and to get workmen to dig for them."

This is the first reference of stone in connection with the new building. "To build a meeting house," looks at first reading as if there was meeting house to be built elsewhere, or as if Merion meeting was now about to begin building one for itself, but it was only the scribe's awkwardness of expression.

1704, 9mo. (Nov.), 3. "The workmen employed by this meeting to dig stone, desiring to be paid, Edward Rees, and Griffith John are desired to answer them untill friends have an opportunity to collect them." That is, the committee must see the workmen and tell them to wait till the meeting could collect the money. This shows the money was collected as the work progressed, and that payments were made as they came due.

1704, 10mo. 8. It was ordered to collect money "to pay workmen for digging stone to the Meeting house." Here we have the definite article for the indefinite.

1704, 11mo. 5. John Roberts, as the treasurer, reported that he has a balance in hand of 13s. 2d, after advancing money to pay "for digging the Stone to ye meeting House." till it could be collected. He also reported that "a legacy of £6. 2. 8. to the use of the Merion meeting." He had laid it out at interest he reported.

During its building operation, the Merion meeting seems to have but little difficulty in raising money to carry it on, but it is notable that contributions were not asked till after work was done, and to be paid for. There is no evidence that the meeting had any assistance with money from other meetings while paying workmen in early years; but then the men's records are not complete. There is evidence, however, that the Merion meeting helped the Haverford meeting materially towards building its meeting house, in 1701, and that Haverford subsequently replied in kind.*

*The names of some of the members of the Merion meeting, during

WELSH SETTLEMENT OF PENSYLVANIA

these years, are preserved in the extant marriage certificate of Jonathan Jones and Gainor Owen, whose wedding took place in the Merion meeting house, in 1706 as follows:

Griffith Owen.
John Owen. (3).
Martha Owen.
Sarah Owen.
Evan Owen.
Owen Owen.
Robert Owen.
Joshua Owen.
Elizabeth Owen.
Robert Jones.
John Jones. (2).
Richard Jones.
Gainor Jones. (2).
Jane Jones.
Anne Jones.
Ellen Jones.
Edward Jones. (2).
Mary Jones.
Evan Jones.
Elizabeth Jones.
Catharine Jones.
Rees Thomas.
Martha Thomas.
Caleb Pusey.
Cadwalader Roberts.
Edward Roberts. (2).
Robert Roberts.
Rebecca Roberts.
Anne Roberts.
Gainor Roberts.
Elizabeth Roberts.
John Roberts.
Jane Roberts.
Thomas Lloyd.
Gainor Lloyd.
Elizabeth Lloyd.

Robert Lloyd.
Catharine Humphrey.
Rebecca Humphrey.
Daniel Humphrey.
Hannah Humphry.
John Cadwalader.
Martha Cadwalader.
Joshua Salkeld.
David Meredith.
Edward Rees.
Rees ap Edward.
Thomas Evan.
Robert Evan.
Jonathan Wynne.
John Moore.
Edward Griffith.
John Griffith.
Evan Griffith.
Hugh Griffith.
Griffith John.
Robert John.
Mary Orme.
Catharine Orme.
Owen Bevan. (2).
Eleanor Bevan.
William Edwards.
Rees Price.
Jane Price.
John Williams.
Sarah Williams.
Rowland Ellis.
Robert Ellis.
Cadwalader Evan.
Mary Badcock. (2).
Elizabeth Badcock.
Jane ab Edward.

WELSH FRIENDS' MEETINGS

On a single sheet of writing paper, partly burned and badly frayed, and almost illegible, which was found in the oldest minute book of the Merion Women Friends' monthly meeting, there is preserved John Roberts's personal account (somewhat complicated) of the cash contributed towards finishing and furnishing the Merion Meeting House, and the expenditure of the same, up to 10. 4mo. 1717, as below. It will be noticed that stone was not bought, nor masons paid, but that boards were bought and carpentering paid for, and for this reason it seems the work was on the interior, for partitions, gallery, &c., excepting for some shingling. The collections were continued to be taken in 1712 to 12mo. 1713-14, and later. The decipherable figures in this ancient account show that at least £267 were subscribed in money, labor, and materials, but the standing of the account cannot be determined because of the incompleteness of the entries.

1712/13. Merion Meeting House. *Dr*

To John Moore bill for work done	£2.	17.	9
To Edw'd Jones acct for diett, Liquor, board, and other things	(?)	(?)	4½
To Richard Hains acct for 14200 sh[ingles]	(?)	(?)	(?)
To Ellis Pugh acct for 216 at 3/10 pr	(?)	(?)	8
To James Thomas acct for lime	(?)	16.	1½
To John Knowles acct for carpenter work	47.	10.	7½
To Richard Jones bill for sawing	27.	8.	10
To Wm & Edw'd Rob'ts acct for ditto	2.	13.	8
To 28 bus lime & cartage yt Owen Thomas brought	1.	19.	8
To Rob't Jones acct for sundries	5.	9.	2½
To Daniel England acct for boards &c	1.	17.	10
To Rob't Evan for ditto		7.	
To John Conor for 46 bus of lime	1.	14.	6
To John Rob'ts acct for naills &	11.	16.	2½
To Edw'd Rees acct for sundries	25.	10.	2
To Hinges had at Jno Caddw[alader's]		14.	8
To Rob't David for D. Tho acct		16.	
To Owen Rob'ts			2

WELSH SETTLEMENT OF PENSYLVANIA

To Geo Claypoole acct		
To John Jones carpenter acc		
To Thomas Kendall acct		
To Owen Rogers acct	2.	10
To Thomas Lassells acct	6.	10

Meeting House Subscriptions.

John Roberts		Dr	
To Wm Edw'd	£3.	0.	0
To Thomas Jones	3.	1.	2
To Jno Thomas	1.	1.	6
To Geo Scolym	1.	0.	0
To Rob't Evan	9.	10.	0
To Abel Thomas	1.	3.	10
To Robert David	4.	4.	0
To David Price	2.	9.	9½
To Jonathan Cogshall		10.	8
To Robert Lloyd	2.	10.	3
To Robert Evan	1.	5.	1
To Wm Edward	1.	1.	9
To Thomas Jones	2.	18	9½
To Rob't Evan	1.	4.	11
To Jno Rob'ts	5.	0.	0
To A Thomas	(?)	11.	4
[Co]gshall	(?)	9.	4
for R Evans acct	2.	4.	6½
wen acct	3.	15.	0
[Ro]b'ts	3.	12.	0½
To John Griffith	1.	4.	8
To John Roberts	3.	16.	6
Pugh	2.	1.	11¾
To Rob't Evan	1.	4.	3
To Rowland Ellis for R P acct	1.	12.	0¼
[R]ob'ts	(?)	15.	0
	2.		
	2.		

WELSH FRIENDS' MEETINGS

				1.	5.	4
					10.	4½
				17.	8.	0
To Ro	aid			1.		
To Jno Thomas				1.	9.	4
To John Roberts				1.	3.	4
To Rob't Evan				1.	5.	5½
To Owen Thomas for his mothers acct				1.	10.	
To Moses Roberts				1		
To David Price				2.	7.	8
To Abel Thomas &c				1.	16.	4
To Rob't David				4		
		[Roberts' total]		£107.	8.	4½

Dr   Meeting House Subscriptions
1713.

6mo. 6.	To Ball due Ellis Pugh			18.	5.	8
	To Rich'd Jones acct			4.	6.	7
	To Wm & Edw'd Rob'ts			2.	13.	8
	To Ball due to Edw'd Jones			6.	3.	4½
	To John Moore				19.	3
	To Edw'd Rees acct			10.	10.	2
				£41.	18.	8½

To Jno Rob'ts	13.	3.	11			
To Tho Jones	4.	13.	0			
To Sundrie persons	32.	7.	2			
" " "	24.	13.	½			
	£74	17.	1½			
1713. 6mo. 6. Amounting to				£179.	15.	0
subscriptions not rec'd				36.	19.	7½
Subscriptions allready Rec'd				142.	15.	4½
Cadd Morgan				10.	0.	0.
Hugh Tho Bond and interest				17.	8.	0
				£170.	1.	4½

WELSH SETTLEMENT OF PENSYLVANIA

	John Roberts continued	*Dr*		
To David Price			2.	7
To Robert Evan		1.	15.	6
To Owen Rob'ts		1.		
To Rowland Ellis		2.	5.	
To Rachel Rob'ts			10.	
To Rob't David		1.	10.	
To Jona Cogshall		1.		
To Rob't Roberts		1.		
To Edw'd Roberts		5.		
To Abell Thomas			10.	0
To Haverford Meeting		16.	2.	
To Rees Howell		3.	15.	
	Sum	34.	10.	1
1713/4. 12mo. 12.	The amt of ye other	107.	8.	4½
		£141.	18.	5½

	Cr.	£	s	d
By Rich'd Jones		5.		
By ditto		4		
By cash for shingles &c		15.	1.	6
By naills		1.	0	10
By Jno Knowles Carpenter		11.	0.	9¾
By James Thomas		5.	7.	6
By naills			10.	
By ditto		3.	18.	4½
By James Thomas		2.	19.	10½
By Tho Rees on ditto acct		8.	4.	
By naills		3.	16.	6
By Ellis Pugh & to his order		8.	7.	4¾
By Jno Knowles carpenter		27.	3.	10¾
By Francis			5.	8
By Board[s] from D[aniel] Eng[land]		1.	15.	4
By naills			2.	4
By ditto			17.	

WELSH FRIENDS' MEETINGS

By Boa[rds and] naills	1.	11.	2½
By /46 c (?)/	1.	14.	6
By	1.	1.	
	£103.	17.	10
Ey Edw'd	10.		
By naills		4.	
By Boards & naills		14.	7
By ditto		8.	8
By Jno Jones carpenter	6.	2.	11½
By Jno		14.	8
By Th	6.	7.	6
By Ge		1.	9
By Lap (?)	6.	10.	
By Edward	8.		
By cash lock		2	
By John [carpe]nter	10.	10.	8
By Wm	5.		
12 mo. 12. 1713/4	£158.	15.	2¾

1713/14. 1mo. 12. *Dr.* John Roberts.	£.	s.	d.
To John Rob'ts cash [sub]scription	1	1.	
To Robt lloyd		9.	9
— mo. 14. 1714. To cash of his son being		7.	6
— mo. 8, 1715. To David Harry for 2 years interest			
— mo. 13 " To Wm * * * * * [interest on] Bond		4.	
To Rees Wms acct for do 2 yrs int		5.	
— 4mo. 3. To Matthew Rob'ts acct	2.	2.	
1715/16. 12mo. 22. To David Price acct	2.	0.	1
1716. 6mo. 9. To Jane Bedward Husbands legacy	2.		
1716/17. 12mo. 2. To Row'd Ellis	1.		
	21.	15.	4

[547]

WELSH SETTLEMENT OF PENSYLVANIA

1717. 4mo. 10. Ball without or beyond interest to Jno Rob'ts by the above acct	4.	7.	0
	£26.	2.	4
1713/14. 12mo. 12. *Cr.*			
By Ball of our acct settled then as by the other side	16.	16.	9¼
1714. 2mo. 7. By Edw'd Jones Jun'r for [B]all acct	1.	4.	
By Evan Owen for [Bal]l acct		15.	
By Jno Jones acct ca[sh in] full		10.	9½
By John Moore acct		16.	
7mo. 4. By Daniel England for boards	1.	15.	
9mo. 2. By Owen Rogers acct	1.	3.	4
By Moses [Roberts] for Tho Ball		3.	6
By Tho Pugh in full		5.	1
10mo. 15. By naills 11 ½ lb @ 10d pr		9.	7
1714/5. 11mo. 15. By 2 lb do at 9d pr		1.	6
1715. 6mo. 20. By 11 lb naills		8.	3
6mo. 27. By 193 foot boards		15.	6
1716/7. 1mo. 30. By Josiah Lawrence		18.	
	£26.	2.	3¾

"Memorandum to Enquire if there is not 1. 0. 11d. of Jno. Rob'ts subscription not paid towards the interest."

It appears from the following entries in the minutes of the Radnor monthly meeting that the Merion meeting called in its loans to be used in paying its building bills.

1713, 3. 8mo. "Merion friends having proposed to have some money that was formerly lent to Rees Howell, which is £5, old currency, £4 thereof belonging to the Merion

Friends. Also £10 that was lent to Joseph Evans, which is now at interest. Monthly Meeting agreed that Merion Meeting shall have these sums to be used towards finishing their meeting House."

And from the same minutes, of the Monthly Meeting "held at the Merion Meeting House, 12, 9mo. 1713," "Five pounds, old currency, formerly lent to Rees Howell, transferred to the Merion Meeting, towards finishing their meeting House. Paid to John Roberts."

Now, as to the acquisition of the lands where the Merion graveyard is located, and where the meeting house stands. Briefly, it may be seen from the following abstracts from deeds, that the deed for the oldest portion of the graveyard was dated 20 August, 1695, eleven years after Hugh Roberts and Robert David selected a site for the Merion burial lot, and that the deed for the meeting house lot was dated 20 March, 1714, twenty-five or more years after the erection of the stone meeting house was begun, and apparently in the year it was finished and paid for.

Exemplification deed, dated 20, 6mo. 1695, (Phila. Co. Book VII, p. 156).

"Edward Rees, of the Welsh Tract, yeoman," for five shillings, sold and conveyed to Robert Owen, Edward Jones, Cadwalader Morgan, and Thomas Jones, all of Merion, "in trust for the use of the Merion preparative meeting," "one-half acre and six square perches of Land," thus described,

"Running, Westward, by Hugh Roberts's land, 11½ perches; Southward, by the said Edward Rees's land, 7 perches, and about 12 feet; Eastward, by the same land of Edward Rees, 11 perches, and Northward, by the said Edward Jones's land, 7½ perches. Being a part of said Edward Rees's land."

The grantor gives and guarantees "free liberty of ingress, egress and regress in, to, and from said piece of ground," and stipulated that it is to be only "to the use of the people of God, called in scorne Quakers, who are members of the Haverford monthly meeting in the Welsh Tract, for only

WELSH SETTLEMENT OF PENSYLVANIA

a burying place, and for no other use whatsoever." Witness to the signature of Edward Rees, who marked E R, were John Roberts, Robert Jones, David Hugh, and Griffith John. This deed acknowledged in open court, Philadelphia, 11 Dec. 1697, Recorded 6. 2mo. (April), 1698.

It may be noticed from this description, that there was no "road to the ford" at this time, along the north side of the "old graveyard," and over Hugh Roberts's property. Sometime in the last century, ten feet were added to the west end of the graveyard from the meeting house lot.

Some think that the date of this deed, the earliest connected with the Merion meeting, is what suggested to the meeting trustees of 1829, when they repaired the building, to put up the date tablet: BUILT IN 1695.

It appears by the Monthly Meeting books, that there was a graveyard near the Merion Meeting House, which was older than the oldest part of its private burial ground.— "Rees' Gift," as there are entries of burials, stating that certain interments were made in "the ould grave yard, Owen Roberts." This as late as in 1716. And, that before 1700, there are entries of removals of bodies "from ye ould grave yard, Owen Roberts," to the grounds now used.

This "ould grave yard" is a mystery now. It may have been either a private burial lot on his father's, Hugh Roberts, and subsequently his plantation, which they permitted outsiders to use, and from which all bodies were eventually removed, because the Roberts' deeds never mention any lot reserved for a graveyard, as was the custom. This, Owen Roberts, 1677-1733, was the Friends' minister's third child, and the land he received from his father, with a dwelling house, lay along the "road to the ford," and near the meeting house, and adjoined Rees' land.

Or, this may have been the site for the Merion Meeting's graveyard selected by Hugh Roberts, in 1684, and it was abandoned, and reverted to the Roberts estate, when Rees gave land more advantageously situated for Merion's graveyard, which is presumed by many to have been the spot

WELSH FRIENDS' MEETINGS

where he buried his child in 1682 (but unfortunately for this idea, Rees did not own this land till in 1691, and if there was an old graveyard here it most likely belong to Dr. Jones), and was the reason for the expression in the "1714 deed," hereafter, "beginning at the northwestermost part of the old graveyard," else, how account for this expression, if there was only one graveyard? This site certainly became the most desirable in the township for the Meeting House, as it is near four highways. Yet, from the wording of Rees' deed, there was no probability of such an advantage.

Here follows an abstract of the earliest deed, conveying by the retiring trustees, to the trustees of the Merion meeting, the lot on which they had built their stone meeting house, recently completed.

There was an indenture of the usual lease for one year, dated 19, 1mo. 1714, from Edward Rees, Robert Jones, Meredith Davies, and Rees Price, to Edward Jones, Thomas Jones, and Robert Roberts, but it was not acknowledged, nor recorded.

In the recorded deed of release, dated 20 March, 1714, of "Edward Rees, Robert Jones, Meredith Davies, of Plymouth township, and Rees Prees (or Price), son and heir apparent of said Edward Rees," [the trustees of the Merion preparative meeting], to "Edward Jones, Thomas Jones, Robert Roberts, son and heir apparent of John Roberts, maltster, the trustees appointed by the meeting," the consideration being "£3, of lawful money of America," the land thus conveyed is described:

"Beginning at the North Westernmost part of the *old* Grave Yard, thence South 80°, West 14½ perches, to a corner stone; thence South 58°, East by line dividing the Meeting House Land from other Land of the said Edward Rees, 28 perches, to a corner Black oak tree, by the line dividing the aforesaid Meeting House Land from the Land of Robert Jones; thence North 14°, West to the said Grave Yard Pales, 11 perches; thence West 85°, along the said

WELSH SETTLEMENT OF PENSYLVANIA

Pales 5 1-3 perches; thence North 15°, West by the end of the said Grave Yard, 7¾ perches to the beginning. Containing ¾ of an acre and 23 square perches of Land, and originally part of the tract of said Edward Rees." Witnesses, Rowland Ellis, Griffith Robert, Moses Roberts, William Walter, David Jones, and Jonathan Cockshaw. This deed was not recorded till 2 May, 1746, by Robert Jones and Rees Price, the survivors of the grantors. (Phila. Bk. G. VII. fo. 131.)

At what date, after 1695, this irregularly shaped lot was conveyed by Edward Rees to the trustees, is unknown at this writing. Including the graveyard, at this time the land of the meeting formed an isosceles triangle. By there coming to be two highways intersecting on the west end of Dr. Jones' property, namely, "the road to the ford" in the Schuylkill, (now called Meeting House Lane), between the lands of Dr. Jones and Hugh Roberts, and another, long only known as "a settled road," subsequently the Lancaster Road, (now Montgomery Ave.), between Dr. Jones's property and some of Edward Rees's, a sharp, narrow point of land was formed, and of the tip of this, Edward Rees bought about two acres, in 1691, which purchase is mentioned in the confirmation patent to him in 1704. Probably, Mr. Rees had a definite idea when he bought this point what he was going to do with it, for in 1695, we have seen that he conveyed about 86 square perches of it to the Merion meeting for a graveyard, and probably the lease, or refusal, or option, or even the title in fee, on 143 square perches for the site of the new stone meeting house. The remaining land, about 139 square perches he had conveyed to Robert Jones, J.P., (a son of John ap Thomas), in 1709.

It is from the fact that Edward Rees was the grantee for this point of land in 1691, that it is presumed the foundation of the stone meeting house was begun about that year, under some understanding with Mr. Rees about the lot. There was nothing at any time to prevent the Merion Friends building their meeting house of stone at that time,

WELSH FRIENDS' MEETINGS

even if they did not finish it till in 1714. There was an abundance of stone in the neighborhood, the same it was built of. And it certainly was substantially built, of well selected stone, and adhering cement. Its stone walls are two feet through, standing 14 feet to the over-hanging roof. The length of the building being 36 feet, with the southwest part, or the nave, 20 by 24 feet. The master-builder was the architect, but his name has not been preserved in connection with this building.

By these two deeds, it may be seen that the Merion meeting now owned, in the graveyard ½ acre and 6 perches, and in the house lot ¾ acre and 23 perches. The balance of the point, "about one acre," as said, Rees sold to Robert Jones. The irregularity of the "consideration," is notable, as it was, in 1695, five shillings for half of an acre; three pounds, in 1714, for three-quarters of an acre, and one pound in 1709, for "one acre," which is the lot now occupied by the General Wayne tavern.

The next transfer of the Merion meeting house and lot, from trustees to trustees of this Meeting, was in 1747, thirty-three years after the finishing of the meeting house. This was done, by deed dated 18. 3mo. 1747, which was recorded at Philadelphia, 12 Dec. 1748. (Deed Book D, XV. fo. 327). Robert Roberts, of Merion, being the only survivor of the trustees acting on 20 March, 1714, by this instrument, conveyed, (his wife, Sydney Roberts, joining in the deed), the lot on which the meeting house stands in fee to the newly appointed trustees, namely James Jones, of Blockley, Robert Jones, of Merion, and John Roberts, of Merion, miller. The lot was described as follows: "Beginning at the Northwardmost corner of the Grave Yard, thence South 79° 30', West 14¼ perches, to a corner stone; thence South 57°, East 28 perches, to a corner; thence North 14°, 30', West 11 perches and 2 feet; thence South 85½°, 5½ perches; thence North 15°, West 7 perches and 13 feet to beginning. Containing ¾ of an acre and 24 perches, being part of land formerly in possession of Edward Rees."

WELSH SETTLEMENT OF PENSYLVANIA

This description was probably from a new, recent survey, as this one does not correspond with that of 1714, and was one square perch less.

In 1763, Mr. Joseph Tunes gave the Merion Preparative Meeting about 6162 square feet of land, adjoining the graveyard land given, in 1695, by Edward Rees, on its east end. He gave it "for a burying place for indigent Friends of this meeting, and for others who were approved by the Merion Preparative Meeting."* This deed of gift, dated 1 Dec. 1763, recorded 7 Jan. following, was from "Joseph Tunes, of Lower Merion tp." "to Edward Price, yeoman, and John Roberts, miller, both of Lower Merion tp., and David George, yeoman, of Blockley tp., trustees." This gift lot was described:—"Beginning at the Northermost corner of the graveyard wall, thence by the said wall, South 17°, East 7¾ perches, to the Southeast corner thereof; thence by the land of said Joseph Tunes, North 78°, East 3 perches, to a corner stone; thence North 17°, West 7¾ perches, to another corner stone, on the South side of the Road, leading to the ford in Schuylkill river; thence by the said road, South 78°, West 3 perches, to the beginning." "Containing 23 square perches of land." Consideration, five shillings. "The trustees must have this ground walled, or fenced, and they and their successors to keep said wall in repair." Witnesses to the deed, James Jones, James Moore, and Abraham Tunes.

This lot was a portion of the inherited farm John Jones, (youngest son of Dr. Edward Jones, deceased), and his wife Mary, conveyed by a deed dated 15 Oct. 1741, "to Anthony Tunes, late of Germantown," for £812, Pensylvania money, described, beginning at a white oak corner, in the line of John Roberts, thence by the land of Hugh Evans, N. 67°, E. 165 per., thence N.W. 48 per., thence N. 70°, E. 40

---

*In earlier days, the Merion Friends were not so particular in separating the rich from the poor, as "John Morgan, a poor man, and a charge to ye Township," was buried in the regular ground of Merion Meeting, in 1718.

per. to a white oak; thence S.E. 52 per., (the three last mentioned courses running by Rees Price's ten acres of meadow, called "Clean John"); thence by said Hugh Evans land, N. 68°, E. 88 per., thence by Richard George's land, N. 66°, E. 173 per., thence partly by said Richard George's land, and land of Thomas Davids, N. 33°, 79 per., thence by said Thomas Davids' land, S. 75°, W. 97 per., thence N. 25°, W. 60 per., thence N. 80°, E. 4 per., thence by Rees Price's land N. 15°, W. 24 per., to the Road; thence along the same Road, dividing this land from land of Edward Price, S. 78°, W. 141 per., to the Meeting House ground; thence by the same S. 15°, E. 36 per. and ¾; thence by the Road to Haverford, S. 72°, W. 76 per., thence by Rees Price's land, S. 25°, E. 30 per., thence S. 70°, W. 158 per., to a corner chestnut tree; thence S. 20°, E. 37 per., thence by land of John Roberts, S. 25°, 39 per., S. 39°, E. 22 per., S. 41°, E. 20 per., S. 26°, E. 16 per., and S. 7°, E. 12 per. to beginning. In all 402 acres and 142 perches of land, late the estate of Dr. Edward Jones.

Mr. Tunis resided on this property till his death, 20. 5mo. 1762. He married at the Merion Meeting, 5 Dec. 1718, Mary, daughter of John Williams, and had nine children, whose births are recorded at this meeting. (For an account of some of his descendants, see Jordan's "Colonial Families of Philadelphia," p. 1556).

Mr. Tunis' second son, Joseph Tunis, 1736-1773, inherited land from his father, and conveyed, by deed of 1 April, 1768, some of it, adjoining the Merion Meeting land, to Robert Holland, a tanner, who by deed dated 25 Oct. 1785, conveyed 40 acres of the same to Joseph Price, a carpenter, which was bounded:—Beginning at a stone by a black oak tree on the south side of the Lancaster road, and on the west side of a road leading to Darby, thence by side of said Darby road So. 8°, W. 23¾ per., to a corner stone by said road; thence by land now of John Dickinson, So. 70°, W. 226 per., to a corner stone; thence by land of John Price, N.W. 14 4/10 perches, to a corner stone; thence No. 70°, East,

WELSH SETTLEMENT OF PENSYLVANIA

141½ per., to another corner stone; thence by same No. 25°, W. 31 per., to a stone in middle of the road leading to Haverford; thence along said road No. 72°, East 76 per., to a stone; thence by Meeting House land, so called, No. 15°, 8 per., to a side of Lancaster road, and thence by said road So. 54°, 41 per. to beginning.*

The next transfer of the property of the Merion Meeting from its old trustees to the new ones, was by deed dated 26 Jan. 1786. (Recorded 2 May, 1786, in Phila. Deed Book G. X, fo. 334). By this deed, "Edward Jones, of Philadelphia, James Jones, of Lower Merion tp., Edward Price, of Lower Merion tp., and David George, of Blockley tp.," transferred the three small, adjoining lots, [that of the old graveyard, (Rees' gift), the one the meeting house stands on, and the lot presented by Mr. Tunes,] "to James Jones, Jr., Thomas George, and Amos George, all of Philadelphia, and Jehu Roberts, of Montgomery county." The descriptions of these lots in this deed differ from former outlines.

1. "Beginning and running Westward by the Land of Hugh Roberts, 11½ perches, Southward, by the land of Edward Rees, 7 perches and 12 feet, and Eastward, by the land of the same, 7½ perches." "Containing ½ acre and 6 perches." "By deed dated 20, 6mo. 1695. Recorded in Deed Book E. III. vol. 5, page 5." (This deed book is in the Philadelphia Recorder's office, but this deed is not copied into it. It is given in the office index as on "page 115," but it is not there. It was found in Exemplification Book No. 7, p. 156). "This land was conveyed by this deed, by said Edward Rees, unto Robert Owen, Edward Jones, Cadwalader Morgan, and Thomas Jones, trustees of the

---

*John Price, aforesaid, devised by will, 16 May, 1792, to his three daughters each one acre of land on the end of his plantation, and on the Lancaster Road, and to his son, Edward Price, he devised five acres on the Lancaster Road, and to his brother-in-law, Robert Holland, he gave a life interest in two acres, on the west end of his plantation, and the balance of his estate he left to Joseph and John Price.

Merion Meeting, in fee. All being deceased, and the title being in Jonathan Jones, (son and heir to said Edward Jones, the survivor of the said trustees of 1695), and the said Jonathan Jones also being deceased, and his estate being vested in his son and heir, Edward Jones, the first named party to this current deed."

2. "Beginning at the Northward corner of the graveyard, thence South 79°, West 14½ perches, to a stone; thence South 57°, East 28 perches, to a corner; thence North 14°, West 11 perches and 2 feet; thence South 85°, 5½ perches; thence North 15°, West 7 perches and 13 feet, to beginning." "Containing ¾ of an acre and 24 perches." "Which lot, by deed dated 18. 3mo. 1747, (recorded in Book G. 10., fo. 334), was conveyed by Robert Roberts to the said James Jones, (a party to this 1786 deed), Robert Jones, and John Roberts, in fee. The said Robert Jones and John Roberts being deceased, and the estate hath survived in the said James Jones."

3. And of the other, remaining small lot:—"Beginning at the Northward corner of the grave yard wall, thence by the said wall, South 17°, East 7¾ perches, to the South East corner of the same wall; thence by Joseph Tunes's land," &c, being the conveyance of 23 perches of land from Joseph Tunis, by deed 1 Dec. 1763.

These three parcels of land were resurveyed 28. 10mo. 1783, and found together as follows:—"Beginning at the North corner of the land conveyed by Joseph Tunis for use of a grave yard, thence along the Road from a ford in the Schuylkill to the Lancaster Road, by the grave yard and the Meeting House ground, South 76°, 15', West 28 85/100 perches to a stone in said Lancaster Road; thence down said Road, South 52°, East 28 8/10 perches, to a stone in the Road; thence North 18°, West 11 7/10 perches, to a stone marked in the grave yard wall; thence along said wall, and the land conveyed as above by Joseph Tunis, North 77°,

WELSH SETTLEMENT OF PENSYLVANIA

East 8 9/10 perches, to corner thereof; thence along the line of John Dickinson, North 19°, West 7 75/100 perches to beginning." "Containing 1¾ acres and 16 perches."

John Dickinson, of Wilmington, Delaware, conveyed, in trust to Messrs. Paul Jones and David Roberts, of Lower Merion tp., and Edward George and Joseph George, of Blockley tp., for the use of the Merion Preparative Meeting, by deed of gift dated 21. 11mo. 1801, about one acre, bounded as follows:—"Beginning at a stone in the old Lancaster road, in the line of Mary Streaper's land, thence by her land N. 19°, W. 15¾ perches to the S.E. corner of the wall of the old grave yard; thence by a lot of ground, conveyed for the use of a burying place by Joseph Tunis, deceased, N. 71°, E. 3 perches, to a stone being a corner thereof; thence by said ground N. 19°, W. 7¾ perches, to a stone on South side of a road leading to a ford in river Schuylkill; thence by said road N. 76°, E. 3 8/10 perches, to a stake in said road, being a corner of other land of the said John Dickinson; thence by his land S. 19°. 31 perches, to a stake in Lancaster road, and thence up said road N. 58°, W. 11 perches to place of beginning."

By deed, dated 4. 10mo. 1804, and recorded 10 Sep. 1807, John Dickinson conveyed to the aforesaid trustees, about one acre of land, adjoining the above land, described:— "Beginning at a stone in Lancaster Road, a corner of the land lately conveyed to the Merion Meeting by the said John Dickinson, thence by said ground N. 19°, W. 31 perches, to a stake on south side of a public road leading to a ford in the river Schuylkill; thence down said road N. 76°, E. 4 7/10 perches, to a stone, the corner of other land of said J. D., thence S. 19°, East by said land 37¾ perches, to a stone in Lancaster road; thence up said road N. 58°, W. 8 5/10 per. to beginning."

The next transfer between trustees was in 1817, when James Jones, Jr., and John Roberts conveyed the property of the Merion preparative meeting to Paul Jones, David Roberts, Edward George, and Joseph George. Deed proved

16 June, 1877, recorded at Norristown, (Deed Book, 238, fo. 186). This deed mentions the change of jurisdiction over this meeting from Haverford Mo. Mtg. to Radnor Mo. Mtg.

There was no other transfer of the Merion Meeting property till 28, 3mo. 1846, when the retiring and surviving trustees conveyed the property as held in 1786, to the new trustees. It was forty years after this when the property was next transferred between trustees.

By deed dated 7 April, 1886, Arthur Moore, and the surviving trustees, Edward R. Price, John M. George, and James L. Paiste, to new trustees, viz. Edward R. Price, John M. George, Robert M. Janney, Alfred Moore, Edmund Webster, J. Roberts Foulke, George W. Hancock, and Howard W. Lippincott. The two lots of land received from John Dickinson are each described in this deed, and land adjoining as follows:—"Beginning at the North West corner of the land conveyed to the Meeting by Joseph Tunis for a grave yard, thence along the Road to the ford in Schuylkill; thence to the Lancaster Road, (by the grave yard and the Meeting House ground), South 76°, West 28 perches and a little more, to a stone in the Lancaster Road; thence down this Road South 62°, East 28 perches, and a little more, to a stone in the Lancaster Road; thence North 18°, West 11 perches, and a fraction, to a stone in the Grave Yard Wall; thence along said wall, and the land conveyed by Joseph Tunis, North 77°, East 8 perches and a fraction, to the corner thereof, and thence along the line of John Dickinson, North 19°, West 7 perches, and a little more, to the beginning." "1¾ acre and 16 perches of land." Recorded 4 Sep. 1886.

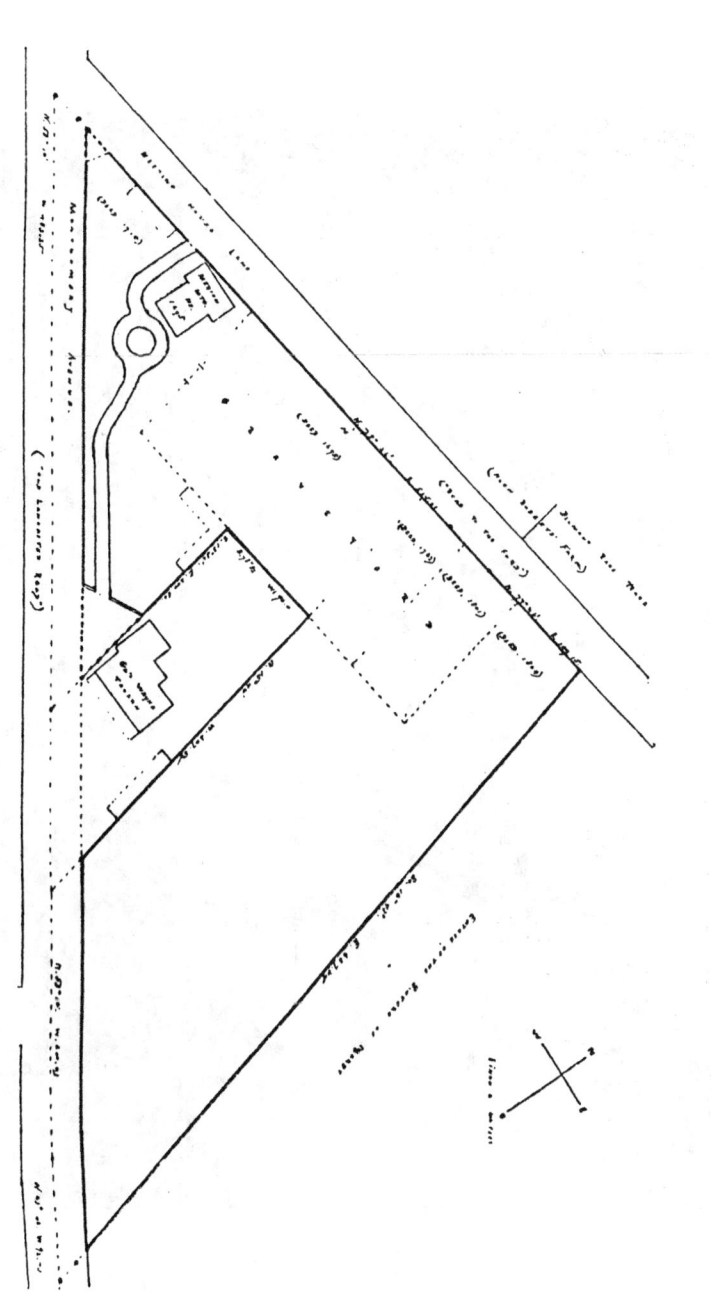

MERION FRIENDS' MEETING HOUSE, IN 1912.

MERION, HAVERFORD, RADNOR

There have been some changes at the Merion Meeting House since its early days. The stable used by the first settlers has long ago been done away with. It may be seen by the deed of Edward Rees to Robert Jones, dated 23. 2mo. 1709, conveying to him the lot where he built his residence, and where the Gen. Wayne Inn now stands, that this stable stood at the southeast corner of the ground Edward Rees gave to the meeting in 1695, exclusively for a graveyard. According to a deed mentioned elsewhere, this "meeting house stable" was in existence as late as 1768. It may be that the first meeting house for Merion Friends stood near this stable, in and before 1695, rather than "just to the east of the present stone meeting house." This latter impression arose from the discovery that at some early period there was a wide gateway in the north wall of the oldest part of the graveyard, east of, and near the meeting house. It may be, that here was a driveway through the graveyard to the stable, and the presumed log-built meeting house.

The roof and chimney of a house which appear beyond the horse-shed, in Sutcliffe's picture of the Merion meeting house, belonged to the school house of the Merion Friends, which has also disappeared. For many years it was the only school house in Lower Merion tp., and stood in a field, back of the meeting house, and across Meeting House Lane, the "road to the Ford." Some old desks and benches are stored on the upper floor of the meeting house, which for sometime was also used as a school room. On some of the desks may be seen their initials cut by pupils of long ago, as "W N 1711," and "D R IV 1802." For years, it is notorious that "schooling" was the simplest, elemental, and that there were no "school books," and all instruction was oral, and this prevailed till after the Revolutionary War.

WELSH SETTLEMENT OF PENSYLVANIA

As to this old school house, there is a deed of gift dated 1 Dec. 1747, acknowledged 12 Jan. 1765, and recorded 10 Feb. 1770, which tells that Rees Price and his son, Edward Price, conveyed to Richard George, Evan Jones, and John Roberts, for five shillings, a lot, 50 by 40 feet, or 2000 square feet, located "by estimate thirty feet North from the Meeting House land." This lot was to be "used only to erect thereon a house, or houses for a school, for such as shall contribute towards building the same, and to such others as the contributors shall approve of." Witnesses to this deed were Hugh Evans and John Price.

A memorandum attached says:—That the master, with the scholars that shall from time to time, and at all times forever, belong to the school intended to be kept on the above granted premises, have privilege of ingress and egress from said land to a spring of water, near said granted ground, on the land of the said Rees and Edward Price, and thereof to satisfy and quench their thirst. Provided always, that if said Rees and Edward Price shall have occasion to build a house over the said spring, then the said master and scholars are hereby privileged and allowed of going lower down the streams issuing from the said spring, to quench their thirst, but never more than fifty perches from the said spring.

Filed with this deed is the following "List of the Contributors towards Erecting a School House on the within Granted piece of Ground, with their respective Subscriptions." The largest contribution was from Evan Jones, whose legacy and subscription amounted to seven pounds. John Price, Gerrard Jones, David Davis, and John Roberts, the miller, each gave five pounds. John Roberts, the carpenter, "surveyed the ground, and writing ye deed, with his subscription in three pounds," gave a total of four pounds. Then John George gave £3. 10. 0, John Righter £3. 6. 2, and the following each contributed three pounds, Sarah Jones, Anthony Levering, Hugh Evans, Richard George, Thomas David, and Robert Roberts, the cooper. Hannah

Williams gave £2. 10. 0, Robert Jones contributed forty bushels of lime, estimated at £2. 3. 4, and the following each gave two pounds, Peter Becket, Lewis Jones, Edward Jones, Owen Jones, Jacob Jones, Daniel Williams, Robert Holland, and Anthony Tunes. The following each gave £1. 10. 0: Abraham Tunes, Lewis Scothern, Hugh Roberts, and John Robinson, and John Thomas, the smith, contributed three days of carting material amounting to this amount. These gave one pound: Edward Williams, John Roberts, Jr., Amos Moore, and Robert Wood, while Edward Roberts, Jr., subscribed only ten shillings. The Preparative Meeting still owns this lot but is never mentioned in the trustees' deeds. Another early school house in this neighborhood is referred to in a deed of Joseph Price, dated 22 Sep. 1804, conveying five acres of land (bought at sheriff's sale 15 Feb. 1803), and a log messuage, or tenement, adjoining the lands of Owen Roberts, William Holget, and William Fritz, from which he reserved five squares of land, on which a school house is built, to the use of said school house forever.

In the Liberties, near by, were two other school houses of early times. One stood on the west side of the old Lancaster Road, below the City Line. It was called the Penn School, and disappeared many years ago. The other was at Jefferson and 57th streets, which became the meeting house of the Orthodox Friends from Merion meeting in 1829.

We have seen that in 1801, and in 1804, John Dickinson gave the Merion Preparative Meeting two small lots, adjoining the graveyard, one was to increase its size; the other was for the site of the dwelling for the caretaker of the meeting house and grounds. This lot is still used for that purpose, and the stone cottage stands on Montgomery Ave., opposite Haverford and Merion Ave. The subscription paper giving the names of those who contributed cash towards defraying the expense of erecting "the stone house, 26 by 18 feet, to cost not less than $800," gives, possibly, the roll of membership of Merion Meeting

WELSH SETTLEMENT OF PENSYLVANIA

in 1804. The trustees at that time were Messrs. Paul Jones, Edward George, David Roberts, and Joseph George. They superintended the work. Those who contributed $50:—James Jones, Richard Jones, Thomas George, and David Roberts; $40, David Jones; $30, Paul Jones, Rees Price, Jon. Robinson, and Owen Jones; $27, Jacob Jones; $20, Giles Jones, Abel Thomas, Joseph George, John Holdgate, Lloyd Jones, and Mary Price; $15, James Jones, Thomas George and Edward George; $12, Elizabeth George; $10, Rebecca Price, Hannah Williams, Rebecca George, R. and H. McIlvaine, A. and M. Jones, Thomas Gavery, George Aston and David Jones; $8, Margaret Cochran, Mary Jones, Ann Jones, Lewis Jones, John Hall, Paul Jones and Lloyd Jones. Some of these increased their original subscriptions subsequently. Among the smaller contributors were Joseph Hayes, David Evans, Nathan Evans, Isaac Hayes, Israel Morris, Elizabeth Rively, Levi Lukens, Marsella Alloway, Charles Jones, Ann Jones, William Hayes, Phebe Hoffman, Jane Walter, Isaac Price, and Thomas Price, "by halling logs to saw mill for pail fence."

Whenever possible, it has been the custom of Friends to build a stone wall around their graveyards, and in reading some of the old deeds for land abutting on the Merion Meeting property, we have seen "the graveyard wall" was frequently a bound, and this was the stone wall there now. But from the "1714 deed" for the land on which the meeting house stands, and from the minutes of the Merion Men's Meeting, we learn that it had a predecessor, "the graveyard pales." It may be presumed the paling fence was erected around the graveyard as soon as the land was acquired, even before deed was passed for it, and that it had become old by 1703, as in the minutes of the Merion Men's Meeting, 3. 10. 1703, it was "ordered, John Roberts to gett someone to secure the grave yard pales," and, 7. 11mo. (Jan.) 1703-4, although bad weather for it, John Roberts, the treasurer, "had the pales fixed," and so reported, and that he had "paid 5 shillings for mending

WELSH FRIENDS' MEETINGS

them, and 12 shillings for nails," and had previously paid 14s. 6d. and had in the treasury £1. 11. 6. He complained "some have not paid their subscriptions towards the meeting house," so it was "ordered they be spoken to."

Pales seemed to be good enough protection till Edward Rees, by his will, 25. 9. 1727, gave the Merion Meeting £10 to be used in erecting a stone wall around the graveyard. This started a fund, quickly raised, and the stone wall was built in 1730, around the "Rees grave yard." But it was not until in 1809, that the stone wall was put up about the gift of lands of Tunes and Dickinson, 357 feet, costing $242. According to minutes, the stone wall has been expensive, and had to be frequently repaired and rebuilt, and especially when the grade of Lancaster road was changed. In 1809, the old wall cost $169.78, and in the itemized bill is a charge of "101 wrought nails @ 10c, $10.10." On 2. 3mo. 1848, "ordered to pay John M. George, treasurer," "to repair the graveyard wall," $280. And again on 10. 2mo. 1859, Edward H. Dickinson, treasurer, was paid "for defraying expenses of repairing the graveyard wall and other property here," $167. On 8. 1mo. 1849, $253.92½ was raised by subscription, and the receiving vault was built below the surface of the lot, at the S.E. corner of the Merion Meeting House. The iron railing about the vault has disappeared.

Although the property of Merion Preparative Meeting passed in 1827-8, and so remains, into the control of the so styled "Hicksite Friends," both branches of the Society of Friends bury their dead in the graveyard of this meeting.

The burial records of the Merion Meeting have been fairly well kept since 1705, and I have had occasion in various instances to go to them for data. There are not many unusual items in these records, and some of them I have noticed elsewhere. Recorded is the burial of the "Dutch woman," no name given, who was poisoned in 1756; Jacob Thomas, who was killed by a wagon of stone passing over his head, in 1807, and the half dozen men killed in the

WELSH SETTLEMENT OF PENSYLVANIA

powder mill. The remaining entry of this class was the burial, 11. 4. 1749, of "one Donelson, killed by the Fall of a Tresal [at] John Robert Matthew's plantation." John Robert Matthew was an early Welsh settler in Merion. He buried his son, Matthew, at the Merion Meeting, 9mo. 6. 1713, his daughter, Susannah, was accidentally drowned, so the record says, without particulars, and was buried here, 4. 6. 1748. Dr. Edward Jones had a servant who was burned to death, and buried here, in 1717. Many servants were buried at Merion, some of them negroes,* but mostly German people, who thus seemed to have been the favorite servants. Some entries of deaths are recorded in the Merion book, but the interments were at Haverford, or Radnor.

It may be seen from the following lists from the records of the surnames of people buried at the Merion meeting house, from the year 1705, that there were few Welsh names, and that this meeting had ceased to be purely one of Welsh Friends twenty-five years after its foundation, and suggests the quick assimilation of the Welsh and English families.

---

*As said elsewhere, Negroes were held and worked as slaves by the Welsh Friends as well as by the English, and in no extant records of the Welsh Friends does it appear that the Welsh were in any way influenced against the "perniciousness of slavery" by the protests of the newly convinced German Friends, therefore, it appears there never was any concerted movement among them to abolish "traffick of men-body." The German Friends have the credit of making the first formal protest, in a document still extant, presumed to have been written by Pastorius, addressed, "This is to ye monthly meeting held at Richard Worrell's." It sets forth the "reasons why we are against the traffick of men-body." The argument being the old "golden rule," or "how'd you like it yourself, if you, or your children were carried off, and kept in bondage." It claimed that all Europeans "are astonished when they hear off that ye Quakers doe here handel men as they handel there ye cattle." It is dated and signed:—"This is from our meeting at Germantown, held ye 18 of ye 2 month, 1688, to be delivered to the Monthly Meeting at Richard Worrell's." Signed by "Garret hendericks, derick up de graeff, Francis daniell Pastorius, Abraham up Den graeff."

WELSH FRIENDS' MEETINGS

Armstrong.
Amos.
Apty.
Bevan.
Beringer.
Bossard.
Bomen (Bowman?)
Balort.
Bedford.
Crockson.
Camberlin.
Creakbeam.
Conlin.
Chapman.
Coultar.
Conrad.
Comley.
Cannel.
Camble (Campbell?)
Claphamson.
David.
Davies.
Dodomite.
Dyer.
Eves.
Edward.
Edwards.
Ellis.
Firth.
Frame.
Francis.
Fisher.
Griffith.
Giger.
Garret.
Harper.
Hughes.
Hamilton.
Henderson.
Humphreys.
Hemler.
Harry.
Hemberger.
Hill.

Hodnet.
Holland.
Henby.
Hover.
Holgate.
Hendricks.
Judgles.
Jordan.
John.
Kite.
King.
Knowles.
Lewis.
Lloyd.
Lee.
Levering.
Latch.
Llewelyn.
Loot.
Morgan.
Mifflin.
More.
Mills.
Musgrove.
Matson.
Millar.
Marks.
McKewson.
Manuel.
Mares.
Miley.
Morris.
Null.
Noble.
Ogleby.
Owen.
Pugh.
Peters.
Palmer.
Pollin.
Pearne.
Pistorus.
Pearson.
Perkins.

Pratt.
Quinn.
Rakestraw.
Robeson.
Robinson.
Robison.
Rogerson.
Rodgers.
Righter.
Reese.
Rewalt.
Roman.
Russel.
Robenson.
Supplee.
Scothom.
Sherrel.
Stuard.
Sunday.
Shutz.
Suitzer.
Schible.
Swaim.
Shiers.
Stadleman.
Streaper.
Streeper.
Tamplin.
Townsley.
Taylor.
Vincent.
Vandern.
Wynne.
Williams.
Warner.
White.
Walker.
Whitloe.
Winter.
Ward.
Whitehead.
Webster.
Winters.

WELSH SETTLEMENT OF PENSYLVANIA

Some of these interments were in "the Strangers's Yard," so they were not Friends, or were not members of this meeting. Besides other early burials in this yard, mentioned elsewhere, were those of Caleb and Joseph, sons of Rowland Richard, buried in 1705, on 1st and 13th, of 5th and 6th months; Hugh George on 26. 1mo. 1714; Ann Walter, on 27. 3mo. 1715; Edward Sion, "living late at Mt. Ararat," on 3. 8mo. 1715; Moses Roberts, on 22. 12mo. 1715-6; Catherine, wife of David Thomas, the mason, 4. 8mo. 1716; and William Shenkin, "aged about 92 years," on 12. 11mo. 1719-20.

Something has already been told of this graveyard itself, but by a ramble through it we have information of people who died in the last seventy-five years, from inscribed head-stones.

Passing eastward on the dividing walk, on the right hand there is first, what a tablet set into the cemetery wall tells is the "Zell Row, 1794-1875," which means that the row of graves along the wall, which in recent years was moved some yards westward, and divides the graveyard from the lawn of the Meeting House, are members of the Zell family, and among them is the grave of "Thomas Ellwood Zell, 1828-1905, A Founder of the Loyal Legion," the society of commissioned officers who served in the Civil War, and were honorably discharged. Next to the Thompson family's graves are twenty-four marked graves of the George family, among them that of Jesse George, the well known Philadelphia philanthropist. A long stretch follows of unmarked graves, and then there are a few graves of the Leedom family with marble head-stones,* and of the families of Hoffman, Yerkes, Jones, Trimble, Smith, Thomas, Bealer, Lynch,

---

*In the minutes of the Concord monthly meeting, held with the Chichester meeting, 7. 1. 1729, "whereas, it hath been upon the minds of some friends of this meeting to suppress all surperflus practices of putting of names and Dates upon Coffins, and it is the mind of this meeting that for the futer friends should decist from all such Idolatrous practices". And in the minutes of the same monthly meeting, 11. 5. 1729, "Agreeable to ye yearly meeting minute relateing to

WELSH FRIENDS' MEETINGS

Lippincott, Hatton, Young, Radcliffe, Du Bree, Carncross, Hansell, Dickinson, Pawling, Huntley, Lockwood, Bond, Wilson, Etc.,

Returning, on the left side of the walk, are the marked graves of Jacobs, Huntley, Jones, Price, Mynick, Leedom, Carncross, Hansell, Anderson, McKeever, Harvey, Schlater, Jones, Thomas, Brookfield, Wainwright, Heston, Hall, Roberts, Zell, Pawling, Evans, Swayne, Sanders, Paiste, Tunis, Oress, Hunt, Moore, Huffman, Trasel, and then a long stretch of unmarked graves, opposite, on the other side of the walk, till the graves of members of the Rutter and Brookfield families, and of Jonathan Jones, *d.* 1821, are passed, then comes the "Roberts Row."

A tablet set into the cemetery wall, along Meeting House Lane, has the legend:—"John Roberts / of Lynn, Carnarvonshire / Wales/ was born in 1648/ Died April 6th, 1724/ and/ his descendants/ are buried opposite/ this tablet/. 1897"/. There are only twelve marked Roberts graves here out of the hundred descendants of the immigrant probably lying in this locality, or in the graveyard. The earliest grave here marked by an old head-stone, sunken to the level of the ground, is that of "John Roberts, Died 1803." The new stones mark the graves of the following of this family:—Algernon, 1751-1815. (He was born 24 Nov. 1750), a lieutenant colonel. His wife (Tacy Warner, is buried next to him); Tacy, 1761-1828; "Sarah, wife of John," 1792-1823; Emily T., 1795-1825; John, 1788-1838; Tacy, 1805-1847; Isaac W., 1789-1859; Lydia, 1783-1862; Mary I., 1816-1865; Gainor, 1791-1868, and William Warner, 1815-1898.

Tombstones, this meeting appoints ****** to advise with these that are concerned in placing Tombstones in order to remove them, and make report to ye next meeting".

Early in the last century, similar opposition to inscribed headstones was so strong in the Merion Meeting that those in sight were laid flat on the ground and covered with earth. Last year, in clearing up the graveyard, and regrading it, many of these stones were again set on end.

WELSH SETTLEMENT OF PENSYLVANIA

Among the burials recorded at this meeting as in this yard, were, 1803, 11mo. 10. "Ann Roberts, (killed by her son Titus), aged about 80"; 1803, 10mo. 8. "Titus's grandchild, 2 weeks old"; 1807, 12mo. 29. "Titus Roberts, Died in Hospital." He died in an asylum for the insane; he was a nephew of Col. Algernon Roberts.

Just beyond the Roberts plot, by the walk, in the ground added to the graveyard by moving the wall some years ago, are the graves of the Levick family, and low marble slabs tell that buried here, in

"Two graves, grass-green,"
are the eminent Friends' minister,

"Samuel J. Levick / Born 8th month, 30th. 1819 / Died 4th month, 19th. 1885"
and his wife,

"Susanna Morris Levick / Born 8th. month, 2nd. 1819 / Died 4th. month, 9th. 1904."

It may be seen that Mrs. Levick "lived to the good old age" of 85 years, and it is remarkable that so many Friends who also attained fourscore years and more were buried in this yard in recent years. For instance, also in 1904, Tacy Ann Jones, aged 85 years, and Paul H. Hoffman, 86 years, in 1900, whose grave is decorated on Memorial Day, as he was a soldier. In other years,

1821. Paul Jones, 84.
1837. Sarah Du Bree, 83.
1843. Mary Tunis, 83.
1847. Jane Huntley, 81.
1852. Mary Bond, 81.
1853. Edward Thompson, 81.
1858. Mary Hall Sanders, 84.
1862. Lydia Roberts, 79.
1868. Gainor Roberts, 77.
1869. Rachel Radcliffe, 87.
1871. Elizabeth Hansell, 78.
1872. Isaac Hansell, 83.
1872. Dr. Joseph Brookfield, 83.
1873. John Thomas, 87.
1873. Jesse George, 88.

1874. Samuel Jones, 85.
1877. Mary Jones, 90.
1878. Elizabeth G. Jones, 77.
1879. Priscilla Tunis, 88.
1879. Rachel Jones, 88.
1881. Mary Price, 97.
1882. Jesse Thomas, 81.
1886. Elizabeth Thomas, 84.
1888. Lewis Yerkes, 81.
1890. Joseph Thomas, 84.
1891. Sarah Thomas, 81.
1892. Emily Radcliffe, 76.
1895. James L. Paiste, 89.
1898. Elizabeth Dickinson, 87.
1898. William W. Roberts, 83.

WELSH FRIENDS' MEETINGS

The earliest decipherable stone records of burials are those of Philip Huffman, died 17 July, 1789, age 61; Edmund Huffman, died ———, 1793, and Beese Thompson, died 14 July 1799, but in regarding the grounds, and resetting sunken stones, several older stones were found in Dec. 1910, engraved "A...... S...... 1783," "H...... S......, 1785," and "Jo.... S...... 1789." They stand three rows from the "Zell Row," but in whose memory they were placed is not known at this writing. However, the meeting records, from 1705, give the names of hundreds interred here, as John, son of Thomas Jones, 2mo. 12, 1706; Catherine, daughter of Thomas Jones, 4mo. 17, 1706; Lewis David, 1mo. 2, 1707-8; Jane, wife of Cadwalader Morgan, 7mo. 19, 1710; Jane, wife of John Griffith, 9mo. 18, 1710; Felix, son of Edward Jones, 8mo. 9, 1714; William Edward, 10mo. 31, 1714; John George, 10mo. 31, 1714; Abraham Musgrove, 11mo. 18, 1714-5; Elizabeth, daughter of Robert Jones, 4mo. 16, 1715; and daughter of John Griffith, 6mo. 1715; John Bevan, bachelor, 11mo. 13, 1715-6; Hugh George, 1mo. 26, 1718; Evan Bevan, 5mo. 15, 1720; and so on, as incorporated in genealogy *super*. From these records it may seem that many of the original settlers of Merion lived there many years, and until the "country "lots" had all become productive farms. For instance, Dr. Edward Jones lived here fifty-five years; Jane, wife of William Edward, for sixty-three years; Robert David for fifty years, and Edward Price for forty-six years.

The earliest extant vital records of the Haverford monthly meeting are not uninteresting, aside from genealogical value, for they tell that the births, if they were all recorded, were not numerous among the members of the meetings of Merion, Haverford, and Radnor, for they did not average four a year in each of the two oldest meetings in the first seventeen years the record was kept, and that there were three births to each death, indicating many young married couples in these meetings. For instance,

WELSH SETTLEMENT OF PENSYLVANIA

From Merion's record, 1684-1690, seven years:—
Births, 0. 3. 2. 5. 2. 6. 1.   Deaths, 1. 2. 0. 4. 4. 2. 1.
From Haverford's record, 1684-1690, seven years:—
Births, 0. 6. 0. 3. 1. 3. 4.   Deaths, 0. 3. 1. 1. 2. 0. 3.

Or, in the same seventeen years, (1684-1700), there were 64 births, and 39 deaths, in Merion, and 59 births, and 26 deaths, in Haverford.

But for some unknown reason, in 1697, there were nine deaths of record in Merion meeting, and in same year, only one in the Haverford.

The earliest births of record on the Merion book are
1682, 9mo. 11. Jane, of Edward and Mabley Rees.
1683, 8mo. 17. Edward, of Edward and Mary Jones.
1683, 12mo. 24. Elizabeth, of Hugh and Jane Roberts.

The earliest burials of record at Merion meeting:—
1682, 8mo. 23. Katharine, of Edward Rees.
1682, 9mo. 16. John Watkin. (Not the man of this name, in p. 137.)
1683, 7mo. 29. Sidney Jones.
" 8mo. 12. Katharine, dau. Robert & Elizabeth David.
" 8mo. 18. Mary Jones.
" 9mo. 5. Elizabeth Jones.
" 9mo. 20. Willia Jones.
" 11mo. 10. Evan John William.
" .... Evan Edward.

In 1702, the entries in the Merion book were in Welsh. The earliest burials at the Haverford meeting were
1684, 9mo. 19. William Sharpless.
1685, 7mo. 29. Margaret, wife of William Howell.
" 11mo. 9. Gwen, wife of Humphrey Ellis.
1687, 5mo. 6. Janet, wife of James James.

George Painter, Thomas John, David Kinsey, and Gobeithia Humphrey, were also buried here in 1687.

There were burials at the Radnor meeting from 3. 11mo. 1686, and the first births recorded were:
1684, 9mo. 12. John, of John and Margaret Jarman.
1636, 5mo. 20. Sarah, of Stephen and Elizabeth Evans.

[572]

WELSH FRIENDS' MEETINGS

There are no very early pictures of the Merion Meeting House extant. The sketchy, and near view of the old house, made by Hugh Reinagle, in 1829, engraved by J. W. Steel, and published by Childs, Philadelphia, 1830, is similar to another picture of it, labelled "Premier Temple de Quakers a Philadelphia," and "Primer Templo de las Cuacros en Filadelfia," "L. Thienon, del., Boiseau, sc." These views have frequently been reproduced. An earlier picture, one including the General Wayne Inn, and surroundings of the meeting house, may be found at page 111, of the printed Journal of Robert Sutcliff, 1804-05. These are herein reproduced, also copy of a wood-cut made about 1833-4.

From these early pictures, it may be seen that the meeting house has not changed in appearance since 1800, and that in the earliest sketch extant, it had the T shape, thus refuting the statement that it was built into its present shape after 1827-8. But by these views, we see that the post and rail fence, with the gate along the old Lancaster Road, has disappeared, and been replaced by a stone wall. Once, a path led from the door of the meeting house straight to this stone wall, where there was a stone built horse-block. After the grounds were altered to their present appearance, and coming to meeting *à cheval* ceased to be necessary, this horse-block of old memories "strolled" up the pike, and has rested ever since in front of the old Price house.

It seems singular now to read a notice of the Merion Meeting House printed fifty years ago like the following, "Merion Meeting House, located in the village of Gen. Wayne, at the head of the West Philadelphia Plank Road, five miles from Philadelphia. It is a stone building, surrounded by buttonwood trees. It is built something like a letter T. The walls are two feet thick. Its longest length is 36 feet. It is 14 feet to the roof, but the end facing the

WELSH SETTLEMENT OF PENSYLVANIA

South West is 24 feet high. Originally, it was stone-pointed, or rough stone, but in 1829, when it was repaired, it was plastered in imitation of large stones."

In the early years of the Merion Meeting, it was visited by many of the best known Friends' ministers, among them John Estaugh, John Richardson, John Salkeld, Thomas Wilson, Thomas Chalkley, and Samuel Bownes, and later, before 1740, by Robert Jordan, Mungo Bewley, John Burton, Paul Johnson, and Samuel Stephens, and subsequently, by Michael Lightfoot, Thomas Gawthrop, Benjamin Trotter, Thomas Brown, Jonah Thompson, John Griffith, Samuel Fothergill, Joshua Dixon, Samuel Jones Levick, and some others.

It may be supposed that the Friends' minister, John Richardson, who sailed from London, and arrived in Maryland, 5. 1mo. 1700-1, visited the meetings in the Welsh Tract, as he was intimate with Rowland Ellis, but he did not say so. But he records in his book:—"I went to visit a meeting in that Part called North Wales, which had not been long planted in that Place, where there was a fine, tender People, but few understanding English. Rowland Ellis was my interpreter. A good meeting it was. Some by interpreter expressed their great Satisfaction in our Visit to that meeting, which heretofore had not been counted as Friends." He left America on 6. 9mo. 1702. This item is useful in that it confirms what has been said of the Gwynedd settlement being more decidedly Welsh than the great Welsh Tract.

The Journal of John Fothergill, a traveling minister, on his second visit to Pensylvania, in 1721, tells, that on 27. 10mo., that year, "I went to Hartford where we had a very large meeting. And on the 28th, "I went to Radnor where was a larger and solidly profitable meeting." And on 29th., "to Merion, where a large number was gathered. I went that evening to lodge with J. Roberts, where I had a good and edifying Session with the old People, many Friends also coming there to see us." Next day, he returned to

WELSH FRIENDS' MEETINGS

Philadelphia. And further, in "The Life and Travels of John Fothergill," (reprinted and sold by James Chattin, in Church Alley, Philadelphia, 1754), on 6. 12mo., 1722, Mr. Fothergill says he was "at a General Meeting for Worship at Haverford, wherein the Lord's Power shook the Earth in many Hearts in divers respects." On the 14th, he was "at Lewis Walker's, in the Great Valley, and had a large meeting out of doors."

Thomas Chalkley, in his published Journal, says, 4mo. 5th, 1724, "I went to Merion to visit an ancient friend, John Roberts, who was sick near unto death, where I again met with John Salgeld. * * * The friend expressed his satisfaction in this visit," and died the next day. "He was a helper of the poor, and a maker of peace in the neighborhood." In 5mo. 1725, Mr. Chalkley was at a Merion meeting, "which was large and solid," and in 2mo. 1726, he writes, the meetings of friends of Haverford, Newtown, Radnor, and Merion "consist chiefly of ancient Britons, who are a religious, industrious, and increasing people." In 6mo. 1726, he attended "the General Meeting at Haverford," and in 9mo. was at a wedding in the Merion meeting house. (James Chattin also published Mr. Chalkley's works, in 1754).

In 1736, John Fothergill made another visit to Pensylvania, saying in his Journal, "some exercise having been upon me some years to visit the Churches in America once more," he came out to a meeting of the ministers and elders at Haverford, on 1st. 12mo., and three days after, he was at the Merion meeting. In his Life and Travels, John Churchman, a public Friend, of Nottingham, Pa., tells, in 1736, of visiting Merion meeting, "where we met our worthy friend John Fothergill, who had great and good service therein."

According to the Journal of John Woolman, a Friends' minister, he visited Merion, Haverford, and Radnor meetings in 8mo. 1758. And William Reckitt, who travelled through America, 1757-9, preaching among Friends, says

WELSH SETTLEMENT OF PENSYLVANIA

that on 12. 4mo. 1759, he attended Radnor meeting, and on 6th day, following, attended the Merion meeting, and went on to Philadelphia. The Journal of Daniel Stanton, a Philadelphia Friend, records, 3. 2mo. 1766, "After our quarterly meeting in Philadelphia, I sat out from home with several Friends towards Haverford. Lodged that night at George Smith's, and was next day at a large meeting at Haverford." He then went on to Radnor and Goshen meetings, which he says were large. From the Journal of Sanuel Neale, we learn that, on 20. 2d mo., 1772, he visited Radnor meeting which "was in a good degree lively, being favoured with the running of the heavenly oil." From the Journal of Job Scott, a travelling minister from Providence, R. I., we learn that on 3d day, 12mo. 1785, he was at Haverford, "a little meeting," and 5. 1mo. 1787, he was at Radnor, and on "6th day, 5th, at Merion, the most satisfactory meeting" he had been at for a long time, and returned to Philadelphia.

Edward Peckover, a Friend from London, travelling in America, tells in his Journal of his visit to "Miriam Meeting," in 12mo. 1742-3, and again in 3mo. 1743, and at the Haverford monthly meeting.

The Journal of Esther Palmer, of Rhode Island, a public Friend travelling with Susanna Freeborn, says she was at Philadelphia, in 9mo. 1704, and "visited the Marion Meeting, six miles from town, on a First-day," and that on Third-day following, they "went from town, with Joseph Glaisaer, to the Harford General Meeting, ten miles from Philadelphia." And in 11mo. following, she again attended the meetings of Merion, Haverford, and Radnor. Her Journal is a mere itinerary, generally without remarks. In 1705, "7th day of ye month & 6 of ye weeck," she "rode eight miles from Jacob Sincock's to the Merion meeting, and returned to town."

In the diary of Robert Sutcliff, a young English Friend, which he kept during his sojourn in and about Philadelphia, in 1790-1806, there are several interesting items about the

WELSH FRIENDS' MEETINGS

old Merion Meeting, for he spent many weeks visiting Friends in Merion, while yellow fever was epidemic in the city, in 1792-3 and later. Among the people he became acquainted with there, besides some mentioned below, were Peter Andrews, Henry Bowman, Elizabeth Cogshall, Elizabeth Bird, Joseph Paul, Sarah Harrison, the widow George, and Mary Price, who was, he says, about eighty years old, and always walked to the Merion Meeting House, about a mile from her house. He tells, 20. 7mo. 1806, that her daughter-in-law (unnamed), "who is a descendant of the Lloyds of Dollebran," owned "a deed from Charles Lloyd, and a female of the name of Davies, to a person of the name of Humphreys." "It was for 5,000 acres [bought] from Penn for £100, the same land, were it inclosed, now sells for £12 per acre."

Mr. Sutcliff frequently attended the Friends' Merion Meeting, and once visited a great camp meeting of Methodists near it, which he records was attended by a "great number of Negroes, and many of them in handsome carriages." He also attended Friends' Meeting at Radnor, and "dined at J. H.'s, and spent the evening at O. J.'s. This Friend was one of those who suffered banishment on account of supposed attachment to the British during the revolution. His sister [see p. 76], told me that on William Penn's arrival in America, he lodged at her great-grandfather's in Merion. At that time her grandfather was a boy of twelve years old," and Sutcliff then tells the anecdote of the boy peeping at Penn and seeing "the great man praying in private of his bed room," which has often been repeated, but with the old Llewellyn house, at Haverford, as the scene.

Should it be presumed that this happened at the time of Penn's second visit to his Province, in 1700-1, and that O. J. refers to Owen Jones, Sr., 1711-1793, sometime treasurer of Pensylvania, who was a conspicuous Tory, (see p. 76). and that Mr. Sutcliff was visiting him in 1792-3, then this Mr. Owen's sister was misinformed, or got the incident "all wrong," because one of her grandfathers (Dr. Jones),

WELSH SETTLEMENT OF PENSYLVANIA

was about 43 years old in 1700-1, and her other (Robert Owen), had then been dead about three years. Or, of her four great-grandfathers, only one (Dr. Wynne), came to Pensylvania and he was dead eight years, in 1700-1. If the spying happened at the time of Penn's first visit, 1682-3, the story is no more reliable, as her grandfather, Dr. Jones, was about 25 years old, and her other grandfather had not come to the Province. If the O. J. was Owen Jones, Jr., 1745-1825, the treasurer's son, and he was the one who "suffered" banishment, and one of his six sisters was Mr. Sutcliff, informant, then her grandfathers, Jonathan Jones, 1680-1770, and Hugh Evans, 1682-1772, could either of them have been the peeper in 1700-1, and two of her great-grandfathers, Dr. Edward Jones, 1657-1737, and Thomas Evans, 1651-1738, could have been Penn's host that memorable night, with everything in favor of the episode happening in this Jones family, but, of course, only during Penn's second visit to the Province.

Sutcliff tells also of a visit to the Haverford Preparatory Meeting, on 12. 10mo. 1805, on his way from the Radnor Prep. Mtg. to the Merion Prep. Mtg., and says that at the early settlement of this meeting, "Friends of Philadelphia went every third First-day to attend it, most of them coming on foot, a distance of ten miles." (Before the R. C. Church of St. Denis was erected in Haverford tp., south of Ardmore, the earliest church of the denomination, the Catholics living in what was the Welsh Tract, walked to St. Patrick's Church on 20th street in the city, for worship). And, continuing as to Haverford, Mr. Sutcliff wrote, "amongst the rest, William Penn used to come on horseback, and would occasionally take up a little bare-footed girl behind him, to relieve her when tired." Out of this item grew the story related by Thomas Clarkson, a biographer of Penn, that once little Rebecca Wood, "says Sutcliff," walking alone from Darby to Haverford Meeting, was taken up behind him by William Penn, and so carried to the Meeting.

Mr. Sutcliff, in entry of 14. 6mo. 1806, tells of attending

WELSH FRIENDS' MEETINGS

Merion Meeting, and listening to the preaching of the celebrated Friends' minister, James Simpson, and his impression of him. He records "Mr. Simpson is only a broom maker; he is thin, and upwards of six feet high; his visage is very long, and his face of an Indian complexion, with small, quick eyes, corresponding, and to appearances, he may be about eighty years of age. In the gallery, he commonly wears a dark colored cap, fitting closely to his head, and over his shoulders, a long dark colored cloak." At this Meeting, he says there was a unusually large attendance— "a senator, four judges, and four magistrates" were in the congregation, "who all behaved in a becoming manner." He recorded that the boys and girls attended the Merion Meeting in hot weather, without shoes or stockings. And that "a number of men Friends also in the upper seats, sat without their coats and stockings, having long cotton trowsers which came down to their shoe tops." And that there was also one young man, who sometime appears in the ministry acceptable, had on a striped cotton jacket and trousers, and a drab hat. A costume which appeared strange to the Englishman.

Mr. Sutcliff says he visited, 29. 6mo. 1806, "J. J. [brother to R. J.] and his wife, aged 95 and 89 years respectively." "One of her sisters is of the same age, and another sister in her 85th year." J. J. told he had "often heard his father speak of having seen the foundations laid of the first house built in Philadelphia." Mr. Sutcliff mentioned many other people but by initials only, as B. J., and "his country residence, just above the Falls of the Schuylkill"; Dr. H., who resided near the Merion Meeting House; D. J., J. Z., H. B., R. B., P. W., who was a German paper maker; and "O. J. and his mother-in-law, and her ten daughters."

In 1805, Mr. Sutcliff introduced the following item as an example of neutrality. A relation of his, W. B., who had a large stone house above Norristown, with 300 acres on the Schuylkill, extending to Perkiomen, he says, formerly owned by a Friend from London, named Vaux, who built

[579]

WELSH SETTLEMENT OF PENSYLVANIA

the house. When Vaux lived here during the American war, being in full view of the American encampment at Valley Forge on the opposite side of the Schuylkill, "he had frequently the company of Gen. Howe. One day it happened that he had Howe to breakfast with him, and Gen. Washington to tea."

On 10. 6mo. 1805, Mr. Sutcliff records "to Radnor monthly meeting at Merion. A couple who were about to be married, for whose accommodation the meeting at Merion was agreed to be held on 5th day, instead of 6th. After meeting, dined at J. H.'s. On 31st. 8mo. he was five days visiting at Merion, and in 9mo. he was there for three weeks. On 21 9mo., he says, "visited P. A. and his wife at H. Bowman's. They are an ancient couple of plain, honest Friends, both in the ministry." "The grandfather, Edward Andrews, of P. A. became a friend in a remarkable way; he was a fiddler, living on the sea coast, in the Jerseys, and after playing for a dance, returning home, found a skull on the sand, buried it, and the reflections convinced him." On 4. 10mo., Mr. Sutcliff says he attended the Merion meeting with Elizabeth Coggerhall and Elizabeth Bird, and went with them to the house of a young man who had been disowned for taking up arms, but who had lately been reinstated. And on 5. 10mo. 1805, "went with Joseph Paul, in his carriage, to see a large encampment on the Ridge Road, of poor people who had fled from the city on account of the yellow fever. Thence to William Hamilton's to see his plants."

Like the Friends of the Merion Preparative meeting, those of Haverford built their stone meeting house by degrees, slowly, and by contributions. The first stone house for public meetings was built in 1697-1700. In 1800, it was rebuilt, retaining part of the original structure, and has been added to, and on the whole, stands a substantial structure, built along plain lines peculiar to Friends' meeting houses.

WELSH FRIENDS' MEETINGS

There is good reason to believe that the Haverford Friends had a meeting house, built of dressed logs, almost co-existent with that of Merion, although "Harfod Town" was only a sparsely settled neighborhood up to 1690. The monthly meeting, when in rotation it met with the Haverford Friends, met at the home of John Bevan, according to the minutes, and it may be supposed the earliest weddings took place at private houses. The first marriage of record on the book of the Haverford Monthly Meeting, was that of Humphrey Ellis and Gwen Rees, on 10. 12mo. (Feb.) 1683-4. But it is not recorded with which preparative meeting it took place. But Lewis David and Florence Jones were married "at the Haverford meeting" 20. 1mo. 1689-90, and Rees Thomas and Martha Awbrey were married on 19. 4mo. 1692, "at the Haverford meeting," so it would appear there was a public meeting place for Haverford as early as Feb. 1689-90.

Admitting that Thomas Ellis's home was in Haverford, we have in a letter written by him at Dublin, Ireland, on 13 June, 1685, telling his correspondent the news from the Welsh Tract, as he knew it at the time he left here, in February, 1684-5. He wrote, "we have our burying place where we intend our meeting House [shall be built], as neer as we can to the Center" [of Haverford tp.]. He also tells that there were fifteen families living there, when he left, and eight others expected to arrive soon. There is no reason to doubt that this house was built when and where Mr. Ellis said, as we have from the minutes of the Haverford (Radnor) Mo. Mtg., "Att our monthly Meeting held at Haverford, ye 10th of ye 11th month, 1694." * * * "William Howell, William Jenkins, John Lewis, David Maurice, and David Lawrence, are ordered to gett a Stable made adjoining to this meeting House." This is certainly good proof that there was a public meeting place here. What kind of a building it was is unknown, but it does not appear to have been durable, if built only ten years, for, from the minutes, of the monthly meeting, held

WELSH SETTLEMENT OF PENSYLVANIA

with Haverford Friends, in 11mo. 1695, we learn a committee was appointed to inspect and consider what way will be most convenient, to rebuild, or to repair this meeting house (the one the men were meeting in), and what the cost would be in each case. No report of this committee, if made, is on record. It may be supposed that by 14 Jan. 1696-7, it was not yet decided which it was better to do, build or repair, as the minute of this date says that David Lewis "accounted to the monthly meeting he had received £5 from Maurice Llewellyn, in part of a legacy from Margaret Howell towards the Repairing or Rebuilding of ye Meeting House at Haverford." But from the next minute on this subject, it may be seen that the Haverford Friends decided to build.

1697-8, 1mo., a committee was appointed by the monthly meeting to get contributions of cash money "to assist Haverford friends to build their Meeting House." And at the next monthly meeting, in 2mo., another committee was named "to consider what charges the building of the Meeting House at Haverford in every respect shall come to, and bring an account thereof in writing against the next meeting." At the next monthly meeting, 3mo., this committee reported that the cost would amount to at least £158. Thereupon, another committee was appointed to bring the subscriptions of the Merion and Radnor Friends towards the building expenses of the Haverford meeting, to the next monthly meeting. And in 4mo. 1698, the committee reported it had "received from Radnor meeting, £5. 15. 0; Newtown meeting, £8. 0. 0; Merion meeting £32. 10. 0, and from Friends in the Upper End of Merion, £9. 10. 0. total £55. 12. 0." This was a large sum for the Merion Friends to contribute when they were themselves paying for a meeting house, yet in addition to this subscription, the women's meeting of Merion contributed £4. 13. 7, "towards building Haverford meeting House," and, again the extant book of minutes of women's monthly meeting, 20. 8mo. 1701, held at Haverford says, "The women friends of Merion contri-

WELSH FRIENDS' MEETINGS

buted £6. 13s. towards building Haverford meeting house." And by entry of 11. 7mo. 1701, the Merion men had increased their contribution to £33. 16. 2. The minute also says that these subscriptions from Merion were all paid. From the minutes of the men's monthly meeting, 11. 4mo. 1702, "informed that assistance was required towards finishing the meeting House at Haverford, and it was decided to lend the £10 left by John Humphrey (towards the printing "The Sons of Jacob in Welch), to be returned when desired." From these items, it may be seen that the experience of the two preparative meetings of Merion and Haverford, were about the same when building, and at the same time, only the Merion meeting did not get the deed for its "house lot" till in 1714, and the Haverford meeting trustees had their deed bearing date 7. 1mo. 1693-4, which was earlier even than the date of the deed to the Merion Friends for their graveyard land, which was in 1695.

In Radnor Town there was no necessity for a public meeting place for Friends before 1717, when erection of the present stone building was considered, the "town" being thinly settled, and dwellings scattered. But, as soon as families of Welsh Friends settled in far away Radnor, religious meetings were held at the dwellings of John Jermon and John Evans. The first wedding of record in this township and preparative meeting, took place at the home of Mr. Evans, on 2. 3mo. 1686, between Richard Ormes and Mary Tyder, both of this township.

When there was a sufficient number of Welsh Friends in Radnor Town, David Meredith formed and completed the organization of the Radnor preparative meeting, and it took the place of the Schuylkill preparative meeting in the Haverford monthly meeting. Through his efforts, it is presumed, the Radnor meeting house was erected. Of this event in Radnor, the minutes of the Haverford monthly meeting record, on 10. 8mo. 1717, "A letter from our friend, Benjamin Holme, to this meeting, recommending to their consideration the stirring up of Friends in the

WELSH SETTLEMENT OF PENSYLVANIA

building of the meeting house at Radnor, and with a desire that we should be concerned." This was approved, and a committee of the members of the monthly meeting was appointed, David Morris at the head, "to assist in the contrivance of the building thereof." At the next monthly meeting, "Radnor's new house" was again considered, but the erection of the house was not begun till the following spring. At the monthly meeting in 9mo. 1718, it was reported as partly completed; but in 4mo. 1721, it was not all finished, and the work on it was then only partly paid for, therefore, a committee was appointed by the monthly meeting to try and obtain cash contributions to help along the Radnor Friends, but in 5mo. 1723, the labor was not all paid. During the Revolutionary War, this meeting house was for a time occupied as soldiers' quarters and a hospital, by the Americans.

Up to 1700, there were apparently no inhabitants of Merion who were not Friends, either Welsh or English, the reason being that the original purchases of land were in large lots, and the settlers well able to hold their grants, and not cut them up into small farms, and sell them, till in the second and third generations.

It was the contrary in Radnor, and partially so in Haverford, and the small farm lots soon attracted many non-Quakers, especially those who built up the Welsh congregation of the Church of England in Radnor "town." As early as in 1700, this was a mission visited by the Rev. Evan Evans, the rector of Christ Church in the city, when services were held at the house of William Davis. As the register of St. David's P. E. Church begins with a baptism in 1706, it is presumed it was about that time the congregation had its first church, and that it was a log one standing on the farm of Mr. Davis (which in late years was the estate of Tryon Lewis), and that the ruins of a log building on the place may have been those of the church edifice which preceded the present stone building. There is an extant letter from the Rev. Mr. Evans to the S. P. G. F. P., dated

WELSH FRIENDS' MEETINGS

Sept. 1707, telling of services which he conducted "in the Welsh language at Radnor once a fortnight for four years past." It was not till seven years after this that the church had its first rector sent to take charge of the congregation. During these intervening years, the Rev. John Clubb, a Philadelphia school teacher, conducted the services, and preached at Radnor, as a missionary. The first graveyard of St. David's was at the junction of the Reeseville and Sugartown roads, where it was originally, or on 7 Sept. 1714, intended to build the present church, the corner stone of which was laid with ceremony, on 9 May, 1715. Up to 1765, the church had no floor, and the gallery was built in 1772. The first rectory, or "vestry house" was built in 1767, where a school house stood, but the present one was not erected till in 1844. During the Revolutionary War the church was without a rector, and closed, excepting that like the Haverford meeting house it was used by the American soldiers.

Before these Welsh Episcopalians had a minister, or their church, they seemed to prefer being wed by Friends' ceremony than by a Justice of the Peace, or the missionary, hence there are some marriages of non-Friends on the books of the Haverford Monthly Meeting, as, for instance, the marriage (certificate dated "Haverford, the 17th day of the Ninth month, in the year 1687") of "Daniel Thomas, late of Haverford, aforesaid," and "Eleanor Vaughan, of the same," "came to the meeting of God, called Quakers," and were married according to Friends' form. This certificate was signed in the usual Friends' custom, by Lewis David, Eleanor Lawrence, Daniel Thomas, James Thomas, Sarah Rhydrth, Eleanor Thomas, David Lawrence, Given Thomas, Morris Llewellyn, Francis Price, John Richard, Sarah David, David Lawrence, Mary Llewellyn, Richard Hayes, and David llyllynn.

It is hardly within the scope of this work to more than refer casually to the unfortunate division, without bringing forward the particulars in the matter, in the Merion prepa-

WELSH SETTLEMENT OF PENSYLVANIA

rative meeting, which occurred in 1827-28, and was brought about by the injection of the theories and teachings of Elias Hicks, when the meeting was separated into two bodies, both members of the Society of Friends.

Ancient Friends to-day recollect hearing that olden time neighbors, birthright members of the Merion meeting (and it was possibly so in the other Welsh Tract preparative meetings), who held different views on the serious matter of doctrine and belief, or the tenets of their religion, the wedge that split every Friends' meeting, became estranged, and their social intercourse was interrupted, and that, at first, after the majority of this meeting was convinced that Friend Hicks was right in his claims and teachings, the two sections, the majority and the minority members, continued to use the Merion Meeting House for worship, alternately, each in a manner after its own convictions. It is related, that while all sat together, the so-called "Hicksites," their leaders being John and Joseph George, and Edward Price, would first hold their meeting for worship, then adjourn, close the shutters, shut the doors of the meeting house, and go home, leaving the minority, who came to be designated as "Orthodox Friends," protesting vociferously in darkness. Then these would open the door and shutters, and hold their services. But the feeling became too intense for such a condition to last long, and the two bodies met in the old meeting house at widely different hours and days, till, it is tradition, the "Hicksites" changed the locks on the doors, and the minority could not get the use of the house, or, till the Orthodox minority could no longer "suffer" such humiliating conditions, and, under the leadership of Jesse and David George, Israel Wister, and Henry Morris, retired in a body, leaving the property, and the ancient meeting house, with its memories equally dear to them, in possession of the Hicksite majority. But they took with them some of the old records of the meeting, the treasurer's accounts, &c., and these are still preserved in their vault, at their library, instituted in 1742, No. 142 N. 16th Street, Philadelphia.

WELSH FRIENDS' MEETINGS

This branch, the seceding members of the Merion Meeting, transferred their meetings for worship and business to a little stone school house, built about 1732, and standing till recently, in the woods, near where 57th and Jefferson streets now intersect, which they used till about 1882, or till the death of Mr. Henry Morris, the last survivor of the "seceders." In an article by Mr. George Vaux, a venerable "Orthodox Friend," in "The Friend," 12. 9mo. 1896, tells a little more of the period of this unpleasant episode in the entity of the Merion Meeting. He says, in 1827, at the time of the separation, the Radnor Monthly Meeting consisted of five particular meetings, namely, Merion, Haverford, Radnor, The Valley, and Charlestown, and out of the 445 members of the monthly meeting there were only 70 of them who were "Orthodox," and naturally all of the meeting houses, and properties were retained by the "Hicksites." Those holding to the Trinitarian belief, as above said, retired from the Merion meeting to the little school house above Hestonville. And those from the Haverford meeting retired to meet at private houses, and eventually met at a meeting house they erected in 1837, near Haverford College. These two Orthodox Meetings had a monthly meeting up to 1865, when they united with the Western District of the Philadelphia Monthly Meeting of the "Orthodox" branch of the Society. After the decease of Henry Morris, the Hestonville Meeting, as the Merion seceders' meeting was known, was "laid down," but that of the "Haverford Friends (Orthodox)," still lives. Some of the records of the original meetings of the Welsh Friends are preserved in the vault of the Friends' Library, at 15th and Race streets, Philadelphia. By mutual arrangement, both branches of the Friends have had the old books in each other's keeping copied for themselves.

On the afternoon of the 5th. 10mo., 1895, "the bi-centennial celebration of the erection of the Merion meeting house," the pioneer House of God west of the Schuylkill river, was celebrated with appropriate ceremonies in a large

WELSH SETTLEMENT OF PENSYLVANIA

tent erected on the lawn on which the historic building stands, a full account of which may be found in the Philadelphia newspapers of that time, and in two little books, handsomely gotten up. It was estimated that upwards of 2,000 people visited the old meeting house that day. Both sections of the Society of Friends attended because the early history of the Merion meeting is the heritage and glory of each. The subject of this commemoration was first introduced at a meeting of the Radnor monthly meeting, on 11. 4mo. 1895, and the celebrations was held under its auspice, Mr. Robert M. Janney being selected as chairman of the committee of arrangement and program.

The ceremonies were simple, and began with a paper read by Miss Walker, of Chester Valley, sketching briefly the annals of the Merion meeting. It is of interest to note here that Miss Walker, speaking of the desire for "an independent State" the Welsh Friends had to surrender after considerable of a struggle, as related before, said, "this relinquishment was only accomplished through a stern sense of duty, and was done, as Friends say, 'greatly in the cross,' after the failure of Griffith Owen, and others, to convince the Commissioners." Miss Walker was followed in the program of the day by the reading of an appropriate poem by Dr. James R. Walker, of Philadelphia. Dr. Allen G. Thomas, of Haverford College, read a paper, entitled "What the Friend has done," in which he told of the good and useful deeds inaugurated and accomplished by the Friends. Dr. Francis B. Gummere, also of Haverford College, read a poem, which was followed by a service of meditation, and a prayer. The literary part of the day's function closed with an address by Mr. Isaac H. Clothier, who spoke of the work and principles of the Society of Friends. The meeting house was temporarily converted into a museum, and relics and mementos of the olden time of the neighborhood were displayed, together with old certificates of removal, old marriage certificates, deeds for local lands, &c. At the time of the celebration, there were not a dozen

WELSH FRIENDS' MEETINGS

families of Friends which attended meetings in the old Merion house, and at this writing, there are not that many, and it is over seventy-five years since a wedding of record took place within its walls, but burials in the old graveyard are frequent.

This is, you may have seen, an annotated compilation of facts concerning the removal of the Welsh Friends to Penn's province. Assembled, they have told of the promises made to them as inducements to remove; their disappointment that they were not kept; how they adjusted themselves to their defeat, and, throughout their troubles with Penn, and his agents in his province, and for years after, that their leading men, their ministers and elders, were always noted for good influence in provincial civic affairs, and for this reason deserve the prominence they hold in the annals of the Province, and the Commonwealth.

But this was not the only end aimed at. It was to relate and to record the *personnel* of the Welsh settlers; the locations of their first purchases; their early experiences in their new homes, matters interesting always to descendants, and something about their Meetings; but particularly concerning the Merion Preparative Meeting, and its place of worship, the oldest meeting house in America.

The method followed, I can only hope has been satisfactory to a majority of the readers. The viewpoint of the events of the past with "the eyes of to-day," should not necessarily distort them. However, human nature was the same then as now. The "high ideals" of olden times still have place; morals have only shifted. What was "wrong" then, from our viewpoint, does not obtain now. What is "wrong" now-a-days was never even imagined then. The "Christian sense of Sin" was the same in the 17th as in the 20th century. Only the "Golden Rule" has accumulated more "exceptions," and "creature comforts" are better, at least they seem so, now-a-days.

I had no idea when, on that
"Fair First-day morning,"

WELSH SETTLEMENT OF PENSYLVANIA

I made my first acquaintance with the old Merion meeting house, which I then visited out of curiosity, that it would become the cause of such arduous labor as I have since experienced. However, it has been facinating, this self-imposed task as one of the chroniclers of its annals, and this strange to say, for I have no Welsh blood, nor am I a Quaker, or a descendant of one. I say this all in extenuation of the selection and reproduction of some statements which I do not imagine will be pleasant reading to everyone.

APPENDIX

Page 26. "No where was persecution [of Quakers] more severe" [than in Wales]. The Welsh Quakers "stood it all heroically, and when William Penn offered them a haven of rest, they found an honourable way of escaping the trials which seemed practically endless. But they loved their old country; its language and customs, and a committee of them obtained from William Penn the offer of a Barony, where they could have a new Wales, and, as they hoped, a government of their own, unmixed with alien influences". (See pp. 442-3, "The Quakers in the American Colonies", by Rufus M. Jones, Isaac Sharpless, and Amelia M. Gummere, 1911).

Page 27. An exception can be given to this statement, for Lady Anne Conway was prominent as a Quakeress in time of Mr. Fox. She was the daughter of Sir Heneage Finch, speaker of the House of Commons, died in 1631. She married (his first wife), in 1651, the Hon. Edward Conway (son and heir of Edward, Viscount Conway, of Ragley), who succeeded his father in 1655, and in 1679, was created Earl of Conway. Lady Conway's brother, Heneage Finch, 1621-1682, was created Earl of Nottingham, and was Lord Chancellor.

Page 80. The location of the Merion meeting house was rather on the northeastern line, than corner of Rees's first land.

Page 80. The deeds of 1695 and 1714, have cleared up all doubt as to on which lot the Merion Meeting House was built.

Page 96. "Elizabeth William Owen" (not "Katherine Robert") was the wife of Robert Pugh, Gent., and mother of Hugh Roberts. See pp. 125-6.

Page 98. The six lines at the foot of this page were badly pied by pressman, and should read:

In Radnorshire, he visited Roger Hughes; at Lanole, Edward Jones, David Powel, Thomas Goodin, near Llwyn-du. From North Wales he travelled to many places in South Wales, then back to Merionethshire, in the North, where he visited Lewis Owen, near Dollegelley, then to Bala, and "Penllyn where I was born and bred," and visited there his old friend, Robert Vaughan, and then made another pilgrimage through Wales.

WELSH SETTLEMENT OF PENSYLVANIA

Page 110. At the top of this page, between the third and fourth lines, should be the lost line:
Goch of Byrammer, in the parish of Cerrig y druidion.
Page 110. Thomas Ellis and Hugh Roberts filed Memorials as to John Thomas with the Haverford Mo. Mtg.

Page 117. The difficulty that the heirs of John Thomas had in getting a bonus lot in the city, as in the following petition, is an example of what other Welshmen experienced.

"The Case of Robert Jones in Relation to a high Street Lot appurtenant to his father's purchase Stated.

May it please the Proprietor.

My father John Thomas and Edward Jones for themselves and Company in 7ber in the Year 1681 purchased 5000 acres of Land in this Province of which Quantity my father's part was 1250 acres.

In the year 1682 Edward Jones arrived here with several others of that Company by whom my father sent some Effects and agreed with them to make some provision for him against his intended coming and on the 18th of the 2d Month 1683 The proprietor issued his Warr^t to the Surveyor Genl to lay out to my father a front lot on Delaware proportional to his purchase of 1250 ac as afores^d.

In the beginning of the year 1683 my fathers intended Voyage hither was prevented be Death But his Widow and family about 20 in number arrived here in November 1683 and found one half of the purchase taken up in the place since called Merion and some small Improvement made on the same where we then settled And as we were soon after informed a lot was laid out in the City on Delaware front by one Richard Noble a Deputy Surv^r in pursuance of the Warr^t afores^d soon after wch s^d Noble left these parts and on Enquiry no Return found of the s^d Lot the Warr^t also was mislaid and not found for several Years during wch interval one Herriot (If I mistake not) possess^d himself of the lot laid out to us as afores^d.

On the 16th of 7ber 1684 the Comm^{rs} granted a Warr^t to my mother for the high Street lot appurten^t to the purchase afores^d.

About the Year 1692 the Warr^t for the front lot being found we thereupon applied to the Comm^{rs} for relief but upon enquiry the Surv^r alleged there was no vacant front lot on Delaware the s^d Comm^{rs} therefore issued their Warr^t dated the 24th. 10th M^o 1692 to the Surveyor to lay out to my Mother a Lot of 50 foot front on Delaware second Street adjoining John Griffiths wch lot was laid out accordingly.

But the High Street lot we were told fell at Skulkil and we refused to accept of it there it being as we conceived without any one president that our front lot should lie on Delaware and our High Street lot on Skulkil.

APPENDIX

About the year 1700 the Second Street lot laid out to us as afore^{sd} was again taken from us, but on the 6th: 2^d M^o. 1702 the Comm^{rs} granted us another Warr^t for a Second Street lot in lieu of the former, but of 34 foot broad, no more (as we supposed) being then vacant and to compensate its deficiency in breadth, a small lot of 20 ft broad on third Street was joined to it, and afterwards confirmed to us by patent But no high Street lot has yet been laid out to us

I therefore desire the proprietor would be pleased to grant a Warr^t for the high Street lot in such manner as has been usual to other purchasers."

Robert Jones's mother, whom he mentions above, (and of whom in page 117), was known in her widowhood by her maiden name, after Welsh custom, as well as by her husband's name, "Katharine Robert" and "Katharine Thomas." Her certificate of removal which she brought over, and is preserved with Merion Meeting MSS, it may be seen was more than the usual, formal indorsement from one meeting to another.

"To all whom it may concern:

Whereas, Katerin Robert, of llaithgwm, in ye County of Merioneth, widdow, hath declared before us her intention in order to her and her families removal to Pensilvania in America, wee thought it convenient to certify in her and their behalfe yt she is one yt received the truth for these ten years past, and that hath walked since answerable to the truth according to her measure. She is a woman yt never gave occasion to ye enemies of truth to open their mouths against ye truth which she owned; her children taught and educated in the fear of the Lord from their infancy Answerable to ye duty of parents, both professing and possessing ye truth.

from our mens & womens
meetings ye 18 of 5mo. 1683.

Robert Owen, Cadd Lewis, Richard Price, Edward Griffith, Elizabeth William Bowen, Elizabeth John, Margaret Cadwalader."

As stated in page 121, this Robert Jones married (11 May, 1693), Ellen Jones, sister-in-law to Mrs. Katharine Jones, (p. 270), whose certificate of removal is also among the Merion Meeting archives. In a few years, these two remarkable pioneer women, related to each other by consanguinity in their native country, became more closely connected by subsequent intermarriages between their descendants. In this connection, it is interesting to know that Mr. Lewis Jones Levick, of Bala, Philadelphia, has a handsome cabinet made by combining, without changing, the two sea-chests, handsomely carved, which were brought to the New World by these two ladies, "the two Katharins". The chest of Katharine Robert, or Thomas, carries her initials: K R 1664.

WELSH SETTLEMENT OF PENSYLVANIA

Page 121. "1756, Aug. 30. Robert Jones, Dr.
On acc't his purchase.
The Estate of Jo Williams.
To the Gulph Mill & plant'n
sold him this day at Vendue,—1005
Pd for Deeds & recording   1. 7.6.

£1006. 7.6.

Pd Cash £290, (& by 5 Jan. 1757, had pd all but 14.18.9, bal due). it is paid".

Above item from the "Jones Papers", (in the Levick collection), where may be seen the marriage certificate of the above Robert Jones and Ellen Jones, with seventy-five signatures. Their wedding took place at the house of Katharine Thomas, 3. 11. 1693. Also marriage certificates of James Jones, of Blockley, and Hannah Hayes, dau. of Richard, 10. 8mo. 1727, (and the birth dates of their children); and of Jonathan Jones, (son of Jonathan and Gainor Jones), and Sarah Jones, (dau. Thomas and Ann Jones), dated 8. 11mo. 1741; and of Evan Jones, (son of John Pugh), and Hannah (Davis) Jones, dau. of Hugh David and Mary Elizabeth, in 1712, and also of Lewis Jones and Katharine Jones, dau. of Thomas Jones. dated 29. 10. 1732 (and births of their children).

Page 129. Sidney Rees's father was "Evan Rees", of Penmaen.

Page 160. In the Book of Memorials of the Haverford Mo. Mtg. may be read the memorial prepared by John Humphreys as to Robert Owen, and his wife, Jane. He said, "They were the man and woman to my knowledge that first opened the door for a reformation of religion in the country (Merionethshire) where they lived, after the Civil War between King and Parliament began." Rowland Ellis also testified as to their worth:—"After the time of Oliver and Richard Cromwell, Robert was commissioned captain of the militia, and governor of Bewmares, a seaport town upon the Irish coast." But when Robert Owen was required to take the Oath of Allegiance and Supremacy, he refused, and was imprisoned for —— years. His wife then was the mother of nine sons, and her relatives, "yt then bore ye chieffest sway in ye whole county," urged her to prevail on her husband to yeild, and save his estate for his children, but she declined to interfere. Robert and Jane died within five days of each other, in 5mo. 1685.

Page 167. Line 18 from bottom should be, "and married his second wife" (?). See pp. 168-9.

Page 168. Line 7 from bottom, omit comma between "sensible" and "she".

Page 178. Line 2 from bottom, should be "Ruabon."

APPENDIX

Page 179. Will of "Daniel Medlicott, of Haverford," signed in the presence of Stephen Evans, John Roberts, and Daniel Meredith, 16. 7. 1688, was proved at Philadelphia, 20 March, 1697-8. He left his estate to his wife, Martha, and mentioned his daughter, Mary Medlicott, and overseers Edward Jones and Francis Howell. He had property "near Schoolkill beyond the Gulff". His widow, Martha, married James Keite (his second wife), who died in 1713.

Page 181. I do not know who was the compiler of the pedigree, so cannot speculate on its authenticity, or reliability, and this, too, since no authorities are given for important statements made, nor are the sources of the information cited, but there is a "long distance" pedigree of Dr. Thomas Wynne printed in page 618, of Jordan's "Colonial Families of Philadelphia." It says that the Doctor was the son of Thomas ap John Wynne, and that "he was born in parish of Yskeiviog, near Caerways, Flintshire." The Doctor's immediate pedigree as given, runs,

"John ap Rees ap John Wynne" married at Bodfari church, 29 Oct. 1588, Grace Morgan. (It is not known when either died). "Their only son,"

"Thomas ap John Wynne," lived on Brovedog farm in Yskeiviog parish. He was *bapt.* at Yskeiviog par. church 20 Dec. 1589. (His wife's name not given). (According to the Doctor's statement, his father died about 1638). "He had five sons. His third and fourth were,"

3. John Wynne, *bapt.* at above church, 13 April, 1625. He came to Pensylvania with his brother, and lived in Sussex county.

4. Dr. Thomas Wynne, *bapt.* at above church, 20 July, 1627.

Page 182. Line 5 from top, should be "Gwydir."

Page 191. Line 13 from top, should be "Mary Southworth."

Page 236. The certificate of removal of Rowland Ellis and his wife was read in the Haverford Mo. Mtg., 12. 6mo. 1697. It appears that meetings for worship were held at his house during the cold weather of 1713-4, and for weddings also.

Page 284. See The Cosmopolitan Magazine, March, 1909, for further concerning the Hank-Lincoln pedigree.

Pages 294-6. The "Awbrey" pedigree is reproduced from Dr. Jordan's "Colonial Families of Philadelphia", (pp. 139-40), and Glenn's "Merion in the Welsh Tract." But the pedigree of "Aubrey, of Llantrithyd, in Glamorganshire", in Betham's "Baronetage", vol. II. p. 137, reproduced from the pedigree compiled by Vincent, the Windsor Herald, of Elizabeth's reign, differs somewhat, as follows, from the one here reproduced:—

(No. 6). THOMAS AUBREY, lord of Aberkinrigg and Slough, [who was the son of Thomas Aubrey, lord of Aberkinrigg, &c. (and

WELSH SETTLEMENT OF PENSYLVANIA

his wife Joneda, dau. Traherne ap Einion, lord of Commott, descended from Lord Brouham, of Brecknock, "who had thirty children"), son of William Aubrey, (and Margaretta, dau. Sir William Gunter), second son of Sir Reginald Aubrey, a knight in the train of Bernard de Newmarch, in his expedition into Wales, 1094, and for services on this occasion received the grant of part of the great manor of Aberkinrigg and Slough, son of "Saint Aubrey", a companion of The Conqueror, 1066], who m. a dau. of Saint Andrew Carew, (son of Egan, Baron Carew, son of Edmund, Baron Carew, and his wife, Elizabeth, dau. of Rhys ap Tudor King of South Wales), and had,

(No. 8). THOMAS AUBREY, lord of Aberkinrigg and Slough, who m. Nesta, dau. of Owen Gethin, a descendant of Blethin, lord of Brecknock. From this man to No. 14 the pedigrees are similar.

Betham, following out the family of Hopkin Aubrey, (13), says he had five sons, and that Thomas Aubrey, second son, was the father of William Aubrey, LL.D., Regius Professor of Law at Oxford, and that (14) William Aubrey, the fifth son, was seated at Ballege, but gives only William's issue by his wife, a dau. of Maddock ap Traharne, of Maddock.

Page 300. Four years after his arrival in America, Edward Foulke wrote in Welsh an account of his removal. It is the only account of this emigration written by one of the Gwynedd Company known to exist, and it is more circumstantial and precise than almost any other referring to any of the Welsh settlers in Pensylvania. With this is a brief genealogy of Edward Foulke, written by himself, all in the British language:—

"I, Edward Foulke, was the son of Foulke ap Thomas ap Evan ap Thomas ap Robert ap David Lloyd ap David ap Evan Vaughn ap Griffith ap Madoc ap Jerwert ap Madoc ap Rihrid Flaidd, Lord of Penllyn, who dwelt at Rhiwaedog.

"My mother's name was Lowry, the daughter of Edward ap David ap Ellis ap Robert, of the parish of llanvor, in Merionethshire.

"I was born on the 13th of 5th month, 1651, and when arrived at mature age, I married Eleanor, the daughter of Hugh ap Cadwallader ap Rhys, of the parish of Spytu, in Denbighshire. Her Mother's name was Gwen, the daughter of Ellis ap William ap Hugh ap Thomas ap David ap Madoc ap Evan ap Cott ap Evan ap Griffith ap Madoc ap Einion ap Meredith, of Cai-Fadog, and she was born in the same parish and Shire with her husband. We lived at a place calle Coed-y-foel, a beautiful farm, belonging to Roger Prince, Esq., of Rhiwlas, Merionethshire aforesaid. But in process of time, I had an inclination to remove with my family to the Province of Pensylvania; and in order thereto, we set out on the third day of the 2nd

APPENDIX

Month, A. D. 1698, and came in two days to Liverpool, where, with divers others who intended to go the voyage, we took shipping the 17th of the same month, on board the "Robert and Elizabeth," and the next day set sail for Ireland, where we arrived and staid until the first of the 3rd month, May, and then sailed again for Pensylvania, and were about eleven weeks at sea."

Page 356. "A political governor ran a county line through their Tract, and devided their State interests. * * * * The powers, both civil and ecclesiatical, conspired to break their unity." ("The Quakers in the American Colonies.")

Page 372. "It was impossible to give them [the Quakers of the Welsh Tract] a complete government, and complete possession of the soil. Saxon ideas would creep in, and Saxon men would marry their daughters, and while their countrymen at home retained the Welsh customs, in a generation or two, they were lost "in Pensylvania. ("The Quakers in the American Colonies.")

Page 513. This matter of buying "the right to affirm", also was noticed as follows by the Falls Meeting, Bucks Co., in 1726. "The Governor and General Assembly of the Province having passed a law for the ease of Friends relating to a solemn affirmation, the getting of which to be confirmed hath cost some Friends considerably, it is therefore agreed that a free contribution be made".

Page 525. In this connection, it may be observed that in early days it was compulsory that men Friends wear their hats in meetings. For instance, because Thomas Atkinson, Sr., 1663-1739, when attending Bridgeton (or Mt. Holly) preparative meeting, would sit in meetings with his hat off, Restore Lippincott reported him to the Burlington Mo. Mtg., for "violation of usuage". Thomas made some satisfactory explanation, and the matter was dropped.

INDEX

WELSH SETTLEMENT OF PENSYLVANIA

"Ye *Labour* and ye *Patience*, ye *Judgement* and ye *Penetration* which are required to make a *Good Index* is only known to those who have gone through with this *most necessary* and *painful*, but *least praised* part of a publication."—(William Oldys, 1687.)

N. B. The names in the following pages are not included in this Index—423-426; 456-457; 448-486; 490-493; 517-518; 541-548; 563; 566-569; 571.

PARTIAL INDEX OF NAMES.

Abel. Thomas, 154
Abraham. Daniel, 347
" Enoch, 490
" Isaac, 490
" James, 490, 491
" Joseph, 130
" Noah, 490
" Sarah, 490
Adams. John, 443
Addihl. William, 455
Albin. Thomas, 347
Alexander. Henry, 452
Alice v. James Lewis, 498
Allen. Benjamin, 283
" Sarah Catherin, 160
Allen. William, 435
Allin. Mrs. Philip T., 294
Andrews. Edward, 579
" Peter, 576
" Roger, 191
Andrew. Shrieve John, 319
Anhurs. Charles, 480

Ann. John Vaughan, 292
Anthony. Richard, 319
Arndt. 474
Armes. Richard, 259
" Thomas, 261
Armett. Richard, 419
Arthur. Charles J., 481
" Robert, 262
Ascue. John, 97
Ashbridge family, 135
Ashbridge. George, 136, 211
Ashbridge. Phebe, 211
Ashcombe. } Charles, 51,
Ashcom. } 52, 67, 71, 88, 366
Aston. } George, 438, 442
Ashton. }
Astor. Mrs. Ava W., 294
Atherton. Grace, 210, 211
Atherton. Henry, 211
" Jennet, 211
Atkinson. James, 122
" Thomas, 597

Atlee. George B., 274, 285.
Aubrey. } Barbara, 163
Awbrey. }
" Barbara, 289
" Elizabeth, 172
" Gwalter, 295
" Hopkin, 295
" Jenkin, 295
" Martha, 172, 294, 296, 520
Awbrey. Morgan, 295
" Richard, 295, 296
Awbrey. Thomas, 172, 295, 296
Awbrey. William, 167, 168, 171, 172, 295, 296
Aull. James, 289
Bache. Sarah, 521
Bacon. Charles L., 73
" Charles W., 73
" David, 420
Bailey. Robert, 420
Baird. Mrs. Edgar W., 284
Baird. Henry C., 284, 294

[599]

WELSH SETTLEMENT OF PENSYLVANIA

Baird. James, 449
Baldwin family, 473
Ball. John, 196, 232, 261
Barker. Thomas, 368
Barnes. Alice, 189
" John, 189
Barrett. Hugh, 481
Bartlett. Walter, 98
Bartram. Edward, 420
" George, 420
" Isaac, 451
Basset. Catharine, 289
" Thomas, 289
Bate. Humphrey, 224
Bealer. Jacob, 130
Beardsley, Alexander, 146
Becket. Peter, 561
Bedford. Gunning, 419
" William, 420
Bedward. William, 85
Beirne. Rich. F., 300
Bell. Mrs. John T., 289
Bennstone. } John, 301
Benson. }
Berenger. Raymond de, 285
Besse. Joseph, 185
Bethel. Major John, 455
Bettaly. } Humphrey,
Bettly. } 178, 191
Bettle. Mrs. Sam'l., 283
Bevan family, 166, 167
Bevan's house, 162
Bevan's land, 163
Bevan. Andrew J., 289
" Ann, 103, 170
" Awbrey, 169
" Barbara, 167, 170
Bevan. Catherine, 170
" Chas., 163, 168, 169, 170, 255
Bevan. Elinor, 221
" Elizabeth, 170
" Evan, 103, 168, 169, 170, 221, 257
Bevan. Henry C., 170, 289
Bevan. Jane, 169
" John, 25, 33, 95, 98, 103, 117, 124, 138, 163-170, 171, 191, 199, 203, 204, 218, 221, 226, 232, 244, 245, 249, 254, 255, 256, 258, 260, 261, 263, 288, 289, 294, 317, 318, 366, 371, 383, 384, 433, 498, 500, 503, 505, 506, 510, 513, 515, 529, 533, 580
Bevan. Jr. John, 163, 168, 169

Bevan. John L., 170
" Mary, 319
" Richard, 168, 490
Bevan. Stephen, 223, 530, 251, 259, 261
Bevan. Thomas, 168
" Walter, 289
" William, 235, 319, 502
Bevan. William E., 289
Bicking. Frederick, 456
" Richard, 456
Biddle family, 159
Biddle. Alexander, 283
" Arthur, 283
" Jr., A. W., 283
" Charles M., 283
" Clement, 159, 420
Biddle. James W., 283
" John, 159, 420
" John B., 283
" William, 283
Bingley. William 242
Bird. Elizabeth, 576, 579
Bispham. Mrs. J. B., 294
Blackford. Mrs. Eugene, 283
Blackham. Richard, 275
Blackstone, 97
Blackwell. Gov. John, 143, 352, 353, 359
Blair. Mrs. A. B., 283
Blunstone. } John, 353,
Blunston. } 358, 529
Bohun. William de, 285
Bond. Elizabeth, 103
" Joseph, 87
Bonsell. Edward, 419
Boone. Andreas, 350
Boteler. Sir William, 286
Boude. Thomas, 440
Boudinot. Elias, 453
Boulton. Job, 65
Bourge. John, 241
Bowle. John, 174
Bowman. Henry, 576, 579
Bowne. John, 232
" Samuel, 101
Bowen. Evan, 271
" John, 173, 180
" Mary, 197
" Owen, 98
" Thomas, 107
Boyle. Capt. James, 468
Bradford. Andrew, 152
" William, 526
Brascy. Thomas, 386
Briggs. David, 452
Bringhurst. James, 419
" Joseph, 420

Brinton. Ann, 230
" Elizabeth, 230
" William, 230
Broadber. Will, 163
Brock. John, 189
Brockes. Samuel, 275
Brooke. Hugh Jones, 133, 296.
Brooke. Hunter, 133
" Jr.. Hunter, 296
" Nathan, 216
" Mrs. Nathan, 296
" William T., 133, 296
Brown. Martha M., 190
" William. 174
Browne. Sir Anthony, 288
" Sir Thomas, 288
Browning. Charles H., 159
Browning. Edward, 73, 130
Browning. Sr., Mrs. Edw., 283
Browning. John, 527
Bryan. George, 474
Buck. William J., 535, 539.
Buffstin. Levin, 98
Bullock. Anna E., 274
Burge. John, 25, 196, 197, 232, 249, 253
Burnyeat. John, 29, 240
Burr. John, 159
Bury. Richard, 442
Buse. Arthur, 204
Buttall. Martha, 189
" Jonathan, 189
" Nathaniel, 185
" Samuel, 188, 189
Buzby. Mrs. Duncan L., 289
Cadwalader family, 107, 109
Cadwallader David ap Hugh, 276
Cadwalader ap Evan, 267, 271, 269, 301
Cadwalader Rhys Lloyd, 290
Cadwalader Thomas Hugh, 111, 283
Cadwalader. Dr. Ch. E., 74
Cadwalader. Edward, 107, 537
Cadwalader. Gen. George, 74

[600]

WELSH SETTLEMENT OF PENSYLVANIA

Cadwalader. Hannah, 73
" John, 73, 74, 77, 84, 109, 138, 190, 192, 193, 275, 276, 280, 283, 299, 457, 530
Cadwalader. Gen. John, 74
Cadwalader. Judge John, 74
Cadwalader. John L., 74
" Col. Lambert, 74
Cadwalader. Margaret, 96, 593
Cadwalader. Mary, 73
" Morgan, 107
" Rebecca, 73
" Richard M., 74
Cadwalader. Sarah, 107
" Thomas, 73, 84, 122, 198, 271
Cadwalader. Dr. Thomas, 74
Cadwalader. Gen. Thomas, 74
Campanius. Rev. John, 321
Campanius. Thomas, 321
Canby. Mrs. Edward T., 284
Caner. Harrison K., 133 296
Carew. Edmund de, 295
" Sir Edgar de, 295
Carew. John de, 295
" Nesta de, 295
Carlisle. Abraham, 471, 473
Carpenter family, 146
Carpenter. Samuel, 97, 146, 222, 356, 357, 529
Carpenter. Preston, 294
Carpley. Mary, 218
Cassel. Hernell, 275
Casby. James, 283
Cassatt. A. J., 444
Castner. Jacob, 449, 450
Chadwick. William, 429
Chalkley. Thomas, 72, 275
Chambers. Benj., 146, 164, 196, 199
Chambers. Colonel, 238
Charles ab Evan, 163
Charleton. Sir Edward, 293
Chase. Mrs. P. B., 294
Chattin. James, 574
Chaworth. Sir Patrick, 285
Cherleton. Sir Edward, 297

Cherleton. Joan de, 293
" John de, 297, 299
Chew. Samuel, 74, 193
" William, 193
Chichester. Mrs. G. M., 284
Childs. Allen, 284, 300
" George Wm., 165
Chorley. John, 189
Churchman. Mrs. C. J., 294
Churchman. John, 527
Clapp. B. Frank, 130
Clancy. Widow, 275
Clare. Gilbert de, 297
" Richard de, 281
Clark. Major, 466
" John, 171
Clarkson. Thomas, 577
Claypool. George, 420
" James, 400, 420
Claypool. Joseph, 420
Clayton family, 508
Clement. John B., 283
Clothier. Isaac H., 587
Cloud. William, 260
Clubb. Rev. John, 584
Coates. Edward H., 133
" George M., 133
" Henry T., 133
" Joseph H., 133
" William M., 133
" Lt. William, 454
Cobb. William, 428
Cochran. George, 74
" Travis, 74, 294
" William, 74
" Major William, 456
Cochran. Wm. Greene, 74
Cock. Peter, 68
Cockshaw. Jonathan, 552
Cofing. Jacob, 275
Cogshall. Elizabeth, 576, 579
Coke. Thomas, 347
Coleman. Jacob, 428
Colket. George H., 133, 296
Collet. George, 201
Collins family, 146
Collins. Jr., Henry H., 294
Collins. Wm. M., 294
Comfort. Howard, 73, 190, 300, 284
Compton. Capt. John, 64
Conarroe. Mrs. G. M., 283
Conway. Lady Anne, 591
Cook. Francis, 100
" Joel, 449
" William, 98

Cooke. Richard, 214, 217, 222, 223, 226, 228
Cooke. William W. J., 274
Coopland. John, 98
Coppock. Jacob Jonathan, 104
Corson. Charles F., 73
" Joseph K., 73
" Robert R., 73, 190, 284
Corn. Richard, 214, 216, 224, 226
Corn. William, 216, 226
Coulton. Lydia, 455
Cowpland. Caleb, 135
Cox. Martha, 103
Craffot. Thomas, 275
Craven. Ann, 482
Creakbeam. Philip, 264
Cresson. James, 300, 420
" William, 73
Croft. Samuel, 429
Crosby. Richard, 178, 191
Cross. Mrs. Arthur D., 170, 289
Crossman. Capt., 68
Crothers. Mrs. Stevenson, 190
Cuarton. Richard, 149, 257, 447
Cuarton. William, 146, 149, 257, 446
Cully. Hugh, 130
Cummings. A. B., 479
Cuthbert. Thomas, 420

d'Aregon. Princess, 283
d'Audley. Hugh, 297
David ap Evan, 213, 221, 289
David. Harvey Rees, 275
David ap Rees, 200
David. Anne, 22, 261
" Caleb, 164
" David, 164, 256
" Ebenezer, 163
" Elizabeth, 221
" Edward, 198, 224, 226, 255, 271
David. Ellis, 54, 55, 57, 59, 80, 84, 97, 105, 133, 275, 387, 493
" Harry, 221
David. Evan, 173, 488
" Hugh, 154, 164, 220, 229, 256, 488, 594
David. Janne, 263
" Jenkin, 86, 173
" Joan, 229
" Jonathan, 164
" John, 111, 166, 323, 490, 537

[601]

WELSH SETTLEMENT OF PENSYLVANIA

David. Katherine, 257
" Lewis, 153, 164, 165, 166, 195, 197, 203, 229, 232,, 249, 254, 256, 258, 384, 391, 490, 515, 582, 584
David. Llewellyn, 173
" Margaret, 96, 108, 154
David. Martha, 164
" Meredith, 225
" Morgan, 227, 245
" Owen, 21, 22, 114
" Philip, 323
" Richard, 56
" Robert, 21, 54, 55, 57, 58, 83, 84, 104, 116, 120, 127, 208, 257, 258, 261, 387, 421, 458, 499, 506, 549, 570, 571
David. Sarah, 221, 584
" Samuel, 164
" Thomas, 147, 179, 261, 275, 491, 561
David. Treharn,204, 263, 498
" William, 216, 221, 259, 261
Davie. John, 114
Davies. Amos, 149, 151, 152, 221
Davies. David, 89, 117, 149, 151, 175, 218, 230
Davies. Edward, 312
" Ellis, 115, 152
" Evan, 149, 150
" Katherine, 218
" Margaret, 33, 55, 141, 145, 147
Davies. Maurice, 84
" Meredith, 551
" Mireck, 488
" Richard, 24, 25, 29, 33, 104, 112, 127, 149, 150, 151, 153, 174, 177, 183, 185, 213, 227, 249, 251, 255, 522, 524, 532
Davies. Robert, 371, 384
" Thomas, 146, 222, 225, 226, 231
Davies. William, 178, 215, 217, 218, 223, 224, 225
Davids. David, 248
" Ellis, 532
" Meredith, 257
" Thomas, 78, 555
Davis. Benjamin, 253, 490
" David, 84, 135, 161, 249, 255, 561

Davis. Ellis, 84
" Elizabeth, 84
" Evan, 215
" Hannah, 594
" Isaac, 451, 456
" Jane, 84
" James, 487
" John, 275, 457
" Katherine, 161
" Lewis, 204
" Margaret, 142, 149, 249
Davis. Meredith, 225, 445
" Morgan, 202
" Owen, 319
" Richard, 124, 177, 179, 249
Davis. Robert, 47, 48, 79, 82, 84
Davis. Thomas, 84
" William, 158, 251, 258, 583
Day. ——, 260
Day. John, 249
" Richard, 73
" Mrs. Richard H., 300
Deemer. Dr., 274
de Ganay. Countess, 294
Deshler. David, 283
Dewees. Lt. Samuel, 455
d'Invilliers. Mary, 274, 285
Dickinson. ——, 260.
Dickinson family, 146
Dickinson. Edward H., 564
Dickinson. James, 98
" Jonathan, 101
" John, 193, 448, 449, 556, 558, 559, 562
Dickinson. Philemon, 74
" Samuel, 193
" Sarah, 107
Diffenderffer, 532
Dillard. Henry, K., 133, 190, 296
Dilwyn. George, 475
Dixon. James, 430
Downing family, 473
Downing. Jane, 212
" Sarah, 211
" Richard, 211
" Thomas, 211
" Thomasine, 211
Drexel. John R., 133
Drinker. Elizabeth, 464, 475
Drinker. John, 420
Duckett family, 508

Duckett. Mary, 498
" Ruth, 506
" Thomas, 174, 433, 436, 438, 498, 499, 500, 503, 505, 506, 507, 509, 510
Duer. Mary Ann, 160
" Capt. William,160
Dunbabin. Alice, 189
" Margaret, 189
" Samuel, 189
Dunlap. Jr., Thomas, 283
Durkee. Mrs. Augustus W., 294
Dynham. Sir John, 288
Edward David Ellis, 300
Edward ap John, 64, 85
Edward Jones David, 216
Edward ap Rees, 63, 64, 79, 311, 445, 446, 462
Edward ap Richard, 253
Elisha David Owen, 298
Elizabeth William Bowen, 593
Elizabeth William Owen, 126, 591
Ellis ap Hugh, 213, 384
Ellis ap Rees, 234
Ellis Rees Lewis, 287, 298
Evan ap Edward, 89
Evan Gwilim Yohan, 288
Evan Harry Morgan, 319
Evan ap Hugh, 267, 268, 276
Evan ap John, 289
Evan John Evan, 166
Evan John William, 56, 137, 213, 215, 220, 571
Evan ap Rees, 136
Evan ap Rees Gôch, 109
Evan Robert Lewis, 155, 301
Eardley. Jeremiah, 452
Evan Thomas Lloyd, 299
Evan ap William, 213, 215, 221
Evan ap William Powell, 152, 498, 531
Eckley. John, 124, 171, 256, 350, 354, 356, 357, 361, 363, 481, 512
Eckley. Sarah, 171
Edge. Jacob, 135
Edmundson. William, 270
"Edward Jones & Co.," 63
Edward. David, 220
" Evan, 85, 517, 571
Edward. Hugh, 224
" Jane, 135
" John, 47, 48, 91, 222, 499, 517

[602]

WELSH SETTLEMENT OF PENSYLVANIA

Edward. Thomas, 85
" William, 47, 48, 54, 55, 89, 91, 138, 369, 384, 499, 570
Edwards. Alexander, 161, 261
Edwards. Edward, 262, 257
Edwards. Elizabeth, 269, 271
Edwards. Ellen, 246
" Evan, 21,
" Humphrey, 260, 261
Edwards. Lowry, 262
" Margaret, 107, 108, 161, 262
Edwards, Martha, 161
" Morris, 490
" Peter, 204, 213, 217
Edwards. Sarah, 245
" Thomas, 161, 173, 224, 323
Edwards. William, 54, 71, 79, 100, 174, 178, 179, 248, 439
Ehret. Alvin, 192
Ellet family, 146
Ellet. Charles, 294
Elliott. C. J., 489
Ellis ap Hugh, 224
Ellis Rees Lewis, 180
Ellis William Hugh, 301
Ellis family, 146
Ellis. Ann, 235, 239
" Bridget, 239
" Cadwalader, 96, 97, 100, 101, 133, 198, 271, 493, 387
Ellis. David, 80
" Edward, 220, 271
" Eleanor, 245, 287
" Elizabeth, 82, 239, 240
Ellis. Ellis, 82, 152, 154, 202, 204, 218, 227, 244, 245, 255, 256, 258
Ellis. Ellin, 115, 154, 220, 240
Ellis. Evan, 152, 221, 239
Ellis. Francis, 319
" Gemima, 132
" Griffith, 532
" Henry, 256
" Humphrey, 196, 201, 215, 218, 232, 244, 245, 253, 258, 391, 435, 488, 503, 582

Ellis. Jane, 225, 462
" John, 451
" Lyddie, 220
" Lidia, 488
" Margaret, 239, 461
" Mary, 132, 498
" Morris, 224
" Rachel, 239, 244, 245
Ellis. Rebecca, 239
" Robert, 106, 225, 235, 240, 461, 498
Ellis. Rowland, 49, 82, 95, 97, 106, 115, 124, 134, 135, 149, 150, 151, 152, 153, 154, 156, 157, 180-192, 200, 213, 214, 215, 219, 220, 221, 224, 225, 231, 233, 247, 251, 256, 264, 285, 287, 296, 298, 309, 314, 318, 317, 316, 354, 369, 387, 458, 461, 462, 480, 481, 498, 503, 511, 515, 516, 528, 552, 573, 594, 595
Ellis. Jr., Rowland, 215, 231, 234, 235, 239, 309
Ellis. Thomas, 25, 82, 87, 90, 97, 120, 124, 153, 154, 196, 197, 199, 202, 204, 215, 221, 224, 225, 227, 231, 240, 249, 254, 250, 251, 255, 256, 260, 261, 314, 318, 371, 498, 499, 509, 513, 582, 592
Ellis. William, 152, 221, 239, 256
Ellis. William Robert, 275
Emlen family, 146
Emlen. Ellen, 294
" Jr., Mrs. George, 294
Emlen. Samuel, 475
Endon. David, 233
England. Philip, 390, 439
Erwis. William W., 287
Espen. James, 452
Evan John Evan, 166
Evan John William, 132
Evan. David, 177, 191, 203, 219, 221, 224, 230, 236, 258, 276, 371
Evan. Edward, 216
" Griffith, 72, 79, 105, 106, 136, 137
Evan. John, 89, 154, 302
" Morgan, 232
" Philip, 215, 218, 258, 371, 498
Evan. Rees, 49, 7, 79, 83, 97, 99, 105, 106, 115, 122, 129, 136, 137, 154

Evan. Robert, 107, 112, 126, 247, 267, 268
Evan. Stephen, 256
" Thomas, 267, 268
Evans family, 161, 233
Evans. Alice, 161
" Allen, 287
" Caleb, 215, 514
" Cadwalader, 107, 159, 240, 268-92, 284, 287, 302, 324
Evans. Charles, 163
" Daniel, 199
" David, 152, 158, 215, 216, 447
Evans. Deliah, 216
" Edmund C., 287
" Edward, 229, 319
Evans. Eleanor, 105
" Elizabeth, 84, 161, 240
Evans. Evan, 158, 215, 216, 222, 323, 528, 583
Evans. Evans, 240, 319
" Glendower, 287
" Gwen, 215
" Hartman K., 287
" Howland, 287
" Hugh, 76, 78, 107, 134, 135, 158, 173, 180, 222, 225, 237, 264, 284, 291, 437, 483, 555, 561, 577
Evans. Jane, 134, 161, 222, 240, 280
Evans. John, 152, 214, 215, 216, 218, 221, 225, 226, 231, 239, 240, 246, 249, 250, 251, 255, 256, 258, 275, 287, 371, 433, 473, 486, 509, 532, 582
Evans. Jonathan, 425
" Joseph, 476, 549
" Joshua, 215
" Katharine, 447
" Lowry, 76, 225, 284
Evans. Manlius G., 287
" Margaret, 240
" Mary, 161, 199, 215, 216
Evans. Nehemiah, 456
" Oliver, 476
" Owen, 223, 268, 284
Evans. Peter, 455
" Rees, 120, 532
" Rowland, 240
" Robert, 21, 84, 106, 107, 129, 130, 222, 225, 263, 268, 284, 324
Evans. Sarah, 161, 447, 271, 284

[603]

WELSH SETTLEMENT OF PENSYLVANIA

Evans. Sidney, 158
" Stephen, 222, 223, 227, 228, 384, 498, 571, 595
Evans. Susanna, 76, 158, 291
Evans. Thomas, 122, 133, 264, 268, 284, 324, 577
Evans. William, 438
" Wm. Elbert, 287
Eves. George, 264
Ewer. David, 391
Faddery. Richard, 230
Fairman. John, 371
Faulkner. Cap't., 440
Fergusson. Mrs. A. C., 294
Filler. Andrew, 420
Finch. Sir Heneage, 591
Fincher. Francis, 438
Finchner. John, 386
Finger (widow), 503
Fish. John, 249
Fishbourne. William, 103
Fisher family, 189
Fisher. Francis, 386
" Mary, 115
" Sydney G., 343
" Thomas, 189, 190
Fitzalan. John, 288
" Sir Richard, 293, 285, 288
Fitzalan. Sir Thomas, 288
Fleming. Charles, 98
Fletcher. Gov. Benj., 328, 392
Floid. Robert, 96, 134
Ford. Philip, 241, 388
" Jr., Philip, 404
" Robert, 260
Fornari. Marquise, 283
Forster. B., 174
Ffoulke of Gwynedd, 298, 301, 302
Foulke. Amos, 76, 158, 291
Foulke. Caleb, 76, 274
" Edward, 224, 247, 267, 268, 276, 300, 302, 596
Foulke. Ellen, 274
" Frank, 73, 133, 190, 300
Foulke. G. Rhyfedd, 300
" Hugh, 273
" Jane, 302
" Linford, 300
" Margaret, 240
" Mary, 175
" Owen, 176
" J. Roberts, 300, 559

Foulke. Susanna, 240
" Dr. Richard, 73, 300
Foulke. Thomas Lloyd, 300
Foulke. Wm. Parker, 300
Fox. George, 23, 28, 110, 189, 241, 242, 346, 347, 409, 411
Fox. James, 258
" Mrs. de Grasse, 283
Francis. Mrs. Tench, 294
Franklin. Benjamin, 521
" William, 521
Frazier. Alexander, 420
" Joseph, 420
Freeborn. Susanna, 575
Frishmuth. Mrs. J. C. W., 283
Fritz. William, 562
Fuller & Holme, 266
Fuller. Jacob, 267
" Joseph, 267
Furby. Thomas, 242
Furness family, 260
Galloway. Samuel, 97
Gallowell. Elizabeth, 98
Gardner. Peter, 438
Gardiner. Mrs. W. H., 294
Garrett. Evan, 391
" John, 130
" Thomas, 134, 491
Garrett. William, 197
Garrigues. Samuel M., 201
Gee. John, 267
" Thomas, 174
George. Amos, 87, 451, 556
George. David, 107, 130, 174, 256, 437, 438, 483, 517, 554, 556, 585
George. Edward, 87, 100, 129, 437, 438, 452, 456, 483, 558
George. George, 257
" Hugh, 567
" Jane, 100
" Jesse, 100, 158, 452, 456, 567, 475, 517, 585
George. John, 86, 561, 585
George. John M., 559, 564
George. Joseph, 558, 585
" Rebecca, 100
" Richard, 78, 100, 121, 438, 483, 555, 561
George. Jr., Richard, 129
" Thomas, 452, 556

George. (Widow), 576
" William, 490
German. John, 215, 226, 391
Gibbons. John, 260
Gillis. David, 456
Gilpin. Thomas, 469
Glaisaer. Joseph, 575
Glenn. Edward A., 77, 160
" Lewis A., 160
" Lewis W., 160
" Col. Thomas A., 160, 284, 360
Goldsborough. Louis M., 294
Good. Elizabeth, 350
" John, 275
Goodin. Thomas, 98, 591
Goodwin. Robert, 262
Goodson. John, 104, 219, 308
Gorman. John, 384
Govett. Annesley R., 289
" Robert A., 289
Graeme. Dr., 104
Graff. Andrew, 440
" Jacob, 440
Graham. John, 74
Gray. John, 451, 475
" Samuel, 283, 451
Greaves. Charles, 429
Green. Robert, 354
Grey. Elizabeth de, 293
" Sir Henry de, 293, 297
Grey. Sir John de, 293, 297
Griffith ap John, 121
Griffith John Evan, 96, 136, 137
Griffith. David, 226
" Edward, 22, 54, 55, 83, 96, 97, 105, 118, 179, 257, 276, 593
Griffith. Edmund, 261
" Evan, 121, 275, 539
Griffith. Griffith, 454
" Harry, 490
" Hugh, 83, 96, 97, 115, 105, 262, 267, 268, 505
Griffith. James, 262
" Jane, 498
" John, 121, 130
" Katherine, 261, 264
Griffith. Lewis, 201
" Mary, 115
" Sibill, 286
" Susan, 161, 261
" Thomas, 54, 55, 252, 275, 319
Griffith. Sir William, 286

[604]

WELSH SETTLEMENT OF PENSYLVANIA

Griffiths. John, 592
Griscom. Clement A., 141, 294, 283
Griscom. Lloyd C., 294
Gronow. Lewis, 452
Growden. Grace, 365
" Joseph, 229
Gruffydd ap Cynan, 294
Gruffydd ap Einion, 290
Guest. John, 82, 420
Gummere. Amelia M., 591
" Dr. Francis B., 587
Gummere. Rich. M., 294
Gunter. Thomas, 295
Gwyn. Hugh, 286
"Gynn." Dr. Thomas, 178, 179
Habard. David, 203
Habart. Ann, 203
" John, 203
" William, 203
Hacker. Edward, 294
Hagy. Hannah, 429
Haines. Mrs. Franklin T.
" Humphrey, 432
" John, 493
" Mrs. R. B., 294
Hallins. Dr., 182
Hallowell. Thomas, 420
Hambright, 474
Hamilton. William, 579
Hancock. George W., 559
Hand. General, 440
Haney. Daniel, 218
" Hugh, 218
Hank. Jane, 269, 284
" John, 271, 284
" Nancy, 284
" Sarah, 269
Hankinson. Samuel E. D., 74
Hanmer. Griffith de, 301
Hanson. John, 531
Hardy. Jr., Mrs. Wm. J., 294
Hardiman. Abraham, 165
" Hannah, 199
Harper. Henry S., 133
Harris. Daniel, 161, 230
" Hugh, 161, 230
" Joseph, 145
Harrison family, 146
Harrison. Mrs. C. C., 294
" James, 222, 260
Harrison. John, 211
" Joseph, 119
" Richard, 237, 437, 458, 462
Harrison. Jr., Richard, 460

Harrison. Sarah, 576
" Thomas, 460
Harriss. Thomas, 319
"Harriton" farm, 236, 461
Harry ap Rees, 222
Harry family, 230
Harry. Abigail, 230
" Daniel, 225, 230, 249
Harry. Evan, 152, 218, 219, 224, 228, 229, 230, 236, 243, 251, 257, 262, 264, 323, 446, 447, 503, 540
Harry. Henry, 230
" Hugh, 230
" John, 230, 235
" Lewis, 230
" Rees, 81
" Samuel, 438
" William, 230
Hart, 474
Hart. John, 386
" Nicholas, 481
Harvey. Edward, 468
Hastings. John, 203
" Jonah, 86
Havard. David, 203, 222, 257
Havard. Dinah, 490
" John, 122, 173, 256, 488
Havard. Mary, 222
Havid. John, 122
Haxett. Michael, 186
Hayes. Benjamin, 76, 158, 199
Hayes. Elizabeth, 199, 269
Hayes. Hannah, 198, 269, 271, 594
Hayes. Issat (Iseult), 198, 270
Hayes. John, 163, 198
" John Russell, 15
" Jonathan, 82, 196, 514
Hayes. Joseph, 198, 232
" Mary, 198
" Richard, 158, 165, 166, 195, 198, 204, 215, 217, 232, 256, 258, 391, 488, 491, 528, 584, 594
Hayes. Jr., Richard, 197, 198, 270
Hayes. 3d, Richard, 198
" Capt. Thomas, 95
Hearne. Sarah, 498
Heath. Susanna, 272
Height. Jonathan, 178
Hendericks. Garret, 565

Henderson. John G., 480
Hendric. Evan, 391
Henten. Rees, 196
Herbert. Morgan, 153
" Sir Richard, 296, 297
Hesson. William, 482
Heston. Abraham, 443
" Col. Edward, 443
Heth. Susanna, 272
Hibbard. Josiah, 159
Hickok. Mrs. F. N., 294
Hicks. Elias, 409, 585
" William, 274
Higginson. Rev. John, 186
Hill. Richard, 146, 515
Hilling. Jone, 197
" Henry, 197
Hinton. James, 86
Hiltzheimer. Jacob, 439, 440
Hodnut. Garret, 487
Hoffman. Edward F., 74
" Jacob, 456
Hogg. Ann, 81
Holcroft. Elias, 186
Holgate. Matthew, 455, 498
Holgate. William, 456, 562
Holand. Alianore, 293
" Sir Thomas, 297
Holland. Benjamin, 456
" John, 124, 201
" Joshua, 201
" Robert, 448, 449, 561, 555, 556
Hollowell. Elizabeth, 98
Holme. Benjamin, 582
" Thomas, 35, 41, 50, 52, 67, 254, 260, 349, 367
Hone. John, 74
Hood. Jr., John, 420
" Jonathan, 77
Hooding. Joan, 503
Hoopes. Daniel, 491
Horner. Benjamin, 420
Hoskins. Martha, 103
" Mary, 158
" Dr. Richard, 158
House. Mary (Wright), 521
Howard. William, 517
Howe. General, 466, 467, 470, 492, 579
Howel Lloyd David, 301
Howel. David, 208, 275
" Francis, 202, 227, 254

[605]

WELSH SETTLEMENT OF PENSYLVANIA

Howel. Mary, 164
" William, 164, 199, 201, 203, 499, 503, 506, 509
Howell. Daniel, 244
" David, 323
" Edward, 166
" Elizabeth, 203
" Francis, 200, 245, 371, 384, 595
Howell. Humphrey, 532
" Jenkin, 166
" John, 49
" Jonathan, 211
" Joseph, 158
" Margaret, 202, 203, 581
Howell. Mary, 164, 203
" Mireck, 166
" Philip, 147, 148, 207, 208, 216, 260, 261
Howell. Rees, 502, 548, 549
Howell. Rowland, 200
" Samuel, 135
" Susan, 203
" Thomas, 166, 202, 203, 229, 254, 257, 318, 319, 509
Howell. William, 164, 169, 195, 196, 198, 204, 226, 227, 230, 245, 256, 219, 222, 354, 258, 358, 371, 384, 391, 510, 582
Hubbs. John, 240
Huber. Mrs. Stiles, 294
Hudson. Susanna, 159
" William, 159
Hugh Cadwalader Rhys, 300, 302
Hugh ap Edward, 276
Hugh John Thomas, 21, 70, 89, 106, 108, 127, 498
Hugh ap Robert, 96, 111
Hugh Thomas David, 301
Hugh ap William, 276
Hugh. Agnes, 115
" Ann, 220
" David, 121, 196, 250, 255, 256, 257, 447, 550
Hugh. Ellis, 171, 481
" Evan, 267, 268
" John, 261, 267, 268
Hugh. Owen, 323
" Robert, 257, 276
" Roger, 256
" Sibill, 286

Hughs. Ellin, 300, 302
" Ellis, 302
" Jane, 302
" John, 153
" Martha, 488
" Mary, 90
" Richard, 438
" Sarah, 153
" William, 302
Hughs. Charles, 161, 262, 263
Hughes. David, 204, 275
" Elizabeth, 323
" Hugh, 490
" Humphrey, 21, 113
Hughes. John, 324, 485
" Joseph, 111
" Mary, 261
" Morgan, 323
" Richard, 323, 442
Hughes. Roger, 98, 214, 216, 221, 222, 224, 226, 228, 591
Huidekoper, Mrs. H. S., 287
Hulse. Mrs. Charles F., 190, 294
Humphries. Benjamin, 142
Humphrey ap Hugh, 150, 234
Humphrey Hugh Howel, 286, 298
Humphrey Howel Evan, 297
Humphrey John Lloyd, 293
Humphrey. Ann, 153, 154, 180, 220, 234, 287, 298
Humphrey. Benjamin, 81, 82, 122, 150, 151, 153, 180, 181, 203, 220, 230, 258
Humphrey. Charles, 152, 153
Humphrey. Daniel, 152, 153, 174, 181, 204, 220, 229, 244, 251, 255, 256, 258, 488
Humphrey. David, 154, 219, 530
Humphrey. Edward, 153
" Elizabeth, 152, 153, 154, 498
Humphrey. Gabbatha, 152
" Jane, 151, 287
Humphrey. Joan, 152

Humphrey. John, 49, 70, 95, 124, 141, 150, 151, 152, 153, 155, 180, 199, 214, 218, 219, 220, 221, 224, 234, 235, 243, 256, 267, 268, 287, 324, 371, 384, 481, 498, 526, 582
Humphrey, Jr., John, 203
Humphrey. Jonathan, 153
" Joseph, 151, 180, 220
Humphrey. Joshua, 153
" Katherine, 220, 247
Humphrey. Lydia, 152, 153, 154
Humphrey. Mary, 203
" Morris, 83, 97
Humphrey. Owen, 49, 97, 115, 134, 151, 153, 220, 226, 235, 247, 286, 491, 532
Humphrey. Rebecca, 81, 154, 220, 283, 498
Humphrey. Reginald, 154
" Richard, 49, 95, 150, 151, 152, 213, 214, 220, 256, 287, 498
Humphrey. Robert, 152
" Samuel, 81, 82, 95, 150, 152, 153, 155, 181, 234, 245, 287
Humphrey. Solomon, 153
" Tabitha, 151
" Thomas, 153, 180
Humphrey. William, 23, 220, 532
Humphreys family, 95, 150
Humphreys. Ann, 122
" Benjamin, 173, 245, 257, 262, 438
Humphreys. Charles, 429, 466
Humphreys. Daniel, 81, 192, 193, 196, 200, 231, 287
Humphries. Edward, 438
" Elizabeth, 193
Humphreys. Hugh, 262
" John, 156, 203, 227, 229, 350, 509, 515, 516, 594
Humphreys. Joshua, 37, 287
Humphreys. Lydia, 81, 245
Humphreys. Owen, 152, 157

[606]

WELSH SETTLEMENT OF PENSYLVANIA

Humphreys. Rebecca, 285, 287
Humphreys. Samuel, 193, 437
Humphreys. Thomas, 481
" Wm. Penn, 190, 287
Hunt. Benjamin, 82
Hunter. Mary, 216
" John, 216
Hurry. Daniel, 249
Ingels. Richard, 208
Ingram. Walter, 253
Jackson. Edwin A., 274
" Mrs. Levin H., 284
Jackson. Mrs. R. B., 294
James. David, 214, 217, 222, 223, 227, 231, 256, 438, 498
James. George, 217
" Howel, 176, 177, 191, 259, 498
James. James, 217
" John, 22
" Josiah, 487
" Lewis, 241
" Margaret, 214, 217, 223, 227
James. Mary, 217, 227, 228
James. Mordecai, 135
" Philip, 176
" Samuel, 217
" Sarah, 198, 217
" Thomas, 164, 217, 323, 487
James. William, 191, 487
Jance John Morgan, 219
Janney. Robert M., 559, 587
Jarman. (Jarmain. Jarmon, Jermin, Jermon, Jormon). Edward, 275
Jarman. Elizabeth, 226
" Margaret, 226, 255
Jarman. John, 216, 226, 249, 256, 258, 358, 498, 503, 509, 571, 582
Jarman. Sarah, 226
" Thomas, 252
Jenkin ap Havard, 289
Jenkin ap Ievan, 290
Jenkins. Chas. F., 300
" Elinor, 226
" Howard M., 266, 300

Jenkins. Margaret, 201
" Martha A., 284
" Stephen, 201
" William, 25, 86, 198, 200, 232, 241, 249, 253, 254, 258, 261, 371, 358, 510, 580
Jennings. Samuel, 101
John & Wynne, 100, 175, 255
John ap David, 112
John David John, 21
John David Thomas, 196, 199, 275
John Evan Edward, 231, 255
John ap Edward, 21, 48, 55, 70, 71, 78, 83, 84, 86, 88, 261, 262, 269, 271
John ab Evan, 121, 163, 166, 225, 261, 301, 289
John ap Howel, 150
John ap Howel-gôch, 286
John ap John, 22, 24, 25, 27, 28, 29, 33, 104, 110, 120, 124, 149, 150, 181, 175-181, 249, 409
John ap Lewis, 298
John Lloyd Wynne, 293
John ap Owen, 391
John Robert Cadwalader, 92
John Robert David, 111
John Robert Ellis, 257, 520
John Robert Matthew, 565
John Thomas ap Hugh, 21
John Thomas Peggy, 475
John Thomas Thomas, 173
John ap Thomas, 22, 25, 33, 41, 45, 46, 47, 54, 58, 59, 64, 99, 109, 114, 115, 116, 129, 137, 138, 155, 157, 158, 161, 240, 255, 261, 270, 299, 312, 362, 363, 444, 493, 552, 592
John ap William, 131
John. Cadwalader, 262
" Catherine, 133
" David, 83, 96, 105, 241
John. Elizabeth, 96, 115, 116, 593
John. Evan, 49, 96, 163
" Gainor, 49, 96, 155 157

John. Griffith, 54, 57, 59, 83, 97, 101, 102, 103, 105, 115, 132, 137, 138, 156, 257, 498, 532, 539, 541, 550
John. Hugh, 47, 95, 128
" James, 173
" Jonett, 111
" Lewis, 173
" Margaret, 21, 96, 131, 301, 498
John. Rees, 49, 517
" Robert, 21, 224, 268, 276
John. Thomas, 99, 114, 106, 133, 267, 268, 302, 461
" William, 72, 95, 461
Johnes. Jonett, 154
" Sarah, 216
Johns. Arthur S., 74
" Priscilla, 283
" Richard, 283
" Thomas, 259
Johnson. Rev. Richard, 236, 239
Jones, of Llwyn-Gwrill, 517
Jones, of London. Edward, 219
Jones, of "Mt. Ararat," 542
Jones. Anne, 121, 161, 225, 447
Jones. Aquilla, 77
" Awbrey, 156
" Benjamin, 448
" Beula, 77
" Cadwalader, 54, 59, 100, 122, 275
Jones. Christopher, 425
" Daniel, 99, 256
" David, 86, 97, 107, 115, 121, 154, 163, 165, 174, 198, 203, 222, 225, 236, 249, 269, 270, 439, 490, 532, 552
Jones. Dr. Edward, 25, 33, 41, 42, 45, 46, 47, 53, 55, 58, 60, 63, 64, 78, 79, 83, 92, 104, 107, 116, 117, 120, 121, 124, 130, 138, 147, 155, 158, 161, 172, 191, 193, 199, 203, 231, 245, 249, 250, 257, 261, 263, 264, 270, 291, 311, 312, 313, 368, 385, 387, 421, 445, 447, 493, 499, 503, 509, 516, 520, 540, 549, 551, 555, 556, 565, 570, 576-577, 592

[607]

WELSH SETTLEMENT OF PENSYLVANIA

Jones. Edward, 73, 98, 148, 174, 208, 214, 216, 222, 225, 226, 430, 454, 556, 557, 561, 591
Jones. Jr., Edward, 54, 55, 57, 58, 71, 77, 78, 80, 83, 88, 89, 91
Jones. Elizabeth, 77, 91, 92, 102, 122, 154, 447
Jones. Elizabeth M., 190
" Elizabeth W., 269, 272, 273
Jones. Ellen, 121, 225, 270, 447, 593, 594
Jones. Ellis, 214, 216, 221, 223
Jones. Evan, 73, 77, 89, 91, 120, 132, 134, 135, 264, 323, 387, 438, 447, 493, 498, 537, 561, 594
Jones. Ezekiel, 77
" Florence, 580
" Fred. Rhinelander, 74
Jones. Gabriel, 89
" Gainor, 129, 154, 594
Jones. Gerrard, 122, 135, 153, 425, 446, 447, 561
Jones. Griffith, 121, 136, 174, 260, 275, 317, 318, 319, 362, 385, 439
Jones. Hannah, 76, 158, 291, 490
Jones. Henry, 249
" Hugh, 48, 54, 56, 57, 59, 90, 91, 106, 108, 216, 246, 225, 257, 309, 371, 385, 487, 500
Jones. Jr., Hugh, 216
" Isaac, 269, 272, 271
Jones. J. Awbrey, 77
" Jacob, 77, 130, 158, 475, 487, 488, 561
Jones. James, 198, 269, 256, 271, 553, 554, 556, 557, 594
Jones. Jr., James, 458, 556
Jones. Jr., James Lewis, 130
Jones. Jane, 76, 216
" Janne, 135
" John, 73, 76, 77, 78, 121, 135, 146 165, 224, 309, 318, 319, 452, 554
Jones. Jonathan, 70, 73, 75, 76, 77, 81, 102, 121, 155, 156, 158, 173, 192, 199, 264, 291, 447, 456, 485, 557, 577, 594

Jones. Jr., Jonathan, 77, 121
Jones. Jonett, 154
" Joseph, 225, 312
" Katherine, 102, 122, 158, 198, 246, 261, 593, 594
Jones. Lewis, 121, 158, 257, 561, 594
Jones. Lowry, 76, 77, 122, 134, 247, 291, 312
Jones. Lydia Griffith, 507
Jones. Rev. Malachi, 487
Jones. Margaret, 135, 252
Jones. Martha, 70, 74, 283
Jones. Mary, 73, 76, 103, 158, 199, 503
Jones. Matthew, 163, 256, 259, 275, 455
Jones. Moses, 319
Jones. Owen, 76, 130, 135, 156, 158, 291, 425, 478, 490, 561, 576, 577
Jones. Col. Owen, 76, 156, 528
Jones. Jr., Owen, 468
" Paul, 122, 558
" Penelope, 77
" Peter, 237, 257
" Price, 369, 385
" Priscilla, 102
" Prudence, 77
" Rebecca, 76, 130, 158
Jones. Rees, 48, 56, 106, 107, 131, 132, 138, 161, 216, 257, 289, 291, 298, 385, 387, 498
Jones. Richard 54, 57, 15, 132, 134, 135, 137, 222, 225, 231, 247, 319, 387, 456, 517
Jones. Robert, 54, 59, 60, 81, 84, 91, 102, 103, 117, 121, 129, 132, 136, 153, 156, 164, 165, 173, 180, 222, 225, 229, 247, 255, 257, 262, 267, 268, 270, 437, 444, 446, 448, 467, 493, 529, 538, 540, 550, 551, 552, 553, 557, 592, 594
Jones. Jr., Robert, 447
" Roger, 146
" Rufus M., 591
" Salvenas, 77
" Samuel, 319
" Sarah, 76, 92, 135, 594

Jones. Sidney, 571
" Silas, 447, 448
" Solomon, 149, 151
Jones. Susanna, 76
" Tacy, 448
" Thomas, 21, 54, 59, 73, 77, 80, 86, 91, 100, 107, 118, 120 120, 136, 141, 142, 148, 149, 158, 192, 214, 216, 217, 224, 249, 257, 262, 309, 362, 364, 447, 493, 498, 499, 537, 539, 549, 551, 556, 594
Jones. Walter, 118
" William, 47, 48, 57, 99, 104, 106, 136, 181, 268, 500
Jones. Woodruff, 294
Jordan. Jr., Francis, 289
" Dr. John W., 169, 289, 595, 555
Jordan. Walter, 289
Junkin. Thomas, 490
Keen. John, 419
Keite family, 508
Keite. James, 595
" Martha, 179
Keith. Mrs. Charles P., 284
Kelly. John, 107
" William, 204, 232, 253
Kenderdine. Margaret, 226
Kenderdine. Thomas, 226
Kensey. Elizabeth, 283
Kinchner. Francis, 174
Kinsey. David, 214, 217, 249
Kinsey. John, 249, 527
Kissack. Robert, 468
Kite. Jr., Isaac, 452
Krickbaum. Col., Conrad, 457
Kynaston. Humphrey, 293
Kynaston. Margaret, 293
" Lady Mary, 296
Kynaston. Sir Roger, 293, 297
Lafayette. General, 450, 467
Landreth. Jr., Mrs. B., 294
Lardner. Lynford, 454
Latch. Rudolph, 130
Lawrence. Ann, 142
" Daniel, 164, 166, 244, 256, 488

[608]

WELSH SETTLEMENT OF PENSYLVANIA

Lawrence. David, 87, 165, 198, 199, 200, 204, 218, 227, 245, 258, 358, 384, 503, 510, 582, 584
Lawrence. Eleanor, 87, 245, 584
Lawrence. Henry, 86, 87, 164, 165, 166, 245, 246
Lawrence. Margaret, 245,
" Mary, 158
" Rachel, 245
" Rebecca, 87
" Thomas, 87, 225, 245
Lawrence. Wm. Thos., 86
Leacey. Col., 238
Leacock. John, 130
Le Fevre. Mary, 283
Lee. Elizabeth C., 284
" Henry, 284
" J. Collins, 284
" Richard Bland, 284
Lee. Richard Henry, 284
" Robert E., 284
" Robert N., 481
" Zaccheus C., 284
Lehnman. Thomas, 223
Le Strange. Lord John, 290
Levering. Anthony, 433, 561
Levick. Anna Lucile, 274
Levick. Charles Mather, 274
Levick. Ebenezer, 272, 273
Levick. Elizabeth W., 274
Levick. Florence, 274
" Henry Lewis, 274, 285
Levick. Dr. James J., 19, 24, 27, 109, 117, 161, 272, 275
Levick. Jane Foulke, 274
Levick. Lewis Jones, 22, 109, 114, 118, 268, 269, 274, 285, 363, 593
Levick. Louise Jamart, 274, 285
Levick. Mary Sabina, 274, 285
Levick. Samuel Jones, 269, 272, 273, 285, 569, 573
Levick. Jr., Samuel J., 274
Levick. Susanna Morris, 569

Levick. Suzanne, 274, 285
Levick. William E., 274
" William Manlove, 273
Lewis ap David, 25, 33
Lewis John Griffith, 298
Lewis Robert Owen, 298
Lewis Sion Griffith, 234
Lewis. Abraham, 232
" Alice, 196
" Amos, 165, 204
" Ann, 165, 253
" Benjamin, 230
" Betty, 203
" Cadwalader, 118, 593
Lewis. Caleb, 164
" Daniel, 226, 435
" David, 152, 164, 199, 217, 230, 232, 256, 258, 263, 391, 488, 490, 581
Lewis. Davis Lewis, 247
" Edmond, 165
" Eleanor, 230
" Eliza, 480
" Elizabeth, 165, 197, 201
Lewis. Ellen Ann, 165
" Ellis, 122, 240, 271, 298
Lewis. Enoch, 165
" Evan, 165, 178, 452, 475, 502
Lewis. Francis, 323
" George, 323
" George H., 247
" Griffith, 152, 180, 221
Lewis. Hannah, 166
" Mrs. Hy. Carvill, 300
" Henry, 165, 173, 195, 197, 199, 200, 204, 215, 221, 230, 253, 255, 256, 258, 269, 270, 318, 366, 371, 433, 488, 499, 507, 508
Lewis. Jr., Henry, 196, 197
Lewis. Howell, 132
" Isaac, 122, 451
" Jr., J. Howard, 133, 296
Lewis. James, 24, 98, 165, 166, 196, 271, 487
Lewis. Jr., James, 197
" Jesse, 165
" John, 195, 196, 209, 204, 229, 256, 258, 384, 582

Lewis. Jr., John, 195, 196, 258
Lewis. Jonathan, 164
" Joseph, 166,
" Josiah, 229
" Katherine, 166, 271
Lewis. Levi, 165
" Lewis, 165, 178, 197, 502, 505
Lewis. Lydia T., 165
" Margaret, 173, 197, 203, 503
Lewis. Martha, 164
" Mary, 164, 178, 230
Lewis. Morgan, 106
" Nathan, 165
" Osborn G. L., 247
Lewis. Owen, 115, 132, 152, 154, 180, 198, 219, 220, 221, 224, 235, 243, 271, 298
Lewis. Jr., Owen, 219, 224, 236
Lewis. Peregrine, 165
" Philip, 229
" Ralph, 95, 163, 164, 196, 204, 218, 232, 245, 256, 258, 261, 498
Lewis. Rees, 298
" Robert, 132
" Ruth, 164
" Samuel, 164, 176, 197, 198, 200, 232, 256, 265, 391, 488
Lewis. Jr., Samuel, 176
" Samuel B., 247
" Sarah, 229, 166
" Stephen, 229
" Thomas, 203
" Tryon, 165, 583
" William, 95, 164, 165, 166, 199, 218, 237, 247, 256, 258, 461, 462, 502, 504
Lewis. Jr., William, 165
Liddom. Abraham, 451
Lightner. 146
Lincoln. Abraham, 284
" Thomas, 284
Lippincott. Howard W., 559
Lippincott. Mary, 170
" Restore, 597
" William, 420
Lisle. Henry, 420
Litzenberg. Simon, 485
Livingston. Mrs. John H., 287
Llewellyn ap Edneyfd, 290

[609]

WELSH SETTLEMENT OF PENSYLVANIA

Llewellyn. Alexander, 98
Llewellyn. Andrew, 271
" Ann, 153
" David, 151, 173, 202, 204, 232, 245, 488, 584
Llewellyn. Griffith, 153, 173, 248, 289, 437
Llewellyn. Hannah, 201
" John, 204
" Mary, 153, 173, 584
Llewellyn. Maurice, 196, 530, 581
Llewellyn. Morris, 153, 199, 202, 201, 204, 227, 229, 232, 249, 255, 258, 263, 371, 391, 584
Lloyd. Charles, 24, 33, 25, 29, 52, 55, 75, 80, 124, 131, 141, 142, 145, 149, 150, 183, 185, 249, 292, 293, 294, 576
Lloyd. Judge David, 146, 147, 148, 219, 225, 228, 229, 447, 514
Lloyd. David, 129, 147, 165, 216, 247, 251, 260, 298, 317, 318, 364, 405
Lloyd. Deborah, 183
" Edward, 241
" Elizabeth, 143, 248
Lloyd. Evan, 248, 256, 290, 293
Lloyd. Francis, 202, 222, 227, 245
Lloyd. Gainor, 247
" Gwen, 247
" Hannah, 247
" Howard W., 184, 247
Lloyd. Col. Hugh, 247
" Jane, 248
" John, 72, 79, 105, 106, 136, 137, 143, 214, 217, 218, 222, 223, 226, 228, 248, 261, 293, 452
Lloyd. Joseph, 222
" Katharine, 293
" Launcelot, 481
" Lowry, 135, 247, 264
Lloyd. Mrs. Malcolm, 294
Lloyd. Mary, 222
" Rev. Morgan, 23, 189
Lloyd. Patience, 146
" Rees, 84, 135, 247

Lloyd. Richard, 135, 247, 248
Lloyd. Robert, 72, 79, 105, 106, 122, 134, 135, 137, 138, 156, 246, 247, 257, 264, 290, 291
Lloyd. Sampson, 149
" Sarah, 247, 248
" Wm. Supplee, 247
Lloyd. Gov. Thomas, 52, 55, 75, 80, 99, 124, 141, 143, 145, 147, 149, 155, 174, 183, 188, 210, 219, 225, 237, 242, 292, 294, 298, 317, 318, 319, 350, 351, 352, 356, 357, 402, 406, 445, 447, 458, 493
Lloyd. Thomas, 47, 48, 56, 86, 134, 136, 137, 138, 151, 222, 246, 247, 290, 291, 292, 296, 364, 366
Lloyd. Jr., Thomas, 247, 248
Lloyd. William, 153, 248
Llwyd. Thomas, 311
Lobdale. Isaac, 420
Lodovicus ap Robert, 114
Logan. Judge James, 147, 191, 208, 268, 308, 347, 398, 405
Longworthy. Sarah, 107
Lort. Elizabeth, 142
" Robert, 261
" Sir Roger, 142
" Sampson, 142
Lower. Thomas, 347
Lowell. Mrs. Jas. A., 294
Lowell. Jr., Mrs. John, 294
Lower. Thomas, 275
Lownes. Hugh, 315
" Jane, 315
" William, 419
Lowry. Gryffyth Vaughan, 300
" John Evan, 231
" Col. Philip, 456
Loxley. Benjamin, 419
Lukens. Jawood, 73, 190, 284, 300
Lutterall, Narcissus, 413
Margaret John William, 131
Mary David Evan, 289
Maurice ap Edward, 109
Maurice Humphrey Morgan, 115
McCall. Archibald, 74
" Col. Geo. A., 74

McCalla. John, 420
McClanachan. Blair, 420
" Charles, 461
McClanachan. Naomi, 461
McClanachan. Robert, 461
McClanachan. Robt. H., 294
McDowell. Samuel R., 465
McKean. Judge Thomas, 470, 473
KcKean. Mrs. Thomas, 289
McMichael. Mrs. C. E. 294
McMichael. Lt. James, 462, 465
MacVeagh. Edmund, 260
" Wayne, 216
Mackay, 474
Macpherson. Eneas, 343
Mahan. Mrs. Alfred T., 287
Malin. Mary, 211
" Joseph, 464
Maltravers. Eleanor, 288
" Lord John, 288
Mansfield. Mrs. Walter D., 302
Marchant. Thomas, 197
Maris. Elizabeth, 178
" George, 82, 159
" Hannah, 159
" Jesse, 159
" John, 165
" Richard, 178
Markham. Dep. Gov. Wm., 67, 69, 347, 356, 392
Marks. James, 487
Marriot. Samuel, 104
Marsh. Richard, 174
Marshall. Christopher, 466, 469
Marshall. Mrs. N. B., 294
Marshall. Samuel, 133, 247
Maruin. Edward, 174
Mather. Charles, 269, 284, 287
Mather. Rev. Cotton, 17, 186
Mather. Isaac, 274
" Joseph, 274
" Mary, 269
" Richard, 274
" Samuel, 136
" Susanna M., 269, 274, 285

[610]

WELSH SETTLEMENT OF PENSYLVANIA

Matlock. Josiah, 419
Matthews. Col., 77
Maud. Margery, 189
" Joshua, 183, 189
Maule. Daniel, 452
Maultsby. John, 394
Maurice. David, 200, 580, 538
Maurice. Edward, 118
" Ellis, 213, 215, 243
Maxwell. John, 452
Mays. John, 166
Medlicot, 124
Medlicot. Daniel, 595
Meigs. Mrs. Arthur V., 73, 130, 190, 281
Mele. Bryan, 242
Mellor. John, 29
Mendenhall. James, 211
Meredith ap Howell, 293
Meredith. Daniel, 231, 371, 595
Meredith. David, 81, 214, 216, 217, 222, 223, 224, 228, 249, 255, 256, 258, 384, 391, 432, 433, 445, 487, 498, 509, 582
Meredith. Jesse, 452
" John, 224, 275
Meredith. Katherine, 224
" Mary, 224
" Meredith, 224
" Richard, 224
" Samuel, 74
" Samuel R., 74
" Sarah, 81, 224, 445
Merritt. Mrs. J. S., 294
Meteer. Ann, 212
" Thomas, 211
" Jr., Thomas, 212
Methey. William, 449
Michinar. John, 275
Middleton. Thomas, 420
Miles. Griffith, 251
" James, 499
" Phoebe, 223
" Richard, 214, 217, 223
Miles. Ruth, 223
" Samuel, 217, 222, 223, 231, 258, 499
Miles. Tamar, 223
Miller. Ann, 442
" Jane, 163
" John, 28
" S. Bevan, 74
Millington. John, 249
Mills. Samuel, 249
Mirick. David, 264

Molineaux. Henry, 176
Montfort. Simon de, 289
Montgomery. William, 81
Moore. Alfred, 559
" Amos, 562
" Arthur, 559
" Deborah. 145
" Edward, 226, 252, 499
Moore. Hannah W., 283
" James, 554
" John, 149, 257, 386, 490, 538
Moore. Mordecai, 97, 122, 146, 183, 249
Moore. Richard, 182, 183, 215, 216, 222, 224, 229, 371
Moore. Thomas, 121
" William, 174
Morce. Mary, 197
Mordant. William, 249
More. John, 218
Morgan. Abel, 454, 457
" Blanch, 218
" Cadwalader, 47, 48, 54, 56, 57, 79, 80, 95, 101, 105, 106, 108, 125, 127, 128, 132, 133, 135, 137, 138, 216, 257, 275, 289, 291, 298, 384, 498, 500, 505, 530, 549, 556
Morgan. Daniel, 437
" David, 197, 227, 257
" Jr., David, 227
" Edward, 218, 248
Morgan. Elizabeth, 227, 263
Morgan. Evan, 227. 425
" Hannah, 216
" Humphrey, 218
" James, 106, 216, 221
Morgan. Jane, 79
" John, 106, 107, 215, 216, 221, 226, 227, 248, 256, 258, 275, 554
Morgan. John Price, 77
" Joseph, 248
" Katherine, 218, 227
Morgan. Lewis, 107
" Owen, 218, 257, 498, 533
Morgan. Rees, 295
" Sarah, 216
" Thomas, 263
" William, 22, 83, 89, 96, 105, 263

Morice. David, 215
Morris. Anthony, 528
" Jr., Anthony, 171
Morris. B. W. Rt. Rev., 294
Morris. Daniel, 159, 222, 231
Morris. David, 198, 203, 215, 225, 583
Morris. Edward, 120
" Ellen, 271, 284
" Ellis, 23, 152, 154, 219, 220, 224, 236, 239, 243
Morris. Evan, 269, 272, 499
Morris. Gainor, 272, 499
" Geo. Anthony, 420
" Henry, 294, 585, 586
Morris. Israel, 174, 439
" James, 457
" Jane, 22
" John, 252, 271, 284, 301, 302
Morris. Joseph, 425
" Joshua, 269
" Levi, 294, 430, 459, 460, 461
" Lewis, 111
" Mary, 203, 269, 274
Morris. Morris, 269, 272, 528
Morris. Sarah, 461
" Thomas, 141, 149
Morson. Mrs. J. B., 294
Mortimer. James, 173, 203
Mortimer. Margaret, 173
Morton. Robert, 466
" Mrs. T. S. K., 294
Mullineux. Nathaniel, 391
Murrey. Col., 238
Musgrove. } Alice, 197
Musgrave. { Gaynor, 488
" Lewis, 197
" Margaret, 197, 198
Musgrove. Peregrine, 200, 232, 241, 243, 271
Musgrove. William, 170
Musser. John, 468
Nancarro. John, 76
Naylor. Mary, 285
Nealson, 148
Neall. Frank L., 294

[611]

WELSH SETTLEMENT OF PENSYLVANIA

Needham. Dr., 182
Neill. Henry, 420
Neilson. Lewis Winthrop, 274
Neilson. Winthrop C., 274, 285
Ness. Robert, 402
Newlin. Elizabeth, 298
Nicholas. Edward, 133, 252
Nicholas. Thomas, 237
" Thomas Jones, 319
Noble. Richard, 592
Noblit. Mrs. C. E., 294
Nordant. Capt., 492
Norris. 146
" Hannah, 237, 458
Norris. Isaac, 101, 146, 237, 294, 405, 406, 458
Norris. Mary, 145
" J. Parker, 294
" Thomas, 130
Odell. Edward, 449
Ogden. Cadwalader E., 287
Ogden. David B., 287
" Gouveneur M., 287
" John, 159
" William, 159
Oliver. David, 499
" Evan, 214, 217, 224, 249, 419, 499
Oliver. Winifred, 252
Orms. { Richard, 178,
Orme. { 179, 191, 215, 503, 509, 510, 529, 530, 582
Osborne. Elizabeth, 260
" Charles, 146
" Peter, 247
Orin. William, 174
Owen ap Evan, 22, 155, 267, 268
Owen ap Hugh, 286
Owen Evan Robert 101
Owen Hugh Evan, 81
Owen Humphrey Hugh, 179
Owen Glendower, 290, 300
Owen. Prince of So. Wales, 280, 294
Owen. Anne, 49, 262
" Captain, 318
" David, 532
" Edward, 47, 48, 55, 72, 83, 95, 103, 142, 180, 213, 421

Owen. Elinor 104
" Ellin, 21, 96, 155, 283
Owen. Elizabeth, 49, 134, 158, 179, 220, 261, 287, 498
Owen. Esther, 158
" Evan, 22, 75, 77, 83, 105, 148, 149, 154, 155, 157, 220, 280, 283, 446, 529, 532, 537
Owen. Gainor, 22, 76, 158, 199, 291
Owen. Dr. Griffith, 25, 83, 104, 160, 161, 177, 188, 191, 219, 317, 318, 319, 385, 387, 421, 493, 529, 587
Owen. Jr., Dr. Griffith, 104,
Owen. Griffith, 55, 75, 101, 197, 229, 245, 261, 368, 371, 378, 383, 384, 498, 503, 509
Owen. Hannah, 159, 160
" Harry, 235
" Humphrey, 49, 115, 132, 152, 180, 220, 221
Owen. Jane, 101, 136, 155, 160, 249, 280, 283, 286, 594
Owen. Jannæ, 96
" John, 49, 84, 104, 132, 151, 157, 159, 180, 220, 257, 287
Owen. Joseph, 309
" Joshua, 150, 151, 157, 180, 231, 257, 287, 498, 520
Owen. Lewis, 98, 104, 115, 152, 154, 160, 213, 215, 220, 224, 236, 243, 532, 594
Owen. Mably, 81
" Owen, 159, 280, 283
Owen. Peter, 21
" Rebecca, 151, 154, 157, 498
Owen. Richard, 149, 151, 152, 180, 221
Owen. Robert, 21, 25, 70, 75, 76, 80, 83, 96, 97, 99, 101, 102, 104, 105, 109, 111, 116, 118, 120, 121, 132, 138, 146, 149, 151, 152, 154, 157, 176, 180, 220, 221, 227, 235, 246, 257, 263, 280, 283, 285, 287, 291, 317, 318, 319, 383, 384, 385, 391, 392, 447, 498, 503,

528, 532, 537, 539, 549, 556, 577, 593, 594
Owen. Jr., Robert, 159
" Roland, 49, 115, 119, 132, 152, 154, 198, 213, 215, 224, 219, 236, 243, 271, 532
Owen. Sarah, 104, 161
" Sidney, 158
" Tacy, 159
" Thomas, 95, 234, 258, 262, 264, 487
Owen. William, 125, 126, 323
Owens. John, 156
Painter. Elinor, 204
" George, 103, 199, 230, 244, 499, 506, 509
Painter. Susanna, 103
Paiste. James L., 559
Palmer. Martha, 77
" John, 130
" Thomas, 130
" William, 77
Pardo. Letice, 197
Pardoe. William, 386
Park. Thomas, 442
Parker. John, 176
Parr. Elizabeth, 189
Parrish. Jr., Edward, 283, 284
Parrish. John, 284
Parry. David, 514
" Edward, 222
" Rev. Harry, 113
" Henry, 143, 222
" Hugh, 222
" John, 165, 488, 514
Parry. Llewellyn, 210,
" Owen, 175, 177
" Robert, 222
" Thomas, 216, 217, 222, 226
Parry. Jr., Thomas, 222
Parsons. Thomas, 174
Paschall. ———, 81
" Benjamin, 420
" Hannah, 283
" Col. Jonathan, 455
" Thomas, 135, 200, 455
Paschall. Jr., Thomas, 201
Paschall. William, 247,
Pastorius. Fra. Dan., 145, 345, 565
Paul. James, 122, 447
" John, 131
" Joseph, 576, 579
Peale. Mrs. Ch. W., 204

WELSH SETTLEMENT OF PENSYLVANIA

Pearce. Joseph, 480
Pearson. Katherine, 173, 203
Pearson. Mary, 173, 203
" Robert, 173
" Thomas, 173, 203
Pearsall. William, 74
Pechin. Col. William, 457
Pemberton. Abigail, 201
" Phineas, 201
Penn. Granville John, 485
Penn. Guilielma, 173
" Thomas, 489
" William, 17, 22, 98, 173, 267
Penn. Jr., William, 124, 173, 422, 506
Penn-Gaskell. Mary, 485
Penn-Gaskell. Thomas, 485
Pennington. John, 124, 422
Pennock. Christopher, 124, 201
Pennock. Nathaniel, 201
Pennypacker. Henry C., 289
Pennypacker. Isaac R., 289
Pennypacker. Samuel W., 170, 289
Penrose. Sarah, 274
Perot. Mary William, 133, 296
Perrot. John, 197
Peter. Rees. 218, 220, 371, 498, 510
Peters. William, 174
Phey. Thomas, 533
Philip ap Evan, 221
Philip ap Ivor, 290
Philips. Mrs. C. S., 283
Phillips. Griffith, 490
" Jane, 222
" Philip, 222, 251
Phillips. Phoebe, 251
Philler. Mrs. W. R., 283
Phillipin. Mary, 199
Pickering. Charles, 188
Pinniard. Marie, 160
Plantagenet. Edmund, 285
Pope. Henry E., 294
Porter. Como. David, 365
Potter. Gen. James, 237, 465

Potts. Arthur, 74
" David, 262
" Thomas, 255
Poultney. Mrs. A. E., 283
Powel. { David, 36, 51,
Powell. { 52, 71, 98, 148, 173, 228, 231, 232, 249, 250, 254, 255, 367, 368, 377, 498, 519, 591
Powel. Elizabeth, 150, 286, 298
Powell. Ellis, 235
" Evan, 252, 499
" Gainor, 498
" John, 150, 252, 319
Powell. Joseph, 254
" Robert, 227, 438
" Rowland, 198, 215, 217, 244, 245
" Thomas, 252, 254, 499
Powell. William, 174, 219, 249, 391, 392, 439
Poyer. John, 153, 200, 204, 229, 232, 241, 249, 253, 255
Prees. Ann, 161
" David, 146, 200, 256
Prees. Edward, 79, 291, 311
Prees. James, 98
" John, 161, 446
" Mary, 161
" Phebe, 161
" Rees, 161, 172, 255, 445
Prees. Richard, 133, 161, 229, 291
Prees. Sarah, 161
" William, 114
Preeson. Capt. William, 161
Preston. Rachel, 145
" Richard, 87
" Samuel, 146
Price. David, 146, 200, 215, 225, 228, 257, 498
Price. Edward, 78, 79, 81, 107, 133, 264, 445, 447, 448, 449, 478, 554, 556, 561, 570, 571, 585
Price. Edward R., 559
" Ellis, 81, 234, 287, 298
Price. Esther, 82
" Evan, 136
" Francis, 584
" Gwenllen, 200, 229

Price. Hannah, 132, 133, 200, 291
Price. Henry, 229
" Isaac, 229, 257, 487
Price. Jr., Isaac, 229
" Jane, 81, 82, 132
" James, 213, 215, 225, 228, 252, 323
Price. John, 81, 200, 449, 456, 556, 561
Price. Joseph, 457, 448, 555, 556, 562
Price. Katherine, 115, 220
Price. Margaret, 229
" Mary, 107, 229, 576
Price. Philip, 229, 237, 257, 481
Price. Rees, 78, 81, 82, 130, 153, 204, 445, 551, 552, 561
Price. Richard, 83, 96, 105, 111, 118, 133, 593
Price. Rowland, 204
Prichard. Edward, 25, 171, 249, 253, 350, 438, 481
Prichard. Elizabeth, 163, 164, 166, 204, 232
Prichard. Katherine, 163, 164, 166, 232
Prichard. Rees, 291
" Thomas, 48, 56, 83, 96, 97, 132, 136, 166
Priest. Edward, 82
Pris. Katherine, 203
Prothero. Evan, 259, 391
Pugh. Ann, 224, 225
" David, 146, 203, 224, 251, 255, 257, 267
Pugh. Edward, 267
" Eleanor, 248
" Elizabeth, 225
" Ellin, 225
" Ellis, 213, 215, 218, 224, 243, 267, 302, 317, 487, 498, 505, 526
Pugh. Evan, 224, 268
" Henry, 225, 248, 264
Pugh. Hugh, 225, 237, 514
Pugh. James, 251, 255, 261
Pugh. Jane, 225
" Jesse, 225
" Job, 225
" John, 302, 491, 594
Pugh. Katherine, 222, 225, 248

[613]

WELSH SETTLEMENT OF PENSYLVANIA

Pugh. Moses, 225
" Richard, 275
" Robert, 96, 125, 126, 225, 501
Pugh. Roger, 225
" Thomas, 225, 275, 526
Pugh. William, 225
Puleston. John, 286, 301
" Robert, 300
Pusey. Caleb, 206, 388, 529
Pusey. Owen, 177
Quandrill. Hannah, 212
" Capt. John, 212
Rees John William, 47, 79, 96, 106, 122, 131, 133, 136, 161, 247, 261, 264, 289, 291
Rees ap Rees, 226
Reinaullt Gruffydd Rhys, 290
Rhys ap Tewdwr, 294
Richard ab Evan, 289
Richard ap Evan, 166
Richard Gryffyth Rhys, 107, 133
Richard Rees Jones, 56, 58
Richard Rhys Grywwyth, 79
Richard Robert Thomas, 126
Richard ap Thomas, 25, 33, 147, 148, 207, 249
Risiart Thomas Rhys, 312
Robert ap Cadwalader, 269, 271
Robert ap David, 48, 63, 64, 79, 82
Robert David Lloyd, 291
Robert ap Evan, 267
Robert ap Griffith, 290
Robert Griffith Evangoch, 299
Robert ap Hugh, 96, 125, 267, 268
Robert John Evan, 115
Robert Owen Humphrey, 103
Robert Owen Lewis, 239, 298
Robert Thomas Morris, 126
Roger ap John, 24, 28
Randolph. Benjamin, 420
Ratcliff. Richard, 98
Rawle. Wm. Henry, 74
Rawlins. David, 97
Read. Harmon Pumpelly, 74
Read. John, 74
" Judge John M., 74
Redman. John, 101
Reece.
Rees. } Daniel, 215, 229
Reese.
" David, 196, 215, 229, 241, 438
Reese. Edward, 22, 47, 48, 53, 57, 58, 60, 71, 80, 81, 82, 102, 105, 138, 146, 154, 216, 223, 239, 257, 264, 289, 291, 298, 312, 446, 447, 448, 499 503, 517, 520, 540, 541, 549, 551, 553, 556, 564
Rees. Eleanor, 215
" Elizabeth, 152, 173, 215, 287
Rees. Ellin, 49
" Ellis, 49
" Evan, 47, 48, 55, 56, 59, 70, 83, 96, 97, 105, 122, 127, 152, 154, 198, 216, 256, 271, 532, 594
Rees. Griffith, 490
" Gwen, 49, 215, 503, 580
Rees. Henry, 215
" Hugh, 115, 152, 154, 220, 221, 532
Rees. Humphrey, 225
" Isaac, 215, 229, 490
Rees. Jane, 291
" John, 56, 173, 215, 223, 226, 229, 490
Rees. Lettice, 229
" Lewis, 215
" Mabley, 571
" Margaret, 215
" Mary, 229
" Miriam, 215, 229
" Philip, 215, 229
" Rebecca, 229
" Rees, 81, 252, 264
Rees. Richard, 54, 220
" Samuel, 199, 215, 229, 371, 488
Rees. Sarah, 229
Rees. Sidney, 122, 129, 594
Rees. Thomas, 164, 176, 199, 215, 217, 229, 256, 257, 258, 261, 490
Rees. William, 452, 490
Reeve. Mrs. Benj. C., 294
Reeve. Mrs. Richard H., 294
Rider. Tryall, 175, 176, 179, 191
Reigert. Adam, 440
Reinald. Humphrey, 152, 180, 220
Reynald. Ann, 105
Reynolds. Humphrey, 49
Rhoads. James, 159
" Dr. Samuel, 294
Rhoads. Thomas, 452
Rhodes. Adam, 391
" John, 391
Rhoderick. David, 149, 150, 257
Rhoderick. Evan, 255
" Thomas, 142
Rhytherch. } John, 141,
Rhydderch. } 142, 149, 150, 498, 508
Rytharch. Rees, 199
Rhydrth. Sarah, 584
Rhydd. John, 149, 150
Rice. John, 498
Richard. Abijah, 452
Richard. John, 82, 163, 164, 232 258, 259, 261, 319, 498, 584
Richard. Maud, 498
" Morris, 262
" Robert, 220
" Rowland, 108, 257, 275, 540, 567
Richard. Thomas, 47, 48
Richards. Bridget, 161
" Hannah, 132, 161
Richards. John, 161, 261, 457
Richards. Lewis, 164
" Lt. Peter, 454
" Susan, 161
" Thomas, 198, 271
Richardson. Charles, 73, 133, 190, 296
Richardson. Joseph, 170
" Samuel, 159, 170
Ridgway. Charles, 133
Right. Henry, 249
Righter. John, 561
Ringgold. Adm., Cadw., 74
Ritchie. James, 454
Rondes. Adam, 198
Rhode. Adam, 208
Roades. Adam, 217

[614]

WELSH SETTLEMENT OF PENSYLVANIA

Robb. Henry B., 74, 190
Robert. Evan, 267, 268
" Ellis, 275
" Gainor, 498
" Griffith, 154, 220, 552
Robert. Jane, 115, 154, 155, 225
Robert. Janne, 220
" John, 101, 198, 225, 226, 271
Robert. Lewis, 220
" Katherine, 86, 117, 498, 593
Robert. Margaret, 154, 220
Robert. Morris, 101
" Roger, 225
" Theodore, 220, 245
Roberts. Aaron, 107
" Abel, 107, 216, 251, 256
Roberts. Alban, 129, 131
" Algernon, 130
" Col. Algernon, 130, 455, 456, 568
Roberts. Algernon S., 130, 283
Roberts. Dr. A. Sidney, 130
Roberts. Ann, 131, 177, 180, 225, 266
Roberts. Awbrey, 103
" Benjamin, 130
" David, 558
" Edward, 100, 103, 130, 154, 180, 490, 517
Roberts. Jr., Edward, 562
Roberts. Elizabeth, 129, 151, 319
Roberts. Ellis, 107, 225, 251, 262
Roberts. Evan, **107**
" Gainor, 47, 56, 70, 84, 86, 95, 96, **106**, 107, 125 **126**
Roberts. George B., 73, 130, 133, 190, 296, 480
Roberts. George T., 130
" Hannah, 180
" Hugh, 21, 25, 47, 49, 53, 54, 57, 59, 60, 70, 80, 80, 84, 85, 86, 89, 95, 96, 103, 110, 116, 117, 119, 120, 122, 125, 134, 136, 137, 138, 147, 148, 150, 154, 155, 156, 160, 166, 170, 176, 207, 208, 219, 234, 241,
246, 257, 261, 262, 266, 280, 283, 284, 317, 318, 348, 368, 371, 374, 383, 384, 385, 387, 391, 421, 425, 433, 439, 445, 447, 498, 500, 506, 509, 510, 515, 517, 529, 549, 550, 556, 533, 562, 571, 591, 592
Roberts. Isaac, 130, 126, 283
Roberts. Jane, 84, 155, 219, 269
Roberts. Jesse, 457
" Job, 269, 272, 285
Roberts. John, 25, 72, 78, 89, 90, 95, 101, 102, 103, 105, 107, 108, 124, 125, 130, 132, 134, 136, 138, 151, 153, 156, 158, 174, 175, 178, 179, 200, 212, 219, 213, 214, 215, 216, 221, 224, 225, 245, 257, 261, 262, 269, 271, 272, 275, 287, 317, 371, 384, 387, 439, 451, 503, 509, 517, 520, 530, 538, 539, 540, 541, 543, 550, 553, 554, 555, 556, 557, 561, 563, 568, 573, 574, 595
Roberts. Jr., John, 76, 129, 130, 180, 247, 269, 272, 284, 562
Roberts. 3d., John, 247
" Jonathan, 130, 458, 460
Roberts. Joseph, 180, 456
Roberts. Katherine, 96, 107, 127
Roberts. Margaret, 84, 129, 239
Roberts. Martha, 73
" Mary, 284
" Matthew, 180, 490
Roberts. Morris, 275
" Moses, 106, 537, 539, 552, 567
Roberts. Owen, 53, 54, 58, 262, 102, 103, 122, 129, 170, 173, 177, 180, 225, 229, 237, 247, 447, 537, 538, 540, 550, 562
Roberts. Percival, 130
Roberts. Phebe, 122
" Phineas, 129, 131

Roberts. Rachel 107
" Rebecca, 180
" Rees, 129, 131
" Richard, 126, 127, 225, 283
Roberts. Robert, 53, 54, 58, 80, 84, 102, 106, 122, 129, 130, 156, 158, 173, 180, 283, 246, 257, 437, 445, 446, 447, 537, 551, 553, 561
Roberts. Roger, 83, 96, 97, 105
Roberts. Sarah, 212
" Sidney, 131, 447, 553
Roberts. Tacy, 130
" Thomas, 265, 456
Roberts. Titus, 131
" William, 180, 247, 256, 257, 261, 456
Robinson. John, 562
" Jr., Mrs. M., 283
Roger. John, 225, 271
Ross. Charles W., 74
Rotheroc. { Rees, 195,
Rothers. { 199, 204, 526
Roules. B., 249
Rouse. John, 347
" Nathaniel, 347
Rowe. Grace, 200
" William, 196, 200, 244
Rowen. Evan, 241
Rowland Edward Humphrey, 235
Rowland. Ann, 154
" Mrs. E. K., 294
Rowland. Henry J., 74
" Hugh, 132
" Thomas, 254
Rowles. Bertha, 244
Royce. Mrs. Ch. C., 283
Rudyard. Thomas, 255
Russell. Elizabeth, 274
" John, 274
Rutter. Samuel, 76
Sandiford. Ralph, 265
Samuel Humphrey Hugh, 81
Samuel. Daniel, 49
" Hugh, 216, 250, 251, 261
Samuel. John, 438
" Joseph, 49
" Lydia, 49
" Margaret, 216
" Rebecca, 49
Sanburn. Daniel, 98

[615]

WELSH SETTLEMENT OF PENSYLVANIA

Sanders. Henry, 253
" William, 104
Saunders. Paul, 509, 510
Scarlett. John, 153
Schley. Cadwalader, 74,
" William, 74
Schrew. George N., 74
Scotharn. Ann, 82
Scothern. Lewis, 562
Scotson. George, 174, 439
Scott. 474
" Mrs. Lewis A., 283
Scott. William, 98
Scourfield. Maurice, 196, 232
Scull. Frances, 461
Sellers. Christopher, 420
" Hannah, 247
" Samuel, 247
" Sarah, 247
Shaner. William, 510
Shank. Benjamin, 481
Sharlow. William, 119, 121, 124, 174, 207, 208, 255, 491
Sharpless. Benjamin, 420
Sharpless. Blanche, 219, 533
Sharpless. Isaac, 17, 372, 487, 591,
Sharpless. William, 261
Sharswood. George, 420
" James, 419
Shaw. Mrs. D. F., 283
" Samuel, 389
Sheetz. Francis, 429
Shenkin. William, 567
Shepherd, 241
Shippen. Edward, 191
" William, 420
Shober. Samuel L., 74
Shoemaker. 146
" Benjamin, 419
Shoemaker. Jonathan, 420
Shone. Hugh, 391
Short. Adam, 188
Sibill Hugh Gwyn. 150
Simons. John, 203, 249
Simpson. James, 578
Simson. John, 174
Sinex. Eli. 212
" John Henry, 212
" Thomas, 212
Sinkler. William, 173
Sion. Edward, 567
Sixmith. Bruen, 189
" Ester, 189
" William, 189

Sixsinth. Lucien, 176
Sixsmith. Bryan, 185
Skone. Margaret, 197
" James, 197
Skurfield. Maurice, 196
Sky. William, 65
Smedley. Hannah, 192
Smith. Abraham L., 73, 190, 245, 283
Smith. Benj. H., 20, 73, 190 245, 283
Smith. Benj. R., 294
" Mrs. Chas. E., 294
Smith. Ch. Perrin, 294
" Francis, 145, 147
Smith. Dr. George, 73, 161, 534, 539
Smith. George, 575
" Henry, 197
" John Jay, 294
" Lloyd P., 354
" Mary, 197
" Michael, 453
" Thomas, 391
" William, 145, 174, 391, 439
Snead. Richard. 386
Snowden. Isaac, 420
" John, 420
Somerset. Henry, 288
Southworth. Alice, 189
" John, 189
" Mary, 176, 179, 189, 191
Sparhawk. Ch. W., 289
Spencer. John, 420
Spray. Christopher, 391
Springet. Herbert, 347
Spruce. John, 437, 438
Stadleman. Jacob, 476
" William, 130, 264, 455, 483
Stafford. Elizabeth, 220
" Sir Ralph; 297
" Richard, 220
" Jr. Richard, 220
Stalker. Thomas, 211
Stampford. Thomas, 503
Stanley. Sir Edward, 293
Stanley. Elizabeth, 293
" Sir Thomas, 286
Stanley. Sir William, 286
Stanley. Thomas, 293
Stansbury. Warren M., 300
Starr. Mrs. Louis, 284

Steel. 202.
" James, 171, 177
Steinmetz. John, 74
" Joseph A., 190
Stephen ab Evan, 217, 218
Stephen ap Evan, 228
Stephens. John, 228, 476
Stephens. Richard F., 74
Stewardson. Mary H., 190
Stewardson. Mrs. Thomas, 190, 287
Stillwagon. Joseph, 429
Story. Enoch, 146, 223, 228
Story. Marcy, 146
" Mary, 146
" Patience, 146
" Thomas, 528, 536
Stout. Elizabeth, 229
Streaper. Abraham, 448
" Mary, 448, 449, 558
Stretcher. Edward, 419
Sullivan. Gen., 238
Sullivant. Joseph, 274
Sutcliff. Robert, 575-6
Swaner. Mark, 347
Sydney. Algernon, 409
" Henry, 409
Symcock. Jacob, 575
" John, 174, 349, 353, 371
Symmons. Thomas, 232
Syng. Philip, 420
Taillefer. Ademar, 289
Taylor. Capt., 97
" Roland L., 74,
" Thomas, 191, 175, 178, 242
Taylor. Jr., Thomas, 178
Thayer. Mrs. J. B., 283
Thomas ap Edward, 114
Thomas ap Evan, 267
Thomas Evan Lloyd, 300
Thomas ap Hugh, 81
Thomas Hugh Evan, 109, 110
Thomas John Evan, 231, 249, 255
Thomas John Thomas, 153
Thomas Llewellyn Owen, 290
Thomas Rees Evan, 133
Thomas ab Richard, 132, 133, 136

[616]

WELSH SETTLEMENT OF PENSYLVANIA

Thomas Richard Evan, 166
Thomas ap Robert, 133
Thomas Robert Lloyd, 299
Thomas Sion Evan, 309, 311
Thomas. Abel, 55, 86, 107, 132, 135, 137, 174, 257, 385, 439
Thomas. Dr. Allen G., 587
Thomas. Ann, 218, 223
" Awbrey, 173
" Cadwalader, 21, 49, 109, 138, 155, 157
Thomas. Daniel, 176, 218, 257, 584
Thomas. David, 223, 323, 457, 567
Thomas. Edward, 98, 141, 142, 150, 173, 230, 247, 262
Thomas. Eleanor, 584
" Elizabeth, 49, 114, 173, 203, 211
Thomas. Ellin, 155, 225
" Esther, 72
" Evan, 87, 164, 173, 195, 196, 199, 232, 261
Thomas. George, 211, 212
Thomas. Given, 584
" Grace, 211
" Hannah, 211
" Henry, 195
" Herbert, 173
" Hester, 173
" Howell, 166
" Hugh, 256
" Humphrey, 249
Thomas. Isaac, 457
" Jacob, 108, 564
Thomas. James, 166, 173, 180, 200, 202, 227, 241, 245, 253, 254, 257, 530, 584
Thomas. Jr., James, 202, 257
Thomas. John, 49, 54, 72, 109, 153, 173, 203, 249, 250, 256, 319, 445, 562
Thomas. John Thomas, 173
Thomas. Katherine, 95, 100, 117, 119, 150, 173, 203, 257, 421, 500, 593, 594

Thomas. Lewis, 319
" Litter, 22, 114
" Lowry, 133
" Margaret, 141, 142, 149, 173, 203
Thomas. Mary, 164, 211, 461
Thomas. Morris, 173
" Nathan, 100, 173, 180, 196, 203, 204, 227, 254
Thomas. Jr., Nathan, 203
Thomas. Owen, 173, 196, 203, 232, 252, 253, 257, 262, 488, 490
Thomas. Rees, 77, 95,, 138, 154, 167, 171, 172, 215, 225, 229, 237, 257, 294, 296, 317, 438, 461, 462, 480, 481, 505, 528 582
Thomas. Jr., Rees, 172
" Robert, 539
" Richard. 55, 71, 100, 229, 319, 493, 539
Thomas. Col. Richard, 210, 211
Thomas. Jr., Richard, 84, 207, 211
Thomas. 3d, Richard, 211
Thomas. 4th, Richard, 211
Thomas. Solomon, 193
" Thomas, 173, 223, 225, 515
Thomas. Watkins, 166
" William, 152, 166, 172, 173, 214, 218, 220, 221, 225, 256, 275, 437, 478, 491, 502
Thomson. Charles, 237, 238, 458, 459, 460, 461
Thomson. John, 460
Thornton. John, 354
Tilghman. Benjamin, 481
Tilghman. Richard A., 73
Todd. William, 429
Toland. Robert, 73, 77
Tongue. Elizabeth, 283
" Thomas, 283
Tounson. Anthony, 197
Townsend. Edward Y., 133
Townsend. Henry Troth, 133
Townsend. John W., 133

Townsend. Richard, 307, 388
Travis. John, 74
Trent. William, 319
Trevor. John, 28
Trimble. John, 211
" Joseph, 211
" William, 211
Troth. William P., 133
Troutbeck. Sir William, 286
Tuberville. Edward, 289
Tunes. ⎫ Abraham, 554,
Tunis. ⎭ 562
Anthony, 78, 264, 447, 483, 554, 555, 562, 557, 558, 559
Joseph, 483, 554, 555
Turnbull. William, 420
Turner. Joseph C., 481
" Robert, 260, 266, 267, 308, 336, 369, 382, 403, 413
Tudor Gryffyth Vychan, 290
Tudor-vaughan, 298
Tudor. Lowry, 290
" Mary, 161, 498, 509
Tudor. Robert, 498
Underwood. John, 478
Up de Graeff. Derick, 505
Up den Graeff. Abraham, 565
Usher. Thomas, 354
van Cuelebroeck. Countess, 294
Vaston. John, 350
Vaughan, of Rhuddalt, 290
Vaughan. Catharine, 289
" Edward, 49, 157
Vaughan. Eleanor, 584
" Jane, 103, 161
" John, 180, 319
Vaughan. Robert, 99, 103, 118, 119, 120, 122, 154, 160, 161, 198, 262, 271, 591
Vaughan. Sir Roger, 288
Vaughan. Thomas, 119
" Watkin, 288
" William, 296
" Sir William, 289
Vaughn. Gawen, 109

[617]

WELSH SETTLEMENT OF PENSYLVANIA

Vaux. 146, 578, 579
" George, 460, 461, 486, 586
Vaux. Mrs. Richard, 294
Vernon. Randall, 354, 358
Vernon. Rebecca, 134
Vincent. Robert, 264
Vroom. Garret, D. W., 474
Vychan. Gryffyth, 290
Wager. Philip, 440
Wainwright. 146
" Clement R., 289
Wainwright. Francis K., 289
Wainwright. John, 478
" Jonathan, 420
Wainwright. Wm. J., 294
Wake. Lord John, 292
Waker. (Vaikaw, Walk-er)
" Mary, 203
" John, 55, 252
Walker. Lewis, 200, 203, 217, 505, 574
Walker. Dr. James R., 587
Wallis. Philip, 257
Waln. 146
" Edward, 294
" Mrs. Jacob S., 294
Walter. Ann, 567
" John, 177
" Richard, 54, 55, 59, 83, 84, 257, 517
Walter. William, 552
Warley. Jr., Daniel, 239
Warner. Col. Isaac, 130, 455, 456, 482
Warner. John, 174, 437, 509
Warner. Tacy, 130
" William, 69, 174, 391, 439, 455, 482
Watkin. Edward, 275
" John, 47, 48, 54, 136, 137, 571
Watkins. John, 48, 57, 99
Watkins. Richard, 226
Watson. John, 226
Watts. Bridget, 261
" Elizabeth, 261
" Hannah, 262
" Jean, 261
" Thomas, 252

Wayne. Abraham, 420
" Gen'l Anthony, 449
Wayne. Thomas, 120
Weaver. John, 146
Webster. Edmund, 559
Welch. James, 420
Welles. John, 275
Wells. John, 456
West. Joseph, 159
Weston. Deborah, 197
Wetherill. Elizabeth, 272
" Isaac, 430
" Joseph, 419
" Mary, 272
" Samuel, 419
Wharton. 146
" Daniel C., 294
" Joseph, 160
" Rachel, 204
" Robert, 245, 256, 488
Wharton. Jr., Thomas, 237, 465
Wheeldon. Isaac, 176
Wheeler. Andrew, 128, 219, 294
Wheeler. S. Bowman, 190, 294
Whitall. Jr., John M., 284, 300
White. Richard, 241
Whitpain. John, 104
" Richard, 171
Wiges. Henry, 98
Wilcox. Barnabas, 119, 174, 433, 439, 499, 506, 507, 509
Wilhelmi. Mrs. L., 294
Will. 474
Willcox. Joseph, 506
William ap Edward, 48, 63, 64, 79, 80, 84, 85, 92, 99, 121, 216, 245, 248, 311, 312, 421, 439, 445
William ap John. 104, 267
William ap Owen, 96
William Robert Ellis. 275
William Thomas Hugh, 275
William. David, 229, 520
William. Edward, 447, 515
William. Elizabeth, 96
" Evan, 232, 258
" Hugh, 276
" John, 22, 49, 56, 57, 80, 115, 133, 215, 220

William. Robert, 54, 55, 59, 147, 148, 257
Williams, of Cae Fadog. 301
Williams. Anthony, 240
" Charles, 190, 283
Williams. Daniel, 87, 425, 456, 561
Williams. Edward, 87, 246, 257, 264, 487, 562
Williams. Jr., Edward, 87
Williams. Eleanor, 87
" Elizabeth, 70, 86, 114, 115, 225
Williams. Ellen, 87, 284
" Ellis, 71, 284, 301
Williams. Evan. 163, 260
Williams. Gwen, 302
" Hannah, 561
" Hugh, 191, 215, 216, 225, 490
Williams. Humphrey, 262
" Isaac, 451, 455
Williams. Jane, 87
" John, 105, 106, 231, 237, 244, 246, 251, 257, 555, 594
Williams. J. Randall, 190.
Williams. Joseph, 87
" Katherine, 86
" Lewis, 248
" Lumley, 252, 499
Williams. Margaret, 260
Williams. Mary, 87
" Rees, 519
" Robert, 71, 86, 208, 493
Williams. Sarah, 87
" Susanna, 225
" Thomas, 114
Williamson. John, 275
" Robert, 275
Willing. 146
" Edward S, 294
" Jacob S, 284, 300
Willing. Mrs. Richard, 294
Willis. Jacob, 260
Wilson. George, 97
" Henrietta, 274, 275
Wilson. Isabella G., 284
" Major John, 476

WELSH SETTLEMENT OF PENSYLVANIA

Wilson. William H., 481
Winsor. Mrs. J. D., 283
Winsor. Mrs. W. D., 283
Wister. Alexander W., 73
Wister. Daniel, 76, 77
" Israel, 585
" Israel J., 73
" John, 156, 469, 478
Wister. Col. Lewis, 156
" Dr. Owen Jones, 73
Wister. Rodman, 73, 190, 283, 291
Wister. Dr. Thomas, 294
" Wm. Wynne, 73
Witmer. A., 440
Wood. Ann, 159
" Eleanor, 169
" George, 169
" Mrs. Howard, 283
Wood. John, 169
" Joseph, 119
" Rebecca, 577
" Robert, 562
" William, 119, 124, 174, 207, 208, 349
Wood. Mrs. W. A., 294
Woodville. Jr. Wm., 74

Woodliffe. Nathan, 226
Woods. William, 439
Worm. William, 264
Worrell. John, 221, 230
" Mary, 230
" Peter, 230
" Richard, 565
Wynne. Elizabeth, 116, 188, 189, 192
Wynne. Hannah, 153, 192, 193, 287
Wynne. James, 192
" John, 21, 77, 113, 174, 181, 192
Wynne. Sir John, 182
" Jonathan, 174, 177, 178, 184, 190, 188, 192, 439, 466, 483, 537
Wynne. Martha, 192
" Mary, 73, 192, 193
Wynne. Morris, 152
" Owen, 112
" Rebecca, 189, 193
Wynne. Sarah, 192
" Sidney, 192, 193
Wynne. Thomas, 153, 182, 249, 255, 443

Wynne. Dr. Thomas, 25, 33, 72, 73, 104, 120, 138, 153, 161, 164, 175, 189, 210, 257, 287, 291, 317, 466, 507, 517, 577, 595
Wynne. Lt. Thomas, 456, 466
Wynne. Tibitha, 193
" William, 182
Wyatt. Mrs. Walter S., 283
Yardley. William, 356
Yeates. Jasper, 412
Yerkes. Mary, 449
" Titus, 428, 449
Yocum. James, 73
" Th. Corson, 300
Young. David, 449, 450
" David Oram, 450
Young. Harriet, 449
" Capt. Llewellyn, 455
Young. Matilda, 449
" Peter, 100
" Rees, 449
" Sarah, 146
Zane. Robert, 267
Zell. John, 456
" Thomas Ellwood, 567

SUBJECTS.

Ab and ap interchangable, 85
Aberkynfrig, 295, 296
Aberystwith, 240
Abington tp., 122, 200, 253, 487
Academyville, 433, 484, 488
Adventurers for Pensylvania land, 25
Aged Friends of Merion, 569
Agreement between Dr. Jones and John Thomas, 117
Alfred, King of Dublin, 295
Almeley par. Hereford, 350
American Civil War, 15
"American Historical Register," 158, 457
"Americans of Royal Descent," 159, 282, 284
"American Weekly Mercury," 265
An execution at New Castle, 170
Angouleme, Count of, 289
Annals of Welsh settlers, 305
"Annerch ir Cymru," 152
An old certificate of removal, 154
An old inventory of personalty, 157
"Antiquity of the Quakers" pamphlet, 134
An unconventional love story, 523-4
Apostles of Quakerism in Wales, 24
Ardmore, 75, 77, 119, 141, 150, 151, 155, 160, 427, 475, 478, 479, 480, 485
Arms used by Dr. Wynne, 183
"Art of Ingeniously Tormenting," 20
Arranging the Welsh settlement in Pensylvania, 20
"Articles of Conditions and Concessions," 26
Artois, Count of, 285
Arundel, Earl of, 285, 288, 293
A surprise for the Welsh, 35
Ashland Heights, 421
Athensville, 478, 479
A Welshman's farm, 236
Awbrey pedigree, 595
Autobiography filed with Merion Meeting, 166
Autobiographies of founders of Merion Meeting, 63, 128
Bala, 25, 35, 47, 63, 65, 67, 75, 79, 85, 86, 96, 98, 118, 120, 121, 125, 126, 133, 155, 160, 161, 192, 301, 309, 434
Ballotting methods, 361, 362
Baltimore, Md., 284
Baptist congregation, 486, 487
Baptist graveyard, 456
Barber-surgeon, 64
"Baronial Assembly," 373
"Barony" idea, 337, 340, 342
Bashford Quaker Meeting, 28
Beauchamp, 285
Beaumaris Castle, 23, 160, 161
Beginning of Quakerism in Wales, 23
Belmont Driving Park, 433

Belmont Heights, 421
Bequests to the Haverford Prep. Mtg., 165, 198, 200, 203, 227
Bequests to Merion Prep. Mtg., 84, 86, 101, 120, 129, 173, 180, 203
Besse's "Sufferings of the Quakers," 24, 29, 115, 266
Bettws y Coed, 21, 48, 104, 176
Bevan as an itinerant minister, 167
Bevan's Land Patent, 163
Bible of David Jones, 271
Bible of John ap Thomas, 118
Bi-centennial of Merion Mtg. House, 586, 587
Bicking graveyard, 456
Birmingham tp., 230
Bishop of London, 19
Black Horse Tavern, 238, 442, 465, 467
Blacksmith's Day Book, 275
Bleddyn-cynfyn, king of Powis, 282, 290, 297
Blockley tp., 69, 77, 85, 100, 121, 130, 158, 192, 198, 208
Blockley, Worcestershire, 69
Blockley and Merion Wagon Road, 436
Blue Anchor tavern, 82, 153
"Blue plush sidesaddle," 87
Bodeon, 286
Bonus city lot, 592
"Bonus land," 179, 304
Books in the Welsh Tract, 81
Boult and Tun inn, 65
Bounds of Thomas and Jones land, 52
Bounds of Welsh Tract, 488
Bowman's Bridge, 434, 443
Branas Uchaf, 290, 299
Brecknockshire, 29, 172, 296
British invade Merion, 466
Bromfield, Lord of, 281
Bronvadog, 120, 184
"Brookfield" farm, 216
Browning's "Americans of Royal Descent," 159
Browning's "Colonial Dames of Royal Descent," 159
Browning's "Magna Carta Barons," 159
Bryn Gwyn, 284
"Bryn Mawr" farm, 134, 150, 180, 233, 236, 237, 246, 247, 285, 287, 296, 298, 457, 462
Bryn Mawr, 86, 150, 153, 165, 180, 213, 216, 247, 287, 298, 480, 481
Bryn Mawr College, 153, 236, 458
Buck Inn, 442, 464
Building Merion Mtg. House, 533-540
Bull and Mouth Mtg., 400, 413
Burge's Tract, 438
Burlington Mo. Mtg., 90, 497, 499, 530, 597
Burials at sea, 118, 183, 234

[620]

WELSH SETTLEMENT OF PENSYLVANIA.

Buying Royal assent, 515
Byllings, 22
Byllings's land customers, 267
Cabinet P. O., 480
Cae Fadog, 301
Cae Mor, 109
Caerwys, 25, 33, 178
Caer y Nwch, 298
Caerdiganshire, 195, 222
Caermarthenshire, 68, 98, 161, 163, 200, 213, 253, 254
Caernarvon Castle, 286
Caernarvonshire, 126, 127, 176, 213, 300, 301
Caifadog, 284
Cantre Seliffe, 295
Cardiff Mo. Mtg., 166
Castle Br'th, 195, 202
Cause for trouble between the Welsh Friends and Penn, 26
"Cave dwellers," 315
Cayrowe, 295
Center Mtg. Hs., Phila., 509
"Central Pensylvania" R. R., 479
Certificates of removal, 532, 593
"Chalkley Hall," 72
Chalkley's Journal, 574
Changes in first purchases, 57
Character of the deeds to the Welsh, 58
Chattam. Kent, 201
Cherry Lane, 155
"Chestnut Hill," 100, 103
Chester, Pa., 63
Chester Welsh Tract, 209
Chester Creek, 80, 84, 86, 104, 119, 128, 135
Chester Co. line matter, 349, 596
Chester Mill, 389
Chester Mo. Mtg., 501, 504
Chester Valley Friends, 505
Chichester Mtg., 230
Chichester property, 119
Chiefs of the "Welsh Nation," 373, 384
Christ Church, Phila., 158, 323
Chuckatuck Friends Mtg., 98
Church Road, 156, 232
Churchman's Journal, 574
Cilltalgarth, 21, 22
City Liberties, 394
City Line Road, 136, 128, 130, 204, 232, 465
"Clean John Meadow," 101, 102, 447, 555
Clerk of Haverford Mo. Meeting of ministers, 120
Cloddan Cochion, 233
Clwye, 295
Clynn, 132
Coalter's Ferry, 420
Coates's Cave, 315
Cobbs Creek, 69, 80, 100, 201, 208, 428
Coch Willym, 301
Cocdiowrid, 293
Coed y Foel, 300
Collena, 166, 289
Colonial architecture, 389
"Colonial Dames of Royal Descent," 159, 302
"C. L. & P. R. R." 476
Columbia Railway, 443, 476, 479
Columbus Inn, 443
Comforts of Welsh Friends, 320
Commissioners' Welsh Minutes, 196, 207

Committee representing Welsh Friends, 25
Comond, 295
"Company No. One," 45, 63, 312, 387
"Company No. 7," 522
Compensation of surveyor, 251
"Concealed land," 387
Concord Mo. Mtg., 521, 567
"Conditions and Concessions to Adventurers for Land," 136
Conditions to purchasers of Land, 35
Conestoga Road, 438
Confirmation of deeds, 508
Confiscated Welsh lands, 422
Congress of Nations, 273
Conshohocken Hill, 53, 489
Continental Army in Merion, 463-4
Convent of the Sisters of Mercy, 14
Conway. Earl of, 591
Cooperstown Road, 232, 484
Cornwall. Earl of, 280
Cornwallis. Earl of, 451
Cors y Gedol, 290
Coulter Ave., Ardmore, 478
"Country stores," 319
County Tax, 258
Court in Fenel Hill, 292
Cowyn, 126
Crossforth, 209
Crum Creek Road, 232
Cryniarth, 301, 282
Cumberland Valley, 17
Curles, Va., 98
Cwm Pennaner, 299
Cydros, 290, 292
Cyfanedd, 120
Cymcydmaen. Lord of, 281
Cynlas, 21, 85, 133
David's Mill, 201
David's land. Lewis, 195
Davies's Journal. Richard, 233
Davis' Queen's Head Inn, 308
Darby Mill, 389
Darby Creek, 232
"Darby Mill Creek," 349
Darby Road, 174
Darby tp., 82
Darby, Pa., 169
D. A. R. monument, 465
Death of John Roberts, 574
Debate with the Bishop of St. Asaph., 143
"Declaration of Denial," 318
Decline of purchasers, 254
Deed for Merion graveyard, 549
Deed for Merion Mtg. House lot, 551
Deed for Merion Mtg. land, 557
Deed to "first purchaser," 195
Deed to second purchaser, 195
Deeds to the Welsh, 45
Deeds to "first purchasers" of Pen. land, 34
"Delaware County," 229
Delaware settlements, 17, 18
Denbighshire, 22, 24, 25, 73, 118, 151, 161, 175, 176, 181, 287, 299, 301, 302
Dermot. King of Leinster, 295
Description of a skirmish at Bryn Mawr, 238
Devizes. Wiltshire, 171
Devon. Earl of, 280
Devonshire House. London, 28
Discharging a servant, 87, 90
Disgust of the Welsh, 88

WELSH SETTLEMENT OF PENSYLVANIA

"Dishonorable marriages," 263
Disorder at funerals, 519
Dissart, 214
Dividing the Welsh tract, 335
Dr. Jones's letter, 26 Aug. 1682, 50
Dr. Jones's party, 84, 85, 87
Dock Creek, 82
Docklow par. Hereford, 350
Dolgelly, 22, 98, 114, 132, 233, 235, 239, 591, 161, 234
Dolgelly Quart. Mtg., 115
Delgelly Prep. Mtg., 126
Dolgyn, 23, 239
Dolgun Vchn, 213, 243
Dolgules, 131, 160, 260
Dolobran, 25, 29, 33, 149, 150, 183, 233
Dolobran Hall, 141, 142, 293
Dolobran Quart. Mtg., 150
Dolserre, 25, 48, 103, 104, 131, 152, 160, 180, 213, 220, 240, 260
Dolyserre Quart. Mtg., 152, 499
Downingtown, 211, 212
Duck Creek, 104, 160
Duckett's Prep. Mtg., 500
Dutch, 17, 18
Dutch "Articles of Freedom and Exemption," 26
Dutch land plans, 33
Dutch Settlement, 373
Dutch West India Co., 26
Dyffryn Mawr tp., 101, 196, 199, 200, 201, 244, 253, 254, 293
Dyffrydan tp., 233, 239, 298
Dynullo, 177
Dwnn's "Visitations" in Wales, 280
Eagle, 479, 480
Eagle Road, 256
Eagle Tavern, 443
"Englesfield" farm, 482
Earliest burials at Merion, 571
Earliest burials at Haverford, 571
Earliest extant minutes of Welsh Mo. Mtg., 502
Earliest Friends' Mtgs., 497
Early Days in the Welsh Tract, 305
Early deeds did not give location of land, 50
Early delegates to Quart. Mtg., 503
Early inventory of an estate, 157
Early Marriage Certificate of Welsh Friends, 76
Early Mtg. clerks, 503
Early maps of the Welsh Tract lands, 50
Early marriage certificate, 157
Early Patentees, 255
Early "peace makers," 503
Early Philadelphia merchant, 319
Early "politics," 360
Early settlers in Haverford tp., 153
Early surveyor's mark, 201
Early tavern keeper, 146
Early use of Friends' marriage ceremony, 152
Early Welsh books in Pa., 151, 152
Early Welsh letters, 309, 312
Eastmoor, 142
East Town tp., 491
Eckley annoys the Governor, 362
Economic features, 319
Edermon, 301
Education of a 17th century physician, 182
Edward I. of England, 292, 297, 298

Edward, the Black Prince, 293
Edwards' Ford, 433
Eglwysilan, 163, 164
Ellis's advice to emigrants, 396
Ellis's description of "Haverford Town," 242
Elm P. O., 450
Emral manor, 300, 301
End of the "Welsh Barony," 386
English tongue, 19
Equal division of land among Welsh children, 123
Evansburg, 323
Evans's house, 162
Evil reports about Penn's projects, 39
"Eyton Park," 118
Exchange Money, 425
Exiled Friends, 468
"Exiles in Virginia," 469
"Explanation of the City and Liberties," 333
Extent of the Welsh Tract, 36
Exterminating wolves, 258
"Fairhill" farm, 146
"Fair Maid of Kent," 292
Fairmount Park, 100
Falls Mo. Meeting, 597
Falls of Schuylkill, 51, 137
Families and lands of first arrivals, 63
Families and lands of second arrivals, 93
Farms divided, 88
Faulty surveys, 128
Fayette Co., Ky., 284
Ferdinand III. of Castile, 29
Ferry franchise, 390
Feudal Barons of Powis, 297
Fire-flies, 322
First birth in the Welsh Tract, 82
First brick house in Phila., 187
First "cave dwellers," 65
First death in the Welsh Tract, 82
First Friends' meeting, 308
First grist mill, 308
First homes of settlers, 306, 313, 314, 315, 316
First homicide, 514
First land laid out in the Welsh Tract, 45
First marriage in the Welsh Tract, 125
First Mo. Mtg. in Phila., 187
First settlers of Merion tp., 137
First Pa. Assembly, 187, 317
First Pa. real estate agents, 27
First Phila. counterfeiter, 188
First physicians in Pa., 104
First public school, 317
"First purchaser's" deeds, 179
First use of the Friends' marriage ceremony, 152
First Welsh child born in Radnor tp., 223
First Welsh deed confirmed, 53
First Welsh Friends to arrive, 64
First Welsh grantees Penn's social equals, 27
First winter of Pa., 313, 314
Fisher's Island, 190
Flat Land Ford, 489
Flight of Congress, 464
Flintshire, 25, 33, 120, 178
40,000 acres engaged, 26
Ford Road, 130, 434
Ford vs. Penn, 397

WELSH SETTLEMENT OF PENSYLVANIA

Foreman of first grand jury, Phila., 197
Fort Albany, N. Y., 77
Fox's Journal, 23
Fox's Pa. lands, 347
Fothergill's Journal, 573-4
Founders of Haverford Prep. Mtg., 95
Founders of Merion Prep. Meeting, 63, 175
Founding Merion Mtg., 46
Friends and their hats, 526, 528
Free Society of Traders, 116, 158, 400-1
Friends and the "Oath," 514
Friends' archives, 63
"Friends' customs," 374
Friends' ferry troubles, 390, 392
Friends imprisoned in Welshpool, 142
Friends in Md., and Va., 97
Friends' Intermeeting library, 489
Friends meeting in a "Steeple house," 29
Friends' ministers, 573
Friends of Merionethshire, in 1679, 49
Friends patrons of printing, 526
Friends' Public School, 75
Friends' "sufferings," 18, 20, 266
Friends' Testimonies, 274
Friends' Yearly Mtg of Wales, 28
F. and A. Masons, 457
Freemasonry in the Continental Army, 457
Free Society of Traders, 17, 89, 400
Fron-Goch, 101, 120, 155, 157, 271, 301
Fronween, 120, 122
"Frame of Government," 348
Frankfort Company, 345
French Creek, 80, 131
Frog Hollow Run, 430
Furnishing the Haverford Meeting House, 152
Gadfa, 286
Gardner family, 508
Gardner's house, 162
Garretsville, 484
Garrig's house, 162
Garthlwich, 141, 149
Garthygn fawr, 24, 132, 235
"Geilli yr Cochinid," 118
Genealogical letter, 291
General Wayne Inn, 12, 427, 437, 444, 446, 449, 467, 478, 560, 572
General Wayne Inn lot, 553
Gen. Wayne P. O., 479
Geologists' theories, 488
George family, 86, 567
"George's Hill" farm, 100
George's house. E., 162
George's house. D., 162
George's house. R., 162
Germans' experience, 380
Germans' grievances, 345
German Friends, 510
German "barony," 347
"German Immigration into Pa.," 532
German settlers, 145, 532
Germantown Mtg. 529
Giving public notice, 520
Gladwyn, 435, 484
Glamorganshire. 25, 33, 163, 166, 168
Glanlloidiogin, 133, 291
Glan y Llyn, 290, 292
Glascombe, 214, 224, 227
Glascram, 214, 227
"Glanrason" farm, 119, 121, 122, 447
Glenn family, 160

Glenn's "Merion in the Welsh Tract," 159, 160
Glenn's Road, 155
Gloucester. Duke of, 293
" Earl of, 297, 298
Glyn Taway, 295
Glyndyfrdwy, 290, 299, 300
Gyna y Maen-gwyn, 297
Goshen tp., 35, 51, 54, 55, 64, 71, 80, 83, 84, 86, 88, 101, 104, 108, 119, 122, 123, 128, 133, 134, 176, 178, 211, 214, 229, 236, 237, 492
Goshen Meeting House, 104
Goshen Prep. Mtg., 575
Gosnell, or Gosnold, 399
Goushill. Sir Robert, 285
Gov. Lloyd and Pastorius, 145
Gov. Lloyd and the Welsh Friends, 145
Government Mill, 388
"Governor's Miller," 223, 306, 388
Grainianoc, 281
Grand Army of the Republic, 15
Granting manorial rights, 343
Graves, 192
Gravestones, 14, 567
"Graveyard pales," 551, 563
Graveyards. 506, 507
Great Meadows, 192
Great Valley, 177, 197
Greave, 192
Green Tree Ins. Co., 435
Griffith family, 121
Griffith of Gwyn, 295
Griffith's house, 162
Griffith. Prince of So. Wales, 281
Griffith. Prince of No. Wales, 281
Grimrod's mill, 430
Griscom family, 141
Growth of Philadelphia, 308
Grubbing the city, 393
Gulf Hill, 489
Gulf Mill, 216, 237, 436, 489, 594
Gulf Road, 102, 237, 433, 434, 436
Gwanas, 213, 243
Gwern y Brechtwyn, 290, 292
Gwern Eyel Ismynydd, 48, 52, 105, 115, 120, 127, 137
Gwy Meeting House, 19
Gwydir House, 182, 184
Gwyddelwern, 290
Gwynedd tp., 19, 38, 92, 99, 105, 107, 132, 239, 240, 248, 284, 287, 300, 301, 302, 323, 324, 499, 505
Gwynedd Prep. Mtg., 135, 263
"Gwynedd Welsh," 266
Hambright's Inn, 442
Hamhanghobycholgen, 223
Hank-Lincoln pedigree, 595
"Harfod Town," 16
Harlech Castle, 301
Harris family, 230
Harrison family, 457
Harrison School House, 458
"Harriton" farm, 435, 457
"Harriton" graveyard, 237, 456, 457, 459
Haverford and Radnor, 357, 363
Haverford burial ground, 242, 580
Haverford College, 153, 201, 204, 245, 432, 478
Haverford Friends, 385
Haverford Friends' School, 81

[623]

WELSH SETTLEMENT OF PENSYLVANIA

Haverford Mo. Mtg., 20, 63, 79, 83, 90, 151, 301, 498, 501, 503, 504, 529, 531, 550
Haverford Mo. Mtg. and the "Oath," 515
Haverford M. M. "Book of Memorials," 594
Haverford Mo. Mtg. ferry, 391, 393
Haverford Mtg. records, 570
Haverford Mtg. House, 204, 242, 256, 432, 435, 579, 580, 581, 582
Haverford Mtg. stable, 580
Haverford Mill, 198, 389
Haverford Prep. Mtg., 82, 499
Haverford Road, 69, 165, 167, 174, 232, 483
Haverford and Darby Road, 204
Haverford and Merion Road, 72, 78
Haverford School, 245
"Haverford Street," 167, 204, 232, 256, 431, 432
"Haverford Town," 1682, 499
Haverford tp., 16, 81, 87, 141, 150, 153, 163, 164, 165, 166, 171, 173, 195, 196, 228, 229, 244, 253, 254, 287, 480
Haverford tp., 1715, 488
Haverford West, 23, 198, 222, 243, 253
Haverford West Mtg., 271, 529
Havod vadog, 117
"Head-land," 259
"Head-rights," 259
Hearne family, 508
Hendri Mawr, 109, 161, 198
Hendri Mawr Mo. Mtg., 122, 271
Heng Wert, 103, 160, 161
Henllan, 222
Henry III. of England, 285, 288
Henry VII. of England, 286
Henry I. of Navarre, 285
Herring Creek, Md., 237
Hertford, Earl of, 281, 297, 298
Hestonville Prep. Mtg., 586
"Hicksites" and "Orthodox," 585
"Hicksite Friends," 15, 534, 536
High Street Ferry, 438, 464, 466
Hiltz's Journal, 462
Hirnant, 141, 149, 150
"History of Haverford College," 414
"History of Proprietary Government in Pen." 241
Historical Society of Pa., 20, 24, 97, 109, 117, 118, 156, 157, 214
Holand, Sir Thomas, 293
Holme's census of the Welsh Tract, 355
Holme's land, 250
Holme's Map of Pa., 119, 124, 249, 255, 354, 355, 359, 381, 499
"Homeworth" farm, 485
Hood and Scarf Inn, 241
House furniture, 319, 320
Houses along the Lancaster Road, 1750, 162
Howel-dda, King of Wales, 280
Howell family, 158
Howell, of Nannau, 297
Hugh Roberts as a minister among Friends, 97
Hugh Roberts's party, 87, 95, 105, 131, 160, 166
Hughs, of Gwynedd, 302
Hughs's house, 162
Humphreys's house, 162, 466
Humphreysville, 153, 428, 480
Ideal asylum, 20

Ieuf Howel Adar, 290
Ilminston, 270
Ilwyn y Branar Mtg., 114
"Immigration of Irish Quakers into Pa.," 266
Impressed servants, 262
Independent "Welsh State," 372
Indians, 306, 310, 316, 321
Indian Chief Wingbone, 53
Indian Creek, 100, 208
Indian fields, 17, 306, 368
Indian grantors, 53
Interviewing Penn in London about land, 115, 116
"Inverie Barony," 343
Iscoed, 290, 300
Ismynydd, 105
Issa, 177
Itinerant Mo. Mtgs, 510
James's Lane, 438
Jenkintown, Pa., 201
John, King of England, 289, 300
John ap Edward's servants, 87, 89
John ap Thomas MSS., 109, 114, 118
Jones family, 89, 91, 105, 134
Jones family Bible, 116, 118
Jones pedigree, 109
Jones' house, 162
Jones' letter, 335
Jones' land, Dr. Edward, 71
Jones, Sketch of Dr., 64
Journal of the Friends' Historical Society, London, 24, 241
Journal of Hugh Roberts, 97
Jsoregenan, 243
Junior Anti-Slavery Society, 273
John ap Edward's servants, 87, 89
Karbardamfyneth, 252
"Keith disturbance," 318
Kennett tp., 298
Kentucky, 17
Kent, Earl of, 292, 293, 297
Kiltalgarth, 47, 48, 74, 79, 96, 109, 120, 125, 127
Kimbolton, Hereford, 350
King of Prussia, 489
Kinnison's Run, 438
Lancaster, Earl of, 285
Lancaster Av. Improvement Co., 443
Lancaster Road, 60, 71, 78, 80, 84, 92, 100, 102, 119, 136, 174, 204, 431, 432, 435, 436, 437
Lancaster Road in war times, 462, 466
Lancaster Turnpike, 167, 440, 441
Land advertising, 18
Land Commissioners' Minutes, 54
Land deeds of John and Wynne, 34
Land deeds of Thomas and Jones, 34
Land owners along the Lancaster Road, 1773, 174
Land scarce in 1683, 311, 312
Land scarce, 325
Land speculation, 235
Land values in Haverford, 258
Land values in Merion tp., 257
Land values in Radnor, 258
Larue Co., Ky., 284
Last Prince of Wales, 289
Lea, Herefordshire, 142
Leaders in Welsh Tract, 373, 384
Leedom family, 567
Leedom's Mill, 198
Leicester, Earl of, 285, 288, 300
"Letitia Penn Tract," 178

[624]

WELSH SETTLEMENT OF PENSYLVANIA

Letter of Dr. Jones, 65
Levering's Ford, 463
Levering's Map of Merion, 487
Levick family, 165, 569
Levick's "Recollections of Her Early Days," Mrs., 272
Levick MSS., 594
Liberty Land, 85, 88
Libertyville, 478, 479, 484
"Life of Samuel Jones Levick," 273
Lightner family, 146
"Lilac Grove" farm, 468
"Line Waggon Co.," 441
Liverpool, 83
Llethgwn, } 127, 129
Llaithgwm, } 22, 25, 47, 65, 96, 109, 116,
Llanbister, 214, 224, 227
Llanbynin, 152
Llandboyden, 253
Llancillio, 22, 200, 202, 254
Llandaff registry, 168
Llandderfel, } 22, 85, 109, 114, 299, 300
Llandervel, }
Llandewy Velfry, 25, 33, 165, 195, 271
Llandigley, 227
Llandovery, 281
Llaneingan, 126
Llanelwith, 222
Llanelyw, 172, 206
Llanegryn, 22, 152
Llanfawr, 107, 114, 301
Llaufillyn, 143
Llan Glynin, 48, 131, 157, 213, 220, 221
Langunllo, 214
Llanllidiog, 85
Llangadog, 295
Llangerig, 100, 226
Llangower, 48, 134, 137
Llangotten, 22
Llanole, 98
Llan Rwst, 176, 282
Llansilin, 293
Llantgervel, 22, 113
Llantrissent, 163, 166
Llantwit Vardre. 149, 150, 163, 170
Llanuwchllyn, 299
Llanvachreth, 213, 531
Llanvawr, 21, 25, 75, 96, 97, 108, 125, 133, 300
Llanvihangel Rhydyithon, 214
Llanvihangel Velgyen, 214
Llanwddyn, 150, 151, 152, 243, 286, 499
Llanwenog, 195
Llanwthin, 141
Llan y keaven, 195
Llardevy, 197
Llaulanread in Elvel, 224
Llavodgyfaner, 120
Llaythgywm, 21, 33
Llewellyn's house, 162
Llewellyn the Great, 290
Lloyd and Davies' land, 151
Lloyd annoys the Governor, 357, 362
Lloyd. Att'y for the Welsh, 356
Lloyd's difficulty with Penn's deputy, 143, 144, 145
Lloyd's land, 56, 83, 147, 234
Lloyd, of Cydros, 292
Lloyd, of Dolobran, 293
Lloyd, of Dyffryn, 293
Lloyd, of Gwern Brychwyn, 292
Lloyd, of Gwerny Brechtwyn, 299
Lloyd, of Upper Plasin, 292

Llun, 127
Llwyn-du, 98, 150, 151, 152, 157, 179, 180, 286, 591
Llwyn y Brauer, 21, 102
Llwyn-Grevill, 132, 150, 234
Llwyn-howell, 296
Llyn, 126, 281
Llyndeddwydd, 96, 125, 126
Llnyniarth, 301
Locating Phila., 41, 42
Locations of Haverford farms, 256
Locations of Radnor farms, 256
Log cabin home, 118
Logan family, 146
Logan's opinion of "the palatines," 347
London Gazette, 186
London Yearly Meeting, 24
Londonderry, 266
Longevity, 272
Long Is., N. Y., 101
Louis VIII. of France, 285
Long Welsh pedigree, 110
Lower Burying Ground, 507
Lower Merion Academy, 487
Lower Merion tp., 422, 426
Lower Mill Creek, 428
Lownes's Cave, 315
Lutherans' church, 485
Lutheran church graveyard, 456
MSS. of John ap Thomas, 47, 64
McCalla's Store, 477
McClennachan family, 146
Macchinleth, 161, 230
Machanlleth, 220
Machynlleth, 240
Mackenzie's "Colonial Families," 283
"Maencoch," 197
Magistrate's Court, 529
"Magna Charta Barons and their American Descendants," 159
"Magna Charta" Sureties, 281
"Magnalia," 17
"Main Line" (P. R. R.), 147, 419, 479
Malin's Graveyard, 211
Manhinteth, 161
Manumitting, 265
Map of Haverford tp., 204
Map of Haverford tp., 232
Map of "Liberties," 1773, 174
Map Merion Mtg. land, 30, 560
Map of part of the Welsh Tract, 60
Map showing the Merion and Haverford Meeting Houses, 194
Map: "Thomas and Jones Tract," 1692, 376
Map of "Thomas and Jones Tract," 1700, 376
Map: "Thomas and Jones Tract," 1750, 162
Map: Thomas and Jones Tract, 1850, 416
Map of "Welsh Tract," 494
March. Earl of, 293
Marchnant Issa, 141, 149
Marriage Certificates, 594
"Married out," 262
Marris family, 159
Marple tp., 163, 164, 196, 232, 255
Masonic "Army Lodge," 457
Mass. Friends, 531
Mass. "sharp laws," 17
Matson's Ford, 430, 463, 466, 489
Maud coat of arms, 183

WELSH SETTLEMENT OF PENSYLVANIA

"Measures to regulate the Welsh Tract," 58
Meeting House Lane, 11, 434, 443
Meetings separate, 585
Melfod, 141
Members of Merion Mtg., 1706, 541-2
Merchantable things in Phila. in 1682, 68
Meredith's house, 162
Merionethshire, 23, 33, 48, 65, 75, 79, 81, 82, 85, 96, 103, 104, 107, 109, 116, 120, 125, 126, 129, 131, 150, 151, 152, 155, 157, 160, 161, 179, 213, 220, 224, 233, 240, 243, 287, 291, 298, 300, 301, 499
"Merion in the Welsh Tract," 63, 159, 160
Merion, 92, 132, 479
Merion adventurers for lands, 63
Merion and Haverford Road, 204
Merion Associators, 455
Merion's creeks, 430
Merion Ford, 432
Merion Friends, 385
Merion Friends' first meetings, 99
Merion Friends' first weddings, 99
Merion Furnace, 430
Merion in 1850, 484
Merion land holders, 58
Merion militia, 455, 456
Merion Mill Creek, 389, 429
"Merion Mo. Mtg.," 501
Merion post-offices, 427
Merion soldiers, 454
Merion Square, 484
"Merion Street," 431, 432, 436
Merion, the richest tp., 426
"Merion Town," 16, 499
Merion township, 11, 16, 24, 54, 55, 117, 214, 217, 236, 237, 250, 253, 291, 312, 421
Merion Troop, 454
Merion villages, 427
Merionville, 479
Merion wood ranger, 419
Merion Preparatory Meeting, 24, 63, 76, 79, 80, 82, 89, 85, 86, 451, 529, 530, 549
Merion Mtg., 1806, 578
Merion Mtg. archives, 85
Merion Mtg. burials, 429, 565, 566
Merion Mtg. burial records, 564
Merion Mtg. caretaker's house, 562
Merion Mtg. Graveyard, 14, 73, 80, 83, 84, 86, 102, 446, 448, 549, 554, 567
Merion Meeting House, 11, 20, 42, 72, 74, 75, 80, 81, 83, 84, 119, 125, 156, 162, 434, 438, 442, 443, 444, 445, 462, 463, 465, 478, 483, 487, 528, 5 3, 550, 572, 591
Merion Mtg. House pictures, 572
Merion Mtg. land, 60, 78, 549, 553, 557, 558
Merion Mtg. minutes, 263, 533, 535, 540
Merion Mtg. school, 487
Merion Mtg. school house, 560, 561
Merion Mtg. stable, 446, 448, 560
Merion Mtg. stone walls, 563
Meteer family, 473
Middle Ferry, 174, 390, 393, 436
Middle Town tp., 178
Mile Stones, 435, 442
Mill Creek, 69, 80, 100, 208
Mill Creek Road, 155, 179, 433

Mill on Darby Cr., 198
Mills, 388
Mills taboo to the Welsh, 389
Ministers' notices of Welsh Tract Mtgs., 573-4-5
Miscin, 289
Money to print a book in Welsh, 151
Montfort, Simon de, 300
"Monthly Meeting" as a Court, 345
Mo. Mtg. authority, 511, 513, 518, 519
Mo. Mtg. legislation, 512, 513
Mo. Mtgs. of Wales, 25
Montgomery Ave., 71, 80, 92, 102, 119, 151, 153, 156, 433, 434, 436
Montgomery Castle, 296
Montgomeryshire, 24, 33, 100, 141, 146, 149, 150, 161, 220, 226, 230, 233, 240, 301
Moore family, 146
Moravians' "barony," 343
Morgan's Corner, 479, 480
Morris family, 146
Morris, of Brin Gwin, 301
Morris' Woods, 458
Mossom, 95, 209
Mothvey, 213
"Mount Ararat" farm, 119, 121, 255, 447, 567
Mt. Mellick Mo. Mtg., 298
Mt. Holly Meeting, 597
Mount Joy Manor, 422
Names of Merion land owners, 1734, 424-5
Names of Merion residents, 1690, 423-4
Names of Merion taxables, 1780, 426
Names of Welsh Friends, in 1688, 371
Names of Welsh Friends, 1693, 301
Names of Welsh settlers, 517
Nannau, 161, 298
Nant Lielding, 21, 48, 85, 108, 132, 136
Nantmell, 102, 214, 252, 499
Nant y Friar, 290, 299
Narberth, 23, 72, 92, 118, 119, 155, 195, 197, 270, 432
Neale's Journal, 575
Neath, 289
Negroes, 265, 565
New Amsterdam land rule, 368
New Church parish, 214, 223
New Castle, Del., 81, 104, 229
New Kent Co., Va., 97
"New Merion," 63
Newport, R. I., 187
Newton tp., 210
New Town Prep. Mtg., 501, 504
New Town tp., 35, 165, 177, 178, 208, 221, 237
"New Wales," in Pa., 25
Non-Quaker Welsh, 308
Non-Quakers in the Welsh Tract, 372
Northampton, Earl of, 285
North Carolina, 211
North Valley Hill, 489
"North Wales," 239, 266
North Wales, King of, 294
North Wales Friends, 573
North Wales people, 275
Official Grave Digger, 509
Oldest house in Merion, 156
Oldmixon's opinion of Welsh settlers, 318
Origin of Penn's plans, 374
Oswestrie, 65
"Ould Grave Yard Owen Roberts'," 102

WELSH SETTLEMENT OF PENSYLVANIA

Other "Welsh Tracts," 37, 265
Overbrook, 85, 99, 432, 439
Overbrook Farms, 86
Over-lapping surveys, 366
"Over-plus" land, 197, 226, 267, 333
Owen family, 158, 159
Owen House, 156, 528
Owen, of Dolserau, 160
Owen, of Duck Creek, 160
Owen, of Merion, 154, 160
Owen, of Vron Gôch, 154
Oxford P. E. church, 323
Palmer's Journal, 575
Paoli, 479, 480
Paoli Inn, 443
Paoli massacre, 492
Paschall's Landing, 450
Passengers in the ship "Vine," 161
"Patroon concessions," 33
Paying for Merion Mtg. House, 536-537
"Peace Maker" of Phila., 197
"Peace" Society, 273
Peckover's Journal, 575
Pektang Road, 438
Pembroke Quar. Mtg., 75
Pembrokeshire, 23, 25, 33, 142, 165, 195, 197, 241, 270, 499
Penarth, 150, 286
"Pencoyd" farm, 106, 122, 126, 127, 168
Pencoyd Iron Works, 421, 430
Penllech, 281
Penllyn, 47, 82, 90, 98, 105, 109, 116, 121, 122, 285, 290, 591
Penllyn Mo. Mtg., 79, 83, 96, 97, 105, 117, 127, 133
Penmaen, 21, 22, 48, 83, 114, 122, 129, 136, 302, 311, 594
Penn and his agents "boom" his province, 40
Penn and Ford, 241
Penn and the Germans, 345
Penn and the Jesuits, 409
Penn and the Welsh, 331
Penn's arbitrariness, 335
Penn's anger, 330
Penn's annoyances, 330
Penn's appellations, 327
Penn's authority, 328, 342
Penn as a courtier, 406
Penn as a feudal prince, 344
Penn a fugitive, 411, 413
Penn blackmailed, 403
Penn's Charter, 327
Penn's Commissioners answer Welsh complaints, 382, 385
Penn's "Conditions," 334
Penn courting, 524
Penn's deeds to the Welsh Friends, 52
Penn's desire to favor the Welsh, 36
Penn's "Experiment," 330
Penn experiments with deputy-governor, 143
Penn's "Free Colony," 18
Penn's first colonists, 41
Penn's first surveyor, 41
Penn's first visit to Pa., 42, 82, 186
Penn's first "weather report," 314
Penn's grist-mill "trust," 388
Penn's hat pin, 528
Penn's "House of Lords," 254, 344
Penn's inducements to buy his land, 25
Penn's "interests" badly looked after, 396

"Penn-Logan Correspondence," 101
Penn's Land advertisements, 22
Penn's land patents to Welsh Friends, 34, 35
Penn's land plans, 33
Penn's land titles, 333
Penn looks for "overplus land," 369, 387
Penn loses ferry and mill rights, 392
Penn's manors, 341
Penn's manor. Letitia, 422
Penn's estate. Letitia, 490
Penn's method of selling his land, 38
Penn's Milling Co., 308
Penn's models, 341
Penn's Nemesis, 397
Penn's "Order of Nobility," 344
Penn's ostentation, 329
Penn's personal sales, 253
Penn's phantasm, 335
Penn plans to get Welsh lands, 367, 368
Penn's promise to Hugh Roberts, 384
Penn's promises to the Welsh Friends, 26
Penn's promises, 327, 330
Penn's "Province business," 330
Penn's regard for certain Welsh Friends, 318
Penn selling land, 20
Penn's "subtil undermining" of the Welsh, 379
Penn's surveys, 334
Penn, "the Jacobite Quaker," 410
Penn's title to land he had sold, 52, 53
Penn's treatment of the Swedes, 332
Penn's unfairness, 332, 333, 334
Penn's vacillation, 348
Penn's verbal concessions to the Welsh, 26
Penn's visits to Welsh Tract, 528, 529, 577
Penn vs. Ford, 405
Penn's word the Law, 334
"Penn Cottage," 485, 528
Penn School, 562
Pennsylvania, or "Pensylvania," 20
Pa. documents, 328
Pa. Loan Office, 425
Pen. R. R., 72, 75, 92, 132, 155, 171, 478, 484, 507
Pennyckland, 178
Penrhyn Castle, 286
Pen y Chyd, 151, 287
Pen y Clwyd, 178
Penytklawe, 178
Persecution of Welsh Quakers, 21, 110, 111, 112
Persecuting the Friends, 185, 591
Petition of Welsh as to lands and rights, 378
Peytyn wyn, 288
Phila. City Line, 84
Philadelphia in 1682-3, 66, 145, 310, 312
Philadelphia in 1754, 420
P. B. & B. M. Turnpike Co., 444
Phila. Mo. Mtg., 75, 497, 499
P. & R. R. R., 483
Philip III. of France, 202
Pickering's Journal, 463
Pike Stage Co., 441
"Pioneer Fast Line," 478
Pioneer Welsh Friends, 20
Pioneering, 17, 18

[627]

WELSH SETTLEMENT OF PENSYLVANIA

Plantation of Ulster, 341
Plas Ifa, 22, 181
Plas yn Yale, 118
Plow Inn, 442
Plymouth settlement, 108
Political development, 371
Poor surveying, 223, 229
Port Kennedy, 489
Porthaml, 288, 289
Powell family, 531
Powell's Ferry, 435
Powell's head-rights, 252
Powell's land, 250, 251
Powell's map of the Thomas and Jones land, 88
Powell, surveyor of Welsh Tract, 251
Pownall's Journal, 420, 442, 445
Powis Castle, 293, 297
Powis, King of, 290
Powys Fadog. History of, 290
Prees, or Price pedigree, 133
Presbyterians, 458
Prescoe, Lancashire, 104, 161
Preston family, 146
Price Family, 229, 462, 465, 467
Price property, 119
Prices in 1698, 316
Primogeniture not recognized by the Welsh, 123, 373
Prince Llewellyn Griffyth, 300
Prince Theodore-mawr, 295
Progenitor of the Haverford Mo. Mtg., 27
Prominent Welshmen, 317
"Proprietary Government in Pa.," 333
Proprietor's Mill, 388
Protection against creditors, 521
Protheven, 287
Proud's description of the Welsh settlers, 305, 306, 316
Provence. Count of 285
Province Island, 190
Prynes Castle, 286
Public highways, 431
Public library, 489
Pugh's "Annerch ir Cymru," 152
"Pugh District," 251
Pugh of Gwynedd, 302
Puritans' Settlement, 373
Quaker apostle, 23
Quakers' hats, 597
Quaker patriots, 453
"Quaker School Boy," 17
Quaker soldiers, 455
"Quaker Tories," 453
Quality of the first Welsh settlers, 95
Quality of the settlers of the Welsh Tract, 279
Quality of the Welsh immigrants, 305, 317, 318
Quit-rent disputes, 335, 381
Quit-rent, when due, 384
Radnor & Chester Road, 232
Radnor Friends, 385, 452
Radnor Mtg. House, 438, 582, 584
Radnor Mo. Mtg., 20, 24, 451, 475, 501, 502, 517, 526, 580
Radnor Prep. Mtg., 81, 108, 510, 529, 576
Radnorshire, 98, 161, 176, 214, 222, 223, 226, 228, 252, 499
"Radnor Street," 256, 431
"Radnor Town," 16, 82, 499

Radnor township, 19, 81, 106, 107, 165, 172, 178, 191, 214, 217, 218, 221, 225, 228, 231, 253, 254, 311, 312, 322, 480
Rattle snakes, 322
Reason for division of purchases, 51
Reckitt's Journal, 574
Red Hill, 489
Rediston, 98
Redstone, 23, 241
Redstone Mo. Mtg., 499
Red Lion Inn, 427, 443
Reesville, 479
Regnal years, 45
Regulating courtship, 520
Regulating weddings, 520, 521
Relationship to each other of the first settlers in the Welsh Tract, 137, 138
Reserved mill-land, 388
Rhiwabon, 120
Rhiwlalon. Prince of Powys, 281
Rhiwlas, 155, 282
Rhonds's house, 162
Rhuddalt, 29, 299
Rhys. Prince of So. Wales, 281
Richard II. of England, 292
Richard Davies Co., 150
Richard Davies' land, 213, 233
Richard Thomas' land, 207
Richards family 452
Richland Prep. Mtg. 272, 273, 274
Richardson's Journal, 573, Ridley Creek, 101
Ridgway Family, 146
Right to affirm, 597
Road to the Ford, 445
Roads in the Welsh Tract, 430
Robert Owen's stone house, 156
Roberts family, 96, 107, 125, 134, 146, 568
Roberts, of Lynn. John, 498, 568
Roberts, of the "Vane Mill," John, 130, 151, 178, 179, 180, 257
Roberts, of "Woodlawn," John, 92
Roberts, the Tory—John, 180, 468-475
Roberts. John, (maltster), 56, 57, 59, 127, 120, 218
Roberts. John, (shoemaker), 54, 56, 57, 59, 220
Roberts. John, (wheelwright), 180
Roberts of "Pencoyd," 106
Roberts, of "Woodlawn," 272
Roberts's acc't of cost of finishing Merion Mtg. Hs., 543
Roberts' graveyard, 550
Roberts' house, 162, 483
Roberts' Mill, 433
Roberts' opinion of some first settlers, 395
Rosemont, 171, 256
"Rosemont" farm, 77, 172, 480
Rowden, 189
Ruabon, 22, 25, 28, 33, 120, 178, 181
"Rules of the Road," 440
St. Asaph registry, 79, 109, 133, 291, 301
St. David's P. E. Church, 19, 323, 583
St. Harmon, 214
"St. Mary's" farm, 75, 77, 119, 156,
Salem, Mass., 187
San Marino, 372
Sassafras Prep. Mtg., 527
Saunders family, 508
Scandalous idea of Friends' meetings, 28

[628]

WELSH SETTLEMENT OF PENSYLVANIA

School houses, 562
Scott's Journal, 575
Schuylkill river, 430
Schuylkill Marshes, 174
Schuylkill Masonic Lodge, 457
Schuylkill Prep. Mtg., 174, 390, 439, 500, 507, 508
Scull & Heap's map, 162, 482, 483
Scull's house, 162
Seating land, 334
Seeing Penn praying, 576
Selecting a help-meet, 522
Sensational, fictitious letter about Penn, 186
"Servants," 259
Servant's certificate, 87, 261
"Servants" in Merion, 261
Servants' land, 128, 259
Servants' references, 205
Settling differences, 520
Sevenoch Friends' Mtg., 98
Several "John Roberts" in the Welsh Tract, 125
Shardlow, Sharelow, Sharlow, Sherlo, 207
Sharlow's land, 447
Ship Inn, 442
Ships, "Endeavour," 188; "Lyon," 64, 83, 85; "Morning Star," 95, 105, 117, 119, 125, 150, 166, 209, 263; "Submission," 189; "Vine," 104, 131, 160, 161, 230, 505; "Welcome," 182, 186, 189, 307, 499; "William," 252; "William Penn," 309.
Shoemaker family, 146
Sign of the Bull Inn, 438
Sisters of Mercy, 14, 437
Sketch of Hugh Roberts, 96
Sketch of John Bevan, 166
Sketch of John Cadwalader, 74
Sketch of John Roberts, 125
Sketch of John Thomas, 109
Sketch of Richard Davies, 233
Sketch of Richard ap Thomas, 209
Sketch of Robert Owen, (from Dolyserre), 160
Sketch of Robert Owen, (from Vron Goch), 154
Sketch of Rowland Ellis, 233
Sketch of Thomas Ellis, 240
Sketch of Dr. Thomas Wynne, 181-190
Small farms customary among the Welsh, 123
Smallpox germs scattered, 183, 187
Smith's "History of Delaware Co.," 243
Social quality of Wolsh and English Quakers, 27
Society of Free Traders, 116, 158, 400
Sonby, 290
Sorrel Horse Inn, 443, 466
South River country, 18
South Wales. Prince of, 294
Spread Eagle P. O., 480
Spread Eagle Tavern, 443
Spring Fair of Phila., 202
Spytu, 300
Stackpole, 142
Stadleman's house, 162
Stadleman's Inn, 442, 443
Stafford. Earl of, 297, 299
Stage drivers, 442
Standing of first Welsh land grantees, 27
Stanton's Journal, 575

State Road, 434
"State in Schuylkill," 455, 482
Stockdale's "Great Cry of Oppression," 266
Subscribers towards finishing Merion Mtg. Hs., 545
"Sufferings of the People Called Quakers," 185
Sufferings of Welsh Friends, 24
Suggestions to emigrants, 38, 39
Survey charges, 67
Survey map of the Welsh Tract, 37
Surveyor's prices, 52
Susquehanna Land Co., 422
Sutcliff's Journal, 572, 576-79
Suttrick, King of Dublin, 295
Swan Lum's land, 128
Swansea, 23
Swanson family, 69, 311
"Swart More," 28
Swedes, 17, 18
Swedes' Ford, 463, 464, 489
Swedes' lands, 128
Swedish Settlement, 373
Swedish settlers, 382
Tal y Llyn, 295
Tancarville. Earl of, 293, 297
Tawrynydd, 298
Tenbigh Friends' Mtg., 98
Tenby, 29, 200, 201, 253
Telcha, 163
The election of 1689, 361
"The Pa. Farmer," 272
"The Phila. Friend," 73, 189
"The Friends' Library," 233, 243
The Lloyd & Davis Grant, 142
The pioneer "land company," 41
The position of the Welsh Tract, 420
The seven streets of Phila., 394
The Story of Philip Ford, 397
The Upper Ferry, 390
The Welsh community short lived, 138
The Welsh Utopia, 375
Thomas & Jones Co., 55, 83, 255, 387, 445
Thomas & Jones' deeds, 49
Thomas & Jones' grantees, 137
Thomas & Jones' Patent, 45
Thomas & Jones land distributed, 50, 51
"Thomas & Jones Tract," 87, 88, 355, 430, 483, 500
Thomas family, 161, 172, 173
Thomas' house, 162
Thompson family, 457, 567
Three Tuns Tavern, 442
To furnish Haverford Mtg. house, 152
To print a book in the Welsh language, 151
Toland family, 77
Toll Gates, 440
Tories in Merion, 468
Township constable, 492
Township officers, 335
"Township village," 335
Townships formed, 335
Townships in Welsh Tract, 488
Traditions in Merion, 467
Transportation charges, 252
Trawsfynedd, 298
Tredomen, 289
Tredyffrin tp., 491
Trefgarned, 290, 300
Tregaron, 176

[629]

WELSH SETTLEMENT OF PENSYLVANIA

Treverigg, 33, 98, 163, 166, 168, 169, 280
Treverigg Friends' Mtg., 166, 261
Trevor, 22
Trevor Iszn, 23
Tribes of Gwynedd, 292
Trouble in getting land laid out, 67
Trouble over "bonus land," 218
Troubles over taxes, 364
Tudor-mawr, Prince of So. Wales, 281
Tunis's house, 162
Tunis' Ordinary, 447, 467
Turner's advertisement of Pa., 336
Tuyn y nant, 83, 127
Tyddyn Tyfod, 79, 290, 291, 299
Tyddyn y Gareg, 106, 154
Tyddyn y Garreg Quart. Mtg., 272, 499
Tyddler y Gareg, 132, 235
Ucheldre, 48, 85
University of Pa., 475
"Unseated Lands," 377
Upland, 41, 63, 64
Upper Branas, 292
Upper Dublin tp., 159
Upper Merion tp., 422, 489
Upper Mill Creek, 102
Upper Side of Bucks Mo. Mtg., 400
Uwchland tp., 35
Vaenor, 216
Valle Crucis Abbey, 28
Valley Forge, 450, 489
Valley of Virginia, 17
Van Lear family, 473
Vaux family, 146
Vehicles, 435
Vernon Tavern, 442
Villa Nova, 256, 479, 480
Vital records, 571
Virginia head-rights, 259
Voting places, 428
Vron Goch, 21, 22, 282
"Vron Goch" farm, 287
Wainwright family, 146
Walker family, 452
Wallbrook, 141, 145
Wain family, 146
"Walnut Grove" farm, 160
Waloons Settlement, 373
War times in Merion, 465
Warner's house, 162
Warrant to survey the land of the Welsh, 35
Warwick, Earl of, 285
Washington, Gen., 238, 450, 451, 452, 462, 463, 464, 467, 471, 489, 579
Watson's "Annals of Philadelphin," 181
"Wayn Mill," 151, 178, 287, 433
Wayside Inn, 449
"Weekly Mercury," 394
Welsh and Chester Mo. Mtg., 502, 504
Welsh appeal from Commissioners to Penn, 384
Welsh ask to be confirmed in their rights, 370
Welsh Baptists, 266, 286
"Welsh Barony," 414, 587
Welsh "bonus land," 394
Welsh book-seller, 275
Welsh chimera, 380
Welsh customs and laws, 19, 337, 374
Welsh defend their rights, 366
Welsh descendants of kings, 280
Welshmen's desires, 512
Welsh emigration, 322

Welsh-English church services, 323
Welsh Episcopalians, 19, 323, 583
Welsh estimate of Penn., 379
Welsh families, 19
Welsh ferryman, 390
Welsh ferryman imprisoned, 392
Welsh foresight, 516
Welsh Friends, 16, 17, 18
Welsh Friends at Phila. Quart. Mtg., 508, 509
Welsh Friends before Penn's Commissioners, 383
Welsh Friends buy 30,000 acres in Pa., 34
Welsh Friends decline to be in Chester Quart. Mtg., 363
Welsh Friends' expectations, 26
Welsh Friends' grievances, 339
Welsh Friends' kin, 19
Welsh Friends Mo. Mtg., 501
Welsh Friends' Pedigrees, 279
Welsh Friends' protest, 370
Welsh Friends' rights, 331
Welsh Friend writers, 526
Welsh get their land deeds confirmed, 386
Welsh given city lots, 387
Welsh helping the needy, 530
Welsh ignore the Executive Council, 361
Welshmen ignored, 337
Welsh inspect newcomers, 431
Welsh interviewing Penn in London, 24, 25
Welsh land trustees, 34
Welsh lands pay Penn's debts, 385
Welsh language, 18, 511, 517, 571, 573, 584
"Welsh lots," in Phila., 225, 228
Welsh Mtgs. aid each other, 581
Welsh Mtg. houses, 431
Welsh Monthly Mtg., 421, 533
Welsh Mo. Mtg. variously called, 24
"Welsh mortgage," 401
Welsh names for R. R. stations, 480
Welsh non-taxable, 352, 355
Welsh pedigrees, 279
Welsh petition about their Meetings, 371
Welsh physicians, 25
Welsh Presbyterians, 487
Welsh pride, 516
Welsh purchase as a "barony," or "state," 26
Welsh Quaker emigration to Pa., 16
Welsh Quaker land companies of Pa., 33
Welsh representatives, 317
Welsh reservation in the city 395
Welsh Roll of Honour, 25
Welsh state their grievances, 370
Welsh tell what was promised them, 379
Welsh tell why they came, 378
Welsh troubles over extra, or bonus land, 305
Welsh Tract, 24
Welsh Tract acreage, 34
Welsh Tract affairs, 327
Welsh Tract "as one Barony," 35
Welsh Tract "Assembly," 513
Welsh Tract bisected, 352
Welsh Tract census, 1690, 381
Welsh Tract deeds, 339
Welsh Tract dimensions, 488

WELSH SETTLEMENT OF PENSYLVANIA

Welsh Tract during French-Indian war, 454
Welsh Tract during the Revolution, 238, 450
Welsh Tract laid out, 36
Welsh Tract Friends' Meeting, 499
Welsh Tract not surveyed, 35
Welsh Tract opened to non-Quakers, 383, 385
Welsh Tract Planters, 249
Welsh Tract schools, 487
Welsh Tract "streets," 431
Welsh Tract to-day, 421
Welsh Tract town-meeting, 392
Welsh Tract townships, 419
"Welsh Tract" of Chester Co., Pa., 171
Welsh use Latin, 84
Welsh women Friends, 530
Welsh Yearly Mtg., 24
Welshpool, 24, 33, 146, 213, 233
Wern Fawr, 81, 109, 110
West Chester, 51, 210
West Chester Pike, 232, 435
West Haverford, 479, 480
West Jersey Land Co., 22
West Laurel Hill Cemetery, 421
West Phila. Plank Road, 443, 572
West Town tp., 171, 491
West Whitland tp., 211
Wharton family, 146, 160
What emigrants should take to Pa., 68
Wheeler's Blockley land, 131
Whipping Welsh Friends, 115
White and black servants, 263, 264
White Hall Inn, 432, 435, 478, 479, 480
White Horse Inn, 442, 464
White Lamb Inn, 443
Whiteland tp., 200, 202, 210, 211, 490
Whitehough manor, 28
White Marsh tp., 284
Whitford Garne, 25, 207, 209
"Whitford Lodge," 211
Whitpain tp., 92
Why Penn allowed the Welsh to be badly treated, 397
Wicaco, 41, 50
Wight's "Quakers," 266
"William Penn & Co.," 388
William Penn Charter School, 318
William Penn Inn, 449
Williams family, 85, 105
Williams' house, 162
Willing family, 146
Willistown tp., 401
Wind-mills, 389
Winter of 1697-8, 316
Wister property, 119
"Wister's Woods," 77
Woman executed by fire, 170
"Woodlawn" Farm, 272, 285
Woolman's Journal, 574
Worcester, Earl of, 288
"Work for a Cooper," pamphlet, 181, 184
Worminghurst, 34
Wresting Welsh land, 377, 380
Wrexham, 22, 28, 176, 185
Wynne, or Chestnut Street, 188
Wynnefield, 443
Wynne's house, 162
"Wynne" pedigree, 184, 595
"Wynnestay," Farm, 184, 192, 466, 483
Wynnewood, 77, 150, 151, 155, 164, 165, 167
"Wynnewood" Farm, 75, 77, 156
Yale family, 118,
y Danyfaen, 301
Yestradtywy, 281
Young & Holmes's powder mill, 429
Yshute, 282
Yspytty, 300, 302
Zell family, 567

[631]

www.ingramcontent.com/pod-product-compliance
Lightning Source LLC
Chambersburg PA
CBHW070003010526
44117CB00011B/1416